THE
ASIAN AMERICAN
ENCYCLOPEDIA

THE ASIAN AMERICAN ENCYCLOPEDIA

Volume 4

Korean Methodist Church of Honolulu – Philippine Scouts

Editor
Franklin Ng

Managing Editor
John D. Wilson

Marshall Cavendish
New York • London • Toronto

Published By
Marshall Cavendish Corporation
2415 Jerusalem Avenue
P.O. Box 587
North Bellmore, New York 11710
United States of America

∞ The paper in these volumes conforms to the American National Standard for Permanence of Paper for Printed Library Materials, Z39.48-1984.

Library of Congress Cataloging-in-Publication Data

The Asian American encyclopedia / editor, Franklin Ng.
p. cm.
Includes bibliographical references and index.
Contents: v. 4. Korean Methodist Church of Honolulu—Philippine Scouts.
1. Asian Americans—Encyclopedias. I. Ng, Franklin, 1947- .
E184.O6A827 1995
973′.0495′003—dc20 94-33003
ISBN 1-85435-677-1 (set). CIP
ISBN 1-85435-681-X (vol. 4).

First Printing

PRINTED IN THE UNITED STATES OF AMERICA

Contents

THE
ASIAN AMERICAN
ENCYCLOPEDIA

Korean Methodist Church of Honolulu: Founded as the KOREAN EVANGELICAL SOCIETY in 1903 and renamed the Korean Methodist Church in 1905. Many of the Korean immigrants who came to Hawaii as laborers were Christians. Some, having served as preachers, established worship services throughout the sugar plantations of Hawaii; in time these churches became the center of the Korean community.

The Korean Evangelical Society in Honolulu was formed under the leadership of Ahn Chung-su and Woo Byong-kil. They held church services in a building on River Street in Honolulu. The Korean Methodist Church was dedicated two years later, becoming the first Korean church in Hawaii. The Reverend John Wiwadman was the superintendent, and the Reverend Hong Sung-ha was the first of a dozen ministers.

The church established the KOREAN COMPOUND School for boys in 1906, followed by a seminary for girls in 1914. Both were combined into the Korean Christian Institute, with Syngman RHEE serving as principal. Rhee, in a disagreement over church and school structure, later led eighty church members to form the Korean Christian Church.

While communicating the tenets of Christianity, the church also assisted its members in other ways. Being (for a time) the only Korean institution in Hawaii, it served as a center for the Korean community. The church employed many educated Koreans who could not otherwise find professional work outside the community because of racial discrimination.

Until 1945 one of the Korean Methodist Church's greatest concerns was Korean national independence from Japan. The church and school played an important role by providing funds and patriotic fervor on behalf of the cause. In later years the church concentrated more on the social, educational, and cultural activities in the community. Not only was the church instrumental in educating Korean immigrants in English, history, and American culture; it also established classes for Hawaiian-born Koreans.

Korean Methodist Church of San Francisco: Founded in 1905 as the KOREAN EVANGELICAL SOCIETY and renamed the Korean Methodist Church in 1911. A movement to organize church services in San Francisco began in 1905 during a period of progres-

Korean Methodist Church congregation, San Francisco, 1920. (The Korea Society/Los Angeles)

sive growth in the number of Koreans becoming Christians. Under the leadership of Mun Hyong-ho, the Korean Evangelical Society was started on Ellis Street. His successor, Ryang Ju-sam, a theology student enrolled at Vanderbilt University, carried the Korean community through the San Francisco earthquake of 1906 and established a new church in a three-story building on California Street. Ryang also created the first Korean newspaper, *The Korean United Church News (Hanin Yon Hop Kyobo)*, which later became *The Great Guidance News (Diado-Bo)*. He returned to Vanderbilt to finish his studies and later became the first Korean Methodist bishop in Korea.

The Korean Methodist Church was established under the pastorship of the Reverend David Lee, who also served as president of the KOREAN NATIONAL ASSOCIATION (KNA). Lee served in both capacities until his death in 1928. With Whang Su-sun as minister, the church moved to a new site on Powell Street. The Korean Methodist Church was the first Korean church on the mainland United States and the first funded by joint contributions from the American Mission Association and the Korean community.

The functions of the Korean Methodist Church included serving the social, educational, and cultural needs of the Korean community. Also, up until 1945 the main goal for many Korean church members was Korean independence from Japan. Although church growth was slow because of the immigrant exclusion laws, the church still assisted Korean immigrants with practical instruction, jobs, advice, and counsel. It helped new Korean immigrants adjust to American life. The church also founded language schools to help educate second- and third-generation Koreans to appreciate their Korean heritage.

In May, 1994, the church was approved for the National Register of Historic Places.

Korean music and dance: Because of a discriminatory immigration process and racism, Koreans in the United States historically have been not only preoccupied with the struggle to survive economically in a capitalist system, but also faced with the complexities of a fragmented cultural identity. Music and dance draw inspiration from cultural forms indigenous to Korea have helped to sustain a sense of cultural identity for Korean Americans. The expression of Korean identity through music and dance performance takes on significance in a nation where mainstream institutions do not support the perpetuation or development of Korean culture, and political and economic structures do not guarantee visibility or success.

Early Period in Hawaii. Korean laborers were recruited to come to Hawaii between 1902 and 1905. More than seven thousand Koreans immigrated to Hawaii during this period, of whom more than six thousand were adult males. (See KOREAN IMMIGRATION TO THE UNITED STATES and KOREANS IN HAWAII.) Later, between 1905 and 1924, a few hundred political refugees (fleeing Japanese rule), about three hundred students, and some one thousand "picture brides" came to Hawaii. Many of the women were better educated and much younger than their husbands—whom most had known only through photographs prior to their arrival in Hawaii. Differences in class background between these first-generation Korean men and women may explain a lack of evidence of much participation by early immigrant women in the performance of music or dance, which were considered inappropriate for respectable women in Korea. Women who danced and sang were likened to the low-class *kisaeng* (female entertainer) or *mudang* (shaman). After long hours in the sugarcane fields, and at celebrations and ceremonies such as *Chusok* (Harvest Moon Festival) and *Ku Chung* (New Year), Koreans gathered to feast, with the males drinking liquor, dancing, and singing Korean and American songs. Instruction in Korean dance and

Man performs a Korean folk dance, the Farmer's Dance. (Korea National Tourism Corporation)

Korean American girls in Penfield, New York, practice a Korean folk dance. (Don Franklin)

music was offered by several early immigrants, including Yong Ha Chai, a former priest who had studied dance and music before leaving Korea in 1905.

In 1922, the KOREAN NATIONAL ASSOCIATION of Hawaii founded the cultural organization Nam Pung Sa. Active until 1927, the association supported the teaching of court dance and music with instruments and costumes imported from Korea.

Ha Soo Whang did much to foster Korean music and dance in Honolulu beginning in the 1930's. A social worker affiliated with the International Institute of the Young Women's Christian Association (YWCA), she founded the Hyung Jay Club, which swerved Korean women from all backgrounds. At the Honolulu Academy of Art, Whang staged traditional court and folk dances, as well as enactments of Korean customs, such as the traditional wedding ceremony. Korean songs were accompanied by community musicians, including Hung Sup Kim, Kyung Sik Ko, Han Bong Pak, Young Sun Choy, and Yong Ha Chai. Other performances featured Western art music on piano, or piano-accompanied arrangements of popular Korean folk songs such as "Arirang." Club members learned Korean dance as well as Hawaiian hula and Polish folk dance. In 1940, Mu Yong Dan was formed so its members could focus on Korean dance, but by the late 1940's the organization had disbanded.

Halla Pai Huhm, the woman who shaped Korean dance in Hawaii after 1950, was raised in Tokyo, where she was trained in dance by her cousin, the renowned Ku Jha Pai. When Huhm began teaching in Honolulu in 1950, most of her students were Japanese Americans. By 1960, she had opened a studio in Pawaa, where she taught children of the Korean community as well as those of other ethnicity. The first major studio recital, "Korean Dances and Dances of the Orient," included not only Korean dances but also Japanese, Chinese, Okinawan, and Filipino dances, in which Halla Huhm herself performed. From 1961, she taught Korean dance as a faculty member of the University of Hawaii's music department.

Post-1965 Period. The IMMIGRATION AND NATIONALITY ACT OF 1965 ended the inequitable national-origins quota system that had been in place since the 1920's. As a result, there was a significant increase in Korean immigration to the United States. Immigrant families settled not only in Hawaii and California, but also in the urban centers of New York, New Jersey,

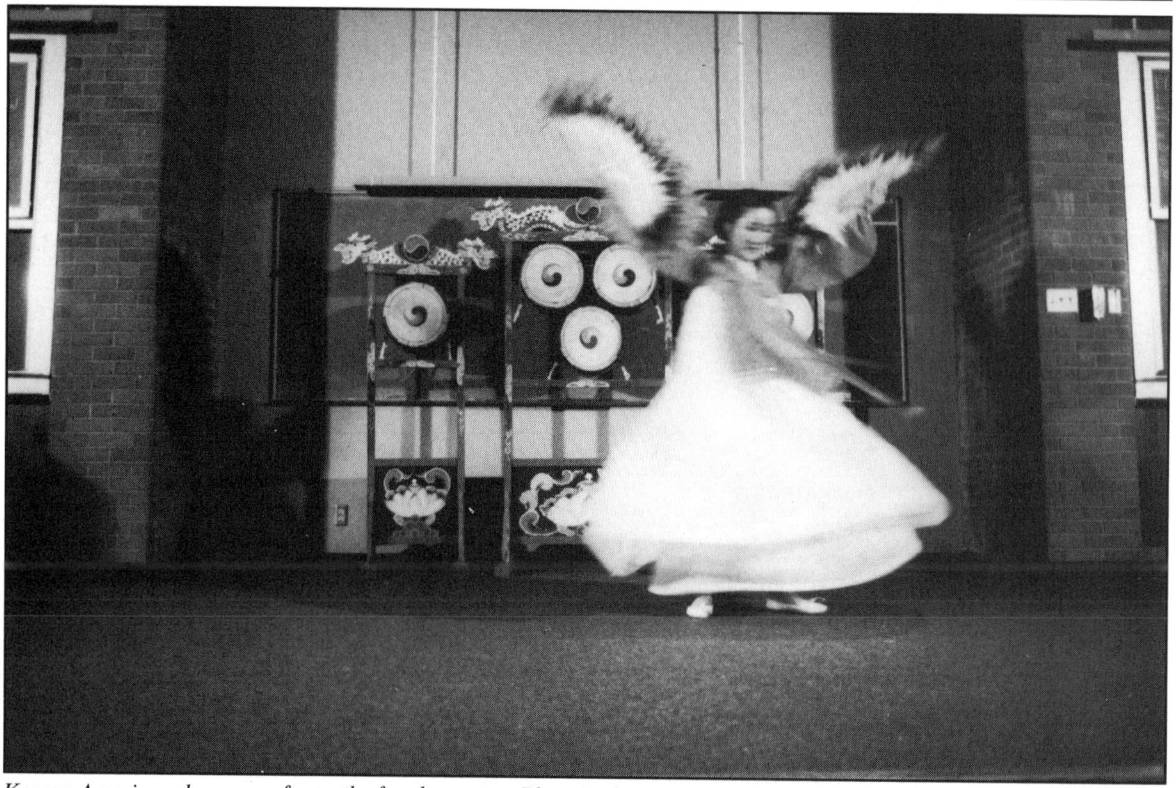

Korean American dancer performs the fan dance at a Phoenix shopping center in 1988. (The Korea Society/Los Angeles)

Connecticut, Massachusetts, Pennsylvania, Illinois, Ohio, and Michigan. To some extent, interest in traditional Korean music and dance was supported by a significant population increase, as well as by a growing political and cultural consciousness on the part of people of color in the United States. In Hawaii, this awareness began in the early to mid-1970's, coinciding with the cultural "renaissance" in South Korea. Most Koreans, however, were preoccupied with making a living instead of asserting their Korean cultural identity. While a majority of the first wave of post-1965 Korean immigrants were college-educated, including a sizable number of professionals, many were unable to find jobs in the professional fields for which they were trained. Forced into self-employment in high-risk, low-income small businesses such as green groceries, fast food restaurants, laundries, and other service occupations, Koreans have generally avoided the performing arts. While there is evidence of gradually growing interest, particularly among the youth as they grapple with issues of identity construction, cultural expression through music and dances is the focus of a relatively small group of artists concentrated in Hawaii, California, the New York/New Jersey area, and in the Midwest.

In Hawaii, the Halla Pai Huhm Studio remained the center for Korean dance. Recitals focused on the studio's Korean dance repertoire—including dances to popular folk songs such as "Arirang" and "Toraji," *Mu Gi* (Exercise Dance), *Putchae Chum* (Fan Dance), *Kum Mu* (Knife Dance), *Puk Chum* (Drum Dance), *Sol Changgo* (Hourglass Drum Dance), *Sung Mu* (Monk's Drum Dance), *Chunaengjun* (Nightingale Dance), and *Salpuri* (Shaman-inspired female dance). Mary Jo Freshley (Pai Myong-sa is the studio name given to her by Huhm) has been studio instructor since 1973. Yun Hi Joo (whose studio name is Pai Mu-sun) taught at the studio from the late 1970's into the 1980's.

In 1974, Kum Yon Sung and Yung Hee Ji, master musicians of *minsok ak* (folk music), moved to Hawaii from Korea. Sung was designated South Korea's Human Cultural Treasure Number 23 for *kayagum* (12-string plucked zither), and Ji was designated Human Cultural Treasure Number 52 for *sinawi* (small improvisational music ensemble). Until the late 1970's, they taught Korean music in Honolulu with the assistance of their daughter, Soon Ja Choi, who played *kayagum and taught dance, and son-in-law, Kyung Man Choi, who played changgo* (double-headed, hourglass-shaped drum) and *piri* (double-reed aerophone). Sung taught *kayagum sanjo* (semi-improvisational music accompanied by *changgo*), *kayagum pyong chong* (singing accompanied by the zither), *minyo* (folk singing), and also her own compositions. Ji, a master musician as well as dancer, taught *changgo* drumming, *haegum* (bowed 2-stringed fiddle), and other *sinawi* instruments—including *piri*, *taegum* (transverse flute), *kayagum*, *komungo* (6-stringed zither plucked with a stick), *ajaeng* (bowed 7-stringed zither), and *ta ak ki* (percussion instruments) including *puk* (double-headed barrel drum), *ching* (large flat gong), and *kkwaenggwari* (small flat gong). Their studio closed with the death of Ji in 1980, and after the death of Sung in 1986, the rest of the family left Hawaii for the Los Angeles area.

Byong Won Lee, a professor of ethnomusicology, has taught at the University of Hawaii since 1974. The most prominent ethnomusicologist of Korean music in the United States, Lee's research ranges from Korean Buddhist *pompae* (chanting) to the development of traditional music in Korea, and music in Yan Bian, the Korean autonomous region in the People's Republic of China. Lee plays *tanso* (high-pitched end-blown flute), *taegum*, *puk*, *changgo*, and *kkwaenggwari*.

Ensemble groups in Hawaii include several *nongak* (farmers' music) groups—largely consisting of senior citizens—which have been active in the Wahiawa and Kalihi-Palama areas of Oahu, celebrating the major Korean holidays such as *Chusok* and *Ku Chung*.

Pansori (dramatic song genre accompanied by the *puk*) was the focus of an award-winning Korean film released in 1993, *Sa Pyon Jae*, which greatly moved Koreans and Korean Americans alike. Nevertheless, the dramatic song form is not performed by many in either Korea or the United States. Chan Eun Park, resident of Honolulu, is the only known *pansori* artist in the United States. What sets Park aside from *pansori* performers in Korea is that she has a background in Western theater and she is fluent in English as well as Korean. Her education makes possible her unique bilingual performances of such stories as "Shim Chlong" (The Filial Daughter). While she uses English to enhance accessibility for a non-Korean-speaking audience, she otherwise makes no conscious effort to alter the tradition. However, while the structure is unchanged, by definition the *pansori* form—like most other Korean performance forms—allows for some improvisation within the boundaries of the song and

Korean American college students perform the traditional mask dance at the 1991 Los Angeles Koreatown Festival. (The Korea Society/Los Angeles)

Korean Senior Citizens League performers play traditional Korean musical instruments on Festival Day, Los Angeles. (The Korea Society/Los Angeles)

dramatic narration structure.

Others who choreograph in the modern dance field include Sin Cha Hong, who travels between Hilo, Hawaii and Seoul, and Trina Nahm-Mijo, a third-generation Korean American who lives in Hilo. Nahm-Mijo's work includes "Wheels" (danced by wheelchair-bound dancers); "Children of War," and "To Omoni" (To Mother).

The best known group in the *pungmulpae* (outdoor band music and dance) genre, Samulnori, has a following in Hawaii and the continental United States. The Seoul-based group, led by Duk Soo Kim, has taught workshops in the United States, including the states of Hawaii and New York. The ensemble's name derives from the four basic instruments played—the *changgo*, *kkwaenggwari*, *puk* and *ching*. (*Samul* means "four things," and *nori* means "to play.") *Samulnori* has become a generic name for groups now playing in Los Angeles, Hawaii, Chicago, and in the New York/New Jersey area.

In Los Angeles, where the largest Korean American community resides, Don (Dong Suk) Kim—a *kayagum* specialist—founded a professional performing group in 1973 called the Korean Classical Music and Dance Company. A graduate of the Korean Classical Academy and Seoul National University, he later studied ethnomusicology at the University of California, Los Angeles (UCLA). Kim founded his company because he felt that the Korean American community needed traditional music and dance to increase its visibility and to maintain its ethnic heritage. In 1993 the company gave some two hundred performances, many of which were in the California school system. The company has performed at the Santa Barbara Bowl, and at the annual festival, Hankuk Eui Nal, which began in 1973. Kim also hosts two radio shows on Korean music.

Although Kim manages a professional company, most other Korean dancers and musicians do not make a living from the performing arts. Even the professional-level traditional musician, Byung Sang Lee, and his wife, musician and dancer Yoon Ja Ji, are dependent on their fast-food business for their livelihood, and manage to perform about five times a year. The son-in-law and daughter of Kum Yon Sung and Yung Hee Ji, they moved to Orange County in 1979, where they teach *kugak* (traditional folk Korean dance and music, literally "national music") during their free time. Byung Sang Lee teaches both *chung ak* (classical music) and *minsok ak*. More specifically, he teaches *kagok* (classical singing) and *minyo*, *taegum sanjo* and *taegum sinawi*, and gives instruction in *changgo* and *tanso*. Yoon Ja Ji teaches dances including *Kamyun Chum* (double mask dance), *Hwa Kwan Mu* (Crown Flower Dance), *Pu Chae Chum* (Fan Dance), *Sung Mu*, and *Salpuri*. To interest their son Sang Yun (Daniel), and daughter Chul Hee (Ruth) in Korean traditional music, Lee, a devout Christian, founded a *samulnori* group called Hosanna Kugak Sun Kyo Tan (Hosanna Traditional Music Mission Team) in 1989. About ten other *samulnori* groups have sprouted up in the Los Angeles and Orange County area. In the early 1970's, a group of Korean performing artists formed Je Mi Kugak Won (Korean Traditional Music and Dance Institute) with Ye Kun Lee as president and Byung Sang Lee as vice-president. In 1980, a new group was formed by Lee and others, called Je Mi Kugak Huyp Hwe (Korean Traditional Music and Dance Association).

Other California-based artists include Ki-ha Lee, a resident of Los Angeles. Trained in ballet and modern dance as well as traditional Korean dance, Lee choreographs modern work using traditional Korean dance vocabulary to express her personal experiences as an immigrant woman in works such as "Crossing." Hi-ha Park, based in Santa Monica, was a musician and dancer at the Korean National Classical Music Institute from 1963 until she came to the U.S. in 1966. She holds an M.F.A. in dance from UCLA, where she taught in 1975; she also taught in the music department at the University of California, San Diego, in 1984. She was initiated as a *mudang* in 1981. She conducts workshops, lectures, and performances which focus on *Mu-a* (no-self) through her *mudang* practices and shaman dances, integrating sound and movement improvisation.

The Midwest. In the Twin Cities area of Minnesota there is a Korean American population of more than 12,000, about 10,000 of whom are Korean adoptees. The Theater Mu theater company has begun to meet some of the cultural needs of these youth. The company was founded in 1992 by Dong-il Lee, Rick Shiomi, Diane Espaldon, and Martha Johnson, with the hope of creating a means of building an Asian American community in the Twin Cities. Performance pieces developed and premiered by Theater Mu include "Han Puri" by Dong-il Lee, "Grace" By Diane Espaldon, Rose Chu, and Sophia Kim, "Kotgam" by Andrew Kim, "Mask Dance" by Rick Shiomi, "Mistaken Identity" by Sara Dejoras, and "Woman Warrior" by Lily Tsong.

Now residing in Madison, Wisconsin, Peggy Myo-Young Choy has a perspective on dance and choreography that reflects her background as a third-generation Korean American who grew up in Hawaii's multiethnic context with roots in a Korean community. In 1992, five days after the Los Angeles uprising, she produced, directed, and performed in "Rooted in Our Bones: Afro-Asian Arts Dialogue," a festival which brought together performers of Asian and African American ethnicity. Participants included Madison organizations, the Mary Bethune Club and the Pacific and Asian Women's Alliance, Winae Kang, poets Shoua Vang, Sophea Mouth, Ger Thao, and Kalamu ya Salaam, and composer Fred Ho. Choy's "Seung Hwa: Rape/Race/Rage/Revolution," choreographed in 1993, is a suite which includes "Sajin Shinbu/Picture Bride," "Chongshindae/Comfort Woman," "En Chong Kerr," and "Seung Hwa" (transcendence after great suffering).

The Korean Culture and Resource Center (KCRC), serving Chicago's Korean community of about fifty thousand, was founded in 1986 by largely bilingual college students of the "1.5 GENERATION" (Korean Americans born and at least partly schooled in Korea), some of whom were involved in the democracy movement in Korea. Its goals include participatory education (Korean history, immigrant history); promotion of cultural identity through music, dance, arts, and theater; community service; and research. *Il kwa nori* (literally "work and play"—dance and music which includes *samulnori* ensemble practice) is taught in workshops. Started by KCRC's director Nam Hee Lee, along with Mihae Kim and Tae Hun Park, *il kwa nori* is performed on public occasions including cultural nights and international fairs.

New York/New Jersey Area. Most of the Korean music and dance activity on the East Coast takes place in New Jersey and New York. Among the most innovative artists is Sun Ock Lee, master of traditional Korean dances, including *Sung Mu* and *Salpuri*. Trained by teachers such as Mei Bang Lee, Young Sook Han, Chun Heung Kim, Sook Kim, and Sa Sup Chun, Lee first learned modern dance, including Graham technique, and ballet from Cho Kim Paik in Korea. Moving to the United States in 1969, she was a member of the All Nations Company from 1972 to 1974, and performed extensively under the auspices of the Asia Society from 1974. She earned a Ph.D. degree in art from New York University in 1984. Since the mid-1970's, she has developed Zen Dance (*Son Mu*)—a form of movement meditation rooted in Korean *Son* (Buddhist meditation)—and founded her Zen Dance Company in 1976. Other artists active in the New York/New Jersey area include modern dancers Myung Sook Chun, Myung-Soon Kim, and Young Soon Kim and traditional dancers Yoon Sook Park and Ah-Shon Jung. Korean dance and music organizations include the Korean Performing Arts Center and the Korean Traditional Music Institute of New York. New York-based musicians include Sang Won Park, who plays the *kayagum*, and contemporary musician Jin Hee Kim, who plays the *komungo*.—*Peggy Myo-Young Choy*

SUGGESTED READINGS: • Lee Byongwon. "Contemporary Korean Musical Cultures." In *Korea Briefing, 1993*, edited by Donald N. Clark. Boulder, Colo.: Westview Press, 1993. • Nishiguchi, Ann Kikuyo. "Korean Dance in Hawaii: A Study of the Halla Pai Huhm Korean Dance Studio." Master's thesis, University of California, Los Angeles, 1982. • Riddle, Ron. "Korean Musical Culture in Los Angeles." *Selected Reports in Ethnomusicology* 6 (1985): 189-196. • Sutton, R. Anderson. "Korean Music in Hawaii." *Asian Music* 19 (1987): 99-120.

Korean National Association (KNA): Organization formed in the United States in 1909 to promote and protect the rights of Koreans and to advance the cause of Korean independence from Japan. On February 1, 1909, the KNA, or Tae-Han Kungminhoe, was organized in San Francisco and Honolulu, merging all the existing Korean organizations and becoming the representative group of the entire Korean population then residing in North America. Consisting of the North America Regional General Assembly in San Francisco and the Hawaii Regional General Assembly in Honolulu, the KNA assumed the role of a semigovernment among the Koreans in Hawaii, maintaining its own police and even collecting poll taxes. In its early years, the KNA came under the strong influence of AHN CHANG-HO and PARK YONG-MAN.

In 1915, the controversy surrounding the way in which Syngman RHEE gained control of the KNA of Hawaii started long bitter disputes within the Korean community between those who supported Rhee and those who supported Park. Thereafter, the KNA of Hawaii acted independently of the KNA of North America. Under the domination of Rhee, its name was changed to Korean Residents Association of Hawaii in 1922. With the decline of Rhee's influence, however, it was renamed the KNA of Hawaii in 1933.

In the meantime, the KNA of North America gradually weakened after its leader, Ahn Chang-ho, moved to China in 1919, and the split with Rhee made it even less effective as a united Korean organization. In 1937, a new leadership took over control of the KNA of North America and, together with its counterpart in Hawaii, played the leading role in supporting the Korean independence movement through financial, diplomatic, and other efforts. In 1953, having witnessed the territorial division of Korea, the KOREAN WAR (1950-1953), and Rhee's virtual dictatorship in South Korea, the KNA of North American adopted a new bylaw asking its members to work for the establishment of a genuinely democratic government and the reunification of Korea. With the passing of the first generation of Korean immigrants in the United States, the KNAs of North America and Hawaii gradually lost their vigor, although they continued to maintain their headquarters in both Los Angeles and Honolulu.

Korean National Revolutionary Party of Los Angeles: Organization concerned with Korean political issues and U.S. policy toward Korea. The evolution of the organization reflected the complexity of Korean nationalist politics in the United States.

The party had its origins in the 1930's as a grassroots movement among Koreans in Los Angeles, who demonstrated at the Japanese consulate there after Japan invaded China in 1937. In 1939, a small group of Korean Americans founded the China-Aid Society, to aid Chinese refugees and support Korean independence fighters based in China, who engaged in espionage and guerrilla actions against the Japanese.

In 1941, the China-Aid Society changed its name to the Korean Volunteer Corps Aid Society in China. The Korean Volunteer Corps, headed by Kim Won Bong, united the leftist factions among Korean independence fighters. Kim had been one of the founders of the Korean National Revolutionary Party, a coalition of Korean independence groups formed in China in 1935. In Los Angeles in January, 1943, the Korean Volunteers Corps Aid Society in China became the American chapter of the Korean National Revolutionary Party.

In September of 1943, the party began publishing a weekly newspaper, *The Korean Independence*. After World War II, the paper's editorial stance was strongly critical of U.S. policy in Korea and sympathetic to North Korea. The Justice Department began deportation proceedings against several party members, including Diamond Kimm, whose case—*KIMM V. ROSENBERG* (1960)—went to the Supreme Court. In 1955, the party disbanded.

Korean nationalist politics in the United States: The politics of the Korean nationalists in the United States involved largely the struggle to regain the political independence of Korea from Japanese rule. Altogether about ninety-five hundred Koreans came to the United States between 1899 and 1932. Of these, about seventy-three hundred went to Hawaii between 1903 and 1905. The arrivals of the early Korean immigrants in the United States coincided with the demise of Korea when Japan annexed the country in 1910. The loss of Korea's independence made almost all the Koreans in the United States ardent nationalists, and the United States became an important center for Korean nationalist activities. One can divide the politics of the Korean nationalists into three periods: up to 1910, from 1910 to 1945, and from 1945 onward.

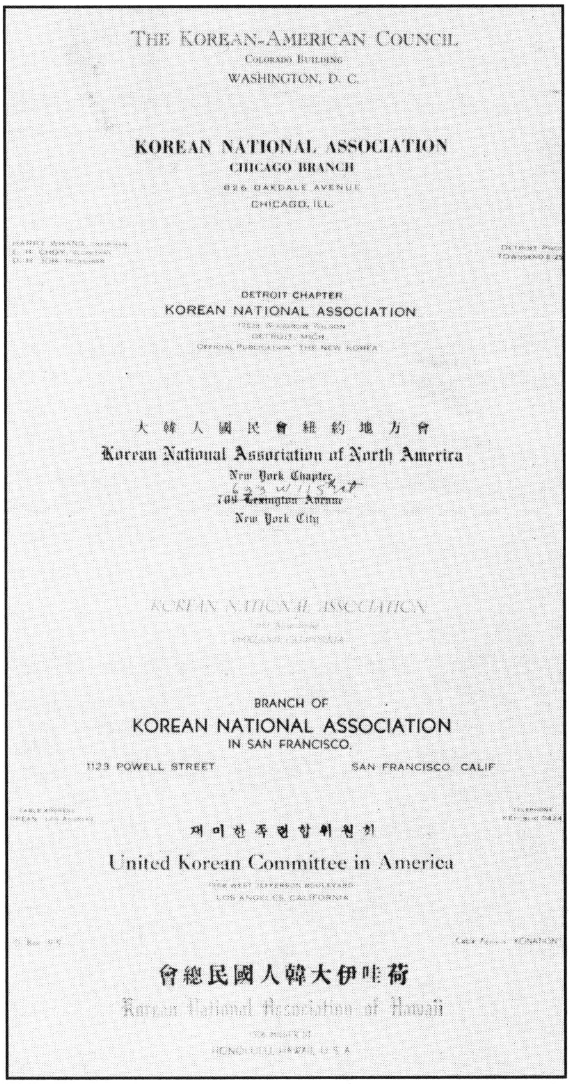

Korean National Association letterheads from branches across the United States. (The Korea Society/Los Angeles)

The First Period. The period before 1910 witnessed the appearance of many Korean organizations formed to promote the welfare of Korean Americans. In 1909 the KOREAN NATIONAL ASSOCIATION (KNA) was formed as a unifing organization of these various groups. In 1905 Yun Pyong-gu and Syngman RHEE, representing the Koreans in the United States, attempted unsuccessfully to plead the Korean cause to President Theodore Roosevelt, as he convened the peace conference to conclude the Russo-Japanese War. In 1908, at San Francisco, Chang In-hwan and Chon Myong-un assassinated Durham W. Stevens, an American working for the Japanese government as a spokesman justifying the Japanese domination of Korea.

The Second Period. In July, 1910, as the annexation of Korea by Japan became imminent, the KNA adopted a resolution calling on all Koreans in the United States to take "hostile actions" against Japan and appealing to the Korean emperor to resist the Japanese to the end. After Japan annexed Korea in August, 1910, military camps were set up at several places in the continental United States and Hawaii to train young Koreans to fight the Japanese. The leading figure in these endeavors was Park Yong-man, who later clashed with Rhee when Korean independence forces established a provisional government in exile.

The outbreak of the MARCH FIRST MOVEMENT in Korea in 1919 prompted a flurry of activities by Korean nationalists. In April, under the guidance of So Jae-pil (Philip JAISOHN), the Korean Liberty Congress was held in Philadelphia for three days to publicize the Korean cause, culminating in a parade leading to Independence Hall. This congress organized the Korean Information Bureau, which published *Korean Review* from April, 1919, until 1922 and many pamphlets reporting Japanese atrocities and calling for Korean independence. The bureau also actively worked to enlist American supporters in the League of the Friends of Korea. In August, Rhee, acting as the president of the newly created Korean provisional government, established the Korean Commission in Washington, D.C., to work for winning public support for Korean independence, especially among the leaders in the U.S. government, particularly in Congress. As a result of these activities, Senators Selden P. Spencer of Missouri and George W. Norris of Nebraska separately raised the Korean question on the Senate floor in June and July of 1919 favoring the cause of the Korean nationalists. In the same year Rhee issued public bonds in the name of the provisional government to raise funds for the nationalist struggle.

In 1921-1922, during the Washington Disarmament Conference, the Korean Commission prepared a forty-four-page "Brief for Korea" to appeal for Korean independence. Also, Jaisohn had a sympathetic talk with President Warren G. Harding and Secretary of State Charles Evans Hughes on the inhumane Japanese policies in Korea. The Korean Commission also attempted, albeit unsuccessfully, to present to the Washington Conference the Petition of the Korean People's Representatives signed by the leaders of many social and religious organizations in Korea.

In spite of these dedicated efforts, discord and schisms often developed among the Korean leaders because of differences in their personalities and divergence in their approaches to achieving the goal of independence. The KNA and the Tongji-hoe (Comrade Society) were the two largest organizations, the latter supporting Rhee and the former opposing him. With the call for a united effort against Japan by all the Korean organizations, however, the Convention for the Koreans Abroad was held in Honolulu in April, 1941, and organized the United Korean Committee in America to wage an all-out struggle against Japan. Following the Pearl Harbor attack, the United Korean Committee was successful in obtaining for the Koreans residing in the United States exemption from the Alien Registration Act of 1940 and from the freezing of their assets by the federal government. Although its attempt to gain recognition of the Korean provisional government as the legitimate government of Korea was not fruitful, the United Korean Committee successfully lobbied to hoist the Korean national flag in several

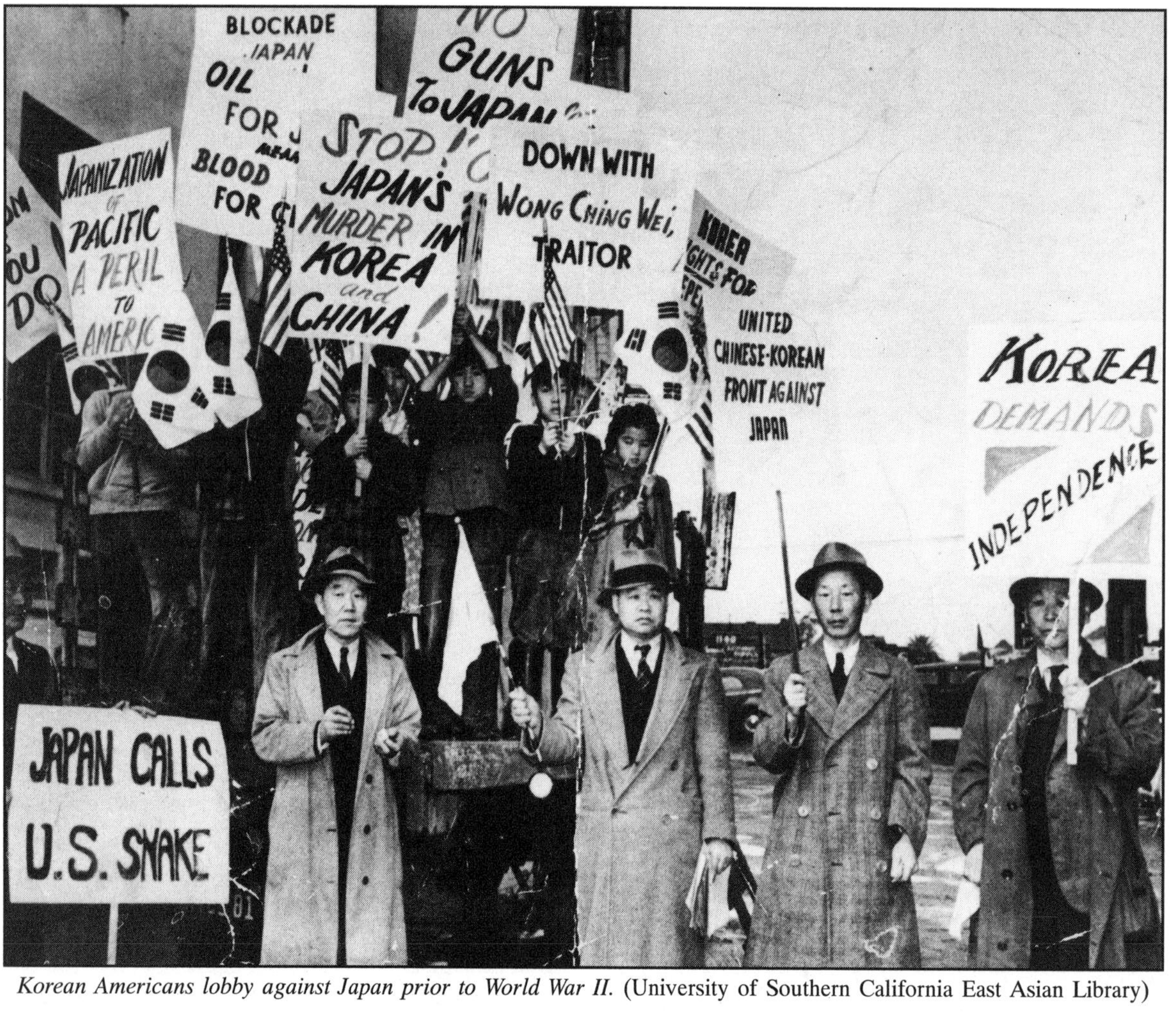

Korean Americans lobby against Japan prior to World War II. (University of Southern California East Asian Library)

Protesters in Los Angeles Koreatown encounter police after they attempted an impromptu march down Olympic Boulevard protesting the government of Chun Doo Hwan. (The Korea Society/Los Angeles)

cities, including Los Angeles, Chicago, St. Louis, and Pittsburgh in 1943 to demonstrate Korean determination in the war against Japan. The committee also raised from the Korean immigrants $26,265, which was presented to President Franklin D. Roosevelt in 1943. In April, 1945, when the United Nations Conference was held at San Francisco, delegates from several Korean organizations worked unsuccessfully to have Korea represented at that meeting.

The Third Stage. After the liberation and division of Korea in 1945, the efforts of the Korean nationalists in the United States were directed largely toward bringing about the reunification and democratization of Korea. With the passing of the first generation (pre-1945) of Korean immigrants to the United States, however, the social backgrounds of the Koreans in the United States underwent significant changes. Between 1950 and 1964, 14,366 Koreans came to the United States, most of whom were either students or brides of American servicemen. After the IMMIGRATION AND NATIONALITY ACT OF 1965, the number of Korean immigrants increased rapidly, most of them seeking new economic opportunities. Although they were preoccupied with settling down in the new cultural environment, they did not lose sight of the political situation in Korea, and a number of them continued to demand the democratization and liberalization of the Korean government. In 1992 a political event of major importance for Koreans in the United States took place when Jay KIM was elected to the U.S. House of Representatives as a Republican in the 41st District of California, thus becoming the first Korean American ever to be elected to Congress.—*Yong-ho Choe*

SUGGESTED READINGS: • Choy, Bong-youn. *Kore-*

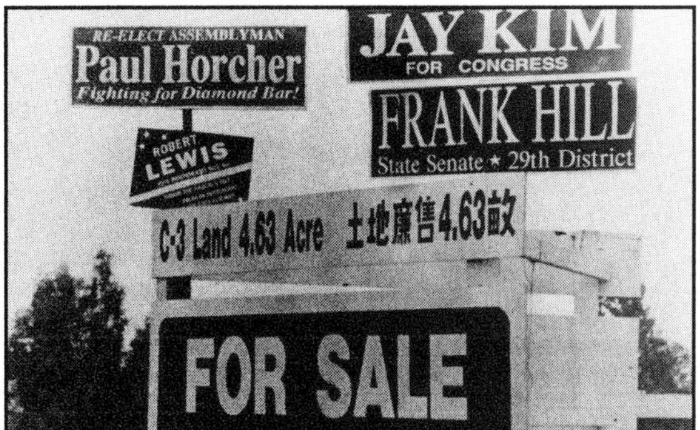

Campaign sign promotes Jay C. Kim for the U.S. Congress. (Korea Times)

ans in America. Chicago: Nelson-Hall, 1979. • Kim Won-yong. *Chaemi Hanin 50-nyon sa* (Fifty-year History of the Koreans in the United States). Reedley, Calif.: Charles Ho Kim, 1959. • Lee, Chong-sik. *The Politics of Korean Nationalism*. Berkeley: University of California Press, 1963. • Lyu, Kingsley K. "Korean Nationalist Activities in Hawaii and the Continental United States, 1900-1945." *Amerasia Journal* 4: 1-2 (1977). • Pang Son-ju. *Chaemi Hanin ui tongnip undong* (The Independence Movement of the Koreans in the United States). Chunchon, Korea: Hallim University Press, 1989.

Korean provisional government: Government in exile set up in China in April, 1919, by the Korean nationalists to fight for the restoration of Korea as an independent nation. Following the March First movement of 1919, the provisional government was organized in Shanghai to proclaim Korea as an independent nation. It was to be a unified government embracing all Korean groups fighting for Korea's independence and would coordinate and give overall direction to further nationalist activities. It also adopted a provisional constitution, declaring itself as a republic and guaranteeing equality and freedom for all Koreans.

Syngman Rhee promotes a general election for Korea in 1947. (AP/Wide World Photos)

Syngman Rhee was chosen as the first president, while Yi Tong-hwi was selected as the premier, along with several prominent nationalists in cabinet posts. A secret network of communication systems was to be organized in every province and county in Korea to establish a liaison with the provisional government. Also, the Korean Commission was created in the United States at the direction of Rhee to work for Korean independence. Many Koreans residing in the United States contributed generously to help finance the commission's activities.

Once the momentum created by the March First movement was gone, discord developed within the provisional government, rendering it less effective as a unified government. In 1932, under the direction of Kim Ku, Yi Pong-chang threw a hand grenade toward the Japanese emperor in Tokyo, and Yun Pong-gil set off a bomb in Shanghai, killing or wounding several Japanese dignitaries. These two bombing incidents caught the attention of the Chinese Nationalist leaders, who thereafter provided financial and other assistance to the provisional government, then under the leadership of Kim Ku. On December 10, 1941, following the Pearl Harbor attack, the provisional government issued the declaration of war against Japan and organized the Korean Restoration Army in 1942 to fight the Japanese. In 1945, the members of the provisional government returned to Korea only as individual citizens, and attempts to be recognized as a representative government were not successful. In 1948, when the Republic of Korea was inaugurated in South Korea, with Rhee as its first president, it was acknowledged as the spiritual successor of the provisional government.

Korean residents' associations: Usually nonprofit fraternal organizations found throughout the United States. These groups have flourished particularly in the wake of the Immigration and Nationality Act of 1965, under which many Koreans have come to the United States.

Korean special events: There are numerous traditional festive days and modern national holidays observed in Korea throughout the year. All the centuries-old traditional festive days are based on and celebrated by the lunar calendar, which was utilized in Korea until the beginning of the twentieth century. Most national holidays of recent origin are based on historical events and are observed by the solar almanac. Some of the modern holidays discussed below are observed only in South Korea, reflecting the political and cultural differences between the South and the North since the post-World War II division of Korea.

Traditional Festive Days. Sol (Lunar New Year's Day) means the "first day of the year." This New Year's Day of the lunar calendar is celebrated as one of the most important traditional events of the year. All family members, dressed in their best clothes or in colorful traditional clothes (*hanbok*), observe a memorial service devoted to the souls of their ancestors. Young people offer deep bows to the elders in the family and go around the neighborhood to offer similar greetings to their older relatives and acquaintances. In greeting one another, people exchange wishes for the new year. After these ancestral ceremonies and greetings, men may play *yut* (four-stick game), boys may fly kites, and women may ride a *nol* (Korean seesaw).

Taeborum (Day of Great Full Moon) is the day of the first full moon of the year, which falls on the 15th day of January by the lunar calendar. Early in the morning all members of the family, including children, drink wine, which is believed to improve the drinker's hearing. *Yakpap*, boiled rice mixed with various fruits and sweets, is served so that those who eat it may be free from tumors during the rest of the year. Families crack open various kinds of nuts or blast firecrackers to exorcise harmful spirits, insects, and animals. After dinner people climb a nearby hill to greet and say their wishes to the first full moon of the year. Whoever sees the full moon first is considered the most lucky. In the evening, under the moonlight, people play a variety of traditional games, including *Kanggang suwollae* (Korean circle dance).

Hansik (Day of Cold Feast) is the 105th day after the winter solstice (Tongji). Family members eat cold food and keep their rooms unheated throughout the day. They observe a memorial service at the graves of their ancestors early in the morning and tidy up the surroundings of tombs.

Tano is May 15 on the lunar calendar. During this ancient agricultural festival, people pray for good crops, a bountiful harvest, and protection from disaster. They wash their hair with iris water in the morning as a good luck charm. In the afternoon men may engage in *ssirum* (Korean wrestling).

Chusok, or Hangawi (Korean Thanksgiving Day) is a harvest moon festival that falls on August 15 on the lunar calendar. It is celebrated as enthusiastically as

Many Korean Americans dress in the Korean national costume to celebrate the lunar New Year.

Many Koreans make and eat Songpyon (rice cakes) on Chusok, Korean Thanksgiving Day. (Korea National Tourism Corporation)

Sol. As a celebration of the harvest, people thankful for the bounty of the earth prepare a table laden with newly harvested crops, including grain, fruits, nuts, rice cakes, meat, and wines.

Tongji (Winter Solstice Day) is the shortest day of the year, falling on or about December 22 on the solar calendar. This day calls for preparation of patchuk, which is rice gruel boiled together with red beans. Some of this gruel is pasted on the gate or wall as a charm against the gods of plague.

Modern National Holidays. New Year's Day (January 1) is a nationwide observance. The first two days of the New Year by the solar calendar are official holidays, although most people, especially in agricultural communities, still prefer to celebrate the Lunar New Year's Day.

Independence Day (March 1) commemorates the Korean Declaration of Independence on March 1, 1919, and the independence movement against Japanese colonial rule. The Korean people, led by thirty-three representatives, demanded immediate independence for Korea. Demonstrations against the Japanese took place throughout the country for more than a week.

On Arbor Day (April 5), all celebrants are asked to perform acts beneficial to the environment. According to the nation's reforestation program, which is trying to restore denuded forests and develop forest resources, people should go out to a nearby hill or field to plant seedlings on this day.

April 8 on the lunar calendar is believed to be the birthday of the Buddha. Solemn rituals are held at Buddhist temples across the country during the day, and paper lanterns are displayed and carried in parades on streets at night. According to the old customs, the believer in Buddhism is required to hang as many lanterns as the number of members in his family.

CHILDREN'S DAY (May 5) was originally founded to instill patriotic spirit into the hearts of Korean children under Japanese colonial rule. On this day the various parks and recreational places, including zoos and amusement parks, are open to children free of charge.

Memorial Day (June 6) is set aside to remember the loyalty of those people, who lost their lives serving the nation, including those who died in war.

Constitution Day (July 17) is held to commemorate the proclamation of the Constitution of the Republic of Korea (South Korea) on July 17, 1948. The constitution was prepared by about two hundred representatives of the people, who had been elected at the first general elections held under United Nations (UN) observation on May 10, 1948.

Liberation Day (August 15) commemorates the restoration of national independence from thirty-five years

(1910 to 1945) of Japanese colonial rule.

Armed Forces Day (October 1) observes the founding of the South Korean national armed forces in October, 1948. Many colorful military programs are displayed on the streets, seas, and air.

National Foundation Day (October 3) recalls the mythical founding of the Korean nation in 2333 B.C.E. by the legendary god-king Tangun, who is believed to have established the Kingdom of Ancient CHOSON in that year.

Christmas (December 25) is celebrated in South Korea as in the West.—*Jae-Bong Lee*

Korean American child visits with Santa Claus. (James L. Shaffer)

SUGGESTED READINGS: • Choe, Sang-Su. *Annual Customs of Korea: Notes on the Rites and Ceremonies of the Year*. Seoul: Seomun-dang, 1983. • International Cultural Foundation, ed. *Customs and Manners in Korea*. Seoul: Si-sa-yong-o-sa Publishers, 1982. • *Korea: Its People and Culture*. Seoul: Hakwon-sa. 1970. • Korean Overseas Information Service. *A Handbook of Korea*, 6th ed. Seoul: Seoul International Publishing House, 1987. • Nilsen, Robert. *South Korea Handbook*. Chico, Calif.: Moon Publications, 1988.

Korean students: The study abroad movement in modern Korea began at the start of the twentieth century among Korean students who wanted to modernize their country. The history of the movement may be divided into four periods: the early modernization period, 1876-1910; the Japanese colonial period, 1910-1945; the postliberation period, 1945-1965; and the post-1965 immigration period.

Early Modernization Period, 1876-1910. In 1876 Korea was forced to accept an unequal treaty with Japan, which had begun to develop colonial interests in Korea. Soon after the treaty, a group of thirteen Korean young men was sent to Japan in the summer of 1883 for military training. One of them was So Jae-pil (Philip JAISOHN), who returned to Korea in 1884 after his education at the Toyama Military School in Japan to participate in the Emeute of December, 1884. After the failure of the Emeute, So fled to Japan and subsequently came to the United States as a political exile. He later attended Lafayette College in Easton, Pennsylvania, and then The Johns Hopkins University, where he received his medical degree. He was probably the first person of Korean ancestry who received an American university degree.

Prior to So's study in America, Yu Kil-chun had come to America in 1883 as a member of the Korean Mission to the United States led by Min Young-ik. Yu had originally gone to Japan as a student attendant of a member of the Gentlemen's Tour Group dispatched by King Kojong of Korea in 1881. He decided to stay in Japan to study but was probably asked to serve the Korean Mission as an indirect interpreter for Percival Lowell, who was serving as an American secretary to Min Young-ik. Lowell employed a Japanese, Miyaoka, as his interpreter. It is quite possible that Yu was asked

Korean Students Enrolled in American Colleges and Universities by Selected Academic Years

Year	Number	Percent*
1980-1981	6,150	2.0
1985-1986	18,660	5.4
1987-1988	20,520	5.8
1988-1989	20,610	5.6
1989-1990	21,710	5.6
1990-1991	23,360	5.7
1991-1992	25,720	6.1

Source: Institute of International Education, *Open Doors*, 1980-1992.

* Indicates percentage of all foreign students enrolled in American colleges and universities.

Korean American college student chats with her instructor after a nutrition lecture. (James L. Shaffer)

to come with the mission as an interpreter for Miyaoka. Lowell was able to communicate in English with Miyaoka, who communicated in Japanese with Yu Kil-chun, who then interpreted in Korean for Min. Yu Kil-chun stayed in Salem, Massachusetts, to attend the Dummer Academy between 1883 and 1884.

Other students followed them to the United States to pursue further studies. In 1888, Yun Chi-ho came to America to attend Vanderbilt University. Kyu-sik Kim, who served as president of the Interim Legislative Assembly in Korea after the country's liberation in 1945, came to America to attend Roanoke College in 1897, graduating from the college in 1903. In 1902 AHN CHANG-HO came to America to study in San Francisco. Two years later, Syngman RHEE, who became president of the Republic of KOREA in 1948, came to the United States to attend Harvard and Princeton, graduating from the latter in 1910 with a Ph.D. degree in political science. He was probably the first person of Korean ancestry to graduate from an American university with a Ph.D. degree. Other Korean students who came to America before Japan's annexation of Korea as a colony in 1910 were Pak Cho-hun, Chong Han-kyong, Paik Il-kyu, Kim Chang-ho, Kim Hyon-gu, and PARK YONG-MAN, among others.

Many of them returned to Korea after their education in America and became involved in social and political activities aimed at modernizing Korea in the years before 1910. After 1910 some of them went into exile and came to America to continue their involvement in the Korean independence movement. Those who stayed in their country resisted Japanese colonial administration initially but were later coerced into cooperation by Japanese authorities. Yun Chi-ho was one of these people.

Japanese Colonial Period, 1910-1945. During this period of harsh Japanese colonial rule, many forces working together or separately pushed young Koreans out of their country and brought them to the United States. First, patriotic Koreans resisted Japanese colonialism and worked to strengthen Korea by organizing the people for education, economic self-sufficiency, and national consciousness. Japan's response to these efforts was swift and without mercy. Japan brought drummed-up charges against many Korean intellectuals, accusing them of plotting to assassinate the Japanese governor-general, and arrested 105 Korean leaders. This incident is known in Korean history as *Paek-o-in sagon*, or the "105-person incident." Many were tortured into confessing involvement in the plot. After this incident many patriotic Koreans left their country and came to America; two of these were Ahn Chang-ho and Chang Ri-wuk.

Still others fled from Korea after the suppression of the MARCH FIRST MOVEMENT in 1919, when Koreans throughout the country rose up to protest the harsh treatment they had received from the Japanese. Again, Japan's response to this mass rebellion was quick and ruthless. They killed women and children and imprisoned thousands. After the uprising many Koreans gave up any hope of gaining their nation's political independence soon and fled to America by way of China or Europe.

Others were allowed by Japan to come to America for their education. The number of Korean students who were sent was rather small; nevertheless, this was a significant departure from Japan's previous policy banning Koreans from leaving the country. Included among these students, who were usually called *Sindo haksaeng* (students who came over recently) by Koreans in America, were O Chon-sok and Kim Whalnan, both of whom became prominent later in the field of education in Korea after Korea's liberation. O became minister of education, while Kim served as president of Ehwa Women's University.

Postliberation Period, 1945-1965. The confluence of many socioeconomic, educational, and political factors contributed to the exodus of large numbers of Korean students, a majority of whom went to the United States for their education during this period. South Korea came under American influence after the end of World War II as a result of the decision to divide the Korean peninsula into two parts along the 38th parallel. The region north of the 38th parallel was occupied by Soviet troops, the region south of the parallel by American troops. The United States established a military government in South Korea that lasted until 1948. The American dominance over Korean society was felt particularly in the field of education. Many Korean students wanted to come to America to learn advanced science and technology as well as social sciences and the humanities, none of which was readily available in their country's schools.

The KOREAN WAR (1950-1953) created other conditions that attracted Korean students to American colleges and universities. During the war, which lasted for three years, many educational facilities were destroyed, and well-trained teachers were not available. Under these circumstances, American colleges and universities established educational exchange programs to assist their Korean counterparts by accepting Korean students for advanced studies. Schools such as

Graduates of the University of Dubuque, Dubuque, Iowa. (James L. Shaffer)

George Peabody College, the University of Michigan, Florida State University, Pittsburgh University, the University of Minnesota, and the University of Hawaii developed specialized programs for Korean students and Korean university faculty members. By the end of the 1964 academic year, there were a total of 4,202 Korean students in the United States. A total of 2,129 students were studying liberal arts, while the rest were studying natural sciences.

Post-1965 Immigration Period, 1965-1992. By the end of 1965, different socioeconomic, educational, and political forces began to work in Korean society. These forces compelled large numbers of Koreans, Korean students in particular, to emigrate to the United States. During the decade 1955 to 1965, Korean society experienced a high rate of unemployment, particularly among college-educated people, and many young aspiring Koreans wanted to leave Korea for better opportunities in the United States. This had not been available prior to the passage of the IMMIGRATION AND NATIONALITY ACT OF 1965. With the passage of this more liberal U.S. immigration law, college-educated Koreans emigrated in search of further education as well as employment. Some of these immigrant families had college-bound students who were reported as foreign students since they did not have U.S. citizenship status.

In the four decades after the end of the Korean War, Korean society experienced a high rate of population growth. The South Korean population more than doubled during this time, thus putting a great deal of pressure on the country's institutions of higher education. One of the ways used by Korean colleges and universities to cope with large numbers of applicants is to administer entrance examinations given both by the state and by individual institutions. Some universities have had five or six times more applicants than they can admit. Many of these students came to America to continue their education.—*Hyung-chan Kim*

SUGGESTED READINGS: • Choy, Bong-youn. *Koreans in America*. Chicago: Nelson-Hall, 1979. • Hong, Sok, ed. *Hanguk hyondae sa* (A Modern History of Korea). Seoul: Korean Education Research Institute, 1993. • Kim, Hyung-chan. "American Influence on Korean Education." *Educational Perspectives* 21, no. 4 (Winter, 1982): 27-32. • O, Chon-sok. *Hanguk Sin kyoyuk sa*. Soul Tukpyolsi: Hyondae Kyoyuk Chongso Chulpansa, 1964. • Thamos, John Alsop. *Korean Students in Southern California: Factors Influencing Their Plans Toward Returning Home*. Ann Arbor: UMI, 1981.

Korean War (1950-1953): Fought between North and South Korea, in which the United States along with fifteen other nations participated under the flag of the United Nations on the side of South Korea while the People's Republic of China (PRC) took part on the North Korean side. The war cost the lives of an estimated five million people.

Background. In 1945 Korea was divided along the 38th parallel by the United States and the Soviet Union. In 1948 the Republic of Korea (South Korea) was established with the support of the United States while the Democratic People's Republic of Korea (North Korea) was organized with the blessing of the Soviet Union.

Cause. The Korean War started on June 25, 1950, when North Korea launched a surprise general attack all along the 38th parallel with the intent to bring South Korea under its rule. Although there are controversies over the question of who actually started the war, the evidence, including testimonies given since the end of the Cold War by several former high North Korean officials who defected to the Soviet Union, leaves little doubt that North Korea was guilty of starting the war.

Spearheaded by more than two hundred tanks, the North Korean troops stormed southward seizing control of Seoul within three days. Ill-equipped and undermanned, the South Korean military was utterly unprepared to cope with the North Korean attack as the North Korean military was armed with vastly superior weapons, including tanks supplied by the Soviet Union. The confused and incompetent leadership exhibited by the high officials of the South Korean government and its military command during the early days of the war brought near disintegration of the South Korean government.

U.S. Reaction. Believing the Soviet Union to be behind the North Korean invasion, the United States decided that its global interest was at stake and that the security of the "free world" was being endangered. President Harry S Truman firmly believed that the North Korean aggression had to be stopped by force if necessary. The Korean War thus became the first testing ground for the newly formulated containment policy of the United States. At the initiative of the United States, the Security Council of the United Nations adopted a resolution requesting its member nations to "furnish such assistance to the Republic of Korea as may be necessary to repel the armed attack and to restore international peace and security in the area." It was under this mandate that the United States dispatched air, sea, and land forces to Korea under the

U.S. Marines advance through Inchon, Korea, after landing on the west coast of Korea near Seoul in 1950. (AP/Wide World Photos)

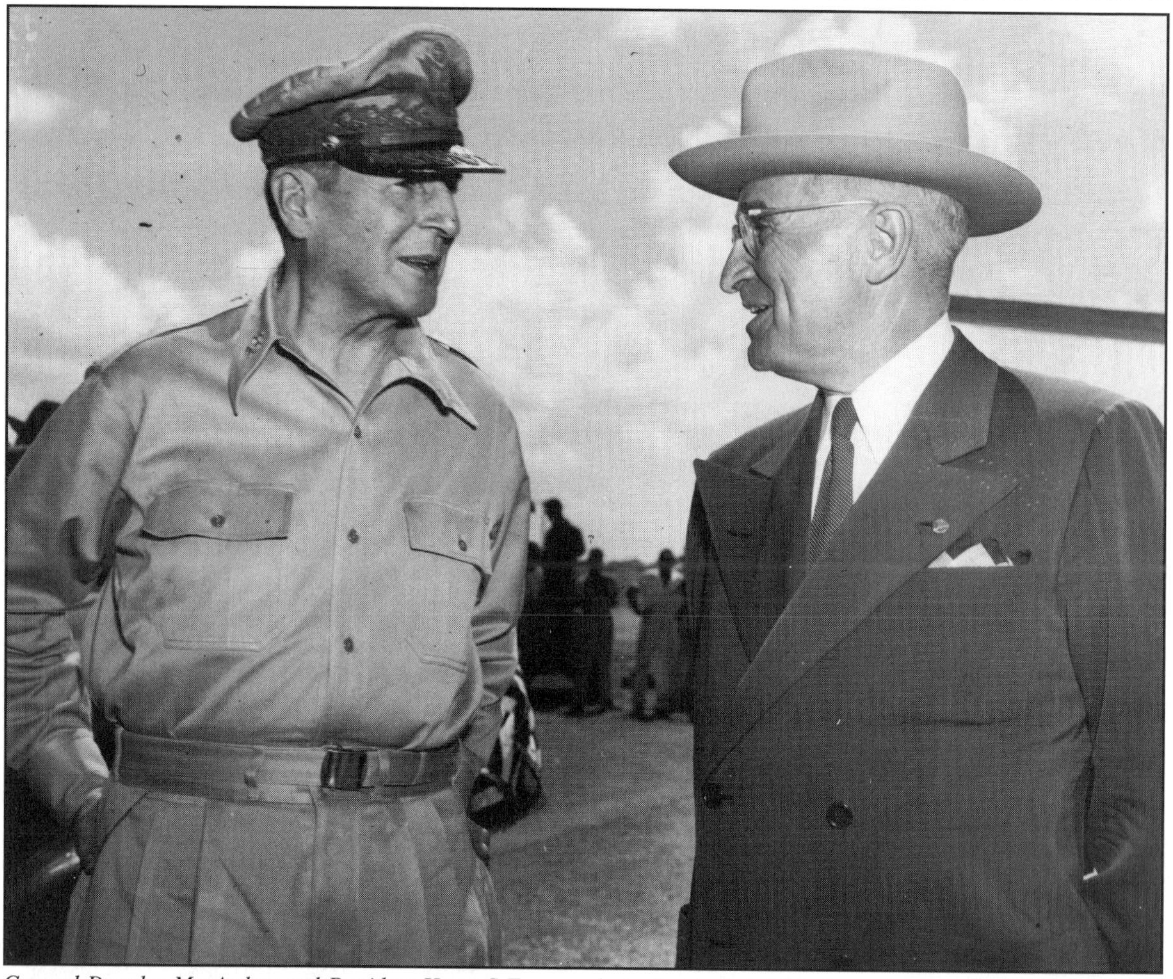

General Douglas MacArthur and President Harry S Truman chat prior to their historic conference on Wake Island. (AP/ Wide World Photos)

command of General Douglas MacArthur, who became the commander-in-chief of the United Nations Command (UNC).

War. In spite of the direct military intervention by the United States, the North Korean troops forced the American and South Korean ground troops to retreat to the Pusan perimeter in the southeastern corner of the Korean Peninsula by early August, 1950. There the North Koreans made several determined but unsuccessful attempts to push the UNC troops to the sea. In the meantime the UNC was reinforced with five American divisions and additional troops dispatched from fifteen other nations. On September 15, 1950, the UNC troops made a daring amphibious landing at Inchon, effectively cutting off the North Korean command, supplies, and communications and completely reversing the tide of the war in the UNC's favor.

Chinese Intervention. As the UNC troops marched toward the 38th parallel, the PRC issued warnings not to cross the parallel. Ignoring such warnings Truman authorized MacArthur to conduct military operations north of the 38th parallel with the objective of destroying the North Korean armed forces. After occupying Pyongyang, the North Korean capital, the UNC troops rushed toward the Yalu River. Meanwhile, undetected by the UNC, during October China had stealthily sent more than 200,000 troops into Korea in the name of the "Chinese People's Volunteers." In late November, when the UNC ordered its troops to advance in the final push for victory, they encountered an ambush by the Chinese troops, who in turn launched a counterattack that forced the UNC troops to retreat in great confusion to south of the 38th parallel. The Chinese military intervention added a new dimension to the Korean War that heightened the international tension even more.

Cease-Fire Negotiations. Regrouped under the new command of General Matthew B. Ridgway, the UNC ground troops launched a series of new offensives in the spring of 1951, pushing the battle line to north of the 38th parallel, where the fighting gradually stalemated. At the suggestion of Jacob Malik, the Soviet ambassador to the UN, cease-fire negotiations started between the UNC and the North Korean/Chinese command at Panmunjom in July, 1951. Although it was obvious that neither side desired to prolong the war, they could not agree upon several issues. One of the most difficult obstacles was the issue of the prisoners-of-war exchange. After long and tedious negotiations, which were interrupted on several occasions, the cease-fire terms were finally agreed upon and were formally signed in July, 1953. His desire to reunify the country under the South Korean government having been frustrated, South Korean President Syngman RHEE refused to commit his government to the terms of the cease-fire agreement.

Significance. Internationally the Korean War marked the beginning of tense relations in the Cold War confrontation between the two superpowers, the United States and the Soviet Union. It resulted in delaying for some time the possibility of reconciliation between the United States and the newly created PRC. It also led the United States to shift its policy toward Japan as to the rebuilding of that country's political and economic base as a bulwark against the spread of communism in Asia. Within the Korean Peninsula the war had the effect of deepening the animosity between North and South Korea, making it all but impossible to have a peaceful dialogue for many years to come. With the end of the war whatever reservations there might have been regarding the issue of the legitimacy of both regimes was removed, and each regime was able to exercise its firm control over its population, thus perpetuating the division of the country.—*Yong-ho Choe*

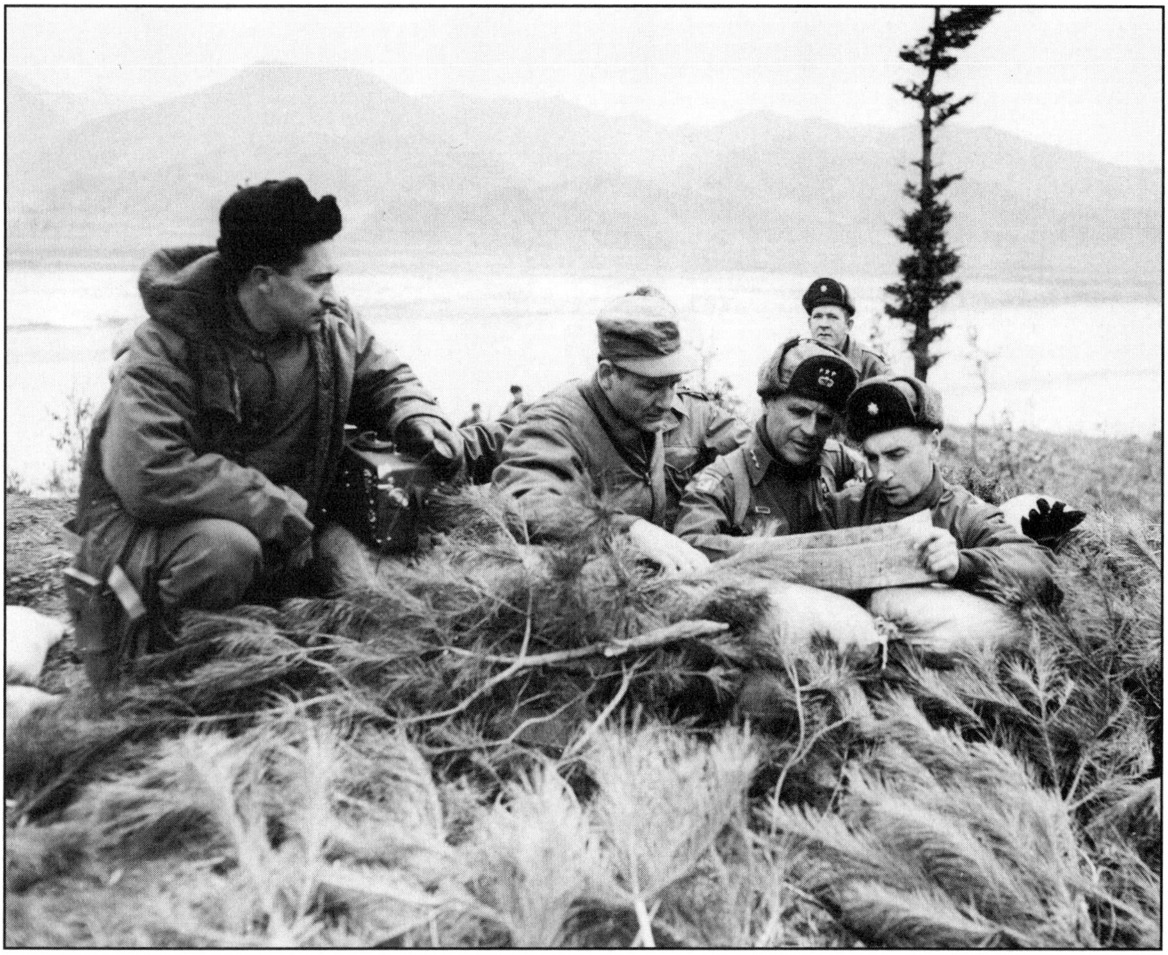

General Matthew B. Ridgway inspects a map indicating frontline positions abandoned by the Chinese. (AP/Wide World Photos)

SUGGESTED READINGS: • Appleman, Roy E. *South to the Naktong, North to the Yalu*. Washington, D.C.: Department of the Army, 1961. • Cumings, Bruce. *The Roaring of the Cataract, 1947-1950*. Vol. 2 in *The Origins of the Korean War*. Princeton, N.J.: Princeton University Press, 1990. • Matray, James I., ed. *Historical Dictionary of the Korean War*. New York: Greenwood Press, 1991. • Merrill, John. *Korea: The Peninsular Origins of the War*. Newark: University of Delaware Press, 1989.

Korean war brides: Korean women who emigrate to the United States as wives of U.S. servicemen stationed overseas since World War II. Korean war brides are one of the major social consequences of the occupation of the southern half of the Korean peninsula by the U.S. military government (1945-1948) and of the continuous U.S. military presence in South Korea since the Korean War (1950-1953). Since 1950 tens of thousands of Korean women have immigrated to the United States as wives of U.S. servicemen. There has been, however, a glaring lack of accurate data on their socioeconomic and demographic characteristics and the patterns of their adjustment to American culture and society in general and to prejudices against interracial marriages in particular. Available studies generally paint negative pictures of Korean war brides and pay little attention to the diversity of their social backgrounds, lifestyles, and patterns of acculturation.

Immigration. Although Public Law 271 was passed in December, 1945, to permit servicemen's brides to enter the United States, it made no provision for Asian war brides. It was not until the July, 1947, amendment that Asian women were legally permitted to marry American servicemen and enter the United States. Although the exact number of Korean war brides is unavailable, a rough estimate of the number can be derived from the immigration statistics on Koreans admitted to the United States as wives of U.S. citizens. According to the *Annual Report* published by the U.S. Immigration and Naturalization Service, one Korean woman was admitted to the United States as a wife of a U.S. citizen in 1950, when the Korean War broke out. A total of 2,636 women had immigrated to the United States as wives of U.S. citizens by the end of 1960. Since then a steady stream of Korean women has con-

Family prays together. (Don Franklin)

tinued to emigrate to the United States as wives of U.S. citizens, mainly because of the presence of a large U.S. military force in Korea. Approximately 100,000 Korean women entered the United States as wives of U.S. citizens between 1950 and 1990. These women constituted a major social category of Korean immigration to the United States until 1965, when the Immigration and Nationality Act abolished the long-standing inequitable quota system discriminating against immigrants from Asia.

Interracial Marriage. In Korean society marriage is regarded as not simply a private matter of the heart but as an important family affair. Traditionally it has been one of the prerogatives of the parents to arrange marriages for their children, and proper family backgrounds of the intended couple were considered more important than love for a successful marriage. Thus when interracial marriages between Korean women and American servicemen first began to occur, the social response of the Koreans toward such love-match marriages was extremely negative. Women who dated and married American soldiers were stereotyped as prostitutes. Prejudice against women in "international marriages"—as Koreans refer to marriages between a Korean and a foreign national—has lingered on both in Korea and in Korean immigrant communities in the United States.

Prejudice against interracial marriages, however, was also strong in American society, where antimiscegenation laws legalized social discrimination against interracial marriages. For example when the California law prohibiting interracial marriages of nonwhites to whites was repealed in 1948, it was the first time that a state had found antimiscegenation laws unconstitutional, and it was not until 1967 that the U.S. Supreme Court, in the case of *Loving v. Virginia*, ruled antimiscegenation laws unconstitutional. Reports from social casework counselors indicate that the U.S. Army's policy toward interracial marriages is to discourage them. The administrative procedures involved in an American soldier marrying a Korean national, for example, may take from several months to two years. Thus many soldiers are unable to complete the process before they leave Korea, aggravating the anxieties of the initial marital adjustment process for the Korean American couple.

Bok-Lim C. Kim finds that Korean war brides led happier and more satisfying lives while their American husbands were stationed in Korea than in the United States. Some major reasons include the buying power of the husband's wage in the Korean economy, many military privileges such as the access to the post exchange and commissary to purchase luxury items, and the psychological support the wife receives from her relatives and friends, which all contribute to the couple's feelings of adequacy, acceptance, and even superiority. Once the couple moves to the United States, however, various problems of adjustment ensue, affecting their marriage.

Typology. The scant literature on Korean war brides deals mostly with those who came to the United States in the 1950's and 1960's and suggests that they came generally from the lower stratum of Korean society. Bascom Ratliff and his associates as well as Kim, for example, wrote that many Korean war brides were prostitutes when they first met their American husbands. They also stated that the educational backgrounds of war brides were very meager. It should be pointed out, however, that the average number of years of schooling for all Korean females was 2.92 years in 1960 and 4.72 years in 1970. As Chon S. Edwards, a war bride of the early 1950's, points out, Korean war brides, especially younger ones who came to the United States after the 1970's, come from diverse social backgrounds, and the patterns of their adjustment in the United States are varied.

Korean war brides may be divided into three basic types: professionals who actively contribute to American society with their expertise and skills as professors, teachers, nurses, and so forth; full-time housewives, some of whom find the time and energy to carry out volunteer work for their local communities and to play the role of Korean cultural ambassadors toward their American friends and acquaintances; and working women in various retail and service industries.—*Chunghee Sarah Soh*

Suggested Readings: • Berwick, Stephen W. F. "From Chongnyangni to Northfield: The Story of a Korean Immigrant to America." *Korean Culture* 12, no. 1 (1991): 34-38. • Edwards, Chon S. *Nado hangukui ttal* (I am also a daughter of Korea). Seoul: Mirae Munhwasa, 1988. • Kim, Bok-Lim C. "Casework with Japanese and Korean Wives of Americans." *Social Casework* 53, no. 5 (1972): 273-279. • Kim, Sil Dong. "Interracially Married Korean Women Immigrants: A Study in Marginality." Ph.D. dissertation. Ann Arbor: University Microfilms International, 1981. • Ratliff, Bascom W., Harriett F. Moon, and Gwendolyn A. Bonacci. "Intercultural Marriage: The Korean-American Experience." *Social Casework* 59, no. 4 (1978): 221-226. • Shin, Eui-Hang. "Interracially Married Korean Women in the United States: An

Analysis Based on Hypergamy-Exchange Theory." In *Korean Women in Transition: At Home and Abroad*, edited by E. Y. Yu, E. H. Phillips, and E. S. Yang. Los Angeles: Center for Korean-American and Korean Studies, California State University, Los Angeles, 1987.

Korean Women's Patriotic Society (also, Taehan Yoja Aekook-dan): Coalition of Korean American women's organizations formed by early Korean immigrants in 1919 in Dinuba, California. It was the result of merging San Francisco's Korean Women's Society, Sacramento's Korean Women's Association, and Los Angeles' Women's Friendship Association. The society's main objectives included working with the KOREAN NATIONAL ASSOCIATION (KNA) to support the independence movement, raising funds, boycotting Japanese goods, and providing aid to needy Koreans in the United States and Korea.

Korean Youth and Community Center (KYCC): Community-based, nonprofit social services agency established by Korean Americans in 1975. Originally known as the Korean Youth Center, it began as an outreach project of the Asian American Drug Abuse Program in response to the growing concern that immigrant youths from Korea were gravitating toward gangs. In 1977 the center established its own advisory board, and in 1982 it was incorporated as an independent, nonprofit agency. In 1992 the organization was renamed the Korean Youth and Community Center. Over the years the agency has evolved into one of the largest centers serving Korean Americans in Los Angeles.

The KYCC functions as an important social outlet for many Korean Americans. The center is divided into five units to provide recreational activities, family services, job training and placement, and health education. The business unit organizes such efforts as Koreatown beautification and recycling projects, the counseling unit provides individual and family counseling, and the employment unit offers services in employment counseling and referrals, as well as summer job-training programs. The center's two education units provide school enrollment information services, a tutorial program, and a substance abuse prevention program.

Each of these units has defined goals to reach the Korean community effectively. The employment unit, for example, offers high-risk youths an opportunity to gain valuable on-site job training and skills in small business management. The education units offer academic assistance and skills-building activities to Korean American youths and their parents with limited English skills. The programs are particularly designed to help recently immigrated Korean American youths assimilate into the American school and social systems.

Under the leadership of Bong Hwan Kim, who became the director of the center in 1988, the KYCC's vision has expanded to encompass the larger multiethnic Los Angeles community. The KYCC has played an active role in building bridges between the Korean American and African American communities. The center also has initiated a housing development project to ease overcrowded living conditions for many Latino as well as Korean immigrants.

Korean Youth Military Academy: Military training center for Korean Americans, established in Hastings, Nebraska, in 1909. It was founded by PARK YONG-MAN, a Korean political activist who graduated from the University of Nebraska in the same year. Park's ultimate goal was to win Korea's independence from Japan. The academy was on a farm, where the cadets worked during the day and received military training in the evening. Starting with twenty-seven Korean cadets at the Nebraska academy, Park established four additional training centers, located in Claremont and Lompoc, California, Kansas City, Kansas, and Superior, Wyoming. In 1919, a similar center, a school for pilots, was established in Willows, California. (See FIRST KOREAN INDEPENDENCE AIR FORCE.)

Koreans in China: Ethnic Koreans in China live mostly in China's northeast region, Manchuria. The region, separated from the Korean peninsula by the Yalu Jiang and Tumen rivers, is the birthplace of the Hahn Koreans. The Yanbian Korean Autonomous Region in Jilin Province is where the greatest number of Koreans live.

Korea's oldest kingdom, Koguryo, controlled most of present Manchuria, the Chinese northeastern territory, until the kingdom's capital was moved in 427 C.E. to Pyongyang, from the Guknaesung in Manchuria. Korean kingdoms were never able to recover the vast, strategic territory from their powerful neighbor, the Han Chinese. Contemporary Koreans living in China are descendants of those who migrated to lightly populated Manchuria since the eighteenth century. Those early agricultural immigrants, mostly refugees of political instability and periodic famines, introduced irrigated rice farming to the region.

It was under the Japanese colonial rule, the period of 1910-1945, that Koreans built their strong presence, particularly in southern Manchuria. The political refugees seeking freedom from the Japanese colonial oppression built many Korean communities in the border region. There, in relative freedom, the Korean settlers engaged in anti-Japanese campaigns, from mainly unarmed protests during the 1910's to well-organized guerrilla warfare during the 1930's. They were the pillar of the Korean military resistance against Japanese colonial rule. For supporting the Korean independence movement, Korean residents suffered greatly. Still they adamantly supported the national cause, providing sanctuaries and logistical support for the resistance movements until the surrender of Imperial Japan in 1945.

After Korea's liberation in 1945, many Korean residents in China returned to Korea. Others who lived mostly in southern Manchuria chose to remain in China. In 1952, the People's Republic of China designated the Yanbian region as a Korean autonomous territory where all administrative agencies were headed by ethnic Koreans. Based on the 1990 census, there are 1,920,597 ethnic Koreans in China. The majority of them live in the three provinces of the northeast region: Jilin, Heilongjiang, and Liaoning. Small numbers of Koreans are found in the nation's major cities, such as Beijing and Shanghai.

Koreans in Hawaii: For nearly three-quarters of a century, until changes were made in the immigration laws in the 1960's, the small Korean community in Hawaii represented the largest concentration of Koreans in the United States. This community was characterized by a high degree of anti-Japanese feelings and Korean nationalism, a history of divisiveness, and a commitment to a better life for their children.

The Immigration Process. Seven thousand Koreans arrived in Hawaii between 1903 and 1905 to form the first community of Koreans in the United States. Most were adventurous single young men in their twenties whose prospects in Korea were not promising and for whom Hawaii offered the possibility of a better life. Their desire to leave Korea just before it was absorbed by Japan coincided with the interests of the HAWAIIAN SUGAR PLANTERS' ASSOCIATION to employ Koreans to offset the Japanese workers, who represented fully two-thirds of the plantation labor force.

The sugar planters were aided in their attempt by the American Minister to Korea, Horace ALLEN, who saw in the immigration of Koreans to Hawaii an economic link between Korea and the United States. Allen attempted to forge such links in the hopes that the United States would begin to take a political interest in Korea and reverse the hands-off policy which had characterized U.S. policy since relations were begun in 1882. Allen hoped that an active U.S. policy in Korea would help maintain Korea's independence in the face of increasing Japanese interest in the peninsular nation. As a consequence, Allen showed himself willing to interfere in Korea's domestic politics to persuade the Korean emperor to allow Koreans to leave. He also acquiesced in the violation of American immigration laws in assisting the planters in recruiting Koreans for work before they had left Korea and prepaying their passage to Honolulu.

Korean immigration came to an abrupt end in 1905 as a result of Japanese opposition. As Koreans arrived in Hawaii and were used to keep wages on the plantations low, Japanese in Hawaii left in increasing numbers for California, where wages were twice those in Hawaii. The influx of Japanese to California from Hawaii triggered calls for a Japanese Exclusion Act—an action potentially devastating to the proud nation of Japan, which saw itself as an equal to the United States. Tokyo concluded that the only way to prevent passage of such an act was to prohibit Koreans from going to Hawaii. In that way, wages for Japanese in Hawaii would rise to such a level that the economic urge to go to California would disappear and so too would calls for a Japanese Exclusion Act. And since Japan had a predominance of influence over Korea as a result of its victory in the Russo-Japanese War (1904-1905), it could manipulate the Korean government to do its bidding and keep Koreans from leaving for Hawaii. When Japan established a protectorate over Korea in late 1905 and then annexed Korea in 1910, Japan's domination became complete.

From the Sugar Plantation to the City. The sugar plantations in Hawaii were the first stop for most of the early Korean immigrants, as well as for many Japanese, Filipino, and Chinese immigrants. The work was arduous and low-paying (about 75 cents per day). Moreover, the Koreans neither liked nor were particularly adept at plantation work. And yet, unlike the Chinese and Japanese, half of whom returned to their native land, most of the Koreans chose to remain in Hawaii. There were two reasons for this. First, despite the hardships of Hawaii, they had left a country which was in a state of chaos, oppression, and maladministration. Second, soon after they arrived in Hawaii, their nation was colonized by Japan, rendering them, in a

Korean-American Club, 1927.

sense, stateless. But while the Koreans were determined to remain in Hawaii, they were also determined to leave the plantations. In fact, Koreans left the plantations faster than any other ethnic group in Hawaii's history. Being largely from the port cities of Korea, where they had toiled in urban-style occupations, Korean immigrants were not accustomed to agricultural work and soon sought out the city—primarily Honolulu—where they were more comfortable. And, given the socioeconomic structure of Hawaii, by leaving the plantation, Koreans had begun their first step up the socioeconomic ladder.

The Korean Nationalist Movement. As the Korean men moved to the city they were joined by "picture brides" sent from Korea between 1910 and 1924 and providing fresh evidence of Japanese domination of Korea. Because many of the immigrants and their new brides had been associated with Christianity, Korean churches soon became the focal point of the Korean community. Closely linked to the churches were nationalist organizations and their leaders, whose aim was to end Japan's rule over Korea. In these organizations, the spirit of unity was rarely to be found. Rival leaders, with separate churches, organizations, and newspapers competed for the hearts and pocketbooks of the Koreans in Hawaii. For example, by the early 1920's the followers of Syngman Rhee had coalesced into the Korean Christian Church and the Tongji-hoe (Comrade Society), while those opposed to Rhee could be found in the Korean Methodist Church and the Korean National Association (Tae-Han Kungmin-hoe). Despite attempts to unify the independence movement, these divisions would remain until Korea was finally liberated from Japanese rule in 1945 and beyond.

The Second Generation. Equally compelling to the Korean immigrants was the problem of raising a family while at the same time maintaining one's family economically during the hard times of the depression in the 1930's, especially since Koreans tended to have large families. Many had found their niche in the Hawaiian economy by operating small businesses: tailors' shops, laundries, small grocery stores, and the like. By the 1940's, most of the first generation had established themselves in small businesses in the city and, having survived the Great Depression, concentrated on the education of their children, who were American citizens since they had been born in Hawaii. Even though most of the immigrants from Korea did not possess a higher education, their high regard for education was transferred to their children, who were encouraged to excel in school. As a result, many second-generation Koreans went on to college or professional training.

While the academic achievements of the second generation were a source of pride to their parents, there were tensions over differing values. Because the second generation had grown up in Hawaii, their values were more Western than those of their parents, who had grown up in Confucian Korea. The second generation was, in general, more egalitarian in its outlook, while the parents continued to view the family and society in a more hierarchical way. Perhaps most vexing for Korean parents was the tendency for Koreans of the second generation to choose spouses from other ethnic groups—even Japanese, whom the first generation regarded as the enemy.

After World War II, as their first-generation parents retired or passed away, this second generation—highly educated and high technology literate—entered the ranks of the skilled and professional work force. In addition, there were more opportunities available to them than had been available to their parents because many racial barriers had been removed. By the early 1970's, Koreans in Hawaii had the highest income and the lowest unemployment rate of any ethnic group in Hawaii.—*Wayne Patterson*

SUGGESTED READINGS: • Pai, Margaret K. *The Dreams of Two Yi-Min*. Honolulu: University of Hawaii Press, 1989. • Patterson, Wayne. *The Korean Frontier in America: Immigration to Hawaii, 1896-1910*. Honolulu: University of Hawaii Press, 1988.

Koreans in Japan: The more than 700,000 Koreans in Japan constitute approximately 85 percent of the alien residents in the country. The immigration of Koreans to Japan in large numbers started after the annexation of Korea by Japan in 1910. The Japanese colonial policy deprived many Korean farmers of their lands. Because of geographical proximity, many displaced workers from South Korea migrated to Japan, whereas most migrants from North Korea went to the Northern part of China.

Whereas before 1939 the economic dislocation in Korea because of the Japanese colonial policy pushed a large number of Koreans to Japan, during the seven-year period between 1939 and 1945 more than 800,000 Koreans were involuntarily brought to Japan as labor and military conscripts. Most Korean conscripted laborers were engaged in coal mining in Japan, which was considered unattractive by the Japanese because of wretched safety provisions, low wages, and poor working conditions. When Japan was involved in the Pacific War in and after 1941, many young Koreans were forced to serve under the Japanese military draft. The Korean population in Japan in 1945 was close to 2 million, and almost two-thirds of them went back to Korea after the end of the war. Consequently, almost all current Korean residents in Japan are migrants from Korea before World War II and their descendants.

The Japanese government has not recognized Koreans as a minority group. Instead, it has treated Koreans as aliens who have to be either naturalized and invisibly assimilated into Japanese society or repatriated to Korea. Naturalized Koreans are required to give up their Korean names and are discouraged from maintaining the Korean language and Korean customs. For this reason, most Koreans in Japan have chosen to remain as unnaturalized aliens, although an overwhelming majority of them were born in Japan. The Japanese government labels unnaturalized Koreans as "long-term aliens," which means that their permanent residence in Japan is never guaranteed. The Koreans who maintain their alien status are subject to all kinds of discrimination. Until 1992, they had been required to file alien registrations with fingerprints. Alien Koreans are not eligible for pensions and other welfare benefits, although they pay regular taxes. They are not eligible for many occupations, including government positions and public school teaching.

Approximately 150,000 of the Koreans in Japan are loyal to the Communist regime of the Democratic People's Republic of Korea (North Korea). This community, centered in Osaka, is a vital source of hard currency for North Korea. A *New York Times* report (November 1, 1993) estimated that Koreans in Japan send $600 million or more a year to North Korea.

Koreans in Mexico: At the start of the twentieth century, Mexico was undergoing major social changes in its economic and political institutions. These changes eventually led to the Mexican Revolution of November, 1910. Many peasants had been uprooted from the land and had left villages in search of a better life in cities. This migration of Mexican peasants came at a time when Mexico was in great need of workers to maintain its world leadership in sisal hemp production. Mexico was responsible for more than half the world's hemp production at this time. It was during this period that an Englishman known to Korean immigration historians only by his last name, Mayas, came to Korea after he had agreed with Mexican landlords to recruit Asian laborers. He had tried to recruit laborers in Japan and China without much success.

Labor Recruitment. Mayas came to Korea and collaborated with a Japanese, Daisho Kannichi, who was at that time running a corporation, the Continental Development Company, in Korea. They began the work of recruiting Koreans on October 15, 1904, and sent out advertisements stating that laborers would be working for a period of four years in Mexico and would be able to accumulate sizable wealth. Korean laborers were assured of their return to Korea. A total of 1,033 Koreans were recruited this way during a four-month period.

The group of laborers left Korea on March 6, 1905, for Yokohama, Japan, where they were transferred to an English ship that carried them to Salina Cruz, located on the Pacific coast of Mexico, on May 16. The group consisted of 802 men (two men died during the voyage), and 231 women and children. The group boarded a train to be taken to Veracruz, then went by ship to their final destination, Merida, Yucatan.

Upon arrival in Merida, the group was divided into twenty-four smaller work teams, and each team was sent to such haciendas as Chenche, Buenavista San Francisco, Santiago An Antoinio, and Santa Rosa. Korean workers lived in work camps established in each hacienda; working conditions were poor. Many Korean workers died because of malnutrition and bad weather conditions. What made their work worse was an excessive production quota that kept them at their jobs for more than twelve hours a day. A male worker received thirty-five cents a day, a youth only twenty-five cents a day.

Permanent Settlement. When their contract expired in April, 1909, some workers remained on sisal hemp farms, as they had been unable to save enough money to return to Korea. Others decided to go to Cuba in order to work on its sugar plantations. A total of 288 Korean workers left for Cuba in March, 1921. Others left hemp farms and moved into Merida, where they began to run small businesses. By the end of World War II, more than half of all persons of Korean ancestry in Mexico lived in Merida.

According to "The Present Conditions of Koreans in Mexico," a handwritten report prepared for the present author by Korean embassy staff in Mexico on March 18, 1976, a total of 24 survivors from the original immigrant group were located. Of these, fifteen were men. Seven of them lived in Mexico City, 7 in Tijuana, 2 in Juarez, 2 in Coazocoalco, 1 in Ariaga, 4 in Merida, and 1 in Torreon. In 1976 there were approximately 1,000 persons of Korean ancestry in Mexico. One hundred Korean families with about 500 people lived in Mexico City, while Tijuana had 60 Korean families with 250 people. Merida had 10 Korean families in 1976. Most persons of Korean ancestry living in Mexico are now citizens of Mexico.—*Hyung-chan Kim*

SUGGESTED READINGS: • "Koreans in Mexico." *Korea Times*, April 28, 1974. • Lee, Gu-hong. *Hanguk imin-sa* (A History of Korean Immigration). Seoul: Chungang sinso, 1979.

Koreatown: Los Angeles is the "capital" of Korean America not only because the city has the largest Korean population in the United States but also because it has Koreatown, the only Korean territorial community, comparable to Chinatown, in the country. Located

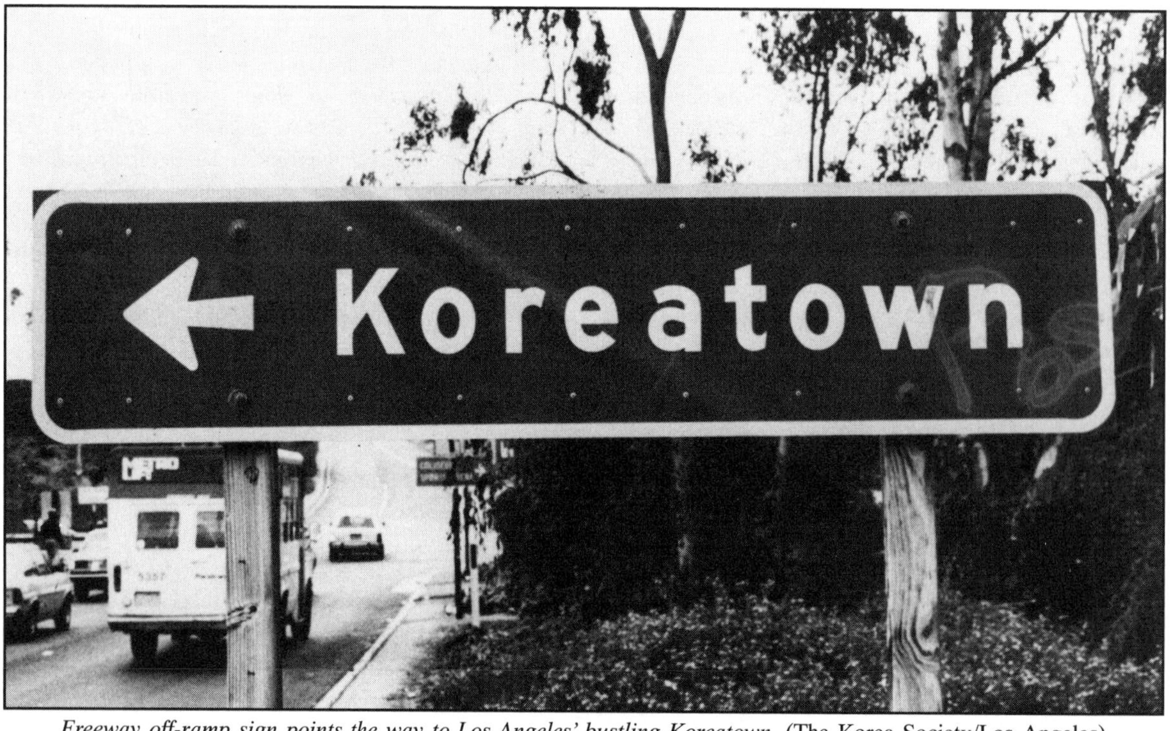

Freeway off-ramp sign points the way to Los Angeles' bustling Koreatown. (The Korea Society/Los Angeles)

about three miles west of downtown Los Angeles, Koreatown covers approximately twenty square miles. Koreatown is bounded by Beverly Boulevard to the north, Jefferson Boulevard to the south, Crenshaw Boulevard to the west, and Hoover Street to the east.

Origin and Development. The establishment of the Olympic Market at the corner of Olympic Boulevard and Hobart Street in 1969 was the beginning of Koreatown. Following this market, many other Korean restaurants, gift shops, and other ethnically oriented stores opened up along Olympic Boulevard. The increasing number of Korean stores paralleled the residential concentration of Koreans in Koreatown. Koreatown became the residential and commercial center for Los Angeles' Korean American community. Nearly 40 percent of Koreans in Los Angeles City are concentrated in Koreatown.

In the early 1960's, Koreatown was a working-class white neighborhood, with Caucasians making up more than 90 percent of the residents. The racial composition of Koreatown has, however, been drastically changed since 1965 by the influx of Latino and Asian immigrants. According to an analysis of the 1990 U.S. census by *The New York Times*, the majority of the population in Koreatown was Latino and more than one-third was Asian. Almost all Latinos in Koreatown are recent Mexican immigrants. Although a large proportion of Koreans in Los Angeles reside in Koreatown, Koreans make up only about 15 percent of the Koreatown residents. This strongly contrasts with Los Angeles Chinatown, where the Chinese constitute the majority of the residents.

Many new Korean immigrants with language difficulty settle in Koreatown partly because ethnic food and other ethnically oriented services are conveniently provided and partly because employment in Korean-owned stores is available. Koreatown also attracts a large number of temporary visitors from Korea and illegal immigrants, who can find employment in Korean restaurants, gift shops, garment factories, and travel agencies located inside or near Koreatown. Yet most of the Korean residents consider Koreatown, which has an exceptionally high crime rate and low-quality schools, a place for temporary residence. Once they live in Koreatown long enough to get adjusted to American society, many of them move to suburban areas. Only elderly Koreans tend to live in Koreatown for a long period of time. Many elderly Koreans live there, away from their adult children, who live in suburban areas where better education is offered.

A Commercial Center. Koreatown is not only a residential but also a commercial center for Los Angeles Koreans. As of 1992, approximately thirty-two hundred Korean-owned businesses were located in Koreatown. This does not mean that Koreatown Koreans are more entrepreneurial than Koreans in other areas of Los Angeles. In fact, a 1986 survey showed that fewer Koreatown Koreans were self-employed than Koreans outside it. This indicates that many Koreans who live outside Koreatown have businesses there. The vast majority of Korean businesses located in Koreatown offer Korean cuisine, Korean groceries, Korean books and magazines, and services with a distinctive Korean cultural flavor. Koreatown has a large number of Korean restaurants and night clubs. Many Korean immigrants who speak little English establish Korean restaurants and other food service businesses in Koreatown. Because of excessive competition, Korean restaurants in Koreatown provide better food and service for lower prices than Korean restaurants in other parts of Los Angeles. Also, there are many businesses in Koreatown that provide professional services, since Korean immigrants with language difficulty usually depend on Koreans for professional services. These establishments include accounting firms, law firms, doctors' offices, real estate companies, insurance firms,

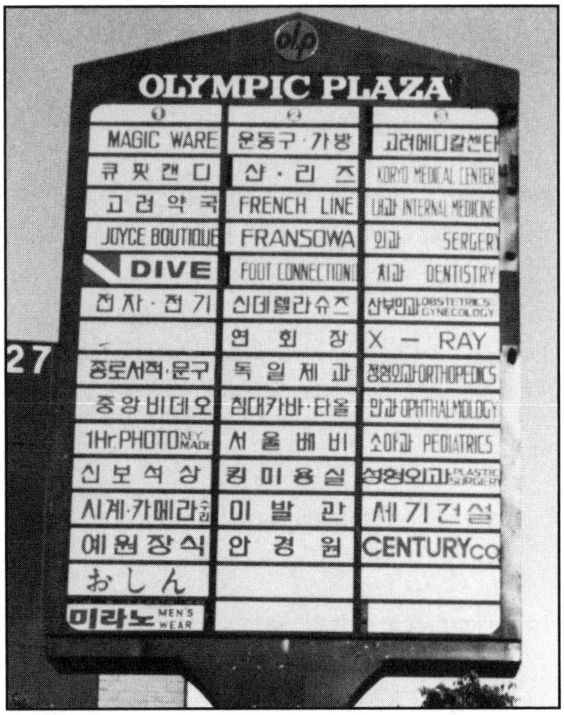

Olympic Plaza in Koreatown, Los Angeles, contains a wealth of Korean American businesses. (The Korea Society/Los Angeles)

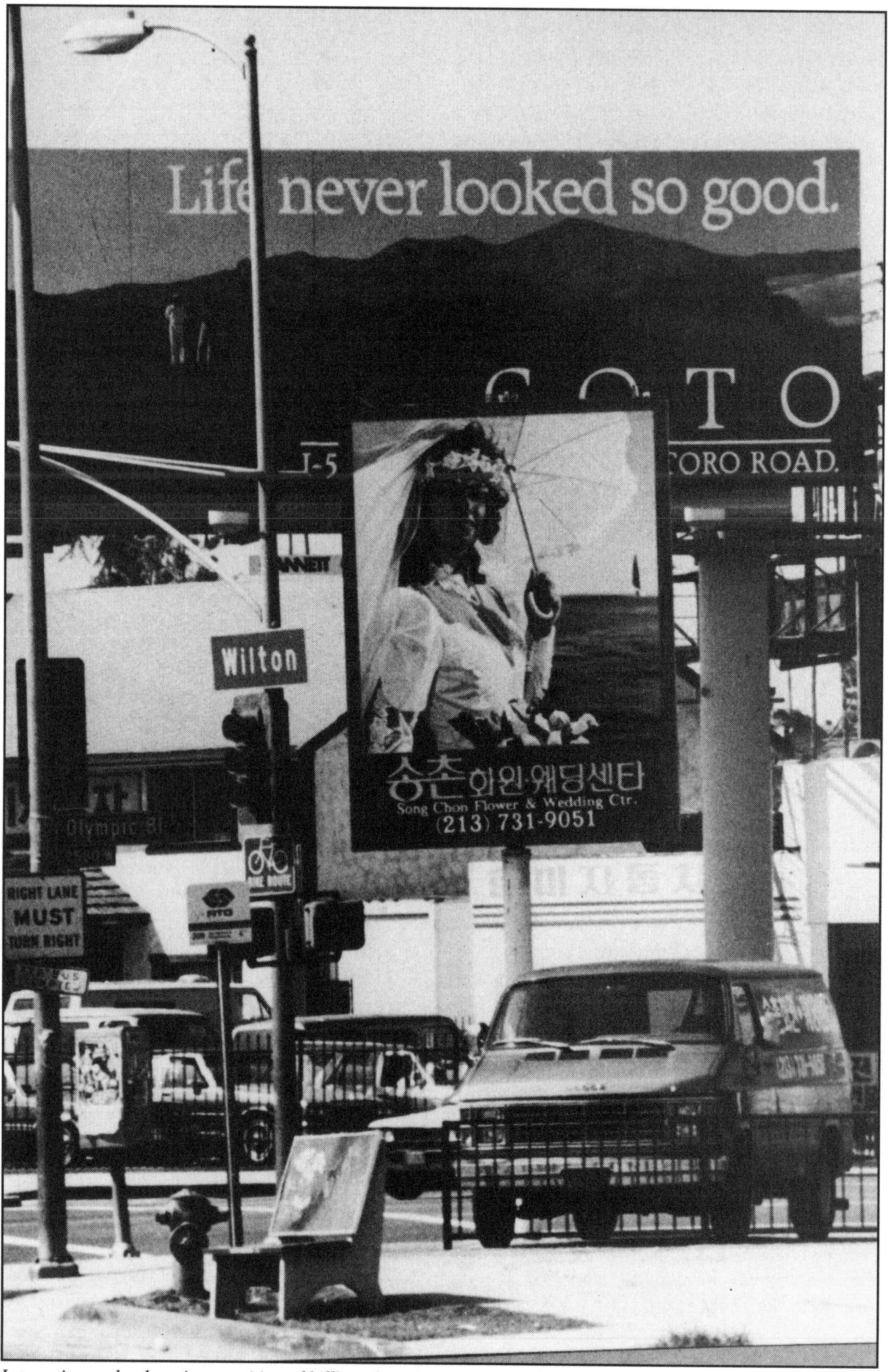

Interesting and upbeat juxtaposition of billboards in Koreatown, Los Angeles. (The Korea Society/Los Angeles)

and travel agencies.

More than three hundred Korean-owned stores in Koreatown were targets of destruction during the 1992 Los Angeles riots. (Altogether, between 2,000 and 2,500 Korean businesses in the Los Angeles area were destroyed during the riots.) Moreover, the destruction of many Korean stores inside and outside Koreatown during the riots affected the Koreatown economy. Restaurants and night clubs in Koreatown depend very much on Korean visitors from all over the Los Angeles area and Korea. Having seen Korean stores in Koreatown targeted for destruction during the riots, however, many Koreans are reluctant to visit Koreatown at night. In addition, Korean accounting firms, law firms, and ethnic media in Koreatown that depended largely on Korean businesses outside Koreatown lost many customers after twenty-three hundred Korean stores were destroyed during the riots.

Koreatown mixes commercial and residential areas. Zoning restrictions have severely hampered Koreatown business development. Although dozens of small shopping malls have been established in Koreatown, they lack parking space. Traffic congestion, scant parking, and lack of English-language signs have made it difficult for non-Korean customers to shop and sightsee. For these and other reasons, Koreatown is not well known to non-Koreans. In a marketing survey, only 12 percent of respondents in Los Angeles reported that they knew the location of Koreatown, whereas the vast majority of them knew the locations of Chinatown and Japantown.

Social and Cultural Activities. Koreatown is also a social and cultural center for Los Angeles Koreans. The Korean Federation of Los Angeles, the central organization of the Los Angeles Korean community, and all eight major business associations, including the Korean Chamber of Commerce of Los Angeles, have their offices in Koreatown. The KOREAN YOUTH AND COMMUNITY CENTER, the Korean Family Counseling and Legal Advice Center, and other Korean social service agencies are also located in Koreatown. Three Korean ethnic dailies and more than ten Korean ethnic magazines have their central offices in Koreatown. Korean business associations, social service organi-

Spectators observe Koreatown Parade, Koreatown, Los Angeles. (Alon Reininger/Unicorn Stock Photos)

zations, and other social clubs hold their regular seminars, meetings, and parties at offices and restaurants there. Many Koreans living in other parts of Southern California often come to Koreatown restaurants for wedding receptions, birthday parties, New Year dinners, and so forth. There are eight motels and hotels in Koreatown, and two of them hold professional conventions almost every month. Koreatown hotels also accommodate many visitors from Korea and other parts of the country.—*Pyong Gap Min*

SUGGESTED READINGS: • Light, Ivan, and Edna Bonacich. *Immigrant Entrepreneurs: Koreans in Los Angeles, 1965-1982*. Berkeley: University of California Press, 1988. • Min, Pyong Gap. "Korean Immigrants in Los Angeles." In *Immigration and Entrepreneurship*, edited by Ivan Light and Parminder Bhachu. New York: Transaction Publishers, 1993. • Yu, Eui-Young. " 'Koreatown' Los Angeles: Emergence of a New Inner-City Ethnic Community." *Bulletin of Population and Development Studies* 14 (1985): 29-44. • Yu, Eui-Young, Earl Phillips, and Eun Sik Yang, eds. *Koreans in Los Angeles: Prospects and Promises*. Los Angeles: Center for Korean-American and Korean Studies, California State University, Los Angeles, 1982.

Korematsu, Fred Toyosaburo (b. 1920?, Oakland, Calif.): Exclusion order violator. Korematsu's life changed after Japan attacked Pearl Harbor on December 7, 1941. First, he lost his welding job when the Boiler Makers Union expelled all of its Japanese members. Next, he lost his freedom when he was arrested for violating the exclusion order. Finally, he lost his Italian American fiancée because of the pressure involved in having a relationship with a Japanese American.

Korematsu never intended to be a hero. That label was bestowed upon him years later. In March of 1942 he intended to take advantage of the brief period of the so-called voluntary evacuation—a time when Japanese Americans could leave the West Coast without permission from the Army. Engaged to be married at the time to Ida Boitano, Korematsu attempted to hide his Japanese features by having plastic surgery done on his eyes and nose so that the two of them could live

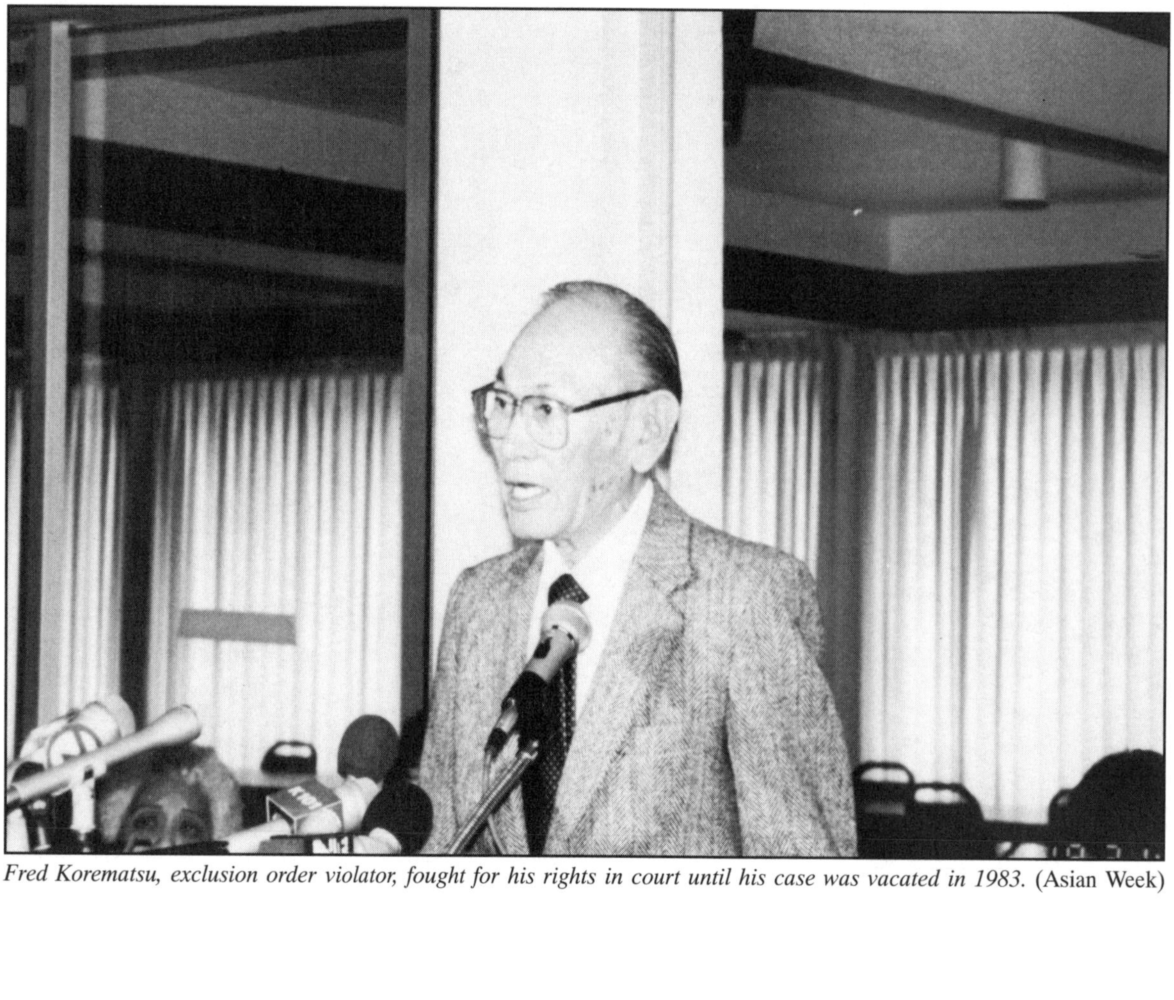

Fred Korematsu, exclusion order violator, fought for his rights in court until his case was vacated in 1983. (Asian Week)

Fred Korematsu chats with attorney Dale Minami, who represented him in his coram nobis case. (Asian Week)

more peacefully in the mostly white Midwest. His plan, however, encountered difficulties when the Army terminated the "voluntary evacuation" program on March 27, 1942.

On May 30, 1942, with his parents and brothers interned at the Tanforan Assembly Center along with other Japanese Americans, Korematsu was arrested in San Leandro for violating the exclusion order. At first he attempted to claim that he was of Spanish-Hawaiian origin. His story, however, quickly crumbled when the draft card he produced as identification proved to be false. Shortly thereafter Korematsu revealed his identity and vowed to fight his case in court. Since the Northern California American Civil Liberties Union (ACLU) was seeking a test case for the exclusion order, Korematsu proved to be a very willing volunteer.

On September 8, 1942, Korematsu stood trial with ACLU attorney Wayne Collins at his side. As expected he was found guilty as charged and sentenced to five years probation. Collins filed an appeal, and Korematsu eventually rejoined his family at Tanforan. On February 19, 1943, the one-year anniversary of EXECUTIVE ORDER 9066, he joined fellow resisters Minoru YASUI and Gordon K. HIRABAYASHI before the court of appeals. Once again he lost his case and another appeal was filed—this time to the Supreme Court.

In the end Korematsu's conviction was upheld by the Supreme Court by a vote of six to three on December 18, 1944. Because the government had suppressed evidence that showed that the exclusion order and other measures taken against Japanese Americans were unwarranted, however, Korematsu's case was vacated on November 10, 1983, through a petition for a writ of *CORAM NOBIS*.

Koryo Dynasty (935-1392): The line of hereditary rulers in the Koryo Kingdom founded in 918 by Wang Kon. The modern Anglicized name "Korea" was derived from "Koryo." The Koryo Dynasty, which consisted of thirty-four monarchs, ruled for more than four-and-a-half centuries. Wang Kon was the chief minister to Kungye, a monk who founded a state called "Later Koguryo" in northcentral Korea. Wang Kon overthrew Kungye in 918. In 935, he overran Kyongju, the Silla capital, destroying the Silla Dynasty and uniting once again the divided countries under one rule. In order to enhance his position and legitimize his rule, Wang Kon married a daughter of the Silla royal family. Wang Kon and his successors continued to use the existing Chinese governmental structure of Silla, with its six ministries, and the civil service examination system as a means of selecting officials. The country was divided into provinces, prefectures, subprefectures, and districts.

Social classes in Koryo consisted of hereditary aristocrats, who monopolized high government offices; commoners known as *yangmin* (good people), predominantly peasants and artisans who paid taxes and provided the government with unpaid labor; and *chonmin* (base people), domestic slaves who could be bought and sold and state slaves who worked in mines, factories, and other government industries.

As had the Silla rulers, the Koryo rulers reconfirmed Buddhism as the state religion, and Buddhism continued to play the dominant role in Koryo life and culture. Buddhist monks were asked to serve as advisors in the government. In the eleventh century the monk Uichon brought back from China the Buddhist sect that later became the predominant force in Korean Buddhism.

In the field of fine arts, Koryo potters created some of the most beautiful pale green celadons, with their elegant and graceful shapes and designs executed in inlaid clay. This inlay technique was one of the most important inventions of Korean potters of the twelfth century. Another remarkable achievement of the Koryo period was in the development of printing art. In the thirteenth century, when the Mongols invaded Korea, the king implored Buddha's divine protection against the Mongols by undertaking the enormous task of carving the entire Buddhist scriptures (the *Tripitaka*) onto wooden blocks for printing. It took fifteen years to complete the project. Korean artisans later developed this printing technique into movable type in 1403, a half century ahead of Johann Gutenberg's invention of printing.

Mongol armies staged a series of invasions of Koryo during the thirteenth century. In 1259 the Mongols forced the Koryo kings to accept Mongol domination. The Koryo king proposed a set of reforms designed to force the invaders and their influence from the court, but his attempts were thwarted.

Toward the end of the fourteenth century, the Koryo government was confronted with one of its gravest problems—the territorial dispute with the newly emerging Chinese Ming Dynasty over the land in the northern and northeastern regions of Korea. The Ming ruler, who had recently overthrown the Mongols, now claimed that the land belonged to China. The Koryo king therefore decided to settle the problem by forceful means and dispatched his troops to the Liaoyang region of Manchuria to fight the Chinese forces. The Koryo troops were led by General Yi Song-gye, who believed that Koryo should not wage a war with Ming China. Amid the internal unrest created by the Ming challenge, Yi Song-gye seized his government's capital city and founded the Yi Dynasty in 1392.

Kosai: Complex system of reciprocal gift-giving at important points in the life cycle that takes place primarily within communities of Japanese American families in Hawaii and on the West Coast of the United States.

When Japanese left their ancestral villages to migrate to North America and Hawaii, they left sources of mutual aid that were traditional in Japan. It is thought that the *kosai* is the result of an effort to re-create the cooperative aid of the home village in the new communities of the United States.

The *kosai* is a set of obligations that participating

Japanese American families must discharge when other families in the *kosai* experience events such as birth, graduation, marriage, and death. Families in the *kosai* who experience the birth of a new household member receive gifts from relatives and close friends, keeping a record of all who gave. They must then await the same event in any of the families who gave and be prepared to give in return at the appropriate time. Graduation from high school or college, marriage ceremonies, and unexpected events such as illnesses and deaths are among the most important *kosai* occasions. A participating family may sometimes feel an economic pinch because of *kosai* obligations.

As the immigrants built communities in the United States, the most important need for mutual aid was funeral expenses resulting from the unexpected death of a fellow immigrant. This part of the *kosai* is called *koden*, which literally means "incense money" and has remained an important part of modern *kosai* among Japanese Americans. The *koden* includes the widest circle of relatives, friends, and acquaintances. As in Japan a careful record is made of all gifts so that obligations can be discharged in the future. In Hawaii even longtime neighbors who are not of Japanese ancestry may participate in this and other aspects of the *kosai*. Gifts of cash pay for funeral expenses and provide an important source of social and economic security.

The *kosai* is an important source of ethnic solidarity in communities of Japanese Americans because it maintains bonds of reciprocal exchange.

Kotonk: Slang term dating from World War II that was used to identify American-born servicemen of Japanese descent. Hawaiian-born servicemen, such as those of the all-Nisei 442nd Regimental Combat Team, coined the term to refer to fellow servicemen born on the U.S. mainland. Allegedly derived from the sound that hollow coconuts make when hitting the ground, the term "kotonk" still carries a somewhat pejorative connotation in comparison to the term "Buddhahead," which came to be associated with Japanese Americans born in Hawaii.

Krishna Janamashtami: Hindu religious festival. It is celebrated throughout India to commemorate the birth of Lord Krishna on the eighth day of the fortnight in *Bhadrapada* (August-September), according to the Hindu calendar. The term *krishna* means "dark," *janam* means "birth," and *ashtami* means "the eighth day of a lunar half month."

One of the most popular and widely worshiped Hindu deities, Krishna represents the eighth incarnation of Vishnu as Supreme God, who periodically descends upon earth in human form to save the world from evil forces, this time to destroy King Kansa, the demonic and tyrannical ruler of Mathura. Krishna's birthday is therefore an occasion for special ceremonies and festivities at Hindu homes and temples.

Though known to the West as the divine teacher, friend, and charioteer of Arjuna in the Bhagavadgita, Krishna is primarily worshiped in the form of a child at Janamashtami. The legends associated with his birth and his childhood pranks, sports, and feats form the focal point of this festival.

The scriptural authorities for Krishna's birth story and early adventures are the *Bhagavata-Purana* (book 10), the *Vishnu-Purana*, (book 5), and *Harivamsa*, or genealogy of Krishna, an appendix to the *Mahabharata*. A vivid account of the celebration of Krishna Janamashtami, with its social and spiritual import, appears in the "Temple" section of E. M. Forster's novel *A Passage to India* (1924).

Since Krishna was born at midnight, devout Hindus keep fast until midnight and pass their time reading or listening to the scriptures or chanting and singing devotional songs. Most temples are decorated for the ceremony, displaying scenes of Krishna's nativity. Episodes from his life are simulated, recited, and sung in different forms with great devotion. Rending notes of the conch announce the birth of Krishna at midnight in the midst of great rejoicing, singing, chanting, and dancing, generated by the ecstasy of devotionalism. After the image of the child Krishna is ceremonially bathed, robed, worshiped, and fed, *prasada* (food first offered to the deity) is offered to all present.

A joyous expression of devotional love, the annual celebration of Krishna Janamashtami signifies to the devout Hindu a symbolic reaffirmation of Krishna's promise of the eternal return given to his friend Arjuna in the Bhagavadgita.

Krishnamurti, Jiddu (May 22, 1895, Madanapalle, Andhra Pradesh, India—Feb. 17, 1986, Ojai, Calif.): Spiritual leader and philosopher. Krishnamurti spread his message of love and space by talking to millions of listeners in public utterances worldwide. Rejecting the authority of all established creeds and religions, he challenged people to shed the tyranny of the past and seek out the truth for themselves in a spirit of open and unfettered inquiry.

Krishnamurti spoke extensively in India, Europe, and America to a variety of audiences, from large

Krishnamurti teaches at the Logan Estate near Bristol, Pennsylvania, in 1932. (Library of Congress)

crowds of thousands to intimate groups of eminent intellectuals. His method of teaching was to start from a blank slate without any presuppositions. Through step by step questioning and a gradual unfolding of thought processes, he tried to show how each individual could seek enlightenment. The mind, he said, had to free itself from the constraints of time and space and regain touch with its own original freedom. He also held that there was no prescribed path to transformation, no spiritual authorities to be followed. This unequivocal rejection of tradition and dogma came from a man who had been hailed from childhood as an incarnation of God.

The Chosen One. Born into a humble Brahmin family, Krishnamurti was the eighth child of his mother, Sanjeevamma, and his father, Jiddu Naraniah, a minor civil servant. The mother, who was considered clairvoyant, died when he was ten. In 1909, the father moved the family from their village to Adyar, Madras, where he had secured a secretarial job with the Theosophical Society. Members of this society, headed by Annie Besant, believed in an occult hierarchy based on Hindu and Buddhist teachings on the universal brotherhood of humanity. At this time, they were preparing for the coming of Lord Maitreya, the messiah and world teacher.

One of the lecturers of the society, Charles Webster Leadbeater, noticed that the boy Krishnamurti had a special aura about him and informed Besant that he had found the "vehicle" for the Lord. Krishnamurti, Leadbeater declared, was the messiah for whom they were all waiting. In reality, Krishnamurti was a scrawny, malnourished child who suffered from severe bouts of malarial fever. As a young man, however, he was described as having a compelling physical appearance of great beauty.

Besant endorsed Leadbeater's "discovery," and Krishnamurti was taken (along with his younger brother Nitya, from whom he refused to be parted) to England to be educated by Theosophical tutors and primed for his calling as the messiah. In 1921, Krishnamurti came back to India ready to begin his mission as a lecturer of THEOSOPHY. For the next several years, he traveled extensively in India, Europe, Australia, and America, gradually evolving his own philosophy and style of teaching.

Jiddu Krishnamurti taught that there is no one prescribed path to enlightenment. (AP/Wide World Photos)

Spiritual Experience. Krishnamurti underwent a major spiritual experience in 1922, when he was staying at Pine Cottage in Ojai Valley, about eighty miles north of Los Angeles. This spiritual experience, which he referred to as "the process," had a profound effect on him and transformed his life. It was followed by excruciating and almost continuous pain in his head and spine. It continued off and on even in later years, though in milder form. In 1925, Nitya died of tuberculosis, leaving Krishnamurti overwhelmed by grief.

Krishnamurti emerged from these experiences with greater enthusiasm than ever for his work. He became head of the Order of the Star of the East, an organization formed in 1911 by Besant to prepare for the Coming. On August 27, 1929, at a huge gathering in Ommen, Holland, Krishnamurti shocked his followers by dissolving the organization. He liquidated his assets, returned to donors the properties he had received, and said, "I do not want you to follow me." Truth, he said, is a pathless land, and organized beliefs are a hindrance to inner liberation.

"You Are the World." Thus began a mission to awaken humanity to the hidden dangers in society and arouse the true potential of the spirit. Krishnamurti believed that world chaos was a projection of individual chaos, outer conflict a reflection of inner conflict. No social reforms or organizations could end this conflict. Only by changing their inner selves could people change the world. He talked of a transformation or mutation in the human psyche, a change in the very brain cells themselves. He often gave examples of concrete relationships, like those between husband and wife, exposing the hypocrisy and selfishness of what is commonly understood as "love." His ideas were difficult to express, but he tried to convey the immediacy of experience, the need for passionate feeling, the importance of giving oneself completely.

Krishnamurti, on a visit to Sydney, Australia, 1934. (AP/Wide World Photos)

Schools for the Young. Education was one of Krishnamurti's chief concerns. He wanted young minds to become alert early, in order to see how conditioning of race, nationality, and other such divisive concepts could lead to conflict. Though he was born Indian, he repeatedly declared that he was of no particular nationality. He created eight schools in India, England, and America as "centers of learning a way of life based not on pleasure but on the understanding of correct action, the depth and beauty of relationship and the sacredness of a religious life." Educational centers in Brockwood Park, England, and Varanasi, India, are among the many institutions founded by Krishnamurti as places where educators and students could learn the art of right living.

Krishnamurti Foundations all over the world propagate his teachings, through books (more than thirty titles) and audio and video tapes. Most of the publications are edited versions of his talks or discussions, or were dictated by him. They include *Tradition and Revolution* (1972), *Krishnamurti on Education* (1972), the series *Commentaries on Living* (1967), *The Wholeness of Life* (1978), and *Mind Without Measure* (1984). He himself wrote "Fifty Years of My Life," an autobiography which he started in 1913 but abandoned after the first few pages, and *Krishnamurti's Notebook* (1976), a daily record of his perceptions and states of consciousness that he started on June 16, 1961 in New York and kept up for seven months. In the notebook, he wrote of his ecstatic states of mind, which he called "otherness," "benediction," and "power."

Krishnamurti died of cancer of the pancreas at Pine Cottage at the age of ninety-one. He is acknowledged as one of the great thinkers of the twentieth century, who opened up a totally new dimension to the field of religious and intellectual inquiry.—*Padma Rangaswamy*

SUGGESTED READINGS: • Jayakar, Pupul. *Krishnamurti: A Biography*. San Francisco: Harper & Row, 1986. • Krishnamurti, Jiddu. *Krishnamurti on Education*. New Delhi: Orient Longman, 1974. • Krishnamurti, Jiddu. *Krishnamurti's Notebook*. New York: Harper & Row, 1976. • Lutyens, Mary. *Krishnamurti: The Open Door*. London: John Murray, 1988. • Lutyens, Mary. *Krishnamurti: The Years of Awakening*. London: John Murray, 1975. Lutyens, Mary. *Krishnamurti: The Years of Fulfillment*. London: John Murray, 1983.

KTAN-TV: Independent television station affiliated with the *Korea Times* of Los Angeles and founded in 1991. Programming, ranging from domestic and world news to entertainment and interviews, is broadcast in Korean but occasionally uses English subtitles for documentaries and dramatic shows.

Kumamoto: Located in central Kyushu (the southernmost major Japanese island), it was the region of origin of many Japanese immigrants to the United States from the 1880's to the mid-1920's. Many of these immigrants came to Hawaii because of an agreement signed between Japan and Hawaii to import Japanese laborers to work on the sugarcane plantations of Hawaii. Kumamoto occupies an area of approximately 2,860 square miles and has a population of about 1,843,000 (1991 estimate). Its capital city, Kumamoto, is famous for its seventeenth century castle and for Suizenji Park.

Kumi: Japanese term that refers to a team or company. The *kumi* system of social organization originated in Hawaii, where as many as twenty households of Japanese immigrants collaborated in group activities such as weddings and funerals.

Kumiai: Cooperative farming arrangement used by Japanese coffee growers in the Kona region of the big island of Hawaii. A term meaning "partnership" or "association" in Japanese, *kumiai* generally referred to a system by which the coffee growers could share responsibilities for common activities involved in raising, harvesting, and selling their crops. These cooperative arrangements were patterned after traditional Japanese farming practices. Because of its similarity to the *kumi* system, usually considered to refer to cooperation in social activities such as weddings and funerals, there is some controversy among scholars over the appropriateness of the term *kumiai* to apply specifically to agricultural activities. The *kumiai* system continued to operate in Hawaii up to the 1930's, when it was abandoned by Nisei farmers more accustomed to American agricultural practices based on competition between growers.

Kung Fu (1972-1975): Dramatic television series depicting a half Chinese Shaolin monk, skilled in the martial art of *gung-fu*, wandering across the American West during the late nineteenth century. The main character, Kwai Chang Caine, was played by Caucasian actor David Carradine. Chinese American actor Keye LUKE played the role of master-teacher Po.

Kunitomo, George Tadao (1893, Kurume, Fukuoka Prefecture, Japan—1967): Educator. With Colbert Naoya Kurokawa and Soen Yamashita, Kunitomo was one of three prominent Hawaii Issei known for advocating the notion that Hawaii belonged to Japan.

Kunitomo went to the United States after being discharged from the Japanese army and enrolled at Oberlin College. Earning his degree in 1923, he sailed to Hawaii and became the first Japanese-language teacher at Honolulu's McKinley High School. After teaching for several years at the University of Hawaii, he returned permanently to Japan, resigning from the university in 1939 to assist foreign students in Japan. During World War II, Kunitomo supported the rise of a new order uniting the nations of East Asia, under Japanese rule and asserted imperial Japan's sovereign right to possession of the Hawaiian Islands. After the war he taught American literature at Tokyo's Aoyama University.

Kuniyoshi, Yasuo (Sept. 1, 1889, Okayama Prefecture, Japan—May 14, 1953, New York, N.Y.): Painter and photographer. Kuniyoshi set out for America in 1906, while still in his teens. He arrived in Seattle and, unable to speak much English and knowing no one, worked a string of odd jobs. After leaving for Los Angeles in 1907, he enrolled at the Los Angeles School of Art and Design, spent three years there, then left for New York to pursue an art career. Kuniyoshi studied and trained at the Art Students League from 1916 until 1920. There he met Katherine Schmidt, another artist, and married her in 1919. He also won the support of a wealthy arts patron, who supplied him with a studio and a place to live.

In the early 1920's Kuniyoshi's career began to fluorish. It was not long before his paintings were being exhibited in galleries all over the city. During this time he also worked as a photographer. Beginning in 1925 his success enabled him to travel widely. In 1931 Japan's National Museum of Modern Art staged an exhibition of his work, for which he was present. Divorced from his first wife in 1932, he married Sara Mazo in 1935.

Throughout the next two decades Kuniyoshi maintained a busy schedule of teaching classes at the Art Students League and exhibiting his works while also playing active roles in various artists associations. During World War II he created posters for the U.S. War Department and publicly criticized Japan's imperialist policies. In 1948 he became the first living American artist to present a solo exhibition at the Whitney Museum of American Art in New York.

Kuramoto, June Okida (b. July 22, 1948, Saitama-ken, Japan): Musician and composer. Born in a prefecture two hours north of Tokyo, Kuramoto emigrated with her family to the United States when she was five years old. After settling in Los Angeles, California, the Okida family became active in a Japanese American organization that helped new immigrants ease their way into life in the United States. At one of the group's social gatherings, Kuramoto heard a performance of the koto, a traditional Japanese stringed instrument that is somewhat similar in sound to the harp. Kuramoto began taking koto lessons with the performer and continued her musical studies through high school.

In college, Kuramoto began to explore ways of combining her interest in contemporary Western musical forms with her talents as a koto performer. Fascinated by the improvisational aspects of jazz, Kuramoto began collaborating with Dan Kuramoto, a jazz flutist and keyboardist. The couple was married in 1971. Their collaboration led to the establishment in the early 1970's of HIROSHIMA, a pop music group known for its blending of traditional Japanese musical elements with jazz and other Western musical rhythms. Working with percussionists Danny Yamamoto and Jess Acuna, *taiko* drum player Johnny Mori, guitarist Peter Hata, vocalist Teri Kusumoto, bass player Dane Matsumura, and keyboardist Richard "Arms" Matthews, the Kuramotos landed a contract with Arista Records and released their first album, *Hiroshima*, in 1979. Grammy nominations and recognition as Best Live Jazz Group by *Cashbox* magazine heralded the band's success.

Artistic differences with the Arista label and the suicide of keyboardist Matthews led the group to sign a new contract with Epic Records before the release of their third album in 1983. The band's lineup was altered, with Michael Sasaki filling in as guitarist and Barbara Long joining as lead vocalist. Hiroshima's fifth album, *Go*, was released in 1987 and spent eight weeks at the top of *Billboard* magazine's Contemporary Jazz Album chart.

After studying musical theory and composition with Brazilian composer Mocair Santos, Kuramoto began to branch into songwriting. In 1989, members of Hiroshima worked together on a theatrical production entitled *Sansei* at Los Angeles' Mark Taper Forum. Inspired by the success of *Zoot Suit*, which depicted the cultural roots of southern California's Latino community, *Sansei* was directly based on the band members' experiences as third-generation Japanese Americans growing up in Los Angeles. In addition to her work with Hiroshima, Kuramoto has recorded, performed, and collaborated with a number of other popular musicians, including Stanley Clarke, Teddy Pendergrass, Ravi SHANKAR, the Manhattan Transfer, and Lou Gramm. Building on her skills as a composer and arranger, Kuramoto has prepared musical scores for television and film.

Kurihara, Joseph Yoshisuke (1895, Kauai, Republic of Hawaii—?): Wartime resister. Born an American citizen, he joined the U.S. Army and served in World War I. When he was interned during World War II, he became incensed that the U.S. government would question the loyalty of a war veteran. He was instrumental in forming militant protests at the MANZANAR relocation center and was sent to the segregated relocation center at TULE LAKE. Renouncing his American citizenship, he moved to Japan in February, 1946.

Kurokawa, Colbert Naoya (1890, Chiba Prefecture, Japan—1978, Japan): Civic activist. Kurokawa was one of three Hawaii Issei known for their efforts to educate and assist Nisei in the islands during the late 1930's and early 1940's. With George Tadao Kunitomo and Soen Yamashita, he also advocated the notion that Hawaii belonged to Japan.

As a youngster Kurokawa was schooled with the idea of becoming a Buddhist priest. While in his mid-teens, however, he abandoned his temple duties and sailed to Hawaii, where he would forge a long career in public service. He enrolled in the Mid-Pacific Institute of Honolulu and earned a degree from Dickinson College in Pennsylvania in 1922. A newly converted Christian, Kurokawa returned to Hawaii and served as educational secretary for a branch of the Young Men's

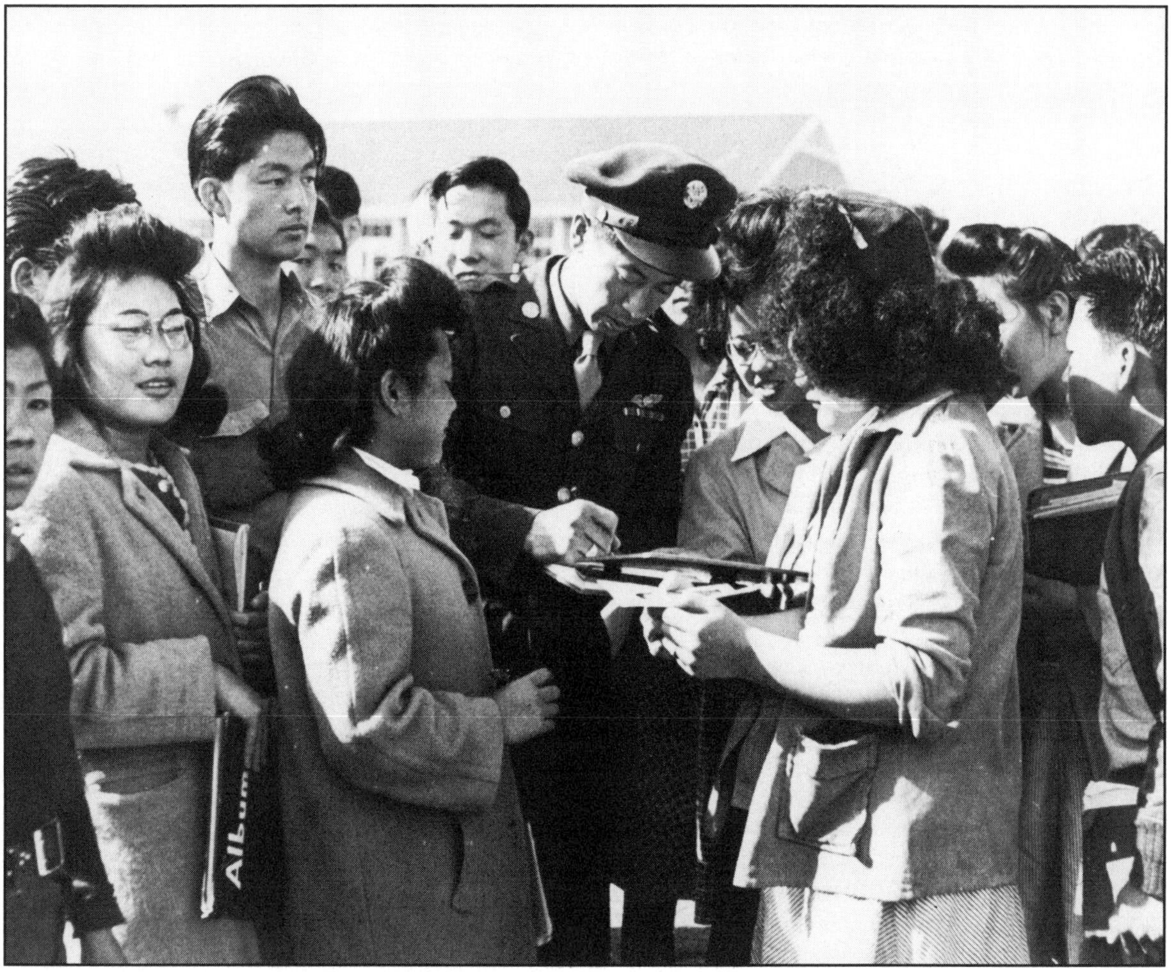

Sgt. Ben Kuroki signs autographs for high school students at Heart Mountain relocation center in Wyoming, 1944. (Pacific Citizen)

Christian Association (YMCA). He was among the first Japanese admitted to membership in the Honolulu Lions Club. In 1926, as a delegate to the national convention in San Francisco, he was instrumental in persuading the Lions to drop the word "white" from its national membership requirements. He also assisted the Japanese consulate in Hawaii as an English-language interpreter. From 1935 to 1939, he taught English in Japan.

During World War II, only days after the Japanese surprise bombing of Pearl Harbor, Kurokawa was either stripped of his U.S. passport by Japanese officials or interned or both. These details are incomplete and somewhat conflicting. Around 1943, a report that he authored was published urging the government of Japan to retake possession of the Hawaiian Islands from the Americans. By the early 1950's, he was again living in Hawaii, but in 1958 he went back to Japan, where he joined a Japanese religious sect.

Kuroki, Ben (b. 1918, Nebr.): Aerial gunner and World War II hero. He enlisted in the Army Air Corps and was assigned to a bomber squadron operating out of England and North Africa. After flying thirty missions, he was sent home to Nebraska. A short while later, at his request, he was reassigned to duty in the Pacific theater and flew almost thirty additional missions against Japan aboard a B-29. *Boy from Nebraska: The Story of Ben Kuroki*, a biography authored by Ralph G. Martin, was published in 1946.

Kuomintang. *See* **Guomindang**

Kusatsu, Clyde (b. Hawaii): Actor. A graduate of Northwestern University with a degree in theater, he has appeared in numerous television and film roles. He was a regular on the television series *Bring 'Em Back Alive* (1982-1983) and the short-lived *Island Son*

(1992). In the 1993 Hollywood-produced film *Dragon: The Bruce Lee Story*, he appeared as a Chinese immigrant on his way to America.

Kwan, Nancy (b. May 19, 1939, Hong Kong): Actor. She is best known for playing the title role in the motion picture *The World of Suzie Wong* (1960). She also appeared in the first Asian American musical, *Flower Drum Song* (1961), and in various television programs.

Kwangju massacre (1980): Brutal suppression of civil unrest in Kwangju, South Korea, by South Korean military forces. The uprising and subsequent bloodbath, a series of events falling between May 18 and May 27, occurred in conjunction with Lieutenant General CHUN DOO HWAN's seizure of political power. Government estimates indicated two hundred people killed. (Human rights groups placed the number at two thousand.)

Following the assassination of South Korean president PARK CHUNG HEE in 1979, the country experienced a period of upheaval. This involved the imposition of martial law, intense maneuvering for political power by various individuals, attempts to forge a new national constitution, and much popular unrest. A central player at this time was Chun, head of the Defense Security Command and the KOREAN CENTRAL INTELLIGENCE AGENCY (KCIA). He was in charge of conducting the assassination investigation but was also at work building his own political power base, backed by the military.

Popular antigovernment resentment began to mobilize, fueled by student strikes that broke out across various university campuses. Among the protestors' demands were the lifting of martial law and the removal of Chun. Chun reacted by arresting several influential opposition party leaders, closing down he universities, barring political gatherings, and imposing censorship of publications and broadcasts.

On May 18 student demonstrators began to defy the new edicts. Government assault forces were ordered to quell the rebellion, killing many. Days later, on May 20, about ten thousand citizens assembled in Kwangju, but the assault forces withdrew from the city the following day, and the rioters took control of it. A crowd of fifty thousand staged a rally in Kwangju on May 25. The army finally ended the revolt on May 27, arresting more than seventeen hundred rioters in the process. Several months later, in August, Chun assumed the presidency.

Among other things, the incident triggered an anti-American backlash in South Korea over the United States' perceived role in the affair. The U.S. military command had allowed South Korean troops from the combined forces to quash the revolt.

Kwong, Peter: Writer and activist. Director of Asian American Studies at Hunter College, City University of New York, and a longtime community activist in New York's Chinatown, Kwong has written some of the most insightful studies of the new immigration. Both in book-length works such as *The New Chinatown* (1987) and in articles and journalistic pieces, he combines historical background with the firsthand observations of a veteran reporter. Kwong is also the author of *Chinatown, New York: Labor and Politics, 1930-1950* (1979).

Writer and activist Peter Kwong. (Asian Week)

Kwuon, Im Jung (b. 1958, Seoul, South Korea): Advice columnist. Arriving in the United States with her family at the age of four, Kwuon grew up in Los Angeles, California, and was reared by parents who adhered closely to traditional Korean values. Kwuon

Korea Times *advice columnist Im Jung Kwuon.* (Korea Times)

experienced emotional pain as she struggled to balance the demands of her family with her desire to fit into American society, and she began keeping a series of diaries to record her private thoughts and impressions. During her senior year at Hollywood High School, Kwuon attempted suicide by taking an overdose of sleeping pills. Although she recovered physically, the incident marked the beginning of a long period during which she searched for a clearer sense of her own identity.

After dropping out of college and feeling rejected by her family and culture, Kwuon sought to escape her problems by using drugs and alcohol. Realizing that she needed help, she went into therapy and decided to move out of her parents' house and return to college. While attending the University of California, Los Angeles (UCLA), in 1985, she met Brian Koziol, a biochemistry professor of Polish descent; the couple was later married. Kwuon graduated from UCLA with a bachelor's degree in sociology and economics in 1989. In 1992, she received a master's degree in counseling psychology at the University of Southern California.

In 1988, Kwuon had approached the editor of the *Korea Times* about writing a column that would address the concerns of readers who, like Kwuon herself, experienced conflicts between Korean traditions and contemporary American values. Although her suggestion was first rejected, in 1990 Kwuon was invited to launch her "Dear Immy" advice column—a popular and controversial column that deals with social and emotional issues that have often been ignored within the Korean American community.

Kye: Korean term that refers to a rotating credit association. The Chinese version is the *hui*, the Japanese the *tanomoshi*.

Kyopo: Korean term for any person of Korean ancestry whose residence is outside Korea. The term typically appears following the name of the country or place of residence, similar to the Japanese term *doho*.

Kyushu: Southernmost of the four main islands of Japan. From the 1880's to 1924, many Japanese immigrated to the United States from six prefectures on Kyushu: Fukuoka, Saga, Oita, Nagasaki, Kumamoto, and Kagoshima. It is the region of origin for so many immigrants because of an agreement arranged by Robert Walker IRWIN, whose friends, the Japanese foreign minister Inoue Kaoru and the importer Masuda Takashi—both from Yamaguchi Prefecture—suggested attracting laborers from the area to work on the sugarcane plantations of Hawaii. Kyushu occupies an area of about 16,225 square miles and has an approximate population of 13,302,000 (1991 estimate).

L

La Brack, Bruce W. (b. July 16, 1941, Troy, N.Y.): Scholar. La Brack is a widely published cultural anthropologist whose many works include pioneering studies of the Sikhs in North America. An example is his book *The Sikhs of Northern California: 1904-1975* (1988). He attended the University of Arizona and Syracuse University, from which he earned a Ph.D. degree in 1980. La Brack held a number of teaching posts, then, in 1986, he was named Professor of Anthropology and International Studies at the University of the Pacific. His academic specializations include South Asian history and ethnology, Sikhs, cross-cultural issues, and postwar Japan.

Laddaran v. Laddaran (1931): California Superior Court ruling that refused to annul the marriage of a Filipino man and a white woman. Estanislao Laddaran filed for annulment of his marriage to wife Emma. The court found that under the state's antimiscegenation statutes the only Asians barred from marrying Caucasians were Mongolians. Since Filipinos were not classified under that category, no laws had been violated. Laddaran's marriage was therefore legally valid. Several years later, in 1933, California lawmakers drafted bills prohibiting intermarriages between Filipinos and Caucasians.

Lahore Conspiracy Trials (Apr., 1915—Jan., 1917): Court hearings conducted by the government of India and charging several groups of Indian nationalists with attempting to wage war against the British crown. The trials were carried out under authority of the Defence of India Act of 1915. The accused, self-identified as working against the repression of British rule on the subcontinent, were eventually sentenced to imprisonment or death.

Lahu: A hill-dwelling people primarily of the southern People's Republic of China (chiefly Yunnan Province), eastern Myanmar, northern Thailand, northwestern Laos, and northern Vietnam. They practice a slash-and-burn style of agriculture and speak Lahu, a language of the Tibeto-Burman linguistic family.

The Lahu refer to themselves as *lahu ya* (*ya* means "son" or "child"). Over time, several different subgroups of Lahu have emerged. The loose, egalitarian structure of Lahu society makes it easy for groups to split off from one another—for example, because of a grievance or in response to the appeal of a charismatic, messianic tribal leader.

Lahu People Groups. Based on purely linguistic criteria, the two basic branches of the Lahu people are the Black Lahu and the Yellow Lahu. The former far outnumber the latter in China and Myanmar, are the more prestigious group, and speak the more prestigious dialect. The split between these two groups probably extends back several hundred years, since the two dialects are now quite different in several important respects. The Red Lahu and the Lahu Shehleh hail from Thailand and are the largest Lahu groups there.

Those Lahu who have come to the United States as political refugees from Laos in the aftermath of the Indochinese wars are Yellow Lahu. Many of these immigrant Lahu are at least nominally Christian, which has probably helped them to assimilate into American life.

History of Lahu Migration. The oldest Lahu settlements are those in China, with the southward movement from Yunnan to Burma (now Myanmar) dating back to the early nineteenth century. In China in the eighteenth and nineteenth centuries, the Lahu gained some notoriety as rebels against imperial Chinese rule. Some moved out of Chinese territory into Burma and then into Laos, partly because of the pacification measures in Yunnan but also because they continually needed new land.

As early as 1837, Lahu had settled in the Shan States of northeast Burma under Burmese jurisdiction, forging links with lowland chiefs by helping to defend the Kengtung Valley and by providing local princes with rice and porters. Yet the Lahu remained fiercely independent and occasionally plundered their Shan neighbors instead of helping them. Lahu migration into Burma continued throughout the first half of the twentieth century, intensifying when the Chinese Communists took over Yunnan.

Lahu immigration into Thailand and Laos has occurred within about the last hundred years. Deteriorating political and economic conditions in the Shan States have forced many Lahu to leave. Yet prevailing conditions in Thailand and Laos threaten to displace Lahu living there as well.

This Lahu American artisan resides in Visalia, California. (Eric Crystal)

In present-day China, the Lahu enjoy the status of one of the fifty-five officially recognized minorities. Since 1953, the Lahu have played a major role in the local administration of the Lancang Lahu Autonomous County in far southwest Yunnan Province, where Chinese and Lahu are the joint official languages. In Yunnan, efforts to integrate Lahu and other minorities into the mainstream of Chinese Communist society have been intense. At the same time, the government has encouraged retention of aspects of Lahu culture that do not conflict with Communist Party philosophy. While some Lahu doubtless have been completely assimilated into Chinese society, it is unlikely that Lahu culture in China will soon disappear.

In the 1970's, a few Lao Lahu who had been closely affiliated with the American military effort arrived in California. Shortly thereafter several hundred Yellow Lahu arrived with a group of mostly Hmong refugees from Laos who settled near Salt Lake City, Utah. By the process of secondary migration, most of these Hmong and Lahu soon relocated to Visalia, a farming community near Fresno, California.

Population Distribution. Like other hill peoples of Southeast Asia, the Lahu live in scattered mountain villages, high above the plains-dwelling majority populations who practice the wet-rice style of farming. The fact that every village community has a different history of relationships with neighboring peoples, both lowlanders and hill folk, means that the Lahu are extremely diverse. They have freely borrowed vocabulary, dress styles, technology, and social, political, and religious ideologies from the literate civilizations on whose peripheries they live.

The most reliable estimate of the total world Lahu population hovers at about 500,000. Chinese census figures count the Lahu population in China at about 300,000—the most of any country. By contrast, the tiny but growing U.S. Lahu population is about 800, clustered in the vicinity of Visalia.

Subsistence Farming. Like other hill tribes, Lahu live basically on what they can grow and produce for themselves. In northern Thailand and southwestern Shan State, rice is the staple crop and the most basic part of the diet. Corn is also cultivated, and hunting and the raising of livestock supply other food. The rice is cultivated in swiddens carved into the steep mountainside by the centuries-old slash-and-burn technique. With no fertilizers, the land used for farming is soon depleted, and the villagers must locate new land in order to survive. Among most non-Christian Lahu villages, the chief cash crop is opium.

In northern Thailand, as population pressure from the lowlands intensifies, the Lahu and other hill tribes find their traditional seminomadic way of life increasingly threatened. It is no longer easy to clear fresh land. Some Lahu have been forced to the lowland areas, joining permanent villages that practice wet-rice cultivation.

Religion. Lahu communities are diverse in their beliefs and practices, reflecting exposure to alien cultures over many decades. In Yunnan some Lahu reportedly are followers of Mahayana BUDDHISM, with Taoist and Confucian elements, prevalent in prerevolutionary China. In Myanmar some Lahu profess Theravada Buddhism.

Lahu traditional religion contains elements of ANIMISM (spirit propitiation), magic and sorcery, Chinese ANCESTOR WORSHIP, and Buddhism. The Lahu believe in an abstract and distant supreme being called Guisha, creator of heaven and earth. They also believe in an assortment of lesser spirits, who are thought to be the children of Guisha.

Among Christianized Lahu, the pastor is the replacement for the priests of Guisha, and there are no spirit-doctors at all. Guisha has been reinterpreted as the Judeo-Christian God by Western missionaries working among the Lahu since the beginning of the twentieth century. One mission agency claimed 28,000 converts in Myanmar and Thailand in 1950. Through the early 1990's, there were about forty Christian Lahu villages in Thailand—some 7,000 people, or more than one-sixth of the Lahu in that country.

Most Lahu living in the United States are Christian. This sets them apart as a separate kind of Lahu, but to a greater or lesser extent they still think of themselves as *lahu ya*.—*James A. Matisoff*

SUGGESTED READINGS: • Fei Xiaotong. "Ethnic Identification in China." *Thai-Yunnan Project Newsletter* 11 (1990): 11-24. • Matisoff, James A. "The Lahu People and Their Language." In *Minority Cultures of Laos: Kammu, Lua, Lahu, Hmong, and Iu-Mien*, edited by Judy Lewis. Rancho Cordova, Calif.: Southeast Asia Community Resource Center, 1992. • Matisoff, James A. *The Dictionary of Lahu*. Berkeley: University of California Press, 1988. • Matisoff, James A. *The Grammar of Lahu*. Berkeley: University of California Press, 1973. Reprinted 1982. • Telford, James H. "Animism in Kengtung State." *Journal of the Burma Research Society* 27, no. 2 (1937): 86-238. • Walker, Anthony R. "The Lahu of the Yunnan-Indochina Borderlands." Ph.D. diss., University of Oxford, 1972. • Walker, Anthony R. "The

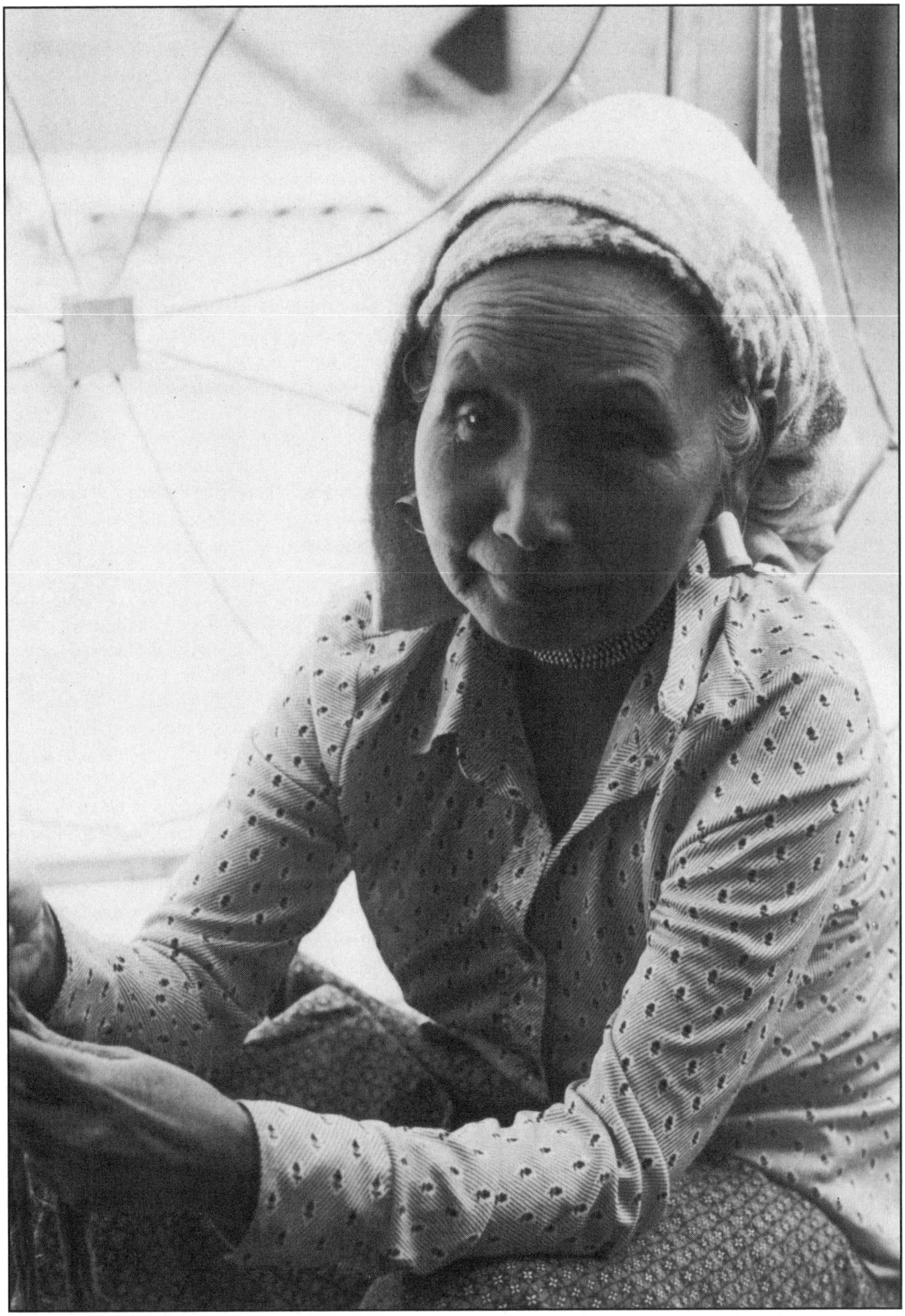

Like this woman, many California Lahu resettled in Visalia after first journeying to Salt Lake City. (Eric Crystal)

Lahu People: An Introduction." In *Farmers in the Hills*, edited by the author. Penang: Universiti Sains Malaysia, 1975. • Walker, Anthony R. "Messianic Movements Among the Lahu of the Indo-Chinese Borderlands." *Southeast Asia* 3, no. 2 (1974): 699-711.

Lai, Him Mark (b. Nov. 1, 1925, San Francisco, Calif.): Engineer and scholar. A mechanical engineer by profession (he worked for more than thirty years at the Bechtel Corporation before his retirement in 1984) and a historian by avocation, Lai is the dean of Chinese American studies. His work is distinguished by its thoroughness and meticulous accuracy, reflecting his knowledge of Chinese-language materials as well as English-language sources.

Among Lai's many books and articles are *A History Reclaimed: An Annotated Bibliography and Guide of Chinese Language Materials on the Chinese of America* (1986) and *From Overseas Chinese to Chinese American: History of Development of Chinese American Society During the Twentieth Century* (1992; in Chinese). He is coauthor of *History of the Chinese in California: A Syllabus* (1969), *Chinese Newspapers in North America, 1854-1975* (1976), and *Chinese of America, 1785-1980: Exhibition Catalog* (1980), and coeditor of *Island: Poetry and History of Chinese Immigrants on Angel Island* (1980), for which he received an American Book Award from the Before Columbus Foundation.

Him Mark Lai, renowned specialist in Chinese American history.

In addition to his work as a researcher and writer, Lai has lectured in Chinese American history at San Francisco State University, where he has been an adjunct professor of ASIAN AMERICAN STUDIES since 1990, and the University of California, Berkeley. He has also served as coordinator or consultant for numerous radio and television programs and productions. A member of the editorial board of *Amerasia Journal* (since 1979) and *Chinese America: History and Perspectives* (since 1986), Lai is a past president of the CHINESE HISTORICAL SOCIETY OF AMERICA and the CHINESE CULTURE FOUNDATION OF SAN FRANCISCO and the recipient of a service award from the ASSOCIATION FOR ASIAN AMERICAN STUDIES for lifelong contributions to Asian American Studies.

Lal, Gobind Behari (Oct. 9, 1889, Delhi, India—Apr. 2, 1982, San Francisco, Calif.): Journalist and patriot. Lal had a long and distinguished career as science editor emeritus for the Heart newspapers and worked in San Francisco, New York, and Los Angeles. He was one of the founding members of the National Association of Science Writers and served as its president in 1940-1941.

Born into a well-to-do Hindu family, he led a privileged life in India and attended an elite missionary school before graduating from the University of Punjab with an M.A. degree in 1908. In 1912, he entered the University of California, Berkeley and was graduated with a degree in the social sciences. He thought of returning to India but got caught in World War I (1914-1918) and decided to work from the United States for India's independence.

In 1925, he joined the *San Francisco Examiner*, where his work on scientific investigation in cancer research won him national recognition. He was also science editor for the *International News Service* and *The American Weekly*. In 1936, he covered the Harvard Tercentenary, for which he along with three other reporters won the Pulitzer Prize. He also received the George Westinghouse Award in 1946 from the American Association for the Advancement of Science for outstanding journalism, and a Guggenheim Fellowship in 1956 for the book *Science in the East and West*. Other books he published are *Joseph Mazzini as a*

Gobind Behari Lal was a longtime science writer for the San Francisco Examiner. (AP/Wide World Photos)

Social Reformer (1915), *Politics and Science in India* (1920), and *Chemistry of Personality* (1932). He traveled widely, lectured around the world, and interviewed some of the most eminent figures of his time, including Albert Einstein, Pierre and Marie Curie. Mahatma Gandhi, Sinclair Lewis, H. L. Mencken, Edna St. Vincent Millay, and Enrico Fermi. His commitment to Indian independence gained for him some of India's highest honors, the Padma Bhushan in 1969 and the Tamara Patra in 1973.

Lal's greatest contribution to journalism was his popularization of science for the layperson and his effort to imbue the general reader with what he called the "spirit of science." He was actively writing for the *San Francisco Examiner* until his death of cancer at the age of 92.

Lam, Tony (b. 1930's): Restaurateur and politician. In November of 1992, Lam became the first Vietnamese refugee to win elective office in the United States. He earned a seat on the city council of Westminster, California, a city thirty miles south of Los Angeles with one of the largest concentrations of Vietnamese Americans in the country. In 1992 Vietnamese in Westminster, Orange County, constituted roughly sixteen thousand of the city's total population of eighty thousand—about 20 percent. Significantly, however, although only about two thousand Vietnamese Americans were registered voters, Lam, a Republican, collected more than seven thousand votes on his way to victory at the polls.

As a youngster growing up in northern Vietnam, Lam worked as a cowherd and singer. Moving south after the country was divided into North and South Vietnam in 1954, he eventually started several successful businesses, amassing a sizable fortune—virtually all of which vanished when Saigon fell to the Communists in April of 1975.

Since fleeing South Vietnam for the United States in the mid-1970's, Lam has worked as a shipping company supervisor, insurance broker, immigration consultant, and advertising executive. His assets include several popular Vietnamese restaurants. Lam has also spent much time assisting Southeast Asian refugees and other ethnic minorities. In 1981 he helped establish the first TET festival, celebrating the Vietnamese new year, in Orange County. In 1990 he led a team of entertainers, including Vietnamese American actress Kieu CHINH, on a goodwill tour of refugee camps in Southeast Asia. Since taking office, he has done much to fight the spread of gang and other criminal activity in Westminster.

Lam was one of several other Asian Americans in Orange County who won elective offices in 1992. Two Korean Americans won city council seats in Garden Grove and Fullerton, while Jay KIM, the Korean American mayor of Diamond Bar, won a congressional seat from the 41st District.

Land tenure in Hawaii: Native Hawaiian life and culture is tied directly to the *aina* (land). Prior to Western contact Native Hawaiians thrived on a land-tenure system based on the unique physical shape of their land boundaries, the stewardship of their chiefs, and the cooperation of the people. The idea of private ownership of land did not exist in Hawaii before Western contact.

The eight main islands were divided into separate kingdoms. Each island was divided into major land divisions called the *ahupuaa*. Most of the *ahupuaa* were shaped like a slice of pie, with the point extending from the mountains and the two sides following mountain tops and ridges down to the lowlands spreading out at the base along the sea. An *ahupuaa* could range in size from 100 to 100,000 acres. Many of the *ahupuaa* were further divided into smaller land divisions called *ili* and *ili kupono* The *ili* were for chiefs who managed the *ahupuaa*, and the *ili kupono*

In traditional Hawaiian society, chiefs and priests directed the clearing of land, cultivating of crops, and other cooperative activities. This illustration shows a heiau temple, c. 1816.

were independent political units managed by other chiefs. The unique shape of the *ahupuaa* allowed the chiefs and the people a right of way to fish in the ocean, to gather products from the mountains, and to raise crops in the rich fertile lands between the mountains and the sea.

Hawaiian society is structured like the pie-shaped *ahupuaa*. At the top (the point) were the *alii ai moku* (chiefs of the entire island, or High Chiefs) and the *kahuna nui* (spiritual advisors or priests. Next were the *alii ai ahupuaa* (chiefs of the major land division) and then the *ahupuaa konohiki* (chiefs of portions of land within the major land division). The backbone of this structure were the *makaainana* (the common people). The chiefs were responsible for distribution of land; all lands given were subject to revocation at will and when conquest or death brought a new *alii ai moku*. The *alii ai moku* did not have personal authority. Their authority, from a Hawaiian religious point of view, came from the gods. In this way, the *alii ai moku* served as a trustee and caretaker for the gods over all land and other resources of Hawaii.

The *makaainana* worked together under the direction of chiefs and priests in clearing land, constructing buildings, cleaning and building irrigation systems, cultivating agricultural crops, building and maintaining fishponds, and other cooperative activities. Each segment of Hawaiian society owed loyalty to those above it in rank. The *makaainana* supported their chiefs and priests with labor and with produce from the land. As a result of their cooperative efforts, the *makaainana* had rights within the *ahupuaa* to hunt, gather plants and herbs, fish, and use parcels of land for cultivation. They were not bound to the land but could move from the *ahupuaa* if treated unfairly by the chief. Since Western ideas of private land ownership did not yet exist, each segment of society depended on one another for survival.

Lansing, Robert (Oct. 17, 1864, Watertown, N.Y.—Oct. 30, 1928, Washington, D.C.): Politician. As the U.S. secretary of state (1915-1920), he negotiated the Lansing-Ishii Agreement (1917) between the United States and Japan, which attempted to reconcile the two countries' policies in China during World War I. Although the agreement recognized Japan's special interests in China, it also reiterated the continuation of the Open Door policy, or the equal trading rights of all foreign nations, in China.

Lansing-Ishii Agreement (1917): Document signed between the United States and Japan. It reaffirmed the relative congenial relationship between the two countries during World War I. Negotiated by U.S. secretary of state Robert Lansing and Viscount Kikujiro Ishii, the agreement reiterated an Open Door policy for the Far East and recognized Japan's special interests in China. Critics claim the document endorsed Japan's imperialistic aspirations in China.

Lao People's Democratic Republic: More commonly known as Laos, homeland of one of the newest Asian American groups. Between 1975 and 1985 more than three hundred thousand Lao people, one-tenth of the Laotian population, fled Laos and were resettled in the United States and other Western countries.

Laos is a small landlocked Asian country bounded on the north by the People's Republic of CHINA, northeast and east by VIETNAM, south by CAMBODIA, and west by THAILAND and MYANMAR. Much of the western border of Laos lies along the middle section of the MEKONG RIVER. Slightly less than half the country's population of about 4,409,000 (1992 estimate) is ethnic Lao. The Lao form the country's dominant political group; the other half is divided among different upland peoples, including the HMONG, Mien, KHMU, and members of various Tai groups.

In 1975, Laos became the Lao People's Democratic Republic. Among the poorest Third World countries, Laos is a predominantly agricultural nation. Only 15 percent of its people live in urban centers. Laos has no railroads and only a limited road network. The capital city of Vientiane is, however, linked by air to the other major towns of the country's sixteen provinces.

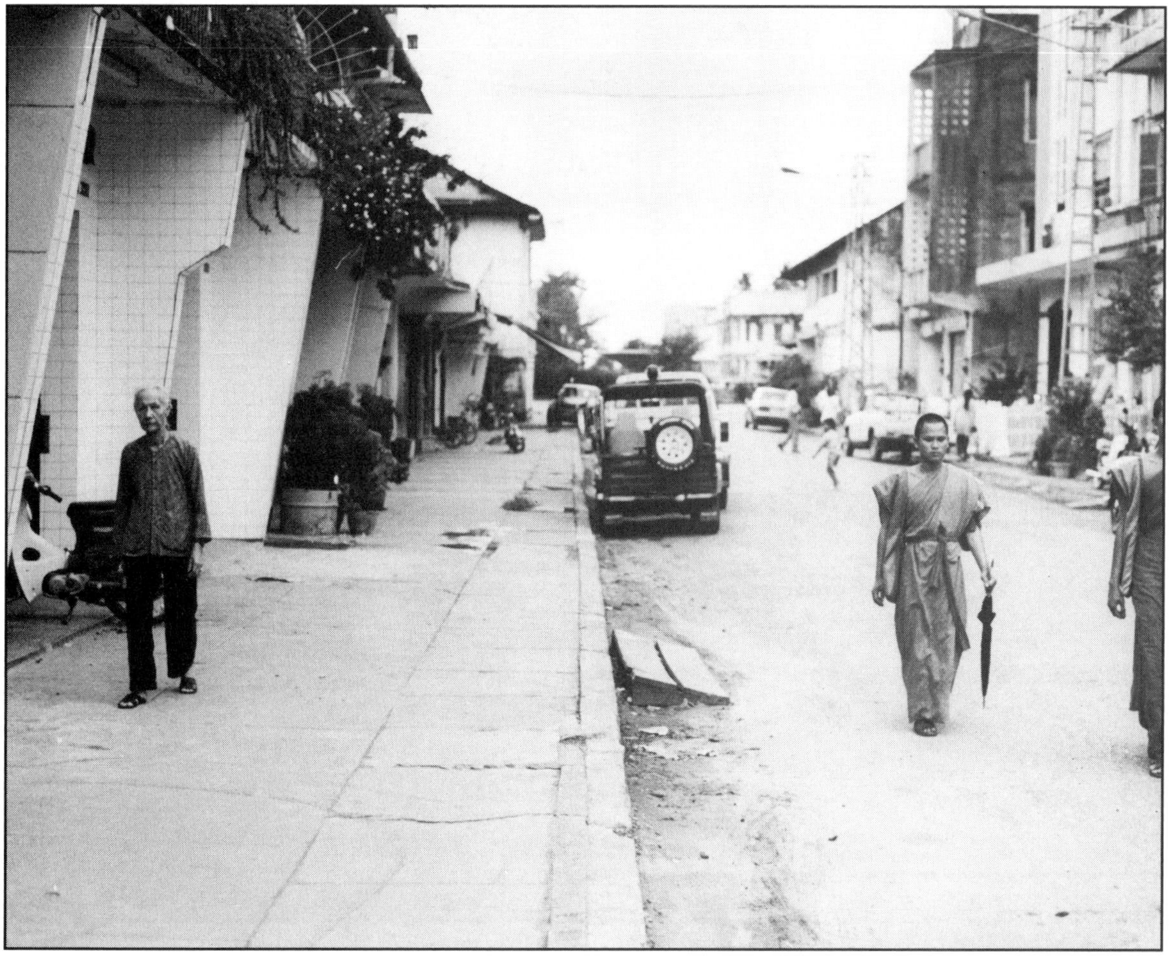

Street scene in Vientiane, Laos, shows the leisurely pace of the Laotian capital city in 1990. (AP/Wide World Photos)

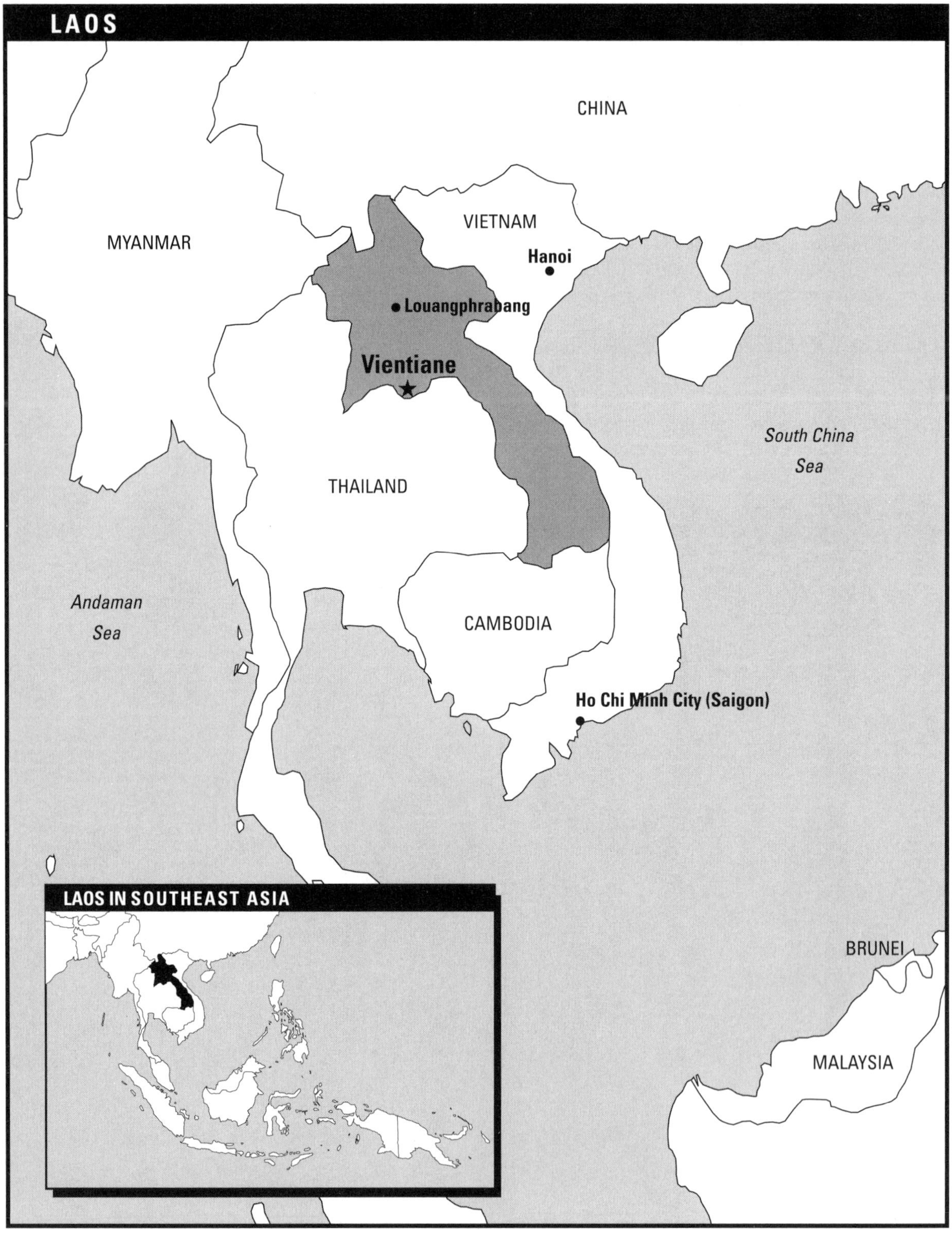

LAOS
CHINA
VIETNAM
MYANMAR
Hanoi
Louangphrabang
Vientiane
South China
Sea
THAILAND
Andaman
Sea
CAMBODIA
Ho Chi Minh City (Saigon)
LAOS IN SOUTHEAST ASIA
BRUNEI
MALAYSIA

Land and People. Laos is a tropical country of approximately 91,400 square miles whose climate is governed by the annual monsoons. Much of the northern part of the country is mountainous and covered with dense jungle. Lower Laos forms a narrow panhandle of descending plateau covered with grassland or thin forest. Several rivers cut across the country, draining west and south into the Mekong, which forms the main artery linking the country together.

Most ethnic Lao live in the fertile lowland river valleys along the Mekong. They belong to a wider language family known as the Tai. Other Tai groups in Laos include the Lue, Black Tai, and Red Tai. The Lao and Tai together account for 56 percent of the population. About 34 percent of the population speaks Austronesian languages and is descended from the indigenous inhabitants of the country. Most, like the Khmu, traditionally live at middle altitudes and practice slash-and-burn rather than wet-rice agriculture.

The Hmong (sometimes called Meo) and Mien (or Yao) began migrating from China to Laos in the mid-nineteenth century. They live at the highest elevations of all Lao peoples. The Hmong are best known to the outside world for raising opium. During the Vietnam War (1965-1975), many fought on the side of the United States, and approximately 115,500 Hmong (or one-third of the total number of Lao refugees who fled Laos) have been resettled in the United States. Hmong and Mien together form about 9 percent of the population of Laos.

Small numbers of Chinese and Vietnamese also live in Laos. Most Chinese left Laos, but those who remained there after 1975 live mainly in Vientiane or other towns such as Savannakhet, Thakhek, and Pakse in southern Laos, where they engage in trade and commerce. Laos has had close ties with Vietnam for many decades, and some Vietnamese, especially in Vientiane, have lived in Laos for generations.

History and Government. By the thirteenth century, Tai peoples had established a number of small independent principalities in Laos. In the fourteenth century, a strong ruler named Fa Ngum united these principalities into the state of Lan Xang, or the kingdom of the Million Elephants. Fa Ngum made Theravada BUDDHISM the state religion; and under his successor, Buddhist *wats* (temples) and schools were established throughout the kingdom.

In the early eighteenth century, Lan Xang split into three separate kingdoms: Vientiane in the middle Mekong River valley, Luang Prabang to the north, and Champassak in the south. In the late eighteenth and early nineteenth centuries, Siam (the precursor to modern Thailand) conquered Vientiane and Champassak and forced Luang Prabang to become a vassal state.

At the end of the nineteenth century, when the French began their colonial expansion in Southeast Asia, they successfully challenged Siamese domination of Laos. The former Lao kingdoms were incorporated into the colonial empire of French Indochina. The Lao had no choice but to accept foreign domination, but in World War II (1939-1945), when Japan occupied Indochina, a Lao nationalist movement emerged. When the French returned to Laos in 1946, they encountered strong nationalist resistance and in 1953 were finally forced to recognize Lao independence.

The Lao nationalist movement had by then, however, split into two factions. The right-wing group was supported by Thailand and the United States, while the Communist PATHET LAO was backed by Vietnam. After prolonged struggles in 1975, the Pathet Lao seized full power. The creation of a Communist-led Lao People's Democratic Republic caused thousands to flee the country.

From 1975 until his death in 1992, Kaysone Phomvihane, a die-hard Communist and longtime ally of the Vietnamese, led Laos. Throughout his years in power, Kaysone and his close associates maintained tight control over the Lao government.

Livelihood and Resources. More than 80 percent of all Lao make a living by rice-farming, fishing, or forestry. In some parts of the country, wheat and corn are also raised. Other crops include cotton, coffee, tea, and tobacco. Laos is rich in mineral resources such as coal, iron, and tin, but these have not yet been exploited on a broad commercial basis.

In the late 1980's, the government began easing control over private enterprise, and foreign-capital investment was encouraged. Thailand, in particular, exports many consumer items as well as machine equipment to Laos; it also purchases Lao timber together with electricity from its Nam Ngum hydroelectric dam north of Vientiane. Japan, Australia, and France also invest in Laos, while world development and relief agencies assist Laos with foreign aid and loans.

Religion and Culture. Almost all ethnic Lao are Theravada Buddhists. Most lowland towns and villages contain a Buddhist temple compound, and the annual festival cycle revolves around Buddhist ceremonies. The Hmong, Mien, and Khmu, by contrast, practice different forms of ANIMISM. Although not Buddhist in origin, the holding of the *baci su khwan*

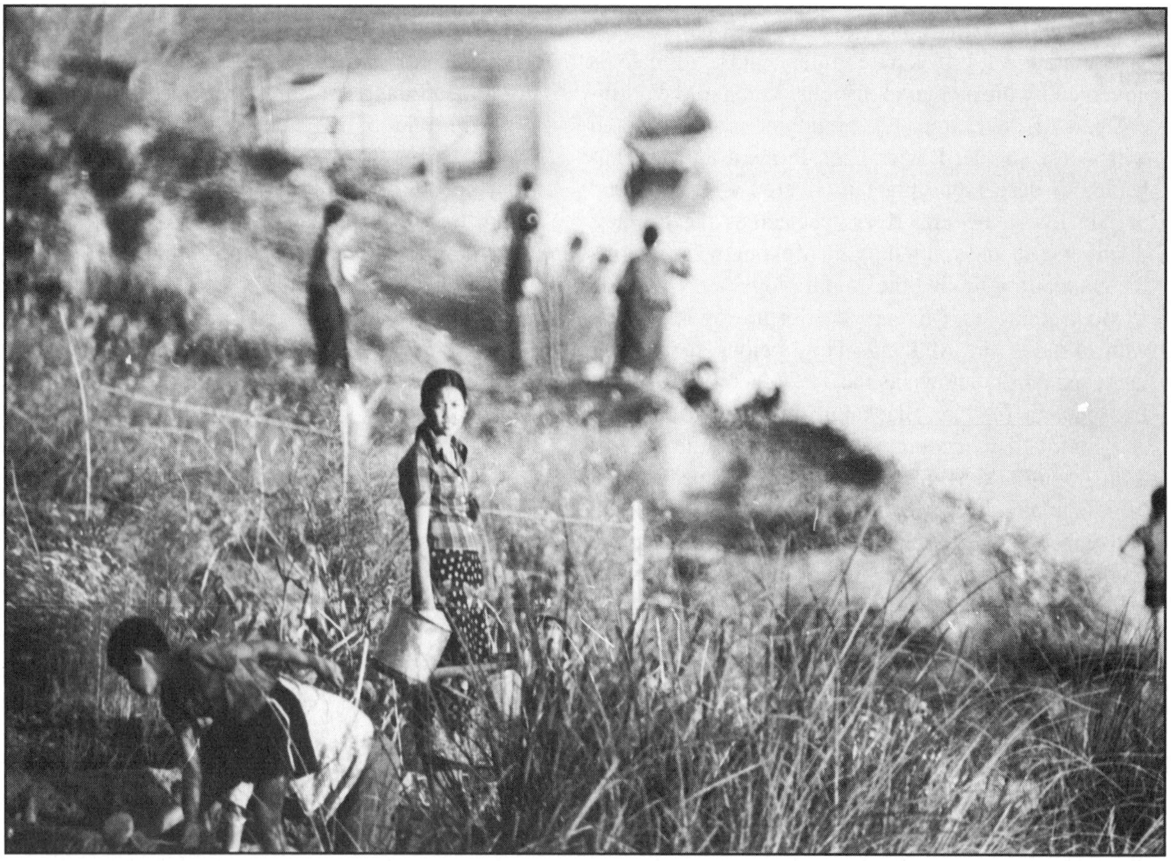

Laotian youngsters tend family vegetable gardens along the Mekong River. (AP/Wide World Photos)

ceremony, in which a person's soul is tied to his or her wrist by white cotton strings on the occasion of a life crisis, is so widespread that it has come to symbolize the lowland Lao people. In the United States, Lao refugees often honor American friends by inviting them to a *baci su khwan* ceremony.

The cultural diversity of Laos is evident among Lao refugee communities. Lowland Lao people in Laos and overseas follow such distinctive patterns as eating sticky rice and playing or listening to the music of the *khaen*, a polyphonic reed instrument. Lao women wear the *sin*, a tubular skirt with an intricately patterned lower border. The Hmong and Mien, in turn, are renowned for their elaborate embroidery and batik work. The Khmu in the United States as well as Laos maintain a rich oral literary tradition. As Laos reestablishes linkages with the non-Communist world, it can be expected not only that overseas Lao will seek to establish business contacts with their homeland but also that cultural ties between refugee communities abroad and communities in the home country will be strengthened.—*Charles F. Keyes and E. Jayne Keyes*

SUGGESTED READINGS: • Condominas, Georges. "Lao Religion." In *The Encyclopedia of Religion*, edited by Mircea Eliade. Vol. 8. New York: Collier Macmillan, 1987. • De Berval, Rene, ed. *Kingdom of Laos*. Saigon: France-Asie, 1959. • Stuart-Fox, Martin, ed. *Contemporary Laos: Studies in the Politics and Society of the Lao People's Democratic Republic*. New York: St. Martin's Press, 1982. • Stuart-Fox, Martin. *Laos: Politics, Economics, and Society*. London: Frances Pinter, 1986.

Lao special events: Lao Americans observe many special events popular in their Southeast Asian homeland. The New Year festival (Boun Pi May) held in mid-April, the traditional beginning of the year, is the most widespread. This high-spirited affair can last several days. Smaller celebrations of annual Buddhist holy days are found in U.S. cities where Lao monks are present. Among the more important are those marking the beginning and end of Buddhist lent (Boun Ok Pansa, Boun Khao Pansa) and the ceremony of offering basic subsistence materials to the monks

(Boun Kathin). The services in honor of the ancestors (Ho Khao Padap Dinh) and the That Luang festival (Boun That Luang), named after the most famous stupa (Buddhist shrine) in Laos, are also noteworthy events. The recitation of the story of Buddha's penultimate incarnation (Boun Pha Vet) is another major annual service. In addition to these seasonal celebrations, family events are often the occasion for community gatherings. The secular and sacred intermingle in these festivities, for at the heart of all Lao celebrations is the ceremony of calling back the souls (*soukhouan*), an animistic ritual to promote health, happiness, and prosperity.

Lao New Year. Gala festivities usher in the Lao New Year. This festival is a legacy from the old royal capital, Luang Prabang, where it became the largest annual event. Several religious ceremonies, including washing statues of the Buddha, take place at the ancient temples (*wats*). Highlights of the New Year festival are the colorful parades and the sacred masked dance of a lion with Pou Gneu and Gna Gneu, the first mythological ancestors of the Lao people.

In the United States, many of these customs are still observed. Water remains a central focus of the events, and pious Lao, practitioners of Theravada BUDDHISM, pour lustral water over statues of the Buddha. Pyramid-shaped hills are built from sand and are then decorated with bright paper banners and candles. Money trees, their leaves fashioned from crisp new bills carefully folded into intricate shapes, are donated to the ancient temples, and caged birds are set free. At home, children perform the ceremony of contrition, asking forgiveness from their elders for any wrongs they may have committed during the year. This is a time of cleansing, rebirth, and renewal.

The New Year festival is also the time for spring cleaning, visiting friends and relatives, and high jinks. Participants douse one another with flower-scented water, and many cover their faces with white powder or charcoal. Holiday festivities may include a beauty-queen contest, a fashion show of costumes from Lao minority groups, and a performance of Lao classical dance. In the evening, celebrants join together in the Lao traditional dance.

Other Annual Festivals. Laos is primarily an agrarian country, and most seasonal celebrations are originally linked to the agricultural cycle. Important events in the Buddhist calendar are now observed on those holidays. By attending religious events and making donations, Buddhists can earn spiritual merit. The term for festivals, *boun*, underscores their religious nature, for this word not only means "festival" but also connotes "to make merit" and "good deeds."

Among the more important ceremonies led by Lao monks in the United States are those marking the beginning and end of Buddhist lent (Boun Khao Pansa, Boun Ok Pansa). Buddhist lent coincides with the onset of the monsoons and ends when the rains have subsided. Another major occasion is the offering of saffron robes and other essential supplies to the monks (Boun Kathin), a service held after the end of the rainy season. At the feast honoring the ancestors (Ho Khao Padap Dinh), money trees decorated with candles, flowers, books, and other donations for the dead are presented to the monks. The celebrations of the That Luang stupa (Boun That Luang) comes in November, at the end of the harvest season. This event originated in Vientiane, the administrative capital of Laos, and today it is the largest annual celebration there. The That Luang, the "royal stupa," built in 1566, is said to contain a relic of the Buddha. At a service held in February (Boun Pha Vet), the tale of Buddha's incarnation as Prince Vessantara, a sterling example of generosity, is recited.

The Soukhouan Ceremony. This ceremony of calling back the strayed souls, also referred to as a *baci*, is an important part of all these annual festivals and is essential for special events in the life of the family and individual. The *soukhouan* ceremony is performed for rites of passage, such as weddings and childbirth, and for times of transition, such as moving to a new house or undertaking a voyage. It may serve to welcome guests or to honor specific individuals. In addition, it is sometimes held to bring good luck to those who have been unfortunate and can serve as a therapeutic rite for those suffering from prolonged illness.

The *soukhouan* reflects the Lao animist belief that humans are composed of thirty-two souls and that each soul governs specific parts of the body. These souls are thought to stray from the body during times of change and crisis, as well as at other times. While they are absent, the person is said to be vulnerable to malevolent spirits.

During the *soukhouan* ceremony, a silver platter containing ritual foods, alcohol, and a bouquet of flowers carefully arranged into a pyramid shape (*pakhouan*) are set out to entice back the missing souls. The ritual officiant (*mokhouan*) chants invocations to the absent souls, inviting them to return if they have strayed. The souls are said to return during the ceremony while white cotton strings are being tied on the participant's wrist, and while wishes for success, good luck, health, and prosperity are exchanged. The return of their souls is thought to help participants to obtain health and good fortune.

The syncretic nature of Lao culture is apparent in the great variety of religious rites and secular festivities observed. Indigenous animistic beliefs still persist and have been combined with brahmanistic practices. Theravada BUDDHISM has been superimposed on this substratum, resulting in a rich and varied culture.—*Therese M. Mahoney*

SUGGESTED READINGS: • De Berval, René, ed. *Kingdom of Laos: The Land of the Million Elephants and of the White Parasol. Translated by Mrs. Teissier du Cros et al. Saigon, Vietnam: France-Asie, 1959.* • *LeBar, Frank M. and Adrienne Suddard, eds. Laos: Its People, Its Society, Its Culture.* New Haven, Conn.: Human Relations Area Files, 1960. • Tambiah, Stanley Jeyaraja. *Buddhism and the Spirit Cults in North-East Thailand.* Cambridge, England: Cambridge University Press, 1970. • Whitaker, Donald P. et al. *Area Handbook for Laos.* Washington, D.C.: Foreign Area Studies, U.S. Government Press, 1972.

Laotian Americans: The term Laotian Americans is used to mean different things in different contexts. For census purposes, "Laotian" refers to those who choose the term as a self-identification. The term "Laotian American" is sometimes used to encompass the diverse peoples of Laos who have come to the United States in the Southeast Asian refugee exodus, including groups such as the HMONG, who are a separate category for census purposes. Ronald TAKAKI, for example, uses

TOP 5 METROPOLITAN AREAS AND STATES OF LAOTIAN AMERICAN RESIDENCE, 1990

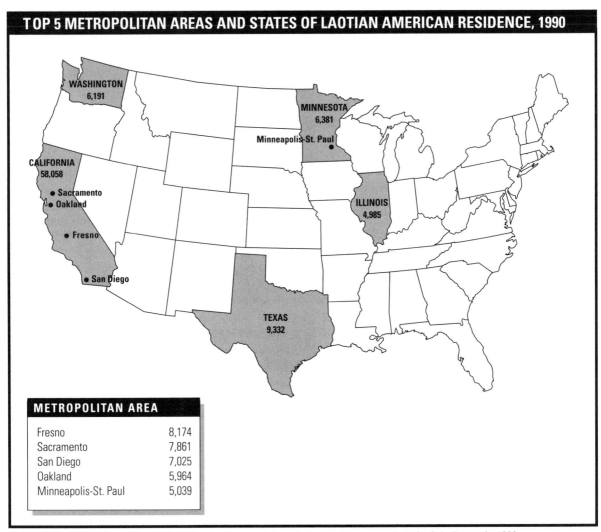

METROPOLITAN AREA	
Fresno	8,174
Sacramento	7,861
San Diego	7,025
Oakland	5,964
Minneapolis-St. Paul	5,039

Source: Susan B. Gall and Timothy L. Gall, eds., *Statistical Record of Asian Americans.* Detroit: Gale Research, 1993.

Laotian woman displays intricate Hmong embroidery at her shop in Merced, California. (UNHCR/L. Gubb)

the term in this way in his influential book *Strangers from a Different Shore* (1989). Laotian American can also be used to refer to the Lao people who have come to the United States, and it is in that sense that the term is used here. The Lao, most of whom are Buddhists, live in Laos and northeastern Thailand. The Lao belong to an important branch of the Tai race, which was established in the thirteenth century along the MEKONG RIVER in Southeast Asia.

Homeland. In terms of its political boundaries, Laos is the creation of the French colonialists. Its borders were established by several treaties that used the Mekong River to separate it from Thailand. These treaties left the ethnic Lao forming less than half of the population of Laos, with considerably more Lao residing in northeastern Thailand. Being the largest ethnic group in Laos and having the most highly organized social and political systems and the highest level of education of any of the Laotian peoples, the Lao are the political and economic elite of Laos. Their religion and culture are the most influential and prevalent in the country. Laos won its independence in 1954. The Lao national movement, however, split into two factions: The right-wing group was supported by the United States and Thailand, while the Communist PATHET LAO were backed by Vietnamese Communists. The Pathet Lao seized power in 1975, causing large numbers of Lao to flee the country.

Immigration to the United States. The main reason the Lao fled their homeland was fear of political persecution, which has been practiced by the Communist government in Laos. Many Lao left because they believed that they had no freedom under the Communist government. Others worried that they were the specific targets of the new authorities because of their connection with the former government. Yet another group left because of economic hardships under Communism. A desire for economic security, however, which has historically been the primary reason immigrants come to the United States, was only a secondary factor for the Lao refugees.

The 1990 census estimated that there are approximately 149,000 Laotians living in the United States. Of this number, 51 percent were in the West, 19.6 percent were in the South, 18.6 percent were in the Midwest, and 6.7 percent were in the Northeast. California had the largest population, with 58,058 Lao, 39 percent of the national total. It was followed by Texas

Laotian American Statistical Profile, 1990

Percentage of Asian American Population
Total Asian Americans: 7,226,986

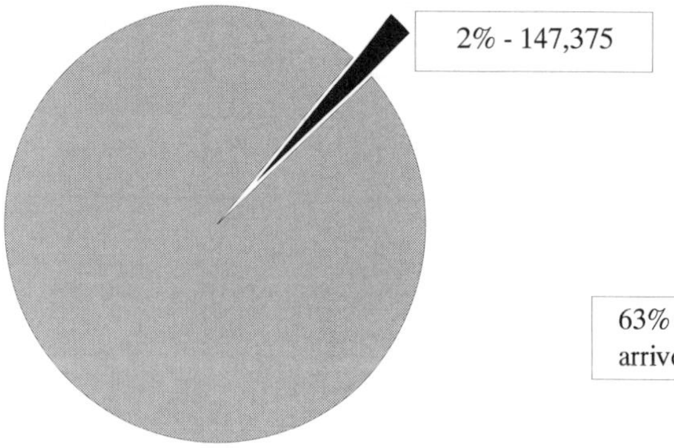

Nativity

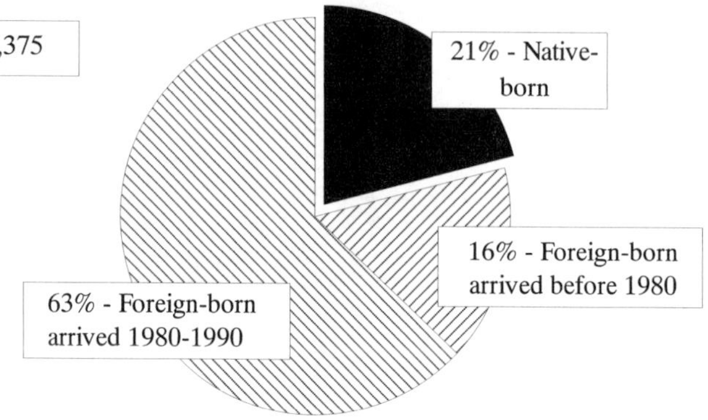

Age in Years

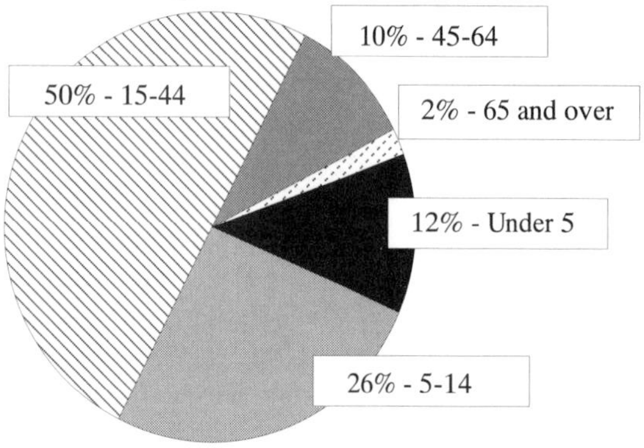

Family Type

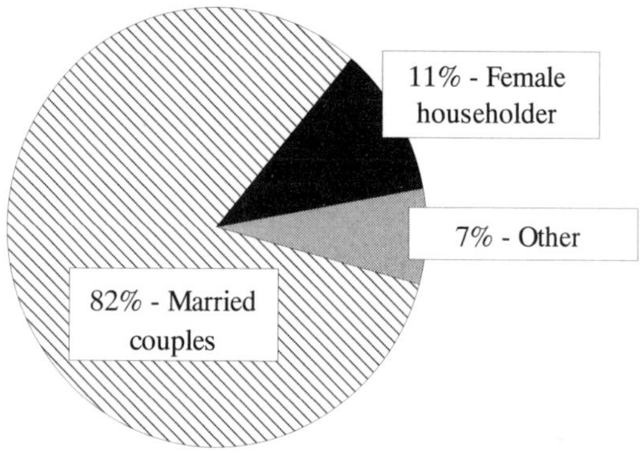

Labor Statistics
Persons 16 Years or Older

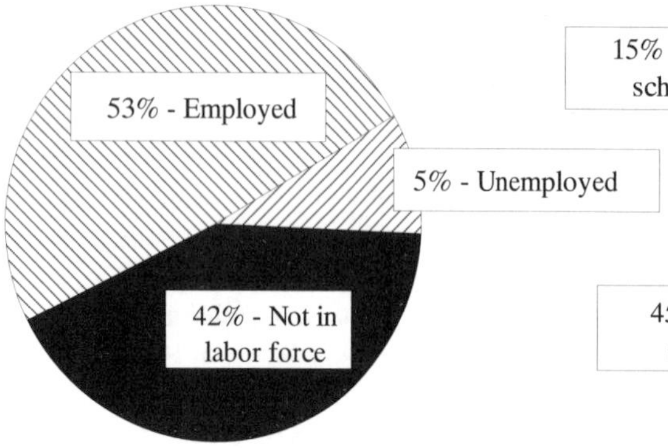

Years of School Completed
Persons 25 Years or Older: 62,521

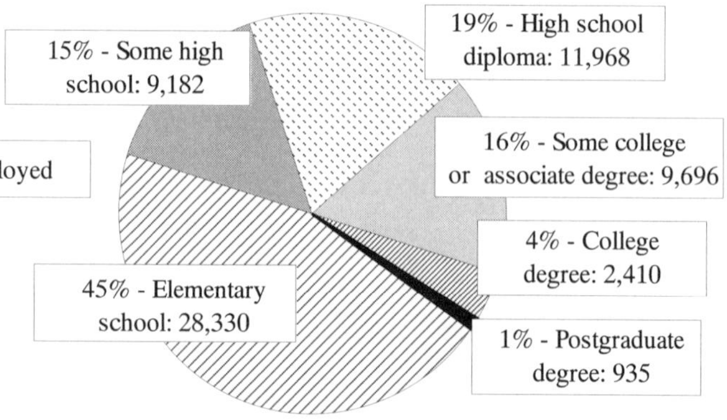

Source: U.S. Bureau of the Census, *1990 Census of Population: Asians and Pacific Islanders in the United States,* 1993.

(with 9,332), and by Minnesota and Washington, each with more than 6,000 Lao.

Religion. The Lao culture is dominated by the traditions and ideology of Theravda Buddhism (one of the two major forms of BUDDHISM). Most Lao think of themselves as Buddhists, accept Theravada Buddhist ideas as part of their beliefs, and engage in rituals sanctioned by Buddhist doctrine. The cult of the *phi* (religious spirits), however, has existed side by side with Buddhism. Together, Buddhism and *phi* constitute the system of belief and practice characteristic of most Lao. *Phi* worship deals with the problems of this world, while Buddhism is oriented to leaving the world. Buddhism is responsible for the formal education of young native Lao. Other popular religious practices include many animist beliefs.

The Laotian lunar year begins in December, but the Lao prefer to think of the year as beginning with the fifth month (April). Traditionally, the end of the old year is celebrated with a procession, prayers, and a long period of festivities. Houses are swept, symbolically indicating the expulsion of evil and marauding spirits that might have taken up residence. On the first day of the year, the bonzes (Buddhist monks) and the people cleanse the Buddha statues with holy water. Streamers of colored paper bearing the signs of the zodiac decorate homes and buildings, and well-dressed Lao visit their friends and relatives.

Cultural Characteristics. There is a great respect for age and authority among the Lao. Individuals are seen as being forever embedded in a web of relationships that center on the family and community. Important cultural values of Lao Americans include educational achievement, a cohesive and harmonious family, and a belief in the value of hard work.

The Lao reckon descent equally through men and women. Behavior between persons of different age, sex, and generation is quite formal. A Lao child behaves in an obedient and respectful manner toward his father, and this type of behavior is obligatory toward all other men. Young people are allowed considerable sexual freedom—as long as they are discreet about it—and considerable freedom of choice is permitted in choosing a spouse.

Laotian Tai, also called Lao, is the language used by the Lao people. Laotian art, poetry, and songs are an integral part of daily life and are closely connected with religious worship. Art works are created and valued for their function in religious rituals and other purposes; they are created to be used, and little thought is given to preserving them for posterity.

As refugees, the Lao experienced the fear of low economic opportunity, low social status, and political persecution. As a result, the Lao people are eager to demonstrate their fidelity to their adopted country.—*Lee Liu*

SUGGESTED READINGS: • Haines, David W., ed. *Refugees as Immigrants: Cambodians, Laotians, and Vietnamese in America*. Totokwa, N.J.: Rowman & Littlefield, 1989. • Harles, John C. "Politics in an American Lifeboat: The Case of Laotian Immigrants." *Journal of American Studies* 25 (December, 1991): 419-441. • Kitano, Harry H. L., and Roger Daniels. *Asian Americans: Emerging Minorities*. Englewood Cliffs, N.J.: Prentice-Hall, 1988. • Strand, Paul J. *Indochinese Refugees in America: Problems of Adapta-*

Occupation

Employed Persons 16 Years or Older	Percentage
Managerial and professional specialty	5%
Technical, sales, and administrative support	15%
Service	15%
Farming, forestry, and fishing	1%
Precision production, craft, and repair	20%
Operators, fabricators, and laborers	44%

Income, 1989

Median household income	$23,019
Per capita	$5,597
Percent of families in poverty	32.2%

Household Size

Number of People	Percentage
1	4.5%
2	8.4%
3	14.0%
4	18.7%
5	20.3%
6	13.8%
7 or more	20.3%

Source: U.S. Bureau of the Census, *1990 Census of Population: Asians and Pacific Islanders in the United States,* 1993.

tion and Assimilation. Durham, N.C.: Duke University Press, 1985. • Whitaker, Donald P. et al. *Laos: A Country Study*. Washington D.C.: Government Printing Office, 1986.

Lasker, Bruno (July 26, 1880, Hamburg, Germany—Sept. 9, 1965, Kitsap County, Wash.): Scholar. Born and educated in Germany, Lasker worked as a social researcher in Manchester and York, England, and coauthored a study entitled *Unemployment—A Social Study* in 1911 before emigrating to the United States in 1914. He was appointed by New York City mayor John Purroy Mitchel to serve on the city's committee on unemployment between 1916 and 1917. Lasker became a naturalized American citizen in 1921 before joining the staff of the Institute of Pacific Relations (IPR) in New York City as a researcher in 1923. In 1928, he accepted a position as secretary of the Southeast Asia Institute. He published *Racial Attitudes in Children* in 1929 and served as editor of *Jewish Experiences in America*, published in 1930. The American Council of the IPR commissioned Lasker to study Filipino immigration to the United States and to prepare a report of his findings within a three-month period in 1931. The report, published as *Filipino Immigration: To Continental United States and to Hawaii*, was among the first to document the pattern of Filipino immigration to Hawaii as well as to the mainland United States. Lasker left the Southeast Asia Institute to serve as a member on the United Nations (UN) Ad Hoc Committee on Slavery in 1946 and worked for the UN until he retired in 1952. A recognized specialist on Southeast Asia, Lasker published several works relating to his field of expertise, including *People of Southeast Asia* (1944), *Human Bondage in Southeast Asia* (1950), and *Standards of Living in Southern and Eastern Asia* (1954), in addition to collaborating with other scholars on a variety of demographic and public-policy studies.

Lau, Alan Chong (b. 1948, Calif.): Poet. With fellow Asian American poets Lawson Fusao INADA and Garrett HONGO, Lau wrote *The Buddha Bandits Down Highway 99* (1978). In 1980, his collection *Songs for Jadina* won an American Book Award from the Before Columbus Foundation. He also served as coeditor for the anthology *Turning Shadows into Light: Art and Culture of the Northwest's Early Asian/Pacific Community* (1982). Lau has received several awards, including a Japan-U.S. Creative Artists Fellowship in 1983.

Lau v. Nichols (1974): Landmark U.S. Supreme Court ruling that failure to supply adequate education to non-English-speaking students violates the Constitution. The opinion declares that some form of BILINGUAL EDUCATION must be reserved for these individuals.

Case Particulars. The case originated on behalf of 1,800 Chinese-speaking students in the San Francisco, California, Unified School District. The plaintiffs alleged that the failure of the school district to provide Chinese-speaking students with full-time English instruction resulted in unequal educational opportunities for them. Consequently such failure violated their rights under the equal protection clause of the Constitution's Fourteenth Amendment, deprived them of equal educational opportunity, and denied them protection from discrimination, a right legislatively provided in the Civil Rights Act of 1964. At the time the school district provided special English-language instruction to 1,050 of the 2,850 Chinese-speaking students who could neither communicate in nor understand the English language adequately enough to function in classrooms. The other 1,800 Chinese-speaking students received no help.

Lau v. Nichols raised the issue of whether non-English-speaking students, situated in national-origin minority groups, received discriminatory instruction if they were taught in a language in which they were not proficient, such as English; such instruction would deny them equality of educational opportunity. This issue clearly surfaced in the plaintiffs' claims: Equality in education includes intangible factors such as language; equality includes an understanding of the language used for classroom instruction; inequality of opportunity results from California's policy of compulsory school attendance, mandated use of English in classroom instruction, and English proficiency as a prerequisite to high school graduation. This discrimination was especially offensive, the plaintiffs claimed, because it targeted Chinese students, a distinct national-origin group.

Judicial Rulings. The U.S. District Court for the Northern District of California, the first to hear the plaintiffs' case, rejected the plaintiffs' allegation that they had been denied equal protection under law and equality of educational opportunity. In language affirmed by the Ninth Circuit Court of Appeals, the district court stated that the Chinese students' rights to equal educational opportunity were achieved by receiving "the same education made available on the same terms and conditions to the other tens of thousands of students in the San Francisco Unified School District."

The case then went to the Supreme Court, which unanimously overturned the lower court's decision. The Court, in an opinion written by Justice William O. Douglas, found that the school district had violated the Civil Rights Act of 1964. By failing to provide English-language instruction to the Chinese-speaking plaintiffs, the district denied these students a significant opportunity to participate in San Francisco's public education program. Public school authorities had therefore violated the act's ban on discrimination based "on the grounds of race, color, or national origin" in "any program or activity receiving Federal financial assistance."

Reversing the previous ruling, Douglas wrote: "Supposition of a requirement that, before a child can effectively participate in the educational program, he must already have acquired those basic (English) skills is to make a mockery of public education." *Lau v. Nichols* underscored the obligation of public school districts in receiving federal funding to provide training in English language skills for non-English-speaking students. Without defining "equality of educational opportunity," the Court reasoned that English language deficiency prevented its realization.

Significance. Lau v. Nichols resulted in the school district's implementation of a bicultural-bilingual program for Chinese-, Filipino-, and Spanish-language groups in the district. The case's significance was, however, far broader than that. *Lau* raised American awareness of the need for bilingual education, resulted

Chinese students do their schoolwork in a New York classroom in 1966, prior to the Lau v. Nichols *decision.* (Library of Congress)

in federal legislation extending the *Lau* decision to all public school districts regardless of the status of federal financial assistance, encouraged federal enforcement activities, and supported the passage of state laws requiring bilingual education. It also produced more lawsuits on bilingual education, principally *Serna v. Portales Municipal Schools* (1974), *Aspira of New York, Inc. v. Board of Education of the City of New York* (1974), and *Rios v. Read* (1977).—*Malcolm B. Campbell*

SUGGESTED READINGS: • Baron, Dennis. *The English-Only Question: An Official Language for Americans?* New Haven, Conn.: Yale University Press, 1990. • Rodríguez, Fred. *Equity in Education: Issues and Strategies.* Dubuque: Kendall/Hunt, 1990. • U.S. Commission on Civil Rights. *Civil Rights Issues Facing Asian Americans in the 1990s.* Washington, D.C.: Government Printing Office, 1992.

Laundry Ordinances: During the late nineteenth century, municipal ordinances enacted by cities and towns in California and the western United States that discriminated against Chinese laundries. The enactment of these Laundry Ordinances was part of the then ongoing ANTI-CHINESE MOVEMENT.

The anti-Chinese movement itself was a regional movement occurring in the West between the 1850's and the 1890's. It condemned the incoming Chinese immigrant as a moral threat to the white majority's cultural hegemony and an economic threat to white jobs and wages. Proponents viewed the Chinese laundries as an unpleasant symbol and decried their physical presence in the central business district and white neighborhoods as morally undesirable.

The enactment of discriminatory Laundry Ordinances, along with periodic outbreaks of boycotts and violent attacks, plagued the Chinese laundry trade throughout the late nineteenth century. The Chinese in response often launched court challenges, testing the constitutionality of the ordinances.

Chinese Laundries. The earliest Chinese laundries began with the influx of Chinese and other nationalities during the California gold rush of 1849. Such establishments sprang up in mining towns, small cities, and urban centers of Northern California. Then, as California and the surrounding region developed, Chinese laundries established themselves in the new communities. By the 1880's the majority of the laundries in California were owned and operated by Chinese.

The laundries were generally small, servicing white customers and providing significant employment for Chinese immigrants. Usually an owner or two partners plus three or four employees worked in the laundry. The owner rarely owned more than the one laundry, usually made only a small profit, and generally viewed ownership as a basis for income security and independence.

The Chinese laundries were originally located in Chinatown, which was often near the central business district of the city. Then, as the cities grew, the laundries often relocated to the central business district, and later to white neighborhoods. Location was dictated by the need for low rent, physical security in times of anti-Chinese violence, and the convenience of their white customers.

The laundry trade became an occupational niche for the Chinese. The low status of the occupation and the early shortage of women kept whites out of the trade, while the rigid discrimination in hiring motivated Chinese toward it. In addition, the availability of credit through Chinese guilds provided the Chinese with the needed capital to start the small business.

Anti-Chinese Activity and Laundry Ordinances. From the onset of the ANTI-CHINESE MOVEMENT, Chinese laundries were a target. During the anti-Chinese violence of 1858 and 1859 in the mining towns of Northern California, several laundries were set upon by protesters, and a few were burned. During an ANTI-CHINESE RIOT in San Francisco in 1877, small bands rampaged through the city, molested Chinese, threatened employers of Chinese, and burned Chinese laundries. During the outbursts of 1885 and 1886, protest, arson, and boycotts plagued Chinese laundries throughout the state.

In addition to the violence and boycotts, many city governments initiated anti-Chinese Laundry Ordinances in response to xenophobia over the increasing appearance of Chinese laundries in the central business district and white neighborhoods. Between 1873 and 1884, San Francisco, a stronghold of the anti-Chinese movement, passed more than a dozen discriminatory Laundry Ordinances. San Francisco passed ordinances forbidding the carrying of laundry on poles (a common Chinese practice), restricting work hours, and establishing harassing licensing requirements.

The cities generally wrote their Laundry Ordinances, using neutral language with no reference to the Chinese, in an effort to avoid violating the U.S. Constitution. In addition they premised their ordinances on a municipality's police powers, which governed the regulation of health, welfare, and safety matters, to enact harassing licensing requirements. The cities used

Chinese hand laundries organized an alliance in New York to challenge high city tariffs and other questionable practices. (Library of Congress)

their zoning powers to restrict the location of Chinese laundries. Last, the cities attempted to use their delegating powers to give local citizenry control over issues of licensing and location.

Of the above tactics, the use of zoning proved the most effective and most difficult to challenge in the courts. Its use was popularized by Modesto, California, which enacted zoning restrictions in 1885 to restrict the growth of Chinese laundries in the central business district and prevent their movement into white neighborhoods.

Court Challenges to the Laundry Ordinances. In 1882, in the case of *In Re Quong Woo* (a circuit court case), Quong Woo, a San Francisco laundry owner, challenged a city laundry ordinance, which required the recommendation of twelve citizens (in the same neighborhood as the laundry) before the issuing of a city permit. Quong Woo had operated his laundry for eight years in the same location and prior to the new ordinance had qualified for all the necessary permits and licenses. Yet despite his efforts, he was unable to secure the citizen recommendations.

The court overturned the ordinance, declaring that the city could not delegate its authority in such a manner, that the ordinance exceeded the city's power to regulate for safety, and that the regulation violated Quong Woo's rights under the most-favored-nation guarantees of the BURLINGAME TREATY of 1868.

In 1886 the U.S. Supreme Court heard the case of *YICK WO v. HOPKINS*, brought by the Tung Hing Tong, a Chinese laundry guild in San Francisco. The Chinese were challenging two San Francisco Laundry Ordinances, which required that a laundry housed in a wooden structure must obtain a city license. At the time the majority of the city's laundries were in wooden structures. During the application process the city denied licenses to all Chinese applicants but approved licenses for all white applicants (except one).

Yick Wo, one of the defendants, had operated his laundry in the same building for twenty-two years, complied with all previous health and safety regulations, and had been approved by the city fire warden and health officer. Yet when applying for the new license, he was rejected.

The Court overturned the San Francisco ordinances, declaring that the law had a right to look beyond the (neutral) language of the ordinance and examine its motives and administration. It then ruled that the Chinese immigrants, as noncitizens, had the same protection as citizens, and that the ordinances had singled out the Chinese as a particular class and thus violated the equal protection guarantees of the Fourteenth Amendment.

As a result of this and other decisions, the Chinese were guaranteed greater protection under the Constitution, and the Chinese laundries gained significant protection from future harassment.—*Lora Wolfe*

SUGGESTED READINGS: • Coolidge, Mary. *Chinese Immigration.* New York: Henry Holt, 1909. • Ong, Paul M. "An Ethnic Trade: The Chinese Laundries in Early California." *Journal of Ethnic Studies* 8, no. 4 (1981): 95-113. • Siu, Paul. *The Chinese Laundryman: A Study in Social Isolation.* New York: New York University Press, 1987. Edited by John Tchen. • Takaki, Ronald T. *Iron Cages: Race and Culture in Nineteenth Century America.* New York: Alfred A. Knopf, 1979.

Laureta, Alfred (b. May 21, 1924, Territory of Hawaii): Lawyer and government official. After earning a B.Ed. degree from the University of Hawaii in 1947, he attended the law school at Fordham University. In partnership with future Hawaii governor George ARIYOSHI, Laureta opened a law practice in Honolulu in 1954. Under Governor John A. BURNS, he became the first Filipino director of the Department of Labor and Industrial Relations. He filled that post from 1963 until 1967, when he left to serve on the state's Circuit Court One.

Le Grand: Fuzzless peaches, also called "Sun Grand." Developed by Kim Hyung-soon, partner of the KIM BROTHERS COMPANY and a 1913 Korean immigrant to California.

Lea, Homer (Nov. 17, 1876, Denver, Colo.—Nov. 1, 1912, Los Angeles, Calif.): Military strategist and political activist. When China was groping for a new direction at the beginning of the twentieth century, Lea worked for the cause of China's reform engineered by KANG YOUWEI under the auspices of young progressive emperor Guangxu and later shifted his support to SUN YAT-SEN's revolution, which resulted in the demise of the imperial rule in 1912. Throughout his short life, he served as an ardent but ineffective advocate for China's national interests.

As a child, he suffered from physical deformity—that is, he was a hunchback and had chronic eye disease. To overcome these difficulties, he read widely and took serious interest in military affairs.

When his father's mining business in Colorado failed because of the early 1890's depression, Lea's family moved to Los Angeles, California, where he was graduated from high school; he later attended Stanford University for two years (1896-1898). Having been a good student, he continued to cultivate his interest in military affairs through his voracious reading about military history and strategy of great wars, especially the American Civil War (1861-1865). During the Spanish-American War of 1898, he served on the California National Guard cavalry troop but not on the front line because of his physical condition. When the war ended, he returned home to Los Angeles to cure his recurring eye disease instead of going back to Stanford.

In 1900, he was commissioned by the BAOHUANGHUI (Chinese Empire Reform Association) in San Francisco to go to China to deliver funds to the reformist troops, direct their military operation in South China, and rescue the imprisoned Guangxu emperor in Beijing, who had supported Kang's unsuccessful reform of 1898. Without any success in China, Lea returned home and, in 1904, established the Western Military Academy for Kang's reform. He worked with Kang from time to time until 1908.

In 1908-1912, Lea supported Sun Yat-sen. In 1910, he met with Sun in Los Angeles to work on the plan to start the revolution in China by raising the necessary funds and forces. When the CHINESE REVOLUTION occurred on October 10, 1911, however, he could not deliver either funds or forces to Sun. Nevertheless, he later tried to persuade high-ranking American and European officials, especially British and French ones, to support the revolutionary government led by Sun. When Sun became the first President of the Republic of China on January 1, 1912, he was appointed Sun's private adviser on military and diplomatic affairs. When Sun gave up his presidency in favor of Yuan Shikai, a strong military leader, Lea returned home because of his sickness and died at the age of thirty-five. He had devoted his short life to China's cause without success.

In his lifetime, he was not successful as a writer either. When PEARL HARBOR was attacked in 1941, however, one of his books, *The Valor of Ignorance* (1909), which had predicted the Japanese attack on the United States, became an instant best-seller. A bright spot of his short, tragic life was his marriage to his longtime secretary, Ethel Powers, with whom he had two sons.

Leadership Education for Asian Pacifics: Nonprofit community organization founded in 1982 to develop and expand Asian Pacific American leadership roles. The organization provides training through its Leadership Management Institute, Community Development Institute, and diversity workshops. In 1992 it established the Asian Pacific American Public Policy Institute, a joint effort with the University of California, Los Angeles, ASIAN AMERICAN STUDIES CENTER.

League of Deliverance: Anti-Chinese labor association formed in San Francisco in 1882. The league was conceived during a California state convention attended by labor and anti-Chinese organizations. One of the founders was Frank RONEY, an Irish labor activist once affiliated with Denis KEARNEY's WORKINGMEN'S PARTY OF CALIFORNIA. It was Roney who, at the helm of the league, spearheaded the drive to boycott the city's store of Chinese-made goods. Handbills and flyers were printed and distributed extolling American-made goods over Chinese goods and urging shoppers not to buy anything Chinese. The movement affected not only the stream of Chinese merchandise but also the large number of Chinese laborers, many of whom lost their jobs because of boycott pressure.

Leasehold system in Hawaii: A lease is a contract right that carries with it the right of possession, which reverts to the fee owner once the lease expires. The right to lease property did not exist in the ancient Hawaiian LAND-TENURE system but was a practice that came from Westerners who settled in Hawaii from about the 1830's onward.

Until the 1840's Kamehameha III continued to claim ownership of all land in Hawaii. With the arrival of more foreigners, he was pressured to grant some guarantees for the security of property to foreigners. In 1835 he and his chiefs signed a fifty-year lease with an American mercantile firm by the name of Ladd and Company. Yet in 1836 he declared that foreigners and natives alike held their plots of land at the will of the king and that he alone had the power to dispossess them. In 1839, after feeling more pressure from foreigners, he granted major concessions in what was called the "Declaration of Rights." This declaration and the 1840 constitution forced the king to surrender his right of arbitrary dispossession of foreigners and native Hawaiians from their lands or building lots but did not require him to relinquish title to the latter.

The Hawaiian government issued a proclamation in 1841 that attempted to persuade foreign landholders to sign written leases for land in their possession unless they already had formal leases. A fifty-year limit was placed on the leases. Yet the government's attempt to execute long-term leases for foreigners failed because the latter opposed leases. They wanted to own title outright and believed that the government's action was an attempt to deprive them of their rights. They applied Western concepts of allodial tenure (a Western term meaning owned without obligation of vassalage or fealty; the opposite of feudal) once they received possession of land and persisted in the belief that the lands belonged to them. The government did not press the leasing issue.

As the land rights of the native people diminished, the rights of Westerners simultaneously increased. As plantation agriculture flourished, concentration of land ownership and control increased. Plantations had purchased considerable quantities of government land and had secured long-term leases on other portions of government and crown lands. Long-term leases at low prices enabled sugar companies to mortgage the land to secure working capital with little risk. By 1890 seventy-six lessees controlled 752,431 acres of crown and government land through leases at an annual rate equaling pennies per acre.

Lee, Ang (b. 1954, Republic of China): Filmmaker. Lee has made films in both the United States and

Taiwan that explore the cross-cultural and generational conflicts arising in Chinese society. The son of scholars, he is the oldest of six children. During the bloody purges of the Communist revolution in the People's Republic of China, his paternal grandparents and many other relatives were murdered for being landlords. Lee's parents then fled with their children to Taiwan, settling there. After failing the Taiwan college-entrance examinations, however, Lee, on the advice of his parents, moved to the United States to pursue his education in 1978. He enrolled at the University of Illinois, Champaign-Urbana, earning a degree in drama. Against his parents' wishes, and impelled by his love for Western films, he decided to become a filmmaker. Subsequently, he earned a master's degree in cinema from New York University.

After seeing *Fine Line*, Lee's award-winning 1984 thesis film, an agent at the prestigious William Morris artists agency agreed to represent him. Several potential projects fell through, however, and Lee continued to work at his craft in relative obscurity until his scripts for *Pushing Hands* (1992) and *The Wedding Banquet* (1993) won top awards at a Taiwan screenwriting competition in the early 1990's. That turn of events persuaded Taiwan's Central Motion Picture Corporation, the country's largest studio, to underwrite *Pushing Hands*, his first feature, which was filmed in the United States but not released there. The story of a retired Chinese master of tai chi chuan who comes to New York to live with his only son, the work won three Golden Horse Awards—Taiwan's version of the Oscars.

Eager to capitalize on this achievement, the company then told Lee to begin shooting his second film. In Taiwan *The Wedding Banquet* (shot for $750,000) surpassed *Pushing Hands* in total box-office receipts—$4 million, making the former the country's most successful film ever released. Another cross-cultural comedy set in Manhattan, and involving a young Chinese businessman who is trying to hide his homosexuality from his overseas parents, the picture collected first prizes at film festivals in Berlin and Seattle and was well-received by American audiences.

Lee began shooting his next film, *Eat, Drink, Man, Woman*, in the fall of 1993. Filmed in Taipei, this Chinese-language picture is about a Taiwanese cook and his three single daughters and revolves around the themes of self-discovery and liberation. The title is based on a Confucian teaching that human behavior is controlled chiefly by the basic desire for sex and food. Lee lives in southeast New York's Westchester County with his wife, Jane Lin, a microbiologist whom he married in 1983, and their two sons.

Lee, Bruce (Lee Jun Fan; Nov. 27, 1940, San Francisco, Calif.—July 20, 1973, Hong Kong): Martial artist and actor. Lee's films contributed to instilling a sense of pride and self-esteem among Chinese internationally.

Named "Jun Fan" by his parents, Lee was given the name "Bruce" by one of the medical staff attending his birth. He began his career in films in Hong Kong at the age of six, appearing in *The Beginning of a Boy* (1946). In his second film, which he made at the age of eight, he was given the stage name "Siu Loong," or "Little Dragon." By the time he was eighteen, he had already appeared in twenty films, including a starring role in *The Orphan* (1958).

In 1954 Lee began studying the martial art of Wing Chun, eventually gaining enough skill to win the Hong Kong Inter-School Boxing Championship in 1958. Later that same year Lee emigrated to the United States.

After a brief stay in San Francisco, Lee moved to Seattle, Washington. He enrolled as a student at the University of Washington, where he majored in philosophy. While there he met Linda Emery and married her in 1964; they were to have two children. Later that same year Lee and his wife moved to Oakland, California, where he began teaching Jeet Kune Do, the Way of the Intercepting Fist.

Lee's art of Jeet Kune Do evolved from his intensive research of various MARTIAL ARTS. He authored *Chinese Gung Fu: The Philosophical Art of Self-Defense* (1963) and the *Tao of Jeet Kune Do*, published posthumously in 1975.

Lee's dynamic performance of his martial skills at the 1964 International Karate Championships in Long Beach, California, brought him the role of Kato in the American television series *The Green Hornet* (1966-1967).

In 1971 Lee and his family moved to Hong Kong, where he made three films with producer Raymond Chow: *The Big Boss* (1971; *Fists of Fury*, 1971), *Fist of Fury* (1971; *The Chinese Connection*, 1972), and *Way of the Dragon* (1972; *Return of the Dragon*, 1973).

In 1972 Warner Bros. Studios agreed to produce Lee's film *Enter the Dragon* (1973). Lee did not live to see its release. His sudden and tragic death, caused by a cerebral edema, was mourned universally.

The film biography *Dragon: The Bruce Lee Story* was released in 1993.

Bruce Lee developed his own version of martial art called Jeet Kune Do. (AP/Wide World Photos)

Lee, Chin Yang (also, C. Y. Lee, Chin-yang Li; b. 1917, Xiaoxia Village, Xiangtan, Hunan Province, China): Writer. Lee was the youngest son in a scholarly family. When he was ten his family moved to Peiping, where Lee finished middle school and then enrolled in Qingdao's Shandong University. During his second year the Sino-Japanese War broke out and Lee fled to Kunming in Yunnan, where he attended National Southwest Associated University and was graduated in 1940. In 1942 he became English secretary to the Chinese Sawbwa in Mangshi on the Yunnan-Burma border and also began writing. When the Japanese invaded Burma in 1942, Lee fled to Chongqing, where his eldest brother encouraged him to leave to study in America.

Lee came to the United States by way of India and enrolled in Columbia University, majoring in comparative literature. The subject did not hold his interest, and following a family friend's advice he changed his major to drama and entered Yale Drama School, where he received an M.F.A. degree in 1947. After graduation he became a columnist for the English edition of the San Francisco Chinatown newspaper *CHINESE WORLD*, taught Mandarin at the Monterey Army Language School, and wrote for Radio Free Asia. During this period his submission of a short story to *Readers' Digest* won first prize and encouraged Lee to apply for permanent residence in America and continue his career as a writer.

During Lee's sojourn in San Francisco's Chinatown he conceived the plot of *Flower Drum Song*, a comedy exploring the conflicts between the old and the young and the Asian and Western ways of life. After a year his manuscript was accepted and published in 1957. The book received a good review in *The New York Times* and became a best-seller. Richard Rodgers and Oscar Hammerstein II put it on Broadway, where it became a hit musical in 1958. Subsequently it was made into a film (1961).

Some of Lee's other works are *Lovers' Point* (1958), *The Sawbwa and His Secretary* (1959), *Madame Goldenflower* (1960), *Cripple Mah and the New Order* (1961), *The Virgin Market* (1964), *The Land of the Golden Mountain* (1967), *Days of the Tong Wars* (1974), and *China Saga* (1987).

Lee, Chol Soo (b. 1953, Korea): Korean immigrant whose experience with the U.S. legal system provided the basis for the 1989 feature film *True Believer*. In 1973, San Francisco police arrested Lee for a murder that he claimed not to have committed, because they were unable to distinguish him from the real perpetrator, who was also Asian. With the support of community activists, his lawyers were able to overturn Lee's conviction.

Lee, Chong-sik (b. July 30, 1931, Korea): Scholar. Immigrating from Korea to the United States after World War II, he published *The Politics of Korean Nationalism* (1963) and coauthored *Communism in Korea* (1972) with Robert A. Scalapino, which received the Woodrow Wilson Award.

Lee, Dai-keong (b. Sept. 2, 1915, Honolulu, Territory of Hawaii): Composer. Lee was a premed student at the University of Hawaii from 1933 until 1936 before switching to pursue music studies full-time. He was awarded a scholarship to study with Roger Sessions in New York from 1937 to 1938 and fellowships under Frederick Jacobi at the Julliard Graduate School from 1938 to 1941 and Aaron Copland at the Berkshire Music Center for the summer of 1941. Lee was also a Guggenheim Fellow in 1945 and again in 1951. A prolific composer, he is well known for his orchestral, symphonic, and chamber music works.

Lee, David (Yi Tae-wi; Korea—1928): Activist. Entering the United States as a political refugee in 1905, he attended the Pacific School of Religion in Berkeley, California. He cofounded the CHINMOK-HOE and KONGNIP HYOP-HOE and was one of the original members of the KOREAN NATIONAL ASSOCIATION, serving as its president from 1913 to 1915 and in 1918. The editor of the first Korean community weekly newspaper, *NEW KOREA*, he invented a typesetting machine for Korean characters in 1915, enabling all Korean publications in the United States to cease using Chinese characters.

Lee, Edward Jae Song (May, 1973, Los Angeles, Calif.—Apr. 30, 1992, Los Angeles, Calif.): Victim of 1992 LOS ANGELES RIOTS. He was the only Korean American among the fifty-six people killed during the riots. The son of parents who immigrated from Korea in 1972, he had decided to answer KOREATOWN storeowners' pleas for help while listening to a Korean-language radio station. He was accidentally shot by a Korean man who mistook him for a looter.

Lee, Evelyn (b. June 25, 1944, Macao): Scholar and health administrator. Executive director of Richmond Area Multi-Services in San Francisco and clinical professor of psychiatry at the University of California,

Edward Lee was accidentally shot while attempting to assist Korean shop owners during the Los Angeles riots. (AP/Wide World Photos)

San Francisco, she is a specialist in mental health and social services. Author of *Ten Principles on Raising Chinese-American Teens* (1988), she has worked extensively with newly arrived immigrants, conducted cultural diversity workshops, and served as program director and consultant to various community and mainstream health agencies.

Lee, Gus [Augustus] (b. 1946, San Francisco, Calif.): Novelist. Lee's life is mirrored in his strongly autobiographical novels, *China Boy* (1991) and *Honor and Duty* (1994). Raised in a largely African American neighborhood in San Francisco, Lee was five years old when his mother died. His father remarried a non-Chinese woman, a harsh figure who sought to "Americanize" Lee with a vengeance. The YMCA became his home away from home; in the boxing program there he gained self-respect, self-defense skills, and a surrogate family. Lee attended West Point and later received a law degree; at the time *China Boy* was published, he

Gus Lee, author of China Boy *and* Honor and Duty. (Asian Week)

was director of attorney education for the State Bar of California. *China Boy*, widely reviewed, was unusually successful for a first novel; *Honor and Duty*, a sequel, was also well received. In 1993, Lee and his family (he and his wife have two children) moved from the San Francisco Bay Area to Colorado Springs, Colorado.

Lee, Jason Scott (b. 1967, Los Angeles): Actor. Reared in Hawaii on the island of Oahu, he attended Pearl High School, where he excelled in volleyball. Moving to California to pursue an acting career, he took courses at Fullerton College and studied under acting coach Sal Romeo at the Friends and Artists Theater Ensemble in Los Angeles. His first film was *Born in East L. A.* (1987). Lee's breakthrough came in 1993, when he starred in *Dragon: The Bruce Lee Story* and *Map of the Human Heart*. In these roles, Lee demonstrated a versatility and range rarely found in a young actor. Equally convincing as the Chinese American martial arts star and as an Inuit Eskimo, Lee received critical acclaim for his performances and established himself as a major draw at the box office.

Lim Poon Lee is postmaster of San Francisco, California. (Asian Week)

Lee, K. W. [Kyung Won] (b. June 1, 1928, Kaesong, Korea): Journalist. As a reporter for the *Kingsport Times & News* (1956) in Tennessee, Lee became the first Korean immigrant investigative journalist of a mainstream daily. The recipient of the first national Asian American Journalists Association Award of Excellence (1987), he has also served as editor of the *Korea Times* English edition and publisher/editor of *Koreantown Weekly* (1979-1982), the first national English-language weekly for Korean Americans. In 1985 he cofounded the Korean American Journalists Association. He is regarded as the dean of Korean American journalists.

Lee, Lim Poon (b. Dec. 19, 1910, Hong Kong): Postmaster. He became the first Chinese American to serve as postmaster in the continental United States at San Francisco, California, in 1966. He served as a sergeant in the U.S. Army, a chair of the California Department of Veterans Affairs, and a board member of the Greater Chinatown Community Service Association and the Chinese American Civic Council. He also testified in 1947 before the U.S. Congress on the effects of the War Brides Act (1945).

Lee, Li-Young (b. 1957, Jakarta, Indonesia): Poet. Lee comes from a distinguished Chinese family. His great-grandfather was Yuan Shikai, president of the Republic of China; his father was Mao Zedong's personal physician before embarking on an extraordinary odyssey that took him finally to a small town in Pennsylvania, where he served as a Presbyterian minister. Lee, who arrived in the United States at the age of six, studied at the University of Pittsburgh, the University of Arizona, and the State University of New York, Brockport. The author of two highly acclaimed volumes of poetry, *Rose* (1986) and *The City in Which I Love You* (1990), he has received numerous fellowships and awards, including a Writer's Award from the Whiting Foundation in 1988 and a Guggenheim fellowship in 1989. *The City in Which I Love You* was the Lamont Poetry Selection of the Academy of American Poets in 1990.

Lee, Ming Cho (b. Oct. 30, 1930, Shanghai, China): Theatrical scenic designer. For more than thirty years Ming Cho Lee has exerted a profound influence on the look and practice of American theatrical scene design. As a youth in Shanghai, Lee studied Chinese landscape painting before emigrating to Hong Kong in 1948, where he briefly considered a career in motion pictures. Realizing that stage design would offer greater opportunities to maintain artistic control over his work, Lee turned his sights to the theater. In 1949 he moved to the United States, where he studied art and theater at Occidental College. After a brief stint at the University of California, Los Angeles (UCLA), graduate school in 1954, Ed Kook, president of Century Lighting, invited Lee to travel to New York to meet the top American scenic designer, Jo Mielziner. Lee assisted Mielziner until 1958, working on the Broadway productions of *Silk Stockings*, *Cat On a Hot Tin Roof*, *Gypsy*, *The Lark*, *New Girl in Town*, and *The World of Suzy Wong*. In 1959 Lee was invited to Baltimore's Peabody Arts Theatre, where he designed his first opera, *The Turk in Italy*; he subsequently spent four years designing nine more operas there. When designer Eldon Elder left Joseph Papp's New York Shakespeare Festival in 1961 to pursue design work elsewhere, Papp hired Lee to replace him, resulting in an artistic collaboration that would last for more than a decade. As the festival's resident scenic director, Lee designed more than fifty Shakespearean productions and American world premieres, including the rock musical *Hair* (1967) and Ntozake Shange's *for colored girls who have considered suicide/when the rainbow is enuf* (1976). Architectural consulting work followed: With Giorgio Cavaglieri, Lee codesigned Papp's influential Public Theatre, creating two distinctive performance spaces, the Anspacher and Newman theaters. In 1978 Lee designed the Astor Court, a permanent exhibit of a traditional Chinese scholar's courtyard, located in the Metropolitan Museum of Art's Asian art wing. Continuing to design extensively for theaters and opera companies around the world, Lee also turned his attention to dance, creating unique designs for choreographers as diverse as Martha Graham, Eliot Feld, Gerald Arpino, and Robert Joffrey.

Often described as a minimalist, Lee is noted for his painstaking work and attention to detail, as well as close collaboration with directors. Throughout his career Lee pioneered innovative techniques and materials, utilizing mylar, multimedia, scaffolding, collage, and sculpture to make bold visual statements. He received the 1983 Tony Award for Best Scenic Design for his work on Patrick Meyers' play *K-2*, for which he created an enormous styrofoam mountain in which actors could actually carve new playing areas as the action progressed.

Lee has also been instrumental in nurturing scores of younger scenic designers. A professor at New York University during the 1960's, he joined the faculty of the prestigious Yale School of Drama in 1970. Through those venues, along with his own New York City-based design studio, he trained new generations of American designers, including Ralph Funicello, Douglas Schmidt, David Mitchell, Marjorie Bradley Kellogg, Karl Eigst, and John Lee Beatty.

Lee, Pius (b. Apr. 14, 1937, Zhongshan, China): Realtor. President of California Realty & Land in San Francisco, California, he served as commissioner of the San Francisco Human Rights Commission (1979-1980), the California State Industrial Welfare Commission (1981-1984), and the San Francisco Police Commission (1988-1992). He was also president of the Chinese Chamber of Commerce (1984-1985) and

Pius Lee is a prominent realtor and has served on various important San Francisco political commissions. (Asian Week)

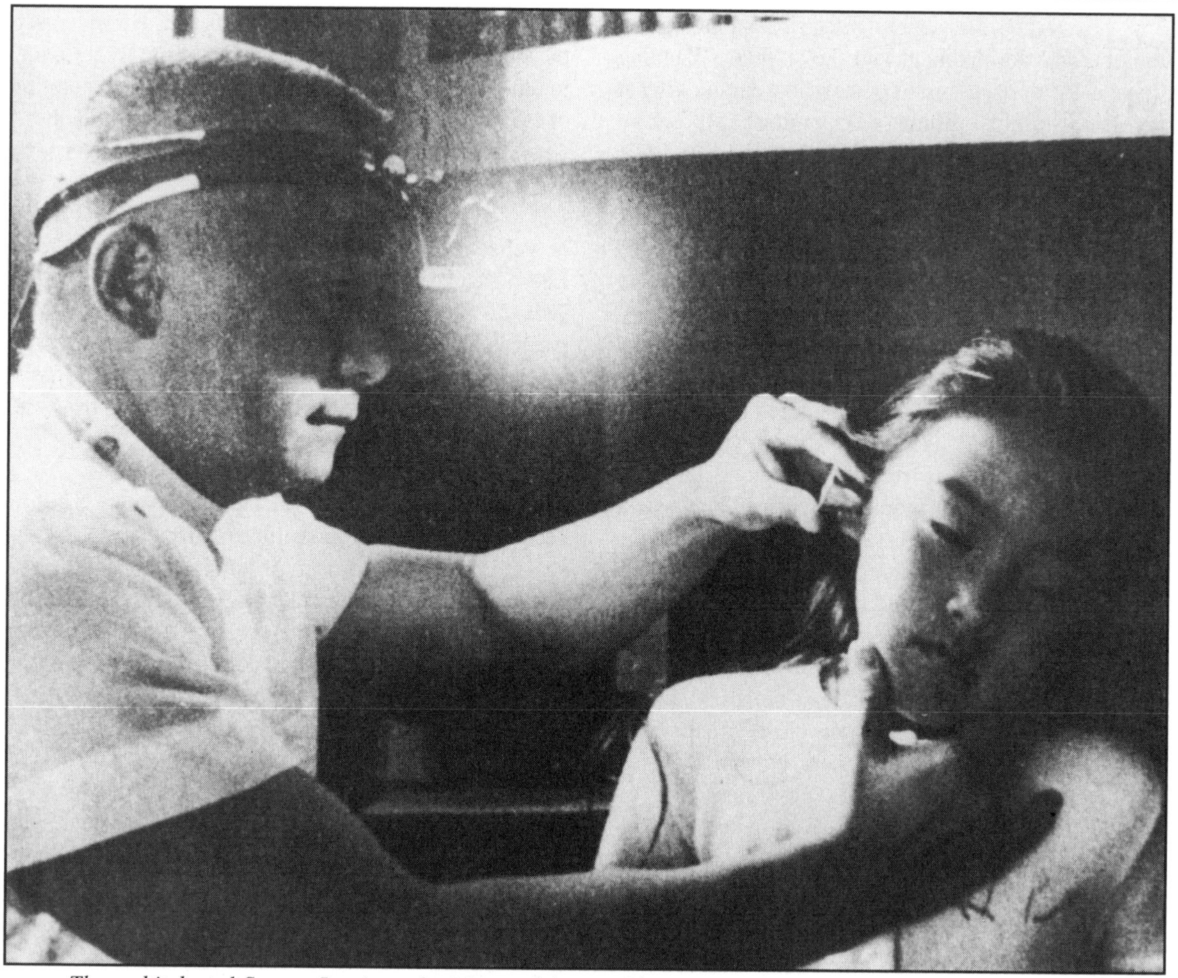

The multitalented Sammy Lee is a physician and former Olympic athlete. (The Korea Society/Los Angeles)

the CHINESE HOSPITAL (1989-1990). He also chaired the Economic Opportunity Council (1965-1968), the San Francisco-Taipei Sister City Committee (1979-1984), the Commission for Economic Development Advisory Council on Asia (1990-1993), and the Hai Sen Benevolent Association.

Lee, Rose Hum (Aug. 20, 1904, Butte, Mont.—Mar. 25, 1964): Scholar. The first Chinese American to chair the sociology department at the University of Chicago, she was actively involved in service organizations that provided relief and social service to people in China during the Sino-Japanese War and World War II. *The Chinese in the United States of America* (1960), a pioneering study, was one of many books that she authored. Also known as Mrs. Glenn Ginn, she earned her B.S. degree at the Carnegie Institute of Technology (1942) and her Ph.D. degree at the University of Chicago (1945).

Lee, Sammy (b. Aug. 1, 1920, Fresno, Calif.): Diver and physician. Born to Korean immigrants who worked on a Hawaiian plantation, he was the first Asian American to win an Olympic gold medal. He received gold medals for platform diving in 1948 and 1952 and a bronze medal for springboard diving in 1948. In 1953 he became the first nonwhite to receive the James E. Sullivan Memorial Award for outstanding achievement in sports. As a medical doctor he became a specialist in diseases of the ear. He was elected to the International Swimming Hall of Fame in 1968 and the U.S. Olympic Hall of Fame in 1990.

Lee, Thomas Henry (b. May 11, 1923, Shanghai, China): Research engineer. Lee came to the United States in 1948 and was naturalized in 1953. He received a B.S.M.E. degree from National Chiao Tung University in 1946 and a Ph.D. degree from Rensselaer Polytechnic Institute in 1954. From 1959 until

1980 he worked for General Electric, managing the research and development and the strategic planning divisions. He was professor of electrical engineering at the Massachusetts Institute of Technology (MIT) from 1980 until 1984, rejoining the school again in 1987. Lee has also held directorships with several private engineering technology and research companies. The holder of at least twenty-nine patents, he developed power vacuum interrupters and was responsible for the production of solid-state HUDC transmission.

Lee, Tsung-Dao (b. Nov. 25, 1926, Shanghai, China): Physicist. Lee is the third of six children born to businessman Tsing-Kong Lee and the former Ming-Chang Chang. In 1945 he fled from the advancing Japanese invaders to Kunming, Yunnan Province. Lee's scientific career began at the National Southwest Associated University of Kunming. There he studied with Ta-You Wu, who obtained a Chinese government scholarship for Lee that allowed Lee to study in the United States in 1946. Lee received his doctorate in 1950 from the University of Chicago, where he studied under Enrico Fermi and became close friends with Chen Ning YANG. The same year he married Hui-Chung (Jeannette) Chin. They have two sons.

Lee worked at the Yerkes Observatory and the University of California, Berkeley, before he was reunited with Yang in 1951 at the Institute for Advanced Study in Princeton. Lee became an assistant professor at Columbia University in 1953 and a full professor in 1956, the youngest on the Columbia faculty.

In 1957 Lee shared the Nobel Prize in Physics with Chen Ning Yang for their penetrating investigations of the parity laws, which led to important discoveries regarding subatomic particles. Lee and Yang were among the youngest ever to receive the Nobel Prize and were the first Chinese citizens to be awarded the prize. Lee has received numerous honors and awards in addition to the Nobel Prize.

Except for the years 1960 to 1963, which he spent as a professor at the Institute for Advanced Study, Lee continued his longtime association with Columbia University. He was named Enrico Fermi Professor of Physics in 1964.

In 1980 Lee established the China-United States Physics Examination and Application (CUSPEA) Program to allow qualified Chinese physics students to study for the doctorate degree at American universities. He would devote much of his energy after 1980 to this program. Lee said that the fellowship for American study, which his Chinese teacher had helped him to obtain in 1946, had changed his life. He organized the program so that similar good fortune might come to others. Influenced by the program and the reputation of Lee and Yang, many of the most talented students in China became physics majors.

Lee, Virginia (b. May 5, 1927, San Francisco, Calif.): Novelist. Born Virginia Yew, she married Howard F. Lee, an accountant, in 1946. Her novel, *The House That Tai Ming Built* (1963), was one of the first to be published by a Chinese American. (Diana CHANG and Louis CHU had published novels earlier.) *The House That Tai Ming Built* received a gold medal from the Commonwealth Club of California in 1963.

Lee Kuan Yew (b. Sept. 16, 1923, Singapore): Political leader. Born into a wealthy family of Chinese descent, Lee won a scholarship to study at Singapore's Raffles College before traveling to England to study law at the University of Cambridge. After graduating with highest honors, Lee was admitted to the bar at the Middle Temple in London in 1950. That same year, Lee was married to Kwa Geok Choo, a Malayan woman who had been a fellow student with him at Cambridge. The couple soon returned to Singapore, where Lee began working as a legal adviser to the Postal Union and several other trade unions, helping them negotiate for higher wages. Eager to initiate political reform in the British crown colony, he became one of the founders of the People's Action Party (PAP) in 1954 and was elected to the colonial legislative council in 1955. After working hard to negotiate for Singapore's right to self government within the British Commonwealth, Lee helped draft a new constitution and won a sweeping victory in the 1959 elections. As prime minister, Lee promoted social and economic reforms, including the emancipation of women and the expansion of local industry. Singapore became a member of the newly formed federation of Malaysia in 1963. In 1965, however, amid rising tensions between Malayans and ethnic Chinese, Singapore was forced to leave the federation and declare its sovereignty.

Under Lee's leadership, Singapore attained extraordinary economic development. As Fareed Zakaria noted in his introduction to an interview with Lee in *Foreign Affairs* 73 (March/April, 1994): 109-126, "In 1965 Singapore ranked economically with Chile, Argentina, and Mexico; today its per capita GNP is four or five times theirs." In 1990, Lee stepped down as prime minister, but as senior minister he still wields considerable influence. He has spoken forcefully of the enduring strengths of Asian values and of the need for Asian societies to find their own way, distinct from Western models.

Lem Moon Sing v. United States (1895): U.S. Supreme Court ruling that aliens within the United States retain the same rights accorded to American citizens; aliens outside the country are subject to the same stipulations governing those seeking to enter. This opinion strengthened the government's authority to resolve with finality matters regarding immigration admission.

Chinese merchant Lem Moon Sing left the United States in 1894 to visit China. He planned to return to California, his home for the past two years. While he was away, congressional lawmakers passed an exclusionary bill that made binding the decrees of U.S. immigration or customs officials in matters pertaining to aliens. Upon returning to San Francisco later that year, he was denied entrance. He appealed to the federal district court for relief, insisting that because he was a legal U.S. resident the new act did not apply to him, but lost.

In affirming the district court's decision, the Supreme Court cited the legal precedent established in *Nishimura v. United States* (1892). There the justices affirmed the power of the immigration inspector to render a final judgment denying entrance to a Japanese alien. Consequently, Lem Moon Sing's petition was not subject to judicial appeal.

Some time later, in *United States v. Ju Toy* (1905), the Court upheld the authority of the immigration bureau to deny entrance even to a Chinese who claimed to be a U.S. citizen. Again the prior administrative decree was declared to be outside the scope of judicial appeal.

Leong, Charles Lai (c. 1911, San Francisco, California—Feb. 23, 1984, San Francisco, California): Journalist. Graduated from Stanford University and San Jose State University in California, he founded the *California Chinese Press* in 1940, an English-language paper for Chinese Americans. Author of *The Eagle and the Dragon* (1976), he wrote for *East/West, Asian Week*, and the *San Francisco Chronicle* and once regarded himself in the 1930's as a "working man, from working people, who has stepped into the sphere of higher education." Leong died of cancer in 1984.

Leong, Russell Charles (b. 1950, San Francisco, Calif.): Writer, editor, and filmmaker. Born in Chinatown, he earned a B.A. degree from San Francisco State College and an M.F.A. degree from the School of Film and Television of the University of California, Los Angeles (UCLA).

Since 1977, Leong has been the editor of *Amerasia Journal*, the leading forum for work in Asian American Studies. His first book of poems, *In the Country of Dreams and Dust*, was published in 1993. In addition, his poems, essays, and stories have appeared in numerous anthologies and journals, including *Aiiieeeee! An Anthology of Asian-American Writers* (1974), *The New England Review*, *Tricycle: The Buddhist Review*, and *Charlie Chan Is Dead: An Anthology of Contemporary Asian American Fiction* (1993). His video documentaries include *Morning Begins Here* (1985) and *Why Is Preparing Fish a Political Act? The Poetry of Janice Mirikitani* (1990). Leong also edited *Moving the Image: Independent Asian Pacific American Media Arts* (1991).

Lesbian issues. *See* **Gay and lesbian issues**

Leung, Peter (b. Mar. 11, 1940, China): Scholar. A lecturer in Asian American Studies at the University of California, Davis, he developed in 1969 the univer-

Peter Leung is a lecturer in Asian American Studies at the University of California, Davis.

sity's first Cantonese-language program. He was a board member of the Sacramento Chinese Community Service Center; organized a festival in Coloma, California, in 1991, to commemorate the contributions of nineteenth century Chinese gold-miners; and authored *One Day, One Dollar* (1984), a book about the Chinese farming experience in Locke, California.

Leung, Tye: Translator. In 1912, she became the first known Chinese American woman to vote in a U.S. presidential election. (Although women were not given the right to vote nationally until 1920, when the Nineteenth Amendment was passed, individual states had given the vote to women before that time. California, where Leung voted in the 1912 election, had extended the vote to women in 1911.) Leung also was the first Chinese American hired to work as interpreter and assistant to the matrons of the ANGEL ISLAND IMMIGRATION STATION in San Francisco Bay. Between 1910 and 1940, the island served as a detention center for Asian immigrants awaiting entry to the United States or deportation back to their country of origin.

Leupp: Prison camp in Arizona, one of two such facilities established by the U.S. WAR RELOCATION AUTHORITY (WRA) during World War II to house so-called troublemakers from other Japanese American INTERNMENT CAMPS, as well as draft resisters. The other such facility was located in Moab, Utah. Officially they were designated "citizen isolation camps." MOAB was the original site, established in December, 1942; in April, 1943, the prison was relocated to Leupp, on Navaho reservation land.

Li, Choh Hao (Apr. 21, 1913, Canton, China—Nov. 28, 1987, Berkeley, Calif.): Biochemist and endocrinologist. Li earned a B.S. degree from the University of Nanjing in 1933. He arrived in the United States in 1935, beginning a fifty-year association with the University of California. After taking a Ph.D. degree from the university's Berkeley campus in 1938, he was a research associate there (1938-1944). From 1944 until 1947 he was professor of experimental biology, becoming professor of biochemistry at Berkeley, and professor of experimental endocrinology and director of the Hormone Research Lab at the San Francisco campus, all in 1950. Li became a naturalized American citizen in 1955.

Li isolated six of eight hormones known to be secreted by the human pituitary gland. In the early 1970's he achieved worldwide acclaim by synthesizing the pituitary human growth hormone, which he had discovered during the 1950's. In 1978 he discovered beta-endorphin, a powerful pain-killing drug manufactured in the brain. Li was also the first to isolate insulin-like growth factor 1, which stimulates the growth of bones and cartilage in the human body. During his lifetime Li was showered with numerous honors and awards.

Li, Victor H. (b. 1941, Hong Kong): Scholar. He earned a B.A. degree from Columbia University in 1961, a J.D. degree from Harvard Law School in 1964, and an LL.M. degree from Harvard the following year. He was honored as the Harlan Fiske Stone Scholar at Columbia Law School in 1964 and as a Fulbright-Hays Fellow in 1965-1966. Li has been a law professor at the University of Michigan Law School (1967-1969), at Columbia (where he began teaching in 1969), and at Stanford Law School (through 1993). From 1981 until 1990 he was director of the East-West Center of Honolulu.

Liang Qichao (Feb. 23, 1873, Xinhui, Guangdong Province, China—Jan. 19, 1929, Beijing, China): Intellectual and political reformer. Considered by some observers to be China's first true modern intellectual, Liang was devoted to the modern transformation of Chinese society. He came of age during a time of grave political turmoil in China and became politically active as a result of the crisis of China's relations with the Western powers and Japan. He met the Chinese scholar and reformer Kang Youwei, and the two of them soon became the leaders of China's intellectual and political reform movement.

In 1898, Liang and Kang led a short-lived movement to restore the Chinese emperor to the throne. This effort was soon defeated, and the two were forced into exile in Japan. To further their political aims, Kang traveled in 1899 to Canada, where he founded the BAOHUANGHUI (Chinese Empire Reform Association), one of the first political parties in Chinese history. At the invitation of this organization, Liang toured Canada and the United States for seven months in 1903. During this trip, he kept copious notes, which eventually became his *Xin dalu youji jielu* (selected memoir of travels in the new world), published in 1904.

Liang's memoir contains valuable demographic information on the Chinese in the United States at the start of the twentieth century, including occupational distribution, Chinese fraternal associations, and his opinions on Sino-American relations. Most important is his assessment of the political consciousness among the Chinese immigrant community. Often ignoring the pernicious effects of American racism and exclusionary legislation, Liang viewed the emphasis on clan and regional loyalties among Chinese immigrants as a main reason for their inability to improve their lot in the United States. On a broader scale, he interpreted this clannishness as a "cultural shortcoming" of the Chinese that hindered their progress in the modern family of nations. Based on his disappointing encounter with the Chinese in the United States, he returned to Asia convinced that the Chinese were unprepared for democratic reform.

Liang returned to Japan and stayed there until after the CHINESE REVOLUTION OF 1911. He served in the new government for a short period and spent his final years pursuing academic concerns.

Liberty Bank: Bank founded by Chinese immigrants in Honolulu, Hawaii, in 1922. A group of fifteen Chinese immigrant merchants wanted a bank to serve their own credit needs and that of the Chinese community. On January 31, 1922, an organizational meeting took place at Sun Yun Wo Restaurant in Honolulu. There these Chinese businessmen made a plan to form a bank. They named it "The Liberty Bank of Honolulu." Application for a banking charter was signed and filed the same day and approved on February 11, 1922.

The newly formed bank, with Lum Yip Kee as its first president, was first located at 75 North King Street at the center of Chinatown in Honolulu. The bank officially opened on February 18, 1922. Within the first three hours of its opening, two hundred accounts were opened by the merchants themselves, their relatives, and other members of the Chinese community.

Although the original depositors were predominantly Chinese, over the years customers and employees began coming from other ethnic groups in Honolulu. The Liberty Bank of Honolulu became the third oldest bank in Hawaii, serving the financial needs of Hawaii's society at large.

Through the Depression years of the 1930's and the World War II period of the 1940's, the bank continued its progress and development. Expansion began in the 1950's with the completion of a new bank building. Between 1953 and 1973 eight branches were opened throughout the island of Oahu.

In June, 1970, the bank's name was shortened to "Liberty Bank" with a new logo. The bank became known for, among other things, its bilingual services. It was able to offer more than sixty different services to its customers. It was also instrumental in establishing and developing many Honolulu business as well as residential communities.

Light, Ivan (b. Nov. 3, 1941, Chicago, Ill.): Scholar. Professor of sociology at the University of California, Los Angeles, he specializes in immigrant self-employment. He is best known for *Ethnic Enterprise in America* (1972), as well as *Immigrant Entrepreneurs* (1988), coauthored with Edna BONACICH.

Ligot, Cayetano: Political appointee. In 1921, Ligot was appointed by Leonard Wood, governor-general of the Philippines, to serve as labor commissioner to oversee conditions faced by Filipino workers on Hawaiian plantations. At the same time, Wood commissioned Hermenegildo Crus, director of the Philippine Bureau of Labor, to prepare a report on labor conditions in Hawaii. Ligot made his own investigative tour of Hawaii and encouraged Filipino laborers to cooperate with their employers in order to strengthen ties between the two territories. As a result of his visit to Hawaii, Ligot concurred with the findings of Crus's report, which dismissed the culpability of the HAWAIIAN SUGAR PLANTERS' ASSOCIATION (HSPA) and placed the blame for labor unrest squarely on the shoulders of Filipino laborers. Filipino workers saw this action as direct evidence of Ligot's collusion with the HSPA and as a betrayal of his responsibility to guarantee the safety and well-being of Filipino laborers.

Liliuokalani, Queen (Lydia Kamakaeha; Sept. 2, 1838, Honolulu, Hawaii—Nov. 11, 1917, Honolulu, Territory of Hawaii): Queen of Hawaii. She was the daughter of Kapaakea (father) and Keohokalole (mother) and the sister of King David Kalakaua, the last ruling monarch of Hawaii. She became queen of Hawaii at the most difficult time in Hawaiian history, and her entire reign was one of trouble, economic depression, political controversy, and eventual overthrow of the monarchy and the Hawaiian Kingdom. She was well educated, dignified, strong willed, mature, full of vigor, and experienced in the politics of the kingdom. Like her brother, she loved music, and she composed beautiful songs, the most memorable being "Aloha Oe" (1898). One of her great contributions was to bequeath her estate to a trust set up to assist Hawaiian children.

Kalakaua died in January, 1891, in San Francisco, California, about a year after the U.S. Congress had

Queen Liliuokalani served as queen of Hawaii during one of the most difficult times in its history. (AP/Wide World Photos)

passed the McKinley Tariff Act of 1890, which devastated the Hawaiian sugar industry and created economic depression in the state. This single factor posed the greatest challenge for the queen, who would rule from 1891 until 1893. The talk among sugar planters, their agents, and businesspeople was no longer simply a reciprocity treaty with the United States but annexation. A secret organization called the Annexation Club concluded that annexation offered the only hope for a stable government in Hawaii. The queen's actions in 1892 to change the Hawaii constitution and to restore more power to the monarchy led to her overthrow in January, 1893. She yielded her authority to the superior force of the United States and was not reinstated as queen. While confined as a prisoner in the former royal palace, Liliuokalani signed a document wherein she formally abdicated all claims to the throne, took an oath of allegiance to the Hawaiian Republic, and stated that she now wished to live her life quietly as a private citizen.

Although the crown lands of the kingdom of Hawaii were taken when Liliuokalani was deposed, her private landholdings were placed in a trust for the benefit of orphan children of Hawaii. The Queen Liliuokalani Children's Center is the result of her trustees' efforts to establish an institution to fulfill the wishes of the queen. In 1946 the Child Welfare Department of the trust was created. In 1952 the Department of Public Welfare licensed the agency as a child-placing organization. By 1987 the center had extended its services to Maui, Kauai, Hawaii (Hilo and Kona), Molokai, and Oahu (Honolulu and Windward Oahu). By 1987 the center was servicing approximately two thousand Hawaiian children statewide yearly.

Lim, Genny (b. Dec. 15, 1946, San Francisco, Calif.): Poet, playwright, editor, and scholar. Born in San Francisco to a family of Chinese descent, Lim moved to New York City to attend Columbia University, where she completed a certificate in broadcast journalism in 1973. She later returned home to study at San Francisco State University, where she earned a bachelor's degree in 1978.

Fascinated by the histories of Chinese immigrants, Lim collaborated with H. Mark LAI and Judy YUNG in translating Chinese calligraphic poems written on the barracks walls at San Francisco's ANGEL ISLAND by immigrants detained upon their arrival in the United States. These poems were published by a small press in 1980 as *Island: Poetry and History of Chinese Immigrants on Angel Island, 1910-1940* and were reprinted

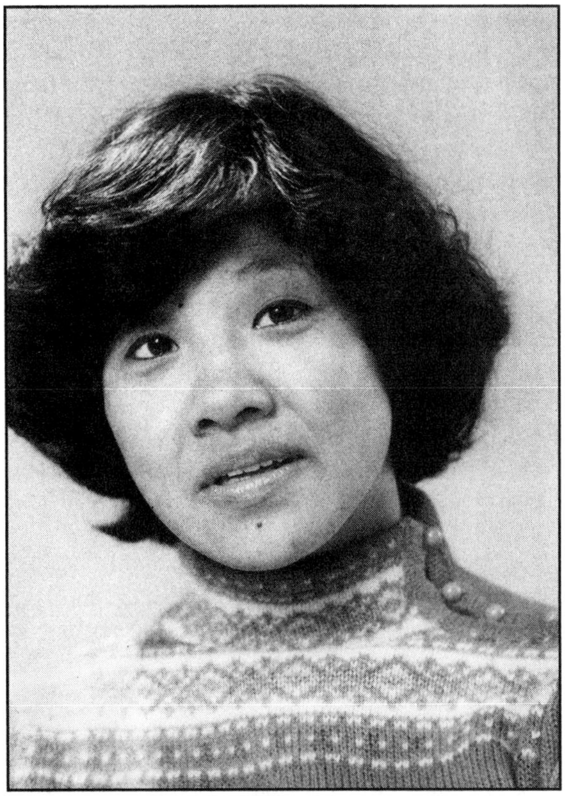

Genny Lim was appointed as poet-in-residence at the Fine Arts Museums of San Francisco. (San Francisco Chronicle)

by the University of Washington Press in 1991. Lim worked as a researcher for the Chinese Women of America historical project from 1981 through 1983 and helped compile and edit *The Chinese American Experience: Papers from the Second National Conference on Chinese American Studies* (1984). Beginning in 1982, she taught as a visiting lecturer in creative writing in the ASIAN AMERICAN STUDIES department at the University of California, Berkeley (and served as assistant editor and feature writer for *East/West* newsletter).

In the early 1980's, Lim published works in several genres that incorporated her research on Angel Island immigrants. *Wings for Lai-Ho*, a bilingual children's story that appeared in 1982, conveys the realities of a Chinese immigrant girl's experience at Angel Island. Her play *Paper Angels*, written in 1982 and produced as an *American Playhouse* teleplay in 1985, portrays the bright aspirations and harsh lives of seven Chinese men and women detained at Angel Island. A later play by Lim, *Bitter Cane* (1989), explores the historical experiences of Chinese laborers in Hawaii through the eyes of a Chinese prostitute owned by the foreman of a sugar plantation.

Since accepting an appointment as poet-in-residence at the Fine Arts Museums of San Francisco, Lim has focused greater attention on her poetry while continuing to explore the full scope of the Chinese immigrant experience in America.

Lim, Shirley Geok-lin (b. Malacca, Malaysia): Poet and scholar. Lim's first book of poems, *Crossing the Peninsula and Other Poems* (1980), was awarded the Commonwealth Poetry Prize. As a scholar, Lim has coedited such influential works as *The Forbidden Stitch: An Asian American Women's Anthology* (1989), which received an American Book Award from the Before Columbus Foundation, and *Reading the Literatures of Asian America* (1992), a collection of critical essays. She has also published *Approaches to Teaching Kingston's "The Woman Warrior"* (1991).

Lin, Maya Ying (b. Oct. 5, 1959, Athens, Ohio): Architect. Lin gained nationwide fame for designing the Vietnam Veterans Memorial in Washington, D.C. Her design was selected in 1981, and the memorial was dedicated in 1982. In 1986, she started her studio practice in downtown New York, after receiving a master's degree in architecture from Yale University that same year.

In 1981, as a twenty-one-year-old architecture student, Lin entered a design contest for the Vietnam Veterans Memorial. The contest was organized by Jan Scruggs, a Vietnam veteran who had established a fund and collected seven million dollars for the contest. Lin's design was selected from a competition that attracted 1,421 entries. The 594-foot monument that she designed, built of polished black granite, has one arm pointing to the Washington Monument and another arm to the Lincoln Memorial. The surface is carved with the names of those who died in the Vietnam War (1965-1975). The memorial triggered some controversy among some veterans and others who found it to be too modernistic and who believed that it

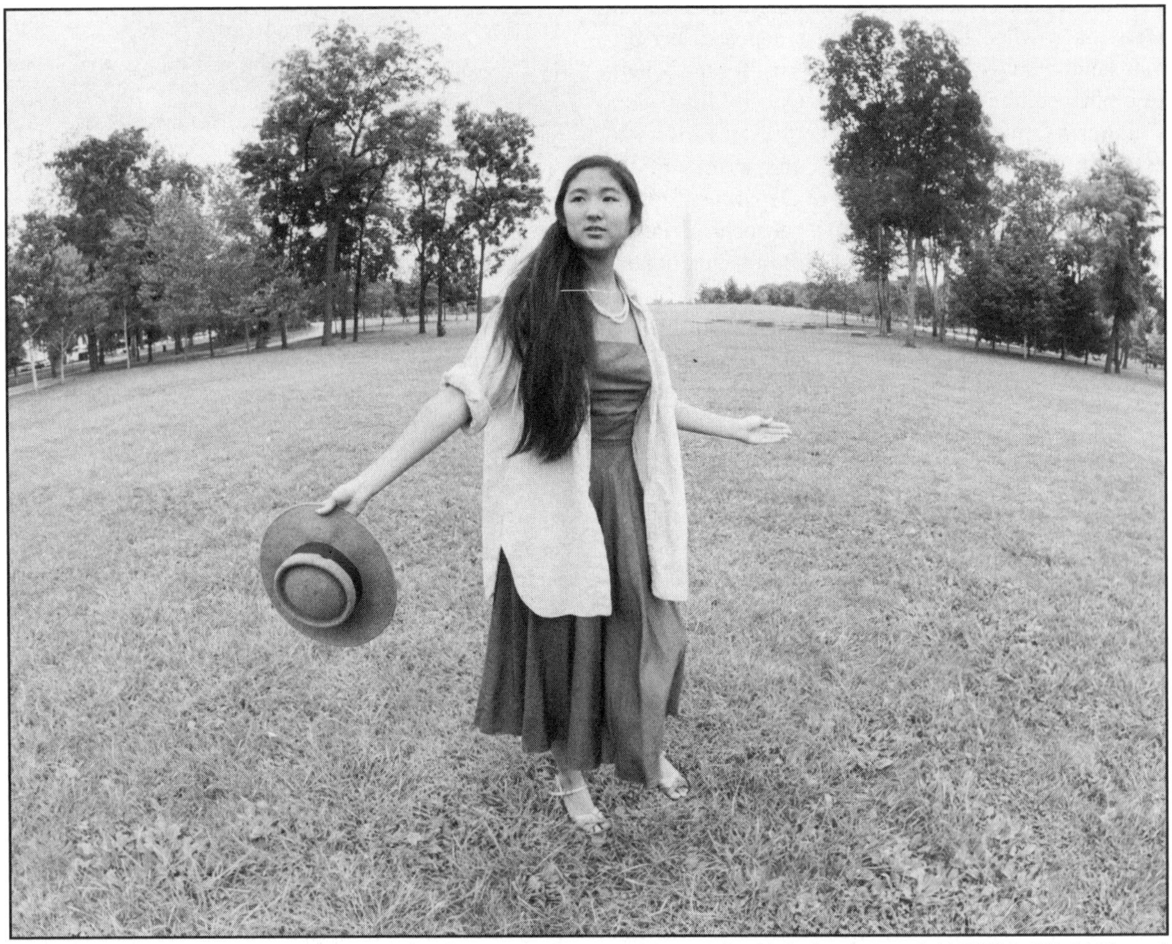

Maya Ying Lin is shown at the site chosen for the Vietnam Veterans Memorial, which she designed. (AP/Wide World Photos)

failed to commemorate properly the men and women who had died, but ultimately Lin's design has been validated by the testimony of thousands who have been deeply moved by it.

In 1989, the Civil Rights Memorial in Montgomery, Alabama, which Lin designed, was dedicated. The monument is composed of a nine-foot-high curved wall and a horizontally laid granite disc on which the major events of the Civil Rights movement are inscribed. Lin's design of the "Women's Table," an outdoor sculpture at Yale University, is dedicated to honor the women of that institution. Among the other projects on which she has worked are the Open Air Chapel at Juanita College in Huntington, Pennsylvania (1989), the Rosa Esman Gallery in New York (1990), the TOPO Topiary Playing Field in Charlotte, North Carolina (1991, with Henry Arnold), and a clock for the renovated Pennsylvania Street Station in New York (1994).

Among the many awards and honors Lin has received are an honorary doctorate of fine arts degree from Yale University (1987), the Presidential Design Award (1988), and the American Institute of Architects Honor Award (1984). Her work has also been shown in many exhibitions.

Lin Sing v. Washburn (1863): California Supreme Court ruling that the state's discriminatory Police Tax—a "measure of special and extreme hostility to the Chinese"—was unconstitutional. A law passed in 1862 imposed a monthly head tax on every Mongolian adult in California who was not employed in the rice, sugar, tea, or coffee industries or had not paid the state's FOREIGN MINERS' TAX. Also known as the "Capitation Tax," it became another means of harassing the Chinese immigrant population. (See CAPITATION TAXES.)

Shortly after the statute was enacted, the San Francisco tax collector assessed a five-dollar sum against Chinese resident Lin Sing. The latter paid the tax but immediately filed suit in state court to challenge the law's validity. Following a judgment in favor of the state, the case went before the Supreme Court, which was asked to decide whether a state could lawfully assume authority that the Constitution had expressly and exclusively reserved for Congress—that of regulating commerce with foreign nations.

Before the bench, California's attorney general argued that the tax was a justifiable exercise of the state's police power and did not impinge upon the Constitution's commerce clause. Upon landing in America and leaving their ships, he claimed, the Chinese left the stream of foreign commerce (federal jurisdiction) and came under state jurisdiction, which encompassed the right to levy taxes.

The Court disagreed, calling on earlier U.S. Supreme Court case law to construct an analogy of the facts at hand. In 1827 the Court had struck down a Maryland statute that taxed foreign goods after they had come ashore and had therefore left the stream of commerce. Since the right to import goods into the states also implied the right to sell them there, the Court explained, a tax on selling was in effect a tax on importing—which only Congress could impose. In light of this conflict of laws, therefore, the Maryland statute could not stand. The California court then declared that the power to regulate foreign commerce encompassed the power to regulate the transport of foreign travelers—in this instance, the Chinese. By this reasoning, then, even as the states could not tax foreign imports, so they could not target foreigners for special taxation. Moreover, merely because foreign goods land ashore does not completely remove them from federal jurisdiction. For the same reason, California could not continue to treat the Chinese differently on the grounds that they have left their ships and come into the state.

This case became the first in which a resident Chinese immigrant went to court to challenge a state statute based on a violation of federal laws.

Lin Yutang (Oct. 10, 1895, Zhangzhou, China—March 26, 1976, Hong Kong): Writer. Lin received his undergraduate education from St. John's University in China and continued his education in the United States in 1919. He also went to Germany, where he received his Ph.D. Upon his return to China in 1922, he joined the faculty of the English department at Peking University. In 1926, he assumed the post of Dean of Humanities at Xiamen University. He worked at the Ministry of Foreign Affairs in Wuhan in 1927. Beginning in 1932, he began to organize and edit literary journals such as *Lun Yu*, which became the name of a school of literary critics. In 1935 he published *My Country and My People*, a book about China written in English. The book was a great success, and shortly thereafter he moved to the United States, where he produced a steady stream of novels, translations, and nonfiction.

Lin Yutang was an important and unique figure in twentieth century Chinese literary history. He has often been described as a master of humor; his writing offers an understanding of life "between tears and laughter." His broad knowledge of Western as well as

Eastern literary traditions enabled him to examine both American and Chinese cultures.

Ling, Amy (b. Beijing, China): Poet and scholar. In 1984, Ling published *Chinamerican Reflections*, a collection of highly personal poems. As a scholar, she wrote *Between Worlds: Women Writers of Chinese Ancestry* (1990), coedited the companion volumes *Imagining America: Stories from the Promised Land* (1991) and *Visions of America: Personal Narratives from the Promised Land* (1993), and edited the essay collection *Reading the Literatures of Asian America* (1992) with Shirley Geok-lin Lim. Ling has served as the director of Asian American Studies at the University of Wisconsin, Madison.

Lion dance: Performance usually given at Chinese Lunar New Year festivities or at other celebrations. Members of martial arts clubs are often the performers. This dance is also used to chase away evil spirits upon the opening of a business establishment. Performers usually hold up a lion's head made out of fabric and bamboo with a colorful fabric body and dance to the beat of a large drum.

Lippmann, Walter (Sept. 23, 1889, New York, N.Y.—Dec. 14, 1974, New York, N.Y.): Journalist. He was one of the most prominent nonmilitary commentators to call for the relocation of all Japanese Americans from the West Coast and for their incarceration. A figure of major influence, he was an associate editor of *The New Republic*, an editor for *New York World*, and a writer for the *New York Herald Tribune*. He was also assistant to the U.S. secretary of war in 1917 and is the author of numerous books on foreign policy.

Little Saigon Radio (KWIZ-FM): Vietnamese-language radio station based in Santa Ana, California, on the air since 1993. The station serves up a mix of music, talk shows, public service announcements, commentaries, and news—including news that Vietnamese Americans in Orange and Los Angeles counties typically cannot obtain through the mainstream media. As a forum for debating controversial issues and a source of important community information, Little Saigon Radio has become an influential voice for Vietnamese Americans throughout the region.

Liu, Daniel S. C. (b. Feb. 13, 1908, Honolulu, Territory of Hawaii): Police chief. The first Chinese American to serve as police chief in Honolulu, in 1948, he was vice president (1957-1963) and president (1963-1964) of the International Association of Chiefs of Police. He received numerous awards for outstanding accomplishments in, and dedication to, law enforcement, including the J. Edgar Hoover Gold Medal Award (1966) and a distinguished service award from the National Police Officers Association (1968).

Liu, Henry Yi (Liu Yi-liang; Dec. 7, 1932, Liu Jia Tai, Jiangsu Province, China—Oct. 15, 1984, Daly City, Calif.): Writer and journalist. The assassination of Henry Liu was an international scandal that greatly embarrassed the government of Taiwan and that probably convinced its leaders of the need to reform and democratize the political system.

Liu had lived in Taiwan and had immigrated in 1967 to the United States, where he became a naturalized American citizen. He eventually settled in the San Francisco Bay Area, writing articles for Chinese-language newspapers as well as books on Chinese politics. In 1984, a revised edition of his critical *Biography of Chiang Ching-kuo*, about the president of the Republic of China (ROC) on Taiwan, was published in the United States.

On October 15, 1984, Liu was shot to death in the garage of his Daly City home. In November, the ROC government arrested Chen Chi-li and Wu Tun, members of Taiwan's largest criminal organization, the United Bamboo Gang. The two admitted to their involvement in the Liu murder and implicated government officials when they alleged that the head of the ROC Defense Intelligence Bureau, Wang Hsi-Ling, had ordered that Liu be killed for defaming Chiang and the nation. Two of Wang's aides were also implicated.

In April, 1985, Chen and Wu were tried and sentenced to life imprisonment by the Taipei District Court; Wang was also given a life sentence by a military tribunal, while his two aides were given jail terms of two-and-a-half years each. Wang denied that he ordered Chen to kill Liu but acknowledged "some moral responsibility" because he had expressed to Chen that Liu should be "taught a lesson."

Years later, U.S. authorities arrested, tried, and convicted a third suspect in the murder, Tung Kuei-sen, a member of the United Bamboo Gang. While serving his prison term, Tung was killed by a fellow prisoner.

The truth of the Henry Liu murder will probably never be ascertained. There were rumors that the intelligence officials had not acted alone as Taipei officials maintained but that higher levels of the government were involved. There were also American press reports

Writer Henry Liu is shown in his china shop prior to his murder in 1984, which allegedly involved the government of Taiwan. (San Francisco Chronicle)

that Liu was a triple agent who collected intelligence for Taipei, Beijing, as well as the U.S. Federal Bureau of Investigation (FBI).

Liu, Pei Chi (Po-chi Liu; b. May 29, 1908): Editor and scholar. Beginning in 1940, Liu was the editor of the San Francisco-based *Chinese Nationalist Daily* (*Kuo Min Yat Po*), an organ of the Chinese Nationalist party. With the assistance of the CHINESE CONSOLIDATED BENEVOLENT ASSOCIATION, he organized the Chinatown Anti-Communist League. In addition, Liu undertook pioneering studies in Chinese American history. His two-volume work *Meiguo Huaqiao Shi* (1976-1981; a history of the Chinese in the United States of America) was based on extensive research in Chinese-language primary sources. While written in Chinese, Liu's history has a foreword in English, and the bibliography includes English-language sources.

Liu, William T. (b. May 6, 1930, Nanjing, China): Scholar. The first Asian American to be appointed to the Chicago Board of Education in 1988, he was the director of the Pacific American Research Centre (1976-1989) and a professor of sociology at the University of Illinois, Chicago until his retirement in 1992. He served on the boards of the Advisory Council of the Asian American Assembly for Policy Research (1977-1984), the Asian Human Services of Greater Chicago (1978-1986), and the ASIAN PACIFIC HEALTH FORUM (1986-1991).

Local: Panethnic identity shared by people in Hawaii with an appreciation of the land, culture, and people of the islands. The notion of "local" transcends ethnic and class differences among Hawaii's people through an emphasis on their collective boundary with nonlocal groupings. "Local" is a relative term defined and expressed in opposition to groups considered as nonlocal, such as *haoles* (foreigners, typically Caucasians), immigrants, the military, or tourists. Over time, the meaning and significance of local identity have changed in response to social and economic changes in Hawaii.

Local identity has its historical origins during the period of plantation labor recruitment prior to World War II (1939-1945). The working-class background of both the Native Hawaiians and the immigrant plantation groups (such as Chinese, Filipinos, Japanese, Koreans, Portuguese, and Puerto Ricans) is the basis of their collective local identity. Together, those groups shared a subordinate social status in opposition to the dominant *haole* planter and merchant oligarchy. Over the years, the local identity gained greater importance through social movements to unionize plantation workers and to wrest political power from the *haole*-controlled Republican Party.

Until the mid-1960's, local identity essentially indicated birth or longtime residence in Hawaii and familiarity with its cultural life-style. "Local" then began to assume a greater significance, representing people with an appreciation of, and commitment to, Hawaii and its people and who thus wanted to retain control of its political and economic future. This change in the meaning and significance of "local" resulted from various external forces of change perceived as detrimental to the quality of life in Hawaii, including increased immigration from the continental United States, substantial immigration from Asia, and the continued expansion of the tourist industry.

The impact of these social and economic changes intensified during the 1980's, particularly with the increased investment by Japanese corporations in tourism development. These forces have contributed to the continuing maintenance and affirmation of local identity. There is, however, among local people a growing sense of marginalization and of powerlessness, an uncertainty that they can regain control of the political and economic future of Hawaii from external sources of change.

Locke: Rural Chinatown founded in 1915. Locke is a California Historical Landmark and is listed on the National Register of Historic Places. It is situated about thirty miles west of the city of Sacramento, on the banks of the Sacramento River. Every year, more than one million tourists visit this last rural Chinatown in North America. With its single paved street, aging buildings, and few Chinese signs, this tiny community reminds people of the unique history of the Chinese associated with the area's agricultural development.

CALIFORNIA

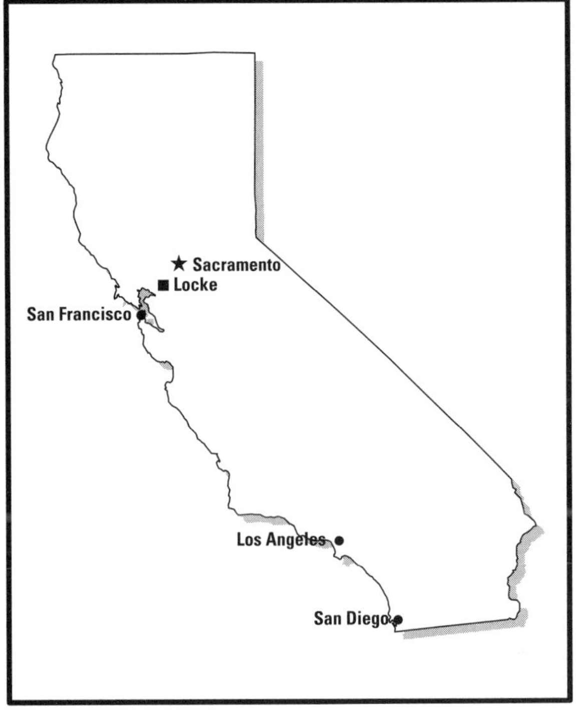

Locke was founded after a fire destroyed the Chinatown in Walnut Grove. Consequently, a group of Chinese merchants, led by Chan Tin-sin and Lee Bing, leased ten acres of land from the local Locke family. A town hall and six buildings were built on the town's Main Street, and other buildings, including the Southern Pacific packing shed and dock, the Star Theater, the Locke Christian Center, Al the Wop Restaurant, and single residences on Key Street were built between 1920 and 1933. Locke, a unique town built by the Chinese for the Chinese, had a population consisting largely of Chungshan people from southern China.

Locke was a lively place from the 1920's to the 1950's. It had a motion-picture theater that showed silent black-and-white films, six restaurants, nine grocery stores, a flour mill, a hotel, and several boarding houses, all catering to Chinese farm laborers. During the harvest seasons, besides its four hundred permanent residents, more than one thousand laborers stayed in the town. In addition to various businesses, the town included gambling houses that operated a lottery. Because lottery tickets were sold almost anywhere in Locke, many people got the impression that Locke was a gambling town.

The town's population began to decline in the

1950's, and by the 1970's, only one hundred retired Chungshan farmworkers lived there. The town and the Locke ranch were sold to a Hong Kong developer who wanted to make drastic changes in the area. Sacramento County and the California state government, however, suggested the preservation of the town's quaint ambience as "living history."

Locke, Gary (b. Jan. 1950, Seattle, Wash.): Politician. First elected to the Washington State House of Representatives (Thirty-seventh District) in 1982, he has served on a number of committees, including House Appropriations and Judiciary. The winner of the 1990 Legislator of the Year award, he was a member of the boards of Kin On Chinese Nursing Home and Asian Counseling and Referral Center, both in Seattle. He earned a B.A. degree from Yale University in 1972 and a J.D. degree from Boston University in 1975.

Congressman Gary Locke of Seattle, Washington. (Asian Week)

Lodge, Henry Cabot (May 12, 1850, Boston, Mass.—Nov. 9, 1924, Boston, Mass.): U.S. senator. At Harvard University he was an instructor in American history, from 1876 to 1879. Following service in the U.S. House of Representatives (1887-1893), he was elected a U.S. senator (1893-1924), during which time he became a prominent conservative Republican leader. He played an important role in the passage of the IMMIGRATION ACT OF 1924, which denied entry to virtually all Asians. In the process he succeeded in persuading other senators who were in favor of either a Japanese quota or a continuation of the 1907 GENTLEMEN'S AGREEMENT to go along with the total exclusion of Japanese.

London, Jack (Jan. 12, 1876, San Francisco, Calif.—Nov. 22, 1916, Glen Ellen, Calif.): Novelist. A writer who led an adventurous life before becoming famous, he was extremely anti-Asian and an outspoken advocate of exclusion of Asian immigration. He subscribed to the idea that Japanese immigrants were going to overtake the state of California by increasing in numbers through their high birthrate.

Lone, John (b. Hong Kong): Actor. Trained as a Beijing opera actor at Hong Kong's Chin Chiu Academy, Lone left the Chinese theater and, in search of artistic freedom, emigrated as a teenager to the United States. His initial theatrical break came when he played "Steve" in David Henry HWANG's 1980 comedy-drama about Chinese American self-identification, *FOB*, at New York's Public Theatre. Lone's performance earned him Drama League of America and Obie awards. The following year, Hwang wrote a play specifically for Lone: *The Dance and the Railroad*, a drama of nineteenth century Chinese railroad workers. Lone directed, choreographed, composed music, and created the character of "Lone" in the play, which was first produced at the New Federal Theatre in New York City and subsequently at the Cricket Theatre in Minneapolis. The artistic association between Lone and Hwang continued when Lone acted in and directed *Sound and Beauty* at the Public Theatre in 1983.

In addition to his distinguished stage career, Lone demonstrated his versatility as a performer in films, as the title character in Fred Schepisi's 1984 *Iceman*; the suave Chinatown organized crime boss in Michael Cimino's controversial *The Year of the Dragon* (1985);

Award-winning actor John Lone. (Nancy Wong)

the pathetic Emperor Puyi in Bernardo Bertolucci's *The Last Emperor* (1987); and as the sexually complex Song Liling in David Cronenberg's film version of Hwang's 1988 hit play *M. Butterfly* (1993).

Loo, Chalsa M. (b. Mar. 7, 1945, Honolulu, Territory of Hawaii): Clinical psychologist and scholar. Loo attended the University of California, Berkeley, and Ohio State University, from which she earned her Ph.D. degree in 1971. Clinical psychologist at the Department of Veterans Affairs in Honolulu and professor of psychology at the University of Hawaii, she has served as executive board member of the ASSOCIATION FOR ASIAN AMERICAN STUDIES and the Chinese Community Action Coalition. Founder of the nonprofit Chinatown Housing and Health Research Project (now the Chinatown Research Center) in San Francisco in 1978 to study the lives of Chinatown residents, Loo is the author of *Chinatown: Most Time, Hard Time* (1991). She has published widely in her field and serves as a consulting editor for assorted professional journals.

Loomis, Augustus Ward (1816, Andover, Conn.—1891): Missionary. In 1859, Loomis, who had previously served as a missionary in China and (in the United States) among the Creek Indians, established a school in San Francisco's Chinatown to teach English and, if possible, win Chinese converts to Christianity. In 1872, the American Tract Society published Loomis' handbook, *English and Chinese Lessons*. In addition to his missionary work, Loomis acted as an advocate for the Chinese American community and promoted mutual understanding between the Chinese and mainstream America.

Lord, Bette Bao (b. Nov. 3, 1938, Shanghai, China): Novelist and journalist. Lord was born in China, the daughter of a Chinese diplomat to the United States. When the Chinese Communists defeated the Nationalists in 1949 and established the People's Republic of China (PRC), the family remained in the United States, and Lord grew up in New York and New Jersey, graduating from Tufts University. From 1985 to 1989 she lived in the PRC with her husband, Winston Lord, during his tenure as U.S. ambassador to China.

Lord's books include *Eighth Moon* (1964), *Spring Moon* (1981), *In the Year of the Boar and Jackie Robinson* (1984), a novel for children, and *Legacies: A Chinese Mosaic* (1990). She is also a widely published journalist.

Lordsburg: Prison camp in New Mexico for enemy aliens, one of four INTERNMENT CAMPS on the American mainland run by the Immigration and Naturalization Service (INS) of the U.S. Justice Department during World War II. Internees were sent to the camps after having been declared national security risks during formal hearings and were subject to deportation at the insistence of the American government. Nondisruptive Japanese evacuees were allowed to live with their families in one of ten RELOCATION CENTERS administered by the U.S. WAR RELOCATION AUTHORITY (WRA).

Los Angeles, Battle of (Apr. 24-25, 1942): Event during World War II, resulting from fears that the Japanese would invade the United States' West Coast. On April 24 and 25, sirens wailed in Los Angeles to signal an "air raid" by Japanese fighters. The city declared a blackout, and U.S. Army antiaircraft fire lit up the sky. Though the incident was a false alarm, the antiaircraft fire damaged houses and buildings, while the commotion caused death by heart attacks and traffic accidents.

Los Angeles County Anti-Asiatic Society: Anti-Japanese exclusionist league formed in 1919. With the passage of the California Alien Land Law of 1913, Japanese immigrants were barred from owning or leasing land. Years later, however, Asian exclusionists began pressing for an even more restrictive statute, and lawmakers offered to amend the 1913 law.

U.S. senatorial candidate James D. Phelan adopted these sentiments into his campaign platform. Phelan, who insisted that Chinese exclusion was the only means of preserving Western civilization, maintained that passage of the amendment would close any legal loopholes evident in the old law.

Numerous California anti-Asian groups such as the Native Sons of the Golden West shared Phelan's ideas and supported his reelection. In the fall of 1919, the jointly organized Anti-Asiatic Committee met in Los Angeles. Two months later, with a roster that included the American Legion and labor unions, it became the Anti-Asiatic Society. Among its declared goals were the preservation of racial purity, the abolition of the GENTLEMEN'S AGREEMENT of 1907, and the enactment of the 1920 amendment.

Los Angeles riot of 1871: Violent uprising in which an angry mob killed nineteen Chinese immigrants. In California economic recessions of the 1850's and 1860's stirred public resentment toward the Chinese. Unemployed white workers blamed them for the loss of jobs and the economic downturn. Bitterness ran especially high in the mining camps and railroad construction sites, two industries with significant numbers of Chinese laborers. As a result, many Chinese lost their lives at the hands of agitators who often went unpunished; Chinese homes, businesses, and other property were also destroyed by angry mobs.

Moreover, political campaigns centered on halting the flow of Chinese immigration into the United States fed anti-Chinese sentiment and provoked public demand for alien-restrictive federal and state legislation. The result was the CHINESE EXCLUSION ACT OF 1882, the first major statutory strike against the Chinese in America. Before its passage, however, public outrage was often expressed in spontaneous rioting, one of the largest examples of which took place in Los Angeles.

The incident actually began when an argument between two Chinese *tongs* escalated into violence in a section of the city. Shots were fired, wounding several bystanders, and a mob of rioters started to form nearby. The latter finally began to turn on the Chinese, who fled but were pursued to their homes and buildings, from which they were driven and then gunned down in the street or shot as they hid inside. Other Chinese were lynched during the four-hour ordeal.

The international response was immediate. The Chinese government issued an official protest, and the U.S. Congress offered to indemnify the victims (the bill was never enacted). Ten rioters were brought to trial; nine were convicted but were freed a year later.

Los Angeles riots of 1992: Civil disturbance that broke out in South Central Los Angeles on April 29, 1992, after the announcement of the verdicts in the first trial of four police officers charged with using excessive force against motorist Rodney King. The rioting spread rapidly. By the time the carnage was over, more than fifty people had been killed and more than 2,000 injured. Property damage exceeded $1 billion.

Neither at the time of the riots nor in retrospect was there any consensus about the causes of the violence. Some observers prefer to describe this civil disturbance as an "insurrection" or a "rebellion," arguing that it was fundamentally an expression of popular discontent with an unjust political and economic system. There has, however, been general agreement that the Los Angeles riots drew attention to the new dynamics of a multiethnic society, undercutting long established theories based solely on a racial polarity of white and black. The riots were a multicultural experience. Of the more than 5000 people arrested within the Los Angeles city limits during the rioting, 51 percent

A shopping mall owned by Korean Americans burns during the 1992 riots in South Central Los Angeles. (AP/Wide World Photos)

were Latino, many of them recent immigrants.

Korean stores and other businesses were particularly hard-hit, and there were indications that long-simmering tensions between African Americans and Korean Americans helped to fuel the violence. Between 2000 and 2300 Korean businesses were significantly damaged or destroyed, with cumulative losses amounting to more than $400 million. Two years after the riots, more than a third of those Korean businesses remained closed.

Lost Battalion: Members of the 3d Battalion of the 141st Regiment of the 36th Division of the U.S. Army caught behind enemy lines during World War II in October, 1944, in northern France near the German border. The all-Nisei 100TH INFANTRY BATTALION and 442D REGIMENTAL COMBAT TEAM—both of the U.S. Army—rescued the battalion after bitter fighting that lasted nearly a week. In all, 800 people died to rescue 211 men.

Louie, David (b. June 19, 1950, Lakewood, Ohio): Broadcast journalist. He became the first Asian American reporter hired by KGO-TV, the San Francisco station owned and operated by the American Broadcasting Company (ABC), and the first Asian American news manager while working at WXYZ in Detroit. The winner of two Emmy Awards, he has served as national president of the eleven-hundred-member ASIAN AMERICAN JOURNALISTS ASSOCIATION (AAJA) and also as president of its San Francisco Bay Area chapter.

Emmy Award-winning broadcast journalist David Louie. (Asian Week)

Louie, David Wong (b. 1954, Rockville Center, N.Y.): Writer. Louie, who holds a dual appointment in fiction writing and Asian American Studies in the English Department of the University of California, Los Angeles (UCLA), is a graduate of Vassar College and the University of Iowa. His first book, *The Pangs of Love* (1991), a collection of stories, was published to great acclaim, winning the *Los Angeles Times* Art Seidenbaum Book Prize for first fiction and the *Ploughshares* John C. Zacharis First Book Award. Louie has also been the recipient of fellowships from the National Endowment for the Arts, the California Arts Council, and the McDowell Colony.

Louie, Sinclair (b. May 11, 1922, Canton, China): Entrepreneur. He came to the United States at the age of ten and later served in the Army under General George Patton during World War II. A longtime contributor to many San Francisco Chinatown charitable organizations, he is the owner of the largest bazaar business chain in the city, including Bargain Bazaar, Canton Bazaar, Ginza, Jade Empire, Empress Fine Arts, Far East Flea Market, and China Bazaar.

Louis, Nikki Nojima (b. Dec. 7, 1937, Seattle, Wash.): Playwright and director. On her fourth birthday Louis was incarcerated at Minidoka relocation center in Idaho. After Would War II, she made a career for herself dancing in the China Doll Shows in Las Vegas and opening for acts such as Liberace. In the 1980's she began writing for regional theaters in the American northwest, including The Exclusion Act (which became Northwest Asian American Theatre) and the Seattle Group Theatre. Her theater works include *Japanese Voices in America* (1985), *Made in America* (1985), *Breaking the Silence* (1987), *Changing Faces* (1988), *Our Mothers' Stories* (1989), *Winds of Change* (1990), *Most Dangerous Women* (1990), *Gold! Gold! Gold!* (1991), *I Dream a World* (1991), and *Island Dreams* (1993). Louis' work is informed by her childhood internment experience and revolves

Filmmaker, teacher, and journalist Felicia Lowe. (Asian Week)

around multicultural themes and issues. Her approach to playwrighting includes oral history, improvisation, and other collaborative creative techniques to create kaleidoscopic visions of the northwest Asian American community, women, and other disenfranchised communities.

Low, Charlie (b. June 9, 1901, Winnemucca, Nev.—1991?): Entrepreneur. The owner of the first bar in San Francisco Chinatown, the Chinese Village, and the well-known Chinese nightclub, the FORBIDDEN CITY, he helped plan the building of the first modern apartment in San Francisco Chinatown in 1927, and established a number of businesses, including a stock brokerage, an insurance agency, a real estate firm, an employment service, and a legal advice office.

Low, Harry W. (b. Mar. 12, 1931, Oakdale, Calif.): State court justice. Before retiring as presiding justice of the California Court of Appeals in 1991, he was deputy attorney general of California and a judge in the superior, juvenile, and municipal courts. He served as president of the San Francisco Police Commission, the National and San Francisco Lodge of the CHINESE AMERICAN CITIZENS ALLIANCE (CACA), and the California Judges Association. He edited *Courts Commentary*, the official publication of the California Judges Association. Low holds B.A. and LL.B. degrees from the University of California, Berkeley.

Lowe, Felicia (b. Dec. 6, 1945, Oakland, Calif.): Filmmaker and broadcast journalist. She wrote, produced, and directed the documentaries *China, Land of My Father* (1979) and *Carved in Silence* (1988). *Carved in Silence* tells the story of Chinese immigrants detained by the U.S. government on the ANGEL ISLAND IMMIGRATION STATION as a result of the discriminatory CHINESE EXCLUSION ACT OF 1882. Her work has been exhibited at New York's Museum of Modern Art, the Whitney Museum, and the Smithsonian Institution in Washington, D.C. Educated at Columbia University in New York and San Jose State University, she also teaches film production and advanced screenwriting at San Francisco State University. An Emmy award-winning journalist, she has reported for KGO-TV and produced for KQED-TV, both in San Francisco.

Lowe, Pardee (George Cooper Pardee Lowe; b. Sept. 9, 1905, San Francisco, Calif.): Writer. Lowe is best known for his autobiography *Father and Glorious Descendant* (1943), the first book-length literary work by an American-born Asian. Named after George C. Pardee, the then governor of California, Lowe was born at a time when second-generation Chinese were still a novelty. His father, Fat Yuen Lowe, was a dry-goods merchant and a leading figure in the Chinese community in the San Francisco Bay area. Pardee Lowe grew up in a predominantly white neighborhood in the East Belleville section of Oakland. His father moved the family there after the earthquake destroyed their old home in San Francisco's Chinatown in 1906. Lowe received a B.A. degree from Stanford University and an M.B.A. degree from the Graduate School of Business Administration of Harvard University. During World War II Lowe enlisted in the Army and served in the Pacific theater.

Portions of *Father and Glorious Descendant* appeared in *The Atlantic Monthly* and *The Yale Review* as early as 1937. Critics found the work rewarding and celebrated it as a solid and significant study of the Chinese American community. The positive response in part reflected the dramatically changed attitude of the American public toward the Chinese. As a result of the United States' involvement in World War II, China became an important ally, and Chinese Americans were deemed a "loyal minority" and enjoyed unprecedented popularity.

Presenting a penetrating account of his life as a second-generation Chinese, Lowe's autobiography represents an important aspect of the common experience of American-born Asians in a period when their fate began to attract the attention of the American public. It is a testimony that reveals Lowe's ardent desire to seek admission into the mainstream society. The thoroughness of Lowe's assimilation is perhaps best evidenced by his marriage to a Caucasian girl from an established New England family during his attendance at Harvard. To avoid interference from his father, Lowe held the wedding in a Protestant evangelical church in Germany; he did not even inform his parents or any Chinese friends of the event until two years later.

The troubled relationship between Lowe and his father constitutes another major theme running through the autobiography. Although in retrospect Lowe acknowledges with gratitude that his father's strength, talent, and ability have given him substance and inspired his continuous pursuit of success in American society, he admits frankly that his father's "stubborn Chinese mind" is a source of constant conflict between the patriarch and his son.

As the first book-length autobiography by an

American-born Asian, *Father and Glorious Descendant* is a significant work. Lowe relates to the audience at a time when the larger society was unaware of the feelings and thoughts of native-born Asians and of their determination to seek a place in American life.

Loyalty oath: Questionnaire designed by the U.S. War Department during World War II to determine the loyalty of Japanese Americans interned in WAR RELOCATION AUTHORITY (WRA) concentration camps. The questionnaire served several purposes: Nisei draft-age males who passed the test made themselves eligible for American military service, while others became eligible for the WRA resettlement program. Those considered to be disloyal were segregated to the WRA camp at TULE LAKE.

Origin. One of the most popular excuses given by U.S. government officials during the war for the exclusion of Japanese Americans was that it was impossible to distinguish immediately the loyal factions from the so-called disloyal. This allegation was untrue according to the government's intelligence agencies, includ-

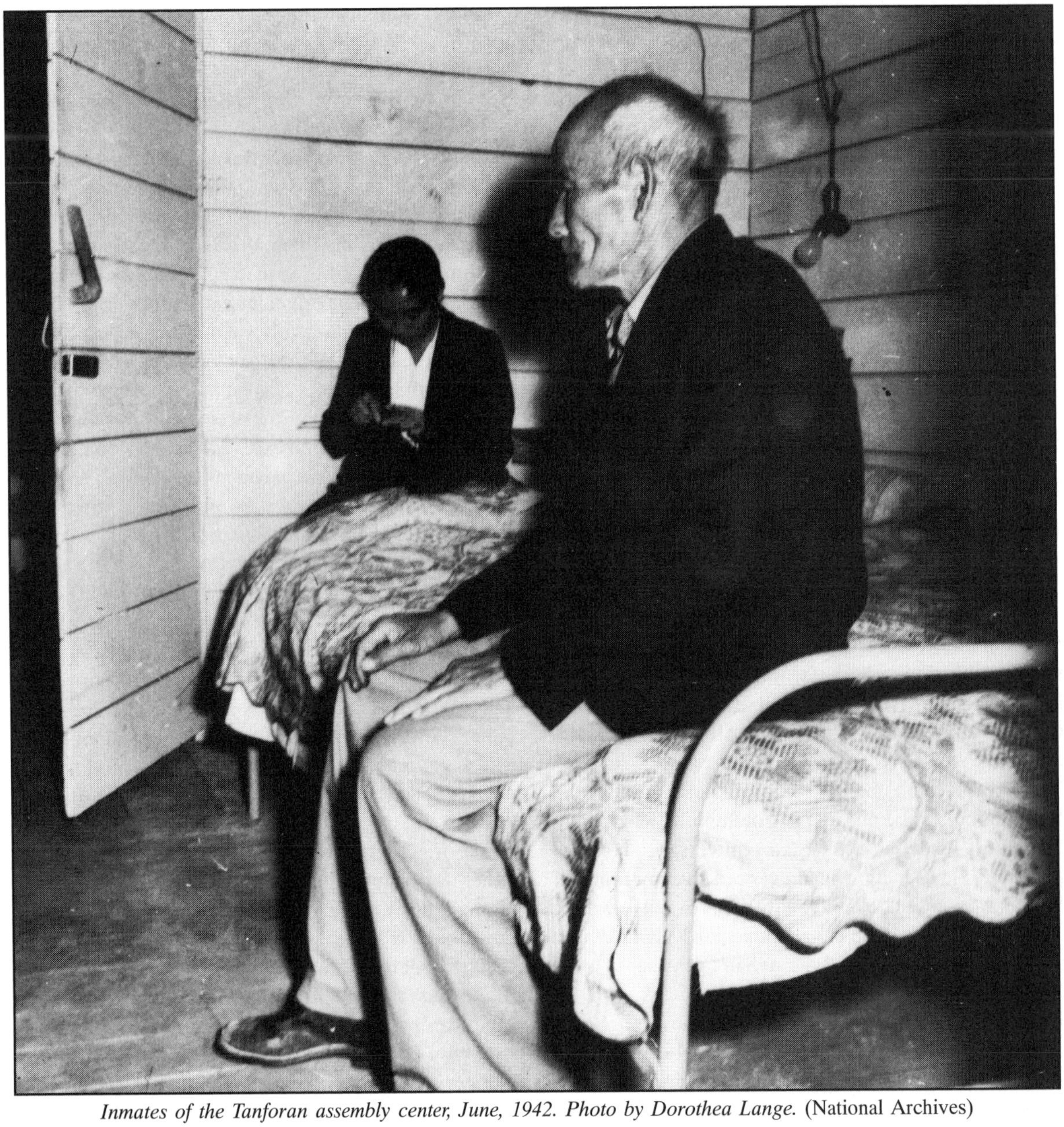

Inmates of the Tanforan assembly center, June, 1942. Photo by Dorothea Lange. (National Archives)

Members of the highly decorated all-Japanese American 100th Infantry Battalion fire a mortar on German snipers in Italy in 1944. (National Archives)

ing the Federal Bureau of Investigation (FBI) and the Office of Naval Intelligence. Truth, however, did not matter in the case of Japanese Americans—especially when it was necessary to rally the country around the war effort.

With Japanese Americans relocated from the West Coast into WRA concentration camps, government officials realized that they could not legally confine them now that they had the time to determine who was loyal. A questionnaire was designed by the War Department for the dual purpose of determining loyalty and finding eligible Japanese American Nisei males for military service. This survey was titled "Statement of United States Citizens of Japanese Ancestry" and was given to all draft-age Nisei males. An almost duplicate form was administered by the WRA for the rest of the internees for use in the planned resettlement and segregation program. This form was called "Application for Leave Clearance."

Controversy. In early February of 1943, the War Department and the WRA began to administer their respective questionnaires. Because of the poor wording and offensive nature of the questions, controversy soon erupted over the surveys. Questions 27 and 28, the "loyalty" questions on both questionnaires, were particularly controversial. On the War Department form, question 27 asked: "Are you willing to serve in the armed forces of the United States on combat duty, wherever ordered?" Question 28 asked: "Will you swear unqualified allegiance to the United States of America and faithfully defend the United States from any or all attack by foreign domestic forces, and forswear any form of allegiance or obedience to the Japanese emperor, to any other foreign government, power or organization?" For many draft-age Nisei, these questions were insulting. How could the government ask them to serve in the military after imprisoning them and their families in concentration camps? How could the government ask them to forswear allegiance to the Japanese emperor when in fact they were loyal American citizens? To the Nisei, a "yes" answer to question 28 could reasonably trick them into admitting an allegiance to Japan that they never had, while a "no" answer would imply that they were disloyal to the United States.

The WRA version of the questionnaire was altered slightly for the first-generation Issei and the female Nisei. Judging from the wording of the questions, however, it was clear that it was not well thought out. Question 27 asked: "If the opportunity presents itself and you are found qualified, would you be willing to volunteer for the Army Nurse Corps or the WAAC?" Question 28 was reformulated as, "Will you swear unqualified allegiance to the United States of America and forswear any form of allegiance or obedience to the Japanese emperor, to any other foreign government, power or organization?" Nisei women found themselves in a bind similar to that of their male counterparts. Question 27 was insulting, while question 28 was confusing, at best. The Issei had an even more difficult time with question 28. Since they were barred by law from becoming naturalized U.S. citizens, a "yes" answer would have forced them to renounce the only citizenship they had and would have made them stateless people. A "no" answer, however, could lead to segregation and ultimate deportation from the United States.

Reaction. Despite the vagueness of the questionnaire, most of the internees eventually answered both questions in the affirmative. The program, however, was far from successful. For example, the Army had originally anticipated that they would be able to recruit 3,000 Nisei men from the camps and another 1,500 from Hawaii for a segregated combat unit in the armed services. As it turned out, only 1,181 (less than 40 percent of their quota) volunteered from the camps while more than 10,000 Nisei volunteered from Hawaii, where they were not subjected to the camps and the loyalty oath.

Many people suffered as a result of the loyalty questionnaire. Those who refused to answer the questions or gave negative answers were labeled "troublemakers" or as "disloyal" and were sent to Tule Lake during September and October of 1943. For many of these people, the questionnaire was the last straw in a growing bitterness toward the United States and the first step on a long road that would end in renunciation of citizenship and in deportation.—*Glen Kitayama*

SUGGESTED READINGS: • Chuman, Frank. *The Bamboo People: Japanese Americans, Their History, and the Law.* Chicago: Japanese American Research Project and Japanese American Citizens League, 1981. • Collins, Donald E. *Native American Aliens: Disloyalty and the Renunciation of Citizenship by Japanese Americans During World War II.* Westport, Conn.: Greenwood Press, 1985. • Drinnon, Richard. *Keeper of Concentration Camps: Dillon S. Myer and American Racism.* Berkeley: University of California Press, 1987. • Irons, Peter. *Justice at War: The Story of the Japanese American Internment Cases.* New York: Oxford University Press, 1983. • Weglyn, Michi. *Years of Infamy: The Untold Story of America's Concentration Camps.* New York: Morrow, 1976.

Luce-Celler Bill of 1946: On July 2, 1946, the U.S. Congress passed Public Law 483, which amended the Nationality Act of 1940. This law (popularly known as the Luce-Celler Bill; also called the Filipino Naturalization Act) permitted the entry into the United States of peoples of India and the Philippine Islands and made both groups eligible for naturalization. Although the Luce-Celler Bill limited Indian and Filipino immigration to the United States by establishing a modest quota of one hundred new entrants per year per country, it was nevertheless the first legislation to overturn exclusionary policies such as the Immigration Act of 1924, which effectively cut off immigration from India and much of greater Asia; the Tydings-McDuffie Act of 1934, which curtailed Filipino migration; and the *United States v. Bhagat Singh Thind* decision of 1923, which declared Asian Indians in the United States ineligible for naturalization.

While immigration and naturalization laws severely restricted Asian Indians in the United States, several American legislators supported their demands for more equitable treatment as residents of the United States. From 1926 to 1928, Senator Royal S. Copeland of New York, Senator David Reed of Pennsylvania, and Representative Emmanuel Celler of New York presented measures before congressional committees endorsing the rights of Asian Indians residing in the United States to become naturalized citizens. In 1939 the India Welfare League, led by Mubarak Ali Khan, addressed a House immigration committee, arguing that the people of the Indian subcontinent were Caucasians and therefore were "white" and eligible for U.S.

citizenship and immigration rights. Although Michigan congressman John Lesinski introduced a law to classify Indians as white people, it was defeated by the 76th Congress in 1939.

Asian Indian organizations and individuals continued to lobby U.S. legislators during the early 1940's. The India League of America, the Indian Association for American Citizenship, and the above-mentioned India Welfare League worked directly with senators and representatives to garner public and congressional support for policy changes regarding citizenship and immigration. In 1944 Representative Clare Boothe Luce of Connecticut and Representative Celler introduced similar bills in Congress to provide immigration quotas and naturalization privileges to Indians.

Congress debated the Luce and Celler proposals along with a rival bill introduced by Senator William Langer of North Dakota. The latter bill focused on providing Asian Indians with citizenship rights but did not include provisions for an immigration quota.

In March, 1945, the 79th Congress held hearings before the Committee on Immigration and Naturalization to consider the Luce, Celler, Langer, and other related bills. In October of the same year, the House of Representatives passed the Celler Bill, which then went to the Senate. During the second session of the 79th Congress, Senator Joseph Ball of Minnesota proposed an amendment to the Celler Bill to include Filipinos and people of Filipino descent. The amended version of the bill was passed in July, 1946.

The passage of the Luce-Celler Bill reflected the prevailing attitudes toward Asian immigration during the 1940's. The United States was not prepared for wide-scale immigration reform. The relatively small quotas designated for Asian countries ensured that there would not be a major influx from countries such as India, China (given a quota of 105 per year in a 1943 measure), or the Philippines. In the first year following the passage of the Luce-Celler Bill, only eighteen Indians were admitted into the United States.

With the advent of World War II and the prospect for decolonization in many parts of Asia and other regions of the world, U.S. foreign policy began to shift. During the war, the U.S. government had looked to Asia for allies in its conflict with Japan. Additionally, U.S. troops had been stationed in India from 1943 until after the war ended in 1945. By the end of the war, some U.S. officials realized that existing immigration and naturalization policies were offensive to soon-to-be independent nations such as India and Pakistan. Policy makers were at least prepared to make some changes, albeit nominal, for the sake of alliance and goodwill.

Ludhiana: City and district in Punjab State, northwestern India. Ludhiana is a major agricultural market and industrial center. Its largest industry is hosiery manufacturing, supplemented by the production of steel and textiles and the processing of agricultural products. Many of the early Sikh immigrants to the United States came from this region. The city contained a population of more than one million in 1991.

Lue Gim Gong (1858, Taishan district, Guangdong Province, China—June 3, 1925): Horticulturist. A self-taught cultivator, Lue came to be widely known as the "Chinese Burbank." He is best remembered for the orange he developed, which bears his name. It became the mainstay of the Florida citrus industry and in 1911 won for him the prestigious Wilder Silver Medal awarded by the American Pomological Society. He made, in addition, other important botanical and medicinal discoveries. At the World's Fairs of Chicago in 1933 and New York in 1939, Lue's bust adorned the Florida Pavilion, attesting the honor accorded him by the state.

Leaving his home in the Taishan district of Guangdong Province, China, in 1870, Lue came to the United States. He landed in San Francisco and went to work in a shoe factory. Next he found himself in North Adams, Massachusetts, after being recruited for work there. At a Chinese Sunday school, he met Fanny Burlingame, cousin of Anson Burlingame, the first American diplomatic envoy to China. Fanny was also a brilliant mathematician and botanist who would significantly influence Lue's life. She invited him to live in her home and treated him like a son.

During his life, Lue returned to his homeland at least once, in 1886. After finding that traditional Chinese society was unreceptive to his Christian beliefs, however, he went back to the United States.

With Lue stricken with tuberculosis, Fanny purchased an orange grove in De Land, Florida. She and her family then left North Adams, taking Lue with them. At the grove, Lue began creating a frost-resistant strain of orange. Recalling how his mother had cross-pollinated plants back in China, he soon was able to produce startling changes and improvements in fruits and plants. He developed a sweet apple that ripened a month earlier than others being cultivated nearby, a salmon-colored raspberry, a peach that ripened shortly before Thanksgiving, and a cherry currant as large as a cherry. A grapefruit also bearing his name was another one of his unique creations.

The merits of the Lue Gim Gong orange were several. It could remain on the tree for up to three years until harvesting time. It was capable of withstanding considerable frost. Its trees bore large crops of excellent, delicious fruit that could be shipped great distances without spoiling.

Fanny willed the grove to Lue upon her death. He was too trusting and honest, however, and growers who bought his budded stock cheated him. Before long, his money dwindled, and he would have lost the grove were it not for a benefactor and friends who came to his rescue. Lonely and sick, he died in poverty. His story is told in greater detail in Ruthanne Lum McCunn's "Lue Gim Gong: A Life Reclaimed," published in the journal *Chinese America: History and Perspectives* (1989): 117-135.

Luke, Keye (June 18, 1904, Canton, China—Jan. 12, 1991, Whittier, Calif.): Actor. He arrived in the United States during childhood. After attending college in Seattle, Washington, he entered the film industry as a commercial artist and poster designer, later serving as a technical advisor on Hollywood films with Chinese themes. After 1934 he appeared in many motion pictures, including *The Good Earth* (1937), *Love Is a Many-Splendored Thing* (1955), and *The Hawaiians* (1970). He also appeared in numerous Charlie CHAN films as the "number-one son." Luke was also well known for his role as the master-teacher in the television series *KUNG FU* (1972-1975).

Actor Keye Luke was best known for his roles as the "Number One Son" in numerous Charlie Chan films and the blind teacher/priest in the TV series Kung Fu. (AP/Wide World Photos)

Luke, Wing Chong (Feb. 25, 1925, Guangdong Province, China—May 16, 1965, Snohomish County, Wash.): Politician. Although he served only one term in office as city councilmember in Seattle, Washington, Luke's influence continues to be felt—both in the quality of life found there and in the diversity of the city's political landscape. Some believe that, if he had not died young in a plane crash, Luke would have gone far in American politics.

Luke's father moved his wife and young son from China to Seattle in the early 1930's, and the family opened a laundry far from the city's Chinatown. Luke soon adapted to his new homeland, however, and became an eager student of many cultures and languages. He also became quite popular, holding numerous elected posts in his junior and senior high schools. When the United States entered World War II, Luke joined the Army and earned a Bronze Star fighting in the Philippines and Korea. While he was serving with valor overseas, however, his family was subjected to harassment in the United States, the victims of misguided anti-Japanese sentiment. (In the eyes of prejudice, all Asians were suspect.) Luke rushed home on emergency leave to help his family relocate.

Returning from the war, Luke became an American citizen, completed a B.A. and an M.A. in political science, and earned a law degree. In 1957, he received an appointment as the State Assistant Attorney General for Washington, and five years later, he decided to run for the Seattle City Council. Despite smear campaigns accusing him of being a communist, he won the seat by a landslide. Luke was a true representative of the people. He campaigned door to door, attended "coffee hours," and continued to work in his family's grocery business after winning the election. Although he was the council's only liberal, Luke's personable style and quick intellect won many political victories. He advocated open housing, cultural awareness, civil rights, fishing programs for city residents, historic preservation, kite festivals, and cross-generational activities. Cultural pluralism and humanism were his passions.

On May 16, 1965, Luke was engaging in one of his

Seattle city councilman Wing Luke was an advocate of humanism and cultural pluralism. (Wing Luke Museum)

other passions—fishing. On his way to a fishing trip with friends, he died when their plane crashed beneath a waterfall on Merchant Mountain. His legacy, however, was not to be forgotten. Honors and dedications abounded, the most important of which was the Wing Luke Memorial Museum, which was later renamed the Wing Luke Asian Museum. The first museum in the United States devoted to Asian Pacific American history and art, it fulfills Wing Luke's dream of cultural understanding and celebration.

Lum, Darrell H. Y. (b. 1950, Honolulu, Territory of Hawaii): Writer. Lum's widely anthologized stories and plays highlight Hawaiian Creole, an English-based creole that draws on the languages of the diverse immigrants who labored on Hawaii's sugar plantations. (For a discussion of pidgins and creoles, see PIDGIN.) Many of his stories are told in the voices of children or young people whose observations explicitly or implicitly criticize the social structure they inhabit. Lum's books include *Sun* (1980) and *Pass On, No Pass Back!* (1990), which received the 1992 Outstanding Book Award from the ASSOCIATION FOR ASIAN AMERICAN STUDIES. He is a cofounder of Bamboo Ridge Press and one of the editors of *BAMBOO RIDGE: THE HAWAII WRITERS' QUARTERLY*.

Lum, Herman Tsui Fai (b. Nov. 5, 1926, Honolulu, Territory of Hawaii): State court chief justice. Lum attended the University of Hawaii and the University of Missouri, from which he earned an LL.B. degree in 1950. Becoming a member of the Hawaii State Bar that same year, he held several legal posts in the public sector until winning appointment in 1967 as a justice of the Honolulu Circuit Court. He then served as senior justice of the state's family court before being named to the Hawaii Supreme Court in 1980. His tenure as chief justice of the state's highest tribunal began in 1983.

Lum, Kalfred Dip (Dec. 25, 1899, Honolulu, Territory of Hawaii—July 3, 1979, San Francisco, Calif.): Scholar and political official. Lum graduated from Honolulu's Kalihiwaena School in 1915, Jackson Chinese Institute in 1917, and Iolani High School in 1919. He was among the first graduates to receive the A.B. degree from the University of Hawaii, in 1922. Lum taught at Min Hon Chinese School in Kalihi, serving as principal from 1920 until 1922, when he became commissioner of Chinese schools in Hawaii.

In 1922 Lum went to the U.S. mainland for advanced studies and received his M.A. degree in political science from Columbia University in 1923; in 1926 he was awarded a Ph.D. degree in government and international law by New York University, after which he joined the faculty of the University of Hawaii as an instructor in political science. He was promoted to a professorship in 1928.

When he was eighteen Lum joined the GUOMINDANG (GMD). Around 1928 he became executive secretary and chairman of its General Branch in Hawaii and concurrently served as president of the Honolulu party organ, *United States News*. In 1931 Lum became Hawaii's delegate to the National People's Conference in Nanjing to draft a provisional constitution for China. In September of the same year the Guomindang government appointed him commissioner of overseas Chinese affairs. Concurrently he became visiting professor at Hangchow Christian College. In November he became Hawaii's delegate to the fourth Guomindang Congress in Nanjing. In 1933 the Guomindang government appointed Lum special envoy to inspect party and overseas Chinese affairs in Hawaii and the Americas. He was visiting professor at New York University in 1933-1934, after which he became professor and head of the department of public administration at Chiaotung University, Shanghai, in September, 1934. In 1935 he was special envoy to inspect Guomindang and overseas Chinese affairs in southeast Asia. In November of the same year he became Hawaii's delegate to the fifth Guomindang Congress and was elected member of the Guomindang central executive committee. In 1937 he was appointed as special envoy to the mainland United States to mediate the power struggle among three party factions.

After that Lum moved to Portland, Oregon, where he managed a hotel. He also headed the CHINA WAR RELIEF ASSOCIATION and raised funds to purchase three airplanes to train Chinese military pilots. After the war he stayed on the West Coast, where he managed hotels and motels until his retirement in 1963.

Lum, Mary (b. New York, N.Y.): Actor. In addition to extensive work with New York City's Pan Asian Repertory Theatre, she has made significant contributions to feminist theater. An original member of New York City's Women's Experimental Theatre Company, she created roles in *The Daughters Cycle* (pr. 1979) and *Women's Body and Other Natural Resources* (pr. 1981) at the Interart Theatre in New York City. During the 1990 *Miss Saigon* (pr. 1989) controversy, she appeared before the New York Human Rights Commission, testifying to the marginalization of Asian American women in the performing arts.

Lum, Wing Tek (b. 1946, Honolulu, Hawaii): Poet. A leading figure in the "local" movement among writers of Hawaii (see TALK STORY CONFERENCE), Lum was educated at Brown University and Union Theological Seminary. He is the author of a highly regarded volume of poems, *Expounding the Doubtful Points* (1987), which received the 1988 creative literature award from the ASSOCIATION FOR ASIAN AMERICAN STUDIES.

Lumpia: Filipino snack food similar to a spring roll and made with beef, shrimp, or chicken. In the Philippines it is eaten during *merienda*—between lunch and dinner—with an assortment of finger foods, coffee, cake, and other sweets. There are several versions of this dish, including *lumpia labong*, made with bamboo shoots; *lumpia* with peanuts; and the most sought after form, *lumpia* with *ubod*, or the heart of the coconut palm.

Luzon: Largest and most important island in the Philippine archipelago and the source of many of the first Filipino laborers to Hawaii. Manila, the nation's capital and largest city, is located there as is Quezon City, the second largest. Situated in the north, the island is 40,420 square miles in size and reported a 1990 population of more than 32 million. In addition to the national language of TAGALOG, other languages spoken there include Ilocano and Bicol.

Lyman, Stanford (b. June 10, 1933, San Francisco, Calif.): Scholar. He received his Ph.D. degree from the University of California, Berkeley. A leading scholar in the field of race and ethnicity in American culture, Lyman has published several studies focusing on Asian American history, including *Chinese Americans* (1974), *The Asian in the West* (1970), and *The Asian in North America* (1977). His book *Color, Culture, Civilization: Race and Minority Issues in American Society* (1994) includes reflections on the Chinese diaspora and other Asian American themes.

M

Ma, L. Eve Armentrout (b. Dec. 28, 1943, Greenville, S.C.): Scholar and educator. She has earned several academic degrees, among them a Ph.D. in modern Chinese history from the University of California, Davis, in 1977 and a J.D. from Hastings College of the Law in 1993. Her extensive career has encompassed such areas of specialization as international and constitutional law, Chinese and Japanese history, and U.S. military history. Publications include *Revolutionaries, Monarchists and Chinatowns: Chinese Politics in the Americas and the 1911 Revolution* (1990), as well as more than two dozen articles in other volumes and such journals as *The Journal of American-East Asian Relations*, *Amerasia Journal*, and *Modern Asian Studies*. Ma was assistant professor of history at Mills College from 1989 until 1991. At Hastings, she served as note editor of the school's *Constitutional Law Quarterly* in 1992-1993.

Asian history scholar L. Eve Armentrout Ma. (William Marshall Ma)

Ma, Yo-Yo (b. Oct. 7, 1955, Paris, France): Cellist. A child prodigy who made his debut in Carnegie Hall at the age of nine, he is regarded as one of the leading cellists of his generation. Reared in a highly musical family, he studied at the Juilliard School and later attended Harvard University. The winner of several Grammy awards, he has made significant additions to the relatively limited cello repertory.

Cellist Yo-Yo Ma is known internationally for his recordings and solo performances. (AP/Wide World Photos)

Macao: Overseas territory of Portugal on the south China coast. Macao, or Macau, is the oldest colony of Portugal in China—it was the first entrepot between traditional China and the Western world and the initial Catholic mission center—and the gambling center of Asia. It is scheduled to revert to the People's Republic of China in 1999.

Macao is situated on the southern tip of the China coast on the western side of the PEARL RIVER and the southern tip of Canton, to the west of HONG KONG. It consists of the Macao Peninsula and two small islands, Taipa and Coloane. Its total area is six square miles, and its climate is semitropical. About 80 percent of its annual rainfall takes place from April to September. Its

total population is about 367,000 (1992 estimate), with the majority being Chinese and the remainder Portuguese, including eleven thousand officials. The official language is Portuguese, but Cantonese, a Chinese dialect, is widely used. The literacy rate is high: 80 percent among the Chinese adults and 100 percent among the Portuguese. Macao has 101 schools (including seven institutions of higher learning), as of 1990. The major religions are Buddhism for the Chinese and Catholicism for the Portuguese.

The imperial Chinese government allowed the Portuguese to use Macao for trade and mission work in 1557. After the Opium War of 1839-1842, Portugal declared Macao a free port and abolished the Chinese customshouse in 1849, thus establishing Portuguese jurisdiction over the territory. In 1887, Macao was ceded from China and formally became a Portuguese colony. In 1951, it was changed into an overseas province of Portugal, with its representatives in the Portuguese legislature in Lisbon, but in 1976 it was given broad autonomy. In 1987, Portugal and China agreed that they would end a four-century-old rule and revert Macao to China by December 20, 1999. Like Hong Kong, Macao, a special administrative district under Chinese jurisdiction, was guaranteed an additional fifty years of noninterference in its way of life and capitalist system, except in diplomacy and defense.

Until 1842, Canton, on mainland China, was the only port open to Western merchants for trade. Western merchants were allowed to trade in Canton only from November to May and were not allowed to live there. Thus western merchants had to establish their own community in nearby Macao, where they would stay until the next trading season. A period of prosperity for Macao followed. When Hong Kong was converted into the British colony in 1842, Macao was no longer the center for either trade or mission work in Asia. Its decline, economic or otherwise, resulted largely from the rise to power of Spain, France, and Great Britain throughout the world.

In the 1990's, Macao is noted for its gambling industry, with several licensed casinos and dog and car races; it is known as the Monte Carlo of Asia. Because of the ban on gambling in Hong Kong and China, Macao monopolizes it for its own benefit. Tourism is another major industry in Macao, along with the hotel and entertainment businesses. In the 1970's, taking advantage of the comparatively cheap labor, overseas Chinese invested in manufacturing industries in Macao. The products are exported mainly to the United States, Hong Kong, France, Germany, and China. As a result, the gross domestic product per capita is $8,000 (as of 1990), with a 12.4 percent annual growth rate. Its trade is on the increase because of the large markets in Hong Kong and China.

McCarran-Walter Act of 1952: Bill passed by the U.S. Congress that codified many existing immigration and naturalization laws. Among its provisions were significant changes in policy regarding Asian immigration and the naturalization of Asian immigrants. Whereas previously only white immigrants and people of African descent were eligible for naturalization—Asian immigrants were categorized as "aliens ineligible to citizenship," although their American-born children were citizens by right of birth—the McCarran-Walter Act, in conjunction with the IMMIGRATION ACT OF 1943 and the LUCE-CELLER BILL OF 1946, removed all racial criteria for naturalization. The 1952 act also removed barriers to Asian immigration.

Japanese and Koreans were the groups most immediately affected by the 1952 act. The Immigration Act of 1943 had repealed the Chinese Exclusion Acts, setting a quota of 105 persons per year for Chinese immi-

The McCarran-Walter Act removed barriers to naturalization that were suffered before 1952 by Asian immigrants to the United States—particularly Japanese and (above) Koreans. (University of Southern California East Asian Library)

gration and making Chinese immigrants eligible for naturalization. The Luce-Celler Bill of 1946 had established annual quotas of 100 for Asian Indian and Filipino immigration and provided for naturalization of Asian Indian and Filipino immigrants.

The 1952 act extended similar privileges to Japanese, Koreans, and other Asian groups. For the first time, the Issei—the first generation of Japanese immigrants, who came for the most part between 1885 and 1924—were eligible to become American citizens. The same was true for the much smaller first generation of Korean immigrants. At the same time, after decades of exclusion, the act permitted new immigration from Japan, Korea, and elsewhere in Asia. Admission of spouses and children as nonquota immigrants and other legislative provisions allowed for immigration that considerably exceeded the tiny quotas. For example, between 1950 and 1964, Japanese immigration to the United States exceeded 60,000, even though Japan's annual quota was only 185.

While the McCarran-Walter Act continued the shift in policy toward Asian immigration begun with the acts of 1943 and 1946, it did not overhaul the national origins system established by the IMMIGRATION ACT OF 1924, which favored immigrants from Northern and Western Europe. That system remained in place until the landmark IMMIGRATION AND NATIONALITY ACT OF 1965.

The 1952 act, sponsored by Senator Patrick A. McCarran of Nevada and Representative Francis E. Walter of Pennsylvania, barred entry into the United States of Communists and members of Communist-front organizations, and provided for the deportation of immigrants or naturalized citizens who joined or belonged to Communist or Communist-front organizations. It also allowed for the deportation of a number of other categories of aliens, eighteen in total, including those convicted of illegal entry into the U.S., those committing a crime against people, property, or the government, and those committing drug offenses. The deportation provisions also stipulated that naturalized Americans would lose their citizenship if they resided abroad for five years or three years in their country of birth or nationality.

Passed at the height of the Cold War, this bill, which distinguished between native and naturalized citizens, was intended to deny citizenship to aliens who did not transfer permanent allegiance to the United States and to protect the nation against Communist infiltration and subversion. In later years critics charged that it was frequently abused to settle political scores with writers, artists, and others who, while clearly posing no real threat to the security of the United States, were denied admission under the 1952 act's provisions.

McCarthy, Nobu (b. 1938): Actor. McCarthy was discovered by a Hollywood agent in Los Angeles' Little Tokyo district and was encouraged to audition for a film role. Despite her lack of fluency in English, she came to the attention of a director on the Paramount studios lot and was cast as the female lead opposite Jerry Lewis and Sessue Hayakawa in *The Geisha Boy* (1958). After her film debut, McCarthy appeared in a string of unremarkable Hollywood films, including *Tokyo After Dark* (1959) and *Walk Like a Dragon* (1960), opposite James Shigeta and Jack Lord. Typecast for the most part in stereotypical submissive roles, McCarthy found little challenge as a film actor.

In the 1970's, McCarthy joined the EAST WEST PLAYERS, an Asian American theater company, and began to find more fulfilling roles. She appeared in the 1976 television film *Farewell to Manzanar*, based on Jeanne Wakatsuki Houston's adaptation of her book of the same title, and opposite Pat Morita in the Hollywood film *The Karate Kid, Part II* (1986). She was

Nobu McCarthy rose to fame as the female lead opposite Jerry Lewis and Sessue Hayakawa in the 1958 film The Geisha Boy. (Asian Week)

cast as the female lead opposite noted Japanese American actors Sab Shimono and Mako in the film adaptation of Philip Kan Gotanda's *The Wash* (1988). In 1989, McCarthy succeeded Mako as artistic director of the East West Players.

McCarthyism: Political term used to describe unwarranted and unverified allegations of subversion. In early 1950 U.S. senator Joseph R. McCarthy of Wisconsin charged that Communists had infiltrated the Democratic administration of President Harry S Truman at the highest levels. Claiming that the U.S. State Department employed 205 card-carrying subversives, McCarthy made additional incriminations in which he utilized unsubstantiated accusations, partially true statements, and politically motivated smears.

McCarthyism's origins stem from the allegations of General Patrick J. Hurley in 1945. As American ambassador to China, Hurley believed that he had arranged an accord between the forces of Chiang Kai-shek and Mao Zedong, thus ending the Chinese civil war. Suspicions between the two parties soon undermined the agreement, but Hurley charged betrayal and blamed foreign service officers in the U.S. embassy for the renewal of hostilities. Since some embassy personnel had questioned Hurley's understanding of China's internal conflict, the ambassador demanded their removal from his Chonging mission.

The defeat of Chiang's government by the Communists in 1949 shattered the American government's anticipation of a friendly regime in China. With the advent of a new adversary, Americans saw their World War II victory thwarted by the unexpected appearance of a powerful Communist threat on the Asian mainland. Moreover the Alger Hiss spy case and the North Korean Communist invasion of South Korea the next year contributed to a sense of betrayal and led partisan Republicans to claim that the Truman Administration was responsible for the fall of China and other foreign policy blunders.

A lengthy and merciless probe for those behind Chiang's collapse was supported by the China lobby, a varied collection of Chinese Nationalist backers. Helped by Congress and Senate Republicans out to embarrass the Truman Administration, a witch-hunt begun by McCarthy was later promoted by Democratic Senator Pat McCarran and his Subcommittee on Internal Security of the Senate Judiciary Committee.

Even though most China specialists had been exonerated of McCarthyite charges by 1953, the search for alleged traitors carried into the Republican Administration of Dwight D. Eisenhower. His secretary of state, John Foster Dulles, yielded to extremist Republican demands to purge the Department of State, and many China-experienced foreign service officers were discharged.

The consequences of McCarthyism were a shattering of morale for the foreign service's Asian experts. Since innocent misjudgments, mainly about Chiang's defeat, were perceived as deliberate Communist subversion, diplomats became cautious when reporting on events abroad. Their whitewashing of disagreeable situations for fear that their reputations would be irreparably disgraced misguided policy makers and probably abetted the United States' involvement in the Vietnam War.

McClatchy, V. S. [Valentine Stuart] (Aug. 28, 1857, Sacramento, Calif.—May 15, 1938, San Francisco, Calif.): Newspaper publisher and writer. McClatchy was co-owner and publisher of *The Sacramento Bee* from 1884 to 1923. He was also an opponent of Japanese immigration into the United States; his involvement with exclusionist organizations helped eliminate immigration and land ownership/leasing rights for all Japanese aliens not eligible for U.S. citizenship.

In 1883, upon James McClatchy's death, his two sons (V. S. and Charles K.) assumed responsibility for their father's two newspapers in Fresno and Sacramento, jointly acquiring ownership of both soon thereafter. The two brothers worked together until V. S. sold his interest in 1923. As publisher V. S. sought to build up the business by bringing it into the Newspaper Publishers Association and by helping to found the West Coast branch of the Associated Press. In 1919 he also lobbied Congress and the Department of the Navy to open its transpacific radio channels to news dispatches from East Asia and the Philippines (formerly channeled through British interests in London).

McClatchy believed that immigration from China and Japan jeopardized American life along the Pacific Coast. He lamented that Asian immigrants would never assimilate into the mainstream and that their lower standard of living, their willingness to work for low wages, and, particularly, their high birth rate would soon overwhelm the European-American community. At one point, McClatchy predicted a Japanese population of one hundred million residing in the United States by the year 2063.

McClatchy devoted himself tirelessly to the exclusionist cause. He spoke widely and wrote voluminously, authoring books, pamphlets, and magazine articles espousing his views.

He opposed the GENTLEMEN'S AGREEMENT (1907), negotiated in settlement of the San Francisco School Board crisis of 1906, because delay in its implementation allowed thousands of Japanese immigrants to enter the United States. He criticized particularly the "loop hole" that the agreement contained permitting Japanese "PICTURE BRIDES" to join their immigrant husbands (thus contributing to a population explosion).

McClatchy actively supported the Alien Land Law of 1913 and championed the California state referendum leading to the Alien Land Law of 1920. In 1921 and again in 1924 he pleaded his case before congressional committees considering the exclusion of Japanese "aliens ineligible for citizenship" from immigration rights as part of legislative language eventually adopted in the IMMIGRATION ACT OF 1924.

McCloy, John Jay (Mar. 31, 1895, Philadelphia, Pa.—Mar. 11, 1989, Stamford, Conn.): Assistant secretary of war. A graduate of Amherst College and Harvard Law School (1921) who was an enormously influential policy maker and administrator in a career that spanned much of the twentieth century, he played a key role in the internment of Japanese Americans during World War II and exercised civilian control over the military legal staff within the War Department.

McCreary Amendment of 1893: Legislation passed by Congress to amend the terms of the GEARY ACT OF 1892. The Geary Act had prohibited all Chinese from entering the United States and required that all existing legislation restricting immigration from China be extended for a period of ten years. The act also contained provisions requiring Chinese laborers and other immigrants already residing in the United States to carry a certificate confirming their residence; those found without proof of residence could be arrested and immediately deported. Although they had been given a one-year grace period in which to register for certifi-

The McCreary Amendment extended the deadline for Chinese laborers to register for a certificate confirming their status as resident "laborers," which was restricted to those employed in skilled and unskilled manual jobs, such as mining. (Asian American Studies Library, University of California at Berkeley)

The term "laborer" referred to miners, launderers, fishermen (above), loggers, and other manual workers. (Asian American Studies Library, University of California at Berkeley)

cates, many Chinese residents still had failed to apply for certificates within this period. Congress quickly passed the McCreary Amendment on November 3, 1893, in order to extend the registration deadline for another six months. Those arrested for deportation after this period were granted the right to a hearing before a judge. The amendment provided detailed definitions of employment status that imposed artificial distinctions within the Chinese community. The term "laborer" was designated to refer to those employed in skilled and unskilled manual jobs, including mining, laundry work, fishing, logging, and railroad construction. The term "merchant" was reserved for those individuals who were employed solely in purchasing and selling merchandise at a fixed location. Those who found outside employment as manual laborers were deemed ineligible for merchant status.

McCune-Reischauer romanization: One of the four major systems used to transcribe Korean writing into the Roman alphabet. Such transcription systems (or "transliterations" as they are sometimes called) are used in both Korea and abroad for a number of very important reasons. The Korean language today is written in both borrowed ideographic Chinese characters and phonetic syllabary called *hangul.* Even though Chinese characters are increasingly being replaced by *hangul*, neither writing system is especially accessible to foreigners. One thing transcriptions do is to allow foreign students and travelers to pronounce Korean names and words (at least to some degree). There are, however, many other uses. For example, Roman transliterations allow Western librarians to catalog Korean books and authors. In Korea, computer programming, word processing, and telecommunications can be highly simplified if handled in a Roman alphabet.

The McCune-Reischauer romanization is one of the older transcription systems, being developed in the late 1930's by two scholars from Harvard University. There are several other competing systems, each with their own strengths and weaknesses. These include the Yale system, devised and promoted by scholars publishing out of Yale University, as well as a system officially sanctioned in South Korea and a rather different one used in North Korea (as these two transliterations carry political overtones, they never use each other's transcriptions). Also different linguists and textbook authors often modify an existing system or develop a totally new one.

When designing a transcription system, several critical decisions have to be made. One major choice is deciding how close to actual pronunciation the system is to be (as opposed to how correct it is in terms of pure linguistic theory). For example, in most languages sounds "assimilate": They blend together depending upon the sounds around them (in English "want to" being pronounced as "wanna" is a simple example). The Korean *hangul* alphabet, however, is phonemic and ignores such changes. That is, it writes sounds always in one single way, even though, depending upon the environment, they may actually be pronounced differently. (This is similar to English, where many plural *s* sounds at the ends of words are actually said as *z* even though the words are not spelled that way, as in "cars" or "beds.") The major way that the McCune-Reischauer romanization differs from most other systems is that it is intended to represent sounds as a person might hear them, and not as they are actually written in the *hangul* syllabary. For example, the Korean word for "shoes" is actually pronounced as "kuDu" (and spelled that way in McCune-Reischauer romanization) even though a letter-by-letter transliteration from the *hangul* would be something like "kuTu."

The McCune-Reischauer romanization, however, has its own drawbacks. Many extra diacritical marks are needed to write Korean in the McCune-Reischauer system accurately (that is, special symbols such as accent marks or the circumflex "wedge" over vowels must be added to the normal letters). This can be cumbersome, because forgetting to add an apostrophe, for example, can make a difference in the meaning of a word. Also this transcription does not especially match the way words are written in the native alphabet. It is for these reasons that many linguists prefer the more scientific (though less transparent) Yale system.

In spite of all its shortcomings, the McCune-Reischauer romanization system will probably survive for some time to come. The main reason for this is that many Western libraries, particularly the Library of Congress, have used this system for many years. At this point it would be an enormously time-consuming and expensive task to convert to some other transcription system, even assuming a better one could be devised and internationally accepted.

McCunn, Ruthanne Lum (b. Feb. 21, 1946, San Francisco, Calif.): Writer. She authored the award-winning *Thousand Pieces of Gold* (1981), a biographical novel from which the 1991 movie of the same name was based; *An Illustrated History of the Chinese in America* (1979); *Pie-Biter* (1983); *Chinese American Portraits: Personal Histories 1828-1988* (1988); and other works. Educated at the University of Texas and San Francisco State University, the daughter of a white American father and a Chinese mother, she writes about the experiences—both personal and historical—of Asian Americans. In 1984 she won an American Book Award from the Before Columbus Foundation for *Pie-Biter*.

MacKenzie, Frederick Arthur (1869-1931): Writer. Sponsored by the Korean Commission, he wrote *Korea's Fight for Freedom* (1920), which received praise in England and influenced the formation of the League of the Friends of Korea in 1920.

McWilliams, Carey (Dec. 13, 1905, Steamboat Springs, Colo.—June 27, 1980, New York, N.Y.): Writer and editor. McWilliams was educated in law at the University of Southern California and worked for ten years as a commercial lawyer in Los Angeles. During that period, with encouragement from editor and writer H. L. Mencken, McWilliams wrote his first periodical articles, most of which concerned literary subjects, for Mencken's *American Mercury*. In 1929 McWilliams published his first book, a biography of American writer Ambrose Bierce.

By 1932 McWilliams had abandoned his literary interests in favor of California politics, which was then marked by a variety of social protest movements growing out of the Great Depression. He was deeply impressed by the Depression-era revival of the American labor movement and by farm labor strikes in California. These events attracted McWilliams' attention to the liberal social causes that he thereafter advocated and reported.

Between the late 1930's and mid-1940's McWilliams' work focused on ethnic discrimination and social injustice, especially in California. His *Factories in the Field* (1939), probably his best-known book, documented the history of migrant farm labor in California. This work was especially important to Asian American history because it was the first time that the participation of immigrants from Japan and the Philippines in California's farm economy had been documented in such a high-profile fashion. *Factories in the Field* was followed by *Ill Fares the Land* (1942), which concerned national aspects of the farm labor problem.

There were, however, political consequences for McWilliams after he finished *Factories in the Field.* Earl Warren, later chief justice of the U.S. Supreme Court, campaigned for governor of California by vowing to remove McWilliams from his position as California's commissioner of immigration and housing, an office created in response to the farm labor problems of the 1930's.

McWilliams' work during the 1940's included four influential studies of American racial and ethnic minorities: *Brothers Under the Skin* (1943), which described racism as a national problem and advocated remedial legislation; *Prejudice* (1944), which concerned the internment of U.S. citizens of Japanese descent during World War II; *A Mask for Privilege* (1948), a history of anti-Semitism in the United States; and *North from Mexico* (1949), a history of Mexican migration to what is now the United States.

McWilliams also wrote two important social histories of California during this period. The first, *Southern California Country: An Island on the Land* (1946), focused on the exploitation and boosterism that transformed desert Los Angeles into a major urban area. Long considered a key study of the region, the book has powerfully influenced subsequent California historians. A second book about California, *California: The Great Exception* (1949), has also endured.

McWilliams was appointed West Coast editor of *The Nation* in 1945. He was invited to New York in 1951 for a brief project. He remained, and in 1955 he became editor of the magazine, a post that he held until his retirement in 1975. This was an important time for the liberal periodical, since it included the time of the Civil Rights movement, the Vietnam War, and the Watergate political scandal.

Magnuson Act. *See* **Immigration Act of 1943**

Maha-shivaratri: Annual one-day festival celebrated by Hindus. The Sanskrit term *Maha-shivaratri* means "great night of Shiva." The festival is celebrated on the fourteenth day of the dark fortnight of the month of *Phalguna* (February-March), so the festival usually occurs about March 1.

What follows is one of the most sacred days of the Hindu calendar. Pious devotees of the god Shiva often fast for the entire twenty-four hours and spend the night before the festival day singing devotional songs in an all-night vigil. The festival day usually includes a visit to the temple, or to multiple temples, for the auspicious viewing (*darshan*) of the temple's images of Shiva. These images include representations of Shiva both in human form and in his symbolic representation of the *linga*, a cylindrical object of stone or metal. The *linga* is typically decorated with paint, flower petals, and bilva leaves and is bathed in milk and honey as a ritual event to honor Shiva. Even Hindus who are not devoted to Shiva, who instead worship Vishnu or the Goddess, often participate in this festival in honor of Shiva, whom they may regard as the most exalted devotee of their own god.

A myth found in several Sanskrit texts known as *Puranas* tells the origin of this festival. An evil hunter once inadvertently dropped water on a Shiva *linga*, caused some bilva leaves to fall on it, and stayed awake all night, going without food for a day. In this fashion, he honored Shiva, however unintentionally, and went to heaven as a reward. Should others of better character and better *Karma* similarly honor Shiva, they will be rewarded as well.

Shiva is an ancient Hindu representation of divinity, often worshiped as the god of Yoga and of the performing arts, such as drama and dance, by Hindus who believe in multiple gods. Many Hindus, however, regard Shiva as God, the sole creator and destroyer of the world.

Mahesh Yogi, Maharishi (Mahesh Prasad Varma?; b. 1911?, Madhya Pradesh, India): Meditation teacher. He introduced TRANSCENDENTAL MEDITATION (TM), a simple form of mantra meditation, to the West. Through a combination of skillful presentation, personal charisma, celebrity endorsements, and fortuitous timing, he became the most successful meditation teacher in history, initiating, with the help of teachers whom he trained, several million Westerners.

The details of Maharishi's life are not readily discovered, and even TM teachers generally do not know his given name. This obscurity seems to be a result of both Maharishi's disregard for the significance of biography and the Indian practice of discarding personal name and history when one becomes a monk. His sketchy official biography states that Maharishi was graduated from Allahabad University with a degree in physics in 1942. Around this time, he met his guru, Swami Brahmananda Saraswati, a noted scholar and religious leader. For thirteen years, Maharishi served

The Maharishi Mahesh Yogi was in large part responsible for introducing transcendental meditation (TM) to the West. (AP/Wide World Photos)

his guru, going into retreat in the Himalayas upon his master's death. In 1958, Maharishi left his cave and set out to transform the world.

The Spiritual Regeneration Movement, the Students' International Meditation Society, and the Maharishi European Research University are only a few of the organizations that Maharishi formed to propagate his teachings. Maharishi International University in Fairfield, Iowa, offers academic degrees along with advanced meditation practice. From the beginning, Maharishi has seen TM as a panacea for the problems of the modern world. He initially claimed that if 1 percent of the world practiced TM, a new age would dawn. Later, based on insights he drew from theoretical physics, he asserted that if the square root of 1 percent of the world's population (roughly seven thousand persons) practiced the TM Sidhi program in the same place at the same time, the world would be at peace, crime would decrease, everyone would spontaneously follow natural law, and an "Age of Enlightenment" would manifest itself.

In the 1990's, Maharishi was living in Holland, appealing to national governments to fund his peace-through-meditation plans, opening Ayurvedic medicine clinics, and starting construction on "Vedaland," a theme park outside Orlando, Florida. In 1992, Maharishi's Natural Law Party ran candidates for the presidency and vice presidency of the United States.

Mah-Jongg: Western version of a Chinese game, resembling gin rummy, that is played with tiles. These playing tiles look like dominoes but are engraved with Chinese symbols and characters. The object of the game is to acquire sets of tiles. Mah-Jongg is thought to have originated in China sometime during the nineteenth century, each Chinese province having its own style of play and dialect name for it. Joseph P. Babcock, an American living in Shanghai, is credited with bringing the game to the West following World War I. He introduced changes to make it more adaptable to Westerners.

Mail-order brides: Overseas Asian women who correspond with prospective husbands through a mail-order bride company. The marketing of Asian mail-order brides is practiced on a wide scale. In 1979, agencies promoting sex tourism and mail-order brides began operating in the United States. Asian mail-order bride businesses sell names and addresses of women to their American clients. For a fee, a client may receive catalogs of Asian women, along with their photos and brief descriptions. Once the fees are paid and selections are made, correspondence between the couple begins; what happens after that is up to the couple. These women are seeking American men as pen pals or as future husbands. Many are hoping to escape the poverty of their homelands.

Advocates and Opponents. John Broussard is the owner of Cherry Blossoms, a typical mail-order bride business. In 1986, a six-month subscription to a complete set of catalogs from Cherry Blossoms cost $250. For an additional fee, the company would attempt to find the client a suitable wife. In 1986, Broussard reported receiving a hundred letters a day from Asian and other women. He publishes about seven hundred pictures every month in his catalog. He reports that men have about a 5 percent chance of finding a wife through his service. Of three thousand Cherry Blossom marriages taking place since 1986, Broussard says that he is aware of about two dozen divorces. He believes that the best evidence that most of these wives are happy is that they have become his chief recruiting agents.

Kathleen Barry is a leading opponent of the Asian mail-order bride industry. In her book *Female Sexual Slavery* (1984), she shows how sexual slavery is connected to rape, the Asian mail-order bride industry, incest, pornography, wife battery, and other forms of exploitation of women. According to Barry, the growing phenomena of organized sex tours, prostitution, and mail-order brides are examples of how women's bodies are being systematically sold. With regard to mail-order brides, she states:

> Marriage by catalogue where brides are ordered by photos is another example of economic and sexual exploitation of poor women. "Happiness without Barriers" and promises of fidelity and docility are some of the slogans used by commercial matchmakers who profit off such marriages. Pictures of women from the Third World with their vital statistics are presented as commodities to male clients. Many of these women are later forced into prostitution.

In 1986, in Honolulu, Hawaii, an Asian mail-order bride was found killed and dismembered. Her husband, an Anglo-American, was arrested, with bail set at $200,000. The couple had met through Cherry Blossoms.

Gladys Symons, of the University of Calgary, has stated that men are attracted to the idea of buying a wife since all immigration, transportation, and other costs run to only about $2,000. As a consumer society, people become translated into commodities easily. For example, in a 1986 television program called "Town Meeting" from Seattle, Washington, Broussard said that the total cost for a mail-order bride is "as much as a good used car."

The Japanese American Citizens League (JACL) believes that the marketing techniques used by the catalog-bride companies reinforce negative sexual and racial stereotypes of Asian women in the United States and that this negative attitude affects all Asians living there. The JACL believes that women are being treated as "commodities," which adds to the "non-human and negative perception of all Asians."

Many people believe that the stereotypes of Asian women can be traced back to U.S. wars in Asian countries. Military bases created markets for prostitution, and many American servicemen were conditioned to seeing Asian women only in a sexual way.

Profile of the Clients and Brides. In a 1983 survey, Davor Jedlicka, a sociologist at the University of Texas, studied 265 mail-order bride catalog subscribers and found that 80 percent of them believed in the stereotype of Asian women as docile and submissive. The general profile of these men was as follows: 94 percent were Caucasian, 65 percent had incomes above $20,000, the average age was thirty-seven, most were college-educated, and the majority of them had experienced bitter divorces or separations.

The Asian women in question are generally born poor and become mail-order brides in order to escape poverty through marriage. Most are ignorant of U.S. immigration laws; many of them miss chances at becoming American citizens and live under an unwarranted fear of being deported, a misconception that may often be promoted by their spouses as a means of controlling these women. Because many of the latter do not speak English, they are unable to call a "hotline" if they are trapped in a situation as a battered wife. JACL representatives have cited meetings with several battered Filipinas who came to the United

Asian women who become mail-order brides are generally seeking to escape poverty through marriage; one survey of subscribers to mail-order bride catalogs found that 80 percent of these men believe in the stereotype of Asian women as docile and submissive. (James L. Shaffer)

States as Asian mail-order brides.

Picture Brides. The Japanese tradition of the "picture bride" was a very different phenomenon because it was an arrangement between people of the same culture and background and who knew each other's cultural expectations. The arrangement was through a *nakodo*, a middleman who knew both families; he received monetary rewards and was responsible for the happiness of the union.

Other Issues. At issue is the question of whether women are being taken advantage of as a result of their poverty. Critics of the business might say that these women are exploited. Advocates might say such women are being saved from a life of poverty or that the women have volunteered for this by writing to mail-order bride businesses. Poverty, however, may have compelled the women to do something that they do not want to do, such as leaving their natal families and countries. Other supporters of this industry might say that mail-order brides become American citizens by marriage and are free to leave their marriages. Yet many Asian mail-order brides do not speak English and do not know their legal rights.

The development of international legal regulations and the requirement that mail-order bride businesses conform to these regulations and those of the International Criminal Police Organization (Interpol) might remedy some of the problems that exist within the industry. There is also no regulatory agency to ensure that the universal human rights of these women are not being violated, nor are the men screened for prior criminal records. Monitoring systems developed by the owners of mail-order bride companies would help to protect the safety of these women in their new homes.—*Patricia Wong Hall*

Suggested Readings: • *Asian Mail-Order Brides.* Video. KOMO Radio/TV, 1986. Barry, Kathleen, Charlotte Bunch, and Shirley Castley, eds. *International Feminism: Networking Against Female Sexual Slavery.* New York: International Women's Tribune Centre, 1984. • Goodwin, Clarissa Garland. *The International Marriage: Or, The Building of a Nation.* Los Angeles: UCLA Special Collections, 1931. • Imamura, Anne E. *Strangers in a Strange Land: Coping with Marginality in International Marriage.* East Lansing: Women in International Development, Michigan State University, 1987. • Larsen, Wanwadee. *Confessions of a Mail Order Bride: American Life Through Thai Eyes.* Far Hills, N.J.: New Horizon Press, 1989. • Taylor, Carol. "Mail-Order Bride." *Good Housekeeping* 210 (February 1, 1990): 62.

Makino, Frederick Kinzaburo (Aug. 28, 1877, Yokohama, Japan—Feb. 17, 1953, Honolulu, Territory of Hawaii): Newspaper publisher and advocate for the Japanese in Hawaii. The third son of an English merchant, Joseph Higgenbotham, and his Japanese wife, Kin Makino, Frederick Makino grew up in the international port city of Yokohama, learning to read, write, and speak both Japanese and English. His father died when he was four years old.

Makino's fun-loving and mischievous ways as a young man led his older brother, then a Yokohama businessman, to send Makino to the Big Island of Hawaii to live with his eldest brother. Makino arrived in 1899, when he was twenty-one years old. In 1901 he moved to Honolulu, where he opened a drugstore. Two years later he married Michiye Okamura.

Makino spoke out for the rights of the Japanese as they encountered racial, social, and economic discrimination. He helped lead a sugar strike in 1909; helped end the practice of forcing Japanese "PICTURE BRIDES," who were already married according to Japanese custom, to undergo an undignified marriage cere-

Frederick Kinzaburo Makino spoke out for the rights of Japanese in Hawaii and founded Hawaii Hochi, *a Japanese-language newspaper that later became the* Hawaii Herald. (Japanese American National Museum)

mony en masse upon arrival in Hawaii; and won naturalization rights for Issei (Japanese immigrant) soldiers who served in the U.S. Army during World War I. Makino also led the court battle challenging anti-Japanese-language school laws and unsuccessfully appealed the murder conviction of a young, deranged Nisei (second-generation Japanese American), Myles Fukunaga.

Dissatisfied with the existing Japanese language newspapers, Makino founded *Hawaii Hochi* (Hawaii news) in 1912 on a shoestring budget. In 1925 he hired George W. Wright as its English-language editor. Wright proved to be a trenchant writer who penned provocative editorials that reflected Makino's views. He wrote, for example, editorials criticizing Hawaii territorial leaders for attempting to discourage the Nisei's educational aspirations and to create a false impression of the opportunities available to plantation workers. The editorials urged the Japanese to behave like Americans and stand up for their rights.

Makino denounced efforts by European Americans to keep the Japanese at the bottom of the socioeconomic ladder and castigated Japanese accommodationist leaders for acquiescing in these efforts. His fighting spirit drew the admiration of the Japanese community and the respect of European Americans.

Actor Mako received a star on Hollywood's Walk of Fame in February, 1994. (Mario Reyes)

Mako (Makoto Iwamatsu; b. 1933, Kobe, Japan): Actor. The son of artist Taro Yashima and his wife Mitsu (also an artist), Mako was left with relatives when his parents immigrated to the United States in 1939 to escape the oppressive militarism then dominant in Japan. Before his parents could bring him over to join them, as planned, war broke out between Japan and the United States. After the war, Taro Yashima had to search for his son in the confusion following Japan's defeat.

Coming to the United States, Mako enrolled as an architectural student at the Pratt Institute in New York. During the Korean War, however, he was drafted into the armed services, and by the time of his discharge he had decided to pursue a career as an actor instead of an architect. Moving to California, he enrolled as a drama student in classes held at the Pasadena Playhouse. After receiving a thorough acting foundation, Mako found a career on screen in a variety of roles and on television in episodes of shows such as *77 Sunset Strip* and *Hawaiian Eye*. His appearance opposite Steve McQueen in *The Sand Pebbles* (1966) earned Mako an Academy Award nomination as Best Supporting Actor.

Despite this recognition, Mako—like other Asian American actors—was largely limited to stereotypical roles. Searching for a new outlet for his talents, he joined forces with a group of likeminded actors, playwrights, and directors to establish the EAST WEST PLAYERS, the first Asian American theater company. East West Players created a forum for presenting drama written and performed by Asian Americans and helped promote a more accurate image of Americans of Asian heritage.

In addition to serving as artistic director of the East West Players, Mako continued to work as an actor, appearing in films such as *Testament* (1983) and *Conan, the Destroyer* (1984) and earning a Tony nomination for his performance in the Broadway production of the musical *Pacific Overtures* (1976). He had a starring role with Nobu MCCARTHY and Sab Shimono in a film adaptation of Philip Kan Gotanda's *The Wash* (1988). Since leaving the East West Players in 1989, he has appeared in the film *Pacific Heights* (1990), opposite Nobu McCarthy, Melanie Griffith, and Michael Keaton, and in the film *Rising Sun* (1993), opposite Sean Connery and Wesley Snipes. On February 1, 1994, Mako was honored with the dedication of a star on the Hollywood Walk of Fame.

Malays in traditional dress stand before a display of scenes from their mother country. (James L. Shaffer)

Malays: Mainly a cultural and linguistic category, Malays are historically indigenous to Southeast Asia and form the dominant population of the Malay Archipelago. Racial classification of this population has been various: generalized mongoloids, southern mongoloids, or the brown race. Such classification distinguishes Malays from the classical mongoloids of Japan, China, Korea, and central Asia on the one hand and the Asiatic/Oceanic negroids on the other hand. Prehistoric reconstructions point to a very complex migration pattern throughout the region, creating diverse theories of racial mixture, linguistic diffusion, origins of food production technology, and the Malays' presumed ultimate descent from *Homo erectus* and later populations.

Predating the impact of the high civilizations of Hinduism, Buddhism, Islam, and Christianity, the indigenous Malay cultures have been gleaned through the study of communities outside these civilizational mainstreams as found in the islands of Sumatra, Sulawesi, Borneo, the Moluccas, and many parts of the Philippines. Their environments vary: highlands, lowlands, and maritime. Sociopolitical integration ranges from tribal to chiefdom; religion, from animism to ancestor worship. Their kinship and descent principles represent every conceivable model: bilateral, matrilineal, and patrilineal. The basic community is a village, regionally known as the *kampong* and often led by a headman or a chief, depending on its size and political autonomy. A *kampong* may consist of thirty to a hundred households. The Malay cultural base can be characterized as follows: bamboo-thatched houses; wooden crafts; sacred trees; respectful attitudes toward elders; and two types of food systems, the yam-sago-taro complex and rice. Ethnographic and historic literature also give diverse accounts of people who ranged from excitable and violent to very peaceful. The Malays' languages belong to the family Malayo-Polynesian, or Austronesia. Their cultures extend beyond Southeast Asia into Oceania, as far as Madagascar and Easter islands.

Malaysia, Federation of: Southeast Asian nation composed of the Malay Peninsula and the states of Sarawak and Sabah on the island of Borneo. It is hot, humid, and rainy throughout the year, and its hilly interior is surrounded by alluvial and swampy coastal plains. It is also one of the richest and most progressive nations in Southeast Asia.

Malaysia has a British-style parliamentary system of government and a constitutional monarch, who is elected by the sultans of the thirteen federated states and who performs only ceremonial functions. Abdul Rahman, a Malay Muslim, was elected as Malaysia's

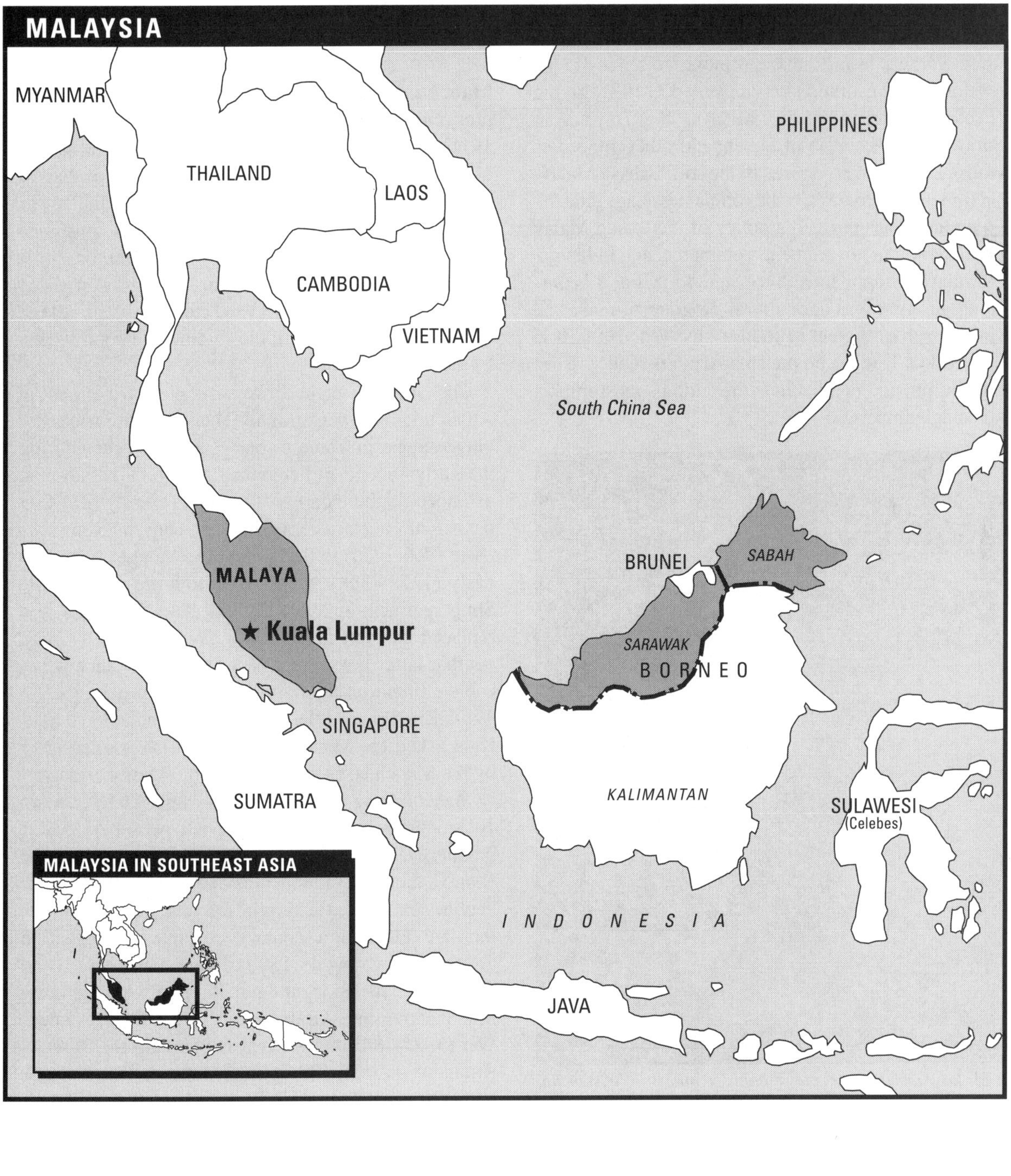

first prime minister in 1957.

With a total area of 127,584 square miles, Malaysia is roughly the size of New Mexico, and about 85 percent of its 18.6 million people (1992 estimate) inhabit the Malay Peninsula. The Malays, who are Muslims, the Chinese, who are predominantly Buddhists, and the Indians constitute 49 percent, 32 percent, and 10 percent of the population, respectively. When the country became independent in 1957, the Malays, the majority of whom are rural farmers, objected to the continued dominance of the public service, commerce, trade, mining, and industry by descendants of indentured workers from China and India. To reduce racial tension, the constitution was amended in 1971, giving special privileges to the Malays, the Dayaks of Sarawak, the Kazadan of Sabah, and other minorities who are *bumiputras*, or sons of the soil. Bahasa Malaysia (or simplay Malay), is the official language, and the government has pursued a policy of increasing Malay participation in government, commerce, and industry.

Malaysia imports rice, the staple food, but it is pursuing an ambitious agricultural program to make the country self-sufficient in food by the year 2000. It is the world's leading producer of natural rubber, palm oil, and tin, and petroleum is the nation's most important single import.

A Malay American girl plays tennis in Madison, Wisconsin. (Mary Langenfeld)

Its vigorous and growing private sectors and its changing attitude toward foreign investment have contributed to rapid industrial expansion since 1990. It exports air conditioners, rubber goods, semiconductors for computers, chemicals, transportation equipment, electrical machinery, textiles, and offshore oil platforms. Kuala Lumpur, the federal capital, is the largest city.

Malaysia's remarkable economic growth can be attributed to the desire of the ethnic communities to set aside their differences in order to promote their common good.

Manchu: Refers principally to a people and their culture; imperial China's final dynasty, the Qing (1644-1911); and the Japanese-controlled nation of Manchukuo (1932-1945). By the end of World War II (1939-1945) Manchukuo had vanished with the downfall of its Japanese patron; the dynasty was consigned to history as an unpleasant reminder to Han or ethnic Chinese of foreign control and to Manchus of irrecoverable glory; and the people and culture became all but invisible through assimilation with the majority Han Chinese.

The Manchus came from a Tungusic tribal and an Altaic linguistic background. Their ancestral tribes begin to appear in Chinese sources as the Jurchen during the early second millennium C.E. By 1115 they had extended the boundaries of the Qin Dynasty (221-206 B.C.E.) into northeastern China, forcing the Song Dynasty (960-1279) to flee south. The Mongol Yuan Dynasty (1279-1368) swept away both the Qin and the Song regimes, but its rule was short-lived and was replaced by the Chinese Ming Dynasty (1368-1644). As that latter government declined, the Manchus became a threat on the northern frontier. When rebel Li Tzu-cheng usurped the throne, Ming general Wu San-Kuei asked the Manchus for help. Li was dispatched by the Manchus, as were Wu and the Ming Dynasty.

Manchu Qing administration spanned 267 years and 10 emperors, created an extended period of peace, prosperity, and cultural achievements (such as the Kangxi dictionary), and presided over both dynastic decline and the extinction of the imperial system. By the late eighteenth century corruption, population growth (from roughly 150 million people in 1741 to 430 million in 1851), and rebellion buffeted the now-Sinicized regime. A half-century later the First Opium War (1839-1842) with Great Britain and the TAIPING REBELLION (1850-1864) nearly destroyed the dynasty, but a reformist Tung-chih Restoration (1861-1874) revitalized the government, defeated the rebels, and began a gradual modernization program. Nevertheless continued foreign troubles (especially China's defeat in the Sino-Japanese War of 1894-1895) and domestic unrest (the BOXER REBELLION of 1900, which also involved foreigners) exposed a dynasty in its death throes, even as nascent Chinese nationalism demanded the expulsion of the "foreign" Manchus. Despite a decade of post-Boxer reforms, the Qing Dynasty fell in 1911.

Under the Republic of China (1912-1949) important Manchus retired to comfortable obscurity, only to be recalled to duty when Japan established Manchukuo and needed Manchu officials to give the government a veneer of legitimacy. By then, however, hundreds of thousands of Han Chinese had migrated to Manchuria, where Japanese economic development produced jobs. Numbering less than three million people, the Manchus soon lost their cultural identity. A prominent but largely empty symbol of Manchu historical existence can be found on the flag of the People's Republic of China, where one of the five stars represents the Manchu people, whose homeland is known as the northeast.

Mandarin: Largest of the seven major dialect groups of the Chinese language. It is spoken almost universally north of the Yangtze River and in Southwest China. The Beijing dialect of Mandarin serves as the basis of Modern Standard Chinese (*putonghua*) and is spoken by about 60 percent of the population. It is obligatory in all schools, though regional dialects are usually spoken alongside it.

Along with the other major Chinese languages, Mandarin is largely monosyllabic, lacks suffixes and prefixes, and is spoken without tenses. The spoken languages are largely mutually unintelligible, but the written forms are uniform, based upon some fifty thousand characters. The earliest writing incorporated simple pictographs in which characters resembled the objects that they represented. As the language became more complex, certain characters or parts of characters came to represent ideas and sounds, as well as objects. Grammatical relationships are established by word order and independent particles. Mandarin usually employs four tones and the use of two or three final consonants. In 1956, 515 simplified characters were adopted, with an additional two thousand in 1964.

The earliest written forms of the Chinese language developed during the Shang Dynasty (traditionally given the dates of 1766-1122 B.C.E. or 1523-1027 B.C.E.). By the Yuan dynasty (1279-1368), an early form of Mandarin became clearly distinguishable in the vernacular literature of the period. Its use has steadily grown because of its intimate association with the capital city of Beijing, post-1919 literature, and modern tendencies toward centralization. Mandarin is also the national language in Taiwan (Republic of China) and the most widely spoken dialect among Chinese immigrant communities in the United States.

Mandarin was also the English term used for high military or civil officials of the Chinese Empire, who gained position through rigorous examination and were never appointed to their home provinces.

Mandu: Fried or boiled Korean dumpling, made of ground beef, scallions, onions, bean sprouts, Chinese cabbage, and tofu. It is wrapped in flour pancakes and seasoned with egg yolk.

Manghokun. *See* **Tiger Brigade**

Manila: Capital of the Republic of the Philippines. Situated on Manila Bay in southwestern Luzon, and boasting one of the world's best natural harbors, Manila is the Philippines' chief port and largest city, with a 1990 metropolitan area population of 7,832,000.

Manila men. *See* **Filipino immigration to the United States**

Manlapit, Pablo (Jan. 17, 1891, Lipa, Butangas, Luzon, Philippines—1969, Philippines): Labor leader. In the 1920's and 1930's Manlapit became known as a leader of Filipino plantation workers in Hawaii. He helped organize the sugar strikes of 1920 and 1924 that inspired Filipino field-workers and antagonized the HAWAIIAN SUGAR PLANTERS' ASSOCIATION (HSPA). A series of prosecutions resulted in his imprisonment and, ultimately, banishment to the Philippines.

Migration to Hawaii. Manlapit completed his primary education at a Lipa City public school established soon after the American occupation of the Philippines. His niece recalls that the Manlapit family originally came from Bataan, moved to Batangas, and then to Manila. The family of six or seven children apparently prospered in the city, where the father, employed in security for an American company, sent the oldest son to a private college. The second son, Pablo, worked briefly as messenger, clerk, and timekeeper in different offices.

Despite his parents' objections, Manlapit left Manila in January, 1910, arriving in Honolulu the following month. He was sent to a sugar plantation on the island of Hawaii (the Big Island), where he worked in the fields for two years. Losing his job after getting involved in a strike, he moved to Hilo, where he tried various ways to make a living, including managing a pool hall. Around June, 1912, he married Annie Kasby, whose mother was German and whose father was a white American homesteader. Their oldest daughter, Alice, was born in 1913. Two years later the family moved to Honolulu. Three additional children (Annie, Sophie, and Pablo, Jr.) were born in Honolulu. To support the family, Manlapit worked as a stevedore, editor of a Tagalog periodical, and janitor/interpreter at the office of attorney William J. Sheldon, where he used his spare time to study law on his own. In 1919 Manlapit was granted a license to practice law in the district courts. He was the first Filipino lawyer to practice law in Hawaii.

Labor Activities. The pre-World War II economy in Hawaii was mainly a plantation system controlled by the HSPA and the powerful BIG FIVE companies, consisting of Alexander & Baldwin, American Factors (Amfac), Theo H. Davies & Company, C. Brewer & Company, and Castle & Cooke. To ensure an adequate labor supply, the HSPA recruited from many countries, including China, Japan, Korea, and the Philippines. Plantation workers demanded better working conditions, leading to the major strikes of 1909, 1920, 1924, and 1937.

In 1919, Manlapit organized Filipino workers to form the Higher Wages Association (not to be confused with the Higher Wage Association organized on Hawaii by Japanese workers some years earlier), which demanded, among other things, a minimum wage of $2 per day, an eight-hour work day, equal pay for men and women, and recognition of the Filipino field-workers' union, the Filipino Federation of Labor. He spoke at meetings in public parks and on government roads and sites nearby but outside the premises of the plantation, from which he was banned. Filipino plantation workers recalled Manlapit as a brave man who delivered speeches without using any notes. Manlapit often stressed that the HSPA should give Filipino workers a fair deal, which he believed to be part of the American tradition and ideal. Leaders of the Higher Wages Association submitted petitions to the HSPA officials, who refused to respond. Thus, in 1920, the Filipino workers decided to strike.

Manlapit had consistently promoted cooperation between Japanese and Filipino workers, and the 1920 strike was the first—and only—multiethnic strike in Hawaii in the pre-World War II period. (See SUGAR STRIKE OF 1920.) The 1920 strike began when Filipino sugar workers at Kahuku plantation ignored Manlapit's advice to delay action and struck for higher wages. Japanese and Portuguese worker later joined the strike. The strike lasted 165 days; its impact was considerably weakened by misunderstanding between the Filipino and Japanese leaders and by the HSPA's hiring of strikebreakers and prosecution of labor leaders. Manlapit avoided prosecution because the HSPA believed that the Japanese had masterminded the strike. Fifteen Japanese leaders were indicted and convicted for conspiracy. The HSPA, anxious about the labor supply in the plantations, continued its surveillance of Manlapit.

The Filipino plantation workers' strike of 1924 occurred over a period of eight months and consisted of loosely coordinated actions on Oahu, Kauai, Maui, and the Big Island. (See SUGAR STRIKE OF 1924.) The executive committee of the Higher Wages Association, composed of Manlapit, George W. Wright, Patricio Belen, Prudencio Gabriel, Emigdio Milanio, Pedro Valderama, and Cecilio Basan, was theoretically in charge of the strike. In reality, local leaders on each island directed activities and managed their strike camps or temporary dwellings for the strikers, who had all been evicted from the plantations. These leaders maintained peace and order at these camps, organized solicitation drives for food, and caught fish in the ocean. Manlapit himself took charge of the strike camps on Oahu.

On September 9, 1924, a confrontation in Hanapepe, Kauai, resulted in the death of sixteen strikers and four police officers. More than one hundred strikers were arrested. Manlapit himself was on another island when the confrontation erupted. The massacre occurred because the fully armed police officers and security forces panicked and overreacted to what they had considered provocations from the strikers. This incident weakened the strike and probably led to Manlapit's conviction on a subornation of perjury, a charge lodged months before the Hanapepe massacre. According to Manlapit's defense lawyer, Manlapit became a convenient scapegoat.

For almost two years Manlapit served his sentence at the Oahu Prison. He was later disbarred from law practice. While in prison he requested a pardon from Governor Wallace R. Farrington and a reinvestigation of his case, sending along affidavits attesting that the HSPA had paid the witnesses to testify against him.

The editor of the *Hawaii Hoichi* asked Manuel L. Quezon y Molina, Philippine Senate president, to support Manlapit's request for pardon. No support ever came from the Philippines, however, and Farrington rejected Manlapit's request. Manlapit's family began to suffer hardships; his wife and daughters did laundry work to keep the family alive. In March, 1927, Manlapit was given a parole that became controversial because it required that he leave Hawaii. Following friends' advice he sailed for California several months later.

From 1927 to 1932 Manlapit was in Los Angeles and other areas in California, where he participated in Filipino affairs, including a brief membership with the Filipino Federation of America, a stint as business manager for a Filipino newspaper (the *Los Angeles Observer*), and campaigns to organize a union of Filipino agricultural workers. The Los Angeles police placed Manlapit under surveillance as a communist. In April, 1932, he returned to Hawaii with Antonio A. Fagel, whom he had met in California and persuaded to get involved in organizing workers.

Road to Exile. Together with Fagel and another labor leader, Epifanio Taok, Manlapit revived the Filipino Labor Union. Once more he spoke at rallies on Oahu and the neighboring islands, advocating basically the same changes that the strikers had demanded in 1924. The HSPA continued to regard him as a dangerous agitator. In July, 1934, Manlapit was arrested and charged with a federal crime for asking a high fee from a Filipino army veteran who needed assistance in applying for a loan from the U.S. Veteran's Bureau. A federal jury convicted Manlapit the following October. Financially unable to continue the litigation, Manlapit reportedly requested that the court suspend sentence and offered to leave Hawaii. In October, 1934, he sailed back to the Philippines alone as his wife and children chose to stay in Hawaii.

Sugar plantation workers, Oahu, circa 1916. (Library of Congress)

Manlapit left a legacy of union consciousness in Hawaii. Fagel took the Filipino union underground and helped lead a successful strike in 1937 at Puunene plantation on Maui. Among the strikers in Puunene was young Carl Damaso, who would become president of the International Longshoremens' and Warehousemens' Union (ILWU) in postwar Hawaii. In the Philippines, Manlapit served in the administrations of presidents Manuel Roxas y Acuma and Elpidio Quirino. In 1954 he offered his services to a labor group, the Philippine Labor Unity Movement. He died in poverty in 1969 because, according to his second wife and son, he was honest and did not enrich himself while working for the Philippine government. Moreover, as he had done in Hawaii, he opened his house to workers in need and contributed his personal money to assist strikers and their families.—*Melinda Tria Kerkvliet*

SUGGESTED READINGS: • Alcantara, Ruben R. *Sakada: Filipino Adaptation in Hawaii.* Washington, D.C.: University Press of America, 1981. • Beechert, Edward D. *Working in Hawaii: A Labor History.* Ethnic Studies Oral History Project, University of Hawaii at Manoa. Honolulu: University of Hawaii Press, 1985. • *The 1924 Filipino Strike on Kauai.* Manoa: Ethnic Studies Program, University of Hawaii, Manoa, 1979. • Manlapit, Pablo. *Filipinos Fight for Justice: Case of the Filipino Laborers in the Big Strike of 1924.* Honolulu: Kumalee Publishing, 1933. • Okamura, Jonathan Y., et al., eds. *The Filipino American Experience in Hawaii.* Social Process in Hawaii, vol. 33. Manoa: Department of Sociology, University of Hawaii, Manoa, 1991.

Manoa Lin Yee Wui: Earliest Chinese association in Hawaii, founded in 1854. It supervised burials in a plot of land in Manoa Valley, secured more land to develop a cemetery, and arranged for Chinese immigrants to send the bones of their dead relatives back to China for burial. Organized by a group of Chinese merchants, the association was chartered by the Hawaiian government in 1889 as the Chinese Cemetery Association of Manoa (Manoa Lin Yee Wui).

Manong: Filipino term meaning "uncle" or "revered elder." The term is used to refer to the more than 100,000 Filipino men who came to the United States between the early years of the twentieth century and the mid-1930's, when anti-Filipino agitation and the effects of the Great Depression led to severe restrictions on Filipino immigration. A majority of the manongs came to the United States in the 1920's. A largely bachelor society, they were primarily farm laborers—Filipinos made significant contributions to the development of organized labor among farmworkers—although some found work in urban centers. In addition to low pay and difficult working conditions, the manongs had to contend with antimiscegenation laws and other forms of discrimination and racial prejudice.

Manzanar: First of ten U.S. government camps under the administration of the WAR RELOCATION AUTHORITY (WRA) used to house Japanese American evacuees during World War II. Officially the camps were designated as "relocation centers." Incarcerated in these camps were more than 120,000 Japanese, approximately one-third of whom were law-abiding Japanese aliens (Issei) denied U.S. citizenship and two-thirds of whom were U.S. citizens (mostly Nisei, but also Sansei and a few Yonsei). Located in central California, the Manzanar site had been used by Paiute-Shoshone Indians for centuries before 1900 and then, roughly between 1910 and 1935, was a tiny Euro-American fruit-growing settlement (*manzanar* is Spanish for "apple orchard").

The camp was established initially by the U.S. Army as an assembly center and managed by the Wartime Civil Control Administration (WCCA) as the Owens Valley Reception Center from March 21 through May 31, 1942. On June 1, 1942, Manzanar was reconstituted as a WRA center, the only one of the assembly centers to be so transformed. The camp's peak population was 10,121, nearly equally divided between male and female, with one-quarter of them school-age children. The overwhelming majority of the internees at Manzanar were drawn from prewar Japanese American communities in Los Angeles County, particularly the city of Los Angeles.

Natural and Physical Characteristics. Situated within the imposing Sierra Nevada range at the base of Mount Williamson, Manzanar experienced a harsh climate of extreme temperatures, high winds, and severe dust storms. The camp proper consisted of a rectangle of about 550 acres dominated by 36 blocks of 504 tar-paper residential barracks for the interned population, most of whom lived within 20 x 25-foot family apartments. This area encompassed communal mess halls, laundry facilities, and latrines, as well as considerably upgraded living facilities for the appointed personnel. Additionally it contained a modern 150-bed hospital, schools, churches, recreational and cultural

The internment camp at Manzanar. (National Archives)

facilities, cooperative stores, and most other amenities found in a "normal" American city of comparable size. Also in this central area were war-related industries (such as a camouflage net factory), an experimental plantation for producing natural rubber from the guayule plant, and the Children's Village orphanage. Immediately outside this main camp were 1,500 acres of agricultural land, which not only made Manzanar self-sufficient in crops, meat, and poultry but also augmented the other WRA camps' food supplies and generated revenue for the Manzanar administration in open-market sales. The camp's core was surrounded by barbed wire and eight sentry towers and manned by armed military police, a battalion of which was quartered a half-mile south of the Manzanar center.

Social and Political History. Although relative peace and harmony generally prevailed within the center, internee resistance to unpopular administrative policies—manifested as work slowdowns and strikes as well as through cultural politics and noncompliance with regulations—was not uncommon. The most dramatic incident of resistance occurred on December 6, 1942. Sparked by the jailing of Harry Ueno—the popular head of the Mess Hall Workers' Union—for beating Fred Tayama—an unpopular internee prominent in the JAPANESE AMERICAN CITIZENS LEAGUE (JACL), whose leaders were widely assumed by internees to be collaborators and informers—the "Manzanar riot" climaxed in the death of two inmates and the wounding of nine others by military police. Its aftermath involved the roundup and ultimate imprisonment (without formal charges or hearings) of Ueno and other suspected "pro-Japanese" advocates and camp "troublemakers" in citizen isolation centers in Moab, Utah, and Leupp, Arizona. The JACL and allied "pro-American" spokespersons and their families were put in "protective custody" and consigned to an abandoned Civil Conservation Corps camp in nearby Death Valley National Monument.

A more pervasive and protracted show of resistance

was set in motion two months later, in February, 1943, when the Army and the WRA imposed a mandatory registration on the adult population of Manzanar and the other centers for the joint purpose of establishing eligibility for leave clearance and securing volunteers for a special Japanese American combat team. At Manzanar only forty-two persons (2 percent of the eligible citizen males) volunteered for military service, while approximately 50 percent of all male citizens and 45 percent of all female citizens either answered no to the so-called loyalty questions on the registration questionnaire or refused to answer the questions. The latter situation led to 1,322 Manzanarians and their families (a grand total of 2,165) being transferred in late 1943 to the WRA's newly established Tule Lake relocation center in Northern California.

With the departure of its "disloyals" to Tule Lake (along with expatriates and repatriates to Japan), an increasing number of its "loyals" entering the U.S. military (following the reinstitution of selective service for Japanese Americans in 1944) and resettling throughout the United States as war workers and college students, Manzanar became a community largely of elderly and youthful residents. Notwithstanding limited self-government and an improved physical appearance and social ambience, Manzanar retained constant reminders that it was a concentration camp: Its residents were not free to leave, its newspaper (the *Manzanar Free Press*) was censored, and its confines were patrolled by armed soldiers.

Post-World War II Development. After its closure, the Manzanar site reverted to its prewar "natural" state, save for four surviving internee-built structures (two 1942 pagodalike stone security posts, a 1943 memorial obelisk, and a 1944 auditorium), plus scattered remnants of the constructed and botanical environment. Beginning in 1969, annual pilgrimages to the site have been held under the sponsorship of the Manzanar Committee, a Los Angeles-based community activist group. Manzanar was declared a state historical landmark in 1972 and a national historical landmark in 1985. On March 3, 1992, U.S. president George Bush signed into law the Congress-established Manzanar National Historic Site, providing government purchase of the site and National Park Service administration, under the Department of the Interior, for preservation and historical interpretation.—*Arthur A. Hansen* and *Alan Koch*

Suggested Readings: • Adams, Ansel. *Manzanar*. With photographs by Ansel Adams and commentary by John Hersey. Compiled by John Armor and Peter Wright. New York: Times Books, 1988. • Embrey, Sue Kunitomi, ed. *The Lost Years: 1942-1946*. Los Angeles: Moonlight Publications, 1972. • Embrey, Sue Kunitomi, Arthur A. Hansen, and Betty Kulberg Mitson, eds. *Manzanar Martyr: An Interview with Harry Y. Ueno*. Fullerton, Calif.: Japanese American Project, Oral History Program, California State University, Fullerton, 1986. • Garrett, Jessie A., and Ronald C. Larson, eds. *Camp and Community: Manzanar and the Owens Valley*. Fullerton, Calif.: Japanese American Project, Oral History Program, California State University, Fullerton, 1977. • Hansen, Arthur A., and Betty E. Mitson, eds. *Voices Long Silent: An Oral Inquiry into the Japanese American Evacuation*. Fullerton, Calif.: Japanese American Project, Oral History Program, California State University, Fullerton, 1974. • Houston, Jeanne Wakatsuki, and James D. Houston. *Farewell to Manzanar*. Boston: Houghton Mifflin, 1973.

Manzanar incident (1942): Mass protest staged by Manzanar relocation center internees. During the evening of December 5, Fred Tayama of the Japanese American Citizens League (JACL) was beaten by several assailants. He later identified one of these as Harry Ueno, a camp cook and an outspoken critic of the JACL. Ueno was promptly arrested by camp authorities, but numerous Manzanar internees were angered by the arrest and staged a mass demonstration in protest the next day. As negotiations for his release lingered on, the protestors grew restless and impatient; as some of them moved to take matters into their own hands, Tayama and other suspected *inu* became the targets of mob wrath. Soon, military police arrived on the scene and began firing tear gas into the crowd to quell the riot; when that failed, shots were fired at the agitators, immediately killing at least one and injuring others.

Manzanar pilgrimages: Return of Japanese Americans to the World War II internment site in central California. The pilgrimages began in the late 1960's and early 1970's when Asian American activists sought to redress the racism, discrimination, and suffering endured by interned Japanese Americans. The first journey to Manzanar occurred on December 27, 1969.

Mao Zedong (Dec. 26, 1893, Shaoshan, Hunan Province, China—Sept. 9, 1976, Beijing, People's Republic of China): Political party leader. He was the leader of the CHINESE COMMUNIST PARTY (CCP) and a major twentieth century political figure who founded, after winning the civil war (1945-1949) against the Guomindang (GMD), the People's Republic of CHINA on October 1, 1949. As the undisputed leader of the CCP for forty years, he shaped the course of pre- and post-revolution China. His theoretical contribution to Marxian communism made Marxism-Leninism a relevant and appealing doctrine to peasant societies of Asia, Africa, and Latin America.

Mao Zedong, leader of the Chinese Communist Party, the revolutionary who founded the People's Republic of China upon winning a civil war with Taiwan in 1949. (AP/Wide World Photos)

Born into a poor peasant family (though his father later became moderately affluent, Mao received primary education in Shaoshan, his native village, and secondary education in Changsha, the provincial capital. In 1911, he joined the revolutionary army that overthrew the Qing Dynasty, and in 1920 he considered himself a Marxist; he was one of the thirteen members present in Shanghai when the CCP was founded. After the breakdown of the CCP-GMD alliance in 1927, Mao and a revolutionary group established the Jiangxi Soviet in 1930, but continued GMD attacks forced the Communists out of Jiangxi Province. In the ensuing Long March (1934-1935), he rose to command the CCP, a position he maintained for the rest of his life.

Mao placed high value on production efforts even in the midst of revolutionary war (1937-1945). His land reform program, announced in 1950, was popular and successful. He also adopted a Soviet-style Five-Year Plan in 1953. His Great Leap Forward (1958-1959), however, which was aimed at creating a communist society through the abolition of private land, the creation of communes, and the bringing of industries to the countryside, failed miserably. During the Cultural Revolution (1966-1976), he sought, through his chosen Red Guards, to cleanse the party and government of bourgeois values and bureaucratic degeneration. Between 1971 and 1976, his wife, Jiang Qing, dominated the ideological and cultural scene in China.

After Mao's death, the Gang of Four was arrested, tried, and given long prison sentences. His successors, especially Deng Xiaoping, have reversed his revolutionary policies in domestic and foreign affairs. They nevertheless recognize him as a great revolutionary and Marxist theorist who led the Communist Party and China in the right direction until the Great Leap Forward period.

March First movement (1919): Nationwide uprising that broke out in the capital city of Seoul, Korea, on March 1, 1919. The movement erupted as a national plea for independence and survival in the face of the intolerable and oppressive policies of the Japanese colonial government then occupying Korea. (See CHOSEN.) As the general public became swept up in the struggle for freedom, more than a thousand mass demonstrations were eventually launched in almost every part of the country. In all, the resistance involved more than a million protestors, thousands of whom died during the bloody and brutal Japanese military suppression that followed. Yet the movement, while achieving some positive results, was greeted indifferently by the world powers and failed to drive the Japanese forces from Korea.

Rising Hopes for Independence. In the aftermath of World War I, an apparent sudden change in the international political climate motivated a group of Korean cultural, religious, and political leaders to launch the fight for independence, both at home and abroad. Prior to the Paris Peace Conference (1919-1920) in Versailles, U.S. president Woodrow Wilson, in his Fourteen Points speech of January 8, 1918, had sketched his agenda for the postwar period. The principles of

An execution of Korean farmers by Japanese police c. 1905. The crime was a protest against the oppressive Japanese policies that eventually led to the March First movement. (The Korea Society/Los Angeles)

humanism, respect for the self-determination of peoples, and international cooperation, he declared, must now become the basis for a new era of world peace. Following Wilson's championing of the concept of the autonomy of nations, Koreans the world over were hopeful that foreign influence, chiefly that of the United States, the preeminent world power, would help loosen Japan's hold on Korea.

Korea's religious leaders and moderate nationalists were particularly inspired by Wilson's appeals for a new age of world humanism and peace. With most of the radical leadership in exile or imprisoned by the Japanese, what remained of the nationalist struggle in Korea fell to the religious community. Church-related organization and assembly had been guaranteed for the purpose of religious freedom and was therefore useful for conducting secret political activities. Encouraged by the presence of exile groups at the peace conference, leaders of the Christian, Chondogyo, and Buddhist churches forged ahead with plans to mobilize national support for an independence movement.

An Opportune Time. In early 1919, as plans for a series of demonstrations began to unfold, movement leaders decided to take advantage of the upcoming funeral ceremonies planned for former Korean emperor Kojong, who had died that January. Rumors of Japanese involvement in Kojong's death intensified anti-Japanese feelings, and many Koreans previously uninvolved in the independence struggle now found themselves suddenly aroused by the emperor's passing. To obtain the widest possible publicity for their cause, protest leaders decided to launch the effort during the time of the funeral, scheduled for March 3, when thousands of mourners would be in Seoul to pay tribute.

In February, as the movement surged forward, its leaders chose to declare absolute independence from Japan, and a declaration of independence was drafted. It proclaimed Korea's liberty and equality among the family of nations unconditionally, with the assertion: "This is the clear leading of God, the moving principle of the present age, the whole human race's just claim." The public demonstrations themselves were to be nonviolent and peaceful.

To avoid discovery by the authorities, the date for the demonstrations was moved ahead two days, from March 3 to March 1. On that day, signatories to the Korean Declaration of Independence sent a copy of the document to the Japanese authorities. At the same time, members of the movement were publicly reading

This parade was held in Dinuba, California, to honor the March 1 incident on its first anniversary. (The Korea Society/Los Angeles)

the statement at Seoul's Pagoda Park and in other townships throughout Korea. Shortly thereafter, demonstrators began marching through the streets shouting "Taehan tongnip manse" (long live an independent Korea). The protests drew people from all walks of life and, in the ensuing months, became nationwide, with Japanese police reporting "disturbances" in all but 7 of Korea's 218 counties.

The movement and its mass popular participation startled the Japanese, who responded with brutal arrests, assaults, and killings, in turn provoking Korean retaliation. Soon, Japanese military reinforcements were summoned to help quell the rioting. Casualty counts for both sides varied widely: Japanese officials reported 553 killed and 1,409 injured, while Korean nationals counted more than 7,500 killed and about 15,000 injured.

Aftermath. The appeal initiated by the March First movement failed to persuade the world powers to intervene on behalf of an oppressed Korea. The movement therefore failed to accomplish its primary objective: to end the hated Japanese colonial rule. Those powers possessing Asian colonies did not want to endanger their own international and domestic political interests and so refused to embrace Wilson's idealistic plan for world peace in Asia.

Short of independence, however, the effort became a catalyst for the expansion of the nationalist movement as a whole. Previously, Korean nationalist activity had consisted of individualized and poorly coordinated efforts overseas and at home. The events of 1919 succeeded in temporarily merging the various movements and groups into a more concentrated and unified coalition in Korea, thereby mobilizing an entire nation to action.

The success of the demonstrations also encouraged the assorted exile groups to organize and conduct independence activities of their own. Thus, for the first time since the Japanese annexation of Korea in 1910, nationalists overseas formed a government in exile to unite the many separate elements and to join with the coalition back home. A Korean provisional government in exile was created in Shanghai in April, 1919, with Syngman RHEE as president.

Finally, the March First independence movement called worldwide attention to the severity of the Japanese imperial rule. The demonstrations were a public relations disaster for the Japanese. Responding to worldwide criticism, the Japanese shifted their colonial policy in Korea toward a looser, more culturally sensitive rule. At the same time, they augmented police surveillance and political controls.

Today March 1 is a national holiday in both North and South Korea, commemorating the historic events of 1919.—*Michael Robinson*

SUGGESTED READINGS: • Eckert, Carter J., et al. *Korea Old and New: A History*. Seoul, Korea: Ilchokak, 1990; distributed in U.S. by Harvard University Press. • Lee, Chong-sik. *The Politics of Korean Nationalism*. Berkeley: University of California Press, 1965. • Lee, Ki-baik. *A New History of Korea*. Cambridge, Mass.: Harvard University Press, 1984. • Nahm, Andrew C. *Korea: Tradition and Transformation—A History*. Elizabeth, N.J.: Hollym International, 1988.

Marcos, Ferdinand Edralin (Sept. 11, 1917, Sarrat, Philippines—Sept. 28, 1989, Honolulu, Hawaii): President of the Philippines (1965-1986). Marcos was born in Ilocos Norte province. He studied law at the University of the Philippines and served in both the Philippine and the U.S. armies in World War II. He emerged from the war as a highly decorated officer. Years later Marcos dismissed persistent allegations that his war record had been fabricated. He claimed that the documentation of his military exploits had been destroyed in a fire.

Marcos' was a liberal member of the House of Representatives (1949-1959) and Senate (1959-1965) but switched to the Nacionalista Party and defeated incumbent liberal Diosdado Macapagal in the 1965 presidential election. Marcos' government was successful in increasing industrial output and agricultural productivity, and despite urban guerrilla activity and the growing Communist and Muslim insurgencies in rural areas, he was reelected in 1969. In 1972, as violent protests mounted against his government, he suspended the constitution and imposed martial law. He adopted a new national constitution under which he became prime minister as well as president. The country remained under martial law until 1981. Marcos maintained close ties with the United States and supported U.S. policy in Vietnam. Opposition to his rule increased during the 1980's because of widespread corruption and ruinous economic policies. His grip on power in the Philippines began to weaken following the assassination in 1983 of Benigno Aquino, Jr., the nation's leading opposition figure, who was shot dead upon returning from exile. Marcos blamed the killing on a professional assassin with ties to the Communists, but the country's opposition movement accused the government of masterminding the murder.

Ferdinand Marcos addresses reporters during a trip to the United States during the height of his power. (Library of Congress)

In the face of increasing unrest at home and new pressure from the United States to enact reforms, Marcos decided in November, 1985, to call a snap election to test his popularity. The decision backfired when the opposition rallied around the presidential candidacy of Corazon Aquino, who had assumed the mantle of leadership from her late husband. The subsequent elections of February, 1986, were marred by fraud. Marcos declared himself victorious, but Aquino initiated a nationwide campaign of civil disobedience in an attempt to topple the government. Marcos' fate was sealed when the nation's two top military leaders resigned a few weeks later and threw their support behind Aquino. Marcos left the country for exile in Hawaii days later aboard a U.S. Air Force plane. Corazon Aquino replaced him as president.

Marcos and his wife, Imelda, had been indicted in October, 1988, by a U.S. grand jury in New York City on charges of stealing more than $100 million from the Philippine government, but Marcos had gained a reprieve in April, 1989, when federal prosecutors declared that he was too ill to stand trial. Imelda Marcos was acquitted in 1991. More recently, the Philippine government began a trial of the Marcoses charging the couple with the "plunder of a nation's wealth." The Marcos' reported wealth—his salary as president was less than $6,000 a year—is in the billions and supposedly includes real estate in Manhattan, entire corporations, and countless foreign bank accounts.

The $365 million Marcos Swiss deposits remain the object of a tug-of-war between the Marcoses and the American government. In 1993 some ten thousand Philippine torture victims began seeking indemnity from the Marcos estate. Honolulu district court judge Manuel Real on September, 1991, declared the Marcos estate, including the Swiss accounts, liable for the human rights victims' indemnification. The jury found the Marcos family guilty of killing and torturing some ten thousand people during a twenty-year period in office.

Marcos died of cardiac arrest at Honolulu's St. Francis Medical Center in 1989. He was buried on October 15 in Honolulu, Hawaii. Marcos' interment came as debate was raging in the Philippines on whether the deposed leader's body should be allowed to be returned to the country for burial in his native province

Opposition to Marcos' rule increased dramatically after the assassination of political foe Benigno Aquino, Jr. (whose dead body is here being lifted into a security van). Many blamed the Marcos government. (AP/Wide World Photos)

of Ilocos Norte. Former president Corazon Aquino had refused to allow the body home for burial. She feared that a funeral would rekindle the admiration of his supporters and make them overlook Marcos' crimes, which probably included the assassination of her husband in 1983.

Marcos personified the double standards by which many Filipinos live. He first sprang to fame, in the best mafia tradition, by being accused at the age of eighteen of murdering his father's political enemy. The killing, which supposedly avenged a family insult, established Marcos as a respected (and feared) "man of honor"; he was acquitted on appeal for lack of evidence.

Marcos wrote *The Democratic Revolution in the Philippines* (1974) and *The New Philippine Republic—A Third World Approach to Democracy* (1982).—*Ceferina Gayo Hess*

SUGGESTED READINGS: • Bonner, Raymond. *Waltzing with a Dictator: The Marcoses and the Making of American Policy*. New York: Times Books, 1987. • Burton, Sandra. *Impossible Dream: The Marcoses, the Aquinos, and the Unfinished Revolution*. New York: Warner Books, 1989. • McDougald, Charles C. *The Marcos File: Was He a Philippine Hero or Corrupt Tyrant?* San Francisco: San Francisco Publishers, 1987. • Rempel, William C. *Delusions of a Dictator: The Mind of Marcos as Revealed in His Secret Diaries*. Boston: Little, Brown, 1993. • Romulo, Beth Day. *Inside the Palace: The Rise and Fall of Ferdinand and Imelda Marcos*. New York: Putnam, 1987. • Seagrave, Sterling. *The Marcos Dynasty*. New York: Harper & Row, 1988. • Youngblood, Robert L. *Marcos Against the Church: Economic Development and Political Repression in the Philippines*. Ithaca, N.Y.: Cornell University Press, 1990.

Marriage matchmaking, Asian Indians and: The tradition of arranged marriages remains popular among Indian immigrants to the United States and, to some extent, among their American-born children; a temporary return to India is often an expected part of the process.

Among the more highly educated Indian immigrants, however, arranged marriages, as well as the observance of other Indian marriage traditions, are in noticeable decline. Many Indians, in both India and the

United States, now marry for "love"—that is, the person of their own choosing; consequently intercaste marriages are no longer rare (except perhaps for Brahmans), and dowries are sometimes dispensed with entirely. Traditionally, the woman's family is obligated to pay the man's family a dowry, with the amount often directly related to the man's educational status. The educational status of the woman also remains important, as her level of education traditionally should be no higher than her husband's.

Arranged marriages are usually negotiated by parents or other close family members, with the well-being and happiness of both prospective marriage partners of primary importance. The matchmaker's role is largely that of go-between, providing an avenue by which either of the principal parties may politely refuse a marriage offer.

The custom of matching horoscopes serves a similar purpose. If the couple's horoscopes match suitably, marriage negotiations may begin, although either family may, for personal reasons, tactfully declare the pair horoscopically incompatible. Conversely, poorly matching horoscopes do not necessarily end the process, for if the marriage is desired, other astrologists may be consulted until horoscopes are satisfactorily matched. Negotiations and meetings then continue until a wedding date (also based on astrological consultation) is set.

In arranged matches the presence of love before marriage is not required—but love often develops later, as individuals thus matched are at least nominally compatible. Additionally much societal and individual angst over dating and selection of safe, compatible partners may be avoided by the practice of deliberate matchmaking. For this reason alone the custom will likely continue among Indian immigrants and their children, disappearing entirely only as families become established in the United States over two or three generations.

Martial arts: Methods of self-defense developed from ancient Asian fighting systems. They utilize physical force and coordination, with or without weapons. The martial arts evolved throughout the world into various schools with varying techniques, teaching methods, styles, and emphases. These arts are now practiced not only for self-defense but also for exercise, health, recreation, and sport. Philosophical and religious themes are significant in many of the forms. There are conflicting theories on the origins of the martial arts, but historical records indicate that such fighting systems existed in many parts of the world at least twenty centuries before the birth of Christ.

Basic Techniques. Weaponless methods used for self-defense and/or attacking include open hand and arm blows; low and high kicks, using various parts of the foot or knees; grappling, locks, holds, twists, and chokes; throws, trips, takedowns, and escapes; blocks and parries; and targeting pressure points or strategic nerve centers. Weapons include swords, spears, sticks, staffs, metal spikes, stones, lances, bows and arrows, chains, sickles, and other hand-held or thrown cutting objects. Many of the ancient combative techniques and weapons have been modified or made nonlethal for the practice of the martial arts as sport, exercise, or recreation. Often, protective clothing is worn, as in Japanese kendo swordfighting.

Colored Belts. While there is no common system of promotion or ranking by colored belts, usually white belt indicates a beginner, a brown belt denotes an advanced pupil, and a black belt indicates a master, and there are degrees within the black belt rank. Colors such as yellow, orange, blue, purple, and green are used for the intermediate ranks. Advancement to the next level of proficiency can be based on *kata* demonstrations, performance in a competition, or a determination by the teacher.

The Major Systems: Karate. The term "karate" means "empty hand," and "karate-do," "way of the empty hand," originated in Okinawa. Gichin Funakoshi, an Okinawa karate master, opened the first karate school, or *dojo* in Japan in the 1920's. The first karate association in the United States was opened by Japanese *sensei* (teacher) Oshima in 1955. The basic techniques used in karate are focused hand and foot blows. Korean karate is called tae kwon do, which means "way of kicking and punching."

The Major Systems: Gung-Fu. This earlier, Chinese form of karate began in a Shaolin monastery in northern China in 520 C.E. It is believed to have been brought there by Indian monk Bodhidharma, who also taught Buddhist philosophies to the Shaolin monks. There are two basic schools of gung-fu: The internal, or soft, school (pa-kua, hsing-i, and tai chi chuan) emphasizes the spiritual or philosophical, while the external, or hard, school (Shaolin Fist, Hung Gar, and Tong Long) stresses kicking and power blows. Tai chi chuan, an exercise popular in China, uses highly stylized movements related to gung-fu.

The Major Systems: Jujitsu, Judo, and Aikido: Jujitsu, or "gentle art," was created from the Japanese art of sumo in 23 B.C.E. and is the forerunner of aikido and

The Japanese art of jujitsu. (Raymond J. Malace)

judo. Originally used in combat by the samurai, jujitsu came to encompass a wide variety of schools and techniques, including kicks, strikes, throws, trips, joint-locking, and swords. Kano Jigoro, a Japanese educator, created judo by synthesizing various systems of jujitsu. In 1882 he began teaching judo, which basically uses throws and grappling. Judo became the sports version of jujitsu and was introduced as an Olympic sport in 1964 in Tokyo. Aikido, or "way of all harmony," was created by Ueshiba Morihei in Japan in the late 1920's in reaction to the physical emphasis in jujitsu. Using holds, locks, twists, and throws, the aikido artist uses an opponent's strength against himself or herself. Aikido aims for the unity of mind, body, and *ki*, the power within each person.

Development in Europe and the United States. Beginning at the end of the nineteenth century, Japanese immigrants to Europe and the United States taught systems of jujitsu and judo. The martial arts were not widely studied by Europeans and Americans, however, until after World War II. The American armed forces occupying Japan after 1945 studied techniques such as judo, jujitsu, karate, kendo, and aikido; U.S. servicemen learned tae kwon do after the Korean War in 1953. When these soldiers returned home, they established martial arts schools and often invited Asian masters to teach in them. The study of Chinese martial arts did not begin until the 1960's, after the easing of U.S. immigration quotas for Chinese.

Martial Arts in American Popular Culture. After World War II American contact with East Asia increased. Once martial arts studios were established in the United States, the centuries-old oral traditions began to take root in a new and fertile environment.

Eastern martial arts first appeared in Western cinema in 1921 in *Outside Woman*, which showed a Japanese servant using jujitsu. The Charlie CHAN series of the 1930's often included Asian-style fighting. *Blood on the Sun* (1945), however, was the first movie in which a Hollywood star (James Cagney) used an Asian

Actor Ralph Macchio performs a karate punch during a practice session with actor Pat Morita; they helped popularize karate in the 1984 feature film The Karate Kid. (Museum of Modern Art/Film Stills Archive)

A high kick in the Korean martial art of tae kwon do. (Raymond J. Malace)

martial art (judo) to overcome an antagonist. Akira Kurosawa's classic *The Seven Samurai* (1956) was the basis for the Western *The Magnificent Seven* (1960). The James Bond thriller *You Only Live Twice* (1967) featured *ninja* for the first time. Other popular media personalities, such as Elvis Presley and James Coburn, also displayed martial arts skills. Younger Americans learned about karate through the film *The Karate Kid* (1984).

One of the earliest karate scenes on American television was in *The Detectives* (1959-1962), in an episode featuring karate master Bruce Tegner. By 1965, series such as *I Spy* (1965-1968), *The Wild, Wild West* (1965-1970), and *Honey West* (1965-1966) regularly featured martial arts. The legendary Bruce LEE played Kato in *The Green Hornet* series (1966-1967). His *Enter the Dragon* (1973) is a cult classic. The popular KUNG FU series (1972-1975) starred David Carradine as a Shaolin disciple in the Old West. In the 1980's martial arts themes penetrated the children's cartoon and toy market with the *Teenage Mutant Ninja Turtles* (1988). Like Chinese restaurants, the martial arts have become a significant element of mainstream American culture.—*Alice Chin Meyers*

SUGGESTED READINGS: • Kauz, Herman. *The Martial Spirit: An Introduction to the Origin, Philosophy, and Psychology of the Martial Arts*. Woodstock, N.Y.: The Overlook Press, 1977. • Neff, Fred. *Basic Jujitsu Handbook*. Minneapolis: Lerner Publications, 1976. • Soet, John Steven. *Martial Arts Around the World*. Burbank: Unique Publications, 1991. • Tegner, Bruce, *Karate: Beginner to Black Belt*. Ventura, Calif.: Thor Publishing Company, 1982. • Williams, Bryn. *Martial Arts of the Orient*. New York: Hamlyn, 1975.

Marutani, William (b. 1923, Kent, Wash.): State court justice. The first Asian American to be named to the bench outside Hawaii or the western United States, he was appointed to the Court of Common Pleas in Philadelphia in 1975. After internment at Tule Lake during World War II, he served in the U.S. Army's Military Intelligence Service (MIS). He earned his A.B. degree from Dakota Wesleyan University in 1950 and his law degree from Chicago Law School in 1953.

Marysville labor camp: Temporary assembly center in Marysville, California, one of sixteen temporary assembly centers set up for the mass relocation of Japanese Americans during World War II. Under EXECUTIVE ORDER 9066 (1942), more than 110,000 Americans of Japanese ancestry were first relocated to temporary centers and later incarcerated in relocation centers administered by the WAR RELOCATION AUTHORITY (WRA). Other temporary centers were in Mayer, Arizona; Portland, Oregon; Puyallup, Washington; and at California locations at Fresno, Manzanar, Merced, Pinedale, Pomona, Sacramento, Salinas, Santa Anita, Stockton, Tanforan, Tulare, and Turlock.

Masaoka, Mike Masaru (Oct. 15, 1915, Fresno, Calif.—June 26, 1991, Washington, D.C.): Lobbyist and political activist. Masaoka grew up in Salt Lake City, Utah, where he attended public schools and the University of Utah. He contemplated a career in politics but was frustrated by the racism that impeded his path. After college graduation and a brief period of work he became in 1941 the executive secretary of the JAPANESE AMERICAN CITIZENS LEAGUE (JACL). He and president Saburo Kido overhauled the moribund organization and recruited many new members. They were responsible for the JACL's exuberantly patriotic assimilationist campaigns, with slogans such as, "Better Americans in a Greater America."

With World War II (1939-1945) on the horizon, Masaoka apparently cooperated with the Federal Bureau of Investigation (FBI) and military intelligence agents as they compiled lists of Issei leaders to be jailed if war should come. When war broke out, those Issei leaders were jailed, and the JACL stepped in to claim community leadership. Masaoka and the JACL counseled Japanese Americans to go quietly into concentration camps as a display of loyalty to the United States. Masaoka himself was not interned. During the war, he was instrumental in restoring to the Nisei the right to be drafted into the armed services. He himself served and was decorated.

After the war, the JACL sent Masaoka to Washington, D.C., as its representative. There, he lobbied for the EVACUATION CLAIMS ACT OF 1948, which gained token compensation for some of the Japanese Americans' property losses. He also worked on behalf of the MCCARRAN-WALTER ACT OF 1952, which allowed the Issei to apply for U.S. citizenship for the first time and provided a tiny quota of Japanese immigrants each year. He formed a private consulting firm in 1952. For the next three and a half decades, he was known as one of the most effective lobbyists in Washington, working on behalf of the JACL as well as various Japanese and American business interests.

By the end of Masaoka's life, a younger generation of activists had largely repudiated his lifework. They especially called into question the JACL's conduct during World War II and demanded redress from the U.S. government for wartime injuries.

Masaoka v. State of California (1952): California Supreme Court ruling that held the state's Alien Land Law of 1920 to be unconstitutional. Haruye Masaoka was an elderly Issei woman to whom her sons wanted to tranfer ownership of a house that they had built for her. Under the land laws then applicable, however, Japanese aliens ineligible for U.S. citizenship (the Issei) could not buy, sell, or be given gifts of real property. Prevented from carrying out their plan, the family then filed a court action to challenge the law's validity, and the judge ruled in their favor based on a finding that the law violated the U.S. Constitution's Fourteenth Amendment.

The state appealed to the supreme court, which upheld the earlier judicial ruling. Citing legal precedent for their finding, the justices pointed to the rule established in *FUJII SEI V. STATE OF CALIFORNIA* (1952), the landmark high court decision that affirmed the right of an Issei to hold title to land in California.

California voters elected to repeal the ALIEN LAND LAWS in 1956. Until then, court opinions such as *Fujii* and *Masaoka* effectively rendered these statutes unenforceable.

M*A*S*H (1972-1983): American television comedy series focusing on the day-to-day lives of the members of the 4077th Mobile Army Surgical Hospital (MASH unit) during the Korean War. The unit consisted of U.S. Army doctors and nurses stationed in South Korea. The popular antiwar series garnered some of the highest critical acclaim ever given a television program; its final original episode, broadcast February 28, 1983, was seen by the largest audience ever to watch a single television show. *M*A*S*H*, starring Alan Alda as Captain Benjamin Franklin ("Hawkeye") Pierce, was based on the hit motion picture (1970) of the same name, which in turn was based on the novel (1968), by Richard Hooker.

Mass, Amy Iwasaki (b. July 5, 1935): Scholar. Amy Iwasaki Mass received her bachelor's degree from the University of California, Berkeley, in 1956 and her master's degree in social work in 1958 from the University of Southern California, after which she was a social worker for various agencies throughout Southern California and in San Francisco. She went into private practice as a clinical social worker in 1970. Mass received her doctorate in social work from the

University of California, Los Angeles, in 1986, and since that time she has served as an assistant professor in the Department of Sociology, Anthropology, and Social Work at Whittier College in Southern California. Professor Mass, the recipient of numerous awards and honors, is particularly knowledgeable regarding the experiences of racially mixed individuals in the Asian American community in general and the Japanese American community in particular.

Massie case (1931): Honolulu, Hawaii, rape case involving a white woman and a group of Asian men. In September of that year, Thalia Massie, wife of a U.S. Navy lieutenant stationed at Pearl Harbor, claimed that she had been raped by a group of local young men—two Japanese, two Hawaiians, and a Chinese Hawaiian. An ethnically mixed jury found the evidence against the defendants inconclusive, resulting in a mistrial. Although subsequently an independent agency hired by the governor of Hawaii vindicated the jury's decision (even Massie's testimony was confused), the white population of the islands felt that white womanhood had been assaulted.

A few days after the mistrial a group of sailors kidnapped one of the Japanese defendants and beat him until he was unconscious. No one was arrested.

Later, informed that new evidence was needed to reopen the case, Massie's mother enlisted the help of her son-in-law and two sailors to force a confession from one of the Hawaiian defendants, Joseph Kahahawai. During the interrogation Kahahawai was shot and killed. Before Massie's mother and her coconspirators could dispose of the body, their car was stopped by police, who had been alerted to the situation by Kahahawai's cousin.

Famous lawyer Clarence Darrow argued the case for Kahahawai's murderers, but the jury had little choice except a guilty verdict. The defendants had admitted to the kidnap and murder of Kahahawai. Nevertheless Darrow blamed the verdict on the ethnic mix of the jury: "Our clients were white, and a white jury no doubt would have acquitted them almost with-

Clarence Darrow (center, white shirt) argued for the defendants in the second trial stemming from the Massie case. (Library of Congress)

out argument." Throughout the United States there were screaming headlines on the case. A columnist cried, "Are we no longer Americans? No longer free and white?" Even Congress was aroused. Pressure was applied to the governor of Hawaii, who then commuted the ten-year sentence to one hour, to be served in his office.

The Massie case put Hawaii on trial; its ability to govern itself was questioned. Although nothing came of it, the Navy strongly recommended that Hawaii be placed under its control. In the aftermath, many islanders began to wonder whether there were two sets of laws: one for the elite and one for the rest of the people.

Masters and Servants Act of 1850: Hawaii state legislation specifying how apprentices and contract laborers in Hawaii were to be treated, with sanctions to be enforced by the courts. It was implemented to help secure labor for Hawaiian sugar plantations.

Masuda, Minoru (Apr. 10, 1915, Seattle, Wash.—?): Scholar. As a professor in the Department of Psychiatry at the University of Washington, Masuda was a specialist in psychophysiology, a branch of psychology that attempts to explain the correlations between physiological processes and human behavior. He earned a Ph.D. degree in physiology from Washington in 1956 and went on to teach there for many years.

Matsuda, Fujio (b. Oct. 18, 1924, Honolulu, Territory of Hawaii): Engineer, scientist, and educator. His parents were immigrants from Japan. In 1943, as a student at the University of Hawaii, he joined the 442ND REGIMENTAL COMBAT TEAM and was assigned to the 232nd Engineers for basic training. The Army selected him to study engineering in the Army Specialized Training Program and later assigned him to the 291st Field Artillery Observation Battalion for combat duty in the northern European theater. He was discharged in December, 1945. He returned to the University of Hawaii in 1946 but completed his undergraduate work at the Rose Polytechnic Institute (now Rose-Hulman Institute of Technology) in 1949. The Massachusetts Institute of Technology (MIT) conferred a D.Sc. degree on him in 1952.

Specializing in the response of structures to nuclear explosions, Matsuda participated in tests conducted in Nevada and the Pacific Islands. He continued structural dynamics research at MIT from 1952 to 1954, at the University of Illinois, Urbana, from 1954 to 1955, and later at the University of Hawaii. He taught at the universities of Illinois and Hawaii from 1954 to 1963. At Hawaii, he served as department chair of the Civil Engineering Department.

Matsuda served as head of the Hawaii State Department of Transportation from 1963 to 1973, being responsible for the financing, planning, design, construction, and operation of the statewide airports, harbors, and highways system. Major projects of his administration include the Interstate and Defense Highway system, the Honolulu Harbor acquisition and consolidation, and the Honolulu International Airport expansion.

Matsuda returned to the University of Hawaii as vice president for Business Affairs in 1973 and became its ninth president in 1974. During his tenure, the university system continued to grow in size, diversity, and quality. The two-year community college system, the upper-division West Oahu and four-year Hilo colleges, as well as the flagship University of Hawaii, Manoa, all made significant progress. In 1984, he retired from the presidency to become executive director of the Research Corporation of the University of Hawaii. He also became a member of eleven prominent local organizations.

Matsuda married Amy M. Saiki in 1949. The couple has three sons, three daughters, and many grandchildren.

Matsuda, Mari (b. Apr. 8, 1956, Los Angeles, Calif.): Scholar. A professor at Georgetown University School of Law, she has been an advocate of critical legal studies, which, among other positions, argues that the First Amendment right of free speech must be balanced with other constitutionally guaranteed rights, including the right of Asian Americans and other minorities to be protected against racist hate speech. She has also taught in the law schools of the University of California, Los Angeles, Stanford University, and the University of Hawaii.

Matsudaira, Tadaatsu (1855—1888): Mining engineer. He came to the United States as a teenager, then went on to earn a degree in civil engineering from Rutgers University. From there he worked for the Union Pacific Railroad and later attended the Colorado School of Mines, eventually becoming the state's assistant inspector of mines.

Matsui, Robert Takeo (b. Sept. 17, 1941, Sacramento, Calif.): U.S. representative. A second-generation Japa-

Representative Robert Takeo Matsui, Democrat from California, was reelected to Congress seven times. (Asian Week)

nese American, Matsui grew up in Sacramento and received his B.A. degree from the University of California, Berkeley, in 1963. Matsui then studied law at the University of California, San Francisco's Hastings College of the Law. After he received his J.D. degree in 1966, Matsui passed the California bar examination and returned to Sacramento to begin the practice of law. Active in community affairs and concerned about issues pertaining to Japanese Americans, he was chosen to serve as president of the Sacramento chapter of the JAPANESE AMERICAN CITIZENS LEAGUE (JACL) in 1969.

Matsui launched his political career in 1971 when he ran for election to the Sacramento city council and was elected as a representative from the city's eighth district. After his reelection, Matsui served as the city's vice mayor from 1977 to 1978. Setting his sights on higher office, Matsui defeated a Republican opponent to win election to the U.S. House of Representatives from California's Third Congressional District in

1978. While in Congress, Matsui served on the House Ways and Means Committee, the Commerce Committee, and the Select Committee on Narcotics Use and Control and served as a congressional liaison with the National Finance Council.

Reelected to Congress seven times, Matsui was one of the leading figures in the fight for government reparations to be awarded to Japanese Americans who had endured forced removal to internment camps during World War II. On August 10, 1988, the reparations bill became law (the CIVIL LIBERTIES ACT OF 1988) and provided internment camp survivors with a tax-free award of $20,000. After declaring his intention in 1992 to campaign for the senate seat vacated by Alan Cranston, Matsui withdrew from the race to spend time with his critically ill father.

Matsunaga, Spark M. (Masayuki Matsunaga; Oct. 8, 1916, Kukuilula, Kauai, Territory of Hawaii—Apr. 15, 1990, Toronto, Ontario, Canada): U.S. senator. Matsunaga was the first of three children of Kingoro Matsunaga, a Japanese who had immigrated to Hawaii and another Japanese immigrant, Chiyono, who had been widowed with four children.

Early Years. On the plantation wage of a dollar a day, Kingoro struggled to support his family. With seven children and a wife who was often unable to work outside the home, the family was so poor that sometimes food was unavailable.

Reduced to the brink of starvation, the Matsunagas moved to Hanapepe where Masayuki, then about eight, acquired the nickname of "Spark," which he later legalized. Although Spark always had to work to help the family, he excelled in school. Because he did well on achievement tests and was usually at the top of his class, he skipped the fourth and seventh grades and entered high school two years ahead of schedule.

He graduated from high school in 1933, during the Great Depression. For four years he continued to work, as stevedore, warehouseman, and grocery clerk.

Spark Matsunaga (right) with President Lyndon B. Johnson in the early 1960's. (Courtesy Matthew Matsunaga)

Senator Spark Matsunaga, Democrat from Hawaii, in 1981. (AP/Wide World Photos)

In 1937 Masayuki entered a Garden Island newspaper subscription contest and won first prize of $1,000. He gave $600 of it to his parents and with the remaining $400 matriculated at the University of Hawaii. He majored in education and attracted attention as a debater and dramatist. In childhood he had spoken the plantation dialect, with its uncouth accent. The passion for self-improvement that was to characterize him throughout life resulted in his winning the Theater Guild Diction Award in his sophomore year.

War Years. When Matsunaga graduated in 1941 war was raging in Europe, Africa, and China and war between the United States and Japan seemed imminent. He volunteered for Army duty in June, 1941. When Japan attacked Pearl Harbor, on December 7, 1941, he was in command of his company in the 299th Infantry on the island of Molokai. When martial law was declared that same day, he became commander of the island. Despite the loyal reputation they had established, on May 29, 1942, he and all other Nikkei were ordered to turn in all guns and ammunition in their possession.

Matsunaga and the others were transported to Oahu and sent to Schofield Barracks, where, in June, 1942, they were organized with Nikkei from other troops into the 100th Infantry Battalion. They were put aboard a converted freighter to sail for a destination concealed from them. They landed at Oakland, California, where they were put aboard trains with drawn shades. At Camp McCoy, Wisconsin, Camp Shelby, Mississippi, and in Africa and Italy, Matsunaga served as platoon leader, company executive officer, company commander, and battalion reconnaissance officer.

In Italy, Matsunaga was advancing up a hill strewn with land mines when a messenger tripped a "teller" mine that wounded Matsunaga below his neck. With artillery shells raining over his men, Matsunaga ignored the wound and continued to advance when the messenger tripped a mine that exploded and sprayed shrapnel fragments, one of which struck Matsunaga in the right thigh, immobilizing him.

Hospitalized but unable to stand the confinement, Matsunaga left and hitchhiked back to his outfit. There his leg swelled so much that he was unable to function as an infantryman. Later he was ordered to return to the United States.

Nikkei Visibility. At Camp McCoy Matsunaga was invited to a welcoming reception attended by more than six thousand people, including the mayor. Chosen to speak as the representative of the veterans, Matsunaga talked about how the fighting spirit of the Nikkei troops had been boosted by a burning desire to prove themselves 100 percent American. When he concluded, an official from the U.S. War Relocation Authority (WRA) asked him to make the same speech throughout the East and Midwest to prepare communities so that businessmen would hire Nikkei from the internment camps.

For months Matsunaga spoke on behalf of the internees, delivering, by his own estimate, eight hundred speeches. Before his speaking tour, a survey of seven hundred businesses in the twin cities of St. Paul-Minneapolis showed not a single firm expressing willingness to hire a Nikkei. After six months of his campaigning every one of the firms had hired Nikkei or indicated a willingness to do so.

In December, 1945, Matsunaga was released from active duty with the rank of captain. For one and a half years he served as veterans' counselor with the Surplus Property Office of the U.S. Department of the Interior and then served for one year as chief of the priority claimants' division under the War Assets Administration.

Rise to Prominence. Matsunaga, however, had his eyes fixed on a political career. As a step in that direction he entered Harvard Law School under the G.I. bill in September, 1948, receiving his J.D. degree in June, 1951. Back in Honolulu he served in the prosecutor's office for two years, joined the then-minority Democratic Party, and worked toward building its influence. In 1954 he was elected to the lower house of the Territorial Legislature. This was the year the Democrats wrested control of the state government from more than fifty years of domination by the Republicans, though Hawaii continued to have a Republican governor. Matsunaga was reelected in 1956 and 1958.

Thereafter, despite failing to be elected lieutenant governor in 1959, Matsunaga began to climb the political ladder. He was elected to the U.S. House of Representatives in 1962, where he served fourteen consecutive years before being elected to the Senate in 1976, a position he still held when he died on April 15, 1990.—*Allan Beekman*

Suggested Readings: • Glazer, Sarah Jane. *Ralph Nader Congress Project. Citizens Look at Congress. Spark M. Matsunaga: Democratic Representative from Hawaii.* Washington: Grossman, 1972. • Hall, Carla. "The Senator and His Space Refrain: Hawaii's Spark Matsunaga Pushing the Potential of Mars." *The Washington Post*, August 13, 1986. • McManus, Larry. "Crucial Talk in Lodge's Office Started Spark's Career." *The Honolulu Advertiser*, October 17, 1964.

• Matsunaga, Spark, and Ping Chen. *Rulemakers of the House*. Champaign-Urbana: University of Illinois Press, 1976. • Reichhardt, Tony. "Mr. Matsunaga Goes to Mars." *Space World* 7-271 (July, 1986): 28. • *Spark Matsunaga, 1916-1990. The Planetary Report* 10 (July 1, 1990): 26.

Matsura, Frank (1874?—June 16, 1913, Okanogan, Wash.): Photographer. An important historical record, Matsura's work captures the flavor of frontier life in the early twentieth century. He arrived in Washington State in 1903. Early on he began shooting pictures of people and places he encountered in and around the old mining town of Conconully, in Okanogan County. He became a professional photographer, working out of his own studio, after moving to Okanogan in 1907. Much of his work is archived at the Okanogan County Historical Society and the Washington State University library.

Mazumdar, Sucheta: Scholar. Mazumdar is a professor in the Department of History at Duke University. She attended the University of California, Los Angeles, earning both undergraduate and advanced degrees there. Among her writings are articles on Chinese history, comparative Asian history, and issues affecting both Asian Americans and women.

Media Action Network for Asian Americans (MANAA): Private watchdog agency, founded by Guy Aoki in Santa Monica, California, in 1992, that monitors the portrayal of Asian Americans in the popular media. In 1993, MANAA presented its first annual Media Achievement Awards.

Mehta, Sonny [Ajay Singh] (b. 1943, India): Editor and publishing executive. The son of a diplomat, Mehta left India to study at Cambridge University in England. After completing his studies he began working in paperback publishing in the United Kingdom. Formerly with Pan and Picador, publishers of paperbacks in the United Kingdom, Mehta moved in 1987 to the prestigious New York publisher Alfred A. Knopf, a division of Random House. He succeeded Robert A. Gottlieb, who became editor of *The New Yorker*. As editor in chief and president, Mehta has brought more bestsellers to Knopf while maintaining the firm's reputation for literary excellence. Vintage Books, a trade paperback house, also falls under Mehta's jurisdiction.

Mehta is a citizen of India but resides in the United States. He is married to Gita Mehta, the author of *Karma Cola: Marketing the Mystic East* (1979), *Raj* (1989), and *A River Sutra* (1993).

Mehta, Ved [Parkash] (b. Mar. 21, 1934, Lahore, Punjab, India, now Pakistan): Writer. A staff writer for *The New Yorker* since 1961, Mehta has written autobiography, social commentary on India, articles and stories for magazines and newspapers, a documentary script, and a novel. Through a sharp focus on his experiences and those of his family, he has provided Western audiences with an intimate and authentic portrait of the complexity of modern India, while his multivolume autobiography, *Continents in Exile*, is a classic of the genre.

Though he often refuses to discuss it, Mehta has been blind since the age of four due to an attack of meningitis. After study at the Dadar School for the Blind in Bombay, India, and the Arkansas School for the Blind in Little Rock, Arkansas, he pursued a distinguished academic career at Pomona College, Oxford University, and Harvard University. Walking without a cane and riding a bicycle, he has always insisted on fully participating in the world of sighted people.

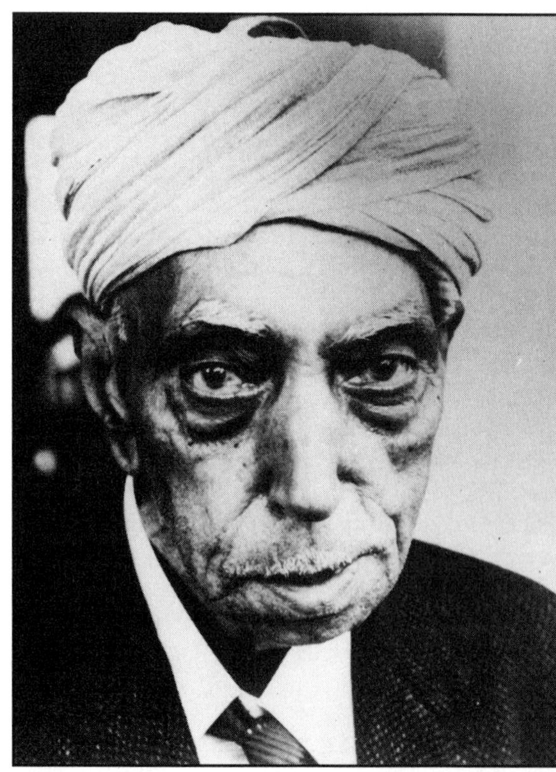

Ved Mehta's writings have ranged from sociopolitical commentary to narratives of the personal experiences of a multiethnic (Indian, British, American) sightless person in a sighted world. (AP/Wide World Photos)

In his autobiographical works, for which he is best known, Mehta has chronicled his family background and his remarkable life with extraordinary fidelity and precision of detail. *Up at Oxford* (1993), the seventh volume of *Continents in Exile*, takes him through his years at Oxford. In his works of social commentary, Mehta has observed and helped explain the profound changes as India has emerged from British rule into independence in the modern era.

A truly cosmopolitan writer, Mehta is a product of many cultures—Indian, British, American. His work is characterized by acute perception, rendered in lucid prose that brings the subject alive for the reader. Some critics have noticed the theme of loss as central to his work—loss of sight, of home, of country, of childhood. Mehta himself has said that, in all the stories of the many lives that he tells, he is trying to communicate the universal that is interwoven with the particular.

Mehta observes, analyzes, and comments on his subjects with astuteness, gentle irony, and affection. With sympathetic objectivity, he has illuminated a part of the real India for a Western audience. To borrow a term used by one of his interview subjects, Mehta has "The Himalayan vision."

Zubin Mehta has received renown as leader of many of the world's greatest orchestras. (AP/Wide World Photos)

Mehta, Zubin (b. Apr. 29, 1936, Bombay, India): Conductor. Mehta was born to Mehli and Tehmina Mehta. His first musical instruction was in violin and piano. He was encouraged to consider a career in medicine, but after leaving St. Xavier's College in Bombay, he entered the State Academy of Music in Vienna, where he studied from 1954 to 1960. At the academy, he played double bass in the school orchestra and studied with Hans Swarowsky, while continuing to explore an interest in conducting. After gaining experience in conducting student orchestras at the Vienna Academy, he entered an international conductor's competition and won the top prize—a year as an assistant to the Liverpool Philharmonic Orchestra. He also conducted in Belgium and Yugoslavia, beginning a lifelong pattern of constant international travel and concertizing.

After serving as a guest or substitute conductor in Vienna, Montreal, and Los Angeles, he was appointed as the director of the Montreal Symphony, a position he held from 1961 to 1967. He held a joint appointment to the Los Angeles Philharmonic Orchestra as an associate conductor, and when he became the music director of that orchestra in 1962, he became the first person in North America to earn the distinction of holding simultaneous appointments with two major symphony orchestras. His position with the Los Angeles Philharmonic lasted until 1978, but when he began, he was the youngest conductor in the United States to have earned such a prestigious appointment. During subsequent years as the director of the New York Philharmonic (1978-1991), he was able to provide opportunities for other young and talented musicians, such as the violinist Midori and the conductor Samuel Wong.

Mehta's most consistent service has been as the director of the Israel Philharmonic, a position that he accepted in 1969. His rapport with this orchestra was such that in 1981, he was appointed Director for Life. Although there was some controversy in Israel concerning his occasional inclusion of Richard Wagner on concert programs, Mehta continued to demonstrate his loyalty to the Israel Philharmonic. During the Persian Gulf war of 1991, he canceled a New York appearance in order to be in Israel, which was under attack.

Meiji Restoration (1868-1912): Coup d'état occurring on January 3, 1868, in which the Tokugawa shogunate, which had ruled Japan in the name of the emperor since 1603, was overthrown by samurai who formally restored political power to the reigning emperor, Mutsuhito. "Meiji," meaning "enlightened rule,"

U.S. president Ulysses S. Grant during a visit to Emperor Mutsuhito in Tokyo. (Library of Congress)

was the reign title adopted by the emperor. "Restoration," referring to the return to imperial rule, followed eight centuries of warrior control over civil affairs. The coup d'état was followed by a brief civil war (Boshin War), but national unity and the centralization of political authority under the emperor were accomplished by 1869.

Causes. Long-term institutional weaknesses, exacerbated by the political and diplomatic crises that followed the United States' efforts to end Japan's policy of seclusion from foreign contact, resulted in the overthrow of the Tokugawa shogunate. Ruling by military force, the shogunate sought to retain political control by preserving the institutional arrangements that had existed in the early seventeenth century, when the Togukawa had come to power. Thus, within the more than 260 domains over which the shogunate exercised control, constraints were placed on commercial development, the daily lives of individuals were restricted according to the socioeconomic status to which they had been born, and efforts to strengthen military defense were prohibited.

Threats of Western invasion, however, which began in the early nineteenth century, raised questions about the capacity of the Tokugawa shogunate to defend Japan. Some advisors to the Tokugawa argued the need to relax the control measures that had kept the rulers of domains financially and militarily weak. Furthermore peasant rebellions, more numerous and more nearly regional in scale than ever before, followed widespread famines from 1833 to 1836. These rebellions seriously disrupted national commercial networks and caused economic dislocations throughout Japan. The shogunate's efforts to implement reform policies from the past were ineffective.

In 1853 the United States made a decisive effort to end Japan's policy of seclusion. One-quarter of the American navy, under the command of Matthew C. Perry, forced the Japanese to accept a letter from the president of the United States to the emperor of Japan demanding that Japanese ports be opened to American trade. Recognizing the inferiority of their naval defenses and the vulnerability of Edo (Tokyo) to blockade, the shogunate feared it could not refuse. Since the principal responsibility of the Tokugawa shogunate was to defend Japan against foreign attack, the threat from the United States constituted a serious blow to the shogunate's authority to rule.

Loyalist Politics. Foreign trade exacerbated inflation, and the presence of Americans provoked anti-Western terrorism, which, in turn, resulted in continued military threats from the United States. The samurai,

Emperor Mutsuhito, to whom the samurai restored power in 1868. (Library of Congress)

frustrated by the weakness of the Tokugawa shogunate, began to assassinate high-ranking officials. Claiming to be "men of high purpose," these samurai defended their actions as demonstrations of their loyalty to the emperor. Loyalists, who tended to be of lower military rank and income, were frustrated with their limited personal opportunities in a time of national crisis. They sought alliances with like-minded men, rallying to the slogan, "respect the emperor; repel the barbarians."

Loyalists dominated politics in the domains of Satsuma, Choshu, and Tosa during the 1860's. Historically opposed to the Tokugawa, these domains competed with one another to provide the leadership to the loyalist movement. They forced the shogunate to concede to their demands for reform in which the imperial court and the most powerful domains would play a larger role in national politics.

Under pressure from the loyalists, the Tokugawa shogunate relaxed restrictions against shipbuilding, the fortification of national boundaries, the purchase of modern armaments, and the training of defense forces. Ostensibly for the purpose of defending Japan against foreigners, these military preparations enabled the loyalist forces to develop the capacity to overthrow the Tokugawa shogunate. Efforts by the shogunate to punish the loyalist-dominated domains for politically subversive activities were unsuccessful.

In 1866 moderates in Choshu and Satsuma proposed a compromise between loyalists and the shogunate in which the Tokugawa shogun would resign his powers (while retaining his landholdings) and work with the other lords of the domains in a new, national structure headed by the emperor. Accepting this proposal, in 1867, the Tokugawa shogun petitioned the emperor to accept the return of political power.

The politics of compromise, however, were overtaken by the efforts of loyalists, who secured from the emperor an edict forcing the Tokugawa shogun not only to give up his political power but also to relinquish his lands. The Tokugawa offered only slight resistance and capitulated on January 3, 1868. Vassals of the Tokugawa in the north continued to resist (the Boshin War), for reasons of economic and political self-interest rather than loyalty to the Tokugawa or opposition to rule by the emperor. They were defeated, however, by forces loyal to the emperor. In 1868 the Meiji emperor issued the Charter Oath, in which he laid claim to undisputed rule.

Consequence. The Meiji Restoration resulted in a break with the political institutions by which Japan had been ruled for the previous eight centuries and offered an opportunity to establish a modern state capable of withstanding the threat of foreign invasion. Exercising authority legitimized by imperial rule, the loyalists who had overthrown the Tokugawa shogunate became the leaders of the new Meiji government. Under the slogan, "rich country; strong army," the Meiji government centralized political authority, promoted industrialization, and established modern social institutions.—*Linda L. Johnson*

SUGGESTED READINGS: • Beasley, W. G. *The Meiji Restoration*. Stanford, Calif.: Stanford University Press, 1972. • Huber, Thomas M. *The Revolutionary Origins of Modern Japan*. Stanford, Calif.: Stanford University Press, 1981. • Jensen, Marius B., and Gilbert Rozman, eds. *Japan in Transition: From Tokugawa to Meiji*. Princeton, N.J.: Princeton University Press, 1986. • Totman, Conrad. *The Collapse of the Tokugawa Bakufu, 1862-1868*. Honolulu: University Press of Hawaii, 1980.

Meiji rice riots: Rural uprisings and disturbances that took place during Japan's Meiji period (1868-1912). Most of these activities occurred in the 1870's and 1880's. In 1873 the Meiji government imposed a land tax of 3 percent of the assessed value of the land. The land tax, paid in cash, provided the government with regular income and the financial base for modernizing the country. The tax proved an onerous burden to most small owner-cultivators. Rural protests broke out in the 1870's as peasants agitated for a reduction in the land tax and for the abolition of the "blood tax" (military conscription). These disturbances were mainly local but reached sizable proportions. Three hundred thousand rural protesters, objecting to the land tax, destroyed almost five thousand buildings in Fukuoka Prefecture in 1873. In 1876 ten thousand rioters in Mie rioted against the high rate of taxation. These conditions contributed significantly to the first wave of Japanese immigration to the United States.

The economic plight of the tenant and small landowner farmers was exacerbated by the deflationary policies of Finance Minister Matsukata Masayoshi. Government policy kept rice prices low. Therefore the farmer had to sell more rice to pay his taxes or rent. Violence broke out in the 1880's, activity now vaguely associated with the Popular Rights movement (Jiyu minken). Some six thousand farmers of Chichibu, Saitama-ken, Gumma, and Nakano prefectures demonstrated against low agriculture product prices, lack of available credit, and government indifference to their situation. Peasants destroyed the homes of landlords and moneylenders and demanded a new government sympathetic to their cause. After ten days of rioting, the uprising was suppressed by government troops and police. Leaders of the farm revolt were sentenced to death.

The rebel farmers had few formal links with the Popular Rights movement or Jiyuto (liberal) Party, led by Itagaki Taisuke. Yet the farmers regarded the movement as an avenue to a fairer, less oppressive system and as congruent with their objective of ameliorating their desperate economic conditions. Itagaki, however, fearing the vehemence and dynamism of the peasant movement, dissolved his party in 1884.

The rural uprisings of the period failed significantly to reduce government and landlord exactions on the peasants. The result was a rise in tenancy from about 23 percent in 1873 to about 40 percent by 1890 and a much lower standard of living for rural Japanese as compared to urban dwellers.

Mekong River: Longest river in Southeast Asia. The Mekong River descends from the eastern Tibetan Plateau to flow for approximately 2,800 miles and drain some 307,000 square miles of land. On its way down to the South China Sea, the Mekong passes through the People's Republic of China, Cambodia, and Vietnam, forming in the process part of the international boundary between Laos and Burma as well as Laos and Thailand.

The Mekong is certainly one of the most mysterious of the world's great rivers. Much of its course remained uncharted well into the nineteenth century, largely because of the remoteness and inhospitable terrains characterizing parts of its course. From 1866 to 1867, the Frenchman Doudart de Lagrée led the first major European exploration of the Mekong River north of Phnom Penh in search of a trade route to China. Although his trip confirmed the difficulty of travel on the Mekong, the river is nevertheless essential to agricultural societies for the rich soil that its floodwaters leave behind. The Angkorian Empire of ancient Cambodia, for example, prospered because of the annual flooding of the Great Lake and surrounding areas. Close to the border of Laos and Thailand is an area known as the Golden Triangle, where much of the world's opium is grown. Further down the lower Mekong basin, the chief crop is rice. Farming in the Mekong Delta of southern Vietnam during the dry season, however, is impossible because of the influx of saltwater from the sea. Despite this fact and the region's limited development, the delta under French rule became a major rice-exporting area in the 1930's. Decades of war interrupted rice production and drastically changed the landscape of the region, but the government of Vietnam is determined to not only revive but also expand into newer areas for farming.

The Mekong River Development Project was initiated in 1957 for the modernization of the Mekong in terms of hydroelectric power, improved irrigation, flood control, and other projects. Though the nations of Laos, Thailand, and Vietnam have shown cooperation, the instability of the region could prove to be a problem.

M.E.L.U.S.: Acronym for both the Society for the Study of the Multi-Ethnic Literature of the United States and that organization's journal. M.E.L.U.S. is devoted to expanding the definition of American literature through the study and teaching of works by ethnic American writers. The idea for M.E.L.U.S. originated with Katharine Newman in 1969. As a professor of American literature at Westchester State University, Pennsylvania, she became aware of the absence of ethnic writers in the canon of American literature. Newman's work began with gradual inclusion of works by African American writers in her classes and in her two anthologies on ethnic literature. Formal recognition of M.E.L.U.S. occurred in 1973 at the Modern Language Association (MLA) convention in Chicago. M.E.L.U.S., as Newman reflects, was "conceived in anger and brought forth into academe in . . . defiance" against the invisibility of ethnic American writers.

The M.E.L.U.S. journal began as a newsletter for a dedicated coterie of individuals who were beginning to teach ethnic literatures in different colleges and universities. These newsletters evolved into a highly respected vehicle for scholarship on ethnic literature. The journal was established at the University of Southern California with Newman as its first editor from 1977 to 1981. Since 1987 M.E.L.U.S. emanates from the University of Massachusetts.

Asian Americans have played important roles in the history of the organization. The works of Asian Pacific writers and the cultures of different Asian ethnic communities were featured from the earliest days of the organization's history. As M.E.L.U.S. became established as a scholarly journal, it featured groundbreaking scholarship on Asian Pacific literature and culture. Furthermore it offered Asian American literary and cultural scholars a space for their critical explications.

M.E.L.U.S. is affiliated with the MLA and the American Literature Association. M.E.L.U.S. panels are consistent features in regional MLA conferences as well as those of other professional organizations.

Menor, Benjamin (b. Sept. 27, 1922, San Nicolas, Philippines): Attorney, politician, and judge. Menor emigrated with his family to Hawaii in 1930 to be reunited with his father, who was a plantation laborer. Menor served in the U.S. Army from 1944 to 1946 before attending the University of Hawaii. After receiving his B.A. degree in 1950, he traveled to the mainland to study law at Boston University. Menor received his LL.B. degree in 1952 and returned to Hawaii, where he passed the bar examination in 1953. He served as a county attorney in Hawaii until 1959, when he went into private practice. In 1962, Menor was elected to the Hawaiian State Senate, becoming the first Filipino American to serve in any U.S. legislature. Menor completed his senate term in 1966 and returned to private practice. He served as a judge on the Hawaii Circuit Court from 1969 until 1974, when he was appointed to serve on the Hawaii State Supreme Court as an associate justice. Menor's appointment made him the first Filipino American to serve on the state's highest court.

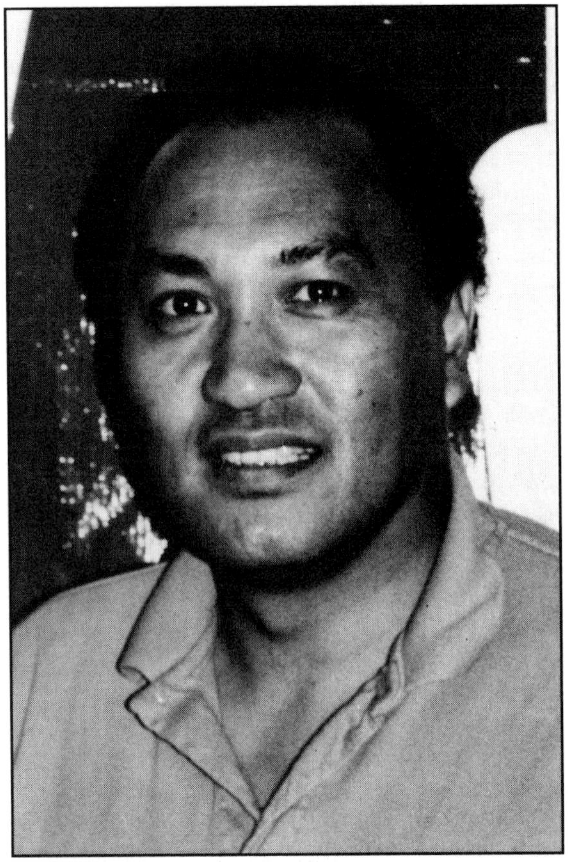

Benjamin Menor was the first Filipino American to serve in any U.S. legislature. (Asian Week)

Merchant Marine Act of 1936: U.S. government legislation enacted to secure employment specifically for Americans during the Great Depression of the 1930's. Signed into law by President Franklin D. Roosevelt in June, the act mandated that ninety percent of the crews on U.S. ships be U.S. citizens.

At the time the act was passed, significant numbers of Filipinos were working aboard American merchant ships. Under the new legislation, then, most would lose their jobs. Especially threatened with dismissal were the Filipino shipworkers of the Louisiana gulf region. In April, 1937, the specter of increased unemployment compelled Louisiana senator Allen Ellender to propose an amendment to the act.

Metcalf, Victor Howard (Oct. 10, 1853, Utica, N.Y.—Feb. 20, 1936, Oakland, Calif.): U.S. government official. He attended Yale Law School, then practiced law on the East Coast before leaving for California. From 1900 until 1904 he was a congressman. He served as secretary of commerce and labor (1904-1906) and as secretary of the Navy (1906-1908) under President Theodore Roosevelt. During California's San Francisco school board crisis (1906), involving the board's newly created policy of educational segregation, Roosevelt sent Metcalf to investigate the conditions of Japanese living in that city. Metcalf believed that California's Japanese community deserved full protection, if not from the state then from the federal government; his report, *Japanese in the City of San Francisco* (1906), urged that the segregation order be withdrawn.

Mi guk saram: Korean phrase that refers to any U.S. citizen who is not of Korean ancestry. It is literally translated as "American person."

MIA issue: Following the war in Vietnam (1965-1975), the fates of U.S. military personnel listed as missing in action were politicized.

The signing of the Paris Peace Accord (1973) resulted in the Pentagon raising the number of MIAs to 2,273, when 1,101 members of the armed forces listed as "Killed in Action/Body Not Recovered" were added to the previous total of 1,172 MIAs. Pilots failing to eject from crashing planes accounted for 81 percent of the original MIAs. The United States has 78,751 MIAs from World War II (1939-1945) and 8,177 from the Korean War (1950-1953). Vietnam's MIAs for the period 1959-1975, including those from both sides, number almost 200,000.

A popular notion grew in the United States after the Vietnam War that MIAs were being held as prisoners of war (POWs) in Southeast Asia, represented by the millions of POW/MIA bracelets Americans continued to wear into the 1990's. A congressional task force was established in 1977, and, in 1982, the POW/MIA flag began to fly over the White House one day per year. Former president Ronald Reagan called the recovery of the MIA's "the highest national priority" and in 1984 proclaimed a National POW/MIA Recognition Day. Despite denial of the existence of live POWs by the Reagan Administration on January 20, 1989, the Bush Administration's Department of Defense in 1990 issued a *POW-MIA Fact Book* stating that the American government assumed that there were still living POWs.

Several films promoted the notion of living POWs: *Uncommon Valor* (1983), Chuck Norris' *Missing in Action* (1984) and sequels, and Sylvester Stallone's *Rambo* (1985) all suggested by the actual POW-hunting of Bo Gritz, a retired Special Forces officer. The United States was struck by what *Time* called "Rambomania," which included the marketing of "Rambo" products and an increased interest in the MIAs.

The issue became news again in July, 1991, when faked photographs of POWs surfaced and several American families claimed the pictured men as their relatives. In 1992, the government of Vietnam turned over to the United States extensive archives pointing toward a clear end to the controversy, paving the way for the United States to lift the economic embargo against Vietnam, which it had previously refused to do, citing as one reason the unknown fate of the MIAs.

Miai: In Japanese culture, a meeting or interview in which a man and a woman meet as potential marriage prospects. The encounter often, but not necessarily, results in a marriage. In the past, it often was a formality to finalize a marriage that the respective parents had previously arranged. The term is most often used in the honorific, as *omiai-kekkon* or simply *omai.*

Miao-Yao languages. *See* **Hmong-Mien languages**

Micronesia. *See* **Pacific Islanders**

Mid-Autumn Festival. *See* **Moon Festival**

Midway, Battle of (June 3-6, 1942): World War II victory for the United States, which sank four Japanese aircraft carriers. It is usually considered the turning point in the war in the Pacific theater.

The Japanese Empire reached its greatest extent in the spring of 1942. By April the Japanese were maneuvering two hundred ships along a line near the Aleutian Islands and Midway Island. With the capture of strategic posts, an outer perimeter would be established providing early warning against any offensive by the United States. More important, Japanese Admiral Isoroku Yamamoto's anticipated seizure of Midway was designed to lure the remainder of the American Pacific fleet into battle.

On May 27, 1942, a Japanese carrier striking force sailed for Midway, followed two days and six hundred miles later by Yamamoto's main group, which included the Midway invasion force. The Aleutian invasion force left Kyushu on May 28. The combined Japanese battle fleet included eleven battleships, eight aircraft carriers, and twenty-three cruisers. Because the Japanese code had been broken, American commanders had been aware that a massive assault was being prepared, though they were unsure of its exact destination until late May.

Aided by this intelligence, American Admiral Chester W. Nimitz decided to strike the Japanese directly. On May 28, a task force left Pearl Harbor, followed two days later by a smaller force. Combined American forces included three aircraft carriers and eight cruisers. Several factors alerted the Japanese to American foreknowledge, but the need for radio silence made it impossible for the Japanese units to consult as they approached Midway. On June 3, Japanese transports were sighted. Both sides knew that enemy fleets were converging, but neither knew precisely the strength or location of the other.

The battle commenced on June 3, about two hundred miles northwest of Midway. The Japanese lost four aircraft carriers and many experienced carrier pilots, while sinking only one American carrier and one destroyer. Thereafter Japan won no major naval engagements in the Pacific. Midway was fought principally by carrier-based aircraft, with the rival fleets never seeing each other.

Mien. *See* **Iu Mien**

Migration, primary: With regard to Asian Americans, refers to immigration from outside the United States and settlement in a first place of residence. This

Leading States of Intended Residence, Immigrants from Selected Asian Countries, 1991

Origin	Total Number	Percentage of Immigrant Population with Intended State of Residence							
		California	New York	Texas	Illinois	Florida	Massachusetts	Washington	All Other States
All countries	1,827,167	40.1	10.3	11.6	4.0	7.7	1.5	1.9	22.9
Total Asian	342,157	-	-	-	-	-	-	-	-
Total Asian*	278,242	35.4	17.4	5.3	4.4	2.5	2.1	2.1	30.8
Bangladesh	10,676	10.0	64.2	3.2	1.1	3.5	1.2	0.3	16.5
Mainland China	33,025	37.1	29.3	2.4	3.5	1.5	3.5	1.7	21.0
Hong Kong	10,427	42.9	22.2	2.9	2.8	2.1	4.3	2.8	20.0
India	45,064	22.8	20.3	5.8	8.5	2.7	2.4	0.9	36.6
Korea	26,518	27.5	19.6	4.2	4.4	1.6	0.9	0.3	41.5
Pakistan	20,355	15.2	36.9	8.9	7.2	4.2	1.2	0.5	25.9
Philippines	63,596	51.4	6.4	2.8	4.6	2.4	0.6	2.5	29.3
Taiwan	13,274	44.0	11.9	6.6	2.8	1.4	2.0	2.0	29.3
Vietnam	55,307	38.9	4.0	9.5	1.7	2.9	3.5	3.4	36.1

Source: United States Immigration and Naturalization Service, 1991, Statistical Yearbook.

Note: 1991 was an unusual year for U.S. immigration in that the total number of immigrants was inflated due to large numbers of legalizations under the 1986 Immigration and Reform and Control Act (IRCA). If IRCA legalizations are not included, the 1991 total was 704,005. Asian legalizations totaled 148,086.

* Includes only those countries listed in the table.

is contrasted with "secondary migration," which refers to migration within the country after the initial immigration and taking up of residence.

"Migration" can be defined as a "permanent" change of residence across a boundary of some significance. Definitions of "permanent" and of the most relevant boundary are always arbitrary and can often not be satisfactorily solved, especially with regard to migration within a country. Regarding *immigration* to the United States, there is no problem of boundaries, but "permanence" remains a problem; we interpret it as accomplished when a person becomes a permanent resident and receives his or her "green card."

Data on patterns of settlement of Asian immigrants can be obtained from two sources: the Immigration and Naturalization Service (INS) and the U.S. Census. Both sources are flawed. INS data are based on the responses of immigrants to the question at entry on intended place of residence; there is no requirement that that place ever be a residence, and there is no follow-up to see if it is. Census data tell us where immigrants live at the time of the census and also provide information about residence five years earlier. However, they do not say where the initial residence was.

Data for 1991 from the INS show the states where immigrants from major Asian sending countries say they will concentrate. More Asians (and indeed immigrants in general) say they will reside in California than anywhere else, but patterns differ depending upon place of origin. Chinese concentrate especially in California, while South Asians are more likely to settle in New York. Filipinos predominantly choose California, while Koreans choose California first but not in such high percentages as Filipinos and Chinese. In general, the states of intended residence mirror the already-existing distribution of Asians within the United States, illustrating a truism in migration: Migrants tend to go to where earlier migrants from the same place have settled.

Migration, secondary: Migration that occurs after immigration. This contrasts with what might be called "primary migration," which is the initial move to a foreign country.

Data on secondary migration cannot be obtained directly from the basic immigration or census sources. The former does not cover movement or residence after arrival. The latter offers information that allows one to track immigrant movement since arrival for those immigrants who were in the country at least five years; however, the exact date of arrival, how many moves were made, and their sequence are impossible to tell.

The secondary migration of most interest with regard to Asian Americans has been that of refugees from Southeast Asia. Those refugees bound for the United States were originally settled in various parts of the country in an effort to spread the burden of assistance and support. It is, however, a fact that migrants, including Asian immigrants in general and refugees in particular, tend to concentrate in certain geographic areas, especially where earlier migrants from the same areas are living. The U.S. government's efforts at distributing refugees around the country were substantially undone by the propensity of the refugees to engage in secondary migration to those places where the largest concentrations already were, especially California. By 1987 California's share of the refugee population was estimated to be 50 percent, and California was the most common place of residence for all three major refugee groups (Vietnamese, Cambodians, and Laotians). Refugees, however, remain less concentrated than other immigrants. Vietnamese are most concentrated in California; Laotians and Cambodians are more often found in urban centers in the Eastern and Midwestern United States.

More general data on all Asian Americans (not merely the foreign-born immigrants) indicate that re-

"Secondary migration," refers to migration within the country after the initial (or "primary") immigration to it from another nation; this Vietnamese American family has migrated within the United States following its primary migration from Vietnam. (David S. Strickler)

gional migration flows mirror those for the total U.S. population: out of the Northeast to all other regions, out of the Midwest to the South and the West, and out of the South to the West. Thus, in addition to being the region that attracts the highest number of Asian immigrants for initial settlement, the West gains from secondary migration as well.

Military Intelligence Service (MIS): Intelligence gathering arm of the U.S. Army during World War II (1939-1945). Many Nisei (especially Kibei) were recruited into the MIS to do Japanese-to-English and English-to-Japanese translation and interpretation, including intercepting radio transmissions, interrogating prisoners of war, and interpreting for civilians in war zones (see MILITARY INTELLIGENCE SERVICE LANGUAGE SCHOOL).

Military Intelligence Service Language School: U.S. operation established in 1941 to train World War II military intelligence personnel. The school was originally the Fourth Army Intelligence School of the Presidio military base in San Francisco, California. With war in the Pacific theater under way, the American military command expanded the school's role in intelligence affairs. The operation was reorganized as the Military Intelligence Service (MIS) Language School and put under the direct supervision of the War Department. When the war ended, the school turned its attention to training students to assist in the rebuilding of Japan.

Although not as celebrated as the 100TH INFANTRY BATTALION or the 442ND REGIMENTAL COMBAT TEAM, the members of the Nisei and Kibei Military Intelligence Service (MIS) played a critical role in World War II. Because of the security oaths they took after the war, their story was not made public until 1979. U.S. Army general Douglas MacArthur's chief of intelligence claimed, "Had it not been for the American Nisei, that part of the war in the Pacific which was dependent upon Intelligence gleaned from captured documents and prisoners of war would have been a far more hazardous, long-drawn-out affair."

MIS recruits were originally trained at San Francisco's Presidio military base. Ironically the MIS Language School had to be moved to Camp Savage, Minnesota, in early 1942 because of the forced en masse removal of Japanese Americans from the West Coast. Japanese Americans already in uniform were the prime source of recruits. Later a number of Japanese Americans from concentration camps volunteered to enlist in the school. A promising group of candidates were the *Kibei*, Japanese Americans who had studied in Japan, since many Japanese Americans were too "Americanized" and did not know Japanese well enough to be trained for military intelligence.

The school's graduates served throughout the Pacific, translating documents and interrogating prisoners. Because of their effectiveness, MacArthur could state, "Never in military history did an army know so much about the enemy prior to actual engagement." When necessary these individuals fought alongside combat troops, although that was doubly treacherous, for too often the former were mistaken for Japanese soldiers.

Because of their language skills, MIS personnel were useful in persuading Japanese soldiers and civilians to come out of caves and other hiding places to surrender. When the war ended, MIS personnel served as interpreters in surrender ceremonies and assisted in the American military occupation of Japan. They were used also in the Korean War because elderly Koreans knew Japanese but not English. Altogether about six thousand Japanese Americans served in the MIS during World War II.

Min, Pyong Gap: Scholar. Min received a bachelor's degree in history (1970) from Seoul National University in Korea, a master's degree in history (1975) from Georgia State University, and doctorates in education (1979) and sociology (1983), both from Georgia State. An associate professor of sociology at Queens College of the City University of New York, Min has published widely both in English and in Korean on Korean businesses in the United States, Korean Americans more generally, and other Asian American topics. Among his many books and articles are *Ethnic Business Enterprise: Korean Small Business in Atlanta* (1988) and "Korean Immigrants in Los Angeles," in *Immigration and Entrepreneurship* (1993), edited by Ivan Light and Parminder Bhachu.

Min, Yong Soon (b. Apr. 29, 1953, Republic of Korea): Artist. Born in South Korea, Min came to the United States with her family when she was seven years old. She attended the University of California at Berkeley, where she received a B.A., an M.A., and an M.F.A. She taught printmaking and drawing at Ohio University from 1981 until 1984. In the mid-1980's she worked at the Asian American Arts Alliance in New York. Recipient of a 1989-1990 artists fellowship grant awarded by the National Endowment for the

Arts, she has executed assorted commissions, working with such materials as glass, mirrors, photography-based imagery, and paper. Her work has been widely exhibited. In 1990 she was named a National Printmaking Fellow at the Rutgers Center for Innovative Printmaking.

In installation pieces such as *Half Home*, *Decolonization*, and *Ritual Labor of a Mechanical Bride*, Min has addressed gender stereotyping, the construction of Asian American identity, and the doubled sense of internal division that many Korean immigrants experience, coming from their divided homeland to the United States. Min's essay "Comparing the Contemporary Experiences of Asian American, South Korean, and Cuban Artists" is included in *Asian Americans: Comparative and Globval Perspectives* (1991), edited by Shirley Hune, Hyung-chan Kim, Stephen S. Fugita, and Amy Ling.

Min Qing (Mun Ching): Progressive San Francisco youth club founded in 1940. The club began as the New Chinese Alphabetized Language Study Society (NCALSS) in San Francisco as part of a movement started in China to eradicate illiteracy by eliminating Chinese characters and replacing them with romanized Chinese. The group rented a basement at 812 Stockton Street that for the next two decades was the center of progressive youth activities. The NCALSS organized musical and dramatic propaganda activities to support China's resistance against Japan. Its members also participated in demonstrations against shipping scrap iron to Japan.

In 1942 the NCALSS and two Chinese youth clubs formed a coalition to stage a drama to raise funds for gifts to Chinese in the armed forces. After the project a Chinese Youth League (CYL) was organized in 1943. The CYL became the most active Chinese youth group, with membership expanding to about a hundred. It published a club newsletter as well as a literary journal, *Zhandou* (battle). It raised funds for gifts to armed service personnel and also sent them publications and letters. Its progressive cultural and literary activities vied with those of the Guomindang's San Min Chu I Youth Corps in efforts to attract Chinatown youth. The CYL also maintained a liaison with progressive groups such as American Youth for Democracy.

In 1946 the CYL reorganized as the Chinese American Democratic Youth League (CADYL, abbreviated as "Min Qing"), which supported the Communist revolution in China and also campaigned for progressive candidates in American politics. In the 1950's the CADYL changed its name to the Chinese American Youth Club (CAYC) and concentrated on educational and cultural activities for its forty to fifty members. Its newsletter was one of the earliest Chinese American publications to use simplified characters. The club also introduced the use of the PINYIN system. The organization was the only Chinatown group regularly giving performances of vernacular dramas, Chinese folk dance, and Chinese songs and choral works. The club finally closed its doors in 1959 when it lost the lease to its headquarters. For a short while it struggled on without a clubhouse as the Haiyan Club.

With hostile relations between the United States and the People's Republic of China beginning in 1950, federal investigative agencies began to monitor the club's activities and to harass members. Although the organization was never officially declared "subversive," during the 1950's some members in the Army had to contest general discharges, and from the 1950's to the 1970's other members had to fight immigration cases.

Minami, Dale (b. Oct. 13, 1946, Los Angeles, Calif.): Attorney. A Sansei, or third-generation Japanese American, Minami became senior partner at the law firm of Minami, Lew and Tamaki, based in San Francisco. He earned a B.A. degree in political science in 1968 from the University of Southern California and a J.D. degree in 1971 from the University of California, Berkeley. He then helped to establish the ASIAN LAW CAUCUS in the San Francisco Bay Area in 1972 to provide free and low-cost legal services to immigrants and other Asian Americans who had been neglected by more traditional legal programs.

Minami is best known for his legal work on civil rights-related issues, including employment discrimination on the basis of race, national origin, sex, and physical disability. As lead attorney in the 1984 Fred T. KOREMATSU *coram nobis* case against the United States, he argued successfully that the U.S. district court should erase Korematsu's forty-year-old conviction for refusing to obey World War II exclusion orders aimed at Japanese Americans. Other major lawsuits include *United Pilipinos for Equal Employment v. California Blue Shield* (1973), resulting in a settlement requiring back pay, English-language program supervisory training programs, and promotion goals and timetables; *Nakanishi v. University of California at Los Angeles* (grievances filed in 1987 and 1988), which, with community pressure, led to granting tenure to Nakanishi and also highlighted widespread ra-

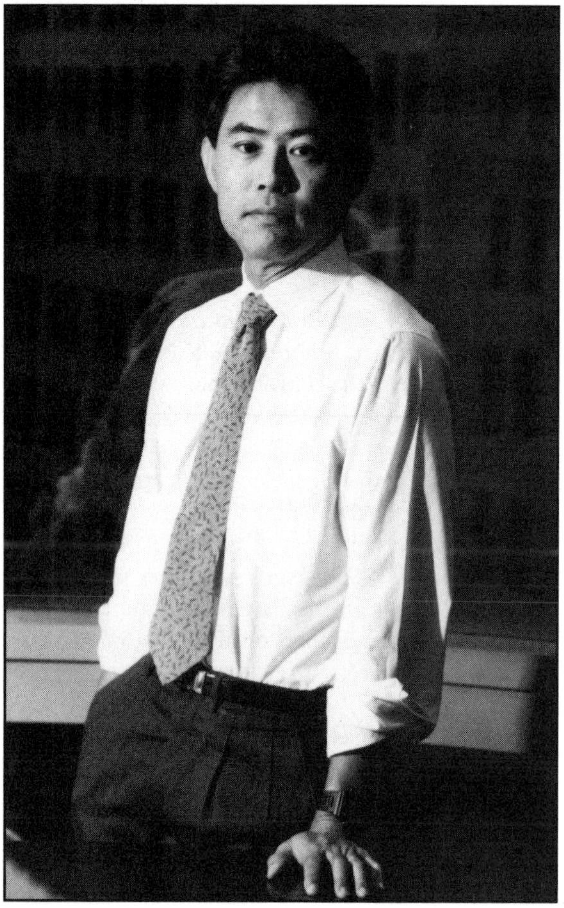

Attorney Dale Minami is known for his civil rights-related work. (Asian Week)

cial discrimination in academia; *Spokane Japanese American Citizens League v. Washington State University* (1978), in which the University agreed to provide an Asian American Studies program and Asian American counselors and recruiters.

Most of Minami's work focuses on personal injury cases, but he also practices entertainment law, representing Asian American newscasters, writers, actors, authors, and athletes, including Olympic ice-skating champion Kristi YAMAGUCHI.

In addition to legal work Minami served on the judicial review committees for the California state bar association (1984 to 1987) and for U.S. Senator Barbara Boxer (1993) and on the state Fair Employment and Housing Commission (1981 to 1984). He also chaired the state Attorney General's Asian and Pacific Islander Advisory Committee, which issued a report on anti-Asian violence (1988 to 1990). He helped found the Asian American Bar Association of the Greater Bay Area and the Asian Pacific Bar of California.

Mindanao: Second-largest island of the Philippine archipelago, located in the southern region. In 1990, Mindanao's land area of about thirty-nine thousand square miles contained a population exceeding fourteen million. Distinguished by its physical geography and Islamic minority, this remote southern island has a unique past setting it apart from the rest of the Philippines.

In addition to its size and odd configuration, Mindanao features an extensive coastline owing to numerous inlets and peninsulas. Many rivers and lakes as well as five major mountain ranges complete the island's topography, including a western chain that contains Mount Apo, the most lofty summit in the Philippines.

Tropical climate causes strong winter rainfall in Mindanao's east and northeast but brief, dry intervals in summer and autumn. The sheltered lowlands of Davao and the Cotabato Valley receive no more than seventy inches of moisture annually. Typhoons seldom strike Mindanao. The island has, however, suffered destructive earthquakes.

Mindanao possesses two large rivers more than two hundred miles in length. The Agusan River runs north through the Agusan Valley to its Mindanao Sea outlet. The Mindanao River and its channels drain the Cotabato Lowland before entering the Moro Gulf.

Mindanao's extractive economy emphasizes corn and coconut cultivation on limestone soils and mining for gold, iron ore, and coal. Surigao del Norte Province in the northeast produces nickel.

The island's population is smaller than the more populous Visayas and Luzon, with the greatest numbers living in Cotabato and Zamboanga del Sur. Yet internal migration from more densely inhabited islands has raised population totals in Davao Oriental and Agusan del Sur.

The race and language of Mindanao's Muslim Filipinos are imperceptible from the majority of the Philippine people. Islam and lifestyle separated both groups after Spanish culture unified lowland Christians. The Muslims are split into diverse religious and linguistic associations, yet their tongues are akin to the speech of southern Luzon and the Visayas. Filipino Muslims as a group remain cohesive and embrace such Islamic practices as slavery and polygamy.

Throughout their history Muslim Filipinos have stoutly defended their autonomy. Spanish and American colonizers failed to pacify them. When the Philippine government encouraged Christian Filipinos to migrate to Mindanao, some Muslims rebelled and formed the Muslim Independence movement. Following hundreds of deaths, Muslim Filipinos, believing that strife was inevitable and favoring secession, created the Moro National Liberation Front.

Mineta, Norman Yoshio (b. Nov. 12, 1931, San Jose, Calif.): U.S. representative. Mineta is a prominent Asian American representing the 13th Congressional District of California, located in Santa Clara and Santa Cruz counties.

Mineta is a Nisei, a second-generation Japanese American. His father, an Issei (first-generation Japanese American), had established an insurance agency in San Jose. During World War II, all persons of Japanese ancestry were removed from the West Coast. Norman Mineta was forced to leave with his family and was placed in an internment camp for Japanese Americans. His family lost its home and the insurance business.

The family eventually returned to San Jose, where Norman Mineta was graduated from San Jose High School. He went on to college at the University of California, Berkeley, graduating with a degree in business in 1953. He served in the U.S. Army as an intelligence officer in Japan and Korea, completing his service in 1956. Serving in the Army Reserves, he became a major. He once again returned to San Jose to work with his father in the Mineta Insurance Agency.

Mineta's return to the San Jose area marked the start of an active participation in business and community organizations. His first public position was as a member of the Human Relations Commission in San Jose in 1962. Mineta was appointed to the Housing Authority of San Jose and the City Council of San Jose in 1967. In 1969 he was appointed vice mayor, serving as mayor of San Jose from 1971 until 1975.

Congressman Norman Mineta. (Asian Week)

As the Democratic candidate, Mineta was elected to the 94th Congress in 1974. He has served on a range of committees and chaired subcommittees such as the Budget Committee; Democratic Policy and Steering Committee; Post Office and Civil Service Committee; Science, Space and Technology Committee; and the Select Committee on Intelligence. For the 101st Congress, Mineta was elected chair of the House Committee on Public Works and Transportation.

Throughout his political career, Mineta has been a significant political leader, particularly because there have been few ethnic minorities and specifically Asian Americans in the positions he has held. Mineta was one of the sponsors of the CIVIL LIBERTIES ACT OF 1988 and testified on its behalf. The bill provided monetary compensation and an apology to those Japanese American survivors who had been incarcerated during World War II because of their ethnic background.

Minh-ha, Trinh T. (b. 1950's, Vietnam): Filmmaker, writer, and composer. Minh-ha is Associate Professor of Cinema at San Francisco State University. She arrived in the United States in 1970 after a year at the University of Saigon. Subsequently, she attended schools there and in Paris while resuming her studies in music and composition, French literature, and ethnomusicology. For three years she was a music teacher at the National Conservatory of Music in Dakar, Senegal.

Minh-ha's body of work has been prolific. Her films include *Reassemblage* (1982), *Naked Spaces, Living Is Round* (1985), and *Surname Viet Given Name Nam* (1989). Published works include *Un Art sans oeuvre* (1981), *African Spaces: Designs for Living in Upper Volta* (1985), *En Miniscules* (1987; poems), *Woman, Native, Other: Writing, Postcoloniality and Feminism* (1989), and "Difference: 'A Special Third World Women Issue,'" an essay that appeared in *Feminist Review* 25 (1987).

Minidoka: One of ten U.S. government camps under the administration of the WAR RELOCATION AUTHORITY (WRA) used to house Japanese American evacuees during World War II. Officially the camps were designated as "RELOCATION CENTERS." The Minidoka camp, located in southern Idaho, opened on August 19, 1942, and closed on October 25, 1945; its maximum population was 9,397. Most of the internees at Minidoka were from western Washington.

Mink, Patsy (Patsy Takemoto; b. Dec. 6, 1927, Paia, Maui, Hawaii): U.S. representative. Mink, a veteran Hawaii politician, was born in the sugar plantation community of Paia. Her parents Suematsu and Mitama Takemoto, were second-generation Japanese Americans. Her father was the first Japanese American awarded a civil engineering degree from the University of Hawaii. He was a land surveyor, rather remarkable at the time considering that most nonwhites were relegated to manual labor.

His position afforded Mink and her brother Eugene a somewhat idyllic—though hardly privileged—upbringing. Mink learned the role that class, race, and social status played in society. Her father, the only Japanese American among an all-white management staff, was denied promotion several times in favor of younger, less experienced Caucasian men. Those experiences helped shape Mink's social and political views.

Mink graduated from Maui High School and the University of Hawaii. She had planned to become a doctor but switched to law, earning her law degree from the University of Chicago in 1951. There she married John Mink of Pennsylvania. Upon returning to Hawaii she was not allowed to practice law because of a residency requirement. She successfully challenged the ruling and passed the Hawaii Bar in 1953.

In 1956 she became the first Japanese American woman elected to Hawaii's Territorial Legislature. In 1964 Mink was elected to the U.S. House of Representatives—the first Asian American woman elected to Congress. She served six consecutive terms before losing a U.S. Senate bid in 1976. Although a lifelong Democrat, her liberal and independent stances often left her at odds with the majority of the party's members.

Mink returned to Hawaii and was elected to the Honolulu City Council. After one term—and an unsuccessful bid for governor—Mink was reelected to Congress in 1990.

Her accomplishments in Congress have been numerous and substantial. She introduced the Early Childhood Education Act, which President Richard M. Nixon vetoed, and authored Title IX of the Education Amendments Act (1972), which prohibited educational institutions receiving federal funds from practicing gender discrimination.

Hawaii's Patsy Mink was the first Asian American woman to be elected to the U.S. House of Representatives. (National Japanese American Historical Society)

In 1976 she filed a class-action suit against the University of Chicago and the Eli Lilly Company after learning that she had unknowingly been given the drug diethylstilbestrol, or DES, while pregnant with her daughter. DES was found to cause cancer in both mother and child The settlement gave the thousand women administered the drug and their DES-affected children free lifetime medical care at the University of Chicago.

Mink also served as an assistant secretary of state under President Jimmy Carter and as national president of the Americans for Democratic Action. She is involved in numerous organizations and has been honored for her contributions to social causes.

Minnick, Sylvia Sun (b. Apr. 26, 1941, Kuala Lumpur, Malaysia): Publisher and city council member. The first Asian American to win a council seat (Fifth District) in Stockton, California, she is the daughter of Patrick P. Sun, the former Chinese ambassador to the Philippines. Author of *Samfow: The San Joaquin Chinese Legacy* (1988), she founded the San Joaquin County Republican Asian Coalition and the consultant firm A Bridge to the Past, and she is the publisher/owner of Heritage West Books in Stockton, California.

Mirikitani, Janice (b. 1942): Poet and community organizer. A Sansei, or third-generation Japanese American, she emerged as a literary voice of the Asian American ethnic pride movement in the late 1960's and early 1970's. Her socially conscious poetry grapples with issues of identity and politics. Among her works are *Awake in the River* (1978) and *Shedding Silence* (1987). She has also edited numerous anthologies, including *Making Waves: Writings by and About Asian American Women* (1989). Containing short stories, essays, articles, and poems, the book is used widely as a resource in public libraries and universities.

Poet Janice Mirikitani emerged in the 1960's as a literary voice for the Asian American pride movement. (Asian Week)

Miss Chinatown: Beauty queen of Chinese ancestry elected annually in various Chinatown pageants across the United States. The first pageant for Miss Chinatown U.S.A. began in 1958 in San Francisco. Before this national competition, there were local pageants in the San Francisco Bay Area during the years 1953 to 1957. Since 1958 the Chinese chambers of commerce from Chinatowns in major American cities such as New York, Los Angeles, Houston, Honolulu, and Chicago host local pageants. The winners are then sent to San Francisco for the national competition. Each year the total number of national contestants varies depending on the participation from local pageants, but there are typically eight to ten contestants. The Miss Chinatown pageant is a part of the Chinese New Year celebration. For that reason the selection of Miss Chinatown U.S.A. usually occurs before the new year has begun, around the end of January or the beginning of February.

All Miss Chinatown contestants must be of Chinese ancestry, be between the ages of seventeen and twenty-six, have never been married, have a high school education, and be a U.S. resident. Titles are given to one Miss Chinatown, four Chinatown Princesses, and one Miss Talent. Prizes include cash, jewelry, scholarships, gifts, and traveling expenses. The newly crowned Miss Chinatown U.S.A. will also act as a media representative for cultural integration and business promotion between the United States and Asia.

Over the years the cost of the competition (training programs, costumes, photo sessions, and so forth) has been paid by local businesses. Each contestant is individually supported by a sponsor, who then pays her expenses. In addition there are general sponsors for the pageant.

The Miss Chinatown pageant, besides acting as a New Year event, is intended to be a cultural awakening of the community, to promote commerce among the Chinese and other ethnic groups, and to bring self-discipline, self-awareness, and confidence to the contestants involved.

Miss Saigon controversy: Vociferous protest spearheaded by Asian American actors, writers, and other activists over the retention of a white actor in a lead role during the New York run of the hit London musical *Miss Saigon* (pr. 1989). The show, an epic success in London, was scheduled to open on Broadway in April, 1991—with acclaimed British actor Jonathan Pryce reprising his award-winning role as the Eurasian "Engineer." Offended by the idea of a white actor in yellowface playing an Asian character, a coalition of Asian American actors and writers, including playwright David Henry HWANG and actor B. D. WONG, vowed to resist the casting.

Miss Saigon is an updated version of the Giacomo

Playwright David Henry Hwang was among many Asian American artists who protested the portrayal of an Asian by a white actor in yellowface during the production of the musical Miss Saigon. (AP/Wide World Photos)

Puccini opera *Madama Butterfly* (pr. 1904). The former tells the story of the doomed romance between Chris, an American serviceman, and Kim, a Vietnamese barmaid and prostitute, during the final days of the Vietnam War. The two meet at a brothel, fall in love, and conceive a child. Soon after, U.S. military forces abandon Saigon, and Chris abandons Kim. He returns to the city three years later with his white wife, Ellen, to search for Kim and the son he left behind. Kim, meanwhile, has remained loyal to Chris: She is now a fugitive, having earlier killed a government official who had tried to force her into marriage. When Chris and Kim are finally reunited in Bangkok, she kills herself, forcing Chris and Ellen to take the boy to a better life in the United States.

By the end of the summer of 1990, advance ticket sales had soared into the millions of dollars en route to the highest advance sales ($35 million) in Broadway history. Actors' Equity, the union representing stage actors in the United States, told *Miss Saigon* producer Cameron Mackintosh to recast the role of the Engineer using an Asian American actor. In August, Mackintosh, backed by much of the American media in his refusal to recast, vowed to cancel the show's Broadway run rather than capitulate to the union. Cancellation would have meant forfeiture of the huge advance—and the more than thirty roles calling for minority actors. Weeks later the union, under intense pressure from producers, the public, and many of its own members to reverse its decision, announced that Pryce would be allowed to play the role after all. Mackintosh then demanded union assurances that no further interference with his casting decisions would be forthcoming.

A few months later more controversy flared when Mackintosh announced plans to retain Filipino actor (and non-U.S. citizen) Lea Salonga in the crucial role of Kim. Actors' Equity again argued that the part should go to an Asian American actor. In a hearing held the following January, 1991, a union arbitrator ruled that Salonga would be allowed to reprise her London role. Shortly thereafter Mackintosh announced the casting of Kam Cheng, an Asian American college student from New Jersey, to share the role with Salonga. (The same arrangement, with a different actor, had been used in London.)

Miss Saigon opened as scheduled, to mixed critical reviews. Audiences, however, flocked to the performances. At the Tony Awards presentation of June, 1991, the $10 million production lost in the category of best musical to *The Will Rogers Follies* (pr. 1991). Pryce and Salonga, however, captured the prizes for best actor and actress in a musical.

Mittwer, Mary Oyama (b. 1907, Fairfield, Calif.): Journalist. In the 1930's Mittwer wrote for various Japanese American newspapers and, under the pen name "Deirdre," was an advice columnist for a Japanese American newspaper in San Francisco, the *New World-Sun*, from 1935 until 1941. As one of a group of Nisei women writers who initiated public discussion on such topics as multiracial relations and gender roles for Japanese American women, she was also one of only a few Japanese American women writers whose works were published in the mainstream American press.

Oyama attended Sacramento High School and San Francisco National Training School (for missionary training) during the 1920's. After studying journalism at the University of Southern California (USC), she began a string of jobs with such well-known Japanese American newspapers as the *Kashu Mainichi*, *Rafu Shimpo*, and *Nichibei Shimbun*. Through her column, which ran under the heading "I'm Telling You, Deirdre," she served her Nisei readers as a kind of guidance counselor on a wide assortment of topics, advising them not only on marriage, dating, and careers but also on the proper etiquette necessary to life in a society dominated and shaped by white Americans. At the same time, mindful of the persistence of racial and gender discrimination, she urged Nisei women to step beyond the restrictive confines of gender roles by becoming more involved in the American political process; encouraged them to become more independent; and underscored the need for all Japanese Americans to forge good relationships with people of other races and cultures. Oyama also wrote numerous articles, interviews, poems, and other works that appeared in assorted Japanese American newspapers and magazines; her pieces were also published in the mainstream journal *Common Ground.*

In addition, Oyama actively promoted the creation and development of a distinct Japanese American ethnic identity as reflected in that community's artistic expression. The League of Nisei Artists and Writers, which she helped to establish, was founded for this purpose. At the age of thirty she married Frederick Mittwer, a compositor for the *Rafu Shimpo* who was part Japanese, part Caucasian. In 1940 Mary Oyama Mittwer was one of twenty-four prominent Nisei writers of both sexes profiled in *Current Life*, a Nisei magazine. Her story is told in Valerie Matsumoto's article "Desperately Seeking 'Deirdre': Gender Roles, Multicultural Relations, and Nisei Women Writers of the 1930s" (*Frontiers* 12, no. 1 [1991]: 19-32).

Miyakawa, T. Scott [Tetsuo] (Nov. 23, 1906, Los Angeles, Calif.—August ?, 1981, Boston, Mass.): Scholar. One of a small group of mainland Nisei born in the first decade of the twentieth century, Miyakawa became one of the first scholars to study the history of Japanese Americans. In 1929, he earned a master's degree from Cornell University, and afterward he went to work as a manager for the New York office of the Japanese-owned Southern Manchurian Railroad Company. His affiliation with this company caused him to be blacklisted by the Federal Bureau of Investigation, because the company was linked with Japanese aggression in China.

In 1951, Miyakawa earned a doctorate from Columbia University, and he went on to teach at Boston University and the University of Massachusetts in Boston. Miyakawa urged Nisei leaders to promote the study of the Japanese American experience in an organized way. In 1962, initially funded by a grant from the Japanese American Citizens League (JACL), the Japanese American Research Project (JARP) was begun, largely as a result of Miyakawa's efforts. Miyakawa served as director of the JARP from 1962 to 1965, overseeing, among other projects, the creation of the Japanese American Research Project Collection, the largest U.S. collection of materials on Japanese Americans. Miyakawa's writings include *Protestants and Pioneers: Individualism and Conformity on the American Frontier* (1964) and "Early New York Issei: Founders of Japanese-American Trade," in *East Across the Pacific: Historical and Sociological Studies of Japanese Immigration and Assimilation* (1972), edited by Hilary Conroy and T. Scott Miyakawa.

Miyama, Kanichi (1847, Yamaguchi Prefecture, Japan—1936): Clergyman. He was educated in Japan and worked there for awhile, then opted to come to the United States. While living in San Francisco, he became a Christian and pastored a church there. In 1887 he left for Hawaii to begin evangelizing Japanese immigrants in the islands as the first Japanese-speaking Christian evangelist.

Miyamoto, Kazuo (1897, Kauai, Hawaii—1988, Honolulu, Hawaii): Physician and novelist. A Hawaiian-born Nisei, Miyamoto completed his undergraduate studies at Stanford University and served in the army during World War I before studying medicine at Washington University in St. Louis, Missouri. During the 1930's, Miyamoto conducted research on public health within the Japanese American community that was eventually published in Japan. After the Japanese attack on Pearl Harbor in 1941, Miyamoto was arrested and imprisoned without trial for nearly one year. Following his release from prison in 1942, Miyamoto volunteered to serve as a physician at the hospital at the Tule Lake relocation center. During his three-year stay at Tule Lake, Miyamoto kept a journal that eventually provided the raw material for his epic historical novel *Hawaii: End of the Rainbow* (1964). The novel chronicles the lives of Japanese immigrant laborers and their families up through the internment experiences of many Issei leaders in Honolulu's Japanese community and their return to Hawaii. After the war, Miyamoto returned to Honolulu, where he resumed his medical practice and continued to publish various books, including *Vikings of the Far East* (1975).

Miyamoto, Shotaro Frank (b. 1912): Scholar. A Nisei resident of suburban Seattle, Miyamoto attended the University of Washington from 1930 until 1932. Originally interested in majoring in engineering, Miyamoto dropped out of school because of lack of

Photographer Toyo Miyatake at his camera. (Japanese American National Museum)

funds. Upon reentering college, he completed his bachelor's degree and went on to receive a master's degree in sociology. His thesis on Seattle's Japanese American community, published as *Social Solidarity Among the Japanese in Seattle* (1939), became a classic in the field; it was one of the first works to study the long-range impact of the restrictive IMMIGRATION ACT OF 1924 on Japanese Americans. After being accepted into the doctoral program at the University of Chicago in 1939, Miyamoto completed his course work in two years. He returned to the University of Washington to accept a teaching appointment while he worked on completing his dissertation.

After the attack on Pearl Harbor in December of 1941, Miyamoto was hired to work as a researcher on the Japanese Evacuation and Resettlement Study (JERS) project headed by Dorothy Swaine Thomas. Interned at TULE LAKE, Miyamoto conducted fieldwork there and, later, in Chicago, where many Japanese Americans resettled. In 1945, Miyamoto returned to join the faculty of the sociology department at the University of Washington, publishing many scholarly articles and continuing to teach there until his retirement in 1980. As a professor emeritus, Miyamoto continued to be active as a scholar. See his article "Problems of Interpersonal Style Among the Nisei," *Amerasia Journal* 13, no. 2 (1986-1987): 29-45; see also *Amerasia Journal* 14, no. 2 (1988): 105-123 for an exchange between Miyamoto and Stanford Lyman regarding this article.

Miyamura, Hiroshi "Hershey" (b. 1926): Korean War hero. As a squadron leader attached to an infantry regiment, he displayed uncommon bravery in defending his men against advancing enemy troops. After more than two years as a war prisoner, he returned to the United States and was awarded the Congressional Medal of Honor.

Miyatake, Toyo (1895, Takashinomura, Kagawa Prefecture, Japan—Feb., 1979): Photographer. During his lifetime, Miyatake was assuredly the most well-known Japanese American photographer living in the United States. He emigrated to the United States in 1909 when his father found work and sent for the family. In the beginning, they lived behind the Shofudo confectionery store that was operated by his father in Los Angeles' Chinatown but later moved to a house on Jackson Street in Little Tokyo.

Toyo Miyatake's interest in photography began at a very young age. Soon after his arrival in the United States, he decided that he wanted to become a photographer. Despite his mother's objections, he had always been interested in art and was determined to learn photography. He signed up for lessons at Harry Shigeta's studio in Little Tokyo and soon discovered that he had found his calling in life. In September of 1923, one year after marrying his wife, Hiroko, he purchased the Toyo Photo Studio in Glendale and worked closely with renowned photographer Edward Weston. By 1926 Miyatake's reputation as a photographer had grown as he won prizes around the United States and also at the London International Photography exhibition. Later he also became known in Hollywood circles through his friendship with dancer Michio Ito and actor Sessue Hayakawa. During this time, however, the studio was constantly in financial trouble.

In the early 1930's, after attempting to open up a studio in Japan, Miyatake opened Toyo Miyatake Studio on the corner of Central Avenue in Little Tokyo. With Hiroko handling the financial end of business, he concentrated on photography, and the studio flourished. Unfortunately, like other Japanese Americans, they were forced to close the business during World War II and were forcibly removed to the MANZANAR relocation center. At Manzanar, where internees were forbidden to have cameras, he took the most haunting photographs of his career using a lens that he had illegally brought into camp and a box that he had constructed to act as the frame. Eventually, he was caught in his activities. Rather than punishing him, however, the camp director realized the historic nature of the photos and made him the official Manzanar photographer for the U.S. WAR RELOCATION AUTHORITY (WRA).

After leaving Manzanar, in November of 1945, Miyatake reopened Toyo Miyatake Studio on First Street in Little Tokyo. Over the years, nearly any Japanese American family living in the Los Angeles area who wanted its portrait done went to him for his professional services. In 1972, following the death of Hiroko in January, he relinquished control of the studio to his eldest son Archie, who was also an accomplished photographer. In the same year, Toyo Miyatake was honored as one of the Pioneers of the Year at the annual Nisei Week festival. More awards followed. In 1976, he was given a Distinguished Service Commendation by the Photographic Society of Japan. Two years later, he served as the Grand Marshal of the Nisei Week parade and was also given an award as the Japanese Artist of the Year. He died at the age of 83.

Miyoshi, Masao (b. May 14, 1928, Tokyo, Japan): Scholar. Miyoshi is the author of some of the most nuanced and penetrating studies of U.S.-Japan relations. He received a B.A. degree (1951) from the University of Tokyo, an M.A. (1957) from New York University, and a Ph.D. (1957), also from NYU. After many years in the Department of English at the University of California, Berkeley, where he became a full professor in 1973, Miyoshi accepted an endowed chair at the University of California, San Diego, where he is Hajime Mori Professor of Japanese, English, and Comparative Literature. Among his books are *Accomplices of Silence: The Modern Japanese Novel* (1974), *As We Saw Them: The First Japanese Embassy to the United States* (1979), and *Off Center: Power and Culture Relations Between Japan and the United States* (1991). He has also published scholarly articles and journalistic pieces on a wide range of topics, including the status of Asian Americans.

Moab: Prison camp in Utah, established during World War II by the U.S. War Relocation Authority (WRA) to house so-called troublemakers from other Japanese American internment camps, as well as draft resisters. The prison camp at Moab, officially designated as a "citizen isolation camp," was established by the WRA in December, 1942. In April, 1943, the camp was relocated to Leupp, Arizona.

Mochi: Japanese dessert made of sweet rice cake, often stuffed with red bean paste; a traditional New Year's Day food served toasted or in broth.

Mochitsuki: Japanese New Year custom in which *mochi* rice cakes are made. In traditional Japan, the women of the community prepared the rice, after which the men pounded it with wooden mallets to soften it; the rice was then formed into cakes. With variations—today, most *mochi* is commercially prepared—Japanese Americans continue to preserve this tradition.

Model Minority: Phrase used to describe Asian Americans, first used in newspaper and magazine articles beginning in 1966. It has since become a popular stereotype of Asian Americans. In academic writing and political discourse the Model Minority thesis is central to debate over whether the government needs to combat racial discrimination actively or whether the persistence of racial inequality has more to do with the culture—the work ethic and habits—of racial minority groups themselves. Proponents of the Model Minority thesis tend to be politically conservative analysts and writers who believe that American society is open and democratic enough for racial minorities to succeed if they try hard enough. Critics tend to be liberal analysts and writers who argue that discrimination and institutional racism continue to bar minorities from competing fully with white persons and that the government has a responsibility to combat discrimination through the development and implementation of social programs.

Model Minority articles describe Asian Americans as hard workers who have been rewarded for their efforts with high college graduation rates, professional jobs, high incomes, and successful family businesses.

The sections that follow include a discussion of the debate over the Model Minority thesis, its origins, historical context, proliferation and development, and impact on Asian American women; criticisms of the Model Minority thesis and how proponents have responded; and some of the effects of the stereotype.

The Debate. Proponents of the Model Minority thesis say the label is less a stereotype than a reality. They believe that Asian Americans, once called "pariahs," are now labelled "paragons" because of their perseverance and hard work. Proponents argue that this dramatic shift in popular image shows that racial discrimination is not a significant obstacle to upward mobility in society. They cite median family income statistics and college completion rates as evidence of Asian American success. As they lament the decline in standards among native-born workers, they praise Asian immigrants for revitalizing the work ethic of which the United States was once proud. Proponents believe less successful groups, particularly African Americans, should follow the example set by Asian Americans.

Critics argue that the Model Minority is a stereotype that conceals important information and is used to discriminate against Asian Americans. They point out that articles celebrating Asian American success include selective statistical data that mislead readers into thinking all Asian Americans are successful and downplay both the persistence of racial discrimination in American society and the reality of class stratification with Asian American communities. Critics also point out that proponents of the Model Minority thesis are often political conservatives less interested in celebrating Asian American success than in providing a rationale for dismantling social programs implemented to combat racial inequality and for preventing the development of new ones.

Proponents of the Model Minority thesis view Asian Americans as hard workers who have achieved professional and material rewards through their efforts. This stereotype is often used to support arguments against special social programs to combat discrimination. (Photo Search Ltd.)

Educational Profile of Asian Americans Compared to Other Americans

Persons 25 Years or Older with 4 or More Years of College, 1990

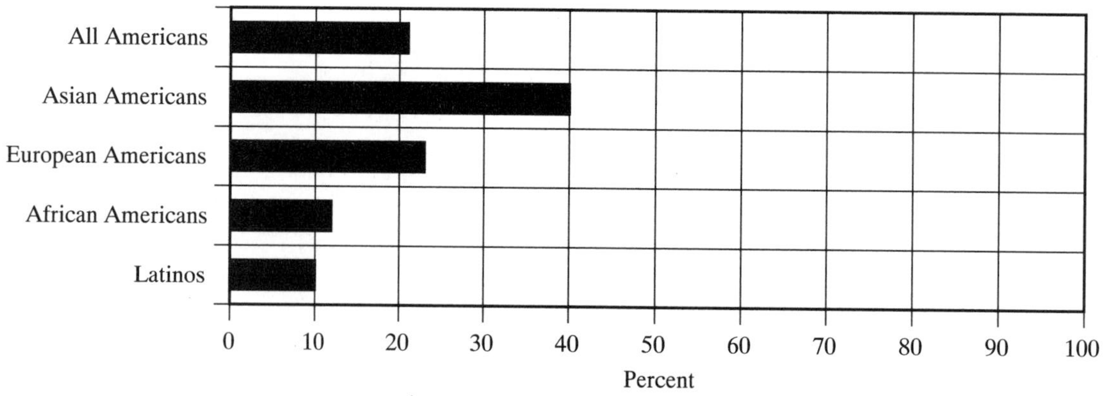

Enrollment in Higher Education, 1990

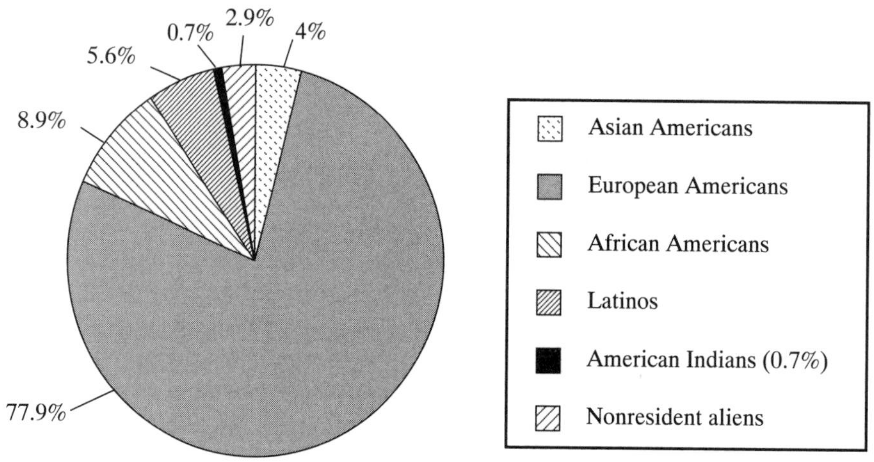

SAT Scores, 1992					
Mean scores on scale of 200-800 on Scholastic Aptitude Tests					
	Verbal	Math		Verbal	Math
All students	423	476	European Americans	442	491
Asian Americans	413	532	Mexican Americans	372	425
African Americans	352	385	Puerto Ricans	366	406
American Indians	395	442			

Sources: Stanley Karnow and Nancy Yoshihara, *Asian Americans in Transition*. New York: The Asia Society, 1992. Susan B. Gall and Timothy L. Gall, eds., *Statistical Record of Asian Americans.* Detroit: Gale Research, Inc., 1993. U.S. Commission on Civil Rights, *Civil Rights Issues Facing Asian Americans in the 1990's*, 1992. *Los Angeles Times*, "Attitudes Toward Asian Americans" in *Crosscurrents*. UCLA Asian American Studies Center 16:2 (fall/winter, 1993).

Critics argue that the underlying political ideology of the thesis is the belief that individuals or groups that do not succeed fail to do so because they simply are not working hard enough and thus have only themselves to blame. Proponents respond by saying that Asian Americans should be recognized for their hard-earned success and upward mobility. They assure critics that this is the only reason why Asian Americans have received so much adulation and deny there is any hidden agenda in the increasing popularity of the Model Minority thesis in public discourse.

Origins. The first time the term "Model Minority" was used was in an article, "Success Story: Japanese American Style," authored by sociologist William Petersen while he was teaching at the University of California, Berkeley. It was published in *The New York Times Magazine* (January 6, 1966). This article set the tone and format for subsequent articles and the development of the Model Minority thesis. Historian Roger Daniels considers it "the most influential single article ever written about an Asian American group."

"Success Story" opens with a comparison of Japanese Americans and African Americans—both of whom have been the object of prejudice and discrimination—the former most notably when interned in concentration camps during World War II. Petersen notes that this kind of treatment usually results in the creation of "problem minorities," characterized by high crime rates, poor health, low levels of educational attainment, poverty, and an "unstable family pattern." Yet, he argues, in the case of Japanese Americans it has had the opposite effect: "[E]very attempt to hamper their progress resulted only in enhancing their determination to succeed."

Petersen says that Japanese Americans outrank others in most measures of success ranging from education to longevity. He seems pleased to note that on the Berkeley campus few Japanese American students were counted among the student activists. He includes quotes from social scientists commenting on the pattern of success and statistics from the 1960 census to substantiate his argument. For example, the median number of years of schooling Japanese Americans completed was 12.2, compared to 11.0 for whites and 8.6 for African Americans. In other areas, too, the achievements of Japanese Americans surpassed those of native-born whites. For example, 56 percent of Japanese American males held white-collar jobs, compared to 42.1 percent of white males. The author also cites Federal Bureau of Investigation Uniform Crime Reports indicating that Japanese Americans committed low numbers of crimes against people and property and a California study which found that Japanese Americans had a longer life expectancy than white residents.

According to Petersen the key to Japanese American success is culture. He explains that Japanese immigrants brought to the United States a work ethic and frugality that is similar to the Protestant ethic. Through a close-knit family and the church, this ethic, along with other traditional Japanese values such as honoring parents, not bringing shame to the family, and placing the family before the individual, are passed down from one generation to the next. The article includes photographs of Japanese American women and men at work, at home, in World War II concentration camps, and on a college campus. One caption reads, "Even in a country whose patron saint is the Horatio Alger hero, there is no parallel to their success story."

The second Model Minority article, "Success Story of One Minority Group in the U.S.," focuses on Chinese Americans and appeared in *U.S. News & World Report* (December 26, 1966). These first two articles concentrated on Japanese Americans and Chinese Americans, respectively, because most Asian Americans living in the United States in the mid-1960's were of Japanese or Chinese descent in part because of discriminatory immigration policies.

No author is named for this article; correspondents reported from San Francisco, Los Angeles, and New York. Although this article does not use the term "Model Minority," it clearly prescribes that less successful groups such as African Americans should emulate Chinese Americans rather than depend on the government for assistance.

The article draws a sharp contrast between how Chinese Americans reacted to discrimination compared to the other groups. According to one expert cited in the article, Richard T. Sollenberger, a professor at Mount Holyoke College who studied New York's Chinatown, "The Chinese people here (in New York's Chinatown) will work at anything. . . . [T]hey don't sit around moaning." The implication is that other groups, namely African Americans, are sitting around complaining when they could and should be working.

Like Petersen's, this article cites culture as the key to success. Chinese immigrants bring with them "the traditional virtues of hard work, thrift, and morality." This, combined with a close-knit family where parents closely supervise their children and children respect their elders, is used to explain how these values are transmitted from one generation to the next.

The Model Minority thesis links "traditional virtues" of hard work, thrift, and morality to Asian family values and culture, thereby linking culture with success. Many find such a conclusion controversial. (Jim Whitmer)

The article includes photographs of Chinese Americans at home, in Chinatown, and in the classroom. One caption reads, "Chinese-American youngsters tend to be obedient and hard-working in the classroom of New York City's public schools. . . ." Another caption describes how strong family ties continue to play an important role in the Chinese American community, "providing its members with a sense of self-reliance and self-discipline."

Historical Context. The Model Minority thesis first appeared at a critical juncture in the Civil Rights movement. There was growing recognition that the pervasiveness and depth of racism required that the government take an active role in combating racial discrimination and its effects. Also, Asian Americans, Latinos, and Native Americans were beginning to unite and join forces with African Americans. On college campuses this new coalition manifested itself in the struggle for ethnic studies.

When Petersen's flagship article first appeared, the movement had recently won two major victories: the passage of the Civil Rights Act of 1964 and the Voting Rights Act of 1965. In the wake of these victories some civil rights activists had been absorbed into the system—employed by the newly implemented Great Society programs. Others were becoming disillusioned with the movement, noting that despite its victories the situation of many African Americans remained unchanged. Part of the original movement was in the process of becoming radicalized, and by spring, 1965, the goal for many activists had shifted from civil rights to Black Power. In this context the introduction of the Model Minority can be seen as an attempt to renew faith in the more moderate demands of the Civil Rights movement, namely integration and assimilation.

Once introduced, the Model Minority thesis gained popularity, and the number of articles proliferated. The thesis fit well with the conservative period that followed the liberal and activist 1960's, particularly the Reagan-Bush years.

The proliferation of the Model Minority in the 1970's took place when the reaction against the philosophy and the programs of the 1960's gained legitimacy and the United States faced a series of domestic and international crises. Many of the crises had racial dimensions: "losing" a guerrilla war in Vietnam to

Asian peasant soldiers, Americans being held hostage by a "fanatical" Iranian leader, "losing" jobs to Southeast Asian refugees and "illegal" Mexican immigrants, being "victimized" by the Middle East during the gasoline shortages, and "losing" the automobile industry to Japan. Conservatives urged Americans to interpret these problems in terms of the United States growing soft and losing its will to be a world leader. The Model Minority coincided with this theme because it graphically illustrated how undisciplined Americans had become.

The Model Minority articles of this period often included sections on white resentment of successful Asian Americans. In the context of fears of losing strength and the will to lead, the focus and significance of the Model Minority shifted from the denigration of non-Asian racial minority groups to concerns about the national "malaise" and anxiety over Japanese and Asian domination. Fears about competing with Asian Americans within U.S. borders and with Japan and other Asian nations in the international arena converged.

The growing connection between the model characteristics of Asian Americans and the fears of Japanese (and other Asian) world dominance did not, however, completely displace the Model Minority's original

Occupational Distribution of Asian Americans Compared to Other Americans, 1990

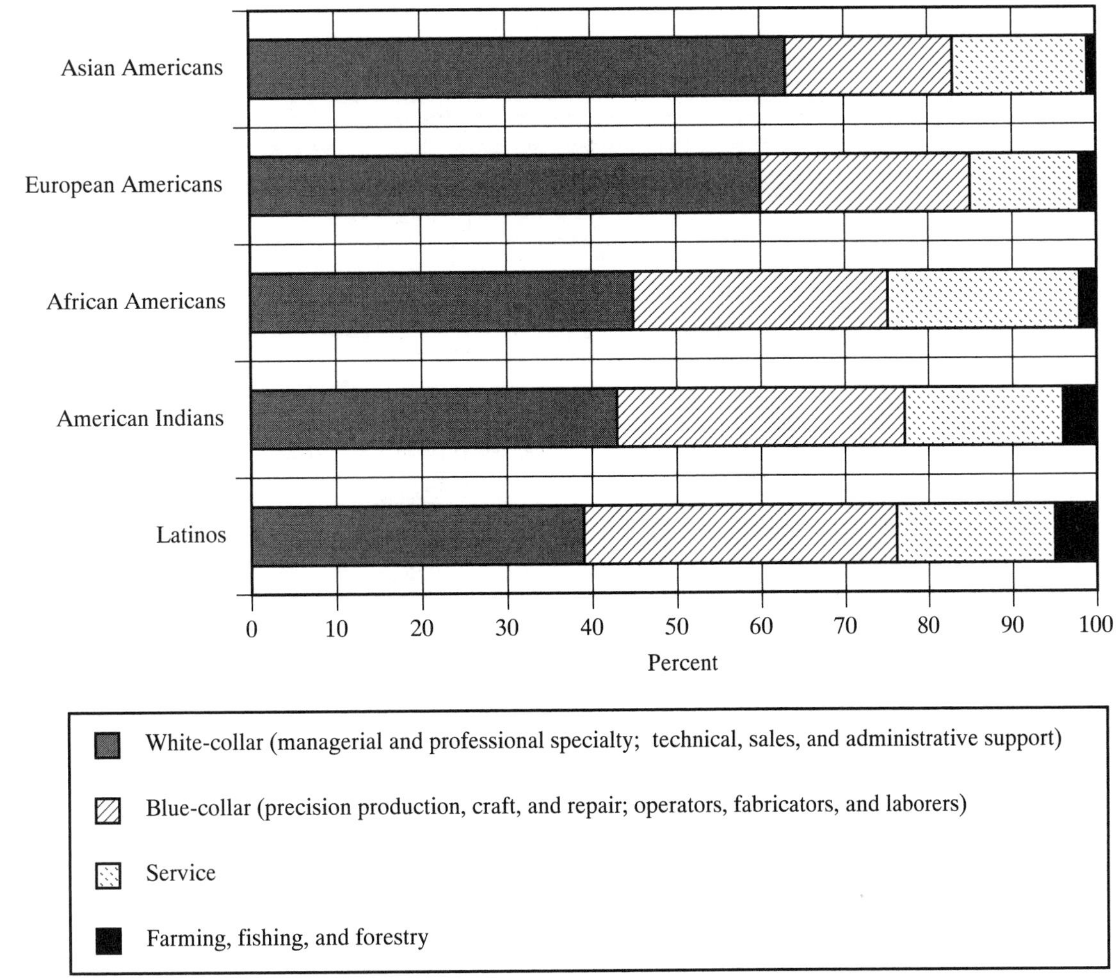

Sources: William O'Hare, "America's Minorities: The Demographics of Diversity." *Population Bulletin* 47:4 (1992). Harry H. L. Kitano and Roger Daniels, *Asian Americans: Emerging Minorities.* Englewood Cliffs, N.J.: Prentice Hall, 1988.

Income and Economic Indicators of Asian Americans Compared to Other Americans

Income and Number of Earners per Household, 1991

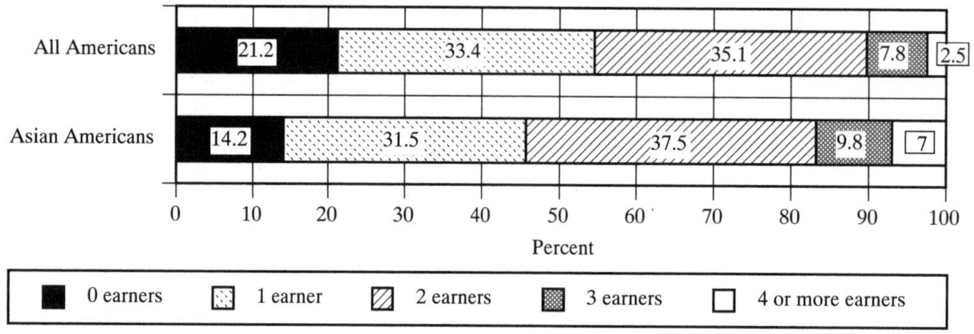

Median Earnings in Relation to Schooling of Full-time Workers, 25 Years or Older, 1990

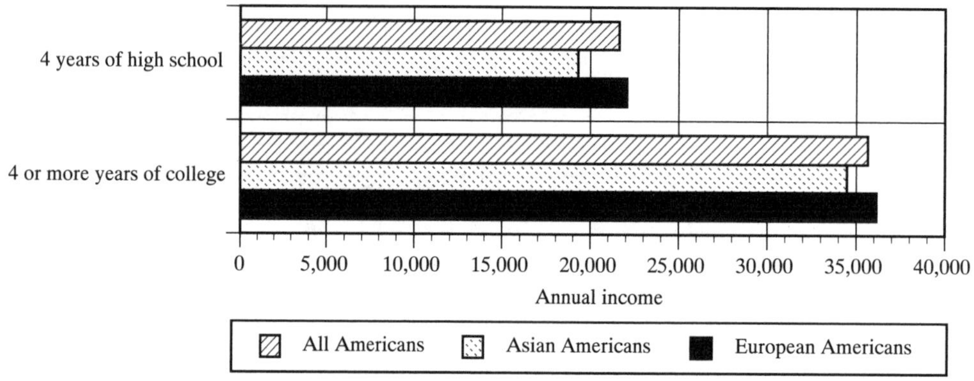

Median Household Income in U.S., 1991

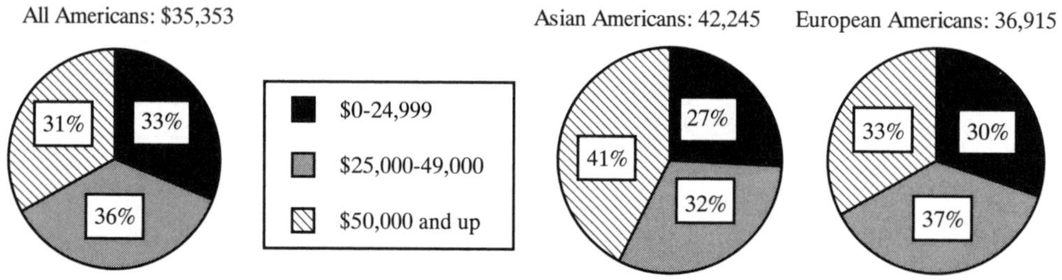

Income and Poverty, 1989			
	All Americans	Asian Americans	New Asian Immigrants*
Median household income	$30,056	$36,784	$26,851
Per capita income	$14,420	$13,638	$10,378
Percent of families in poverty	10.0%	11.6%	20.6%

Sources: Susan B. Gall and Timothy L. Gall, eds., *Statistical Record of Asian Americans.* Detroit: Gale Research, Inc., 1993. Stanley Karnow and Nancy Yoshihara, *Asian Americans in Transition.* New York: The Asia Society, 1992. U.S. Bureau of the Census, *1990 Census of Population: Asians and Pacific Islanders in the United States,* 1993.

* Denotes those who immigrated to the U.S. after 1980.

thrust. Conservative journalists, politicians, and academics continued to use the Model Minority thesis to denigrate other racial minority groups. U.S. president Ronald Reagan, whose administration sought to reduce or eliminate government programs for racial minorities, held Asian Americans up as an example for all Americans to follow and cited their median family income as higher than the "total American average" when he addressed a group of Asian Americans at the White House in February, 1984.

Nathan Glazer of Harvard University, a leading critic of affirmative action, began to incorporate the Model Minority thesis into his writings as a way of supporting his belief in the assimilation theory of race relations when other academics were turning to alternative theories to explain the persistence of racial inequality. Sociologist Peter Rose, a highly regarded scholar of race relations, argued that African Americans and Latinos have taken a "backward" path in their struggle for equality, "signposted with phrases like 'institutional racism' and 'second-class citizenship.' " By contrast Asian Americans, "despite their own continuing encounters with prejudice, will follow the other path" to conduct their lives by "meritocratic principles" rather than "capitalizing on inherited 'disadvantages.'" As posed in *Commentary* (August, 1990), the Model Minority thesis raises the question of "whether even the most debilitating discrimination need incapacitate a people. . . ."

Proliferation and Development. By the early 1980's Model Minority articles referred to "Asian Americans" as an aggregate group and included segments of the population that entered the United States after the first articles had been published: immigrants from South Korea, India, the Philippines, and Taiwan and refugees from Cambodia, Laos, and Vietnam. In some articles the thesis is even applied to Amerasian children.

Like the first two published, these articles cite a culture of self-discipline and self-help as key to Asian American success and use aggregate national statistics as evidence. Articles report that the median family income for Asian Americans in 1980 stood at \$22,075, compared to \$20,840 for white families; in 1990 it increased to \$42,250 for Asian American families, compared to \$36,920 for white families. In 1980, 33 percent of Asian Americans more than twenty-five years of age had completed college, compared to 17.5 percent of white Americans; in 1990 the Asian American proportion increased to 39 percent, compared to the white proportion of 22 percent. The articles also note that the Asian American population is one of the fastest-growing in the United States—ballooning by 120 percent between 1970 and 1980. A study issued by the Population Reference Bureau in 1985 estimated that the Asian American population could reach ten million by the year 2000.

The articles also mention the downside of the Model Minority—the "mixed blessings of achievement" or the "costs" of educational success—but most often in a way that makes the overall thesis of success all the more convincing. One example can be found in "The Drive to Excel," which appeared in *Newsweek on Campus* (April, 1984), an insert to college newspapers. This article first acknowledges that not all Asian Americans are the same—there is great diversity not only in educational attainment but also in ethnicity and acculturation. It then continues: "Some facts, however, are plainly incontestable. Asian American students form the fastest growing segment of American higher education . . . and more often than not at the best universities."

"Formula for Success," published in *Newsweek* (April 23, 1984), employs a similar tactic. The article begins with a description of Willy Chia, who admits that he is not "into school" and would rather "mess around with cars." Yet after acknowledging that Chia is one Asian American who probably will not attain a high degree of education, the article generalizes about the majority of Asian Americans: "From San Francisco's Lowell High School to New York's Bronx High School of Science, Asian Americans pack the honor rolls of some of the country's most highly regarded schools."

By the 1990's Model Minority articles emphasized educational achievement and the successful immigrant business entrepreneur. "The New Whiz Kids," published in *Time* (August 31, 1987), features photographs and biographies of six star students. Fourteen-year-old Michael Rendor De Guzman, who immigrated from the Philippines, is pictured with his mother. The shelves of his family's dining room are said to be crammed with his trophies and awards. Michael says he is highly motivated to excel in school and studies five hours each day.

"The American Way," published in *INC* (September, 1991), highlights Indian-born entrepreneur Vinny Gupta. Gupta is applauded for coming to the United States with the "fresh eyes and fresh convictions" necessary to buy a foundry in the Rust Belt of Ohio and turn it into a facility with annual sales that have soared from less than \$2 million to nearly \$9 million. How did he do it? According to the article "he simply dug into

Proponents of the Model Minority thesis cite the rise in Asian American college students as support for the contention that educational achievement is associated with Asian American culture. (Jim Whitmer)

his business elbow-deep every day." Gupta admits, "Foundries are dirty work." A photograph shows him working next to the men he employs. The caption reads, "Gupta arrives early, stays late, and can often be found alongside his line workers." Gupta's success allowed him to purchase two more foundries.

Steve Hui, founder of Everex Systems, immigrated to the United States in 1967. Before filing for bankruptcy in 1992, his company's annual sales reached $437 million. Hui refers to the thrift, self-discipline, and willingness to defer gratification that he, Gupta, and other immigrant entrepreneurs exhibit as the "refugee mentality." The article describes this attitude as a "truly American ethic" rooted in the "fundamental belief that in the end, one's circumstances are one's own responsibility."

These articles emphasize how the new immigrant has come to the United States with a freshness of American spirit that Americans themselves have lost. They depict new immigrants as the truest of Americans because they will work at anything—much like the immigrants of earlier times. The native-born American is faulted for being too spoiled to take any job. Some articles appear to be using Asian immigrants as a model not solely for other racial minority groups but also for the white majority.

These articles represent a shifting definition of the Model Minority. The line is not as clearly drawn between Asian Americans and other racial minorities; instead, a new configuration of Asian, European, and Latino immigrants is favorably contrasted with the native-born population. Native-born Americans, be

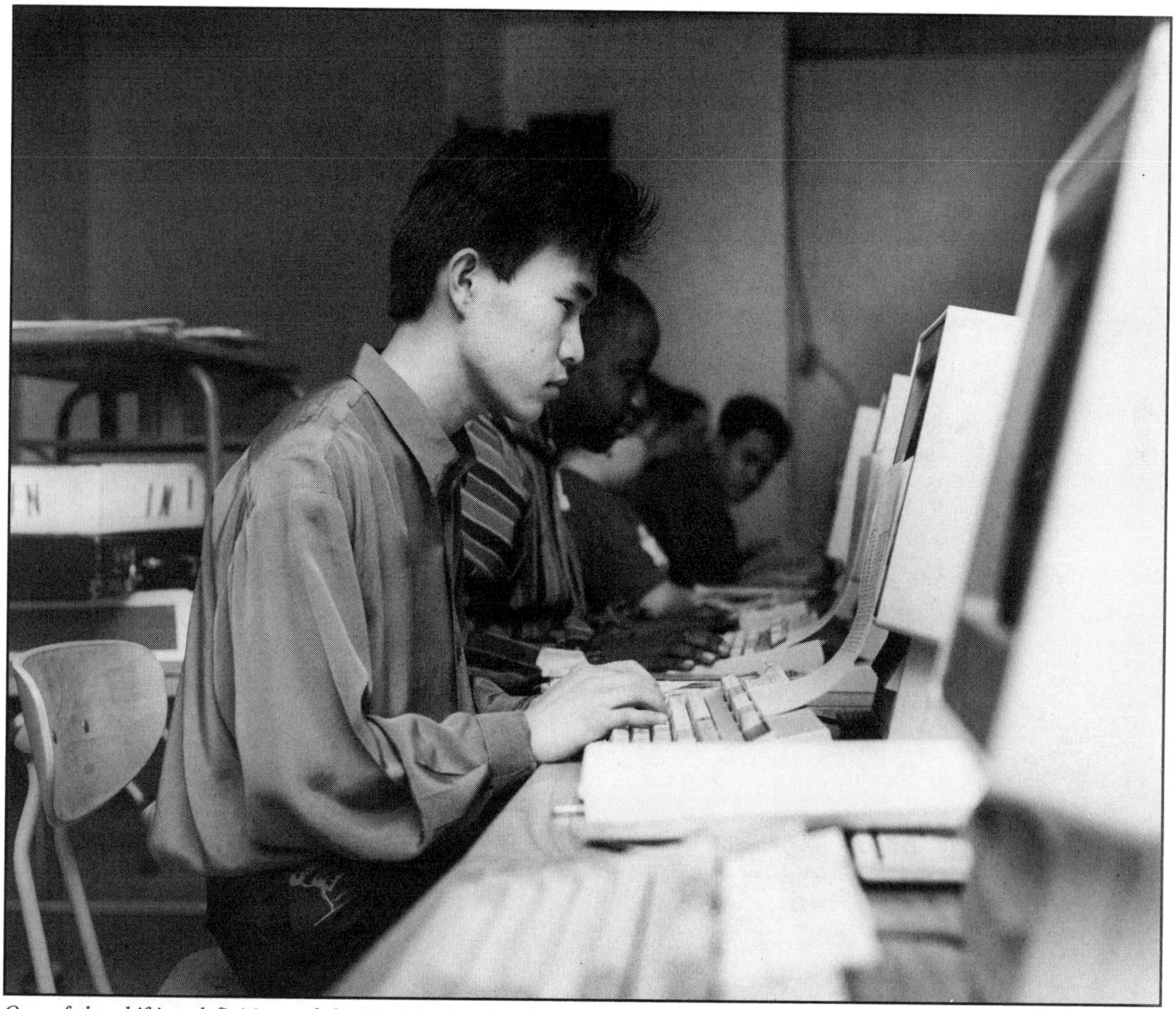

One of the shifting definitions of the Model Minority thesis presents a new configuration of Asian, European, and Latino immigrants favorably contrasted with "native-born" white and African Americans; the latter group is seen as lacking the same work ethic possessed by the former group. Such stereotypes remain open to question. (James L. Shaffer)

they African American or white, are denigrated for not putting in long enough hours or taking their work seriously. In contrast, the new immigrants are credited with "reinvigorating" the United States' "entrepreneurial culture" and are described as "more American in their attitudes and aptitudes than the third-, fourth-, or fifth-generation Americans whose society they joined."

Asian American Women. Proponents of the Model Minority extend their thesis to include Asian American women, who are well-integrated into the articles. They are included in the photographs and mentioned, sometimes by name, within the text. In addition to national television news anchor Connie CHUNG, articles feature other notable women such as writers Bharati MUKHERJEE and Maxine Hong KINGSTON, New York fashion designer Cathy Hardwick, who emigrated from Korea in 1953, and (former) California Secretary of State March Fong EU. Sometimes less well-known women, such as Massachusetts Institute of Technology internist Elaine Shiang, are named or pictured. Shiang is not only a medical doctor but also a wife (married to another medical doctor) and the mother of two young children. She epitomizes the well-rounded successful woman who apparently has not sacrificed marriage or family for her career.

Model Minority articles cite cultural attributes to explain why Asian American women do not seem to face the same gender barriers as white women. In an article in *Fortune* (November 24, 1986), the author concludes that Asian American women have a "psychological advantage" over working women of other races. "Their heritage makes them less susceptible to supermom syndrome, the burnout that threatens women who struggle to reconcile family roles with career aspirations." The article quotes a fifty-one-year-

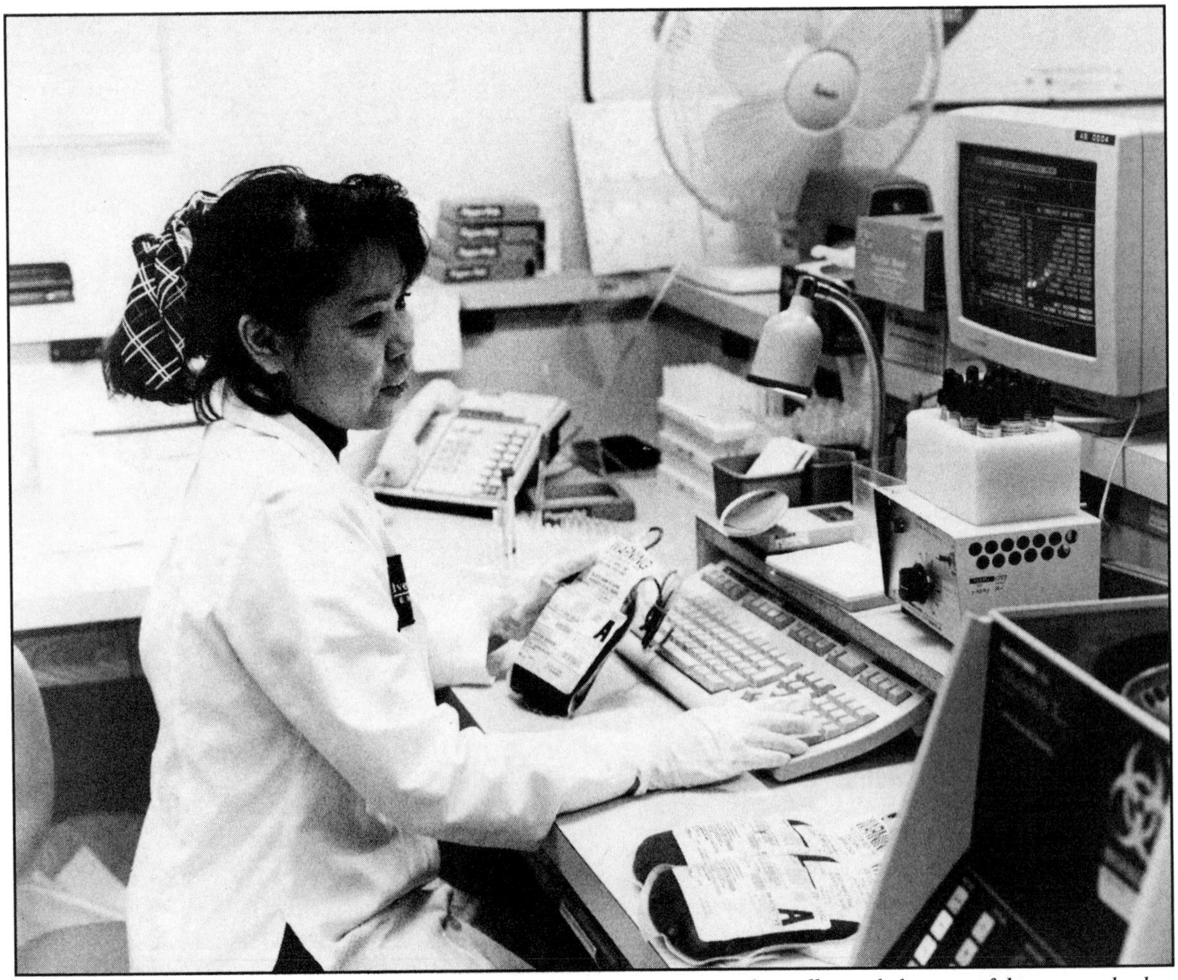

The Model Minority thesis sometimes epitomizes Asian American women as the well-rounded, successful woman who has not sacrificed marriage or family for her career. (Martin A. Hutner)

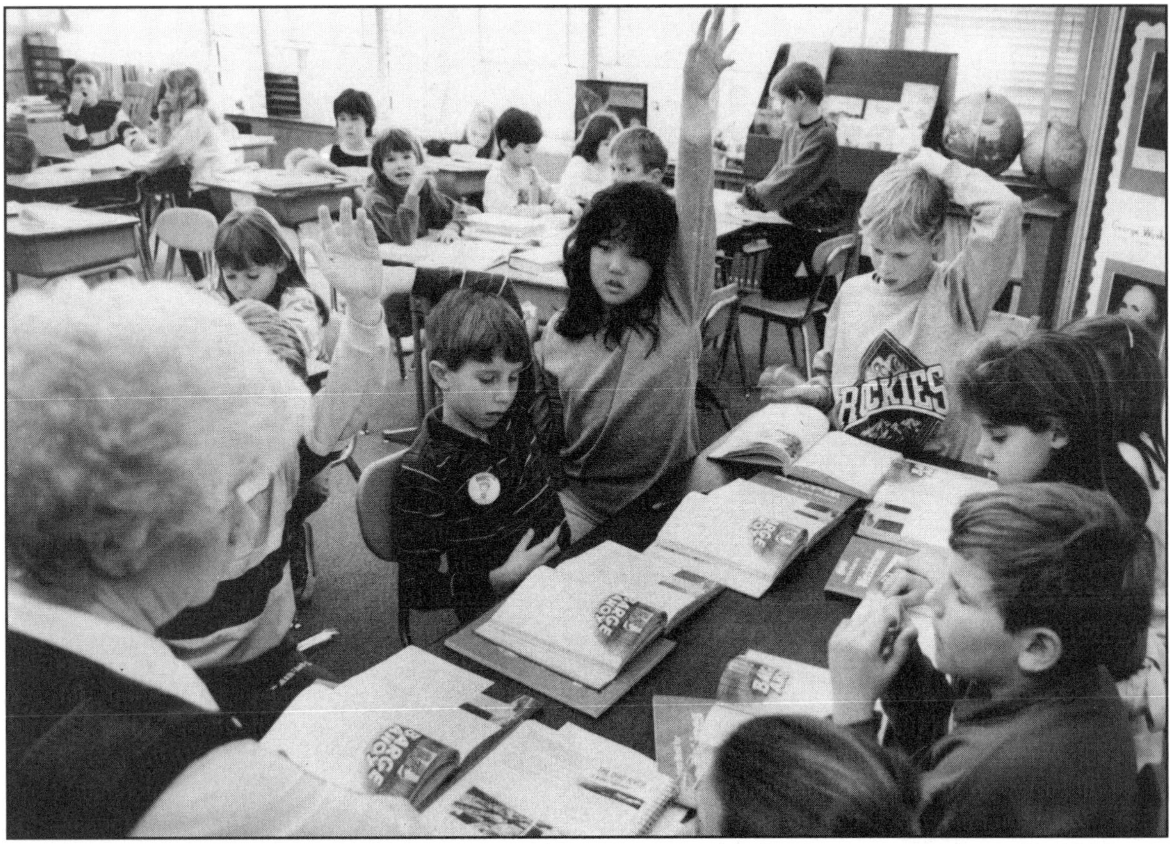

Asian American children are sometimes seen as more achievement-oriented in the classroom, according to Model Minority proponents. (Jim Whitmer)

old Shanghai-born president of a marketing company, who says that in "Asian culture there is no concept of mom taking care of everything" and who proudly announces that she had no qualms about relying upon "nannies" to care for her three sons. Her attitude meets the corporate demand that executives not be too involved with their families and probably stems from her upper-class background, but the author presumes that it is a cultural trait shared by all individuals of Asian descent.

Criticisms. Critics of the Model Minority thesis acknowledge that some segments of the Asian American population have been upwardly mobile but argue that the success of Asian Americans has been deliberately inflated to serve conservative ideological and political interests. Critics argue that proponents of the thesis have an interest in adhering to a vision of the United States as an egalitarian society despite evidence to the contrary. In this sense the Model Minority is central to a much larger debate over the nature of racial inequality and to what extent the government is responsible for intervening and eradicating it.

Critics argue that the statistics used as evidence of Asian American success are misleading. They maintain that the use of aggregate Asian American statistics for a group comprising more than twenty different subgroups masks important differences that can be seen with disaggregated data. For example, in California in 1980 the median income for Vietnamese American men who worked full time was $13,671, and $9,803 for Vietnamese American women. This compares to $20,408 for white men, $12,015 for white women, $15,236 for African American men, and $11,565 or African American women.

Critics also charge that comparing median family income of Asian Americans and white Americans is deceptive since Asian American families tend to be larger and have more working members than white families. Individual income presents a different picture. In 1990 the per capita income of Asian Pacific Americans was $13,420, lower than the $15,270 average for whites. Moreover, the Asian American population is largely urban and concentrated in areas where the cost of living is highest, and where wages and

Asian American children are often stereotyped as "whiz kids," which may not always be the case. (Jim Whitmer)

salaries are adjusted upward, while the white population is more equally distributed between urban and rural and across high and low cost-of-living areas. Even so, when comparing individuals with four years of college in 1990, Asian Pacific Americans earned $34,469 annually, compared to $36,134 for whites. These statistics lead critics to argue that higher family incomes among Asian Americans are more a reflection of unique family, geographic, and residential characteristics than an indication that Asian Americans have entered the most privileged positions in society.

Critics maintain that the continued use of the Model Minority thesis seems to be aimed more at denigrating other groups than praising Asian Americans. Some note that Model Minority articles, with their inclusion of Asian American women, challenge the very underpinnings of the feminist movement and its call to end gender discrimination.

Proponents Respond to Critics. Proponents have responded to critics by conceding that not all Asian Americans have been uniformly successful and then focusing on the success that some Asian groups, namely Japanese Americans, have attained. As Louis Winnick writes in *Commentary* (August, 1990), "It would be foolish and irresponsible to slight the profusion of Asian unsuccesses amid the profusion of successes." The usual descriptions of success follow his disclaimer, including income figures for the various Asian American groups that are higher than the "median family income of their host." Statistics indicating how far below the national average groups such as Vietnamese, Laotians, and Cambodians fall are noticeably absent. No statistics are included to document the "unsuccesses" among Asian Americans.

In "Mything the Point," published in *Reason* (October, 1992), author Thomas W. Hazlett, professor of economics and public policy at the University of California, Davis, responds sarcastically to a front-page article published in *The Washington Post* the previous June entitled, "Myth of Model Minority Haunts Asian Americans: Stereotype Eclipses Group's Problems." He writes, "Have you ever marveled at those successful members of disadvantaged minority groups, those who have somehow surmounted large odds to make it big in America? Aha, you disgusting bigot! . . . Why, you must harbor the soul of a Nazi." He hopes that

African Americans do not become "wealthy like the Asians" because that could "tragically" lead to what he calls the "myth of black success." By the end of the piece he decides that the possibility of "black success" becoming a reality is minimal because "of our current array of social programs and our time-tested system of welfare dependency."

Effects. When used uncritically to renew the belief that "you can make it if you try," the Model Minority potentially affects members of all racial groups. It gives highly educated and well-paid Asian Americans license to look down on the less affluent if the former believe that the latter have simply not worked hard enough. Less successful Asian Americans may blame themselves for their lack of success, even in the face of benign neglect, or may blame severe racial or language discrimination. Asian Americans on the whole may be held up to a higher standard in the classroom and the workplace. African Americans and other racial minority groups, recognizing that they have been unjustifiably measured against Asian Americans, may come to resent all Asian Americans. The same holds true for whites.

From an organizational perspective the existence of the Model Minority limits the extent to which multiracial coalitions can be formed. One political purpose of the Model Minority is an attempt to splinter the unified movement that is developing among racial minority groups, perhaps best illustrated in the 1960's student movement to establish ethnic studies and Jesse Jackson's Rainbow Coalition of the 1980's. The Model Minority continues to drive a wedge between groups who, despite differences, may benefit from combined efforts to combat racial discrimination.

Belief in the Model Minority also contributes to increasing bigotry and violence against Asian Americans. In 1982 Vincent CHIN was beaten to death with a baseball bat in Detroit by two white men whose livelihoods had been adversely affected by the decline in the domestic automobile industry—a decline the industry blames on Japan. When the Model Minority coexists with Japan-bashing, the distinction between a trade-war enemy abroad and the Asian American "whiz kid" becomes blurred in the popular American mind.—*Colleen Fong*

SUGGESTED READINGS:

• Chan, Sucheng. *Asian Americans: An Interpretive History*. Boston: Twayne, 1991. Chapter 9 criticizes the Model Minority from at least seven different vantage points. The rest of the book provides a concise and highly factual overview of Asian American history. A chronology of Asian American history, maps, and archival photographs add to a thorough treatment of the subject.

• Daniels, Roger. *Asian Americans: Chinese and Japanese in the United States Since 1850*. Seattle: University of Washington Press, 1988. The epilogue contains a critique of the Model Minority. Daniels excerpts William Petersen's original article and calls it the "most influential single article ever written about an Asian American group."

• Glazer, Nathan. *Affirmative Discrimination: Ethnic Inequality and Public Policy*. New York: Basic Books, 1975. An early conservative reaction to the government programs that came out of the 1960's, written by an academic. Glazer questions the "justice and wisdom" inherent in the shift from protecting what he calls "individual rights" to "group rights" in an attempt to combat racial discrimination.

• Kim, Kwang Chung, and Won Moo Hurh. "Korean Americans and the 'Success' Image: A Critique." *Amerasia Journal* 10 (October 2, 1983): 3-21. A critique of the success image based on 281 male and 334 female Korean immigrant adults living in Los Angeles that yields mixed conclusions as to the extent to which Korean Americans fit the Model Minority. The bibliography contains pertinent sources from both sides of the debate.

• Omi, Michael, and Howard Winant. *Racial Formation in the United States: From the 1960s to the 1980s*. New York: Routledge & Kegan Paul, 1986. While this source does not specifically address the Model Minority, it provides the ideological and political context of the period in which it was first introduced and the following decades in which it proliferated.

• Petersen, William. "Success Story: Japanese American Style." *The New York Times Magazine* (January 6, 1966). The term "Model Minority" was used for the first time in this article. It set the tone and format for subsequent articles and the development of the Model Minority thesis.

• Rose, Peter I. "Asian Americans: From Pariahs to Paragons." In *Clamor at the Gates: The New American Immigration*, edited by Nathan Glazer. San Francisco: Institute for Contemporary Studies Press, 1985. An example of how the Model Minority thesis can be used by an academic. The author, a sociologist and proponent of the Model Minority thesis, clearly differentiates between Asian Americans who follow "meritocratic principles" and African Americans and Latinos who capitalize on "inherited 'disadvantages.'"

• Takaki, Ronald. *Strangers from a Different Shore:*

A History of Asian Americans. Boston: Little, Brown, 1989. Chapter 12 contains a section, "The Myth of the 'Model Minority,' " that specifically critiques the stereotype. Other chapters provide a personal look at the various Asian groups living in the United States through the use of interview excerpts.

• U.S. Commission on Civil Rights. *Civil Rights Issues Facing Asian Americans in the 1990s*. Washington, D.C.: 1992. This Commission report refers to the Model Minority thesis as the "most damaging" of all Asian American stereotypes and recommends the media make every attempt to provide more balanced coverage. Chapters 2 and 8 discuss how the Model Minority thesis contributes to increasing bigotry and violence against Asian Americans and documents incidents in the 1980's.

• Young, Philip K. Y. "Family Labor, Sacrifice and Competition: Korean Greengrocers in New York City." *Amerasia Journal* 10 (October 2, 1983): 53-71. An examination of one of a number of small businesses Korean immigrants appear to have a "remarkable propensity" to engage in. Rather than finding that these immigrants went into small businesses because of an entrepreneurial spirit, this author found that they did so because they had few other options.

Modified Hepburn romanization: System of Japanese-language romanization, and the one most commonly employed (outside Japan, it is used almost exclusively). It was formulated around 1885 or thereafter by a group of interested Japanese and foreigners as a new and improved system that would replace the traditional writing system incorporating *kanji* and *kana*. Subsequently, James Curtis Hepburn, an American missionary and physician and an adviser to the group, adopted the new form for use by the Japanese-English dictionary that he published. As a result, the system is named after him despite the collaborative way in which it was produced. In Japan, modified Hepburn romanization is known as the "Hyojun" (or Standard) system.

Mody, Navrose. *See* **Anti-Asian violence**

Mohanty, Chandra Talpade (b. Jan. 22, 1955, Bombay, Republic of India): Professor. She holds degrees in English from the University of Delhi and a doctorate in education from the University of Illinois, Urbana-Champaign. She teaches feminist and international studies at Hamilton College and is coeditor of *Third World Women and the Politics of Feminism* (1991).

Mon-Khmer languages: Family of languages spoken mostly in mainland Southeast Asia, especially Cambodia, Vietnam, and parts of Thailand, Laos, and Myanmar. A few Mon-Khmer languages are also spoken in parts of Malaysia, as well as eastern India. There may be as many as one hundred different extant Mon-Khmer languages (not counting the problematic Vietnamese languages), including numerous dialects, spoken by twelve million to fifteen million people.

The Mon-Khmer languages are usually grouped together with the Munda languages of India to form a larger family called "Austro-Asiatic" (just as the European languages are generally collected into an "Indo-European" family). In terms of taxonomy, then, the term "Mon-Khmer" corresponds to levels such as the Romance languages (for example, Italian, Spanish, Portuguese) or Germanic languages (for example, English, Dutch, German) in Europe. Within Mon-Khmer, there are also numerous subdivisions.

The Mon-Khmer language family is named for two important and historically influential languages in western Southeast Asia. Khmer (or Cambodian) is the national language of Cambodia, and Mon is spoken in Myanmar. Eight million people speak Khmer as a first language, while more than half a million Burmese and Thais speak Mon (though most are also probably bilingual in their national languages). The Khmer Empire dominated the region for more than 350 years, leaving spectacular archaeological ruins, such as the old capital at Angkor Thom and various beautiful temples. The Mon states were among some of the oldest in Southeast Asia, extending from Rangoon to Cambodia. By 1757, however, the Burmese peoples had conquered the Mon, incorporating them into the Burmese union.

The major Mon-Khmer languages have writing systems, but many smaller ones still do not. The oldest Mon inscriptions go back to the seventh or eight centuries C.E. The Mon people borrowed a script from southern India a millennium ago and subsequently gave writing to several other Southeast Asian cultures. The Mon script, for example, was borrowed in its essentials by the Burmese. As in India and most other parts of Southeast Asia, the orthographies of the Mon-Khmer languages are in syllabaries rather than in alphabets; in other words, a single symbol represents the sound of both a consonant and a vowel (such as "ko" or "ta") rather than a single sound, as in a letter of an alphabet.

Most Mon-Khmer languages follow a subject-verb-object word order similar to English. The Mon-Khmer

Khmer script appears on the storefront of this Cambodian market in Long Beach, California. (Eric Crystal)

system of vowels, however, is much more complex (with Bru, for example, having more than forty vowels). Also typical is the use of special voice qualities to distinguish between sounds (as in a "breathy" vowel being different from one spoken in a more normal manner). In terms of word structure, suffixes (and to a certain degree, prefixes as well) are rare, but infixes are common; in other words, root words do not often have special endings attached, but these prefixes or suffixes are instead inserted into the middle of the word stem.

The place of Vietnamese as a Mon-Khmer language is complex and controversial. Phonologically, Vietnamese is a monosyllabic tonal language, where the pitch of a syllable (whether said with a rising or falling intonation, for example) makes a difference in the meaning of a word. Most Mon-Khmer languages, however, have words composed of many syllables, and many are toneless. Still, many scholars classify Vietnamese as a Mon-Khmer language because of its morphology and other structural similarities to the Mon-Khmer family. If the Vietnamese languages are included, the number of speakers of Mon-Khmer languages rises to more than sixty-five million.

Moncado, Hilario Camino (Hilarion Caminos Moncada; Nov. 3, 1895, Balamban, Philippines—Apr. 9, 1956, Aguascalientes, Mexico): Social and political activist and messianic leader. Moncado founded the FILIPINO FEDERATION OF AMERICA in Los Angeles in 1925 and served as its first president. Created to improve relations between Filipino Americans and the larger American society, the federation encouraged Filipinos to honor the U.S. constitution and flag and to adopt Christian practices; it evolved to become a quasi-religious organization centered on faith in Moncado's divinity.

Born into a peasant family on the island of Cebu (federation members regard his date of birth as November 4, 1898), Moncado left for Hawaii in 1914 as a recruited laborer (*sakada*) for the Hawaiian Sugar Planters' Association (HSPA). A year later he sailed for San Francisco. He legally changed his name to its present form and moved to Los Angeles around 1920.

The Filipino Federation of America, founded by Hilario Moncado in 1925 to foster good relations between Filipino Americans and the larger American society, evolved into a quasi-religious organization centered on faith in Moncado's divinity. (Filipino American National Historical Society Collection)

Before forming the federation, Moncado had been part of a growing number of self-supported students in Los Angeles who were seeking places of leadership in the Filipino American community. In 1926 he spearheaded a successful Rizal Day celebration in the city to honor Jose Protasio Rizal y Mercado, the Philippine national hero. Now observed annually by Filipino communities the world over, this event launched Moncado's career and boosted the federation's reputation.

Moncado earned a law degree from Southwestern University in 1928, testified before the U.S. Congress in support of Philippine independence, and traveled around the world in 1930. Starting in 1932 he began visiting the Philippines regularly following his decision to enter Philippine politics. In 1938 he married Diana Toy, a well-known Filipino entertainer, to enhance his popularity as a politician. Moncado ran unsuccessfully in 1946 for election as the first president of the newly independent Republic of the Philippines against fellow politicians Manuel Roxas y Acuna and Sergio Osmena. It was to be Moncado's last attempt to run for public office. He and his wife left the islands in 1948 and lived in Los Angeles until 1954, when they chose to leave the United States voluntarily rather than face threatened deportation.

Moncado's success as a leader stemmed from his charismatic personality and his unorthodox methods, which were thought by his followers to be a reflection of his "supernatural" qualities. With the endorsement of Lorenzo de los Reyes, the federation's spiritual teacher, federation members entertained a messianic belief that Moncado was the successor to Jose Rizal as the reincarnation of Jesus Christ. Others, however, admonished Moncado publicly, condemning him of "fakery," ridiculing his "bizarre" organization, and accusing him of personal aggrandizement and of "fooling" his "illiterate" followers.

Montagnards: Indigenous linguistic and ethnic minority living, for the most part, in the mountainous regions of what was previously South Vietnam. Their traditional homelands have been in the Central Highlands, running just southwest of the old demilitarized zone (DMZ)—the dividing line between North and South Vietnam—to the plains just northeast of Saigon. During the Vietnam War in the 1960's and 1970's, this area took on strategic significance as the Viet Cong escalated operations and the North Vietnamese regular army infiltrated the south. Montagnard involvement with the Central Intelligence Agency (CIA) and the U.S. Army, especially with the Green Beret Special forces, which conducted guerrilla warfare and pacification campaigns in the area, brought these relatively isolated villagers into a modern political armed conflict not of their making. Still, many Montagnards fought loyally with their American allies. After the war, the Montagnards became one of the groups that emigrated to North America along with other Southeast Asian refugees.

Terminology. When the French occupied Indochina in the nineteenth and twentieth centuries, they used the term "Montagnard" (meaning "highlander," or "mountaineer") to refer to these non-Vietnamese-speaking peoples living in the central hills and plateaus of southern Vietnam and eastern Cambodia. This was thought to be somewhat less pejorative than the Vietnamese name *moi* or the Khmer *phnong* (both meaning "savage"). The term "Montagnard" continued to be used by Western journalists and government officials to refer to any of these highland peoples who are ethnically and linguistically distinct from lowland Vietnamese. Most highlanders, however, object to the colonial Montagnard label. Instead, they prefer to be called by the name of their own ethnic groups, the name of their village or region, their particular language's generic label for all upland people, or some local word, such as *dega* (first people). In the late twentieth century, the

Jarai phrase *ana chu* (sons of the mountains) was used by many highland people to refer to themselves.

Populations and Ethnic Affiliations. The Montagnards are by no means a single unified people. More than two dozen different language and ethnic groups coexist in an area that fills about half of Vietnam (or about the size of the state of Washington). The highland peoples speak languages from two vastly different linguistic families. About a third of the Montagnards occupy the vast central Darlac Plateau from the cities of Pleiku in the north, to south of the city of Da Lat. They speak Austronesian languages, making them linguistically related to Malays, Indonesians, and Filipinos. These Austronesian speakers form a wedge between two groups from another major language family. To both the north (on the Kontum Plateau) and the south (on the Mnong and Di Linh plateaus) are two groups of highlanders who speak Mon-Khmer languages, making them related to the Khmer-speaking Cambodians. This split seems to imply that the Austronesian-speaking central Montagnards probably arrived in the area after the Mon-Khmer speakers did.

Each Montagnard group may have different customs, lifestyles, kinship systems, and marriage patterns. Most highlanders, however, live in villages (though some highlanders are migratory, leaving a place after several years) and share many cultural practices. These include techniques of swidden rice cultivation, housing styles, hunting patterns, tool and pottery use and construction, and certain animistic religious beliefs. Exact figures on the number of Montagnards are difficult to determine, but estimates run anywhere from eight hundred thousand to more than one million.

Highland Cultural Identity. The problems of the Montagnards—and their difficulties regarding resettlement in the United States—cannot be properly understood without looking at the history of the highland area and the nationalist movement that grew there out of the various Indochina wars. Unlike their lowland Vietnamese and Cambodian neighbors, the Montagnards remained largely unaffected by Chinese and Indian influence. Until the twentieth century, for example, there were no urban areas in the highlands, and the

A Montagnard basket maker in Lam Dong Province. (Eric Crystal)

highlanders had no writing system (except for some Chru who borrowed the Cham script.)

Several scholars believe, therefore, that in spite of linguistic and cultural differences, the highlanders, beginning in the late nineteenth century, have gradually been developing a common ethnic identity. The people, however, who are in political and military control—first the French, and later the Vietnamese—were either unaware of these sentiments or chose to ignore them. Regional nationalist passions developed within an elite cluster of leaders from various groups who tended to intermarry. In 1964, about a year after the overthrow of the Diem government in South Vietnam, several Cambodian and highland nationalist groups began armed resistance under a movement usually known as FULRO (an acronym for the French Front Unifié pour la Lutte des Races Opprimées, or Unified Front for the Struggle of Oppressed Races). Part of their agenda was driving the "expansionist Vietnamese" from their territory and declaring an independent state. Highlanders felt almost equal hostility toward both the South and the North Vietnamese governments.

The French, for the most part, had left the Montagnards alone and had prevented some lowland Vietnamese incursion into Montagnard areas. Many highlanders, then, trusted the Americans when the latter came looking for local support to build a buffer zone in the central mountains and plateaus against the Viet Cong and the People's Liberation Army. Some highland leaders believed that Americans might ultimately help them gain their independence. About forty-five thousand Montagnard irregulars fought alongside American Green Berets. The highlanders developed a reputation among the American military as being some of the most loyal and fiercest fighters in Southeast Asia (as depicted, for example, in Francis Ford Coppola's 1979 film *Apocalypse Now*).

The Vietnam War and Resettlement in America. By the time the Vietnam War ended in the mid-1970's, as many as two hundred thousand highlanders had died, and perhaps as many as 85 percent of the villagers became refugees. The Communist government did not grant the highlanders autonomy but instead brought lowland Vietnamese into the area for economic development. Many FULRO guerrillas continued to fight. Some believed that the Americans would return or at least send military or humanitarian aid. In October, 1992, however, the last FULRO soldiers surrendered to the United Nations (UN) after running out of ammunition and personnel, ending a twenty-eight-year struggle against Hanoi. Under an international agreement, these highlanders were given sanctuary in the United States.

It is difficult to estimate the number of Montagnards living in the United States. Because of their cultural and linguistic diversity, they are sometimes lumped together with other Southeast Asian refugees or are confused with the Hmong or Khmer. Their geographic isolation also prevented many of them from leaving Vietnam. At least several thousand highlanders, however, have come to the United States, many resettling in the North Carolina cities of Greensboro, Raleigh, and Charlotte, near the home base of the U.S. Army Special Forces.

The problem of resettling the Montagnards is a microcosm of the Southeast Asian refugee predicament in general; American guilt and economic pragmatics often collide. The highlanders are fortunate in having many Americans of the armed forces ready to assist them. A warm welcome, however, hardly takes the place of the home and family left behind, nor does it eliminate the linguistic and economic struggles these refugees will face in a new, and totally different, society. Even among the highlanders themselves, there may be great differences in language and culture, and their relationship with other Vietnamese, Lao, and Cambodian refugees is ambiguous. As most observers have noted, however, the highland peoples are extremely resilient and have weathered similar hardships in the past; it is likely that they will survive their new trials as well.—*James Stanlaw*

SUGGESTED READINGS: • Condominas, Georges. *We Have Eaten the Forest: The Story of a Montagnard Village in the Central Highlands of Vietnam.* New York: Hill & Wang, 1977. • Haines, David, ed. *Refugees As Immigrants: Cambodians, Laotians, and Vietnamese in America.* Totowa, N.J.: Rowman & Littlefield, 1989. • Hickey, Gerald. *Sons of the Mountains: Ethnohistory of the Vietnamese Central Highlands to 1954.* New Haven, Conn.: Yale University Press, 1982. • Hickey, Gerald. *Free in the Forest: Ethnohistory of the Vietnamese Central Highlands, 1954-1976.* New Haven, Conn.: Yale University Press, 1982. • Mole, Robert. *The Montagnards of South Vietnam: A Study of Nine Tribes.* Rutland, Vt.: Charles E. Tuttle, 1970. • Stanton, Shelby. *Green Berets at War: U.S. Army Special Forces in Southeast Asia, 1956-1975.* Novato, Calif.: Presidio Press, 1985.

Monterey Park: City in Los Angeles County, California, site of the first suburban Chinatown. Originally called Ramona Acres, Monterey Park was incorpo-

CALIFORNIA

rated in 1916. The city's main thoroughfare, a park, and a school district were named after Richard Garvey, a U.S. Army mail carrier and miner who settled in the area at the beginning of the twentieth century. It is a well-defined community just east of downtown Los Angeles and Chinatown.

In the 1970's, increasingly anxious over future relationships with the People's Republic of China, many people in Hong Kong and Taiwan began looking to the West for resettlement. The established Chinatowns in the United States did not have the residential property to accommodate this wave of émigrés from Hong Kong and Taiwan, most of whom were affluent and well educated. Monterey Park, however, met their needs. The first trickle began in the mid-1970's. The immigrants liked the community, found housing reasonable, and began to open their own businesses. The word was passed to relatives, friends, and business associates, leading to a significant Chinese influx throughout the 1980's. From a bedroom community with vacant commercial properties and a good view of downtown Los Angeles, Monterey Park was transformed into a second Chinatown. New businesses replaced established ones, with Chinese owners catering to the recent arrivals. City blocks were turned over entirely, and Cantonese and Mandarin were regularly heard on the city's streets.

The 1990 census put the total population at about sixty-thousand, with Asians as the new majority. Asians made up 57 percent of the count, with Hispanics at 31 percent and Anglo-Americans at 11.8 percent.

Monterey Park's change of identity led to racial tensions and political strife during the 1980's. Controversies centered on an attempt to make English the official language and the need to have Chinese-languages books in the local library. Other issues included architectural building codes, congestion laws, and moratoriums on new construction. Many residents, upset over the Asian influx and resultant change, moved to other cities. Judy Chu, a Chinese, served as mayor in 1990.

Monterey Park has become the model suburban Chinatown. Its importance will increase as it becomes the cultural, social, and servicing site for the growing number of Chinese and other Asians in the Los Angeles area.

Moon, Henry (Sept. 28, 1914, San Francisco, Calif.—Aug. 2, 1974, San Francisco, Calif.): Medical researcher. Born to early Korean immigrants, he received his B.A. and M.A. degrees in anatomy from the University of California, Berkeley. He graduated from the University of California School of Medicine in San Francisco in 1940, later joined its faculty, then became chair of its Department of Pathology in 1956. He was part of the team that first isolated the adrenocorticotropic hormone (ACTH) and gained fame for his groundbreaking research on arteriosclerosis.

Moon, Sun Myung (Yong Myung Moon; Jan. 6, 1920, Kwangju Sangsa Ri, Pyungan Bukedo Province, Korea): Founder and spiritual leader of the Unification Church. He was the fifth of eight children of a modest peasant family. In 1930 his family converted to Christianity.

Early Years. The young Moon early gave evidence of a profound concern with religion. When he was sixteen years old, he reportedly had a religious experience that convinced him that he had been chosen for special Christian responsibilities. After the completion of his elementary education, Moon undertook the study of electrical engineering at Waseda University in Japan. Throughout this period of study (during the Japanese occupation of Korea), Moon continued his preoccupation with Christianity, in the syncretic form common among Asian converts.

When Korea was liberated from the Japanese at the conclusion of World War II, Moon founded a Pentecostal ministry in Pyongyang. In those early years, he was undistinguished except for the hostility that he generated among the more orthodox Christians and the Communist authorities. He suffered grievously at the hands of his Communist captors and languished in prison until his liberation by the United Nations (UN) forces during the opening phases of the Korean War.

After his liberation, Moon fled to the south and for a time survived as a laborer in the harbor city of Pusan. It was during this period that he fully committed himself to a religious calling. In time, he emerged as a religious leader of uncommon ability, capable of inspiring selfless devotion among an increasing number of followers. On May 1, 1954, Moon founded the Holy Spirit Association for the Unification of World Christianity, Unification Church (Tongilgyo).

Causes. Moon's new church was born out of the apocalyptic chaos that followed World War II. The collapse of the Korean economy, the resultant unemployment and grinding poverty, the erosion of traditional values, the loss of leadership, the massive transfer of populations, and the frightening presence of hundreds of thousands of armed men made the Korean peninsula a natural breeding ground for utopian, mass-mobilizing movements.

In a situation of real and relative deprivation, Korea became the arena for vast political and social movements, including an aggressive Soviet-supported Communism in the north, as well as a host of messianic "new religions" (*shinhung jonggyo*). As an example, Tae Sun Park founded the Olive Tree Movement in the south, a religious cult with traits shared by other new religions in Korea. Members of the new religions lived in communes, engaged in commercial and industrial undertakings, and were dedicated to an ethic of sacrifice and devotion. All these traits characterized the Unification Church as well and would later become matters of controversy for the church.

Doctrines. In August, 1957, the *Divine Principle* (first published in English in 1973) was officially published as a guide to "Unificationist Thought." The *Principle* contains the doctrinal beliefs that define the faith of the Unification Church and is composed of a series of interpretive sermons on Christian theology and eschatology given by Moon over the years.

According to Moon, "God's plan" was deflected from its purpose by Satan's seduction of Eve and the subsequent corruption of Adam. In this manner, what God had intended to be the Perfect Family, the vehicle of human fulfillment, became compromised. Only through redemptive action and sacrifice can God's plan once again shape humanity's destiny. In particular, "central persons" are required to "indemnify" the human race so that God's purposes can be achieved. Moon is believed to be the "central person" in the present time.

Moon teaches that human redemption could only be achieved through the perfection of family life. That redemption would supplement the spiritual salvation that was achieved by the sacrifice of Jesus of Nazareth. The Unification Church serves as a spiritual family for its members. Moon is the "Father" of this redemptive Ideal Family, with the members of the church serving as his "children" through the assumption of "filial" responsibilities of hard work, obedience, and dedication.

According to Moon, in the contemporary world the salvific family finds itself opposed by forces that he identifies with God's enemies. Those enemies are organized among the ranks of the Communist movement. Marxism's traditional atheism, its theoretical objection to the monogamous family, and its support for abortion on demand make it the antithesis of Moon's doctrines. As a consequence, Moon believes that the completion of God's plan requires the abject defeat of the Antichrist of world Communism.

Toward that objective, the Unification Church devoted considerable intellectual and material resources to its anti-Communist crusade. In this manner, an overt political program was added to the church's religious convictions. For some time, the church's crusade was concentrated in the United States, where it lent material support to anti-Communist causes and groups. As the leader of the Free World, the United States was regarded by Moon to be the principal staging area for the ultimate struggle against Communism.

Moon's Personal Life. In 1955 Moon divorced his first wife, purportedly because she did not understand his religious mission. In 1960 he married his second wife, Hak Ja Han, with whom he would rear thirteen children.

In the early 1970's, Moon became deeply involved in the domestic politics of the United States. By that time, the Unification Church was reported to have about 30,000 converts in 120 local branches across America. The rapid growth of the Unification Church, coupled with unconventional practices such as mass weddings, prompted critics to conclude that many young adherents were victims of brainwashing—an allegation that Moon denied.

In 1973, Moon marshaled the resources of the church to defend then President Richard M. Nixon against the charges stemming from the Watergate scan-

Arraigned in 1981 for cheating on his personal income taxes, the Reverend Sun Myung Moon gestures acknowledgment to thousands of supporters. (AP/Wide World Photos)

dal. At almost the same time, the U.S. government, together with various state governments, commenced a series of investigations into the activities of the Unification Church. From 1976 through 1979, hearings on the church's activities were conducted by Senator Robert Dole, by the House Subcommittee on International Organizations, as well as in Ohio, Alabama, Connecticut, Massachusetts, and New York—all of which culminated in federal charges of tax evasion on the part of Moon. Moon was charged with failing to

The Reverend Sun Myung Moon, founder and spiritual leader of the Unification Church. (AP/Wide World Photos)

report the receipt of funds from overseas sources and for failing to pay taxes on a relatively small sum that was used for personal rather than church purposes. Moon was found guilty and was incarcerated from July 20, 1984, to August 20, 1985. Some commentators suggested that the government's case against Moon was merely a pretext for religious and political persecution.

After his release from federal prison, Moon decreased his personal activities in the United States, and church membership declined. The death of one of his sons in an automobile accident deeply affected Moon; thereafter, his special affection for the United States seem to have been displaced by an increasing involvement in Eastern Europe and the People's Republic of China. The collapse of international Communism allowed Moon to initiate a major program of proselytization and recruitment in the former Soviet Union.

Church Membership and Activities. In the early 1970's, after the church had become well established in South Korea, Moon charged his followers with missionary obligations. Japan and the United States became principal targets. By 1975, the Unification Church claimed a "presence" in 120 countries with a membership of 3 million. Through the early 1990's, the church's worldwide membership is reported to be about 1 million. Aside from its religious activities, the church is also a successful international institution engaged in about 150 enterprises, including publishing firms, pharmaceutical production, fisheries, the marketing of ginseng tea, and the manufacturing of arms.

The recruitment and funding successes of the church in Japan and the United States are probably a function of Moon's anti-Communism as well as his emphasis on the salvific role of the family. His message was particularly appealing to American youth who felt alienated from an increasingly materialistic and individualistic society. In Africa and Latin America, although the church is continuing its missionary efforts, it has apparently been less successful.

Like many new churches in the past, the Unification Church has evolved from a small, informal, loosely structured, spontaneously organized cult of believers into a thriving international institution. Unlike other more established religions, such as the Mormon and the Christian Science churches, the Unification Church has not yet proven its durability. Whether it will join the ranks of the established faiths will depend on whether it survives the passing of its charismatic founder.—*Maria Hsia Chang*

SUGGESTED READINGS: • Chryssides, George D. *The Advent of Sun Myung Moon: The Origins, Beliefs, and Practices of the Unification Church*. New York: St. Martin's Press, 1991. • Edwards, Cliff. "Sun Myung Moon and the Scholars." *Dialog: A Journal of Theology* 21 (Winter, 1982): 56-59. • Fichter, Joseph H. *The Holy Family of Father Moon*. Kansas City, Mo.: Leaven Press, 1985. • Moon, Sun Myung. *A Prophet Speaks Today*. New York: HSA Publications, 1975. • Sontag, Frederick. *Sun Myung Moon and the Unification Church*. Nashville: Abingdon Press, 1977.

Moon cakes: Small, round cakes stuffed with delicacies such as sweetened soybean paste, salted duck egg yolks, and shelled melon seeds. The cakes are served especially during the Moon Festival, also known as the "Mid-Autumn Festival," a Chinese tradition.

Moon Festival: The second most important Chinese festival, falling on the fifteenth day of the eighth lunar month. A large percentage of China is agricultural; therefore the Moon Festival touches a great number of people. Even nonagricultural families observe this happy and important occasion. The celebration occurs at the end of the harvest season, when crops have been gathered and stored for future use or sold. Families

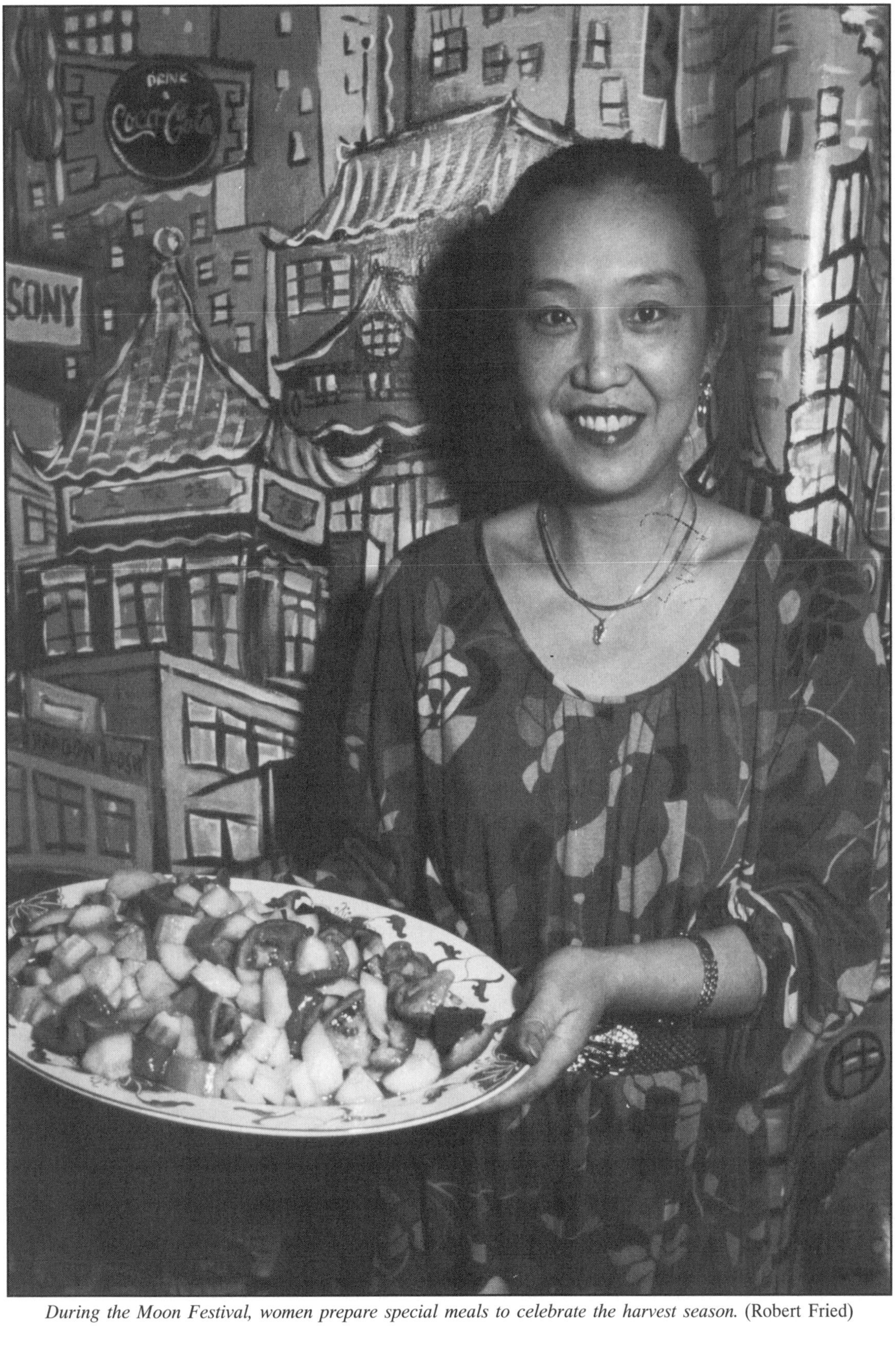

During the Moon Festival, women prepare special meals to celebrate the harvest season. (Robert Fried)

gather and have a fine dinner of specially prepared foods.

The Moon Festival has usually been considered a women's event because they have traditionally performed the rituals associated with it. The women will therefore prepare the special meal and set up the altar to give thanks for the blessings received. An old specialty was snails found on the farms and cooked with a special herb that had a delicate flavor. In modern times another popular dish is a thinly sliced raw fish salad with greens and a special dressing.

Another of the specialties of this occasion, which are mostly purchased in shops, are the moon cakes. These cakes are round in shape with embossed tops. They are filled with various fillings such as lotus paste, black sugar, and fruit and nuts. The center may have one or two salted duck egg yolks, representing a full moon.

The harvest Moon Festival has historically been associated with various legends and folk tales. It is said that when the weather is clear on the night of the festival, one can see the figure of a toad outlined against the surface of the Moon. The figure is Chang-O, wife of a famous legendary archer believed to have lived around 2500 B.C.E. He was given a special pill of immortality in return for some daring deeds he had performed, but he was to prepare himself before taking it. While he was away Chang-O noticed a glow in the house and found the pill. When her husband returned home she quickly hid the pill in her mouth. Frightened, she swallowed it and began to float up toward the sky, eventually landing on the Moon. Chang-O was changed into a three-legged toad, and when she spat out the pill, it turned into a white jade rabbit.

Moxibustion. *See* **Acupuncture and moxibustion**

Mori, Toshio (Mar. 20, 1910, Oakland, Calif.—Apr. 12, 1980, San Leandro, Calif.): Writer and historian. In the introduction to the first edition of Mori's *Yokohama, California* (1949), William Saroyan calls Mori "the first real Japanese-American writer." That accolade was echoed by Japanese American poet and critic Lawson Fusao INADA in the introduction to the book's 1985 edition.

Mori was a Nisei, a person born in America of parents who emigrated from Japan. He grew up in San Leandro, California, and lived all of his life in the East Bay Japanese American community.

Mori had only a high school education. His educational background, however, did not stop him from wanting to make his voice heard in what Inada called "the Occidental world of mainstream American literature." In order to achieve that goal, Mori educated himself by frequenting bookstores and libraries. His reading list was long and comprehensive. More important, he never stopped writing.

During World War II (1939-1945), Mori was interned at the Topaz relocation center in Utah. His experience in the camp was similar to and typical of what 120,000 Japanese Americans went through during the war. Physical confinement, however, did not shake Mori's determination to write about his own people and about what he knew best. He used the opportunity of serving as the camp historian to improve his writing skill.

Yokohama, California, a collection of some of Mori's best short stories, was first published in 1949. The narrative pace of Mori's stories included in the book is deliberate, the description vivid and colorful, and the tone humorous. Mori's thematic preoccupation with the sense of community and his interest in representing the Japanese American culture are two of the main reasons why Inada believes *Yokohama, California* is "the first real Japanese-American book."

Some of Mori's short stories are published and included in periodicals and anthologies, such as *Best American Short Stories of 1943*, *New Directions*, *Aiiieeeee! An Anthology of Asian-American Writers* (1974), *The Big Aiiieeeee! An Anthology of Chinese American and Japanese American Literature* (1991), and *Common Ground*. In 1979, Mori published another collection of short stories, *The Chauvinist and Other Stories*. He also published the novel *Woman from Hiroshima* (1979).

Morimura, Toyo (1854, Tokyo, Japan—1899): Merchant. A graduate of Keio Gijuku (later Keio University) who joined his brother in the family-run business, Morimura traveled to New York in 1876 to promote stronger trading ties with the United States. Along with visiting merchant Momotaro Sato, Morimura founded the Hinode Company in 1876. After his partner returned to Japan, Morimura reorganized the firm as Morimura Brothers and Company in 1879. The firm's business expanded rapidly after Morimura began to focus on importing ceramic and porcelain tableware and decorative goods from Japan to the United States; gross profits for this trade amounted to $100,000 by 1880.

Morita, Pat (b. 1932, Isleton, Calif.): Actor. The child of farm workers who opened a Chinese restaurant, Pat

Actor Pat Morita is familiar to millions for his many roles on television and in films. (Asian Week)

Morita suffered from spinal tuberculosis and was hospitalized much of the time until he reached the age of eleven. He eventually became a department head at Aerojet General Corporation, but he was dissatisfied with his work and left to become a nightclub comedian.

Beginning in the mid-1960's, Morita worked as a television and film actor, appearing in such films as *Thoroughly Modern Millie* (1967), *The Shakiest Gun in the West* (1968), *Midway* (1976), and *Savannah Smiles* (1983), among others. In 1984, Morita played the role of Miyagi in *The Karate Kid*, a popular and critical success that spawned two sequels. For his performance, Morita was nominated for an Academy Award for Best Supporting Actor. In 1987 and 1988, he played the title character in the television crime drama *Ohara*, his second chance at a leading role in a long-running television career. A regular in a number of situation comedies, he starred in the series *Mr. T and Tina* (1976), which lasted less than a full season. Morita has continued to work in films as well; in addition to the *Karate Kid* sequels, he had a starring role in *Captive Hearts* (1987).

Mu yu: Chinese term for young Chinese girls brought over to the United States to live with wealthier Chinese families as maids and nannies.

Mukherjee, Bharati (b. July, 27, 1940, Calcutta, West Bengal, India): Teacher and writer. Born into a prosperous Bengali Brahmin family, she received her early education at Loreto Convent School, Calcutta, and later attended Calcutta University, where she obtained a B.A. Degree in English (with honors) in 1959. In 1961, she received her M.A. degree from the University of Baroda and came to the United States that same year to attend the Writers' Workshop at the University of Iowa, where she obtained her M.F.A. degree in creative writing in 1963.

In 1963, Mukherjee married Clark Blaise, an American writer of Canadian descent. In 1966, she migrated with her husband to Canada, where she got a teaching position at McGill University. In 1969, she earned a Ph.D. degree in English and comparative literature from the University of Iowa. In 1972, she became a Canadian citizen.

During her stay in Canada, Mukherjee became painfully conscious of the country's hostility toward Indians and other Asian immigrants. She recorded her experience with racial prejudice in Canada in her essay "An Invisible Woman" (1981) and also expressed it

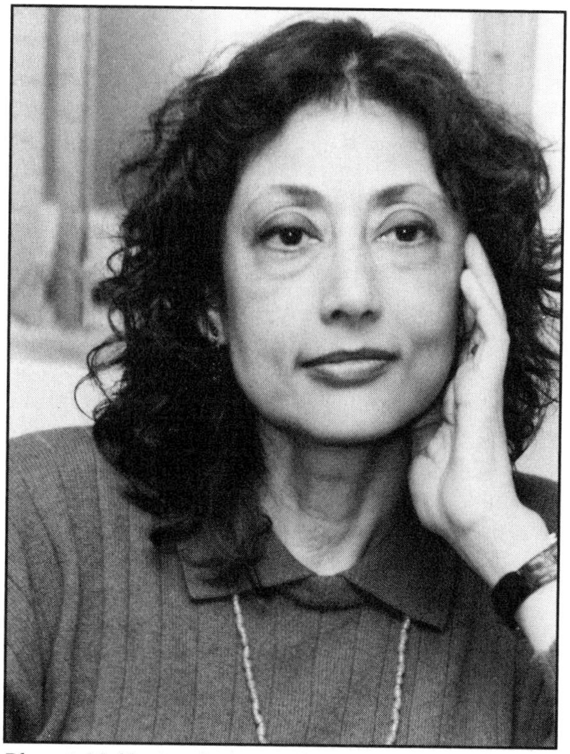

Bharati Mukherjee depicts in her fiction the problems of immigration, expatriation, and cultural identity faced by Third World immigrants in North America. (AP/Wide World Photos)

artistically in some of her short stories.

In 1980, Mukherjee moved to the United States to pursue her career as a teacher and writer and became a permanent U.S. resident. She has taught at several American universities and colleges, including the University of Iowa, Skidmore College, Columbia University, Queens College, and the University of California, Berkeley. A recipient of many grants and awards, she received the 1988 United States National Book Critics Circle Award for fiction.

Mukherjee is the author of several books: the novels *The Tiger's Daughter* (1971), *Wife* (1975), *Jasmine* (1989), and *The Holder of the World* (1994); the volumes of short stories *Darkness* (1985) and *The Middleman and Other Stories* (1988); and the nonfiction works (coauthored with Clark Blaise) *Days and Nights in Calcutta* (1977) and *The Sorrow and the Terror: The Haunting Legacy of the Air India Tragedy* (1987). Her work has received widespread critical acclaim.

Imbued with a diasporic consciousness, Mukherjee depicts in her fiction problems of immigration, expatriation, and cultural identity faced by South Asian and other Third World immigrants in North America and imparts a potent voice to their experiences of trauma and triumph.

Mun Lun School: One of the first two Chinese-language schools in Hawaii. Sponsored and managed by the Bow Wong Wui (Society to Protect the Emperor), the school began instruction on February 4, 1911, with only two instructors. It became the largest and best-equipped Chinese-language school in Hawaii. Its curriculum emphasized traditional Chinese cultural and classical education.

Munemori, Sadao (d. Apr. 5, 1945, near Seravezza, Italy): War hero. Munemori was the only Nisei ever awarded the Congressional Medal of Honor, the United States' highest military honor, and is one of only four Japanese Americans ever to receive the award. He served during World War II, with the all-Nisei 442ND REGIMENTAL COMBAT TEAM. On April 5, he threw himself atop a live German grenade, shielding two other U.S. servicemen but killing himself.

Mung, John. *See* **Nakahama Manjiro**

Munson Report (1941): Secret intelligence report discussing the loyalty of Japanese Americans and aliens to the United States, submitted as the latter was about to enter World War II (1939-1945). From October to November 1941, journalist and businessman Curtis B. Munson conducted an investigation of the Japanese community in Hawaii and the West Coast. Assigned to this project as part of a makeshift intelligence operation for President Franklin D. Roosevelt, Munson gathered data from intelligence officers and his own personal observations. His twenty-five-page report concluded that "there is no 'Japanese problem' on the Coast." Both in Hawaii and on the West Coast, Munson believed, the "big bulk" of Japanese Americans would be loyal to the United States. Munson's conclusion was not new and certainly not surprising—it simply corroborated ten years' worth of intelligence gathering conducted by various government agencies, including the Federal Bureau of Investigation (FBI) and the Office of Naval Intelligence (ONI).

Evidence suggests that the report was shared by the State, Navy, and War departments; yet paradoxically the leaders of all three departments were among the strongest advocates of "evacuation." All three agencies had a full three months to analyze thoroughly the contents of Munson's report yet chose to disregard his conclusions. Roosevelt himself was said to have examined at least a one-page synopsis of the report but commented only on Munson's concerns about unguarded strategic locations. This report, according to writer Michi Weglyn, "was to become one of the war's best kept secrets." Public knowledge of the Munson Report was not released until it was unveiled as evidence at the Pearl Harbor hearings in 1946. It was not until Weglyn's book *Years of Infamy* was released in 1976 that Munson's report became more widely known among Japanese American activists and academics.

Mura, David (b. June 18, 1952, Great Lakes, Ill.): Writer and critic. Mura is a Sansei, a third-generation Japanese American. He is one of the emergent writers in Asian American literature who have started a new literary movement to examine, reexamine, and reclaim Asian Americans' sense of history and identity.

Mura was born and grew up in the Midwest. He graduated from Grinnell College in Iowa and earned an M.F.A. degree from Vermont College. In college he demonstrated his interest in creative writing, especially in poetry. He has published poems and essays in a wide variety of magazines, journals, and anthologies.

Mura's critically acclaimed collection of poems *After We Lost Our Way* was published in 1989. In the book Mura uses powerful yet precise images to celebrate the indefatigability of the human spirit in the face

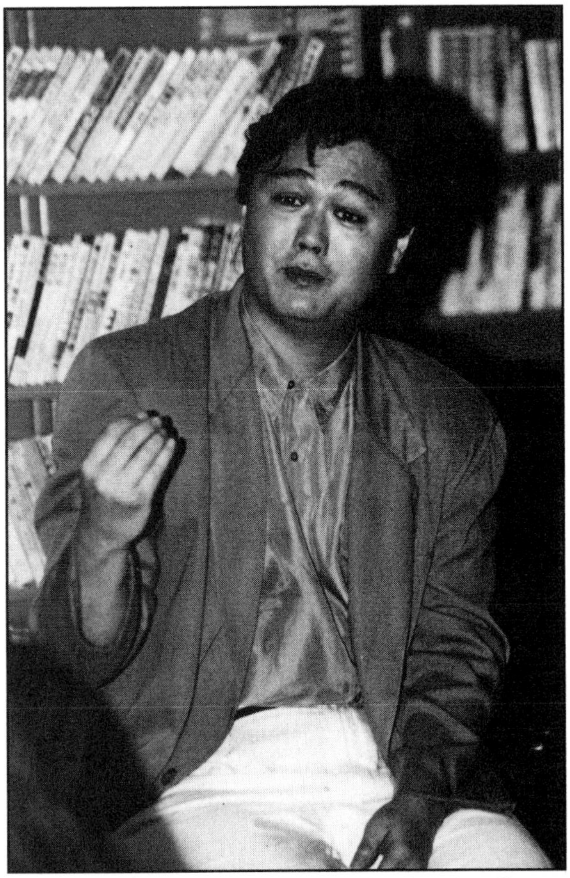

David Mura has helped start a new Asian American literary movement to reexamine and reclaim Asian American history and identity. (Asian Week)

of adversity and peril; the voice of agony and anger is intermingled with that of hope. *After We Lost Our Way* won the National Poetry Series Contest.

In 1984, with the support of the Creative Artist Exchange Fellowship offered by the National Endowment for the Arts (NEA) and the U.S./Japan Friendship Commission, Mura was able to visit Japan. The result of that trip was a semiautobiographical travelogue, *Turning Japanese* (1991). The book won the Oakland PEN Josephine Miles Book Award. In the book Mura describes his journey to the land of his ancestors in search of a "lost center" within his soul. The power of his narrative is generated by his attempt to redefine his ontological relationship with both mainstream American culture and his Japanese cultural heritage.

Mura has received many awards and fellowships. Besides the Creative Artist Exchange Fellowship he has also received an NEA Literature Fellowship, two Bush Foundation Fellowships, a Loft-McKnight Award, and two Minnesota State Arts Board grants.

Mura has taught at the University of Minnesota and in the COMPAS Writers-in-the-Schools program. In 1991 he helped found Asian American Renaissance, a Minnesota-based Asian American arts group. His *A Male Grief: Notes on Pornography and Addiction* was published in 1987.

Murayama, Makio (b. Aug. 10, 1912, San Francisco, Calif.): Medical researcher. After spending ten years of his childhood in Japan, Murayama returned to San Francisco and entered high school. He studied biochemistry and bacteriology at the University of California, Berkeley, earning his degree in 1938. Staying on at Berkeley, he pursued graduate work in biochemistry and nuclear physics.

In early 1943, after the Japanese surprise bombing of Pearl Harbor, more than 110,000 Japanese were placed in relocation centers run by the U.S. government. Although Murayama's family was sent to one of these camps, he was ordered to report to the Manhattan Project in Chicago as a physicist. He was, however, ultimately rejected for being Japanese and throughout the war was closely watched by the Federal Bureau of Investigation (FBI).

In 1953, after obtaining a Ph.D. degree, Murayama began postgraduate work at the California Institute of Technology. There, under Linus Pauling, he performed sickle-cell research, eventually garnering worldwide fame for his discoveries in this specialized field.

Murayama, Milton Atsushi (Atsushi Murayama; b. 1923, Lahaina, Territory of Hawaii): Writer. Murayama was born on the island of Maui to Sawa Yasukawa and Isao Murayama, During his childhood Lahaina was a sleepy fishing village where his early life was occupied with the family fishing business and lazy days of swimming. The Depression years brought about an awareness that his family was sinking into debt. Later he lived on "Pig Pen Avenue" in Puukolii, a plantation camp, once home to more than six hundred residents.

Murayama attended Lahainaluna High School. During World War II he trained at the MILITARY INTELLIGENCE SERVICE LANGUAGE SCHOOL (MISLS) at Camp Savage, Minnesota, and served as an interpreter in India and China. He earned his B.A. degree in English and Philosophy at the University of Hawaii in 1947 and his M.A. degree in Chinese and Japanese at Columbia University in 1950.

Murayama's short story "I'll Crack Your Head Kotsun" was originally published in the *Arizona Quar-*

terly. This resulted in *All I Asking for Is My Body*, originally published in 1975 by Supa Press, his own publishing venture. This book has become a classic; it was reprinted by the University of Hawaii Press in 1988. The *Hawaii Herald* called the work the "only comprehensive literary treatment of the Hawaii plantation experience, an experience which either directly or indirectly affects a very large segment of Hawaii's population." A second novel, *Five Years on a Rock*, centering on the mother of the family whose story is told in *All I Asking for Is My Body*, was published in 1994.

Murayama is also interested in theater. He has written three plays, one of which, *Yoshitsune*, a historical play, was produced by Humukahua in Honolulu, 1982. *All I Asking for Is My Body* has also been transformed into a play and was performed by the ASIAN-AMERICAN THEATRE COMPANY in 1989.

Among the awards Murayama has earned are the Before Columbus Foundation American Book Award in 1980 and the Hawaii Award for Literature in 1991. He resides in San Francisco with his wife and continues to write.

Muzumdar, Haridas [Thakordas] (b. Dec. 18, 1900, Gujarat, India): Author, lecturer, and activist for Indian national independence. Born and educated in India, Muzumdar came to the United States to attend Northwestern University, where he received his B.A. degree in 1925. He went on to complete graduate studies at the University of Wisconsin and was graduated with a Ph.D. degree in sociology in 1930. Throughout the 1930's, Muzumdar campaigned actively in the United States and India for the cause of India's independence from British colonial rule. He traveled to India in 1939 to participate in discussions with Mahatma GANDHI, Jawaharlal NEHRU, and other political leaders before returning to the United States in 1940 to continue his crusade. Once India was granted independence in 1947, Muzumdar chose to remain in the United States. He became a naturalized American citizen and wrote an account of the experiences of the independence movement entitled *America's Contribution to India's Freedom* (1962). Other works focusing on India and Asian Indians in the United States written by Muzumdar include *India's Religious Heritage* (1986) and *Asian Indians' Contributions to America* (1986).

Myanmar, Union of: Country located in Southeast Asia and governed by a military regime. Myanmar was formerly the republic of Burma. The capital city is Yangon (formerly Rangoon). In 1989 Myanmar's total land mass of 261,228 square miles contained an estimated population of almost forty-two million. The country is centered in the basin of the Irrawaddy River and includes surrounding uplands and mountains. It borders Thailand, Laos, the People's Republic of China, India, and Bangladesh. To its south lies the Indian Ocean.

Within the basin are two distinct areas of dense population: the Dry Zone, around and south of Mandalay in Upper Myanmar, with a population of 650,000 people, and the delta, focusing on the capital and major seaport of Yangon, with 2.9 million residents. The Dry Zone has been the historical core area of Myanmar. The annual rainfall of this area is exceptionally low for Southeast Asia, and there is a dry season of about six months. The people are supported by mixed subsistence and commercial farming. Millet, rice, cotton, beans, peanuts, and sesame are major crops. Throughout the twentieth century the Dry Zone has been surpassed in population by the delta. With warm monsoon climate and fine alluvial soil, the delta's commercial rice-farming economy supplies the country's food and export. The old and new core areas are connected by the Irrawaddy River in its function as a water route.

The eleven minority groups reside mainly in the uplands and mountains. Major groups include the Karens, the Shans, the Kachins, and the Chins. Many of them have demanded self-determination in their homelands.

The Burmese follow "the path of the elders," Theravada Buddhism. The country has, however, experienced important social and political changes since its independence from Great Britain in 1947-1948. The brutal, repressive military rule since 1962 has halted the country's development and brought impoverished and exhausted Myanmar to the ranks of the world's poorest countries, although there has been significant economic growth in the 1990's. Many talented and patriotic Burmese have left the country because they could not accept, or be accepted by, the military government. Myanmar's relations with the United States have been friendly but low-key.

Myer, Dillon S. (Sept. 4, 1891, Hebron, Ohio—Oct. 21, 1982, Silver Spring, Md.): Government official. Myer was best known as the director of the WAR RELOCATION AUTHORITY (WRA). To some Japanese American internees Myer was the "great White father"; to others he was a "keeper of concentration camps."

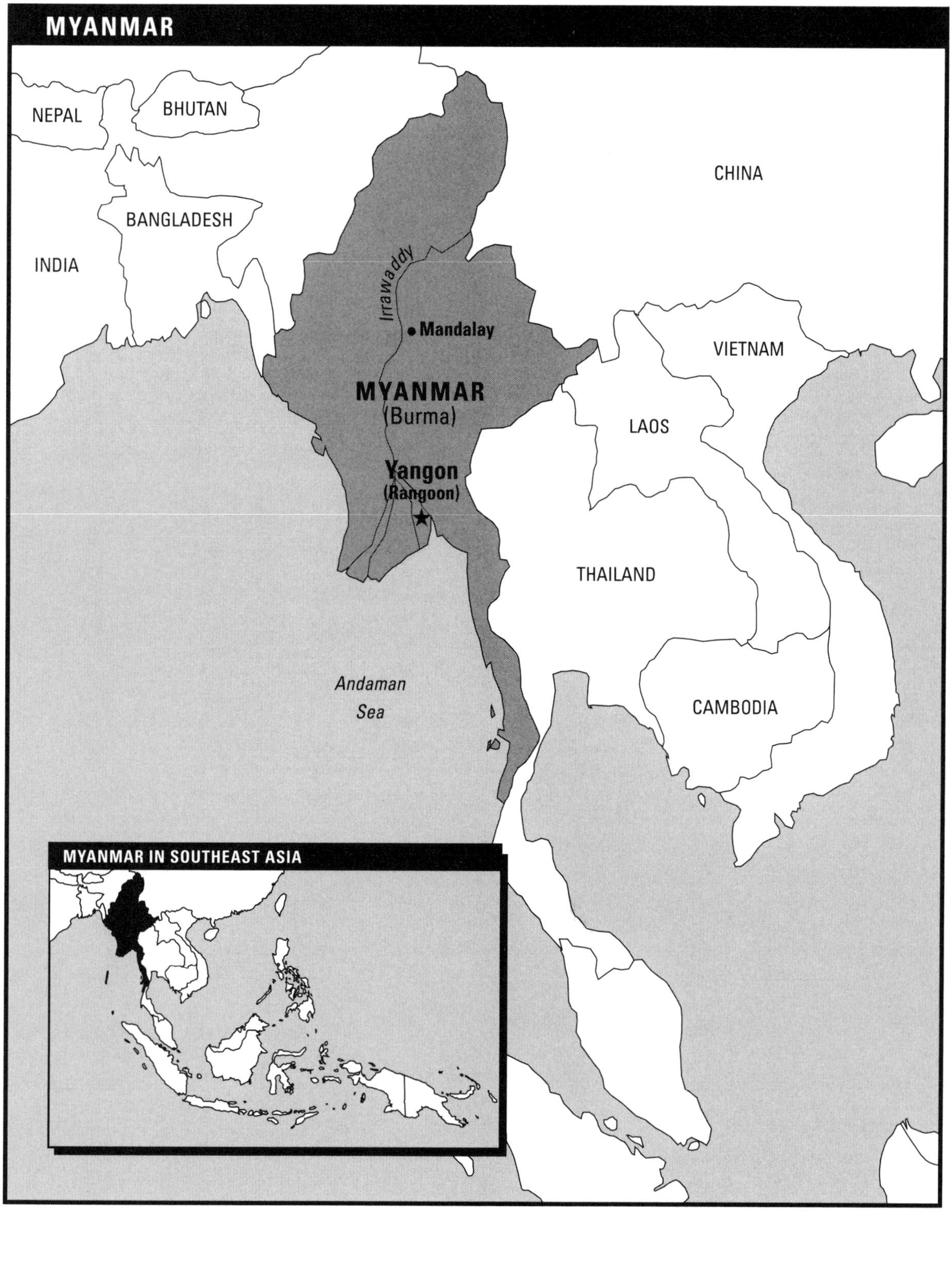
MYANMAR
NEPAL
BHUTAN
CHINA
BANGLADESH
INDIA
Irrawaddy
Mandalay
VIETNAM
MYANMAR
(Burma)
LAOS
Yangon
(Rangoon)
THAILAND
Andaman
Sea
CAMBODIA
MYANMAR IN SOUTHEAST ASIA

Myer abhorred the latter definition and viewed himself as the top administrator of "relocation centers" or "havens of rest and security."

Myer grew up on a rural farm in central Ohio. He attended Ohio State University's College of Agriculture in 1910 and graduated with a bachelor's degree in 1914. In general he led an uneventful life until he started his government career in agriculture. Myer learned the system well and soon became an expert in dealing with politicians and others who could potentially help him. He rose quickly in the government, accepting one promotion after another until he became assistant chief of the Soil Conservation Service in 1938. His big break came on June 17, 1942, when Milton Eisenhower resigned as director of the WRA and recommended Myer as his successor. Myer would remain in charge of the organization for the rest of its existence.

To the JAPANESE AMERICAN CITIZENS LEAGUE (JACL) whose policy of cooperation with the U.S. government made it a favorite son of the WRA, Myer was a benevolent father figure who was a friend to Japanese Americans. In Myer the JACL had a leader who assisted them in gaining acceptance in everyday life. In the JACL Myer found perfect test cases willing to carry out his policy of assimilation.

Myer, however, was not loved by everyone in the internment camps. Those, such as the "no-no boys," who resisted his directives were labeled "troublemakers" and sent to the camp at TULE LAKE. Those considered an extreme threat to Myer and the WRA were sent either to the stockade or to a prison camp located first in Moab, Utah, then in Leupp, Arizona. To those resisters in camp Myer was a prison warden who exhibited little sympathy toward those who wanted their freedom.

After World War II Myer was appointed Bureau of Indian Affairs (BIA) director, largely on the strong reputation he had earned with the WRA. At the BIA he implemented the same policy toward American Indians that he had used so effectively against Japanese Americans.

N

NAATA. *See* **National Asian American Telecommunications Association**

Nagae Lum, Peggy (b. 1951, Portland, Oreg.): Attorney. Best known as lead counsel for the 1984 *CORAM NOBIS* case filed by Minoru YASUI against the U.S. government, she was adjunct professor at the University of Puget Sound School of Law in Tacoma, Washington, specializing in civil rights issues. She also worked at the Seattle law firm of Betts, Patterson, and Mines (1989 to 1991) and the University of Oregon School of Law. She earned her J.D. degree from the Northwestern School of Law at Lewis and Clark.

Nagano, Kent (b. 1950): Conductor. Musical director of L'Opera de Lyons, France, and of the Berkeley Symphony Orchestra in Berkeley, California, Nagano has won several recording awards, including the 1993 Gramophone Magazine Award for Best Opera Recording of the Year for his direction of L'Opera de Lyons performing Francis Poulenc's *Dialogues of the Carmelites*. In 1994, Nagano made his debut at New York's Metropolitan Opera House, conducting the same Poulenc work to great acclaim.

Kent Nagano. (Asian Week)

Raised in California (his grandparents were interned during World War II), Nagano received an undergraduate degree in sociology from the University of California, Santa Cruz. He began to study conducting in graduate school at San Francisco State University. In 1978, after a four-year stint with the Opera Company of Boston, he became the director of the Berkeley Symphony Orchestra. He has also served as director of the Halle Orchestra in Manchester, England, and has held several guest conductorships. His recordings of John Adams' opera *The Death of Klinghoffer* and Sergei Prokofiev's *Love of Three Oranges* received Grammy nominations.

Nagasawa, Kanaye (Isonaga Hikosuke; 1852, Kagoshima, Japan,—1934, Calif.): Wine maker. Isonaga was born into a samurai family in southern Japan. As a youngster he was sent to Europe by his lord to learn more about the West. Since secrecy was required, Kanaye Nagasawa became his new name. Sailing from Japan in 1865, he traveled to England and Scotland and then headed to the United States. Nagasawa and five others accepted employment on a large New York vineyard owned by Thomas Lake Harris, leader of the Brotherhood of the New Life, a spiritualist sect. Although Nagasawa's remaining companions eventually sailed back to Japan, he stayed on with Harris, learning the vintner's trade in New York and later in California. Ultimately, Nagasawa established himself as one of California's leading wine makers; his Fountain Grove wines, produced near Santa Rosa, enjoyed a national reputation.

Nagumo, Shoji (1890—1976): Gardener. Nagumo helped found a gardeners' association in Southern California in the 1930's. After arriving in the United States, he worked as a gardener's helper before launching his own business. When California housing construction flourished in the 1920's, he prospered by building and tending gardens for many new homes. Nagumo was one of the founders of the Japanese Gardeners' Association of Hollywood in 1933. Four years later this organization became absorbed into the

Southern California Gardeners Federation. The autobiographical *Gadena Goroku* (a gardener's essays) appeared in 1960.

Nahm, Andrew C. (b. Mar. 3, 1919, Yonggang, Korea): Scholar. Nahm was educated at Andrews University (B.A., 1951) and Stanford University (Ph.D., 1961). A Research Fellow with the Hoover Institution of Stanford in 1959-1960, he has taught at such schools as the University of Nebraska (1961), Michigan State University (1964), and Western Michigan University (where he began teaching in 1960). His books include *The United States and Korea; American-Korean Relations, 1866-1976 (1979), Korea: Tradition and Transformation, a History of the Korean People* (1988), and *Historical Dictionary of the Republic of Korea* (1993).

Naichi: Abbreviated form of "Naichijin" (people of the homeland). In referring to themselves, the Japanese who went to live in Korea following Japan's annexation of that country in 1910 adopted the term "Naichijin." In Hawaii the term was applied to Japanese from mainland Japan as opposed to those from OKINAWA. By excluding the Okinawans from the meaning of the term, the implication was that Okinawans were not true Japanese.

The Okinawans who came to Hawaii in 1900, fifteen years after the arrival of the first group of Japanese contract laborers, did seem foreign to the other Japanese. The language they spoke, although a Japanese dialect, was unintelligible to the Naichi. Though the Naichi spoke a variety of dialects among themselves, with a little experience they were able to understand one another.

The Naichi believed that some Okinawan customs were marks of inferiority. For example the Okinawan women who were married had tattooed hands. These were a mark of beauty and a source of pride. The Naichi, however, saw tattooing as primitive, aboriginal. Also, the Okinawans raised pigs. In Japan the raising and killing of animals were done primarily by the Eta, the outcasts of society. The Okinawan-Naichi relationship was that of a minority within a minority. Considered inferior by the dominant Naichi, the Okinawans were the targets of ostracism and discrimination. Naichi parents forbade their children to marry Okinawans.

World War II changed the Okinawan-Naichi relationship. Both groups were associated with the Japanese enemy. As Japanese Americans the NISEI (second generation), whether Naichi or Okinawan, had to prove their loyalty to the United States. Members of both groups fought in the war together in such units as the 100TH INFANTRY BATTALION, the 442ND REGIMENTAL COMBAT TEAM, and the MILITARY INTELLIGENCE SERVICE. At the end of the war, Okinawan, as well as Naichi, veterans took advantage of the GI Bill, enabling them to enter various professions and gain respectability.

Many third- and fourth-generation Japanese Americans of Hawaii lack a strong identity as Japanese, whether Naichi or Okinawan. Their primary identities are as Americans and as "locals," that is, as people of Hawaii.

Naipaul, V. S. [Vidiadhar Surajprasad] (b. Aug. 17, 1922, Chaguanas, Trinidad): Novelist and travel writer. Naipaul's grandfather migrated in the late nineteenth century as an indentured laborer from the North Indian state of Uttar Pradesh to Trinidad, where Naipaul was born. Naipaul has lived in England since 1950, when not traveling. First acclaimed as a talented young comic novelist of colonial life in the Caribbean, he has become widely recognized in the English-speaking world as an important commentator on societies of the postcolonial developing world. His views are highly controversial, eliciting praise from British and American critics as distinguished as Irving Howe, who called him "the world's writer," and deeply offending many writers from the countries he criticizes, such as H. B. Singh, who calls him "a despicable lackey of neocolonialism."

Early Fiction. Naipaul has described the years spent writing his first three comic novels, *The Mystic Masseur* (1957), *The Suffrage of Elvira* (1958), and *Miguel Street* (1959), as "an apprenticeship." All three are entertaining and well crafted, though even these early books brought some untoward comments. George Lamming accused Naipaul of depicting life among Indians at the expense of a realistic, multiracial portrayal of Trinidadian society.

Naipaul's fourth novel, *A House for Mr. Biswas* (1961), is a rich, complex novel about an Indian family in Trinidad, the work of a highly talented, maturing novelist (Naipaul was twenty-nine years old when it was published). Naipaul wrote in 1983 that *Mr. Biswas* was "Of all my books . . . the one that is closest to me. It is the most personal, created out of what I saw and felt as a child. It also contains, I believe, some of my funniest writing."

Travel Writing. In 1960 the government of Trinidad

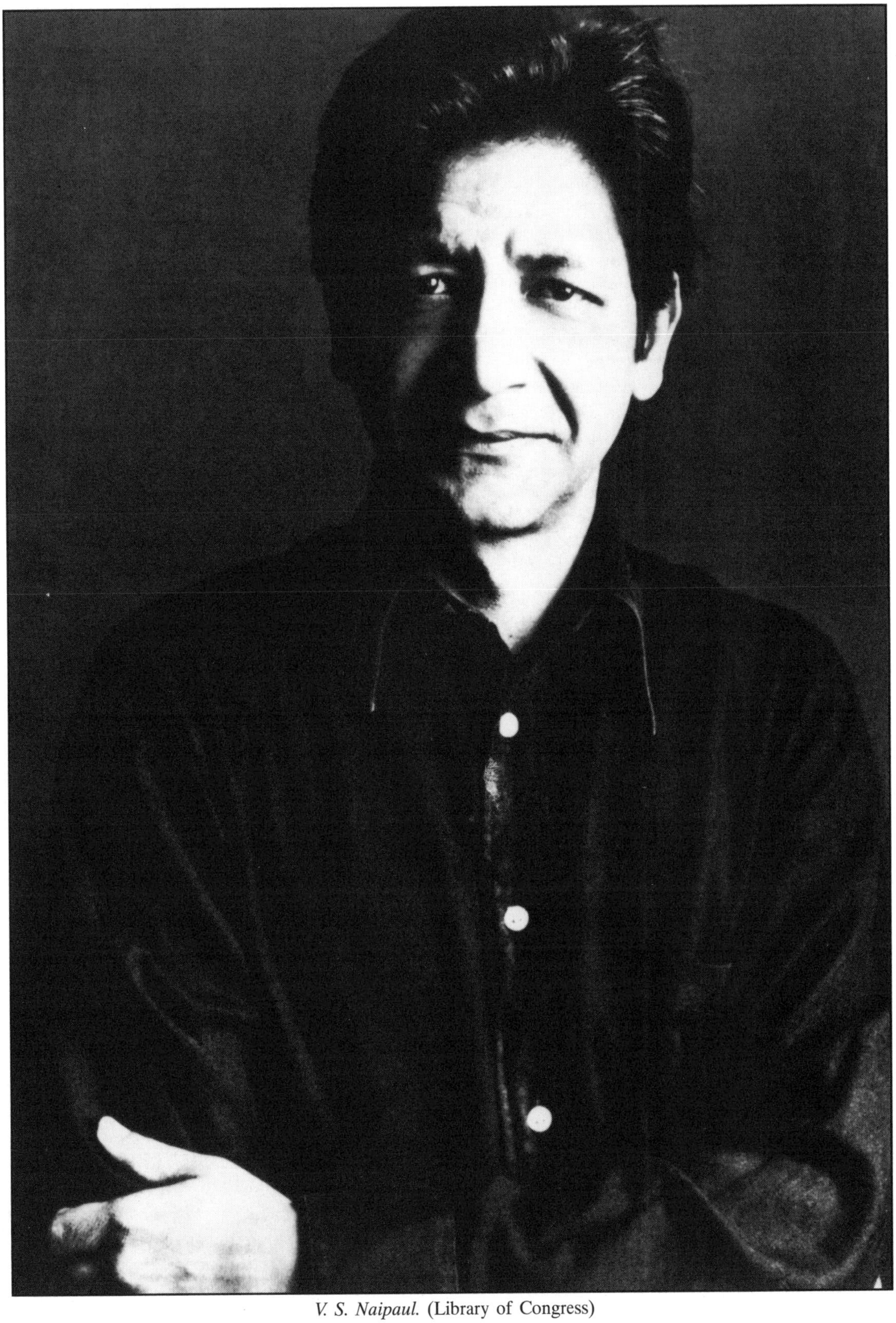

V. S. Naipaul. (Library of Congress)

and Tobago commissioned Naipaul to write a travel narrative about the Caribbean. *The Middle Passage* (1962) inaugurated Naipaul's career as a special, intensely autobiographical kind of travel writer. The West Indies, he writes, "in all their racial and social complexity, are so completely a creation of Empire that the withdrawal of Empire is almost without meaning." *An Area of Darkness* (1964), about his first visit to India, is an alternately scathing and deeply moving account of a year living and traveling in India. In evidence is Naipaul's ability to offend with his trademark unsparing frankness. "It is well that Indians are unable to look at their country directly," he writes, "for the distress they would see would drive them mad." In *India: A Wounded Civilization* (1977), an even more devastating indictment prompted by Indira Gandhi's 1975 Emergency, he nevertheless continues to offer equally characteristic autobiographical reflections. "In India I know I am a stranger," he writes, "but increasingly I understand that my Indian memories, the memories of that India which lived on into my childhood in Trinidad, are like trapdoors into a bottomless past."

The Overcrowded Barracoon (1972) is a collection of Naipaul's essays, including two about the United States: "Steinbeck in Monterey," and "New York with Norman Mailer," about Mailer's campaign for mayor of New York City in 1969. It is a good introduction to Naipaul's style and concerns.

Mixed Genres. Naipaul has continued to publish both fiction and nonfiction, though as his work has developed the boundary between genres has become increasingly blurred. The novels *The Mimic Men* (1967) and *A Bend in the River* (1979) show him at his best portraying characters lost in the postcolonial world. *Among the Believers: An Islamic Journey* (1981) is an account of a trip through four predominantly Muslim countries: Iran, Pakistan, Malaysia, and Indonesia. This book was extremely well timed for sales and for its author's notoriety, seeing print as it did just after the Iranian hostage crisis. Naipaul's appearance on the cover of *Newsweek* on November 16, 1981 greatly expanded his American audience.

Finding the Center: Two Narratives (1984), is a short, accessible introduction to Naipaul, consisting of an exquisite memoir of his childhood and beginnings as a writer called "Prologue to an Autobiography," and "The Crocodiles of Yamoussoukro," which he offers as a glimpse of the travel writer at work, "going about one side of his business: travelling, adding to his knowledge of the world, exposing himself to new people and new relationships."

"An autobiography can distort," writes Naipaul in an essay, ". . . but fiction never lies: it reveals the writer totally." He wrote that about the Trinidadian black nationalist Michael X, but the observation applies superbly to Naipaul himself, who began his career writing fiction, but since the 1970's has concentrated on crafting a highly stylized persona of himself as a displaced, stateless subject of the defunct British Empire. He calls *The Enigma of Arrival* (1987) "a novel," but it is really a brilliant if selectively self-reveling autobiography—Naipaul's consummate attempt simultaneously to reveal and distort. "In 1950 in London, in the boarding house," he writes, "I had found myself at the beginning of a great movement of peoples after the war, a great shaking up of the world, a great shaking up of old cultures and old ideas." The critic Peter Hughes aptly describes *The Enigma of Arrival* as Naipaul's attempt "to write himself into mankind's history"—a description that could be applied with equal justice to *A Way in the World* (1994), a brilliant sequence of historical narratives billed as a novel.

Naipaul and America. In 1984, Naipaul published a long, entertaining account of that year's Republican National Convention (titled "Among the Republicans") in *The New York Review of Books.* Out of that trip to Dallas came an interest in the American South, leading him to write *A Turn in the South* (1989), a remarkably gentle, even uncritical travel book, his only one about a developed country. *A Turn in the South* betrays Naipaul's reluctance to criticize the West, but also signals a turning point in his career; his next book, *India: A Million Mutinies Now* (1991), also displays a hitherto unwonted empathy. *A Turn in the South* is a fresh portrayal of the American South through the eyes of an outsider, who nonetheless recognizes in his subject the New World themes and afflictions of his native Trinidad.

Naipaul and the West. The critic Rob Nixon, in his excellent recent discussion of Naipaul's nonfiction, makes a point central to an adequate understanding of this important, complex writer. Nixon strives to debunk Naipaul's "autobiographical persona . . . as a permanent exile, a refugee, a homeless citizen of the world." Rather drily, Nixon argues that "it would seem appropriate to address the disparity between the energetically defended image of Naipaul as one of history's rejects, someone condemned to concentrated alienation, and his standing as among the two or three most lionized writers resident in England." Many writers of color despise Naipaul. The African American poet Ishmael Reed says Naipaul writes for "the white insecurities market" and offers "a sort of Kiplingesque reassurance that the West is best." The Indian writer and academic C. J. Wallia exclaims: "It's understandable that the Queen knighted him last year—he's England's favorite 19th-century Englishman!"

To all of which Naipaul answers; "It was necessary . . . if I was going to be a writer, and live by my books, to travel out to that kind of society where the writing life was possible. This meant, for me at that time, going to England. I was traveling from the periphery, the margin, to what to me was the center; and it was my hope that, at the center, room would be made for me."

Suggested Readings: • Hughes, Peter. *V. S. Naipaul*. New York: Routledge, 1988. • Nixon, Rob. *London Calling: V. S. Naipaul, Postcolonial Mandarin*. New York: Oxford University Press, 1992. • Theroux, Paul. "V. S. Naipaul." In *Sunrise with Seamonsters: A Paul Theroux Reader*. Boston: Houghton Mifflin, 1985. • Winokur, Scott. "The Unsparing Vision of V. S. Naipaul." *Image* (*San Francisco Examiner* Sunday magazine), May 5, 1991.

Nakahama Manjiro (John Mung; 1827, Nakanohama, Tosa Province, Japan—Nov. 12, 1898, Tokyo, Japan): Sailor and diplomat. At the age of thirteen, Nakahama went to work on a Japanese fishing boat in order to earn money to help support his widowed mother and his four siblings. On January 5, 1841, he sailed on a boat to help catch sea bass; within a week, an enormous storm blew the boat off course. Nakahama was marooned along with the other four fishermen when their boat was wrecked off the coast of a small island in the Pacific. They were rescued six months later by an American whaling ship, the *John Howland*, and were taken to Hawaii. William H. Whitfield, the ship's captain, could not return the fishermen to Japan: Since the beginning of the Tokugawa period, Japan had had no diplomatic contact with the Western world. The government maintained such strict isolation that upon their return, Japanese castaways were put on trial to determine their loyalty and were threatened with possible execution. Hoping to avert this fate, Whitfield found sponsors who would employ the fishermen and offered to take Nakahama

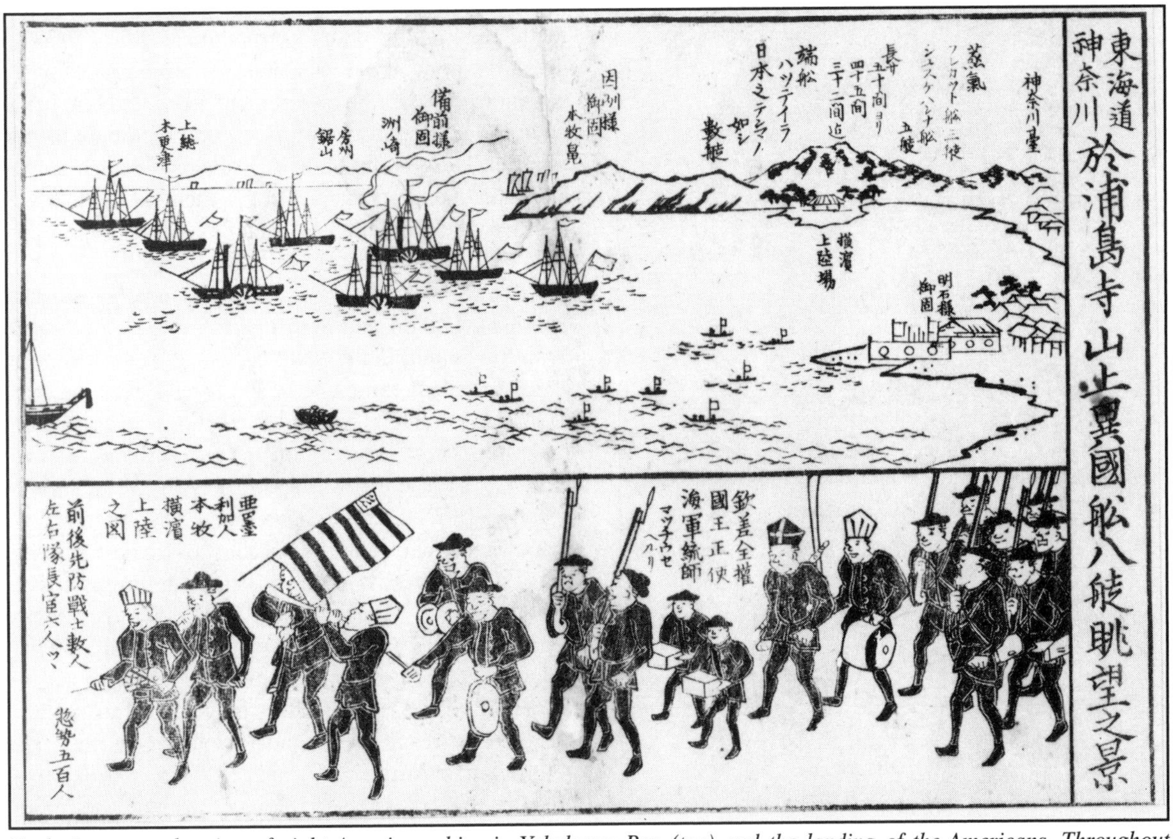

Early Japanese drawing of eight American ships in Yokohama Bay (top) and the landing of the Americans. Throughout the Tokugawa period (1600-1867) feudal Japan had maintained strict isolation from the West. As such, castaways such as Nakahama Manjiro could be executed upon returning to Japan. (Library of Congress)

Commodore Matthew Perry, as rendered by a Japanese artist. (Library of Congress)

back to Whitfield's home in New Bedford, Massachusetts.

Nakahama, who was given the name "John Mung" by Whitfield, lived with Whitfield's family and learned English at a local school. Eventually, he returned to the sea as a crewman on a whaling ship; in 1849, he traveled to California by way of Cape Horn as a crewman on a lumber ship. In 1850, Nakahama left San Francisco for Hawaii to be reunited with his friends and make plans for their return to Japan. After purchasing a small whaleboat and arranging passage on an American merchant ship, Nakahama made plans for his party to be dropped off near the RYUKYU ISLANDS. When they arrived on the island of OKINAWA in January of 1851, they were treated to a feast before being questioned by government officials. Placed under special guard, Nakahama and his friends were eventually put on trial and imprisoned. After they were released in June of 1852, they were officially repatriated and returned to their home villages.

Soon, Nakahama was summoned by feudal officials to serve as a teacher. In 1853, the Tokugawa government invited him to serve as an interpreter in diplomatic negotiations with Commodore Matthew PERRY; upon learning about Nakahama's progressive, anti-isolationist views, the government prevented him from having direct contact with Perry and members of his mission. Despite this setback, Nakahama came to the attention of an important patron, a member of the royal cabinet who appointed Nakahama to advise the government on improving its sea defenses.

In 1857, Nakahama was appointed to be an instructor in navigation and ship engineering at the Naval Training School in the royal capital of Yedo. Because of his excellent command of English, he was selected to serve as an interpreter and navigational instructor on the *KANRIN MARU* expedition—a goodwill mission to America sponsored by the Japanese government in 1860. In 1869, the Meiji government appointed Nakahama to the faculty of the Kaisei-jo Gakko (precursor to Tokyo University) as a professor of English. The following year, he revisited the United States and was reunited with the Whitfields when he visited the East Coast. Nakahama visited London and intended to travel through Europe but was prevented from further travels as a result of a tumor in one of his feet. He returned to Japan in 1871, only to suffer a stroke that impaired his speech and left one of his legs paralyzed. After living for many years with his eldest son, who was a prosperous physician, Nakahama died in Tokyo in 1898.

Nakahara, Ron (b. July 20, 1947, Honolulu, Territory of Hawaii): Actor and theater director. Artistic associate for New York City's PAN ASIAN REPERTORY THEATRE, Nakahara began his directing career in 1979 at Atlanta's Alliance Theatre. His distinguished directing career at Pan Asian included works by Asian American dramatists Ed Sakamoto, Rosanna Alfaro Yamagiwa, Wakako YAMAUCHI, and Jon SHIROTA, as well as Asian playwrights Sha Yexin and Yukio Mishima. Nakahara also acted in numerous Pan Asian productions. Among his most notable performances was "The Child Who Becomes a Dictator" in the 1992 world premiere of Ernest ABUBA's dance drama *Cambodia Agonistes*. A participant on three National Endowment for the Arts (NEA) panels, including an NEA Directing Fellowship, Nakahara acted and directed at such major theaters throughout the United States as Hartford Stage, the Guthrie Theatre, and Actors Theatre of Louisville.

Nakamura, Gongoro (1890, Hanechi, Okinawa, Japan—1965): Lawyer and Issei community leader. Nakamura arrived in Los Angeles in 1906, eventually earning a law degree from the University of Southern California. As an ISSEI, however, he was prevented from practicing his profession. Instead, in the 1920's he joined such community organizations as the JAPANESE ASSOCIATIONS and actively worked to improve conditions for his fellow Issei while advising them on legal matters. During World War II he spent time at the CRYSTAL CITY internment camp in southern Texas. Returning to Los Angeles after the war, he resumed his work in community affairs, assisting Japanese Peruvians, Okinawans, and Japanese Americans displaced by the internment. Nakamura became a naturalized U.S. citizen in the early 1950's.

Nakanishi, Don T. (b. Aug. 14, 1949, Los Angeles, Calif.): Scholar. Cofounder of *AMERASIA JOURNAL* and pioneer in the field of ASIAN AMERICAN STUDIES, he has conducted research on a plethora of subjects including educational policy, electoral politics, international politics, and the impact of mass internment on Japanese Americans. In 1990 he became director of the ASIAN AMERICAN STUDIES CENTER of the University of California, Los Angeles. After the school denied him tenure in 1986, he became a *cause célèbre* for students and community activists during a three-year battle to gain tenure at the Graduate School of Education, which he finally won in 1989. He received his M.A. and Ph.D. degrees in political science from Harvard University. Much of his research has focused on Asian Americans and electoral politics.

Don Nakanishi. (Asian Week)

Nakano, Yosuke W. (1887, Yamaguchi Prefecture, Japan—Kobe, Japan, 1961): Architectural engineer. Educated at the University of Pennsylvania's architectural school, he became an expert on the use of reinforced concrete in the building of large-scale structures. Nakano came to California while in his late teens. Following his formal schooling, he was hired by Philadelphia architectural firm Wark and Company, where he rose to become chief engineer. Over the course of many years, he helped to construct more than two hundred buildings in the United States. He became a naturalized American citizen in 1953.

Nakaoka, Kiyoto Kenneth (Oct. 23, 1920, Los Angeles, Calif.—Aug. 12, 1980, Gardena, Calif.): Mayor. Nakaoka was the first Nisei mayor of GARDENA, a Los Angeles suburb known for its large concentration of Japanese Americans. After earning a B.S. degree at the

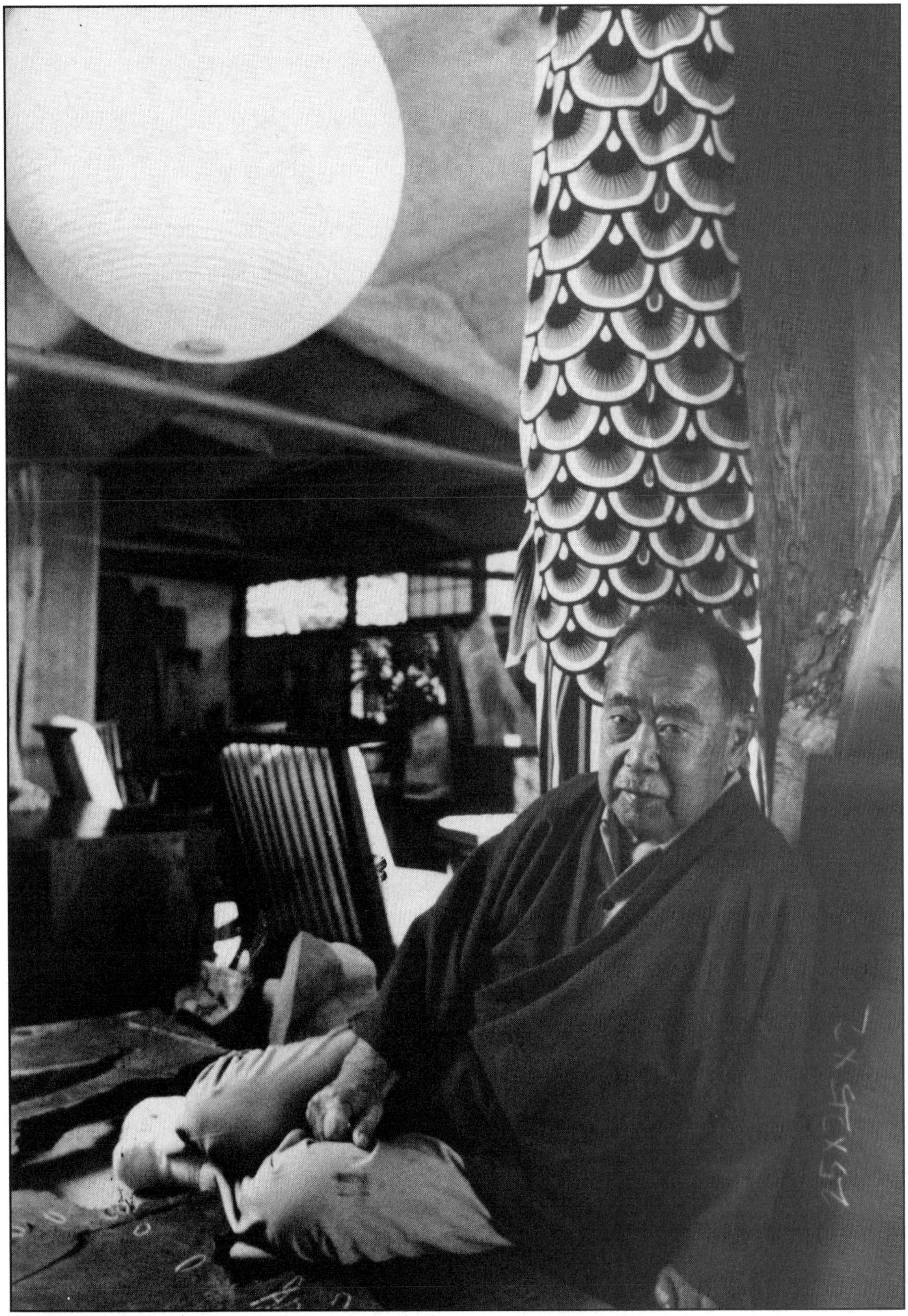

George Nakashima. (Michael Yamashita)

University of California, Los Angeles, in 1944, he did postgraduate work at the Universities of Connecticut and Southern California. He later started his own Gardena realty firm, the Ken Nakaoka Company. Elected to the Gardena City Council in 1966, Nakaoka served three consecutive terms as mayor, from 1968 until 1974. An active member of numerous civic and community organizations, he was named Rotarian of the Year in 1962 and 1968 by Rotary International, the major worldwide service club.

Nakashima, George (1905, Spokane, Wash.—1990, New Hope, Pa.): Furniture maker. Nakashima's handmade wooden furniture collected a number of prestigious honors and awards. The Museum of Modern Art in New York and the Renwick Gallery in Washington, D.C., exhibited his works. The American Craft Museum in Manhattan staged a retrospective of his work in 1989. His major prizes included the gold medal for craftsmanship of the American Institute of Architecture in 1952 and the National Gold Medal presented at the Exhibition of the Building Arts, New York City, in 1962.

Nakashima attended the University of Washington, the École Americaine des Beaux-Arts in Fontainebleau, France, and the Massachusetts Institute of Technology (MIT), where he received a master's degree in architecture in 1929. He also studied architecture and craftwork in Japan and other foreign cities. During World War II he and wife and child were forcibly evacuated to the MINIDOKA relocation center in southern Idaho. Released before the war's end, they settled in New Hope, Pennsylvania, in 1943; Nakashima opened his own furniture business there in 1945, and, as the demand for his work increased, the company prospered. More than a hundred pieces of his furniture perished in a fire that ravaged a Princeton, New Jersey, house in 1989. He died a year later.

Nakayama, Joji: Immigration official. Originally hired as chief inspector of Issei contract laborers on Hawaiian plantations, Nakayama was responsible for monitoring the health of the laborers and served as a liaison between them and plantation overseers. In 1886, the newly established terms of the IMMIGRATION CONVENTION established the Hawaiian Bureau of Immigration, and Nakayama was appointed to serve as head of the bureau's Japanese section. Although ostensibly representing the interests of Japanese laborers in his new post, Nakayama was essentially in the pay of the plantation owners and sided with them on all labor disputes.

Nakazawa, Ken (Dec. 18, 1883, Fukushima Prefecture, Japan—1953): Scholar and writer. Nakazawa was the first Japanese American to teach at a major American university. He came to the United States in 1908 and studied English at the University of Oregon. While there he became a published writer; *Weaver of the Frost*, a collection of short stories, appeared in 1927. The University of Southern California hired him in 1926 to teach classes on Asian culture. His post with the Japanese consulate in Los Angeles resulted in his internment and eventual deportation to Japan in 1942. He was allowed back into the United States ten years later.

Namul: Korean term for vegetable, used as an identifying marker with the names of various vegetables.

Nanak (Apr. 15, 1469, Rai Bhoi di Talvandi, near Lahore, India—1539, Kartarpur, India): First of ten Sikh gurus who established and developed the Sikh religion. Nanak was born into a mercantile family of high standing. For many years he traveled to the Muslim and Hindu religious centers of India and perhaps to other parts of the world as well. By 1520 he had returned from his journey and was living in Punjab. Nanak spent the remaining years of his life in Kartarpur, a village in Punjab, where his numerous disciples gathered to receive instruction on spiritual truth. To them he handed down his teachings in the form of numerous devotional hymns, many of which have survived to this day. Shortly before his death, he named a successor—thereby establishing a practice followed by all but the tenth guru.

Nanjing: Capital of China's Jiangsu Province. It became the province's capital in 1952, and it is located on the southeast bank of the Yangtze River, near Shanghai. It is noted for several industries, including the steel and iron, automobile, and farm equipment industries. Nanjing was founded in 1368 during the Ming Dynasty (1368-1644) and was the empire's capital until 1403. It was chosen in 1928 as the headquarters of the nationalist organization the GUOMINDANG (GMD). The city's population exceeded two million in 1990.

Nanjing, Rape of (Dec., 1937—Jan., 1938): Seven-week period of terror in which the Japanese Imperial Army plundered NANJING, the capital of the Republic of CHINA, raping an estimated 20,000 women, murdering an estimated 12,000 civilians, and killing approxi-

Japanese troops conduct training exercises back in Tokorozawa, Japan. Japanese soldiers raped or murdered more than thirty thousand Chinese civilians during the brutal Rape of Nanjing. (National Archives)

mately 30,000 Nationalist Chinese soldiers.

In July, 1937, the Marco Polo Bridge incident initiated hostilities between Japan and China as the first battle of World War II in the Asian theater. Hostilities rapidly escalated in the area, and Japan had consolidated its control over the region by the end of July. CHIANG KAI-SHEK, the president of the Republic of China, attempting to divert Japan's military campaign in northern China, ordered an attack on the Japanese military stationed at Shanghai. Japan responded by launching a campaign, in an as yet undeclared war, to take Nanjing and force a Chinese capitulation. The Chinese resistance held from August through November, costing an estimated 250,000 Chinese casualties and more than 40,000 Japanese casualties, but ultimately the Chinese Nationalist army failed to withstand the Japanese advance and retreated to Nanjing.

The Japanese army began the siege of Nanjing by dropping leaflets on the city promising that it would treat the civilian population humanely upon the surrender of the city. Demoralized Nationalist troops, who had retreated to Nanjing from Shanghai, murdered local residents and robbed them of their clothing in an attempt to escape the advancing Japanese army. As the Japanese neared the outskirts of Nanjing, the general commanding the Nationalist troops abandoned the city, leaving the Chinese resistance in chaos.

On December 13 the Japanese army entered Nanjing and unleashed its campaign of terror, death, and destruction that left most of the city in ruins. The Rape of Nanjing is burned deep in the memory of all Chinese as the most barbaric episode in the history of Sino-Japanese relations. In Nanjing, the People's Republic of China constructed a memorial and a museum in order to perpetuate the collective memory of what must be ranked as one of the most gruesome incidents of World War II.

Narcissus Festival: Launched in 1950 by the Chinese Chamber of Commerce of Hawaii to preserve Chinese customs and traditions for future generations. The festival was also expected to attract more people to Chinatown. Events included a beauty contest, a banquet, and a flower show. A cooking show was added because many people enjoyed Chinese food and wanted to learn the intricacies of Chinese cooking. This meant encouraging shop owners to import an increased variety of Chinese cooking ingredients.

Since Narcissus blooms profusely during CHINESE NEW YEAR, the name was used for the festival. Today there is much interest in the cultivation of this beautiful fragrant blossom from Chinese imported bulbs.

Family-oriented events such as the open house in Chinatown and the various cultural events provide an opportunity for people to learn about Chinese customs and traditions. LION DANCES are often an exciting feature of the festival, although DRAGON DANCES are not performed because of the small Chinatown area. Many colorful souvenir items are imported from the Far East for sale. Fashion shows have also been successful and attract large audiences. Two shows spotlighted designers from Beijing who used many beads and sequins to produce glamorous garments.

The festival begins with a kick-off party in November, and events run through the first day of February. The events help provide activities for winter visitors to Hawaii. Large businesses as well as individuals help support the festival every year. It has also managed to arouse the curiosity of those outside the Chinese community, while allowing them to get a glimpse of another culture's customs and traditions.

A colorful, formal coronation ball adds dignity to the crowning of the Narcissus Queen by the governor of the state of Hawaii. An extension of the festival is the Narcissus Queen Goodwill Tour of the Orient in June. The group usually numbers about a hundred members who benefit from learning about the land of their ancestors.

Narika: Organization formed in the San Francisco Bay Area in 1990 to assist physically and emotionally abused women. The agency was started by a group of South Asian Indian women who were alarmed at the rising rate of domestic violence among women of Asian Indian origin.

Narita, Jude: Actor. She has developed a loyal audience of both Asian and non-Asian Americans for her deep and personal portrayals of Asian American women. She is best known for *Coming into Passion: Song for a Sansei*, a solo show that explores issues of race and gender facing Asian American women of different ethnicities and generations.

Nash, Philip (b. Dec. 3, 1956, New York, N.Y.): Attorney. Born to a Nisei mother and European American father, he is executive director of the NATIONAL ASIAN PACIFIC AMERICAN LEGAL CONSORTIUM. He cofounded the first Asian Pacific American Heritage Week Festival in New York City (1979), the National Asian Pacific American Law Student Association (NAPALSA), and the AmerAsian League (1986). He has published poetry and articles in *The New York Nichibei*, *BRIDGE*, *GIDRA*, and *The Asian Journal* and advocated Japanese American REDRESS.

National Asian American Telecommunications Association (NAATA): Media arts service organization founded in 1980 to advance the ideals of cultural pluralism in the United States and to promote better understanding of the Asian Pacific American experience. NAATA began in response to the need to address the scarcity of images of Asian Americans and to correct the often distorted and stereotypical portrayals of them in film and television. Its goals include nurturing and supporting Asian Pacific American artists working in film, video, and radio; providing Asian Pacific American communities locally and nationally with access to works by Asian Pacific American media artists; and ensuring that film, video, and radio works by and about Asian Pacific Americans reach mainstream audiences.

With an initial grant from the Corporation for Public Broadcasting (CPB), the nonprofit, tax-exempt association became one of five members of the National Minority Public Broadcasting Consortia, which was created to provide culturally sensitive programming to the Public Broadcasting System (PBS). As the Asian American component, the association acquires, packages, and distributes television and radio programs that reflect the Asian American experience.

Among NAATA's PBS television programs have been copresentations with the national Point of View (POV) series, including Renee TAJIMA and Christine CHOY's *Who Killed Vincent Chin?* (1989) and Steven OKAZAKI's Academy Award-winning *Days of Waiting* (1989). NAATA has also developed special PBS presentations such as Loni DING's *Color of Honor* (1988). In addition, NAATA presented the PBS series *Silk Screen*, which ran from 1983 to 1987 and covered a wide range of styles, subjects, and genres.

NAATA's public radio program offerings have included *Bamboo Radio* and *CrossCurrent*, aired by National Public Radio (NPR) and many community-based stations. These programs have covered refugee resettlement, Japanese American internment in World War II, and the rise of ANTI-ASIAN VIOLENCE.

Over the years the San Francisco-based group has expanded activities and services beyond public broadcasting to include exhibits, workshops, fiscal sponsorships, and research on racial images in mass media. Highlights of these programs include the annual Asian American International Film Showcase, which presents films and videos by Asians and Asian Americans, including students; an audio facility that is housed with radio station KPFA in Berkeley, California, and that offers audio production services for independents and community groups; and grants for new productions by independent film and video producers in various phases of development and production.

CrossCurrent Media, NAATA's nonbroadcast distribution service, provides Asian American films, videos, and audio cassettes to schools, libraries, and universities nationwide. *Network*, NAATA's quarterly publication, focuses on issues pertaining to Asian American media.

National Asian Pacific American Bar Association: Nonprofit, nonpartisan national legal organization representing the interests of Asian Pacific American attorneys and the community on a national level, founded in 1988. The group, comprised of individuals and local, regional, and state bar associations, serves as a national communications network, provides mutual professional support, and represents its members and the community on legal issues.

National Asian Pacific American Legal Consortium (NAPALC): Organization founded in 1993 and based in Washington, D.C., dedicated to protecting the civil rights of Asian Americans. The first national civil rights group for Asian Americans, NAPALC is an alliance of three older organizations: the Asian Pacific American Legal Center (Los Angeles), the Asian Law Caucus (San Francisco), and the Asian American Legal Defense and Education Fund (New York). Among NAPALC's chief concerns are anti-Asian violence, voting rights, and immigration issues. In April, 1994, the consortium issued the first comprehensive national report on anti-Asian violence.

National Chinese Welfare Council: U.S. organization formed in 1957 by Chinatown leaders to work for immigration laws more favorable to Chinese. The U.S. government's investigation of Chinese immigration fraud during the 1950's created a crisis atmosphere in the Chinese community in America. In 1957 Shing Tai Liang of the New York Chinese Consolidated Benevolent Association (CCBA) had conferred with San Francisco leaders on the possibility of convening a conference on anticommunist actions and support for the Taiwan government. It was agreed, however, that in view of the current climate only an agenda on immigration and refugees would draw broad support from the Chinese community. Accordingly a National Conference of Chinese Communities in America was convened in Washington, D.C., on March 3 through 7, 1957. Out of this historic meeting was formed the National Chinese Welfare Council, which membership consisted of CCBAs and similar organizations all over the United States. The principal objective of the organization was to lobby Congress for laws more favorable to Chinese immigration. It also fought for more minority rights and to improve the political position of the Chinese in America.

Many delegates, especially the American-born, advocated a nonpolitical nonsectarian organization, and their opinions prevailed at the first national conference of the council. By the second conference in 1959, however, pro-Taiwan elements had seized control. The latter pushed through resolutions to support a "free China," thus setting the organization's political tone. Wording on the nonpolitical nonsectarian nature of the council was subsequently deleted from the bylaws.

In time some of the council's members began to lose interest. For example, Hawaii did not send any delegates to the fifth (1966), sixth (1969), and seventh (1972) conferences. The organization was also torn by bitter rivalries among the leadership, especially between the New York and the San Francisco CCBAs. A confrontation appeared very early when the San Francisco CCBA refused to recognize the validity of draft bylaws presented by Shing Tai Liang and proceeded to call a meeting of ten regional councils to pass another draft. In 1972 San Francisco refused to send delegates to the seventh conference. This split became permanent when the San Francisco CCBA led the founding of a National Chinese Welfare Council of Western United States on June 7, 1992.

National Coalition for Redress/Reparations (NCRR): Founded in 1980, one of three major organizations that fought to attain redress for injustices committed by the U.S. government toward Japanese Americans during World War II. A grass-roots organization, the NCRR was formed in Los Angeles out of the Los Angeles Community Coalition on Redress/Reparations (LACCRR) and various other Japanese American community groups around the country. The NCRR's primary goal was to provide an alternative voice that was missing in the redress movement. Many members believed that the Japanese American Citizens

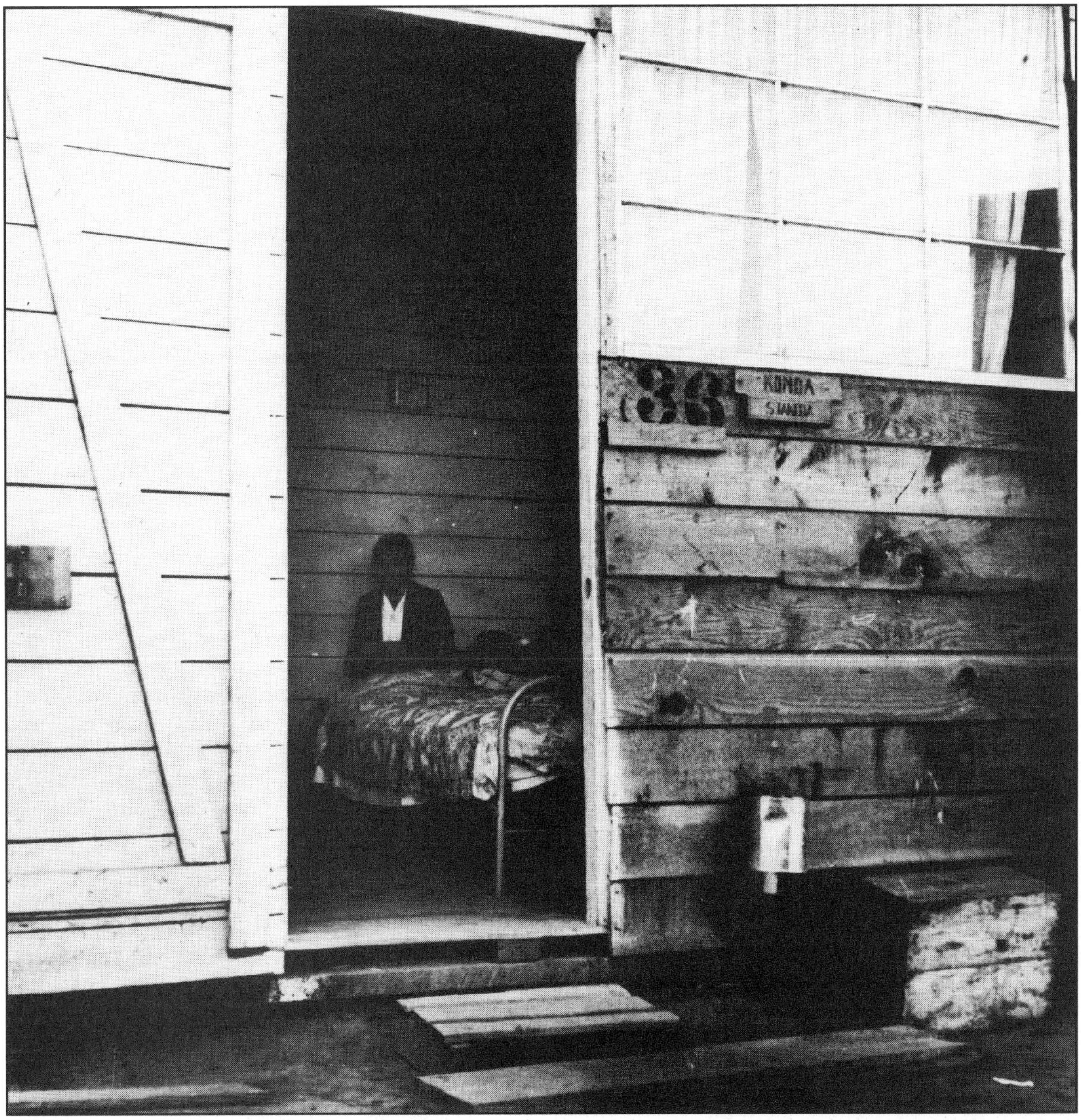

Entrance to an apartment at the Tanforan assembly center, 1942. The forced evacuation of Japanese Americans living on the West Coast during World War II resulted years later in reparations for surviving internees, an effort spearheaded in part by the NCRR. (National Archives)

League (JACL) was not following the wishes of the Japanese American community and needed to be pushed into taking action. At their founding conference on November 15, 1980, the NCRR attempted to form a united front for redress with the JACL and the National Council for Japanese American Redress (NCJAR), but it soon discovered that the path toward unity was often rocky.

One of the primary strengths of the NCRR was its ability to mobilize the members of the Japanese American community and solicit their input. In Los Angeles, the main base for the NCRR, the members of the group ensured that the Commission on Wartime Relocation and Internment of Civilians (CWRIC) hearings were accessible to Japanese Americans and that community members were able to testify about their concentration camp experiences in front of the commissioners. Not surprisingly, most of the witnesses demanded that individual reparations be paid to the Japanese American community—a position the

NCRR had demanded all along. In 1983 those who testified at the hearings were rewarded when the CWRIC recommended to Congress that the government pay $20,000 in damages to those interned in U.S. CONCENTRATION CAMPS during the war. These recommendations were the basis for the various redress bills introduced into Congress over the next few years.

In 1987 the NCRR mobilized a delegation of more than one hundred Asian Americans to lobby for the redress bill in Washington, D.C. From July 25, 1987, to July 29, 1987, the NCRR delegation met with more than one hundred members of Congress and gained many new supporters for the bill. The House of Representatives finally passed the redress bill in September, 1987, the two-hundredth anniversary of the U.S. Constitution. The Senate followed suit on April 20, 1988. After threatening to veto the legislation, President Ronald Reagan eventually signed the bill on August 10, 1988. (See CIVIL LIBERTIES ACT OF 1988.)

The NCRR continued to work on redress appropriations following the signing and ensured that the government kept its promise to pay for damages inflicted on Japanese American camp survivors. In 1990 the group changed its name to Nikkei for Civil Rights and Redress to reflect its postredress priorities.

National Committee for Redress (NCR): Committee created at the 1976 National Convention of the JAPANESE AMERICAN CITIZENS LEAGUE (JACL) to secure reparations from the U.S. government for Japanese Americans evacuated and interned during World War II. The efforts of the NCR spurred the formation of the federal COMMISSION ON WARTIME RELOCATION AND INTERNMENT OF CIVILIANS (CWRIC) and the eventual passage of the CIVIL LIBERTIES ACT OF 1988, bringing the REDRESS MOVEMENT to a close.

The NCR studied the issue of redress for two years and then made its policy recommendations at the 1978

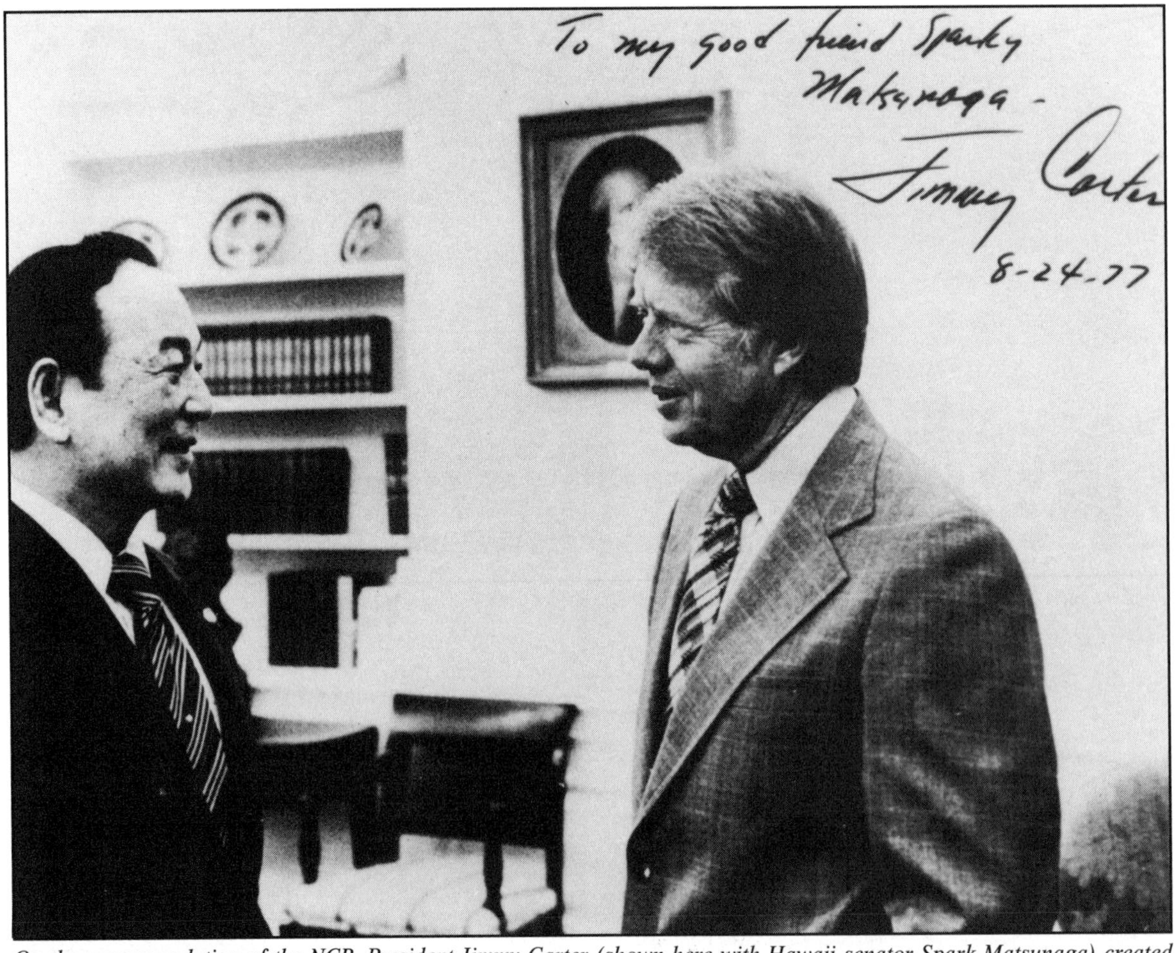

On the recommendation of the NCR, President Jimmy Carter (shown here with Hawaii senator Spark Matsunaga) created the CWRIC in 1980. (Courtesy Matthew Matsunaga)

California senator S. I. Hayakawa ardently opposed the redress movement. (AP/Wide World Photos)

convention. Its guidelines proposed the issuance of federal "block grants," or public funds, to Japanese American community organizations and $25,000 paid directly to each internee. A vote was taken, and the new plan was approved.

In 1979, however, in view of recent California state tax cuts and smarting from strident criticism of the redress campaign by Senator S. I. HAYAKAWA of California, the NCR abandoned its original legislation in favor of asking the U.S. government to form a fact-finding commission to consider and resolve the matter of Japanese American reparation. A revised JACL bill was adopted and presented to the U.S. Congress. Both houses of Congress passed the new bill in 1980, within a few weeks of each other. Shortly thereafter, President Jimmy Carter convened the CWRIC. The following year, the CWRIC heard testimony from about 750 camp survivors in cities across the United States. Testimony was also taken from government officials involved in the incarceration and civilian experts addressing the internment experience. The hearings served to galvanize the Japanese American community, which rallied in support around the call for monetary compensation.

The CWRIC released its findings, *Personal Justice Denied: Report of the Commission on Wartime Relocation and Internment of Civilians*, in 1982. The document concludes that the incarceration was unjustified, the result of wartime hysteria and racial prejudice. The remedies subsequently proposed by the commission included the issuance of a formal apology acknowledging the injustice perpetrated on Japanese Americans during the war and payment of $20,000 to each camp survivor as compensation for losses suffered as a result of the internment. The Civil Liberties Act of 1988, signed by President Ronald Reagan, made these remedies binding and closed the books on the redress campaign. The first payments dispersed under authority of the new law began in October, 1990.

National Council for Japanese American Redress (NCJAR): Organization formed in Seattle, Washington, in May of 1979 for the purpose of obtaining redress for those Japanese Americans who were imprisoned in RELOCATION and INTERNMENT CAMPS during World War II. Other national organizations, such as the JAPANESE AMERICAN CITIZENS LEAGUE (JACL), had decided not to push for the federal government to pay direct reparations to Japanese American survivors of the camps. A breakaway group of JACL members from Seattle came together to establish the NCJAR in order to lobby aggressively for reparations through the introduction of federal legislation that would provide for such payments. The bill that was introduced into Congress through the efforts of the NCJAR had no support from Japanese American congressional representatives, however, and was defeated in favor of a bill establishing a federal commission that would study the wartime experiences of Japanese Americans and recommend solutions to the reparations problem.

In the wake of this defeat, the NCJAR filed a class action suit in 1983 demanding that some $24 billion in damages be paid to Japanese Americans by the U.S. government. Although the case was delayed by a complicated appeals process, the NCJAR was ultimately pleased that the pressure exerted by their suit helped speed the passage of a redress bill in both houses of Congress in 1988. The bill, which awarded $20,000 to camp survivors provided that they waived all rights to

President Ronald Reagan moments after signing the internment reparations bill in 1988. (Ronald Reagan Library)

bring lawsuits for the same claims, was signed into law by President Ronald Reagan on August 10, 1988. (See CIVIL LIBERTIES ACT OF 1988.) Later in October of that year, the Supreme Court ruled against allowing the NCJAR suit, and the organization was disbanded some time later.

National Democratic Council of Asian and Pacific Americans: Membership-supported political organization in Washington, D.C., dedicated to promoting the full representation of Asian Americans in the Democratic Party at all levels of government, formed in 1986. The group worked on legislative issues that included Japanese American redress, immigration, bilingual education, and racial/hate violence and was instrumental in the defeat of two legislative bills in Maryland that would have made English the official language of the state. The organization disbanded in the early 1990's.

National Dollar Stores: Chain of fifty-four retail stores established by Joe SHOONG in California, Washington, Utah, Arizona, and Hawaii. Originally established as the China-Toggery-Shoong Company in 1921, the name was changed to the above in 1928. In early 1938 the stores were struck by more than a hundred Chinese members of the International Ladies Garment Workers' Union (ILGWU) Local 341 (the Chinese Ladies Garment Workers' Union). The laborers wanted wage parity with union workers, who were making several times more money. After thirteen weeks the strike ended, with National Dollar Stores agreeing to a 5 percent weekly pay increase, a $14 per week minimum wage, and paid holidays.

Nationalist Party. *See* **Guomindang**

Nationals: In the United States, "national" means a person owing permanent allegiance to a state; "national of the United States " means either a citizen of this country or a person who, though not a citizen of the United States, owes such permanent allegiance to the United States.

Each state, as part of its sovereign powers, exercises jurisdiction over those persons living in it. Its primary concern is with those individuals who are its citizens, its true members. Legal writers as well as legislators in many countries employ two terms in this connection—"nationals" and "citizens"—and it should be kept in mind that the two may not always be synonymous. "National," in popular usage, has a broader meaning than "citizen" does. Before the Philippines became independent, the inhabitants of the archipelago were nationals of the United States but not citizens. When the Philippines became independent, all Filipinos not naturalized in other countries (including all those born in the islands but residing as nationals in the United States) became citizens of the Republic of the Philippines and lost their status as nationals of the United States. By contrast, a citizen of any country is, at the same time, a national of that country. Today most of the fifteen thousand Samoans in American Samoa are U.S. nationals, not U.S. citizens. They are, for example, not permitted to vote in American presidential elections.

The Importance of Nationality. Because domestic laws of states relating to citizenship vary greatly, the terms "national" and "nationality" are framed with respect to international law. The relationship between state and citizen represents a link through which an individual normally can and does enjoy the protection and benefits of international law. If an individual lacks a nationality tie to a state, he or she is without protection if a wrong is done to him or her by any government, for without this tie no state would be willing to protect that individual against the government that had committed the wrong. Nationality, then, is the bond that unites individuals with a given state, that identifies them as members of that entity, that enables them to claim its protection, and that also subjects them to the performance of such duties as their state may impose on them. The International Court of Justice has held that there must exist a specific link, a genuine connection, between a state and its nationals. This doctrine has, however, been criticized strongly, for each state is free to decide who shall be its nationals, under what conditions nationality shall be conferred, and who shall be deprived of such status and in what manner.

Acquisition of citizenship in the United States is governed solely by the U.S. Constitution and by acts of Congress. Nationality may be acquired through either of two modes: by birth or by naturalization. Most of those living in each of the fifty U.S. states acquire their nationality by the former method, but tens of thousands of persons, as well as individuals singly, have received a new nationality by the second method.

Rules That Govern. By general agreement, any individual born on the soil of a given state of parents who are nationals of that state is regarded as a national of the state in question (the rule of *jus soli*). Based on comity or courtesy rather than on international law, however, children of foreign heads of state, foreign diplomats, and, in a few cases, foreign consular officials are not claimed as nationals by the state on whose soil they happen to be born. Most European states, by contrast, adhere primarily to the civil law principle of the law of the blood (*jus sanguinis*), according to which a child's nationality follows that of the parents, regardless of the place of its birth. Thus, a child born to French parents in the United States would be a French national under *jus sanguinis* as well as an American national under *jus soli*. In the United States that individual would be an American citizen, in France a French citizen, and in Ghana a citizen of both France and the United States (dual nationality). Children born aboard vessels registered in the United States are not however, U.S. nationals under *jus soli*.

Effect of Dual Nationality. Generally, when two states have a claim on a person's allegiance on the basis of birth, the state asserting its primary preference as to principle of law and exercising actual control over the individual is acknowledged by the other claimant to be sovereign over the person in question. Individuals sometimes hold two nationalities concurrently. Thus, a number of Japanese-descent American nationals present in Japan at the outbreak of war with the United States in 1941 were forced to enter the Japanese armed forces. According to American laws, the individuals were nationals of the United States under *jus soli*; but under the prevailing Japanese laws, they were Japanese citizens under *jus sanguinis*.

The problem of dual nationality itself, irksome as it is to both the states and the individuals concerned, has not yet been settled by means of a general international convention. The Convention on Certain Questions Relating to Conflict of Nationality Laws, signed at The Hague in 1930, was a modest beginning. This instrument, to which the United States did not become a party, stated that a person having two or more nationalities could be regarded as a national by each of the states whose nationality he possessed; that a state could not afford diplomatic protection to one of its nationals against a state of which that person was also a national; that in a third state a person having dual nationality should be treated as if he were a national of only one state; and that a person possessing two nationalities acquired involuntarily was entitled to renounce one of them but only with the permission of the state whose nationality he desired to surrender. In general, states today follow in practice almost all those provisions, despite the absence of general conventional rules.—*Ceferina Gayo Hess*

SUGGESTED READINGS: • Hooson, David, ed. *Geography and National Identity*. Vol. 29 in the Institute of British Geographers Special Service Publications Series. Cambridge, Mass.: Blackwell, 1993. • Moynihan, Daniel P. *Pandaemonium: Ethnicity in International Politics*. New York: Oxford University Press, 1993. • Ringrose, Marjorie, and Adam Lerner, eds. *Reimagining the Nation*. Bristol, Pa.: Taylor & Francis, 1993. • Von Glahn, Gerhard. *Law Among Nations: An Introduction to Public International Law*. 6th rev. ed. New York: Macmillan, 1992.

Native American Programs Act of 1974: U.S. legislation that for the first time recognized Hawaiians as a category of native peoples, while providing funds to back activities on behalf of native American groups. Legislation regarding North American natives, American Indians, began in the eighteenth century, when neither Alaska nor Hawaii were part of the United States. In 1971, when Congress passed the Alaska Native Claims Settlement Act to hasten construction of an oil pipeline from Alaska to the Pacific Northwest, Native Hawaiians realized as never before that they had been excluded from programs to advance the status of native American people groups.

Samoan man, circa 1890. Samoans and other Native American Pacific Islanders are eligible for federal programs under amendments to the Native American Programs Act of 1974. (Brigham Young University, Hawaii)

Accordingly some Hawaiian organizations began to lobby Congress for appropriate legislation. In 1974 the Economic Opportunity Act of 1964 was amended; Title VIII of the legislation (the NATIVE AMERICAN PROGRAMS ACT) for the first time identified Hawaiians as a category of native peoples. In 1987 the law was amended to add "other Native American Pacific Islanders (including American Samoan Natives)" to the list of groups. To qualify for entitlements under the legislation, Hawaiians, Samoans, and other Native American Pacific Islanders must prove that their ancestors were living on the islands at the time of contact with the West during the eighteenth century.

The legislation directs the U.S. Department of Health and Human Services to provide financial assistance for research, demonstration projects, and pilot projects aimed at promoting self-sufficiency for native American groups. Funds can go either to public agencies or to private nonprofit corporations, with the federal government generally providing no more than 80 percent of the financing for each project.

Alu Like ("working together" in Hawaiian), a nonprofit corporation, was formed in 1975 to administer the funds by directing needs-assessment surveys in a variety of areas of concern to the Native Hawaiian community. When the surveys found significant social problems among Native Hawaiians, Congress passed legislation to provide additional assistance, including the NATIVE HAWAIIAN HEALTH CARE ACT OF 1988.

In 1987 Title VIII was amended to provide a revolving loan fund, with $3 million from 1988 to 1990. The fund was reauthorized in 1992 for $3 million for an additional three years, matched by an equal amount by the OFFICE OF HAWAIIAN AFFAIRS (OHA), state of Hawaii, which has administered the fund since its inception.

Native Hawaiian Health Care Act of 1988: U.S. legislation enacted in order to provide Native Hawaiians with better overall health care. In 1980 Congress established the NATIVE HAWAIIAN STUDY COMMISSION. Its job was to investigate problems that might require granting reparations to a people who had lost their autonomy when the Hawaiian monarchy fell in 1893. Although the report did not favor reparations, an appendix presented statistics on the dire health status of Native Hawaiians.

In 1984 Congress reacted by commissioning a comprehensive study of the health conditions of Native Hawaiians. In 1986 members of Congress asked the Office of Technology Assessment, which not long ago had produced a report on the health care for American Indians, to provide a comparative perspective on the data regarding Native Hawaiians. The resulting analysis revealed that the health of Hawaiians of mixed blood was slightly worse than the national average; by contrast pure-blooded Native Hawaiians were subject to a wide variety of diseases at a rate that was greater than almost every other ethnic group in the United States.

Accordingly, in 1987 legislators proposed to amend the Indian Health Care Improvement Act (1976) to benefit Native Hawaiians. Under the new Native Hawaiian Health Care Act of 1988, grants of up to $11.25 million were authorized for the establishment of Native Hawaiian health centers incorporating traditional Hawaiian healers and Western-trained health personnel. These facilities would be operated by Native Hawaiian organizations charged with developing programs on disease prevention, health promotion, and primary health services other than in-patient services. Beginning in 1990 up to $4.6 million was authorized to Papa Ola Lokahi, a consortium of health care institutions, to design a comprehensive health care master plan for Native Hawaiians and to administer the centers. The consortium consists of Alu Like (a coordinating body for federal programs), three agencies of Hawaii state government (the OFFICE OF HAWAIIAN AFFAIRS, the Office of Hawaiian Health, and the University of Hawaii), and E Ola Mau (an organization of Hawaiian health professionals).

In 1992 the legislation was reauthorized, setting numerical goals for the reduction of various adverse health conditions by the year 2000 and providing scholarships in health fields to Native Hawaiians.

Native Hawaiian Legal Corporation: Non-profit public interest law firm founded in Hawaii in 1978. The group attempts to reclaim stolen Native Hawaiian lands by tracing land ownership through genealogical research and by supporting Native Hawaiian legal claims.

Native Hawaiians Study Commission: Nine-member commission appointed to conduct a comprehensive study of the questions relating to Native Hawaiian property claims arising from the overthrow of the Hawaiian monarchy in 1893 as well as to provide background information regarding the culture, needs, and concerns of Native Hawaiians. The first commission, appointed by President Jimmy Carter in 1980, was dissolved and replaced by appointees selected by President Ronald Reagan in 1981. Substantial disagreement between the three Native Hawaiian and six nonnative members of the commission over the methodology of the study and its analysis of actual information resulted in the presentation of two separate reports containing conflicting accounts of the role played by the United States in Hawaii's past and its responsibilities in shaping Hawaii's future.

The majority report not only cleared the U.S. government of any direct responsibility for the 1893 overthrow of Queen LILIUOKALANI but also rejected the notion that federal action was necessary to redress the property claims stemming from this event. The minority report, which was written by Kinau Kamalii, Roger Betts, and Winona Beamer, listed fourteen key recommendations. Some of the key points included the recommendation that Congress pass a joint resolution to acknowledge the role of the U.S. government in the overthrow and to announce its intention to grant restitution to Native Hawaiians; that the Senate Energy and Natural Resources Committee and the House Committee on Interior and Insular Affairs work together in consultation with Native Hawaiians to determine an equitable resolution of legitimate claims; that such restitution be subject to formal acceptance by Native Hawaiians; that federal policies concerning the use and possible release of federally controlled lands to native residents be reviewed; that the commission be directed to advise Congress on the status of such lands and be given the authority to declare such lands surplus and available for return to the state of Hawaii; that Native Hawaiians be included in all Native American programs; that a special federal-state study be conducted to assess the needs of Native Hawaiians; and that the definition of Native Hawaiian be expanded to refer to "any individual whose ancestors were the natives of the area which constituted the Hawaiian Islands prior to 1778."

Hearings were held on the islands of Oahu, Hawaii, Maui, and Kauai in April of 1984 to present the commission's findings and to record the responses of witnesses who were invited to comment on these findings. The minority report was particularly important for its airing of issues relating to the movement for sovereignty in Hawaii.

Native Sons of the Golden State (NSGS): There were two organizations that were originally known by this name. The first was formed between June and July, 1875, in San Francisco with John Steinbeck as its first president and was incorporated in March, 1876. By 1880 the original one hundred members had decided to expand their horizons and changed the name to the Native Sons of the Golden West (NSGW). Its purpose, as stated in the original constitution, was for the mutual benefit, mental improvement, and social intercourse of its members. It was formed in order to remember the Forty-Niners, to elevate and cultivate the mental faculties of its members, to rejoice over the prosperity of each member, to improve the condition of its members by helping them to obtain employment, and to extend to its members assistance in time of sickness. The male members had to have a good reputation and a respectable calling and practice temperance. The organization had a Grand Parlor in San Francisco and local parlors, the first one being established in Oakland.

The second organization, the United Parlor of the Native Sons of the Golden State, was founded by Chun Dick, Sue Lock, Ng Gunn, Li Tai Wing, Leong Sing, Leong Chung, and Lan Foy on May 4, 1895, and reorganized by Walter U. Lum, and Ng Gunn in 1904, with new articles of incorporation filed in 1912. Encouraged by an unidentified European-American attorney, a group of native-born Chinese Americans founded this fraternal organization for the purpose of fighting for their rights as American citizens, improving and elevating their position as Chinese Americans so that the foreign-born Chinese would respect them, and accelerating the process of assimilation into American society. They were inspired by and used the patriotic NSGW as their model. Their structure, offices, and constitutions were similar. Both organizations decided to carry out their purpose and aims by selling, renting, leasing, mortgaging, improving, and dealing in real estate and personal property. Both organizations had their main headquarters, or Grand Parlor, in San Francisco and branch parlors throughout California and the Western states.

There was one notable deviation from the NSGW constitution. Disgusted with the bellicose *tongs*, the Chinese Native Sons wanted to exclude them from their membership and included the clause: "It is imperative that no member shall have sectional, clannish, Tong or Party prejudices against each other or to use such influences to oppress fellow members. Whosoever violates this provision shall be expelled from the membership of this organization."

The Chinese Native Sons participated in many community activities for the benefit of Chinese Americans; were concerned with immigration, health, welfare, and education issues; and, most important, encouraged participation in the political process of the United States. Local lodges (Los Angeles, May of 1912; Oakland, June of 1912; Fresno and San Diego, 1914) were established in major Chinese communities in California and were then expanded by 1915 into the CHINESE AMERICAN CITIZENS ALLIANCE (CACA) outside California (Chicago, March of 1917; Detroit, Boston, Pittsburgh, and Portland, February of 1921). In 1929 the organization officially began calling itself the Chinese American Citizens Alliance.

On July 15, 1924, the organization sponsored its own daily newspaper, the *CHINESE TIMES* (San Francisco), the first successful daily newspaper owned, edited, and published by Chinese Americans. By 1929 the *Chinese Times* had the largest circulation among Chinese newspapers published in San Francisco, a position it held for many decades.

Native Sons of the Golden West (NSGW): Organization, called the NATIVE SONS OF THE GOLDEN STATE (NSGS) until 1880, composed of native-born Californians, "a body of young men unparalleled in physical development and mental vigor and unsurpassed in pride and enthusiasm for the land that gave them birth," according to their constitution. Begun in 1875 with one hundred members and with John Steinbeck as president, the NSGW suffered a decline in October, 1877, when one of its investments, the Pioneer Land and Loan Bank, failed. Oakland established a branch parlor in December, 1877, and after some rocky years, the order expanded by 1897 to include some two hundred parlors throughout California and the West. From the start of the twentieth century until the onset of the Great Depression, it was one of the most influential pressure groups in California and included among its members numerous anti-Japanese and anti-Filipino advocates, such as V. S. McCLATCHY (brother of the *Sacramento Bee* publisher Charles McClatchy), who led the JAPANESE EXCLUSION LEAGUE OF CALIFORNIA in the 1920's.

Chief Justice Earl Warren of the U.S. Supreme Court (center), with Senator and Mrs. Spark Matsunaga of Hawaii. As a member of the NSGW, Warren used his authority as California attorney general to strip Nisei internees in the relocation centers of their right to vote. (Courtesy Matthew Matsunaga)

The NSGW worked for numerous anti-Asian causes, including the establishment of a separate school for Asians in San Francisco. In May, 1907, the organization began its monthly publication, the *Grizzly Bear*, and warned of "The Asiatic Peril" in that and every subsequent issue. "Would you like your daughter to marry a Japanese? If not, demand that your representative in the Legislature vote for segregation of whites and Asiatics in the public schools," the *Grizzly Bear* urged. The group also popularized unfavorable images of the "dangerously" sexual Filipino males in the 1920's and took a strong stance against Japanese immigration throughout the Western states.

After World War I the NSGW joined with other similar patriotic as well as labor organizations to oppose the immigration of the Japanese; the group's activities contributed to the passage of the IMMIGRATION ACT OF 1924. In January, 1942, the organization joined the California Joint Immigration Committee (a private organization) and other anti-Japanese groups in pressuring U.S. President Franklin D. Roosevelt to remove "all persons of Japanese lineage . . . aliens and citizens alike from the West Coast." One NSGW member, California Attorney General Earl Warren, was able to disenfranchise the NISEI in the RELOCATION CAMPS on the basis that they had not fulfilled the residency requirement for voting. Then in June, 1942, the NSGW filed a lawsuit, *Regan v. King*, in an unsuccessful attempt to take away citizenship from all Japanese Americans. The Ninth Circuit Court of Appeals ruled against Regan on the basis of the U.S. Supreme Court decision in the *Wong Kim Ark* (1898), case which declared that an American-born Chinese was a U.S. citizen even though his or her alien parents were ineligible to vote. After this failure the NSGW began to agitate for national legislation to disenfranchise the Nisei, and the outcome was the formation of the California Citizens' Association, dedicated to carrying on the campaign for permanent exclusion of the Japanese. This was another failure. After World War II the NSGW turned its attention to other, more positive patriotic activities, such as fund-raising for education.

Natividad, Irene (b. Sept. 14, 1948, Manila, Republic of the Philippines): Academician and political activist. She gained prominence in 1985 when she became the first Asian American to head the bipartisan National Women's Political Caucus. As its national chair from 1985 to 1988, Natividad strongly affirmed that the basic route to power is through politics and that women are increasing their influence over American politics as voters, campaign staff members, and candidates. One of her missions was to transfer the political expertise that women developed on a national level to state and local levels, through workshops focusing on such basics as polling techniques, fundraising, local organization, and strategies for dealing with the news media.

Having earned a B.A. degree in 1971 from Long Island University and M.A. (1973) and M.Phil. degrees (1976) from Columbia University, she was awarded an honorary Ph.D. degree by Long Island University in 1989. Natividad was introduced to politics as a college student in 1968, when she passed out campaign leaflets for Eugene Joseph McCarthy's presidential bid. This experience became the springboard for numerous political and governmental positions including chair of the New York State Asian Pacific Caucus (1982-1984), deputy vice chair of the Asian Pacific Caucus of the Democratic National Committee (1982-1984), representative to the Ferraro Campaign (1984), and Alternate Delegate of the Democratic Convention (1984). She was also an adjunct instructor in the English department at Lehman College and City University, New York (1974), an instructor in the English department at Columbia University (1974-1976), and the director of Continuing Education, both at Long Island University, New York and at William Paterson College, New Jersey (1978-1985).

Natividad has served as founder and president of Asian-American Professional Women, Inc., founding director of the National Network of Asian-Pacific American Women and the Child Care Action Campaign, and executive director of The Philippine American Foundation. She is also the recipient of numerous honors and awards, including the Outstanding Young Woman Award (1978), the Democratic Women's Congressional Council's Women Making History Award (1985), Americans by Choice's Honored American Award (1986), and the Filipino American Women's Network Award. She was also voted one of the one hundred most influential women by *Ladies Home Journal* in 1989.

Natividad has served as director of the 1992 Global Forum by Women (Dublin, Ireland), a gathering of more than four hundred international women leaders from fifty-eight countries to develop strategies to address issues facing women worldwide. She has also served as the chair of the National Commission on Working Women, which works to improve the economic status of working women across the United States. Having campaigned for Bill Clinton and Albert

Irene Natividad. (Filipino American National Historical Society)

Gore in the 1992 election season, she cochaired the Women of Color for Change Committee for Clinton/Gore, a group of African American women leaders representing some twenty four organizations. The group planned fundraisers, rallies, and meetings on behalf of Clinton/Gore. She has testified before Congress on several issues, such as family leave, health care, and judicial appointments of members who did not favor women's issues. President Clinton has appointed her as a director of Sallie Mae, the quasi-governmental corporation that administers student loans.

Natividad is married to Andrea Cortese, director of Digital Communications Services for the Communications Satellite Corporation, and they have a son, Carlo Natividad-Cortese.

Nativism: The belief that native members of a society should be given first consideration with regard to society's resources. There are varieties of nativism. Some nativists call for increased restrictions on immigration, while others want a total ban on new immigration; some believe that benefits for foreign-born residents should be severely limited. Expressions of nativism range from speech to discrimination to violence.

Nativist sentiments have waxed and waned in intensity and influence over the course of American history. The reasoning or support for nativism can range from sheer racism to thoughtful arguments based on economics. Extreme cases of the former hold that nonnative races are genetically inferior; in the United States, such presumptions have been made with regard to Asians, South Europeans, Africans, and others. The psychological and sociological origins of racism cannot be discussed here, but it seems certain that racism against immigrants is more evident and virulent when immigrants are more numerous, when they are quite different from the "natives," and when the economic situation is such that there is competition from the immigrants. All these conditions pertained in the early 1990's, when nativism was on the rise.

More thoughtful arguments in favor of at least limiting immigration have some of the same foundations. Economic arguments, for example, center on the fact that immigrants are perceived as taking jobs from and lowering wages for the native population. Research has been equivocal on this question.

In terms of culture, immigrant groups are seen as "different" and thus—from the nativist perspective—

as threatening "the American way of life." Immigrant groups bring with them different languages, foods, dress, and behaviors. They are especially viewed as introducing values that are seen as not in tune with those of American democratic society.

Compounding the situation, and a basic underpinning of some of the milder nativist arguments, is the fact that immigration was booming in the late twentieth century. The number of immigrants was more than half a million annually for the 1981-1991 decade and in 1989-1991 rose to almost 1.5 million because of the amnesty and legalization provisions of the Immigration Reform and Control Act of 1986. Nativists see such large numbers as undermining American culture and turning the United States into an unstable, fragmented society.

Naturalization Act of 1790: Formally passed as An Act to Establish a Uniform Rule of Naturalization, U.S. government legislation defining the requirements for American citizenship. Under the act, citizenship required two years of residence in the country and was limited to "free white persons."

Creation of the new act originated with President George Washington, who suggested congressional adoption of a uniform naturalization rule. The result was the first in a series of federal statutes under which the right of citizenship was extended only to free whites. In the wake of the American Civil War (1861-1865), the law was amended to allow blacks to become citizens. Asian immigrants to the United States, however, unlike all other immigrant groups, remained excluded from naturalization (although their American-born children were U.S. citizens by right of birth). That policy began to change with the IMMIGRATION ACT OF 1943, which repealed the Chinese Exclusion Acts and made Chinese immigrants eligible for citizenship. The LUCE-CELLER BILL OF 1946 extended the right to Asian Indian and Filipino immigrants, and the MCCARRAN-WALTER ACT OF 1952 conferred it upon other Asian groups as well.

Nee, Victor (b. 1945): Scholar. Professor at Cornell University, he is best known as coauthor, with Brett de Bary Nee, of *Longtime Californ': A Documentary Study of an American Chinatown* (1973), a collection of oral histories about San Francisco Chinatown residents. The book was one of the first to record the lives of Chinese using the voices of the Chinese people. Other books include *Remaking the Economic Institutions of Socialism: China and Eastern Europe* (1989) and *Social Exchange and Political Process in Maoist China* (1991).

Nehru, Jawaharlal (Nov. 14, 1889, Allahabad, Republic of India—May 27, 1964, New Delhi, India): First prime minister of independent India. Born to an affluent Indian family that had originally migrated from Kashmir, Nehru was sent by his lawyer father to do his schooling at Harrow, one of England's exclusive private schools. Later he attended the University of Cambridge. The years he spent in England were the most important in shaping his ideas and attitudes, including his interest in Fabian socialism, his attraction for Western liberal ideas, and his dislike for religious orthodoxy.

Although Nehru started his law practice upon returning to India in 1912, he soon fell under the spell of Mahatma GANDHI, who was launching his mass nonviolent civil disobedience movement for India's independence. Their relationship was strange in many ways: Nehru was skeptical of Gandhi's talk of spirituality but was impressed with his nonviolent approach to India's freedom struggle. As a Gandhian freedom fighter, Nehru first went to jail in 1921 and was imprisoned by the British again a number of times. In prison, he found time to write his autobiography and such books as *The Discovery of India* (1946).

During his struggle for India's freedom, Nehru traveled to Europe during the 1930's and was much impressed by such events as the Spanish Civil War (1936-1939) and the rise of Fascism. When World War II broke out in 1939, he led the Congress Party in offering support to Great Britain and its allies in their struggle against Fascism, provided that London would promise India freedom after the war. Headed by Sir Winston Churchill, who was opposed to granting independence to India, the English government threw Nehru and others in jail.

After the war, India, in 1947, was partitioned into the two independent countries of India and Pakistan. Nehru became the first prime minister of India at the age of fifty-seven. Enjoying unparalleled popularity among all sections of the country's diverse population, Nehru, unlike many other Asian and African leaders, eschewed the temptation of a more authoritarian rule by having India's Constituent Assembly adopt a constitution based on the concepts of equality, freedom of expression, and democracy. Despite the opposition of many religious orthodox groups, Nehru stood firmly for a secular state. In economic policy, he launched the country's developmental programs within the frame-

Jawaharlal Nehru. (AP/Wide World Photos)

Nehru was joined by Yugoslavian Communist leader Josip Broz Tito (shown here) in launching the nonalignment movement on a global scale in 1961. (National Archives)

work of a mixed economy, although publicly he mostly talked about socialism.

In foreign policy, Nehru believed that India—and, for that matter, other Asian and African countries—could benefit most by following a policy of nonalignment. They would be able not only to preserve their independence in an international environment vitiated by the Cold War but also to establish a fruitful economic relationship with both the West and the East. He joined Josip Broz Tito of Yugoslavia and Gamal Abdel Nasser of Egypt in 1961 to launch the nonalignment movement on an international scale. Nehru died while still holding office as India's prime minister.

Nehru's legacy to India and the world has been a mixed one. A great freedom fighter, he also became his nation's builder after independence. Perhaps his lasting achievement was to set India's future course on democratic and secular foundations.

Neo Hom (United Lao National Liberation Front): Shadowy right-wing anticommunist group founded in the United States in 1981. Believed to be controlled by the Hmong General VANG PAO, it attracted much attention in 1989-1991 when its fundraisers were accused of soliciting monthly contributions from Hmong in the United States. These contributions were solicited under a number of pretexts, including an exchange for promised jobs in the government that the Neo Hom proposed to establish in Laos and return air tickets to a liberated Laos.

Opponents of the Neo Hom claimed that such offers took unfair advantage of the many homesick Hmong, most of whom were on welfare, in order to finance the unrealistic ambitions of Vang and other wealthy leaders. Such claims were typically made anonymously because of death threats said to have been issued by the Neo Hom leadership.

Of concern to the U.S. government were unsubstantiated reports that contributions to Neo Hom were demanded from clients of the social service agency Lao Family Community, which had also been headed by Vang from 1979 to 1988. These accusations led to the cutting off of U.S. government funding for the agency's branch in Orange County, California, and the legal separation of the other branches from the national association.

It has never been clear how much money was collected by the Neo Hom or how much of it actually went to fund resistance operations in Laos. Besides the contributions from the refugees themselves, several anticommunist American groups also made donations of "humanitarian" assistance, which in sum meant that the organization had a substantial budget. Nevertheless, the U.S. State Department in 1990 described the threat presented by the Neo Hom to the government of Laos as being insignificant. By the 1990's, however, the Thai government was discouraging any active involvement of Laotian rebels on Thai soil.

Nepal: Independent kingdom in South Asia. It is located along the southern slopes of the Himalayas and is landlocked between two countries: the Tibetan Autonomous Region of China to the north and India to the east, west, and south.

Nepal has an area of 54,362 square miles. Topographically, it is divided into three zones: The mountains in the north, which cover 25 percent of the landmass and have only 3 percent cultivable land; the hill areas, including valleys such as the Kathmandu, which form more than 55 percent of the total landmass, house about 60 percent of Nepal's population, and have only 25 percent cultivable land; and the Tarai area, commonly known as the breadbasket of Nepal, located in the southern belt of the country. The Tarai, a strip of low flatland, covers approximately 20 percent of the

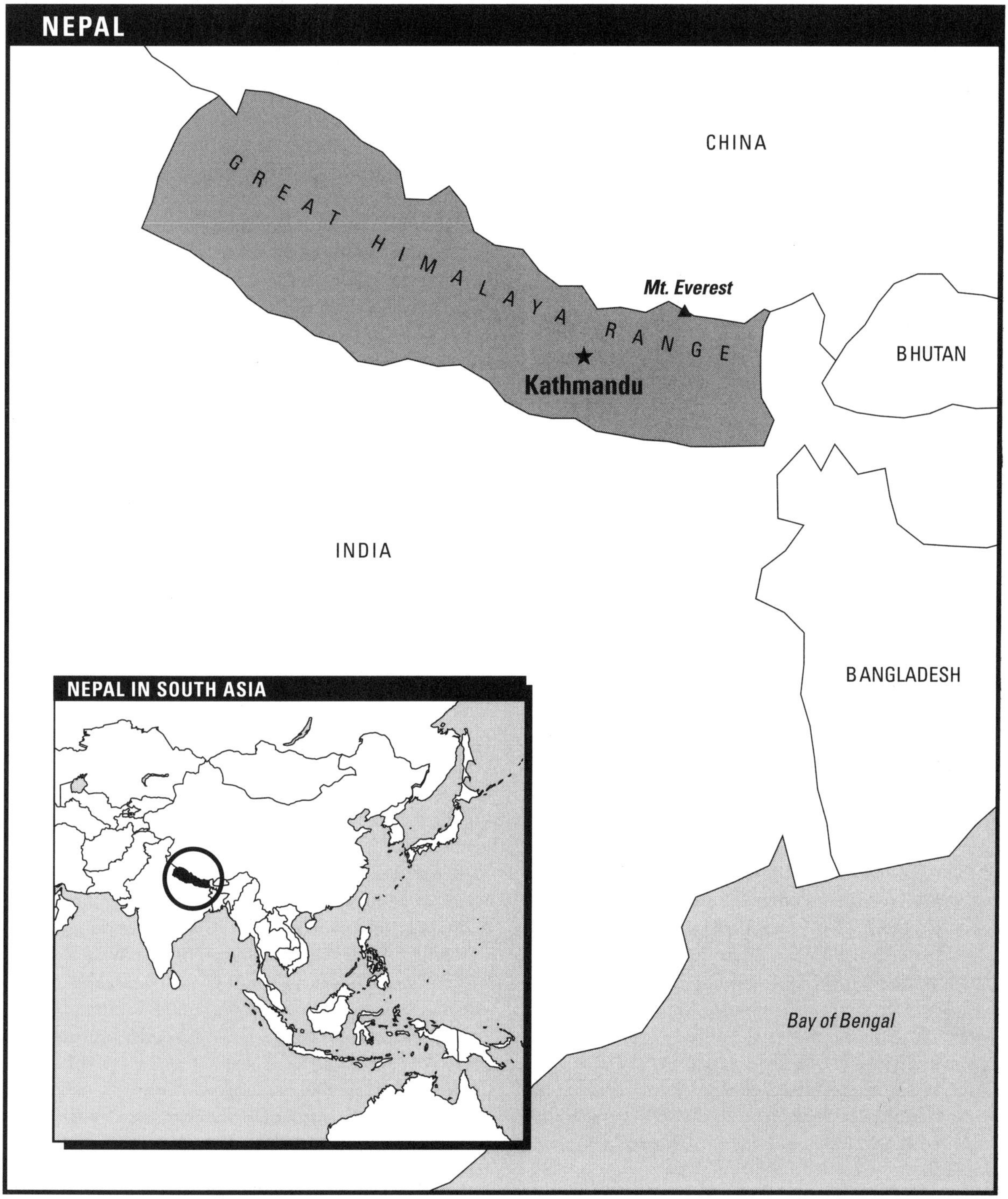
NEPAL
CHINA
GREAT HIMALAYA RANGE
Mt. Everest
BHUTAN
Kathmandu
INDIA
BANGLADESH
NEPAL IN SOUTH ASIA
Bay of Bengal

total land area, houses about 30 percent of the population, and has 70 percent cultivable land.

Nepal's population is overwhelmingly rural. In 1992, its population was estimated to be 19,795,000, of which only 8.3 percent lived in urban areas and 91.7 percent in rural areas. Nepal's population is ethnically and religiously diverse, primarily of Indo-Aryan and Burman descent. Nepalese society is composed of ethnic groups who live in close proximity to one another but remain clearly demarcated by distinctive languages, religions (HINDUISM, BUDDHISM, ISLAM, Christianity, and ANIMISM), race, and historical experiences. Although Nepali is the official language, sixty-four different dialects are spoken in Nepal. The official state religion is Hinduism.

Nepal opened its doors to the outside world in 1951. The land of the majestic Himalayas and the home of the tallest mountain in the world (Mount Everest), Nepal is popularly advertised in tour books as "Shangrila." It attracts tourists from the industrialized world generally out of curiosity and as a source of spirituality. Aside from its reputation as an exotic land, Nepal is also known to be one of the poorest countries in the world. On the basis of 1990 economic and social indicators, Nepal was classified with twenty-five other countries as "least developed," with a per capita income of about $170 per year.

Nepal has a subsistence-level agrarian economy. More than 90 percent of its national income is derived from agriculture. The system of government until early 1990 was called "partyless" PANCHAYAT democracy and was headed by an absolute monarch. The monarch influenced the political, economic, and social arenas of Nepal. The panchayat system of government was a four-tiered pyramid of councils, headed by the monarch, who exercised absolute power. The absolute power of the Nepalese monarchy, however, was challenged in early 1990, resulting in a drastic transfer of power, on April 9, 1990, from the monarchy to the people. After that, the system of government became a parliamentary democracy similar to that of the United Kingdom, with the monarch as head of state and the prime minister as head of the government. The difference in the Nepalese parliament system is that the monarch still retains the right to dissolve the government at any given moment and for any reason.

Network. *See* **Guanxi**

New Americans Conferences (1927-1941): Series of public assemblies organized annually by Hawaii Nisei to examine their place in the future of Hawaii. During the conferences, NISEI from throughout the Territory gathered to hear from the islands' government, business, and community leaders. Ample time was invested in addressing issues of interest to the Nisei and plotting a course of action for their assuming a greater voice in the political and socioeconomic life of Hawaii. The open format of the conferences allowed for the public expression of opinion on these expectations.

The idea for the New Americans Conferences originated with the Reverend Takie OKUMURA. As a Japanese Christian minister in Hawaii, he had since 1924 been urging the Nisei to live as loyal U.S. citizens, become politically active and exercise their right to vote, and stick to agriculture (as the islands' white leadership advised). His goal had been to improve relations between the resident Japanese population and the dominant Caucasian minority. In 1927 he took this "Americanization" campaign a step further when he initiated the first of the conferences as a means of educating the Nisei with these ideals in mind. Fundraising and planning committees were formed, speakers were chosen (mostly prominent whites but including Japanese Americans), and delegates (Nisei only) were invited. A total of more than nine hundred delegates attended the fifteen conferences.

Many of the issues raised and debated at the conferences concerned the inequalities inherent in the prevailing Hawaiian power structure and the means by which they might be abolished. Whether out of racial prejudice or other factors, a significant segment of conference speakers chose to steer a narrow, conservative course, essentially advising the Nisei to live within the established order. To that end, the former encouraged Japanese Americans to be content with jobs in agriculture, to live as those worthy of the privilege of American citizenship, and to do their best to assimilate fully into the larger American society.

Beyond the rhetoric, many Nisei, however diligently they may have tried to prove themselves good Americans entitled to better opportunities, found that, outside agriculture, entry into white-collar professions in Hawaii was subject to a kind of "glass ceiling." They even encountered resistance from the islands' ISSEI employers, many of whom expressed contempt for them and refused to hire them. Moreover, the conferences proved not to be a means of political or socioeconomic empowerment for the Nisei after all. Sensitive to the highly public nature of the discussions, and fearful that negative remarks would brand them as un-American, many Nisei hesitated to express their true feelings even on points with which they vehemently disagreed.

No more conferences were held in the aftermath of Japan's surprise bombing of PEARL HARBOR, Honolulu, in December of 1941. World War II enabled Hawaii's Nisei men to prove their loyalty once and for all. In the postwar period Hawaii's other ethnic minorities formed an influential voting bloc that finally secured a substantial share of political control and established a permanent power base in the islands.

New Delhi: Capital of India. The city is situated within the Indian union territory of Delhi, in northcentral India. New Delhi contained a population of more than 294,000 people in 1991.

New Korea (*Sinhan Minbo*): Weekly Korean-language newspaper first published on February 1, 1909, under the editorial supervision of Choe Chong-ik to serve the San Francisco Bay Area. The paper had been previously published under the name *Mutual Cooperative News* between 1907 and 1908. Its editorial offices were moved from Oakland to San Francisco and later were relocated to Los Angeles after the KOREAN NATIONAL ASSOCIATION (KNA) built its headquarters there. One of numerous papers serving Korean communities in the United States, *New Korea* holds the distinction of having the longest operation of any such newspaper.

New religions. *See* **Shin shukyo**

New Territories: Enclave of GUANGDONG Province, acquired by Great Britain in 1898 on a ninety-nine-year lease and incorporated into HONG KONG. It is the last piece of Asian land claimed by the British. (Hong Kong Island was ceded to Great Britain in 1841 and the Kowloon Peninsula in 1860.) The New Territories occupy an area of about 368 square miles and are formed of the area north of Kowloon Peninsula from Mirs Bay on the east to Deep Bay on the west, including Lantau Island and many other islands. The area's 1991 population was almost 2.4 million.

News Media and Asian Americans: The impact of the news media goes far beyond the pages printed or the minutes aired. Print and broadcast news—along with other media images and treatments—affect how Asian Americans view themselves and how they in turn are viewed by others. The media also have the power to affect how Asian Americans treat themselves and are treated by other people.

Statistics. U.S. census data from 1990 peg the Asian Pacific American population at approximately 2.9 percent of the total population. Projections out of the University of California, Los Angeles suggest that by the year 2000 that figure will reach about 4.0 percent. In California, Hawaii, and the Tri-State region of New York-New Jersey-Pennsylvania, the Asian Pacific American percentage of the general population is much greater.

In 1991 more than 50 percent of newsrooms serving U.S. daily newspapers did not have any Asian Americans, African Americans, Latino Americans, or American Indians working in them. Asian Pacific Americans constituted only 1.5 percent (836) of the total work force (55,700) in the daily newspaper industry. The majority of those journalists were reporters (366) and copy editors (173). Asian Pacific Americans represented only 0.9 percent of newsroom supervisors.

In the radio and television industries, the figures for 1991 reflect a similar pattern. Only 1.3 percent (2,010) of the total number of employees (158,779) in commercial and noncommercial broadcasting were Asian Pacific Americans. Moreover while the percentage had remained the same since 1988, the actual number had decreased along with the general downsizing of the industry.

Unequal Representation. In addition to the general underrepresentation of Asian Pacific Americans in the media, there are some areas where the lack of participation is particularly noteworthy. Most evident is the relatively low number of Asian Pacific American males in the broadcast field, especially as anchors. Journalists and other experts in the field have speculated as to the possible reasons for this. One theory is that the general stereotype of Asian Pacific American males (submissive and passive) does not endow them with sufficient "authority" to present the news. Another theory is that because television tends to imitate and repeat what has worked well in the past, the success of the initial pairing of an Asian Pacific American woman with a (usually) white male co-anchor has encouraged the industry to use the same formula rather than try something different, such as hiring an Asian American male coanchor.

Another area of particular concern is the very low number of journalists—at any level—from certain ethnic communities that constitute Asian Pacific America, especially the more recently established or smaller ones. According to a 1990 study conducted for the ASIAN AMERICAN JOURNALISTS ASSOCIATION (AAJA),

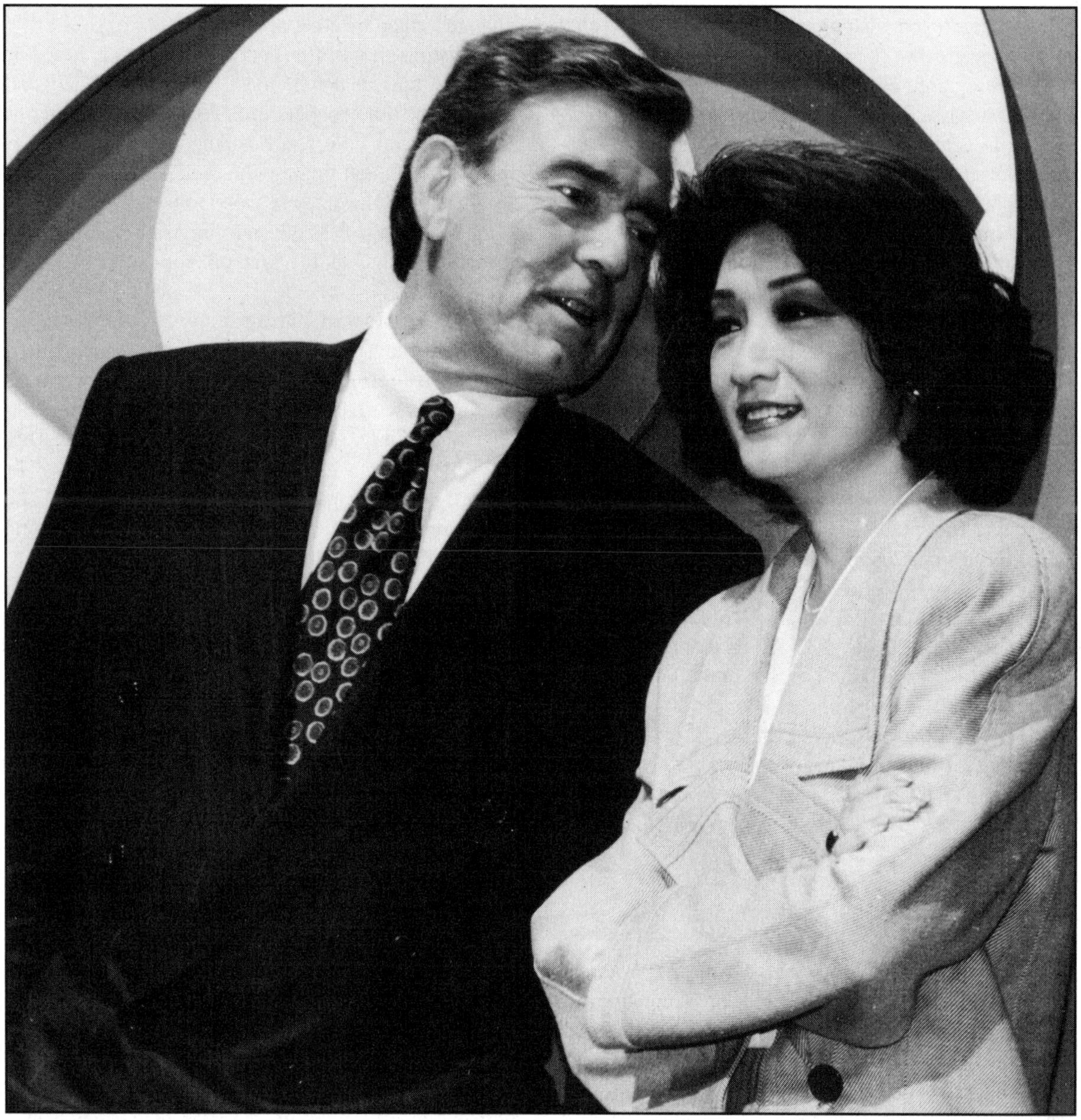

News veteran Connie Chung has risen to become the most prominent Asian American broadcast journalist in the United States. She was named coanchor (with Dan Rather, left) of the CBS Evening News *in May of 1993.* (AP/Wide World Photos)

Chinese and Japanese constitute more than three-fourths—by far the largest segment—of all Asian American journalists, followed distantly by Koreans and Filipinos. The communities least represented include Pacific Islanders and Southeast Asians.

Reasons for this pattern may reflect a pattern common to many immigrant populations. Parents coming to the United States for better opportunities may steer their offspring toward fields that are more financially rewarding and more prestigious than journalism. In addition, for many immigrants and refugees from Asian countries journalism is synonymous with working as the voice of government and not exercising any independent thought, with fear that criticism of the government means sure loss of job and possible loss of life.

Improved Coverage. Increased employment of Asian Pacific American journalists can have a direct impact on the news coverage and content afforded their particular communities. Print and broadcast journalists cannot cover everything that happens; rather they must constantly decide such questions as what stories to cover, where to include them in the newscast or newspaper, and how to cast the issues.

Whether that coverage will reflect more accurately and fairly the increasing diversity of the Asian Pacific American community and its issues, or whether it will focus solely on the unusual and exotic event or person, is largely dependent on the understanding, sensitivities, and resources of the news staff. The more diverse the staff, the more likely it is that coverage will also be diverse, say contributors to *Kerner Plus 25: A Call for Action* (1993), a report issued by Unity '94, a coalition of national journalism associations representing African Americans, Asian Americans, Latino Americans, and American Indians.

Without a staff that can adequately report on the community, news media companies can all too often revert to using stereotypes to identify story ideas, contacts, and interviewees and to influence the tone of a story. For example an inability to overcome language differences may result in perpetuating the image of Chinese as inscrutable and of the Chinese community as mysterious and impenetrable. A lack of understanding that the popular image of all Asian Americans doing well in school is an inaccurate stereotype may result in more stories about outstanding Southeast Asian refugee valedictorians without an acknowledgment of all those students who have dropped out of school.

Journalists in general are charged with the task of taking sometimes complex and sensitive issues from within a community and somehow communicating them clearly enough so that others outside that community can understand them and draw their own conclusions. This role can become even more critical when a community or ethnic group has less access to other resources.

For many Asian Pacific American journalists, their work carries additional responsibilities. These individuals are role models who must provide a highly visible example to others. They must educate not only a reading or viewing public but also their colleagues—and themselves—about the community and how to cover it accurately, fairly, and sensitively.—*Diane Yen-Mei Wong*

SUGGESTED READINGS: • Center for Integration and Improvement of Journalism. *Project Zinger: A Critical Look at News Media Coverage of Asian Pacific Americans*. San Francisco: Asian American Journalists Association, 1992. • Center for Integration and Improvement of Journalism. *Project Zinger: The Good, the Bad and the Ugly*. San Francisco: Asian American Journalists Association, 1991. • Tan, Alexis S. *Why Asian American Journalists Leave Journalism and Why They Stay*. San Francisco: Asian American Journalists Association, 1990. • Unity '94. *Kerner Plus 25: A Call for Action*. Oakland, Calif.: Unity '94, 1993. • Wong, Diane Yen-Mei. "Media Policy: Will the Real Asian Pacific American Please Stand Up?" In *The State of Asian Pacific America: Policy Issues to the Year 2020*. Los Angeles: LEAP Asian Pacific American Public Policy Institute and UCLA Asian American Studies Center, 1993.

Ng, Fae Myenne (b. 1956, San Francisco, Calif.): Writer. In 1993, Ng arrived suddenly on the literary scene with the publication of the novel *Bone*. Critics were taken with her story of Leila Fu and her family in San Francisco's Chinatown, as well as with the novel's story of the old men who worked in the sweatshops, trying to earn enough money to send for their wives and children in China. Ng studied English literature at the University of California, Berkeley, and received her master's degree in writing from Columbia University. She also writes short stories.

Ng, Poon Chew (Ng Poon Chew; Mar. 14, 1866, Guangdong Province, China—Mar. 12, 1931, Oakland, Calif.): Newspaper editor and publisher, clergyman, and public speaker. At a time when Chinese immigration was severely restricted and prejudice against the Chinese and other immigrant groups was high, Ng served as an eloquent advocate for Chinese American concerns.

As a child in a poor Chinese village, Ng was reared by his grandmother, who hoped that he would become a Taoist priest. In his early teens, he was working at a Taoist shrine when one of his uncles returned from California with money and gifts. Ng was determined to go there himself.

Ng reached California in 1881. While employed as a houseboy on a ranch outside San Jose, he learned English at the local Chinese Presbyterian mission. Sometime after his arrival in California, he began to use Chew rather than Ng as his family name or surname.

Chew proved to be a good student. In 1892, after graduation from San Francisco Theological Seminary, he was ordained as a Presbyterian minister. In the same year, he married Chun Fah; they were to have five children.

In 1899, in Los Angeles, Chew began editing and

publishing the first daily Chinese newspaper in the United States, the *Hua Mei Sun Po* (*Chinese American Morning Paper*). In 1900, he moved with his family to San Francisco, where the paper, rechristened *Chung Sai Yat Po* (*Chinese American Daily Paper*), became a leading forum for the Chinese American community.

In the years before radio and television, many Americans—especially outside the big cities— received cultural news from public lectures. As a popular speaker on the chautauqua and lyceum circuits, Chew lectured throughout the United States. He was one of the first Chinese Americans to achieve national recognition.

Chew, who dressed in the Western manner at a time when many Chinese Americans retained their traditional attire, sought to combine the best qualities of Chinese culture with the best of Western culture. In 1905, he went on a cross-country tour to speak out against anti-Chinese discrimination. He addressed the U.S. House of Representatives and spoke personally with President Theodore Roosevelt. Chew was also active in China politics in the United States. He was a strong supporter of the Chinese Republic established by SUN YAT-SEN in 1911; later he supported CHIANG KAI-SHEK's Nationalist Party.

Ng Sheung Chi (b. 1910, Taishan district, China): Folk singer. Born in a small village, Ng grew up to be a farmer. From childhood he was also a singer, and he was often called on to sing at weddings, festivals, and other special occasions. Singing was not restricted to such occasions, however, but rather was a part of the everyday life of people in rural China. In addition to performing, Ng collected songs as he encountered them, helping to preserve a rich local tradition that was threatened by modernity and especially by the repressive Cultural Revolution (1966-1976), during which traditional arts were under attack.

In 1979, Ng immigrated to the United States, settling in New York's Chinatown, where he continued to be active as a singer. In 1992, he was a recipient of a National Heritage Fellowship, awarded by the National Endowment for the Arts to traditional artists who have "made valuable artistic contributions both to their local communities and the country at large." Those who are chosen are truly masters of their art. Ng was the first Chinese American to receive this award.

Ngor, Haing S. (b. 1947, Samrong Yong, Cambodia): Actor and political activist. In 1985, he won an Oscar for Best Supporting Actor for his performance in the role of Dith Pran in the film *The Killing Fields* (1984). He has helped Cambodian refugees at home and abroad and worked for political stability in Cambodia.

Ngor was born into a Teochiu Chinese Khmer family. As a youth, he sold produce and worked on a bus near his village. His father, a merchant with a lumber mill, became wealthy, enabling Ngor to attend school in Phnom Penh and receive his medical degree in early 1975. While completing his degree, Ngor set up his own obstetrics-gynecology clinic and operated part of his father's commercial enterprise. Upon graduation, he was made a captain in the military medical service but was able to continue his private practice. He and his fiancée, Huoy, lived in the capital.

On April 17, 1975, however, the Lon Nol government collapsed, and the KHMER ROUGE took the city, forcing the entire population into the countryside. Ngor and his family initially moved south to the region where they had first lived. He had to disguise his educated background (most of his medical-school classmates would be killed), eventually assuming the role of a *samnang*, a Phnom Penh cabdriver. Within a year, the former urban dwellers in his region were moved to work on the front lines, doing rural reconstruction east of Battambang. Many died or were executed, but Ngor and his wife, Huoy, survived with the help of her fortitude and his rural skills learned as a child.

Still, illness struck Ngor hard, and he was tortured three times: by maiming, fire, and water. During this period, his mother died and his father, brother, and sister-in-law were executed. Hard labor, malnutrition, and the unrelenting terror took their toll. For three years, Ngor suffered in this region, digging canals, farming, building huts, and hauling night soil. His wife subsequently died in childbirth.

The Vietnamese invasion liberated the region in April, 1979, and Ngor moved first to Battambang, then on to the Thai border with surviving family members. Attacked again and again by rebel bands and Thai robbers and rapists, they eventually reached a refugee camp. For almost a year, Ngor worked as a medical technician in Khao I Dang.

In August, 1980, after several years of hardship in Cambodia, Ngor came to the United States as a refugee, going first to Columbus, Ohio, then settling near kin in Los Angeles. There, he started work as a night watchman, then became a refugee counselor with the Chinatown Service Center of Los Angeles. Eventually he was cast for a role in *The Killing Fields*, an opportunity that led to other roles in films and television

Haing Ngor holds the two awards presented to him in June, 1985, by the British Academy of Film and Television Arts at its London ceremonies. He was named Best Actor and Most Outstanding Newcomer for his role in The Killing Fields, *which also snared the prize for Best Film.* (AP/Wide World Photos)

shows. With Roger Warner, Ngor wrote his autobiography, *A Cambodian Odyssey* (1987). In 1989 both he and Dith Pran were allowed to return to Cambodia, their first visit back since leaving the country. Ngor has also written about the plight of refugees worldwide. Meanwhile he continues to work for peace in Cambodia and to work on behalf of refugees, especially children, for whom he has become something of an international spokesman.

Nguoi Viet Daily: Largest Vietnamese-language daily newspaper in the United States, founded in Westminster, California, in 1978.

Nguyen, Dustin (Nguyen Xuan Tri; b. Sept. 17, 1962): Actor. Nguyen, a Vietnamese American, is known best for his role as Officer Harry Truman Ioki in the police drama *21 Jump Street* (1986-1990). The son of professional entertainers, he grew up in Saigon (now Ho Chi Minh City), the capital of South Vietnam. His father was a television producer, director, and actor, his mother an actor and dancer. He attended Saigon public schools, where, because of the pervasive French influence on Vietnamese society, he learned to speak fluent French.

When the North Vietnamese invaded the city in April, 1975, the Nguyen family escaped, eventually ending up in an American refugee camp in Arkansas. There Dustin learned English. After a time, under sponsorship by the Methodist church, the family was sent to Kirkwood, Missouri, and a new life in the private home of a volunteer. Nguyen's father took a job as a dishwasher, his mother as a cleaning lady. Nguyen was enrolled in school and continued his English lessons. He also took lessons in tae kwon do, the popular Korean martial art, becoming Midwestern champion as a teen. After graduating from Kirkwood High School, Nguyen attended Orange Coast College in California, with plans to fulfill his parents' wish that he become an engineer. While there he took an acting class, loved it, and subsequently dropped out of school to pursue an acting career in Hollywood.

By this time Nguyen had legally changed his name and become a naturalized American citizen. He threw himself into the usual round of auditions. Along with many rejections came roles in such popular television

Dustin Nguyen. (Baker, Winokur, Ryder Public Relations)

series as *Magnum, P. I.*, where he made his television debut in 1984, and *General Hospital*, where he enjoyed a seven-month stint. His big break came in 1986 when he was cast in *21 Jump Street*. Since that series ended he has continued to work in film and television. He appeared in Oliver Stone's 1993 film *Heaven and Earth* and the 1994 release *3 Ninjas Kick Back*. In 1993, he became a regular on the NBC television series *seaQuest DSV*.

Off the set, but not far removed from his fictional television role as a police detective, Nguyen has spoken out publicly against drug and gang involvement. He has served as a spokesperson for the now-nationwide DARE (Drug Abuse Resistance Education) program, visiting schools and cautioning young children to say no to drugs.

Nichibei Shimbun: Japanese-language newspaper founded in San Francisco in 1899 by Kyutaro Abiko, a Christian leader of the early Japanese American community. Abiko strongly believed that Japanese immigrants should settle permanently in the United States and become American in their outlook, and the paper reflected those views. The *Nichibei Shimbun* (Japanese American news) was the result of the merger of two already established Japanese-language newspapers. For many years the most influential paper in the Japanese American community, it survives as the *Nichibei Times*, a smaller publication with both English and Japanese sections.

Nichiren (Mar. 30, 1222, Kominato, Japan—Nov. 14, 1282, Ikegami District, in what is now Tokyo, Japan): Buddhist reformer and leader. An active Buddhist proponent in Japan during the Kamakura era, Nichiren would found the Nichiren sect (also called the Hokke or Lotus sect) of Buddhism. Ordained as a monk in the Tendai sect, Nichiren underwent a crisis of faith as he reflected on the social unrest and natural disasters that plagued his time. He came to believe firmly that these problems resulted from a decay of true Buddhism, which, Nichiren held, was embodied in the *Lotus Sutra*. Nichiren strongly denounced the other Buddhist sects (Ritsu, Shingon, Zen, and Pure Land) for their promotion of false teaching. Rather, he proclaimed, the peace and safety of the nation lay in returning to complete devotion to the *Lotus Sutra*. Nichiren was frequently persecuted and exiled, but he attracted a large following, many of whom looked upon him as a *bodhisattva* mentioned in the *Lotus Sutra* who had returned to preach the ultimate truth of the *Lotus Sutra*.

As the primary act of worship, Nichiren devised the *daimoku* (sacred title), a recitation of the phrase *namu myoho renge-kyo* (adoration to the Lotus of the perfect law). Simply reciting this formula unifies one with the power radiating from all the Buddhas mentioned in the *Lotus Sutra* and with the unified Buddha-reality itself. Furthermore Nichiren devised a *mandala* called the *gohonzon*, containing the names of important Buddhas, *bodhisattvas*, and Japanese *kami* arranged around the title of the *Lotus Sutra*. In worship Nichiren adherents chant the *daimoku* before an altar on which the *gohonzon* is placed. Faith in the *Lotus Sutra* is to be shown by the aggressive refutation of other, wrong faiths, a practice called *shakufuku* (break and subdue).

After Nichiren's death various schisms arose among his disciples, resulting in permanent subsects that have continued until this day. In the modern period Nichiren tended to become allied with conservative, nationalistic forces. There also has been a tendency for vigorously growing new religious movements to spring from within Nichiren Buddhism, such as Reiyu-kai, Rissho-Kosei-kai, and Soka-gakkai. Many of these new religious movements rely heavily on popular, lay-oriented religious organizations and activities.

The Byodo In Buddhist Temple of Oahu, Hawaii. Much of modern Japanese Buddhist belief is rooted in the teachings of Nichiren, the thirteenth century Buddhist reformer and leader. (John Penisten, Pacific Pictures)

Nihon Rikkokai (Japan endeavor society): Association established as the Tokyo Workers' Society in 1903 to promote emigration to America. A Japanese Christian organization, the group became the Nihon Rikkokai a short while later and continued to expound the merits of relocating to the West, offering classes on America and publishing travel guides. Even after the GENTLEMEN'S AGREEMENT (1907-1908) banned Japanese immigrant laborers from coming to the United States, the society continued to assist those determined to go anyway by such means as stowing away aboard ships bound for America. Thousands of Japanese migrated to the United States with the group's help.

Niihau, Battle of (Dec. 13, 1941): Battle between a Niihau couple and a Japanese fighter pilot, occurring a few days after the Japanese bombing of PEARL HARBOR. The Battle of Niihau began when Ben Kanahele and his wife, Ella, attacked Japanese Naval Airman First Class Shigenori Nishikaichi, who had crash-landed his disabled Zero fighter plane on Niihau, Sunday, December 7, after participating in the attack on Pearl Harbor.

The most northwestern Hawaiian island, Niihau is about seventy-two square miles in area. It had only 136 residents. When the pilot's plane landed, its wheels snagged on a fence wire, pitching the plane on its nose and knocking the pilot unconscious. While the pilot was unconscious, a resident took his pistol and papers.

Having learned by radio of the Pearl Harbor attack, the island's residents regarded the pilot as a prisoner. The pilot had landed with the hope of being rescued by submarine, but the submarine had been ordered elsewhere. When the pilot realized that he was abandoned, he resolved to die with honor but believed he could do so only after destroying his papers and plane.

A Hawaii-born son of Japanese immigrants, Yoshio Harada, provided the pilot with a shotgun, and the two went on a rampage to regain the missing pistol and papers. They regained the pistol but could not find the papers. Meanwhile, most of the residents had fled at their approach, but the two managed to take Ella and Ben prisoners to assist them in their search for the papers.

At the moment preceding the attack, the group was standing on a boulder-strewn incline, near a stone wall. In an attempt to free themselves, Ben and Ella leaped at the pilot, who fired three times, wounding Ben. Despite being badly wounded, Ben picked up the pilot and dashed him against the stone wall. As the pilot fell stunned, Ella beat his head with a rock, and Ben killed him with his hunting knife. Yoshio Harada then killed himself, ending the Battle of Niihau.

Nijima Jo (1843, Kanda, Edo, Japan—Jan., 1890, Oiso, Japan): Japanese government interpreter. The son of a samurai warrior, Nijima attended school to learn more about Western science and technology, with an emphasis on mathematics and navigation. In the course of his studies, he became determined to visit America. The laws of Japan, however, prohibited Japanese citizens from leaving the country, and so in 1864 Nijima secretly boarded an American ship bound for Shanghai. From there, aboard another American ship, he was able eventually to make his way to Boston. Assisted by the ship's owner, he was enrolled in school.

In 1870 he was graduated from Amherst College. Later he interrupted his studies at Andover Theological Seminary to serve as interpreter for the Japanese government's Iwakura Mission to Europe and the United States. After completing his studies at Andover in 1874, he returned to Japan to start a Christian college, Doshisha University in Kyoto.

Nikkei: Japanese term referring to people of Japanese ancestry who have immigrated from Japan or are the descendants of immigrants. The Nikkei include the Issei, the first generation of Japanese immigrants to other countries, particularly the United States, the Nisei (second generation), the Sansei (third generation), and the Yonsei (fourth generation). In the Japanese American community, the term Nikkei is widely used as a synonym for Japanese American; like Issei, Nisei, and the other generational terms, it is used both as a noun and as an adjective.

Nippon Kan Theatre: Founded in 1910, it was the cultural center of the pre-World War II Japanese American community in Seattle, Washington. The theater had many uses but was unusual in that it was designed to be used for Kabuki performances. Kabuki troupes and political speakers from Japan were featured in the hall, and it also provided the stage for locally produced *shibai*, or theatrical entertainment. Japanese martial-arts competitions, including judo, kendo, and sumo-wrestling matches, were held at the theater along with community activities such as fund-raising events and awards ceremonies. The forced removal of Seattle's Japanese American residents during World War II led to the theater's closure and its repos-

Japanese Kabuki dancer. (Ron P. Jaffe)

session by bank creditors. Attempts to refurbish and reopen the theater in the years immediately following the war failed. In 1969, a white Seattle architect and his wife purchased the building, lobbied for its designation as a national historic landmark, and obtained a grant to restore the theater and redevelop its additional space for office use. After the theater reopened in 1981, it became a popular venue for a variety of Japanese and Western performing arts.

Nirvana: Sanskrit term meaning "extinction"—ultimate goal of Buddhist practice. The basic tenets of BUDDHISM state that the primary problem of existence is that it is characterized by suffering, which is experienced by beings because they are deluded into believing that the self exists in some absolute sense. According to the Buddhist view, nothing exists independently; things exist only in terms of their relationships with other things (for example, the idea of blackness cannot exist independently of the idea of whiteness). The belief that the self exists independently gives rise to a dualistic view of the world in which the self is opposed to other beings and other things. This dualistic view is the source of the problems that beings experience, because when one views other beings or things as being separate, one tends to desire those beings and things that one believes will make one happy. Unfortunately, such happiness is not always experienced, and even when it is experienced, it does not last. Therefore one suffers. In the state of Nirvana, however, the dualism that gives rise to such desire no longer exists. Nirvana is the extinction of the mistaken idea that an absolute self exists, the extinction of the dualistic view of the world, the extinction of desire and suffering. When a being finally experiences Nirvana, that being is no longer subject to the workings of KARMA (essentially, the law that every action has a result) or to the endless cycle of rebirths that unenlightened beings must experience.

Nisei: The second generation of Japanese Americans, and the first generation to be born in the United States. Most Nisei were born between 1910 and 1940. Thanks to their parents' emphasis on education, they took full

Growth of Nisei Population, 1920-1940

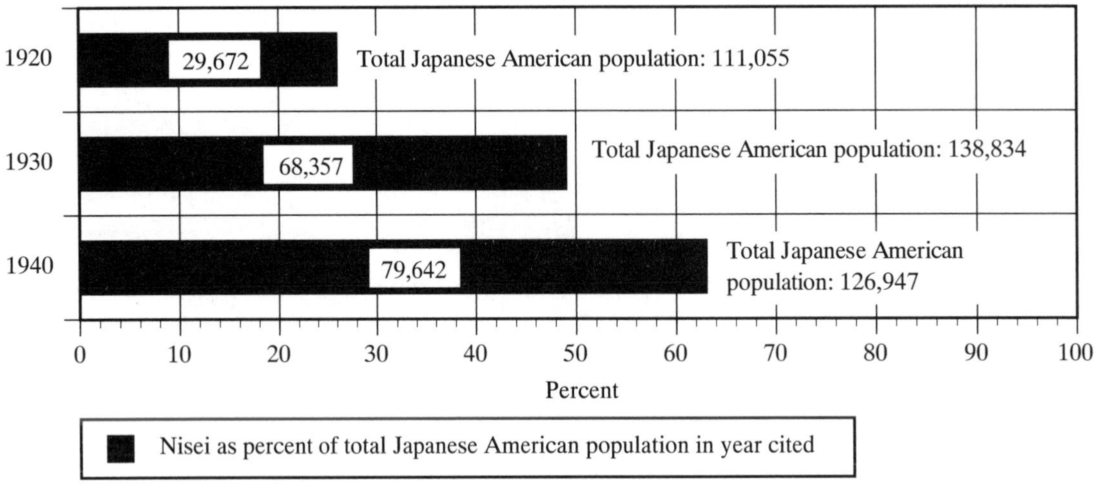

Source: Roger Daniels, *Asian America: Chinese and Japanese in the United States Since 1850.* Seattle: University of Washington Press, 1988.

advantage of the benefits of American education and became much more Americanized than their ISSEI parents. Despite the benefit of English competence and American education, opportunities for the Nisei were severely restricted by prejudice until the end of World War II. After PEARL HARBOR, the Nisei were interned with their parents despite being American citizens by birth. The internment experience gave them a distinct generational identity. In the postwar period, the Nisei made significant inroads into the educational and professional fields previously closed to them.

Between Two Worlds. Because of persisting prejudice, the Issei and their American-born children stayed within their ethnic communities for security and mutual support. Although Nisei children were exposed to American culture through their activities in churches and schools, their friends and peer groups were usually restricted to other Nisei children. Thus, they grew up in a stable ethnic community. Their Issei parents instilled in them traditional Japanese values such as hard work, honesty, obligation, loyalty, obedience to authority, and family honor. To the Issei, these values often conflicted with the more democratic and egalitarian American values to which their children were exposed. Therefore, the Nisei children were usually caught in a dilemma between two distinctly different cultures.

Wartime Experiences. These generational conflicts culminated during the internment period. Living conditions in the camps made it difficult for Issei parents to socialize their children in the traditional Japanese way. Communal living made it easier for Nisei youth to socialize among themselves, away from parental control. Furthermore, the U.S. WAR RELOCATION AUTHORITY (WRA) encouraged English-speaking Americanized Nisei to take leadership roles in the camps. As a result, the Issei had even less control over their American-born children.

During World War II, nearly 30,000 Nisei served in the American armed forces. More than 6,000 worked for military intelligence as translators, interpreters, and interrogators in the Pacific. In 1942, when the U.S. Army decided to form all-Japanese combat units to fight in Europe, many Nisei volunteered for the 442ND REGIMENTAL COMBAT TEAM and the 100TH INFANTRY BATTALION. Despite unjust treatment by their government, the Nisei soldiers proved their loyalty. The 442nd/100th became America's most highly decorated units and gained considerable public recognition.

Nevertheless, some of the Nisei wanted to register their protest to a country that had incarcerated their families and relatives and denied them their rights. In 1944, immediately after the U.S. military had begun drafting Japanese Americans, young Nisei in the HEART MOUNTAIN relocation center started a draft resistance movement that eventually spread to other camps. Altogether, 267 persons from among the camps were convicted of evading the draft, and the leaders were sent to TULE LAKE, a segregation camp for those Japanese who had declared their disloyalty to the United States.

Into the Mainstream. Their contribution to the war, however, helped the Nisei to establish themselves in the mainstream of American society in the postwar years. Soon after being released from the camps, the Nisei moved rapidly into fields from which they had previously been excluded. G.I. Bills helped Nisei veterans gain admission to colleges and graduate professional schools. The expanding postwar economy provided ample opportunities for the educated Nisei. Both in Hawaii and on the West Coast, there were the first signs of change from a Caucasian-dominated system to a more democratic, ethnically diverse system. The Nisei made significant gains in politics, especially in Hawaii.

In 1930, Nisei professionals established the JAPANESE AMERICAN CITIZENS LEAGUE (JACL) to represent and promote the interests of American-born Japanese Americans. Although the accommodationist stance of the JACL regarding the wartime internment has been criticized, the organization helped to overturn the prewar anti-Japanese legislation. With more than 27,000 members, it organized numerous effective campaigns for REDRESS and spurred the formation of the COMMITTEE ON WARTIME RELOCATION AND INTERNMENT OF CIVILIANS (CWRIC) in 1980.

Nisei Membership in Selected Organizations, California, 1979-1980

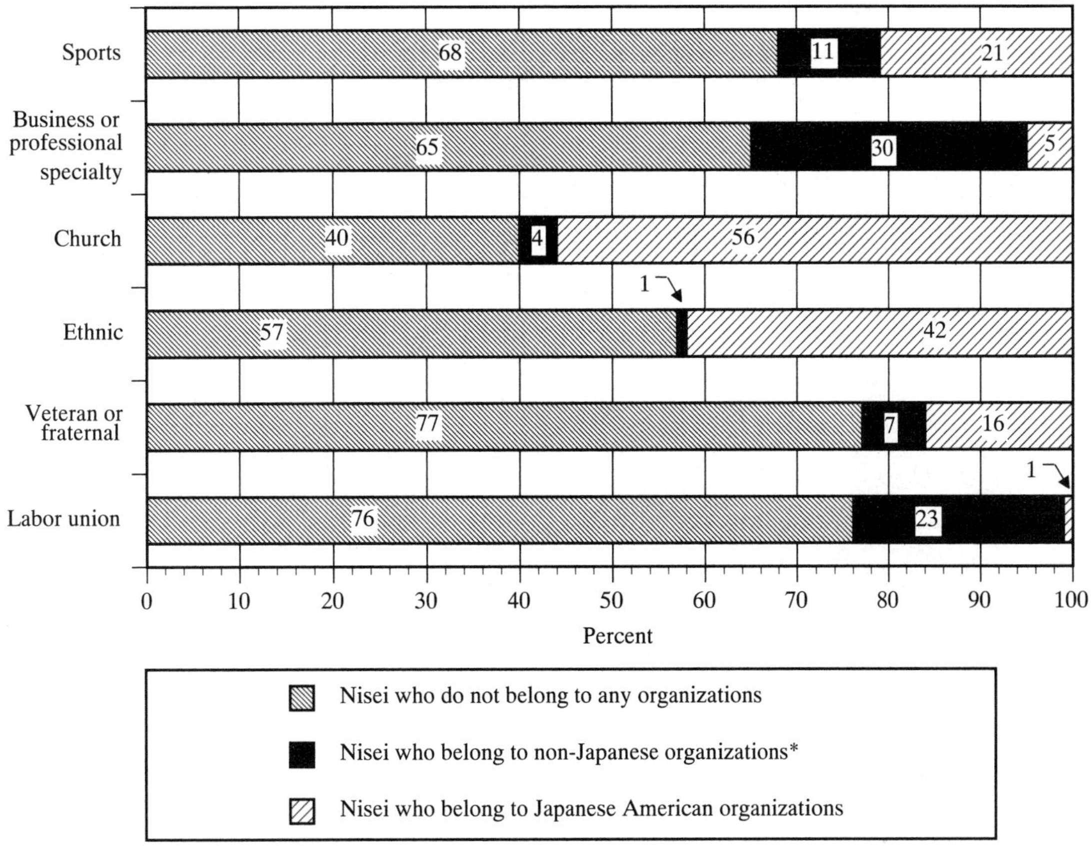

Source: Stephen Fujita and David J. O'Brien, *Japanese American Ethnicity: The Persistence of Community.* Seattle: University of Washington Press, 1991.
Note: Data are from a study of 310 Nisei men in Fresno, Gardena, and Sacramento, California.
* Includes other Asian American organizations.

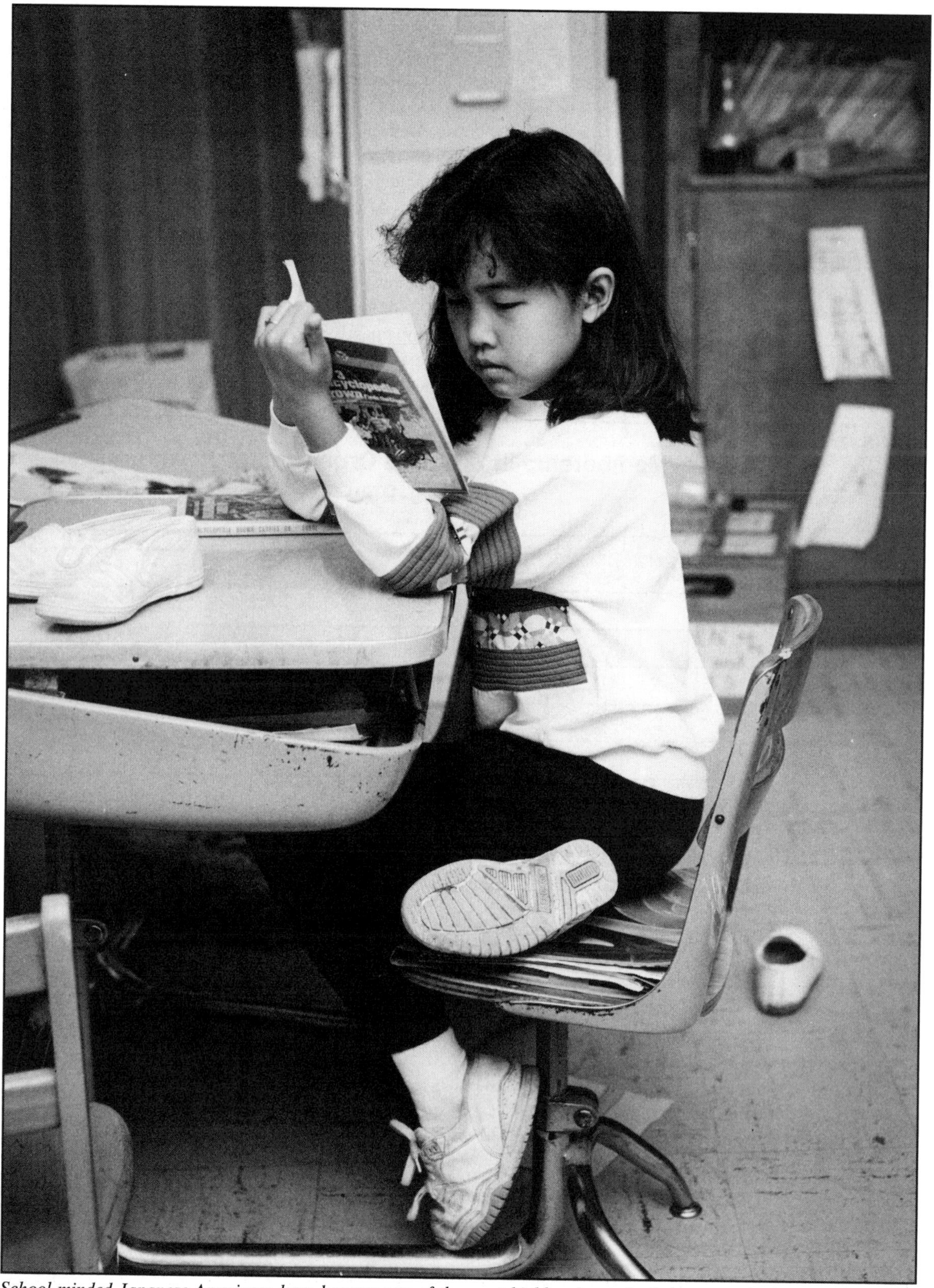

School-minded Japanese Americans have become one of the most highly educated ethnic groups in America. (James L. Shaffer)

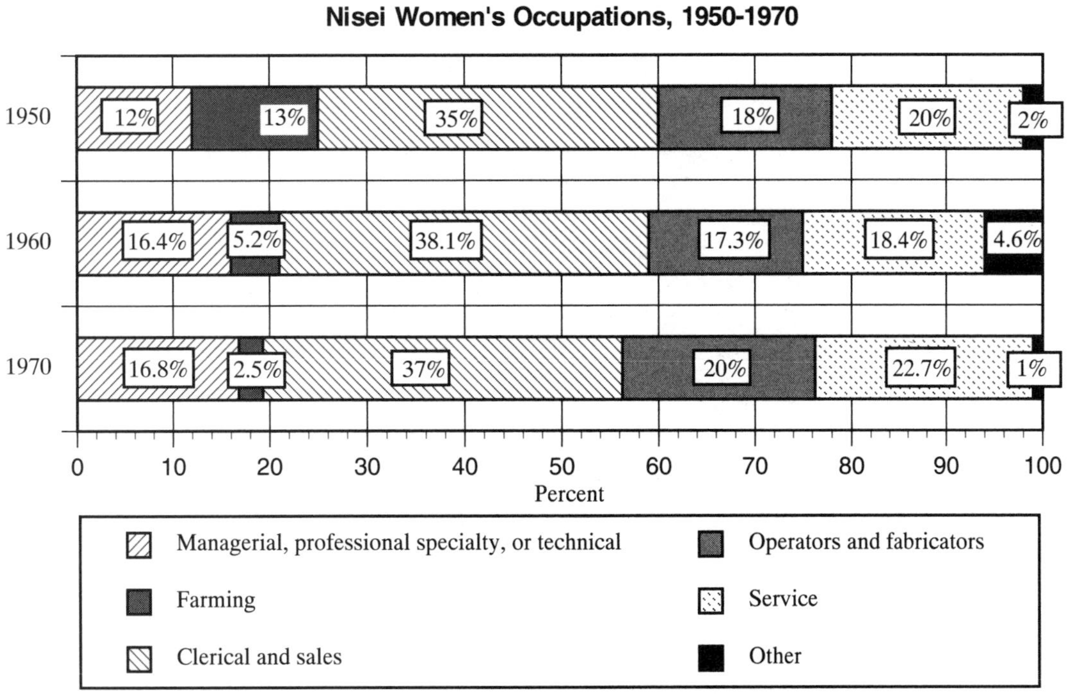

Source: Evelyn Nakano Glenn, *Issei, Nisei, War Bride.* Philadelphia, Pa.: Temple University Press, 1986.

One of the reasons for the Nisei's success in the postwar period is their high educational achievement. Even in 1940, the percentage of college graduates among Japanese Americans was slightly higher than that of Caucasian Americans (5.0 percent versus 4.9 percent). In 1980, 26.4 percent of Japanese Americans were college graduates, compared to 17.4 percent of Caucasians. By 1980, more than one-fifth of Japanese Americans were employed in professional fields. In the 1980's, Japanese Americans were one of the most highly educated ethnic groups in the United States. Yet the Nisei's income level continued to be lower than that of Caucasians with comparable levels of education.

Research on the Nisei's socializing patterns demonstrates the persistence of the ethnic community despite a high level of assimilation. The Nisei maintain close ties with one another in the suburbs, where most of them live. Studies also suggest that the majority of the Nisei still experience a degree of social discrimination. These findings raise serious questions regarding the concept of the MODEL MINORITY, revealing persisting problems faced by the children of Japanese immigrants and their own children and grandchildren.—*Machiko Matsui*

SUGGESTED READINGS: • Daniels, Roger, Sandra C. Taylor, and Harry H. L. Kitano, eds. *Japanese Americans: From Relocation to Redress.* Rev. ed. Seattle: University of Washington Press, 1991. • Fujita, Stephen S., and David J. O'Brien. *Japanese American Ethnicity: The Persistence of Community.* Seattle: University of Washington Press, 1991. • Hosokawa, Bill. *Nisei: The Quiet Americans.* New York: William Morrow, 1969. • O'Brien, David J., and Stephen S. Fujita. *The Japanese American Experience.* Bloomington: Indiana University Press, 1991. • Weglyn, Michi. *Years of Infamy: The Untold Story of America's Concentration Camps.* New York: William Morrow, 1976.

Nisei Farmers League (NFL): Agricultural grower's organization established in 1971. It was formed by local Japanese American farmers in response to César Chavez's United Farm Workers of America (UFW) union picketing ranches in the Fresno area. Throughout the 1970's the NFL was heavily involved in California growers' resistance to the UFW's unionization efforts.

Initially the NFL's membership was almost entirely Japanese American. Soon it became ethnically mixed.

Japanese lettuce picker. Japanese Americans have engaged in agriculture since the earliest period of their arrival in the United States. (Library of Congress)

Since its inception it has been led by Nisei (second-generation) grower Harry Kubo.

Throughout its existence the NFL, like many other agricultural and business organizations, has promulgated a conservative rhetoric. It extols the virtues of free enterprise and self-sufficiency and portrays agriculture as a frequent victim of a liberal press and media. Its positions have led to controversy with liberal elements within the Japanese American community. Nevertheless, in a number of ways the NFL is similar to earlier organizational responses by Japanese farmers with regard to existing conditions.

History of the Japanese in Agriculture. From their initial immigration to the United States at the beginning of the twentieth century, the Japanese have been heavily involved in agriculture, particularly in California. For example, in the Fresno area in the early 1900's, the Japanese immigrants (Issei) constituted 60 percent of the grape harvesting force, some four thousand to five thousand strong during the harvest season. As the Issei soon realized that farm laboring was not going to make it possible for them to accumulate money and return to Japan as wealthy individuals, they sought opportunities in independent farming. As a group they progressed from farmworkers to contract farmers to sharecroppers to lease farmers. Many eventually became farm owners. They did this while being the target of ALIEN LAND LAWS and other forms of discrimination.

One factor that made it possible for the Japanese immigrants to establish themselves in agriculture despite these obstacles was their families. Another was the cohesive communities that allowed the immigrants to make collective responses to the economic and political exigencies that they faced. While wives and children provided cheap labor, the JAPANESE ASSOCIA-

TIONS, agricultural cooperatives, and large number of fellow Japanese in the distribution and marketing arms of agriculture facilitated their laborers' competitiveness in intensive agriculture. This economic infrastructure was destroyed when Pacific Coast Japanese Americans were incarcerated during World War II.

Rise of the UFW. In the post-World War II period, when many Japanese Americans were struggling to reestablish themselves in the cities and on the farms, Chavez began working in the Mexican American community and Larry ITLIONG and Philip VERA CRUZ in the Filipino community to organize farmworkers. Ultimately the Filipino and Chicano groups combined under the banner of the UFW with Chavez as their leader. During the 1960's the UFW succeeded in obtaining numerous union contracts in the grape industry because of its ability to mobilize liberals and, in particular, to resort to the secondary boycott. In this way it was able to bring significant pressure to bear against large corporate growers, particularly those with branded products.

An example of the effectiveness of the boycott, or the threat of it, was the UFW's first successful organizing drive and contract at White Rivers Farm. This huge, five-thousand-acre wine grape operation was the largest in the Delano area. It was owned by the Schen-

Japanese business district, Salinas, Monterey County, central California. (California State Library)

ley Corporation. Because of the potential impact of a boycott of their branded products, Schenley signed a contract with the UFW in 1966 and renewed it in 1968 and 1970.

In 1971 Schenley sold the ranch to the conglomerate Buttes Gas and Oil. The UFW's successor clause maintained UFW representation. Buttes also acquired the Sam Hamburg ranch, a mechanized row crop operation, near Los Banos. In 1972 both the union and the corporation faced numerous pressures. The union wanted to gain representation on the Hamburg ranch and slow down the movement to mechanization of harvesting grapes at White Rivers. Buttes Gas and Oil wanted to rid itself of the control and demands of the union.

NFL Activities. The NFL was contacted by Buttes Gas and Oil after a strike had started at White Rivers. In this situation, unlike that of the NFL ranches, 260 White Rivers workers had walked off their jobs in support of the UFW. After promising not to renegotiate with the UFW, White Rivers management persuaded NFL to bring in workers from the Fresno area. At this time the league was still relatively small and inexperienced. After considerable internal debate, the NFL decided to bus in and protect workers from their area. The importation of these workers and the assistance of the NFL growers was the major reason for the strike's failure.

Other actions of the league during the period when it was fighting the UFW was the formation of a counterpicketing operation called "picket patrol." Ranchers who worked on the picket patrol on a given day would stand between the UFW pickets and the workers inside a ranch. They were kept informed of where the UFW was picketing through the use of a large radio communications network. The NFL also created a legal aid fund to help member farmers with litigation expenses. In disputes over elections conducted by the Agriculture Labor Relations Board, the NFL has frequently provided for farmers' legal expenses.

The NFL also has a Political Action Committee that supports progrower candidates. Many prominent national, state, and local politicians have spoken at league functions. In 1976 Kubo led the statewide growers' organization "Citizens for a Fair Farm Labor Law" that successfully defeated the pro-UFW farm labor law initiative Proposition 14. Along with other grower organizations, the league has actively lobbied against immigration legislation that they see as threatening their members' labor supply. The NFL also continuously sponsors seminars to keep its membership abreast of changes in farming regulations.—*Stephen S. Fugita*

SUGGESTED READINGS: • Fugita, Stephen S. "A Perceived Ethnic Factor in California's Farm Labor Conflict: The Nisei Farmers League." *Explorations in Ethnic Studies* 1 (1978): 50-72. • Fugita, Stephen S., and David J. O'Brien. "Economics, Ideology, and Ethnicity: The Struggle Between the United Farm Workers and the Nisei Farmers League." *Social Problems* 25 (1977): 146-156. • Fugita, Stephen S., and David J. O'Brien. *Japanese American Ethnicity: The Persistence of Community*. Seattle: University of Washington Press, 1991. • Iwata, Masakazu. *Planted in Good Soil: A History of the Issei in United States Agriculture*. Vols. 1 and 2. New York: Peter Lang, 1992.

Nisei Week: Annual festival held in Los Angeles' Little Tokyo during the months of July and August.

The idea for Nisei Week began in 1934 during the height of the Great Depression. At the time, the first-generation ISSEI controlled the businesses in Little Tokyo and catered primarily to other Issei. The second-generation NISEI, many of whom were entering young adulthood, believed that their parents' retail practices needed to be changed. They approached the Issei merchants with the idea of hiring Nisei to work in the stores and also catering to the needs of the Nisei. Nisei Week became a vehicle through which these efforts would be accomplished.

The first Nisei Week was held from August 12 to August 18, 1934. It was a joint venture between the two generations, with the Issei providing most of the funds and the Nisei doing the rest. To many Nisei organizing the event, Nisei Week was more than merely means to attract business back to Little Tokyo; it was also a way of demonstrating to their Issei elders that the Nisei were also capable of handling responsibility in the Japanese American community.

According to Togo TANAKA, who at the time was a budding journalist and later was a successful businessman, events in the first Nisei Week revolved around activities that the Nisei knew best: a parade featuring Japanese *ondo* dancing, MARTIAL ARTS exhibitions, a Japanese TEA CEREMONY, Japanese floral arranging, calligraphy, art shows, and talent programs. Although it initially lost money, Nisei Week showed enough promise to become an annual event. The next year, a beauty pageant was added to the festivities, with Alice Watanabe crowned the first Nisei Week Queen. As the years passed, additional events were added to Nisei Week, and in turn its popularity soared. With the ex-

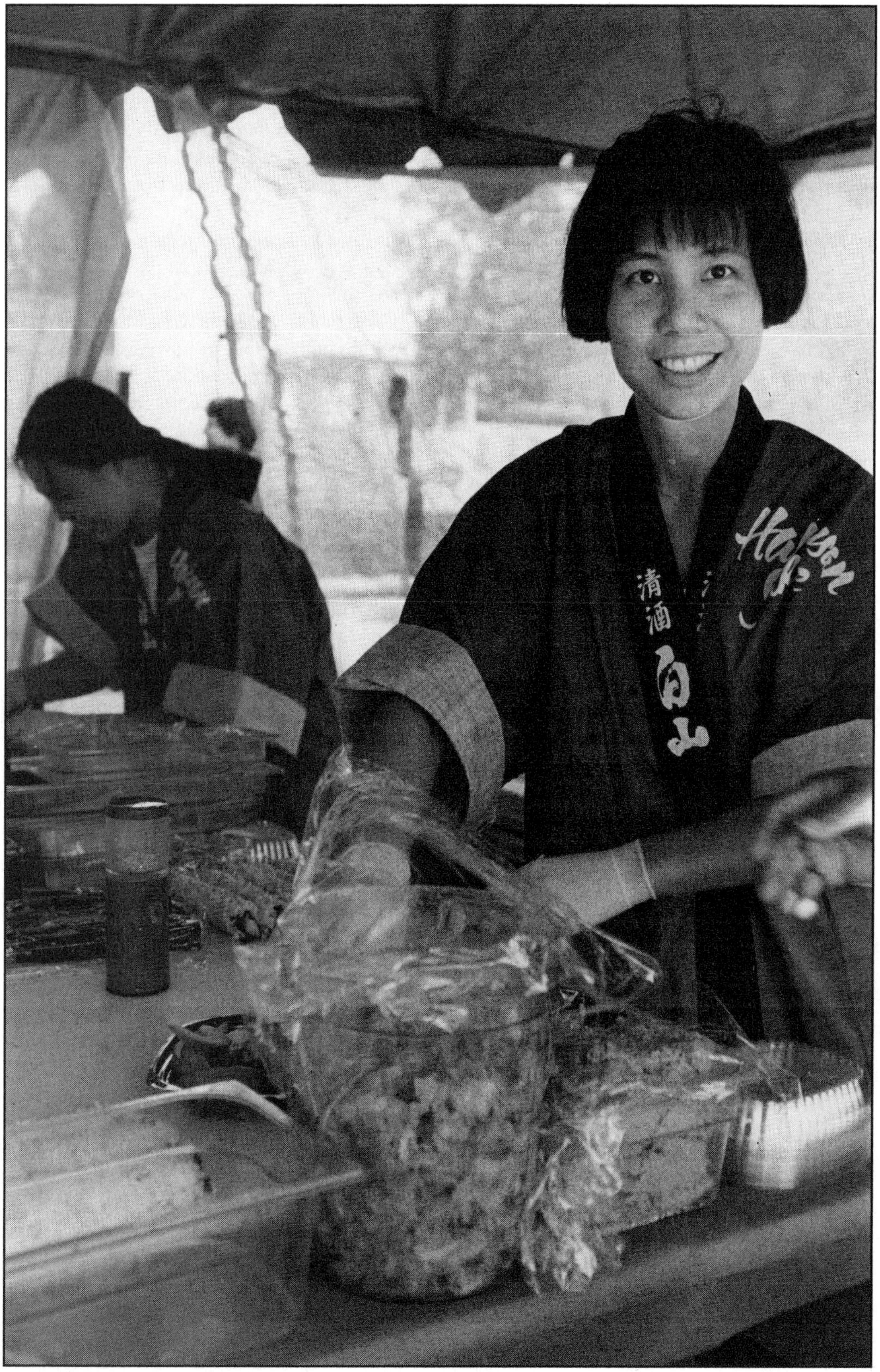

Nisei Week celebrates the various facets of Japanese American culture. (Ben Klaffke)

ception of the years 1942 through 1948, when the festivities were stopped because of the interment of Japanese Americans and aliens, Nisei Week has become an annual summer event. The fiftieth Nisei Week was held in 1990.

Nishikawa, Lane (b. Jan. 24, 1955, Honolulu, Territory of Hawaii): Playwright, actor, and theater director. A solo performer who has won accolades for his pieces exposing and attacking Asian American stereotypes, *Life in the Fast Lane* (1981) and *I'm on a Mission from Buddha* (1989), Nishikawa was a founding member of San Francisco's ASIAN AMERICAN THEATRE COMPANY (AATC), where he also served as artistic director from 1986 to 1989. He has also directed the world premieres of major Asian American theater works, including Philip Kan GOTANDA's *A Song for a Nisei Fisherman*, Milton MURAYAMA's *All I Asking for Is My Body*, R. A. SHIOMI's *Yellow Fever*, and Laurence YEP's *Pay the Chinaman*. In 1993 he assumed the artistic directorship of the AATC for the second time in his career.

Nishikawa v. Dulles (1958): U.S. Supreme Court ruling that restored citizenship rights to an American-born Japanese who had been forced to serve in the Japanese military during World War II. The Court underscored the judicial principle that in expatriation cases, where the punitive loss of citizenship is concerned, the government must prove its case convincingly. Here the government failed to demonstrate that Nishikawa had entered foreign military service voluntarily—without which it could not strip him of his citizenship.

California-born Nishikawa Mitsugi went to Japan in 1939 for further study following his graduation from the University of California. He intended to return to the United States after completing his term of study. Later that year, however, after his father died, Nishikawa had no means of returning home. By the middle of the following year, he had been conscripted into the Japanese army—against his will, as he later testified in court. After the war, he applied for a passport back to the United States, only to be notified much

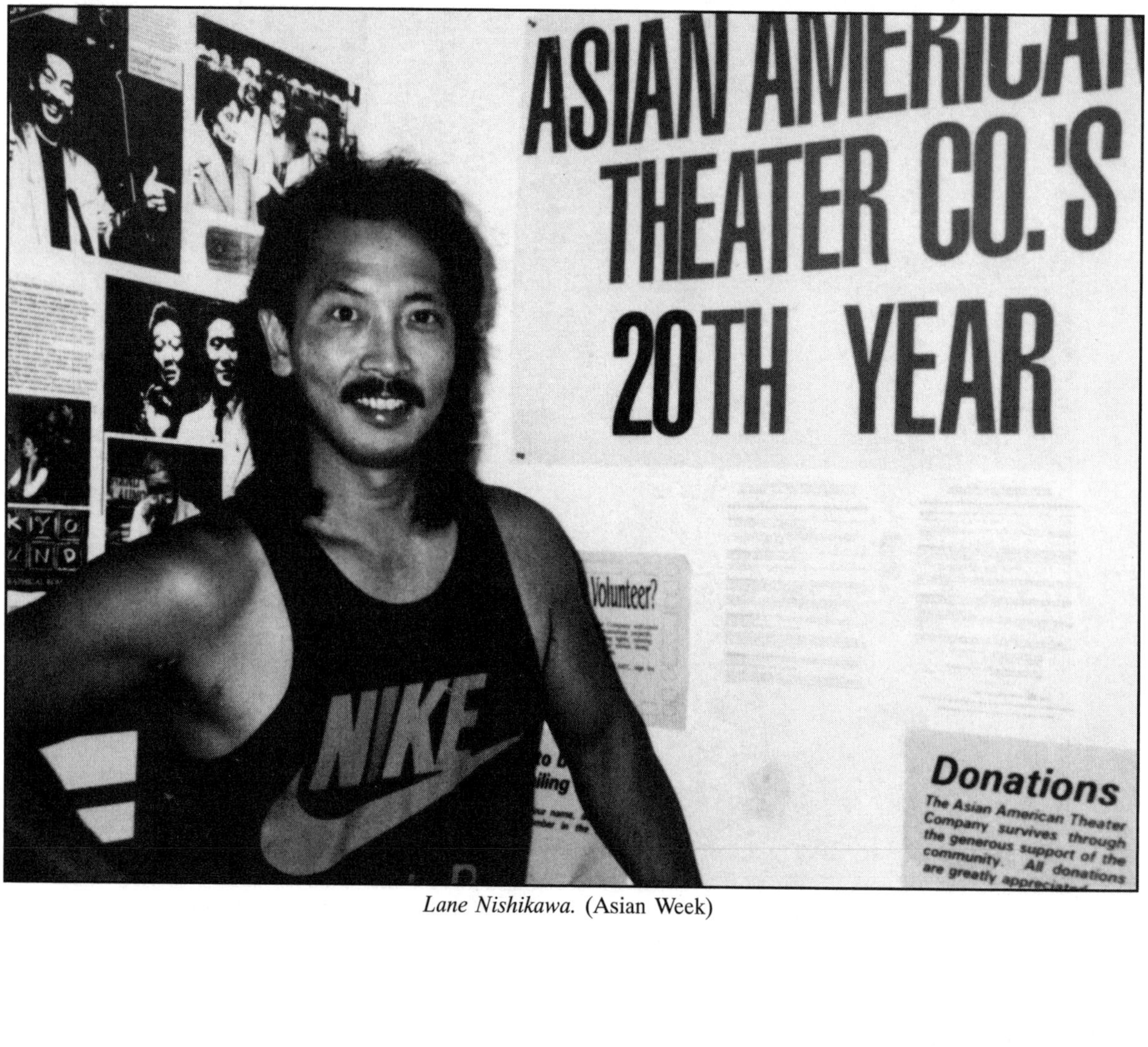

Lane Nishikawa. (Asian Week)

later that his citizenship was being taken away. An appeal to the U.S. secretary of state (John Foster Dulles) was unsuccessful. Following a round of litigation in U.S. district court and the U.S. Ninth Circuit Court of Appeals, both of which ruled against him, Nishikawa took his dispute before the Supreme Court. The Court's majority opinion, finding no proof of voluntary servitude, overturned the earlier decisions and ordered that Nishikawa's citizenship be restored.

Nishimoto, Richard Shigeaki (Aug. 23, 1904, Tokyo, Japan—1950's): Researcher and internee. Nishimoto was the sole Issei member of the JAPANESE AMERICAN EVACUATION AND RESETTLEMENT STUDY (JERS), a special research commission that monitored and evaluated the incarceration of Japanese Americans during World War II. He secretly conducted his fieldwork for the JERS, which operated out of the University of California, Berkeley, under the direction of social scientist Dorothy Swaine Thomas, even while himself interned at the POSTON relocation center in western Arizona. After his release in 1945, he coauthored *The Spoilage* (1946), summarizing the camp experiences of those prisoners labeled "disloyal." Nishimoto's contributions to the project were therefore key to its success.

After being graduated in 1921 from a missionary school in Japan run by the American Episcopal church, Nishimoto went to the United States to join his parents in California. He earned a degree in engineering from Stanford University in 1929, but discrimination prevented his finding a suitable job with an American company following graduation. He moved to Los Angeles, where between 1929 and 1934 he ran an insurance brokerage and served as an interpreter for the Los Angeles courts. After that Nishimoto lived in GARDENA until 1942, when he was evacuated to Poston.

At Poston, Nishimoto became a respected leader among the internees of his particular "block," able to resolve an assortment of personal disputes diplomatically. Over time he rose to a position of power and influence that was recognized throughout the whole camp. At one point he was even made an adviser to Poston officials of the WAR RELOCATION AUTHORITY (WRA), including the project director.

Nishimoto officially began working for the JERS in early 1943. Under cover of secrecy, and with some risk to his personal safety, he was able to relay to the JERS field reports of life inside the camp, updates on internal developments or problems, statistical information, and other personal observations. After his release he went to Berkeley and continued working for the JERS, assuming an even more central role and lending his expertise to the various publications and research produced by the group. Once the commission disbanded, however, he failed to find any suitable academic-related employment; at the time of his death he was working as a night watchman for a San Francisco hotel.

Nishimura v. United States (1892): U.S. Supreme Court ruling that upheld the plenary authority of the immigration inspector to refuse entry to a Japanese woman under a federal statute that allowed the exclusion of immigrants adjudged to be lunatics, idiots, or convicts or deemed likely to become public charges in America. Such sole administrative jurisdiction, declared the Court, is binding on the parties concerned and not otherwise subject to judicial review.

Twenty-five-year-old Nishimura Ekiu arrived in San Francisco from Japan in 1891. Upon landing, she presented her passport, which declared that she was married to a man who had resided in the United States for several years. She told immigration inspectors that she was to meet him in the city upon her arrival. She also had with her the average amount of money possessed by most new immigrants landing in America. Despite her claims, however, she was denied entry and detained by the official on duty.

Nishimura sued the commissioner of immigration, alleging that to allow an administrative officer to decide her status was to deprive her of personal liberty without due process of law, as mandated by the U.S. Constitution. The commissioner countered that she had received the proper hearing required under law and that his decision to reject her application for entry was final. An appeal to a circuit court was similarly unsuccessful. The Supreme Court agreed that under law the immigration inspector was empowered to render decisions that were conclusive and ruled against Nishimura. Among Supreme Court hearings involving those of Japanese ancestry, this was the first.

Nitobe, Inazo (Sept. 1, 1862, Morioka, Japan—Oct. 15, 1933, Victoria, British Columbia, Canada): Scholar and writer. Born in northern Japan to an aristocratic samurai family, Nitobe graduated from Sapporo Agricultural College before attending Tokyo Imperial University, where he majored in economics and English literature. A convert to Christianity as a result of his contact with American missionary teachers, Nitobe traveled to the United States in 1884 to study at Johns Hopkins University and later spent four years at a German university. Nitobe married Mary Patterson

Elkinton, a Quaker woman from Philadelphia, in 1891 before returning to Japan to teach. He published a number of books both in Japanese and in English intended to foster mutual understanding between Japan and the United States.

Nitobe was so disgusted by the passage of the restrictive IMMIGRATION ACT OF 1924 that he categorically refused to travel to the United States until the law was repealed. He did, however, return in 1932 for a lecture tour. The following year he came to Canada as a member of the Japanese delegation to the Banff Conference of the Institute of Pacific Relations; he died while in Canada.

No-no boys: Phrase that characterized draft-age Nisei male internees who answered no to "loyalty" and "allegiance" questions submitted to them by the U.S. government during World War II as part of a draft-registration program. In each of the ten RELOCATION CENTERS, Nisei male volunteers ages seventeen through thirty-seven were asked to register to serve in the Army by first filling out a "loyalty" questionnaire—a screening process to determine draft fitness. Although these men had already been classified by the Selective Service as IV-C, or enemy aliens unacceptable because of nationality or ancestry, they were now being recruited to join the all-Nisei 442ND REGIMENTAL COMBAT TEAM. QUESTION 27 and QUESTION 28 on the "Statement of United States Citizens of Japanese Ancestry" (Selective Service Form 304A), became especially controversial. These asked, first, whether the respondent would be willing to serve in the United States and to perform combat duty, and second, whether the respondent would swear "unqualified allegiance" to and "faithfully defend" the United States while at the same time forswearing allegiance or obedience to the Japanese emperor or other foreign power.

The questionnaire proved to be an unpopular action. Fully one-fourth of about twenty thousand eligible male internees offered a no, a qualified answer, or no response to the "loyalty" and "allegiance" questions. The men who answered no to questions 27 and 28 became known as the "no-no boys." Many chose this path to protest symbolically the violation and loss of their civil rights, as evidenced by the unconstitutional nature of their evacuation and internment. From among the almost twelve hundred volunteers who answered yes, the Army accepted a smaller number who met loyalty and physical standards; the War Department, however, had anticipated three thousand enrollees from the ten relocation camps. In Hawaii, by comparison, where there was no forced displacement and no imposition of a loyalty questionnaire, the ten thousand Nisei who volunteered for combat far exceeded the War Department quota of fifteen hundred enrollees.

The 100TH INFANTRY, or "Purple Heart," BATTALION, formed of Hawaiian Nisei even as their West Coast counterparts were being evacuated to INTERNMENT CAMPS, had a triumphant showing. The draft was reopened, but the loyalty and allegiance questions remained on Selective Service questionnaires. Again, many interned Nisei answered negatively, and few were drafted. Eventually more than fifty percent of all eligible Nisei males would serve in the 442nd Regimental Combat Team.

Noda, Steere Gikaku (1892—1986): Lawyer and state legislator. A pitcher for the ASAHIS, the famous Japanese American baseball team that dominated Honolulu amateur leagues for many years, he later became, in 1917, the first Nisei licensed to practice law in the state courts of Hawaii. While practicing law, he continued his interest in sports, promoting various athletic events. He was elected a Hawaii state representative in 1948 and a state senator in 1959. Noda, in addition to his prominence throughout the Hawaiian Islands, was recognized for his efforts in service to Japan and to the sport of amateur wrestling.

Noguchi, Hideyo (Nov. 24, 1876, Inawashiro, Japan—May 21, 1928, Accra, Ghana): Scientist. His research and persistent battles as a bacteriologist, parasitologist, and immunologist contributed to the advancement of medicine. As a chief advisor to the International Sanitary Board, he led the effort to stem the outbreak of bubonic plague in China. After moving to the United States, he studied snake venom and later invented an innovative method for diagnosing syphilis. This pathfinding research led him to study Rocky Mountain spotted fever and, later, yellow fever. His research of yellow fever transformed him into a global crusader as he conducted a comparative study of the disease's effect on American Indians, Latin Americans, and Africans. He himself contracted the disease and died in Africa.

Noguchi, Isamu (Nov. 17, 1904, Los Angeles, Calif.—Dec. 30, 1988, New York, N.Y.): Sculptor, theatrical designer, and landscape architect. Son of Japanese poet Noguchi Yonejiro and Leonie Gilmour, an American teacher, Noguchi moved back and forth all his life between the cultures of his parents. His work as an artist, stage designer, and builder of artificial landscapes combined elements of both cultures. In his last decades, Noguchi produced work with genuinely multicultural perspectives.

Trained as a sculptor in the United States, Noguchi worked as a studio assistant to Constantin Brancusi in Paris between 1927 and 1929. A modernist influenced by the work of Alexander Calder and Alberto Giacometti, as well as that of Brancusi, Noguchi began to sculpt with a Surrealist's approach to shape, mass, and light that carried over, after 1935, into designs of stage settings for the dance companies of George Balanchine, Merce Cunningham, and Martha Graham. Noguchi's interest in the theatrical use of space developed, by the 1950's, into experimental combinations of sculpture, architecture, and landscape, as in the gardens he designed for the Beinecke Library at Yale University, the United Nations Educational, Scientific, and Cultural Organization (UNESCO) headquarters in Paris, and the Domon Ken Museum in Sakata, Japan.

Noguchi's carefully designed landscapes derived from the traditional monastic gardens of Japan, but like his designs for lamps and furniture and his sculpture, they are metaphors. In them he shaped the earth itself, turning the site of each project into a sculptural object suggesting something about humanity's relationship to the land. Noguchi was not an environmentalist. He was not concerned about danger to the ecosystem. Instead, he focused on earth, water, and stone as materials for his craft. Noguchi's work with landscape design pushed sculpture to its limits and redefined its aesthetic potential for his contemporaries.

In all of his work, Noguchi had an eclectic, multicultural outlook. He studied painting in China in 1929, apprenticed with a potter in Kyoto, Japan, and spent time working in England and Mexico in the 1930's. In 1941, he spent seven months in an internment camp for Japanese civilians at POSTON, Arizona; and from 1952 until the end of his life, Noguchi divided his time between Japan and the United States. He kept a studio at Long Island City, New York, which he opened in 1985 to the public as the Isamu Noguchi Garden Museum, and one at Mure, a village near Takamatsu, Japan.

Noguchi won the Edward MacDowell Medal for outstanding lifelong contribution to the arts in 1982. He was awarded the National Medal of Arts by President Ronald Reagan in 1987. A year later, in 1988, the Japanese government presented Nogushi with the Order of the Sacred Treasure.

Noguchi, Thomas [Tsunetomi] (b. Jan. 4, 1927, Fukuoka, Japan): Forensic pathologist and author. Noguchi's father, Noguchi Wataru, had been a painter before becoming a physician. As a boy of thirteen, young Thomas was inspired someday to study forensic medicine after watching his father endure the rigors of a medical malpractice lawsuit, prevailing when an autopsy cleared him of any negligence. That incident left a lasting impression on the son, who eventually enrolled at Tokyo's Nippon Medical School, graduating in 1951. Equally fascinated by the legal process (having observed it firsthand), during medical school he studied law at night.

In 1952 Noguchi came to California to complete his residency in pathology at Orange County General Hospital. Eight years later he was made deputy medical examiner of the Los Angeles County coroner's office, becoming chief medical examiner in 1967. His years with the coroner's office included the highly publicized investigations of actors Marilyn Monroe and Sharon Tate and Senator Robert F. Kennedy. Noguchi became known throughout Southern California as the "Coroner to the Stars."

Amid accusations of highly unprofessional behavior, Noguchi was fired in 1969 but reinstated several months later. His firing occurred during a time of strenuous political and social agitation by Asian Americans in the United States, particularly in California. During the hearings leading up to the reinstatement, the Japanese American community rose to his defense.

Controversy continued to haunt Noguchi, however, and in 1982 he was demoted as chief coroner after a series of articles published in the *Los Angeles Times* beginning in late 1981 criticized him for administrative mismanagement. Shortly thereafter, he and his wife of twenty-two years, Hisako, were divorced. Subsequently, he accepted a job as deputy coroner at Los Angeles County-USC Medical Center; he also became a professor of forensic pathology at the University of Southern California (USC). Noguchi is the author of *Coroner* (1983), *Coroner at Large* (1985), *Unnatural Causes* (1988), and *Physical Evidence* (1990).

Nomura, Gail (b. Apr. 5, 1948, Honolulu, Hawaii): Scholar. A professor at Washington State University and the University of Michigan, her research has focused on Asian American women and Asian American communities in Hawaii and the Pacific Northwest. She received her Ph.D. degree from the University of Hawaii in 1978 upon completion of her dissertation, entitled, "The Allied Occupation of Japan: Reform of Japanese Government Labor Policy on Women."

Nonresident Indians (NRIs): A classification devised by the government of India to refer to Indians who live outside the subcontinent but retain their citizenship and voting rights. The government extends special tax breaks to NRIs and encourages them to reinvest in India's economy.

North Adams: City in Berkshire County in northwestern Massachusetts, which in the early 1870's had one of the largest Chinese populations east of the Mississippi River. In 1870, about seventy-five Chinese workers, mostly under the age of eighteen, were recruited by Calvin T. Sampson to break a strike in his shoe factory led by the Secret Order of the Knights of St. Crispin. The Chinese signed three-year contracts and lived in quarters connected to Sampson's factory. Although little is known of the everyday lives of the Chinese who were brought to North Adams, there are indications that they were a more visible element in the community than is often expected.

Newspaper and magazine accounts reveal that many of them attended the local churches and Sunday schools, where they took English lessons. A few of them developed relationships with their teachers, with at least one leading to marriage. One Chinese worker was adopted into a North Adams family, and another is known to have married a local woman and opened a store on Main Street in North Adams. Furthermore, evidence indicates that at least two of the workers purchased burial plots in North Adams.

It should also be noted that the Chinese were not the docile workers they were often depicted to be. While most of them renewed their contracts in 1873, they also rioted and went on strike later that same year, disappointed in their working conditions and possibly with the performance of their Chinese foreman.

Records on the Chinese in North Adams are scarce after 1873. It is believed that a number of them stayed in the area for awhile, but that most left for other areas such as Boston. Although the Chinese in North Adams did not leave obvious marks of their stay, they represent an important period in the growth of the Chinese population in the United States.

North Korea. *See* **Korea, Democratic People's Republic of**

Northwest Asian American Theatre (NWAAT): Theatrical company founded in 1972. Along with Los Angeles' East West Players, San Francisco's Asian American Theatre Company, and New York City's Pan Asian Repertory Theatre, the NWAAT of Seattle, Washington, is one of the four "first wave" or pioneer Asian American performance companies established between 1965 and 1978 in the United States.

Under the leadership of Bea Kiyohara, its artistic director, NWAAT was founded as the Theatrical Ensemble of Asians (TEA). In 1978, the company adopted the name Asian Exclusion Act, by which it was known until 1981, when it became the NWAAT. From its inception until 1987, the NWAAT's artists performed in whatever space was available to them. In 1987, after more than a decade of performing without a permanent home while Kiyohara simultaneously led efforts to secure funding, the NWAAT settled in a performance space of its own, the newly designed Theatre Off Jackson, adjacent to the Wing Luke Museum in Seattle's International District.

Throughout its history, the NWAAT has been committed to nurturing the careers of Asian American playwrights, directors, actors, designers, stage techni-

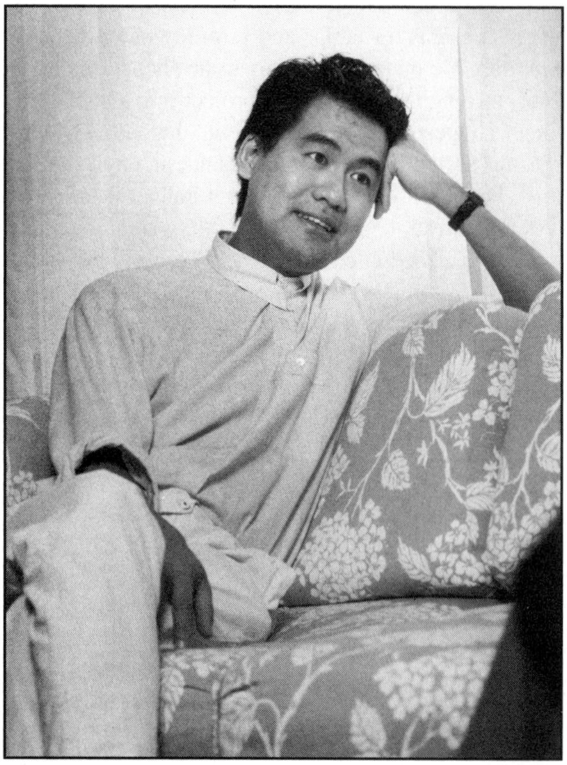

The NWAAT has staged plays by such leading dramatists as David Henry Hwang, a Tony Award-winner. (AP/Wide World Photos)

cians, and arts administrators by creating a public forum in which to hone their skills and share their vision. To that end, NWAAT world premieres have included works by Garrett HONGO (*Nisei Bar and Grill*, pr. 1975); Amy Sambo and Lonny Kaneko (*Lady Is Dying*, pr. 1980); Nikki LOUIS (*Breaking the Silence*, pr. 1986); Gary Iwamoto (*Miss Minidoka 1943*, pr. 1986; revived in 1987); and Jeannie Barroga (*Eye of the Coconut*, pr. 1987). In addition to mounting works by leading Asian American dramatists such as Wakako YAMAUCHI, Frank CHIN, Momoko Iko, David Henry HWANG, Philip Kan GOTANDA, and Rick A. SHIOMI, the NWAAT has contributed to a sense of continuity within the Asian American theater community, providing actors, directors, and designers with opportunities to interpret germinal works of the Asian American theater movement. By producing staged adaptations of Asian American literature by Carlos BULOSAN, Jeffrey CHAN, and John OKADA, the NWAAT has made it possible for those authors to reach wider audiences. The NWAAT has also served as a conduit for cultural exchange with other Asian American communities by importing productions such as Lane NISHIKAWA's *Life in the Fast Lane* in 1982-1983, which Nishikawa developed during the mid-1970's at the Asian American Theatre Company in San Francisco. Finally, as Asian American theater artists have been lured away from Seattle to theater centers such as those in New York and Los Angeles, the NWAAT continued to educate local artists through its own training programs and workshops.

Other performances mounted at the NWAAT have included staged adaptations of literary works by such authors as Carlos Bulosan, the foremost Filipino American writer. (Filipino American National Historical Society)

By developing new works, reviving the "classics" of Asian American theater, and providing an arena in which Asian American performing artists could speak in their own voices, the NWAAT has played a crucial role in educating both non-Asian American and Asian American audiences about the richness and diversity of the Asian American experience.

O

O-bon: Annual Japanese Buddhist celebration to honor the dead. Although this celebration has roots in India, when BUDDHISM spread to Japan via China in the sixth century, the Indian festival became enmeshed with indigenous Japanese festivals and developed into what is now known as *O-bon*. *O-bon* is most usually translated into English as "Festival of Souls," "Feast of the Dead," or "Festival of Lanterns," each of which captures some elements of the occasion. Traditional belief maintains that souls of the departed return to Earth to be with the living during *O-bon*, thus making this a joyous occasion of reunion. During festival activities lanterns are usually placed around temples or on walkways to guide spirits of the departed to the appropriate location.

The term *bon* comes from the Sanskrit *ullambana* (hence the festival is sometimes also known as *urabon*), literally "hanging upside down," and is derived from a story in which the Buddhist disciple Mokuren saved his departed mother from a torture in which she was suspended upside down in the netherworld.

O-bon traditionally lasts from the thirteenth to the seventeenth days of the seventh month, according to the solar calendar (July or August in the lunar calendar). During celebrations, individuals clean grave sites of ancestors and friends and place food offerings there, perform devotions at the family altar in the home (*butsudan*) and at grave sites, recite scriptural verses (*sutras*), attend a special temple service (*segaki*), and light welcome and farewell fires (*mukaebi* and *okuribi*). Communal dancing is an important feature at many *O-bon* celebrations, and at locations close to oceans, rivers, or streams floating lanterns of paper or straw boats with candles on them (*toro-nagashi*) are set adrift to guide departed souls on their return to the spirit world.

As Japanese immigrated to the United States, they brought the *O-bon* festival with them, and wherever Japanese have settled, *O-bon* is still celebrated. In communities with small concentrations of Japanese immigrants, celebrations may simply take the form of activities in the home; in communities with larger immigrant populations, festive all-night dances are held at Buddhist temples. Other immigrant groups from areas in Asia where Buddhism is prominent continue similar traditions that are known by other names.

Obata, Chiura (1885, Sendai, Japan—1975): Artist. Obata studied art rigorously and from an early age in his native Japan before emigrating to San Francisco in 1903. There he found work painting displays in hotels and stores and began exhibiting his paintings, watercolors, and prints widely. In 1931, he began teaching art at the University of California. During World War II he was sent to the Tanforan assembly center in central California and the TOPAZ relocation center in central Utah. At both camps Obata taught art classes in addition to documenting the internment experience in his own paintings. Discharged from Topaz after an attack by another internee required Obata to be hospitalized, Obata moved to St. Louis. In 1949, he and his family returned to Berkeley, where he resumed teaching at the university, attaining the rank of emeritus upon his retirement.

Several of Obata's works from Tanforan and Topaz are reproduced in Deborah Gesensway and Mindy Roseman's *Beyond Words: Images from America's Concentration Camps* (1987), while *Obata's Yosemite: The Art and Letters of Chiura Obata from His Trip to the High Sierra in 1927* (1993) reveals his love for the California landscape.

OCA. *See* **Organization of Chinese Americans**

Oceanic Group: Six Japanese businessmen who came to the United States from Japan in 1876 aboard the *Oceanic*. Landing in San Francisco, they caught a train to New York, their destination. The group's intentions were to establish markets for Japanese goods such as tea and silks, as well as to promote trade between America and Japan.

Odo, Franklin S.: Scholar. The director of the ethnic studies program at the University of Hawaii, Manoa, Odo is a coauthor of *A Pictorial History of the Japanese in Hawaii, 1885-1924* (1985) and coeditor of *Roots: An Asian American Reader* (1971), to which he contributed the article "The U.S. in Asia and Asians in America." Odo is a past president of the ASSOCIATION FOR ASIAN AMERICAN STUDIES.

Office of Hawaiian Affairs (OHA): Trusteeship created by the 1978 Constitutional Convention of the

State of Hawaii. The purpose of the convention was to clarify and implement the trust language of section 5(f) of the state's Admissions Act of 1959 as it applied to Native Hawaiians.

Before 1978 little attention was put on the trust language of section 5(f). The state believed that this section required only that certain proceeds and income must be used for one of the five stated trust purposes; the state chose public education. At the 1978 convention, three new sections were added to the constitution. The first provided that lands granted to the state were to be held by the state as a public trust for Native Hawaiians and the general public. The second formed an Office of Hawaiian Affairs, governed by a nine-member board of trustees, to hold title to all real or personal property as a trust for Native Hawaiians and Hawaiians. The third set forth the powers of these trustees.

The OHA was established to serve all Hawaiians through receiving and administering its share of public land trust funds for the purpose of improving the condition of Native Hawaiians under the Admissions Act. The definition of "Native Hawaiian" is tied to the definition under the Hawaiian Homes Commission Act of 1920. Benefits under that act are limited to those individuals with at least 50 percent Hawaiian blood. Although the OHA amendment lists two beneficiaries of the OHA trust, Native Hawaiians and Hawaiians (less than 50 percent Hawaiian blood), the OHA is restricted to using its public land trust funds solely for the benefit of Native Hawaiian beneficiaries.

The OHA is unique because it combines both a public trust and a government agency. The OHA is a separate state agency and is independent of the executive branch. Its independence is assured by its primary funding mechanism (the public land trust fund). The organization controls its own internal affairs and regulates its own power to acquire and manage property and to enter into contracts and leases. It also has its own elective process by which the board of trustees is chosen.

The OHA's statutory purposes include improving conditions for Native Hawaiians and Hawaiians; serving as the principal state agency for the performance, development, and coordination of programs and activities relating to Hawaiians; assessing the policies and practices of other agencies impacting Hawaiians; conducting advocacy efforts; receiving and disbursing grants and donations from all sources for Hawaiians; and serving as a receptacle for reparations from the U.S. government.

Office of the JACL, 1942, which worked with the ORA to locate survivors. Pictured here is Larry Tajiri, editor of the JACL newspaper the Pacific Citizen. (Pacific Citizen)

Office of Redress Administration (ORA): Office in the U.S. Department of Justice that administered the disbursement of redress monies mandated by the Civil Liberties Act of 1988 and authorized by the U.S. Congress to surviving Japanese Americans and Aleuts who were relocated and interned during World War II. The ORA, in cooperation with the Japanese American Citizens League (JACL) and the National Coalition for Redress/Reparations (NCRR), worked to locate and contact camp survivors, held workshops and established a telephone hotline to answer questions about eligibility, and processed the paperwork necessary to ensure distribution of redress checks. It is estimated that the ORA located some seventy-five thousand eligible recipients, approximately fifteen thousand more individuals than were originally expected to qualify. President George Bush held a ceremony at the White House on October 9, 1990, to present the first redress checks to former camp inmates.

Ogawa, Dennis (b. Sept. 7, 1943, Los Angeles, Calif.): Scholar and businessperson. A professor in the American Studies department of the University of Hawaii and a director of the Japanese American Research Center at the Honolulu Japanese Chamber of Commerce, he is also part owner of the NGN cable television station in Hawaii, which features programs from Japan. He holds B.A. (1966), M.A. (1967), and Ph.D. (1969) degrees, all from the University of California, Los Angeles. He is the author of *Jan Ken Po: The World of Hawaii's Japanese Americans* (1973) and *Kodomo No Tame Ni—For the Sake of the Children: The Japanese American Experience in Hawaii* (1978).

Ohana: According to Hawaiian tradition, a group of households who regarded themselves as related by blood, marriage, or adoption, and who were living in an *ahupuaa* (land division). While some anthropologists believe the term referred in the nineteenth century to a domestic group rather than an extended community, such a community was the basic unit of *makaainana* (commoner) society. Because of the fact that most foods and material resources flourished in different biomes, often some distance apart, exchange among households was necessary in most areas. According to nineteenth century oral tradition, sharing between coast and inland was carried on within the *ohana*. Uncalculating reciprocity, symbolized as *aloha*, constituted the basic value of this community.

Incorporation increased the supply of labor for production of food and materials, given an abundance of land. Hospitality, *hanai* (adoption), meeting others' needs, *laulima* (joint labor), feasting, and entertaining all promoted incorporation and tied members of the *ohana* together. The elder male of the senior branch "was the *haku* ('master'), who directed the activities of the several households, acted as ritual head, and represented the 'ohana before the *alii* ('chiefs')." *Haku* also monitored relations between members and presided over conflict resolution (*hooponopono*: "to set things right" spiritually). Prior to 1819 the sexes were segregated in eating and ritual. While obedience to authority was stressed, equality among those of the same age/sex/seniority was expected. Grandchildren and grandparents, cherished as links to the past and future, shared a special relationship.

The *ohana* today tends to be the household, but it remains the major institution preserving Hawaiian values. Uncalculating reciprocity still defines membership in the extended *ohana*. *Haku* no longer exist, and increasingly women have become the focal point. *Hanai* persists in altered form, and strangers are still widely incorporated. Obedience and equality continue to be stressed in rearing children. Yet the ravages of poverty, landlessness, and individualism have seriously undermined family *lokahi* (solidarity) since the 1980's. Nevertheless *ohana* remains a valued symbol and is applied to civic associations and large groups descended from a common ancestor.

Okada, John (1923, Seattle, Wash.—Feb., 1971): Novelist. Okada is the author of *No-No Boy* (1957), a novel that addressed the deep and bitter divisions within members of Japanese American communities as a result of World War II. The work met with critical indifference but was later celebrated as the first Japanese American novel.

Okada, a Nisei, was born in the Old Merchants Hotel in Seattle. He attended Scottsbluff Junior College. When Okada volunteered for military service with the U.S. Air Force during World War II, Japanese Americans incarcerated in RELOCATION CENTERS were deliberating how to answer "loyalty" and "allegiance" Questions 27 and 28 of the U.S. government's predraft questionnaire. The questions required a simple yes (if loyal) or no answer. Nearly one-fourth of the draft-age Nisei answered with a no, a qualified answer, or no response. Those who answered no to both questions were called "no-no boys." Okada was not one of those. He served until 1946 and was discharged as a sergeant.

Okada received two bachelor's degrees, in English and in library science, from the University of Washington. He continued his studies after World War II at Columbia University, where he received a masters' degree in English in 1949 and met his wife, Dorothy; they were to have two children.

No-No Boy relates the story of Ichiro, who spent two years in camp for being an Asian American and then two more years in jail for answering no to Questions 27 and 28. The protagonist alternately embraces and reviles the duality of his identity as an Asian and an American. During Okada's lifetime *No-No Boy* was a commercial failure; the novel, published in an edition of fifteen hundred copies, failed to sell out its press run. He died in obscurity, at the age of forty-seven, of a heart attack.

After Okada's death Dorothy Okada offered her husband's manuscripts and correspondence to the JAPANESE AMERICAN RESEARCH PROJECT (JARP) at The University of California, Los Angeles (UCLA). After JARP declined to accept his papers, she burned all the documents. Among the things that were destroyed was his second (and unpublished) novel. It was to have dealt with the experiences of the *Issei*, or immigrant Japanese, in the United States. Five years after Okada's death the COMBINED ASIAN-AMERICAN

RESOURCES PROJECT reprinted *No-No Boy*, and the book has since sold out many repeated printings.

Okamura, Jonathan Y. (b. July 22, 1949, Wailuku, Hawaii): Scholar. A research associate at the University of Hawaii's Center for Studies of Multicultural Higher Education, Okamura has published widely on topics relating to Filipino immigration and the Filipino experience in Hawaii; he has also published extensively on topics relating to the Philippines. Among his many works as author, coauthor, editor, and coeditor is *The Filipino American Experience in Hawaii* (1991), and coedited with A. Agbayani and M. Tria Kerkvliet, a special issue of *Social Process in Hawaii*.

Okamura received a B.A. degree in anthropology and mathematics from the University of Southern California (1971) and a Ph.D. in anthropology from the University of London (1983). In addition to his research post at the Center for Studies of Multicultural Higher Education, he is on the affiliate graduate faculty of the department of anthropology at the University of Hawaii.

Okayama: PREFECTURE on the island of Honshu, Japan. It was the region of origin of many Japanese who immigrated to the United States from the 1880's to 1924. Many landed in Hawaii because of an agreement signed between Hawaii and Japan to import Japanese laborers to work on Hawaii's sugarcane plantations. The agreement was arranged by Robert Walker IRWIN, whose friends, the Japanese foreign minister Inoue Kaoru and the importer Masuda Takashi—both from the adjoining prefecture of Yamaguchi—suggested attracting laborers from that area. Okayama is located on the western part of HONSHU (the largest Japanese island) and occupies an area of about 2,738 square miles. Its 1991 population was about 1,929,000. The region's economy is mostly agricultural. Its capital, Okayama City, is a major marketing center.

Okazaki, Steven (b. Mar. 12, 1952, Los Angeles, Calif.): Filmmaker. The son of U.S.-born parents, he graduated from San Francisco State University in 1976. His documentary about a European American interned with Japanese Americans during World

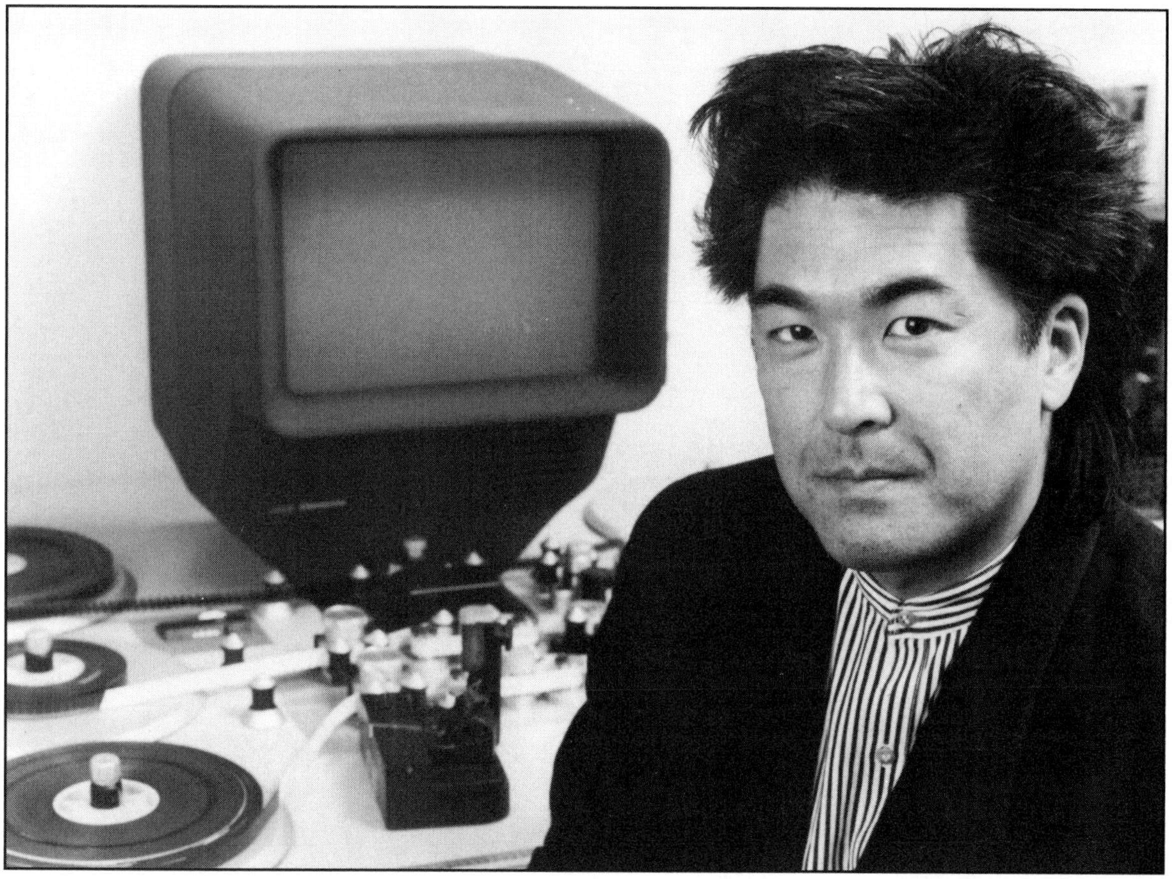

Academy Award-winning filmmaker Steven Okazaki at an editing bay. (Asian Week)

War II, *Days of Waiting* (1990), won an Academy Award; *Unfinished Business* (1986), a documentary about Japanese American wartime internment resisters, was nominated for an Oscar. In addition to children's films, he also produced *Living on Tokyo Time* (1987), a feature film, and a documentary about development in Hawaii, *Troubled Paradise* (1992).

Okei (1852, Japan—1871, Gold Hill, Calif.): Teenage nursemaid. She worked for John Henry Schnell's family in the WAKAMATSU TEA AND SILK FARM COLONY in Gold Hill, near Sacramento, in Northern California. She apparently came to the United States in 1869 with Schnell, who that year brought a group of Japanese immigrants from Wakamatsu, on the Japanese island of Kyushu, to establish an agricultural colony; the colony, however, failed in 1871. Okei died of fever at the age of nineteen, a symbol of the struggle and tragedy of that early farming colony.

Okihiro, Gary Y. (b. Oct. 14, 1945, Aiea, Hawaii): Scholar. His research focused initially on African history but later shifted to ASIAN AMERICAN STUDIES. Having worked with Herbert Aptheker, the legendary leftist historian, Okihiro applied theories of resistance to reexamine Japanese American history and World War II internment. His books *Japanese Legacy: Farming and Community Life in California's Santa Clara Valley* (1985, with Timothy J. Lukes) and *Cane Fires: The Anti-Japanese Movement in Hawaii, 1865-1945* (1991), won awards from the ASSOCIATION FOR ASIAN AMERICAN STUDIES. He is also the author of *Margins and Mainstreams: Asians in American History and Culture* (1994). A professor of history at Cornell University, where he directs the Asian American Studies program, he received his B.A. degree from California's Pacific Union College and M.A. and Ph.D. degrees from the University of California, Los Angeles.

Okimura v. Acheson (1952): U.S. Supreme Court ruling that ordered citizenship rights restored to an American-born Japanese who had been conscripted into the Japanese military and while in Japan had voted in an election. At age four, Hawaii-born Okimura Kiyokura was sent to Japan by his parents, who wanted him to get a traditional Japanese education there. After more than ten years, he returned to Hawaii but a short while later went back to Japan for language study in

Gary Okihiro (left) has done extensive research in Asian American Studies. He is shown here with Don Nakanishi. (Asian Week)

preparation for a teaching post back in the islands.

In 1939, the year that World War II began, Japanese Americans in Japan, especially the KIBEI, were in danger of being forcibly drafted into the Japanese military. As the war extended into the Pacific theater, many Kibei were left stranded behind enemy lines. Some of them would eventually be inducted into service or forced to do things against their will. As a penalty, by order of the U.S. government, many of them would lose their citizenship. To avoid conscription, many Kibei left Japan, but Okimura stayed behind at his parents' request to finish his schooling. After graduation, he taught school for a while at the Japanese government's insistence, then in 1942 was forced to enter the army under threat of punishment. At the war's end, he returned to Hawaii for further studies, and in 1947 he voted in a Japanese election in which popular participation had been heavily encouraged by the American occupation forces then in Japan. Two years later he applied for a U.S. passport but was denied on the grounds that he had relinquished his American citizenship by serving in the Japanese army and voting in the election.

A federal district court handed down a ruling in Okimura's favor, declaring the U.S. government's action against him to be unconstitutional. The opinion found that while the U.S. Congress had sole authority to revoke citizenship received through naturalization, it was barred from withdrawing citizenship conferred at birth and by right of birth. Only one who had actually become a naturalized citizen of another country was subject to revocation. U.S. secretary of state Dean Acheson then appealed to the Supreme Court, which affirmed the district court's decision and concluded that foreign military service under threat of punishment did not justify loss of citizenship.

The ruling in *Okimura* established a legal precedent for subsequent cases involving Nisei who had involuntarily joined the Japanese military.

Okinawa: Largest and most important island of the RYUKYU ISLANDS, an archipelago in the North Pacific Ocean falling between Taiwan and Kyushu, Japan. Okinawa, about 67 miles long and anywhere from 2 to 16 miles wide, covers an area of about 554 square miles. It contains more than 1 million people. Naha, the capital of the Ryukyus, is located there. The island is also the largest in Okinawa Prefecture.

The history of Okinawa shows that although the people are ethnically Japanese, they have had a separate history from Japan for much of their existence.

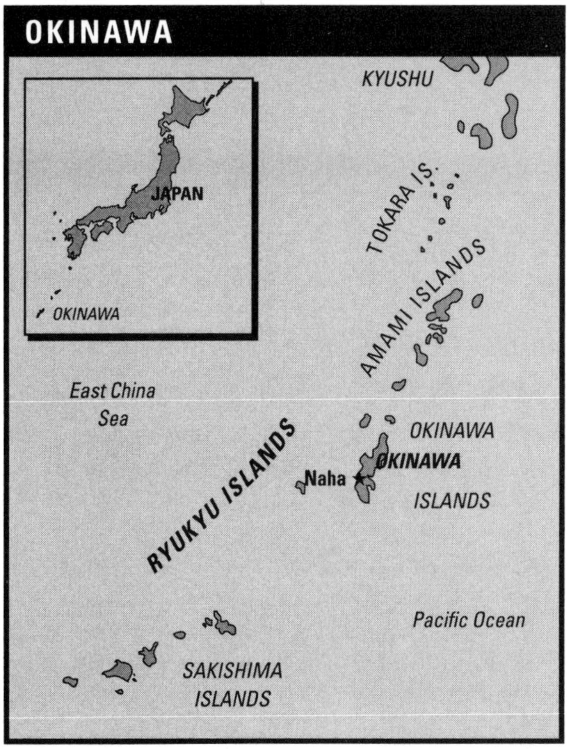

They developed an independent kingdom that entered into a tributary relationship with China that lasted from 1372 until 1872. The Satsuma conquest in 1609 began the integration of Okinawa into Japan. It was during the Meiji period of Japan (1868-1912), however, that it became a truly integral part of that nation.

Early History. The origin of the people of Okinawa is shrouded in mystery. It is hypothesized that some came from northern East Asia via Japan, some from Mongolia via Korea, and others from Southeast Asia via the Philippines or the coast of China. Their language, however, is a Japanese language, and their religion is similar to traditional SHINTO of Japan.

In the twelfth century, after a period of battling warlords, Shunten, Lord of Urasoe, established the first Okinawan dynasty (1187-1259). By the fourteenth century, the island of Okinawa had become three kingdoms: Hokuzan, Nanzan, and Chuzan. In 1372 King Satto of Chuzan sent the first tribute mission from Okinawa to China. Shortly thereafter, Hokuzan and Nanzan followed suit. In 1422 Sho Hashi of Chuzan united the island of Okinawa. The tribute relations with China, however, were maintained. These relations greatly accelerated Okinawa's cultural and political development. When Okinawa was first established, China sent thirty-six families to serve as diplomats, government ministers, interpreters, teach-

During WWII, Japan attempted to use its hold on the island of Okinawa to delay the advance of U.S. forces. Here a Japanese plane is shot down by cannon fire from an American aircraft carrier near the Mariana Islands in June, 1944. (National Archives)

ers, navigators, and shipwrights. In addition Okinawa was permitted to send students to study at the Imperial Academy in the Chinese capital and elsewhere.

Of great economic value to Okinawa was the trade that China allowed as part of the privileges granted through the tributary system. During the fourteenth and fifteenth centuries, Okinawa carried on a lucrative entrepôt trade between China, Japan, and Southeast Asia. For example Southeast Asian spices, such as pepper, and Japanese swords were exchanged for Chinese chinaware and silk, which in turn were sold to Japan for silver and copper.

The tributary relations lasted for five hundred years, from 1372 to 1872. During this time China did not attempt to control Okinawa. China was satisfied to receive the acknowledgment of supremacy from Okinawa and to reserve the right to perform the investiture ceremony when a new Okinawan king ascended to the throne. In other words, the relationship between China and Okinawa was basically ritual, not an actual exercise of overlord dominance.

Conquest by Satsuma. In 1609, Satsuma, a southern province of Japan, invaded Okinawa. The northern islands of Amami were placed under the direct control of Satsuma, and Okinawa was assessed taxes. Okinawa, however, was allowed to keep its royal family and to maintain a façade of independence. The façade of independence was granted because that was the only way for Okinawa to continue its tributary relations with China on which the Sino-Okinawa trade was based. By conceding to China's ritual authority over Okinawa, Satsuma could continue, and control, the Sino-Okinawa trade, from which it now profited. At the same time Satsuma exercised de facto control over Okinawa, requiring that Satsuma approve each new king, regent, and government minister.

Japanese drawing depicting an American naval vessel docked in Japanese waters, circa 1861. Under the Tokugawa regime, Japan remained closed to the Western world until the arrival of Commodore Matthew Perry of the United States in the 1850's. (Library of Congress)

Aboard the USS Missouri, *General Douglas MacArthur signs as Supreme Allied Commander during formal surrender ceremonies in Tokyo Bay, September 2, 1945. In the postwar period American troops occupied Okinawa for nearly thirty years.* (National Archives)

Because TOKUGAWA Japan (1600-1867) was a closed country except for trade with the Chinese and Dutch at Nagasaki, the Okinawa tributary missions to China during this period served as one of Japan's valuable avenues of information on the outside world. It was mainly through Nagasaki and Okinawa that Japan was aware of the impact of Western activity on Southeast Asia and China.

Okinawa Prefecture. In 1853 Commodore Matthew C. PERRY sailed into Naha port. Shortly afterward he went to Edo (now Tokyo) and forcibly opened Japan. In reaction the Japanese established the MEIJI government. The new government ended the tributary relations between Okinawa and China, abolished the Okinawan monarchy, and incorporated the islands into Japan proper.

On March 11, 1879, Okinawa was made a prefecture. It was one of the poorest PREFECTURES in Japan, but initially Japan did not invest in Okinawa to effect significant changes. Many young people emigrated to large cities such as Osaka, Kawasaki, and Tokyo, where there was employment in factories. Others sought a new life in Hawaii, the United States, the Philippines, or South America.

Eventually, with assimilation as its goal, Japan initiated a program of change. Education was emphasized and schools were built. Okinawans were required to learn standard Japanese, because although the language of the Okinawans is a Japanese language, it is unintelligible to speakers of standard Japanese. Another development was the 1903 land reform, which converted traditional communal lands to private lands and made former peasants landowners.

World War II and American Occupation. After the fall of Saipan in July, 1944, thousands of Okinawan civilians were evacuated to Kyushu and Taiwan and about 100,000 Japanese soldiers were sent to Okinawa. The Japanese strategy was to use the island to stop, or at least delay, the advance of the Americans to Japan proper as much as possible.

By April 1, 1945, U.S. marines occupied the center of the islands. The Battle of Okinawa was one of the bloodiest battles of the war in the Pacific, killing more than 120,000 inhabitants, or about a third of the island's population. At the end of the war, in 1945, Okinawa was placed under American military occupation.

Reversion to Japan. On May 15, 1972, after twenty-seven years under American military occupation, Okinawa was returned to Japan. Part of the reason for the reversion was that the American involvement in Vietnam had become unpopular and the role of the United States as "policeman" in Asia was in question.—*Ruth Adaniya*

SUGGESTED READINGS: • Ch'en, Ta-tuan. "Investiture of Liu-ch'iu Kings in the Ch'ing Period." In *The Chinese World Order*, edited by John K. Fairbank. Cambridge, Mass.: Harvard University Press, 1968. • Kerr, George H. *Okinawa: The History of an Island People*. Rutland, Vt.: Charles E. Tuttle, 1958. • Lebra, William P. *Okinawan Religion: Belief, Ritual, and Social Structure*. Honolulu: University of Hawaii Press, 1966. • Sakai, Robert. "The Ryukyu Islands as a Fief of Satsuma." In *The Chinese World Order*, edited by John K. Fairbank. Cambridge, Mass.: Harvard University Press, 1968. • Sakihara, Mitsugu. "Ryukyu's Tribute-Tax to Satsuma During the Tokugawa Period." *Modern Asian Studies* 6.3 (1972): 329-335.

Okubo, Mine (b. 1912, Riverside, Calif.): Artist. Okubo was born into a poor family of seven children. The mother, an artist and calligrapher, encouraged the young Mine to draw and paint. After a year at Riverside Junior College, Okubo enrolled at the University of California, Berkeley, as an art student. Graduating with an M.A. degree, she traveled to Europe on a fellowship. With the advent of World War II, however, she went back to California and, through the federal Works Progress Administration (WPA), was hired to produce murals for the U.S. Army. Following the Japanese surprise bombing of PEARL HARBOR, Honolulu, in late 1941, Okubo's father ended up in the Missoula internment camp in western Montana. Okubo and her brother were sent first to the TANFORAN assembly center and then to the TOPAZ relocation center in central Utah, where she passed the time sketching people, events, and so forth (photographs were prohibited). She also taught art classes and served as art editor for the camp newspaper published daily by the inmates and for the literary magazine *Trek*.

In 1944 Okubo was released from Topaz to work as an illustrator for *Fortune* magazine in New York City, settling there permanently. Two years later she published *Citizen 13660*, a book of ink and rice paper drawings chronicling her camp experiences. Eventually, as she became better known to the American public, her drawings were featured in exhibitions across the United States. From that point on she made her living as a freelance commercial artist based in New York. Later she decided to concentrate exclusively on fine art, staging numerous solo and group exhibitions of her work.

Okumura, Takie (Apr. 18, 1864, Kochi, Japan—Feb. 10, 1951, Honolulu, Territory of Hawaii): Christian minister. Okumura became a Christian when he was twenty-four years old, a year after his marriage to Katsu Ogawa. From 1890 to 1894 he attended Doshisha University Divinity School in Kyoto. In 1894 he arrived in Hawaii on a three-year contract with the (Congregationalist) Hawaiian Board of Missions. After deciding to dedicate his life to mission work in Hawaii, he returned briefly to Japan in 1896 to bring his wife and their three boys to the islands. Another son and three daughters were born to them in Hawaii.

In Hawaii, Okumura established a Japanese-language school, operated a Christian dormitory for

Takie Okumura. (Japanese American National Museum)

Japanese American high school and college students, organized Boys Clubs, and published two periodicals. He also founded the Makiki Christian Church, which grew from a membership of twenty-four in 1904 to more than five hundred in ten years.

Okumura and other Christian ministers performed various services for Issei (Japanese immigrants) such as writing letters for them, teaching night school, mediating plantation disputes and family quarrels, and sending birth, marriage, and death notifications to the Japanese consulate. Since, however, most Issei came from southwestern Japan, where BUDDHISM was strong, converts to Christianity were few.

In keeping with the social and economic agenda of the European American elite, Okumura began a six-year campaign in 1921, visiting sugar plantations across the territory. He held meetings with workers in an effort to Christianize them and discourage them from leaving the plantations. In 1927 he began a series of annual NEW AMERICANS CONFERENCES, which continued for fifteen years. Each year conference speakers told the fifty to eighty adult Nisei (second-generation Japanese American) delegates that white-collar jobs were in short supply and that the only jobs available were on sugar and pineapple plantations or in general farming.

Okumura opposed the court challenge to laws in the Territory of Hawaii that would have abolished Japanese-language schools. Instead he counseled acceptance and restraint.

Okumura was one of the most outspoken of several accommodationist Issei leaders in Hawaii during the first half of the twentieth century, a time of anti-Japanese sentiment and tension between the large Japanese population and the European American community. He was opposed by other Issei leaders who urged the Japanese to stand up for their rights.

Oland, Warner (Werner Ohlund; Oct. 3, 1880, Umea, Sweden—Aug. 5, 1938, Stockholm, Sweden): Actor. He is best known for his portrayal of detective Charlie CHAN in motion pictures, beginning in 1931. He started his career in the theater, working as an actor, set designer, and Strindberg translator.

Olson, Culbert L. (Nov. 7, 1876, Fillmore, Utah—1962): Governor of California. A Democrat, he was a state senator before being elected governor in 1938. After Japan's bombing of PEARL HARBOR, he summoned leaders of the Japanese American community on the West Coast and proposed a special internment plan for the Japanese in California: Japanese American men were to be sent to CONCENTRATION CAMPS in the interior of the state and work for the agricultural industry during the day. Most of the leaders rejected his plan. In 1942 Olson complied with the federal government's evacuation orders.

Olympics in Korea: The summer games of the Twenty-fourth Olympiad were held in Seoul, South Korea, from September 17 to October 2, 1988. More than ninety-five hundred athletes representing more than 160 nations competed.

In the autumn of 1981, the Olympic congress in Baden-Baden decided that Seoul would be the site of the 1988 summer games. Although that clearly was a controversial choice, the only other candidate was Nagoya, Japan. Numerous citizens of Nagoya had campaigned against the selection of their city, because construction for the Olympics would ruin the city's only remnant of park space.

North Korea spoke of a possible boycott unless PYONGYANG was recognized as a cohost city, with

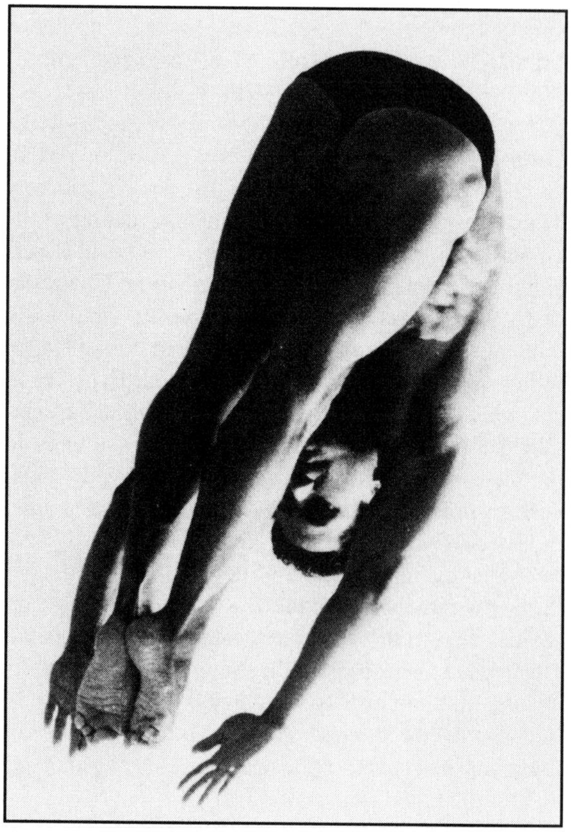

American diver Greg Louganis recorded several firsts at the Seoul Olympics. (Department of Special Collections, University of California at Los Angeles)

Site of the twenty-fourth Olympic Games (summer) held at Seoul, South Korea, in 1988. (Korea National Tourism Corporation)

North Korea hosting half of the events. International Olympic Committee (IOC) president Juan Antonio Samaranch proposed that North Korea host the popular archery and table tennis events, and some of the cycling and soccer competitions. North Korea rejected the offer and, along with Cuba, Ethiopia, and Nicaragua, boycotted the games.

South Korea took every possible security measure in anticipation of terrorist acts during the Olympics. Fortunately there was no violence or domestic strife, and attendance was at the highest number of countries ever for an Olympiad.

The issue of the use of performance-enhancing drugs, such as anabolic steroids, by athletes received unprecedented news coverage. The gold-medal winner of the 100-meter event, Canadian Ben Johnson, was disqualified for using steroids, and the medal was awarded to the American, Carl Lewis, who had finished second.

The total number of medal events was 237. Thirty-one different countries won gold medals. The top four overall medal winners were the Soviet Union, with 55 gold, 31 silver, and 46 bronze; East Germany, with 37 gold, 35 silver, and 30 bronze; the United States, with 36 gold, 31 silver, and 27 bronze; and West Germany, with 11 gold, 14 silver, and 15 bronze.

Some noteworthy "firsts" occurred during the Olympics. American diver Greg Louganis, of Samoan and European ancestry, became the first man to win both the platform and springboard diving events in consecutive Olympics. Table tennis made its first appearance as an Olympic event.

Omatsu, Glenn (b. Cleveland, Ohio): Editor and community activist. Omatsu is a third-generation Japanese American. Beginning in 1985, he served as a staff member of the ASIAN AMERICAN STUDIES CENTER, University of California, Los Angeles (UCLA), he has also served with community and labor groups in Los Angeles and with solidarity networks. At UCLA, he serves as associate editor of *AMERASIA JOURNAL*—the annual bibliographies he compiles are a vital resource for scholars in ASIAN AMERICAN STUDIES and allied fields—and as editor of *CrossCurrents*, the newsmagazine of the Asian American Studies Center.

Prior to his work at UCLA, Omatsu served as assistant editor of the English section of the *Hokubei Mainichi* newspaper in San Francisco from 1971 to 1976, and as chief shop steward for Teamsters Local 986 at a small factory in Los Angeles from 1979 to 1985. He has also been active in community organizing, particularly with the Committee Against Nihonmachi Evictions in San Francisco from 1973 to 1977.

Omatsu has edited two special issues of *Amerasia Journal*—one a retrospective analysis of the Asian American Movement, and another focusing on contemporary Asian American labor organizing. He is the author of "The Four Prisons and the Movements for Liberation: Asian American Activism from the 1960s to the 1990s," in *The State of Asian America: Activism and Resistance in the 1990s* (1994), edited by Karin Aguilar-San Juan.

Omi, Michael Allen (b. Mar. 9, 1951, Berkeley, Calif.): Scholar. A specialist in race relations/politics and coauthor of *Racial Formation in the United States: From the 1960's to the 1980's* (1986), he has taught ethnic studies at the University of California, Berkeley. The winner of Berkeley's 1990 Distinguished Teaching Award, his writings have appeared in *Socialist Review* and *Critical Sociology* and have provided a foundation for scholars who grapple with racial theory and ideology in the United States.

Michael Omi. (Asian Week)

Omoto: Japanese new religion, founded by Deguchi Nao in 1892. The sect is characterized by monotheism, a complex spiritual world, divine revelation, a vision of an imminent new age, and influences from Western spiritualism. During the 1920's and 1930's, membership peaked at about 2,000,000 followers; through 1977, however, levels had dropped to only about 160,000. Omoto worshipers later left to establish such new religions as Seicho no Ie and Sekai Kyusei Kyo.

Omura, James Matsumoto (Utaka Matsumoto; Nov. 17, 1912, Winslow, Bainbridge Island, Wash.—June 20, 1994): Journalist. Born to a Japanese father who had immigrated illegally in order to escape conscription into the Japanese army and had assumed the name Matsumoto in the United States to avoid detection, James Omura grew up in a small town on Bainbridge Island near Seattle, Washington. He dropped out of school at the age of thirteen in search of adventure in Alaska, where he found employment at a salmon cannery. Between 1926 and 1929, he worked at other canneries and was employed as a sawmill worker and a railroad laborer in various western states before returning to Seattle. After trying unsuccessfully to get work as a reporter on the *Japanese American Courier*, Omura went back to school and received his high school diploma.

After graduation, Omura moved south to Los Angeles in 1931, where he took a job as the English-language editor of the *Shin-Nichibei*. Three years later, he headed north and was offered a position in San Francisco as the English-language editor of the *Shin Sekai Shimbun*. During his tenure at that paper, some of his editorials evidently gave offense to leaders of the Japanese American Citizens League (JACL). Omura found himself shunned by certain members of San Francisco's Issei community, and this situation foreshadowed his chilly relations with JACL members during the 1940's. Soon after the newspaper merged with the *Hokubei Asahi* in 1935 to become the *Shin Sekai-Asahi Shimbun*, Omura quit his job and began another long-term stretch of temporary jobs, including stints as a migrant farmworker, a tractor operator, and a warehouse worker in central and northern California. By 1940, he had saved sufficient funds to launch his own magazine, *Current Life*. After marrying and settling down in the San Francisco Bay Area, Omura and his wife worked together to produce the magazine, which particularly focused on social issues and cultural affairs of interest to the Nisei community.

In the wake of the Japanese attack on PEARL HARBOR in 1941, Omura and his wife relocated to the "free zone" state of Colorado and tried to continue their publication. After the magazine folded, they launched an employment agency to help other Japanese Americans who had voluntarily relocated in Denver and other Rocky Mountain communities and were not forced into INTERNMENT CAMPS during the war. Omura attracted attention for his involvement as the only Japanese American not affiliated with the JACL to attend the TOLAN COMMITTEE hearings on plans to relocate Japanese Americans. Although he was unable to prevent the relocation process, Omura continued to speak out on behalf of other Japanese Americans who resisted the government's plans and wrote several editorials as editor of the *Rocky Shimpo* in support of the HEART MOUNTAIN FAIR PLAY COMMITTEE. As a result of his actions in support of the committee, Omura joined them in being brought to trial for aiding and abetting the violation of the Selective Service Act. Unlike his codefendents, however, Omura was found innocent.

When World War II ended, Omura received little attention for his efforts to preserve the civil rights of Japanese Americans during the war. He eventually found employment as a landscaper in Colorado. During the 1980's when the push for REDRESS and reparations for Japanese American camp survivors was brought to national awareness, Omura began to receive greater recognition for his courageous efforts in support of Nisei draft resistance and respect for individual conscience during World War II.

1.5 generation: Term originally applied to Korean Americans who came to the United States with their parents as children or adolescents. Born in Korea but raised in the United States, they have an identity distinct both from that of their parents, who immigrated as adults, and from that of American-born Koreans. The 1.5 generation is an in-between generation. Its members often lack their parents' fluency in the Korean language, yet they may not be fully at home in English. At the same time, there is the potential for this generation to serve as a bridge between the elders and the American-born, conserving elements of traditional Korean culture and identity that might otherwise be lost. Hence the term "bridge generation," another label for the same phenomenon.

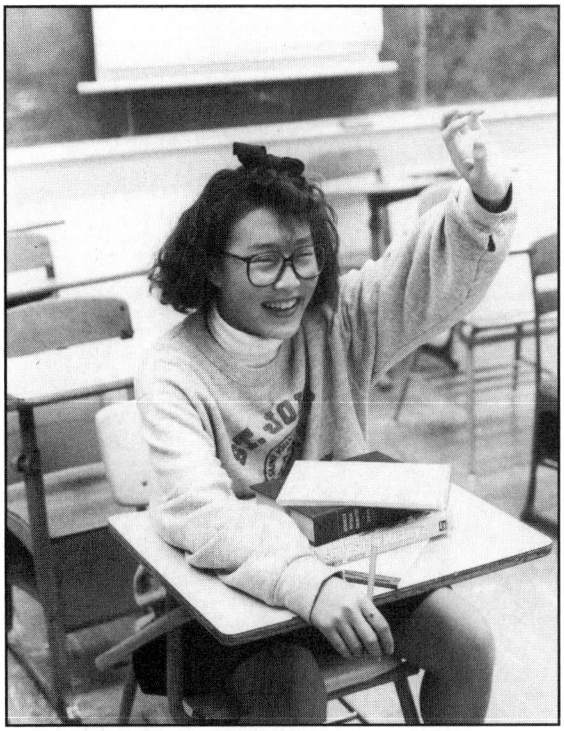

The 1.5 generation encompasses Korean Americans who immigrated to the United States in childhood or adolescence. (Cleo Freelance Photography)

The existence of the 1.5 generation reflects the fact that post-1965 Korean immigration has included many families. The same is true of the post-1975 refugees from Southeast Asia. As a result, the terms "1.5 generation" and "bridge generation" are being applied to Vietnamese Americans and other groups whose experience parallels that of 1.5-generation Korean Americans.

100th Infantry Battalion: The most heavily decorated unit of its size in the history of the U.S. Army, formed almost entirely of Americans of Japanese ancestry from Hawaii. Its thirteen hundred soldiers earned forty-four Silver Stars, thirty-one Bronze Stars, nine Distinguished Service Crosses, three Legion of Merit Medals, two Presidential Unit Citations, and more than a thousand Purple Hearts.

Battalion members called themselves "ONE PUKA PUKA," Hawaiian Pidgin for "one zero zero"; later, because of heavy casualties from some of the most intense fighting seen by American soldiers, they became known as the "Purple Heart Battalion." Yet group spirit was so strong among the 100th that not one soldier deserted his post or went AWOL (Absent WithOut Leave)—except for two wounded soldiers

Japanese Americans, attached to the U.S. Army Signal Corps as residents of Hawaii, assemble at Honolulu's Iolani Palace prior to leaving the islands for the Camp Shelby, Mississippi, Army base. (Hawaii State Archives)

who left their hospital beds to return to combat.

Many Japanese Americans were already in uniform when World War II began following the December 7, 1941, bombing of PEARL HARBOR by the Japanese Empire. Some were part of the Hawaiian infantry company that captured the first prisoner of war (from a small Japanese submarine). Unfortunately an initial wave of anti-Japanese hysteria resulted in the temporary barring of most Japanese American soldiers from U.S. military service. By June of 1942, however, the paranoia had subsided, and the 100th Infantry Battalion was created. After training, the 100th was deployed overseas in August of 1943, joining the 34th Division in North Africa.

Three weeks later the 100th landed at Salerno, where it scored an impressive number of U.S. Army firsts in Italy: They were the first to take German prisoners, the first to destroy a German tank, and the first to take a German emplacement by using a bayonet charge. One of their ranks, Joe Takata, was also the first Japanese American soldier to win (posthumously) the Distinguished Service Cross.

In March of 1944 the 100th landed at Anzio beach and in June became part of the newly arrived 442ND REGIMENTAL COMBAT TEAM, known as the "Go for Broke" unit. The combined group—still nearly all Japanese American—fought in Europe until the end of the war. The contributions of these American servicemen cannot be overstated: They greatly advanced the political and social rights of all Americans, and especially those of Japanese ancestry.

One Puka Puka: Hawaiian Pidgin English nickname for the 100TH INFANTRY BATTALION. *Puka* means "hole" in Hawaiian. The term became the favored designation of the 100th after that regiment went to Europe. It also exemplifies how the 100th used Hawaiian PIDGIN English during radio transmissions to confuse enemies.

Ong, Paul (b. Sept. 6, 1949, Sacramento, Calif.): Scholar. He attended the University of California and the University of Washington; from the former he took his Ph.D. degree in 1983. He has contributed numerous articles on issues impacting Asian Americans, including issues of racial inequality. Also, his demographic analyses have played a major part in reapportionment efforts in Los Angeles. Ong teaches in the Graduate School of Architecture and Urban Planning of the University of California, Los Angeles (UCLA).

Ong, Wing Foon (Feb. 4, 1904, Wing On Li, Guangdong Province, China—Dec. 19, 1977, Phoenix, Ariz.): Businessperson, lawyer, and state legislator. Ong, the first Chinese American to serve in a state legislature in the United States, served two terms in the Arizona house of representatives (1946-1950) and one term in the state senate (1966-1968). For a book-length account of his life, see *Summer Wind: The Story of an Immigrant Chinese Politician* (1986), by Richard Nagasawa.

Onizuka, Ellison (June 24, 1946, Kealakekua, Territory of Hawaii—Jan. 28, 1986, Cape Canaveral, Fla.): Astronaut. A graduate of the University of Colorado, Boulder, with B.S. and M.S. degrees in aerospace engineering, Onizuka entered the Air Force in 1970. He was initially an aerospace flight test engineer; but after pilot training, he spent more than seventeen hundred hours in the air on forty-three different kinds of aircraft.

Ellison Onizuka. (NASA)

Onizuka was selected by the National Aeronautics and Space Administration (NASA) as an astronaut in 1978—becoming the world's first Asian American astronaut—and trained as a shuttle mission specialist. He worked at the Shuttle Avionics Integration Laboratory and was on the launch support crews for the first two space shuttle flights in 1981. He was assigned to the flight crew for the tenth scheduled shuttle mission in 1982, but the mission was canceled. Onizuka was then assigned to the crew of the *Discovery* shuttle mission in January, 1985, on which he was a mission specialist focusing on the launch of a military satellite.

After completion of this flight, Onizuka was assigned to the third and final *Challenger* flight, the one that exploded shortly after its launch from Cape Canaveral, Florida, in January, 1986. His job was to deal with the payload satellite. Other professional members of the crew were Francis "Dick" Scobee, the pilot; Michael Smith, the copilot; Judith Resnick, the flight engineer; and Ronald McNair, a mission specialist. Also aboard were Gregory Jarvis, an engineer, and a New Hampshire teacher, Christa McAuliffe. The *Challenger* exploded over the Atlantic minutes after launch, and Onizuka and his colleagues became the first in-flight fatalities in NASA's space program since the early 1960's.

President Ronald Reagan, who spoke at a memorial for the *Challenger* crew at the Johnson Space Center in Houston, Texas, appointed a presidential commission to investigate the accident. It was chaired by former secretary of state William Rogers.

Onuki, Hachiro (Hutchlon Ohnick; 1849, Japan—1921): Businessman. He arrived in Boston in 1876, later moving to Phoenix. There he was awarded a municipal contract to provide the city with either gas or electric light, or both. He also changed his name to "Hutchlon Ohnick." Later he was named superintendent of the Phoenix Illuminating Gas and Electric Company. He went to Seattle in 1901 and founded the Oriental American Bank.

Opium and the Golden Triangle: The Golden Triangle is located in southeast Asia, where the borders of southeast Myanmar, northwest Laos, and northwest Thailand intersect. This region, which roughly takes the shape of a triangle, is considered golden because of the enormous wealth derived from opium cultivation and heroin processing, particularly after the early 1970's. Historically poor, ethnically diverse, and beyond the effective control of central governments (traditional, colonial, or postindependence), the region produced nearly 75 percent of the world's illicit opium supply in the early 1990's. The drug enterprise flourishes because of foreign demand, but the opium poppy, from which the drug is obtained, also enhances the incomes of impoverished farmers and corrupt officials in the region.

Demand, Profits, and Politics. Before the opium and its derivatives get to the millions of users, mainly in the industrial world, the lion's share of the drug profits has been snared by opium warlords, smugglers, organized criminals, and street dealers. Contributing to the success of Golden Triangle drug enterprises are Cold War contestants permeating the region. Remnants of the Nationalist Republic of China, or GUOMINDANG (GMD) army, who survive financially through the drug trade, provide a particularly apt illustration. The United States, though never directly involved in drug trafficking, supported tribes in the region that did cultivate and distribute opiates, such as the HMONG in Laos, because these tribes fought the Communists during the Vietnam War (1965-1975).

Attempts to eradicate the drug enterprise in the region have had mixed, though mainly ineffective, results. Opium production continued unabated in MYANMAR and nearly so in Laos, and though crop substitution has reduced opium cultivation in Thailand, trafficking there persists. The end of the Cold War has had little effect on Golden Triangle opium ventures: The Americans are gone and a much diminished GMD force remains, but new drug lords have appeared to satisfy the foreign craving for opiates.

Pre-Colonial and Colonial Opium Use. Opium's use is usually traced back to Homeric Greece, but wherever its origin, the drug had made its way east—to Persia, India, and China—at least by the end of the first millennium C.E. On the eve of European explorations some five centuries later, Asian consumers ate or drank opium concoctions, which served both medical and recreational purposes. The Europeans introduced opium smoking and large-scale commercialization of the drug to Asia, notably to those areas along the maritime routes in Southeast Asia. By the beginning of the twentieth century, most of Asia had been colonized, and a significant part of colonial regimes' revenue came from government monopolies. Between 1903 and 1907, French Indochina, which included Laos, obtained 13 to 17 percent of its budget from opium; India, which incorporated Burma, some 6 to 7 percent; and Thailand, which was independent, approximately 14 to 20 percent.

A crop of opium poppies is burned in Ban Na Kong in Laos as part of dedication ceremonies of the government program to develop alternative crops for former poppy growers. (AP/Wide World Photos)

Most of the opium probably came from the world's then two largest producers: China and India. The Golden Triangle's proximity to southwestern China, where most of that country's and a very large part of the world's opium was grown, probably hastened the cultivation of opium as a cash crop in the region. Moreover, China's antiopium crusade in the early twentieth century, the United States' criminalization of drugs after World War I (1914-1918), and the British promise first to end its export of opium to China by 1917 and later to phase out its sale of opium to the colonial regimes in Southeast Asia by 1936 drove a good part of the drug trade underground. Increasingly, illicit planting, transportation, and sales of drugs supplanted the legal enterprises as drug prohibition became the official objective of nations and international antidrug conferences. The rapid development of organized crime following drug prohibition, warlordism in China after 1916, and the breakdown of colonial rule in Asia with the outbreak of World War II (1939-1945) provided remote and autonomous regions such as the Golden Triangle with opportunities to link their highly valued poppy crops with felonious traffickers. It would not be until after World War II, however, that the region would become the global center of the opiate enterprise.

Decolonization and the Cold War. The war had disrupted commercial activity worldwide, and transportation and distribution systems only very slowly reappeared in Asia. Decolonization there involved still more unrest, as returning Europeans attempted to reestablish the status quo ante, failed, and eventually departed by mutual consent or were forcibly expelled. Meanwhile, the on-again, off-again Chinese Civil War reerupted, the result being a Chinese Communist Party (CCP) victory over the GMD and the creation of the

People's Republic of China (PRC) in 1949. The Golden Triangle experienced two consequences: First, opium cultivation, distribution, and use vanished in China after the Communist triumph. Together with the fading of opium activities in now independent India, opium production fell, thus creating a demand that the Golden Triangle began to satisfy. Second, elements of the defeated GMD armies fled across the Chinese border into Burma and remained there to launch incursions, with Central Intelligence Agency (CIA) assistance, into the PRC from time to time. The principal occupation for many of these units, however, was not fighting but the production and distribution of drugs. By the early 1970's, the GMD probably controlled most of the opium traffic in the Golden Triangle.

The Indochinese phase of the Cold War found the United States recruiting the HMONG of Laos to fight both the PATHET LAO and the North Vietnamese. Directed, supplied, and funded by the CIA, the Hmong derived outside income from opium cultivation and sales (some say with CIA direct assistance, an issue still in dispute). The Hmong, however, were involved with drugs before the arrival of the CIA and continued to participate in trafficking long after the Vietnam War concluded. Until the late 1980's, Thailand also contributed to the global drug enterprise, not only by growing and distributing opium but also by processing it into heroin. The Thai government, though, has since embarked on a fairly firm opium eradication campaign, and it is estimated that Thailand produced less than 1 percent of the world's illicit opium by the early 1990's, though trafficking continues to be a problem.

The undisputed drug lord by the late twentieth century was Khun Sa, a Shan-Chinese with a checkered career in Golden Triangle drug ventures. With an army of four thousand to five thousand troops, Khun Sa reportedly controlled 80 percent of the opium in the

This burned out clearing, site of a former heroin factory north of Ban Houei Sai in Laos, reflects the anti-opium policy enacted by the Laotian government in 1971. (AP/Wide World Photos)

Khun Sa, a Shan-Chinese from Myanmar, was indicted by the U.S. government in 1987 on drug-trafficking charges. (AP/Wide World Photos)

region, claiming to be a freedom fighter for the creation of an independent Shan state (now in Myanmar). He has, however, been associated with the killing of the wife of an American Drug Enforcement Administration (DEA) agent and was indicted for drug activities by the United States in 1990. So long as local poverty, instability, corruption, and foreign demand persist, the drug lords have only one another to worry about.—*Thomas D. Reins*

SUGGESTED READINGS: • *Far Eastern Economic Review* (a reliable periodical that has long kept a vigilant eye on drug activities in Asia, including those in the Golden Triangle). • McCoy, Alfred W. *The Politics of Heroin: CIA Complicity in the Global Drug Trade*. New York: Lawrence Hill Books, 1991. • *Report of the International Opium Commission, Shanghai, China, February 1 to February 26, 1909*. 2 vols. Shanghai: North China Daily News & Herald, 1909. • U.S. Congress. House. Committee on International Relations. *Proposal to Control Opium from the Golden Triangle and Terminate the Shan Opium Trade*. Washington, D.C.: Government Printing Office, 1975. • Westermeyer, Joseph. *Poppies, Pipes, and People: Opium and Its Use in Laos*. Berkeley: University of California Press, 1982.

Opium Wars (1839-1842, 1856-1860): Two wars waged during the mid-nineteenth century over trading rights, the result of which won commercial concessions in China for Western powers. China fought two Opium Wars. The First Opium War (1839-1842), also known as the First Anglo-Chinese War, resulted because of an accumulation of political and commercial grievances over more than a century, which were magnified as British trade with China swelled beyond the control of either London or Beijing in the early decades of the 1800's. Opium trafficking was the proximate cause of the war that led to China's defeat and to the TREATY OF NANJING (1842), which installed a Western system of international relations, including the opening of five Chinese ports. Moreover it was China's resistance to the new treaty system, which now involved all Western nations dealing with China, that Britain and France used to justify military operations that became the Second Opium War (1856-1860), Second Anglo-Chinese War, or Arrow War. The treaties ending this fighting further opened China to Western penetration and ultimately established a Western basis for international relations in the Middle Kingdom.

China's Traditional Foreign Relations. China historically viewed itself as the center from which civilization radiated. Foreigners wishing to deal with China were required to acknowledge the supremacy of Chinese civilization by paying tribute. The tribute system required that embassies from abroad ritually present gifts to the emperor and kowtow before him, clearly indicating who occupied the superior position. For outsiders that was the cost of doing business with China. When the Europeans arrived in the sixteenth century, they encountered this system and learned to operate within it. Each tribute bearer was assigned a place of entry; for the Europeans and some others this place was CANTON. By the mid-eighteenth century the BRITISH EAST INDIA COMPANY came to dominate Europe's trade with China, and a new method of doing business emerged, known as the "Canton System." This limited commercial activity to exchanges between Chinese monopolists, known as *hong*, merchants who were organized into a guild (*co-hong*), on the one side and representatives of the East India Company on the other; all business had to be done at the port of Canton; and the British were required to work and live in their

Chinese opium smokers in turn-of-the-century San Francisco. (Asian American Studies Library, University of California at Berkeley)

settlement or factory outside Canton. This cozy trade relationship broke down when Americans, Britons without trading rights in China, and others began evading the Canton System by trading directly, and illegally, with unlicensed Chinese merchants. Much of this trade was in opium.

The First Opium War. Contrary to popular lore, China was not self-sufficient. It imported such things as woolens, metals, and furs from the West, particularly from Britain. Yet until the nineteenth century China ran a large surplus of trade with the West, which purchased tea, silk, chinaware, and other commodities from China. To reverse the flow of bullion the BRITISH EAST INDIA COMPANY began exporting opium to the Middle Kingdom, which became an increasingly lucrative market because of the growing demand for the drug there. Opium exports to China in the early eighteenth century were minimal, only a few hundred chests (133 pounds per chest) per year; a century later the figure was forty-five hundred chests annually; by the 1830's it amounted to approximately ten thousand chests each year. This resulted in an outflow of between seventeen and thirty million taels (a tael equals 1.2 English ounces) of silver annually between 1823 and 1838, the year before war erupted. While silver streamed out, opium addiction sapped physical strength and drained moral substance from China's elite. Moreover, since much of the Western trade with China was being conducted with non-*hong* merchants and all the opium trade was being carried on illegally, the Qing court in Beijing became concerned that it was losing control over the foreigners. The Canton System had regulated their activities but was no longer doing so. Also, since the late eighteenth century the British had been pursuing the idea of diplomatic exchanges on the basis of equality, something China flatly refused to consider. After a heated debate in 1836 over whether to legalize opium, the Qing government came down on the side of prohibition, which involved bringing both Chinese and British (who sold 95 percent of the opium) traffickers under control. In March, 1839, as the opium trade declined, Beijing sent an Imperial commissioner, Lin Tse-hsu, to CANTON to apply the coup de grâce. A week after his arrival, Lin ordered the

British to give up their opium and to discontinue any further trade in the drug. British merchants then transferred their opium to the superintendent of trade, the British official who oversaw trade in China ever since the East India Company lost its monopoly in 1834. In October, 1839, London decided to blockade Canton after China refused to pay for the opium that had been confiscated and burned and also because Lin refused to allow trade to continue unless the British posted bond to ensure no further opium trafficking. In November a clash between the British and Chinese navies began the war.

China proved no match for industrial Britain, and after two years of warfare the Treaty of Nanjing formally ended the conflict. It stipulated that the *cohong* be dissolved; that five ports (Shanghai, Ningpo, Foochow, Amoy, and Canton) be opened for British officials and merchants; that tariffs be fixed and posted; that Hong Kong be ceded to Britain; that communications between Chinese and British officials be on an equal basis; and that an indemnity of $21 million be paid. The next year, 1943, the two nations signed the Treaty of the Bogue, which determined the tariff rates and provided for extraterritoriality. In 1844 China concluded treaties with the United States (Treaty of Wangxia), which conferred upon Washington most-favored-nation status; and France (Treaty of Whampoa), which extended to Paris the right to teach Catholicism. Eventually other Western powers in China acquired most-favored-nation status.

The Second Opium War. China proceeded cautiously after the war, exhibiting a façade of cooperation while surreptitiously acting to emasculate the essence of the treaty system. Eventually this approach failed, since the British wanted to enter the city of Canton, authorized by the Treaty of Nanjing, and wished as well to gain even more privileges through treaty revision (as per the American and French treaties of 1844). Beijing demurred, as did its local officials. When in October, 1856, the British-registered ship *Arrow* was boarded by Chinese officials who proceeded to arrest part of the Chinese crew and to lower the British flag, these acts became the pretext for war. France joined the effort, using the murder of a French missionary in Guangxi Province as the casus belli. The British overran Canton, and a combined British-French expedition north to Tianjin met little resistance, convincing Beijing that negotiations could no longer be avoided. The Treaty of Tianjin (1858), which ended the conflict, provided for a resident minister in Beijing; ten more treaty ports to be opened; travel beyond the treaty ports for foreigners, including missionaries; internal tariffs on foreign goods limited to 2.5 percent; and indemnities for Britain and France. A 5 percent tariff was set at the Shanghai Tariff Conference in October, 1858, and opium imports were legalized upon payment of duty. The following year, when Britain attempted to proceed to Beijing to ratify the Treaty of Tianjin, Minister to China Frederick Bruce insisted on taking an unauthorized route to Beijing, and he and British forces were repulsed at Taku. In August, 1860, an army of twenty thousand British and French troops marched from Taku to Beijing, forced the emperor into exile, and burned the emperor's summer palace. The Convention of Peking (1860) installed foreign ministers in Beijing, increased the indemnity of the Treaty of Tianjin, gave Britain Kowloon Peninsula, provided French missionaries with the right to own property, and in the Supplementary Treaty of Peking awarded to Russia territories north of Manchuria.

Foreign imperialist victory in the Second Opium War, as in the First, forced China to grant further trade and travel concessions to the West. The sum of protracted international disputes led to agreements that became the first of a series of "unequal treaties," concluded during the nineteenth and early twentieth centuries, under which China yielded many of its territorial and sovereignty rights.—*Thomas D. Reins*

Suggested Readings: • Chang, Hsin-pao. *Commissioner Lin and the Opium War*. Cambridge, Mass.: Harvard University Press, 1964. • Fairbank, John K. *Trade and Diplomacy on the China Coast: The Opening of the Treaty Ports, 1842-1854*. Cambridge, Mass.: Harvard University Press, 1953. • Fay, Peter Ward. *The Opium War, 1840-1842*. Cambridge, England: Cambridge University Press, 1975. • Hurd, Douglas. *The Arrow War: An Anglo-Chinese Confusion, 1856-1860*. New York: Macmillan, 1967. • Reins, Thomas D. "Reform, Nationalism, and Internationalism: The Opium Suppression Movement in China and the Anglo-American Influence, 1900-1908." Modern Asian Studies 25 (February, 1991): 101-142. • Waley, Arthur. The Opium War Through Chinese Eyes. London: Allen & Unwin, 1958.

Orderly Departure Program (ODP): International plan that created a legal avenue for Vietnamese to emigrate from Vietnam. It was established in May, 1979, by a Memorandum of Understanding between the Office of the United Nations High Commissioner for Refugees (UNHCR) and the government of Vietnam. Its origins lay in the efforts of the UNHCR

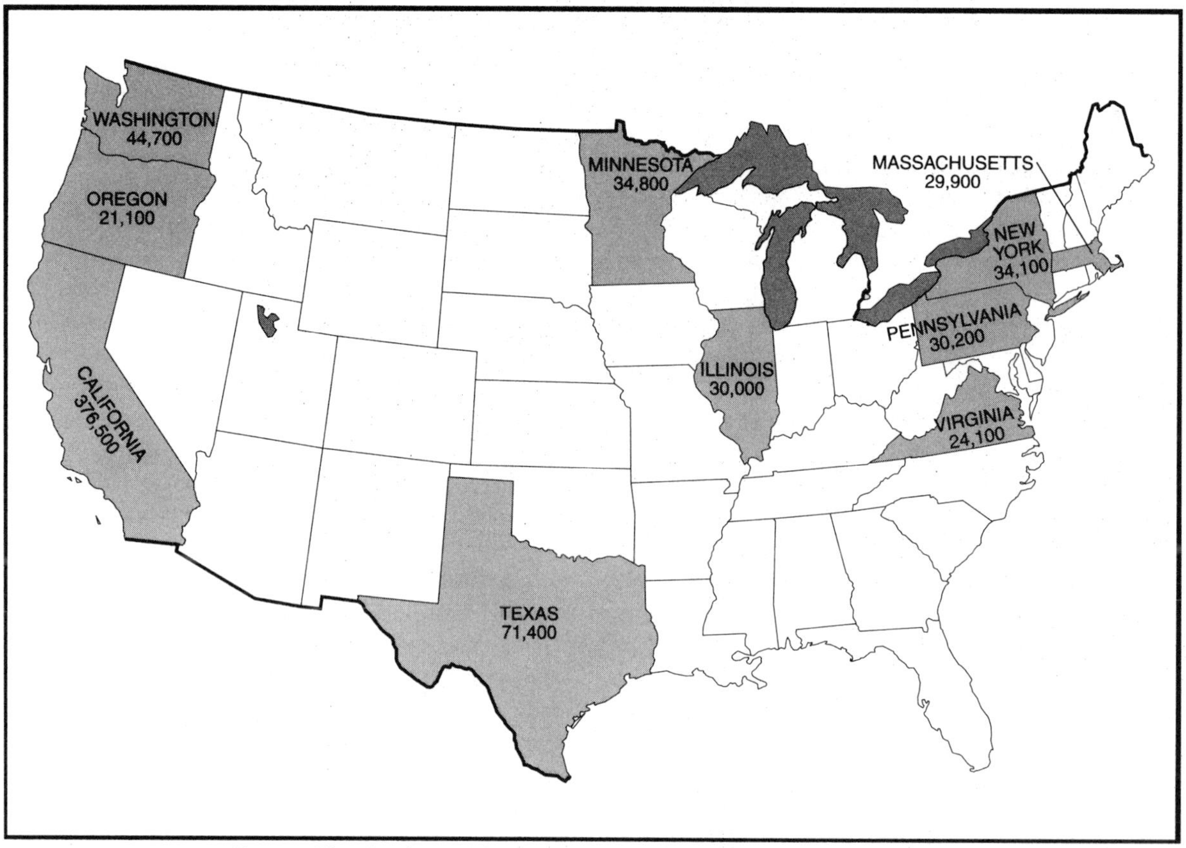

States with a Southeast Asian refugee population of 20,000 or more, 1990.

Source: Data are from Susan Auerbach, *Vietnamese Americans*. American Voices series, p. 54. Vero Beach, Fla.: Rourke Corp., 1991.
Note: Vietnamese refugees constitute about two-thirds of the total Southeast Asian refugee population in the U.S.

and various nations to reduce the huge flow of illegal "BOAT PEOPLE" from Vietnam that had begun so precipitously in the chaos of Indochina during 1978.

The program was meant to allow the Vietnamese government and foreign governments to cooperate in bringing Vietnamese desirous of leaving to these countries. Initially the aim was to allow those Vietnamese who had served the republic in Saigon and were in disfavor to leave. It required that both Vietnam and the host country separately list individuals seeking emigration, the Vietnamese to give an exit visa and the host country an entrance visa.

Through the 1980's the UNHCR, Vietnam, and host countries, particularly the United States, continued to renegotiate the terms of the program. The American government urged its expansion and in 1984 moved to restructure it into three parts. First was the Regular Program covering those applicants linked to the American effort during the war; second was the Asian-American Program for the Amerasian offspring of American fathers and Vietnamese mothers with their close kin; and third was the Political Prisoner Program for those who were or had been in the reeducation camps and their family members. (See AMERASIAN HOMECOMING ACT OF 1987; VIETNAMESE AMERASIANS.)

The 1980's saw the numbers of those leaving Vietnam in the ODP grow steadily. About 2,000 left in the first year (1979), and the number more than doubled the following year and again the year after, reaching around 10,000 for both 1981 and 1982. Finally, in 1983, for the first time more than 1,000 a month emigrated, and the total annual number almost doubled again to 19,000. The year 1986 saw the Vietnamese cut the program, and only 13,000 emigrated in 1987. Thereafter the numbers rose rapidly again and in 1991 reached almost 65,000. The total in the program had come to be more than 300,000 emigrants, yet this was small compared to the overall numbers of people that had fled Vietnam illegally.

The vast majority of Vietnamese leaving via the ODP have come to the United States, flying from Ho

Chi Minh City to Bangkok, then being processed and given orientation at Bataan in the Philippines before coming to America.

Organic Act of Guam of 1950: U.S. government legislation extending citizenship rights to residents of the Territory of Guam. Under the terms of the act, these individuals are free to come to the United States. Many of them have settled in such major cities as Los Angeles.

Organic Act of 1900: U.S. government legislation incorporating Hawaii as an American territory under the control of a self-governing territorial administration. The act limited the right of self-governance to a span of sixty years. It also extended voting rights to Native Hawaiians (but not to Asians) as U.S. citizens and outlawed contract labor. The act provided the islands with a wealth of public capital improvements. During congressional consideration of the bill, with contract labor about to vanish, the HAWAIIAN SUGAR PLANTERS' ASSOCIATION (HSPA) imported thousands of immigrants in anticipation of a labor shortage.

Organization of Chinese American Women (OCAW): Private organization founded in 1977 to lobby for the interests of CHINESE AMERICAN WOMEN and foster awareness of their concerns. The Washington, D.C.-based group, which publishes the quarterly newsletter OACW Speaks, claimed a 1991 roster of two thousand members.

Organization of Chinese Americans (OCA): Washington, D.C.-based association formed in 1973 to address the needs of Chinese Americans and promote their history and culture while advocating their legal rights and opposing harmful stereotypes. Pursuant to this task, the OCA offers a broad assortment of programs and publications such as the bimonthly newsletter Image. The group assisted the passage of the first Chinese American commemorative postal stamp in 1992. It also lobbied the Clinton Administration to enact greater legislative protections for undocumented immigrants and publicly opposed the anti-immigrant policy proposals introduced by California governor Pete Wilson. With the help of the organization, *A Place Called Chinese America*, a chronicle of the Chinese American experience by Diane Mei Lin Mark and Ginger Chih, was published in 1982. In the early 1990's, OCA membership numbered eight thousand, with chapters established in a number of states.

Organization of PanAsian American Women (PANASIA): National nonprofit public policy organization based in Washington, D.C., founded in 1976. It seeks to achieve equal opportunity for Asian Pacific American women by eradicating all forms of discrimination and by ensuring that their concerns are addressed at the national level. The group promotes the accurate portrayal of Asian Pacific American women in the media, strives to eliminate employment barriers, and facilitates and supports women in policy-making positions.

Oriental Development Company (ODC): Semigovernmental agribusiness corporation the Japanese government created to advance its colonization of Korea and other areas. The ODC, or Toyo Takushoku Kabushiki Kaisha, was created as a joint-stock company with capitalization of ten million yen by the Japanese government in 1908. At the same time Japan forced the Korean king to authorize the incorporation of the ODC in Korea, thus making it a joint corporation established by the two governments. The Korean government was obliged to contribute a large amount of land to the ODC. By 1919 the ODC's authorized capital had increased to fifty million yen.

Initially the ODC was organized with two objectives: first, to cultivate new land and to improve already cultivated land in Korea, and second, to promote the settlement of a large number of Japanese farmers in Korea. The second objective derived from the Japanese ambition to establish political and economic control over rural Korea. This objective, however, was not fully realized as the actual number of Japanese households settled in Korea by the end of 1938 was barely above four thousand, with a population of about twenty thousand.

The ODC's operation instead concentrated upon the ownership and management of land in Korea for profitable exploitation. By means of purchase and government conferment, the ODC acquired land in Korea and eventually became by far the largest landowner in Korea. Even after parceling out land to the Japanese settlers, the ODC owned as of 1938 a total of 60,591 *chongbo* (1 *chongbo* is about 2.45 acres), including 35,553 *chongbo* of paddy land and 18,839 *chongbo* of dry field. To cultivate these lands the ODC utilized Koreans as tenant farmers, who in 1938 numbered 78,667, and usually collected at least half of the harvest as rent. Costs of seeds and fertilizers were usually borne by the tenant farmers. In negotiating with the ODC the Korean farmers were in a decidedly disadvantageous position as they had to compete among themselves constantly to obtain tenancy rights. The ODC acquired land largely at the expense of Korean landowners, many of whom became dispossessed or were reduced to tenant farmers. For this and other reasons, the ODC became one of the most resented Japanese agencies in Korea.

Oriental Food Products of California: Company established in Los Angeles by Korean entrepreneur Peter HYUN in 1926. Catering primarily to Los Angeles' growing Asian community, the company tapped into a large market of non-Asian consumers and expanded its line of canned and bottled products to include some twenty-seven varieties of Oriental foods by 1939. Profitable operations helped the company accumulate assets estimated at $2 million by 1958. The company later changed its name to the "Jan-U Wine Food Corporation"; it continued to market its food products into the 1990's. Popular products included soy sauce, vegetables (mushrooms, bean sprouts, water chestnuts), chop suey, chow mein, and various noodles.

Oshogatsu (Jan. 1): Literally "standard month," the Japanese term for "New Year." It is celebrated on January 1, for the Japanese adopted the Western calendar system in 1872. For Oshogatsu many Japanese Americans carry on a number of traditional Japanese customs—often with modification—that are meant to ensure happiness, prosperity, health, and longevity.

On New Year's Eve the more traditional Japanese Americans go to shrines and temples to receive blessings for the new year. They also eat *soba* (buckwheat flour noodles) for health and long life. For New Year's Day a number of customs rich with symbolism are enjoyed. The *kadomatsu* (a bamboo and pine ornamentation that is displayed at the entrance of the home), for example, expresses a wish for a long and happy life. Bamboo represents strength through flexibility because it bends and never breaks, while the pine represents longevity. The pine also represents love and fidelity between two people because the needles come in pairs.

Symbolism, which is often the result of a play on words, is seen in some of the traditional New Year's

The 1993 Nisei Queen (wearing crown) and her court celebrate Oshogatsu in Los Angeles. (Diane C. Lyell)

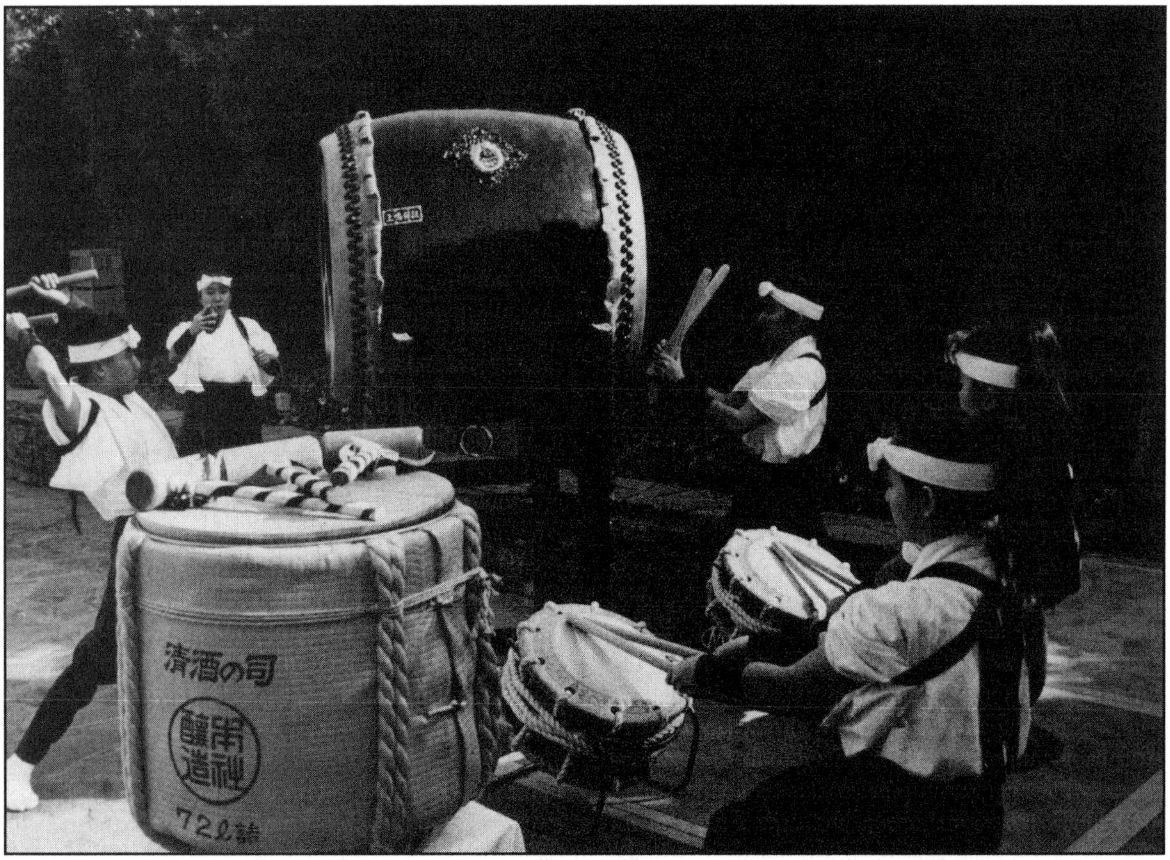

Japanese taiko *drum performance during an Oshogatsu festival in Los Angeles, California.* (Diane C. Lyell)

dishes. For example *kombu* or *kobu* (seaweed) recalls the word *yorokobu*, which means "to be glad." Hence *kombu* symbolizes happiness. *Kazunoko* (eggs of herring) recalls the words *kazu*, which means "number," and *ko*, which means "child." Hence *kazunoko* symbolizes the blessing of many children. *Kuromame* (boiled and sweetened black beans) recalls the words *mame* (perserverance and honesty) and *kuro* (character-building suffering) and so is eaten to foster a strong, honest character.

Food is central to Oshogatsu. Many families begin the day with a bowl of *ozoni*, the traditional New Year's soup, and *mochi* (steamed and pounded rice cake, which symbolizes wealth and fertility). At dinner most Japanese Americans supplement the traditional Japanese New Year's dishes with American dishes such as turkey or ham. In Hawaii other ethnic foods such as *kalua* pig (Hawaiian-style roast pig) or *gau gee min* (a Chinese noodle dish) may be added. Although *mochi* pounding has virtually disappeared, *mochi* is still part of New Year celebrations. Today most families buy the *mochi* or make it themselves.

Osonae: Japanese term for an offering to a buddhist altar or grave.

Ota, Kamado (1884, Yonagusuku, Okinawa, Japan—July 7, 1958): Produce merchant and community leader. Ota left Japan in the early 1900's, headed for Mexico and a job as a contract laborer. In 1904 he worked as a clerk for a coal mining company in Coahuila, northern Mexico, before moving to California the following year and becoming a farmer. He eventually became so successful at farming that, in 1915, he was able to become a founding partner in the Star Produce Company of Los Angeles. Under his guidance the company grew into one of the area's most prosperous produce businesses. Ota also turned his attention to serving the city's Okinawan community, taking highly visible and influential roles in several associations. During World War II the U.S. government closed his business and sent him to an INTERNMENT CAMP.

Ota, Shelley Ayame Nishimura (b. 1911): Novelist. Ota's *Upon Their Shoulders* (1951) was the first novel in English on the Japanese experience in America. The story concerns a Japanese migrant family and its life in Hawaii.

Ota Camp: Filipino community in Waipahu, Hawaii, that was the focus of an antieviction struggle in the early 1970's. The confrontation began in January, 1972, when the 140 residents of Ota Camp were given eviction notices by a real estate development firm that had obtained a lease for the property where their homes stood. This same developer had evicted about 100 Filipino families from Ota Camp in 1968. Filipino families had been renting housing from the landowner, Tatsuichi Ota, for about forty years. After an initial period of distress and despair, the residents organized themselves into the Ota Camp Tenants Association to oppose the eviction.

After holding meetings among themselves, the Ota Camp residents issued their own demands to the Honolulu state and city governments. The tenants demanded to be relocated together as a community, not to have to live in apartment-style housing, and not to be moved out of Waipahu. The community claimed the right to live according to its "cultural lifestyle," which for the residents meant a rural way of life that provided for social interaction among community members and included growing vegetables and raising pigs and chickens.

After several large public demonstrations and much negotiation between the Ota Camp Tenants Association and government officials, the dispute was settled in 1974 through a joint city and state government plan. The plan called for the Honolulu City Council to lease 5.2 acres of city-owned land in West Loch (at the opposite end of Waipahu, away from Ota Camp) to a city redevelopment agency for $1 a year. The agency in turn leased the land to a private developer for the same amount for a period of thirty-five years. With state government financing, the developer built new homes for the Ota Camp residents, who named their new community Makibaka (struggle) Village. The villagers paid nominal rents for their homes, which they were allowed to purchase in 1985 with state government assistance. The Ota Camp struggle represented a significant triumph for local communities in Hawaii that faced similar eviction by developers insofar as it established a precedent of resistance in future confrontations over land and housing.

Ouchi, William George (b. June 28, 1943, Honolulu, Territory of Hawaii): Scholar. An international consultant to several Fortune 500 companies, he became in 1979 a professor at the Graduate School of Management at the University of California, Los Angeles. He earned his M.B.A. degree from Stanford University in 1967 and his Ph.D. in business administration from the University of Chicago in 1972. A Nisei author of several books, including *Theory Z* (1981), *The M-Form Society* (1984), and *Organizational Economics* (1986), he first attracted attention when he wrote about Japanese business practices and how they could be applied to American businesses.

Overseas Chinese. *See* **Chinese diaspora**

Overseas Chinese investments in the People's Republic of China: Following Deng Xiao-ping's economic reform in 1979, China has attracted approximately $26.7 billion direct foreign investments into the country, with approved enterprises reaching thirty-seven thousand in 1991. Roughly 75 percent of foreign investment projects have been financed by overseas Chinese. Most of these Chinese investors trace their roots to either the GUANGDONG or the FUJIAN regions, which is not surprising, considering the fact that these regions were first opened by foreign colonial powers and served as imperial China's liaison with the outside world.

A 1991 issue of *Asian Business* reports that non-Communist Chinese have a combined population of forty six million and are spread all over the world. More than 80 percent of them live in Southeast Asia. Together, they have a gross national product (GNP) of somewhere between $390 billion and $440 billion, representing a per capita GNP of as much as $6,600. The economic growth rate within the overseas Chinese communities is estimated to be at least 10 percent. The distribution of overseas Chinese, though spread all over the world, is concentrated in Asia, with more than 90 percent of them residing there in the early 1980's (mainly in Association of Southeast Asian Nations countries and Hong Kong and Taiwan).

Many overseas Chinese are either refugees or descendants of refugees who fled the mainland for a variety of reasons. From the late nineteenth century to the late 1940's, many Chinese fled China because of economic pressure, political turmoil, and foreign invasion. The defeat of the national regime in 1949 brought Chinese emigration to a new high. In 1949 alone, CHIANG KAI-SHEK and three million members of his political, economic, and military elite fled to Taiwan, while Hong Kong received close to one million refugees.

Heavily commercial Hong Kong street. Much of the world's overseas Chinese population resides in Hong Kong. (Japan Air Lines)

Most of these overseas Chinese are anti-Communist or are unsympathetic to Communist rulers. Many of them were victims, or the descendants of victims, of the Communist persecution. It was not until the 1980's that the Chinese government began to show a limited desire to protect the interests of overseas Chinese. Nevertheless, most of these overseas Chinese remain bound emotionally and culturally to their homeland, China. Many of them continue to be influenced by the traditional idea of "dead leaves falling back to the roots" and believe they are obliged to contribute to their own hometown and home regions, even though they have not been there for years.

When China was first reopened to the West and the global economy in the late 1970's, the Chinese government turned its attention to the overseas Chinese for investment and trade. The overseas Chinese were among the first to answer the Chinese government's call for participating in Chinese economic development. In order to attract overseas Chinese investment, the Chinese government not only offered special incentives but also set up four special economic zones, with each aiming at a particular group of overseas Chinese. Shanzhen was set up to attract Hong Kong Chinese investment, Xiamen for Taiwanese, Shantou for the overseas Chinese in Southeast Asia, and Zhuhai for Chinese living in Macao. Within a decade, steady investment from Hong Kong to Shenzhen transformed the city from a rural town to a booming metropolis with 2.5 million residents.

The Hong Kong Chinese have channeled most of the international investment to China. Taiwan's investment in China has increased rapidly since its beginning in the early 1990's. By 1992, Taiwan's investment in mainland China had reached $4 billion, while Hong Kong's investment in the mainland had grown to more than $10 billion. More than 80 percent of Hong Kong's manufacturing base has been moved to China, and more than 40 percent of Taiwan's overseas investment is in the mainland. Many industries, under the growing pressure of high labor and land costs, have moved their operations to the mainland. The integrative trend of Chinese, Hong Kong, and Taiwanese economies has given rise to the possibility of the eventual emergence of a greater China economic sphere.

Ow, George, Jr.: Documentary filmmaker. The films that he has been involved with include *A Dollar a Day, Ten Cents a Dance* (1984), *Mi vida: The Three Worlds of Maria Gutierrez* (1986), and *Chinese Gold: The Chinese of the Monterey Bay* (1987).

Ow, George, Sr. (b. Canton, China): Entrepreneur. He first came to the United States in 1937, settled in Santa Cruz, California, and helped establish the city of Capitola in California, where in the 1960's he built a large supermarket called Ow's King's Market. A former cow pasture, Capitola and the surrounding Scots Valley developed to include several shopping centers as a result of Ow's vision and tenacity.

Oyakoko: Japanese term connoting indebtedness of children to their parents, as well as filial piety.

Oyama, Joe (b. Sept. 8, 1912, Suisun, Calif.): Journalist. Former president of the Japanese American News Corporation in New York City (1945), he was a board member of the New York chapter of the JAPANESE AMERICAN CITIZENS LEAGUE (1944-1976) and the Japanese American Association of New York. Since his 1976 return to California, he has been published in numerous newspapers, including the *PACIFIC CITIZEN, RAFU SHIMPO, Kashu Mainichi—California Daily News, San Francisco Nichibei,* and *The New World Sun.*

Oyama v. California (1948): Landmark U.S. Supreme Court case which ruled that California's ALIEN LAND LAW OF 1913 was unconstitutional. Nisei and American citizen Fred Oyama legally owned land bought and recorded in his name by his Issei father, who then cultivated the land on behalf of his six-year-old son. Following World War II, California sued the Oyamas, declaring the arrangement an attempt to evade the Alien Land Law, which provided that aliens ineligible for citizenship could not own land. The California Supreme Court found in favor of the state, and the case was appealed to the nation's highest court. Finding that the law's sole intent was "nothing more than outright racial discrimination," the Court held it to be in violation of the equal protection clause of the Constitution's Fourteenth Amendment, which prohibits all such conduct on the basis of race.

Ozawa, Seiji (b. Sept. 1, 1935, Hoten, Manchuria): Conductor. The third son of Japanese parents who had lived in Manchuria and Beijing, Seiji Ozawa began his musical studies when his family moved to Tokyo at the outset of World War II and he began to take piano lessons. He might have had a career as a concert pianist, but when he was fifteen, he broke two fingers while playing soccer, and after that he began to study composition.

Seiji Ozawa. (AP/Wide World Photos)

In 1951, Ozawa entered the Toho School of Music, where, as the school's only conducting student, he studied European and American music with the German-trained Hideo Saito until 1958. In 1959, Ozawa conducted the Japan Radio Orchestra and the Japan Philharmonic Orchestra, and he was named outstanding talent for the year by the magazine *Friends of Music*.

In 1959, he studied conducting with Eugène Bigot in Paris and Herbert von Karajan in Berlin. During his European sojourn, he demonstrated his talent by entering the International Competition for Young Orchestra Conductors and winning first prize, which brought him to the attention of Charles Münch, the music director of the Boston Symphony Orchestra. Later that year, at Münch's invitation, he went to the United States, where he won the Koussevitsky Memorial Scholarship Award for Conducting at the Berkshire Music Center in Lenox, Massachusetts, the home of the Tanglewood Festival.

Leonard Bernstein, conductor of the New York Philharmonic Orchestra, was impressed by Ozawa's performance, and Ozawa became one of three assistant conductors with the New York Philharmonic Orchestra in April of 1960. He made his debut with that orchestra on April 14, 1961. Ozawa was chosen to be the sole assistant conductor for the New York Philharmonic for the 1964-1965 season, and in 1966 he became the Toronto Symphony Orchestra's permanent conductor. He stayed in Toronto until 1970, when he became music director of the San Francisco Orchestra. In 1973, Ozawa took over the musical directorship of the Boston Symphony Orchestra, a position that he continued to hold into the 1990's.

In 1984, Ozawa formed the Saito Kinen Orchestra, an organization created in honor of Ozawa's teacher Hideo Saito, a champion of Western music in Japan. Ozawa, who is regarded as one of the outstanding conductors of his day, is known for the intensity of his performances. In addition to leading the Boston Symphony Orchestra, Ozawa performs as a guest conductor with major orchestras worldwide. He also conducts at least one opera each year, usually at La Scala in Milan, Italy, or at the Paris Opera.

Ozawa v. United States (1922): Landmark U.S. Supreme Court ruling that denied citizenship to a Japanese alien for reasons of race. In handing down its opinion, the Court cited earlier federal legislation extending naturalization rights only to "free white persons" and "persons of African descent" or birth. Being neither, Ozawa was therefore excluded from naturalization.

Japanese citizen Ozawa Takao had lived in the United States continuously since 1894, the year of his emigration. He attended American schools, as did his children, and worked for an American company; the entire family spoke English and were churchgoing Christians. He applied for naturalization in 1914 but was turned away on the sole ground that he was Japanese and therefore, under applicable federal law, ineligible for naturalization. Following unsuccessful attempts at resolution in a U.S. district court and the U.S. Ninth Circuit Court of Appeals, the case went before the Supreme Court. Once there, however, the earlier judicial decisions were affirmed.

The Court's unanimous decision consisted primarily of a definition of the term "white person," statutory language that had appeared in the naturalization laws continuously since 1790. A law passed by the U.S. Congress that year stipulated that only free white persons were eligible for naturalization. That statute was amended in 1870 to apply also to aliens of African birth or descent.

The justices held that the intent of Congress was to

"confer the privilege of citizenship upon that class of persons whom the fathers knew as white, and to deny it to all who could not be so classified." What was required was membership in the Caucasian race. Despite the fact that Ozawa was "well-qualified by character and education for citizenship," he and all those of Japanese ethnicity did not meet the racial criterion. "Of course," the opinion declared, "there is not implied—either in the legislation or in our interpretation of it—any suggestion of individual unworthiness or racial inferiority."

Ozawa closed the chapter on the efforts of Japanese aliens to win their U.S. citizenship in courts of law. Several years later, the passage of the IMMIGRATION ACT OF 1924 effectively halted all emigration from Japan to the United States—a federal policy that would remain in force until the enactment of the MCCARRAN-WALTER ACT OF 1952. Not until then would Japanese in the United States win the right to become American citizens.

Ozoni: Japanese soup of fish stock eaten with sweet rice cakes. It is a popular New Year dish and is eaten for breakfast on the first day of the year for good luck.

P

Pacific Citizen: The official weekly publication of the JAPANESE AMERICAN CITIZENS LEAGUE (JACL), first published in 1929.

The regular issues of the paper keep the members of the more than one hundred chapters in the United States and Japan informed of JACL news and of national and international issues of particular significance. Each year, in the latter half of December, the newspaper publishes a holiday issue of as many as one hundred pages, carrying analyses of the news of the year and biographical and historical articles of particular interest to the NIKKEI.

The *Pacific Citizen* succeeded *The Nikkei Shimin* (the citizen of Japanese ancestry) published by the New American Citizens League, which was founded in San Francisco on October 19, 1928. The New American Citizens League became the JAPANESE AMERICAN CITIZENS LEAGUE. With seven pioneer chapters, the JACL became a national organization for Americans of Japanese ancestry at the first Pacific Coast Nisei (second-generation) conference at San Francisco, held April 5 to 6, 1929.

In 1929 the newspaper began to appear; *Pacific Citizen* became its name in January, 1930. At its second biennial convention in Los Angeles, July 27, 1932, the JACL "adopted" the *Pacific Citizen* as its official publication. From 1933 until 1939 it was published as a monthly.

The Japanese attack on PEARL HARBOR, December 7, 1941, sent the *Pacific Citizen* into a period of particular hardship. The American declaration of war against Japan the following day brought official suspension of publication.

EXECUTIVE ORDER 9066, signed by U.S. president Franklin D. Roosevelt in 1942, made the right of those of Japanese ancestry to remain on the West Coast subject to military edict. The evacuation of the Nikkei began. The last monthly issue of the *Pacific Citizen* was printed in March, 1942. In June, 1942, it resumed publication, as a weekly, in Salt Lake City, Utah.

In October, 1952, the *Pacific Citizen* relocated to Los Angeles, where in 1993 it was still being published.

Pacific Islander American families: Pacific Islander Americans are an extraordinarily heterogeneous group. They include Micronesians such as Marshall Islanders, Melanesians such as Fijians, and Polynesians such as Hawaiians and Samoans. Nevertheless, studies have shown certain similarities in family systems that characterize most Pacific peoples. Pacific Island societies are family societies, and Pacific Islander Americans value their families above almost everything else.

Structure. Pacific Islander Americans commonly understand two definitions of "family." One definition is the nuclear family: father, mother, and children, all living under one roof. In some Pacific languages, the word for this type of family is adapted from English: *famili.* The extended family—*kainga* in Tonga, *aiga* in Samoa, *matavuvale* in Fiji, *te utu* in Kiribati, and *ohana* in Hawaii—is the other definition. It includes grandparents, uncles, aunts, and cousins along with the nuclear family. Both these conceptions of family operate in the minds and lives of Pacific Islander Americans.

A Tongan or Samoan expects to interact with a large kin network and to show automatic generosity to even distant relations. Typically, what belongs to one is available for the use of others. All take pride in the achievements of any family member, and all bear a measure of shame and responsibility for any member's shortcomings. Members of an extended family are likely to live together or nearby. Aunts and uncles are as likely to reprimand a child as are that child's bio-

Masthead of the Pacific Citizen *in 1993.* (Pacific Citizen)

logical parents. The extended family comes together for holidays and to observe milestones such as births, deaths, graduations, and coming-of-age ceremonies. All branches of the family are expected to make their contribution to such occasions. They may also contribute to educational expenses and other needs of an extended family member. The extended family also gathers for more formal occasions that have to do with important decisions affecting the whole group. All these activities are carryovers from the family system as it exists throughout the Pacific.

For those who have been in the United States for a generation or more, however, the strength of the extended family often has begun to wane. Frequently, though individuals understand and value this large family ideal, in practical fact most of their lives are organized around their nuclear families. Although they speak of their families as extended entities and recall large family occasions with fondness, most day-to-day decision making, discipline, and activities focus on the nuclear family as the unit of action.

Pacific Islander Americans value both the extended and the nuclear family. A commitment of loyalty, obligation, and support to both groups is crucial to the Pacific Islander American way of family life.

The Hawaiian Islands contain a variety of Pacific Islander and other nationalities—as may be seen from this photograph of schoolchildren from the Oahu hill country. (David S. Strickler)

Power and Authority. There is a strict hierarchy of power and authority in Pacific Islander American families, with parents taking primacy over children, men over women, and older over younger siblings. Pacific Islander American families are dominated typically by males. Most decisions are made within the nuclear family, and the father makes the final decisions on all significant issues. The mother frequently is accorded some input, often taking the role of intermediary to express the opinions of other family members before the father does the final deciding. Out of respect, the children obey, to the point where they may seriously alter their life plans at their father's command. Sometimes older siblings, brothers in particular, feel themselves deputized to take on the decision-making role. When decisions go beyond the nuclear to the extended family, the male heads of household gather to confer, and the decision is most often made by an elder for the extended family.

Expression of Caring. Pacific Islander Americans describe their families as loving ones, where a great deal of caring is expressed. Yet that caring is seldom expressed in words. "I love you" are words seldom spoken in immigrant families. Parents express their caring by taking care of their children. Children express their caring by obeying, by caring for elderly relatives, and by exhibiting the character qualities that the family values. The love that exists in abundance in these families is expressed not in words but in deeds, gestures, and behaviors. Pacific Islander men display their love by attending to the welfare of their female family members. By contrast, women tend to demonstrate care and concern by doing manual tasks of a nurturing nature. While many Pacific Islander Americans have little difficulty expressing their love for family members to outsiders, they frequently feel inhibited from revealing themselves directly to their families.

Discipline. One of the ways that Pacific Islander American parents express their caring is by disciplining their children. Discipline among Pacific Islanders is intimately connected with caring, and also with respect. For example, the Tongan word *fakaapaapa* evokes an elaborate system of duty, honor, obligation, and security that stands as the rock of stability at the base of Tongan, and Tongan American, society. It is in the context of the value that Pacific Islander Americans place on caring and respect that one must interpret the issue of discipline.

From the perspective of middle-class white Americans, Pacific Islander disciplinary practices seem harsh.

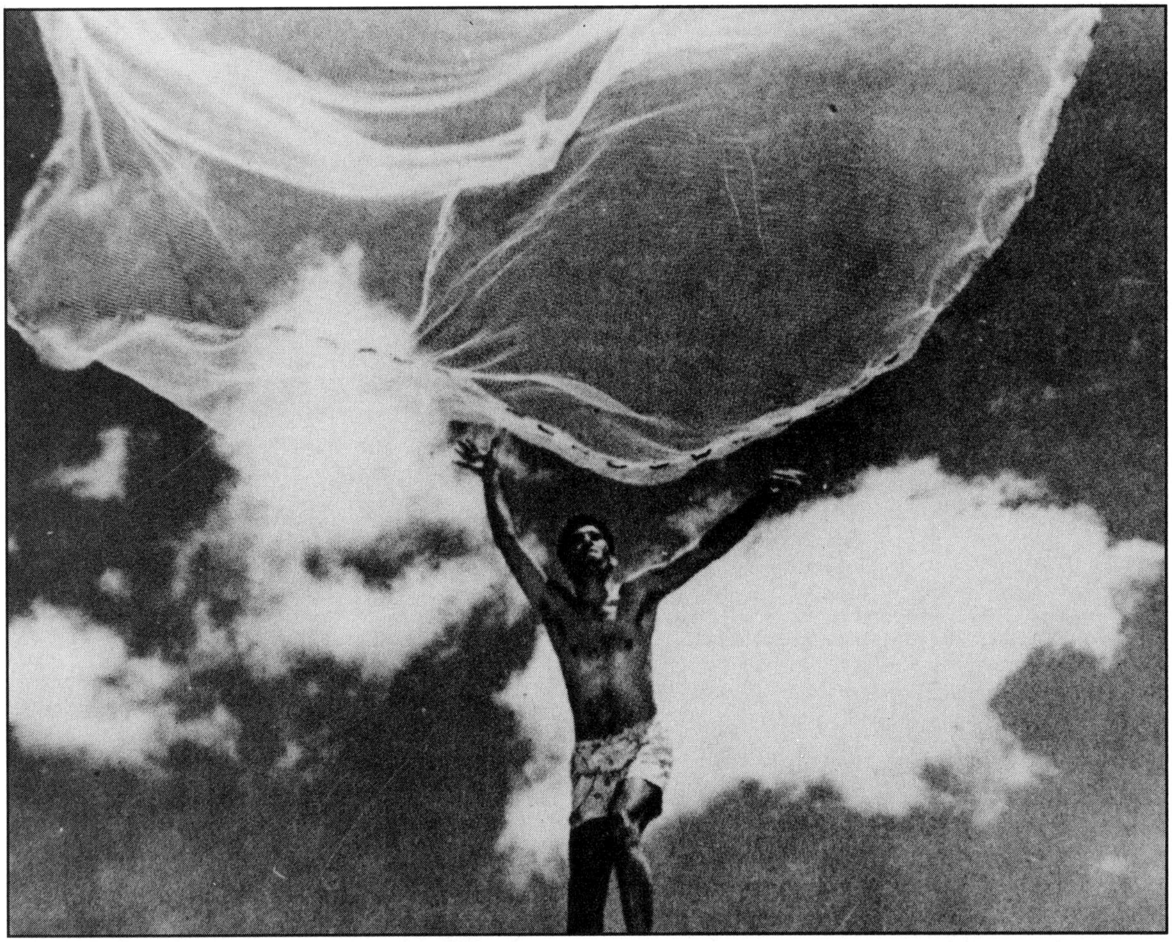

Hawaiian fisherman throwing his net in the traditional manner. (Lyman House Memorial Museum)

Almost always, discipline involves forthright physical punishment. Some non-Pacific Islanders go so far as to label such practices "child abuse." They may not be right. Almost always, it is the fathers who do the heavy hitting, and boys especially are their targets. Girls are hit, too, but not so often and not as hard. Mothers are more likely to scold or to reason with children than to hit, although sometimes they, too, slap or pinch. Seldom does the permission given to aunts and uncles to reprimand a child extend to physical punishment. Similarly, an older sibling's delegated leadership of a younger child rarely includes the right to hit.

Pacific Islander Americans have a somewhat different understanding of this physical punishment than some non-Pacific Islanders might suppose. Almost to a person, they speak in positive terms of the corporal punishment they have experienced, saying such things as, "That's how they show their love to me," and stressing that punishment is necessary for learning to take place.

Physical discipline in Pacific Islander families, then, is a basic means by which parents show the depth of their caring. Children show their caring in return by respect: by obedience, by respecting the elderly, by taking care of their siblings, by not answering back.

Culture Change. European-American culture has negatively impacted the more-traditional Pacific Islander customs, and the results are easily observed. Some Pacific Islander Americans who have spent a decade or more in the United States have begun to express personal feelings at odds with what they experienced growing up in their native cultures. This is especially true in the matter of discipline. Even though they value the punishment they received, islanders interviewed after some years in America said they would exercise a lighter hand on their own American-born children. They would not completely eliminate corporal punishment, but they would first try to talk to the child before resorting to physical discipline. As to decision making, elements of change are also apparent.

Hawaiian man wearing a traditional orchid lei. As of 1990 Hawaiians constitute the largest segment of Pacific Islanders in the United States. (James L. Shaffer)

Pacific Islander Americans interviewed said they would discuss issues with their children, although they would not allow them total freedom to make their own choices. Finally, more and more Pacific Islander Americans are organizing their lives around the nuclear, rather than the extended, family.—*Dianna Fitisemanu, David Hall, Debbie Hippolite Wright, Karina Kahananui, Brucetta McKenzie, Dorri Nautu, and Paul Spickard.*

SUGGESTED READINGS: • Gledhill, Marion. *Growing up: Child Development in the Pacific Islands.* Suva, Fiji: Lotu Pasifika Productions, 1974. • Gray, Ellen, and John Cosgrove. "Ethnocentric Perception of Childrearing Practices in Protective Services." *Child Abuse and Neglect* 9, no. 3 (1985): 389-396. • Handy, E. S. Craighill, and Mary Kawena Pukui. *The Polynesian System in Ka'u, Hawai'i.* Rutland, Vt.: Charles E. Tuttle, 1972. • Jolly, Margaret, and Martha Macintyre, eds. *Family and Gender in the Pacific: Domestic Contradictions and the Colonial Impact.* Cambridge, England: Cambridge University Press, 1989. • Pulea, Mere. *The Family, Law and Population in the Pacific Islands.* Suva, Fiji: Institute of Pacific Studies, University of the South Pacific, 1986. • Shu, Ramsay Leung-Hay. "Kinship System and Migrant Adaptation: Samoans of the United States." *Amerasia Journal* 12, no. 1 (1985-1986): 23-47.

Pacific Islanders: Pacific Islanders are distinct and diverse peoples with varied languages and cultures. There are three major groups: Polynesians, Micronesians, and Melanesians. Since the 1950's large numbers of Pacific Islanders have left their islands to emigrate to the United States. They are a rapidly growing group. For example, their population in America increased 46 percent between 1980 and 1990. Pacific Islander Americans have emigrated for numerous reasons, including better education, employment, and health care. Very little, however, was known about the Pacific Islander population in the United States prior to 1980. These people became part of an invisible minority group. The census reflected this, as it grouped Pacific Islanders as a category of Asian Americans. Individual Pacific Island racial groups were not distinguished, except for Hawaiians.

An overwhelming majority of Pacific Islanders in the United States reside in Hawaii, California, and Washington. The largest groups of Pacific Islanders are from Hawaii, Samoa, and Guam, then Tonga, Palau, and Fiji.

Polynesians. These islanders inhabit the largest geographical area of the Pacific Ocean. They come from islands that extend from Hawaii in the north, Tonga and Samoa in the west, Easter Island in the east, and New Zealand in the south. Other islands in the Polynesian

The early period of American contact with Polynesia included the first missionaries to Hawaii. Hiram Bingham (shown) led the pioneer company of American Congregational missionaries to the islands. (Lyman House Memorial Museum)

Tongan woman (center) in Oregon. (Gail Denham)

group are the Cook, Tahiti, and Marquesas islands.

Traditional Polynesian cultures encompassed similar languages and social organizations. For example, most Polynesian cultures were organized into tribes or extended families, and leadership within these tribes was determined according to genealogy. In addition, many of the Polynesian languages have similar words; for example, the Hawaiian word *aloha* (love and regard) is *alofa* in Samoan and *aroha* in Maori (the indigenous language of New Zealand).

The United States has had contact with Polynesians since the eighteenth century. It began when whaling ships blanketed the Pacific and traded at ports of call throughout Polynesia. Soon after, Christian missionaries spread rapidly, scattering throughout the islands. They were followed by a wave of plantation owners and entrepreneurs who influenced the economy and politics of Polynesia.

The United States exerted its influence mainly in the islands of Hawaii and Samoa. For example, American businessmen played a key role in the overthrow of the Hawaiian monarchy in 1893. By the start of the twentieth century, the Hawaiian Islands had become a U.S. territory and by 1959 had become a state of the Union. The United States also took possession of part of Samoa, now referred to as American Samoa. The U.S. government established a naval base in Pago Pago, the capital of American Samoa, and relied on the U.S. Navy to administer American Samoa until 1951, when the Navy moved its naval base for the Pacific to Ha-

Polynesian Population in the U.S., 1980-1990

	1980	1990	Percent increase
Hawaiians	172,346	211,014	22%
Samoans	39,520	62,964	59%
Tongans	6,226	17,606	183%

Sources: Herbert Barringer, Robert W. Gardner, and Michael J. Levin, *Asians and Pacific Islanders in the United States*. New York: Russell Sage Foundation, 1993. Harry H. L. Kitano and Roger Daniels, *Asian Americans: Emerging Minorities*. Englewood Cliffs, N.J.: Prentice-Hall, 1988.

Pacific Islander American Statistical Profile, 1990

Percentage of Asian American Population
Total Asian Americans: 7,226,986

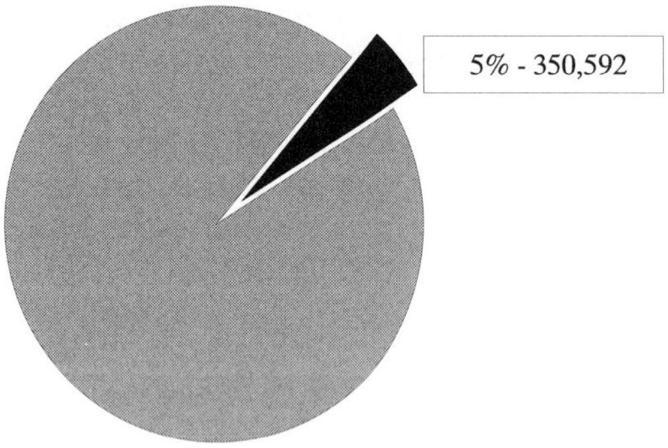

Nativity

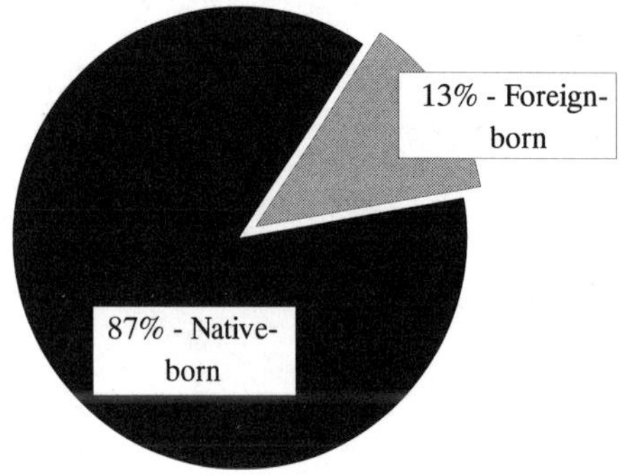

Age in Years

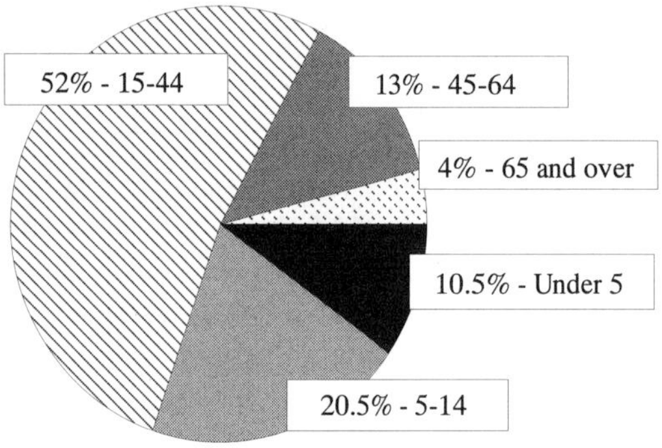

Family Type

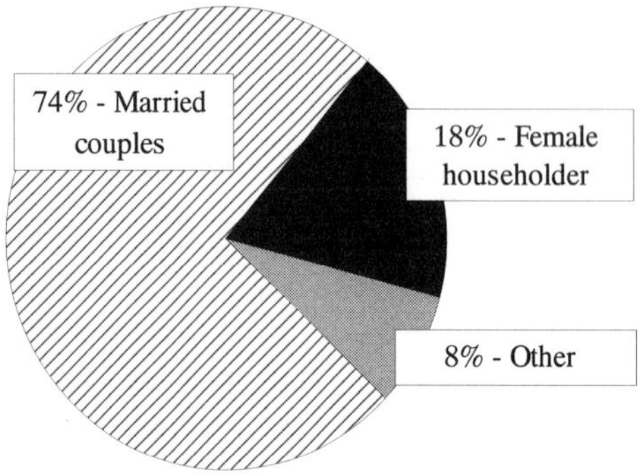

Labor Statistics
Persons 16 Years or Older

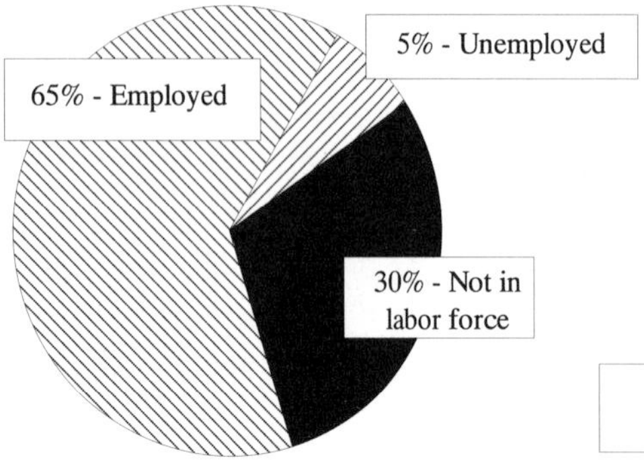

Years of School Completed
Persons 25 Years or Older: 176,021

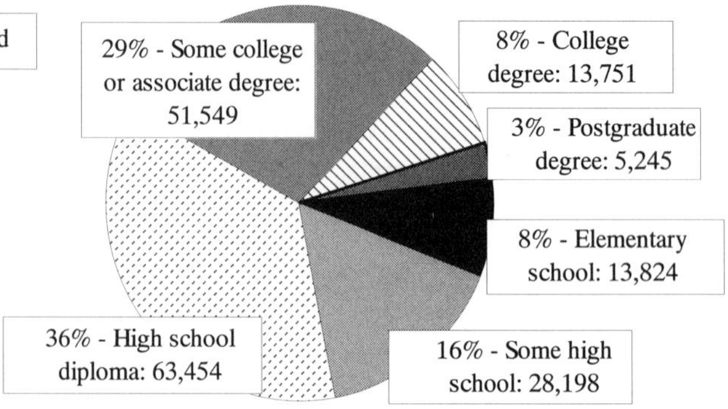

Source: U.S. Bureau of the Census, *1990 Census of Population: Asians and Pacific Islanders in the United States,* 1993.

waii. American Samoa remains a territory of the United States, and those born in American Samoa are U.S. NATIONALS who can freely enter the United States, although they cannot vote in federal elections. Although Western Samoa is an independent nation, a large number of Pacific Islander emigrants to the United States were born there. Many migrate to American Samoa and then to the United States because the standard of living in Western Samoa is low.

Census reports show that approximately 85 percent of Pacific Islanders in the United States are Polynesians. The 1990 U.S. census indicates that HAWAIIANS are the largest group of Pacific Islanders in the United States (211,014), SAMOANS are the second-largest group (62,964), and TONGANS (17,606) are the fourth-largest group.

Micronesians. These people inhabit the islands in the northwest region of the Pacific, which covers approximately three million square miles, roughly the same size as the continental United States (3.7 million). Micronesia comprises more than 2,100 small islands covering a land mass of 700 square miles.

Occupation

Employed Persons 16 Years or Older	Percentage
Managerial and professional specialty	18.0%
Technical, sales, and administrative support	32.1%
Service	19.2%
Farming, forestry, and fishing	2.5%
Precision production, craft, and repair	11.9%
Operators, fabricators, and laborers	16.3%

Income, 1989

Median household income	$31,980
Per capita	$10,342
Percent of families in poverty	15%

Household Size

Number of People	Percentage
1	12.8%
2	21.0%
3	17.7%
4	18.8%
5	13.0%
6	7.7%
7 or more	9.0%

Source: U.S. Bureau of the Census, *1990 Census of Population: Asians and Pacific Islanders in the United States,* 1993.

The major island groups in Micronesia are Guam (a U.S. territory), the Mariana Islands, Micronesia, the Marshall Islands, Palau (a trust territory of the United States for the United Nations), and Kiribati (a former British colony previously known as the Gilbert Islands).

Micronesia has had a series of colonial rulers since 1521, when Spain took control of the Marianas. Spanish rule ended following the Spanish-American War of 1898, at which time the United States acquired Guam as a trust territory and Germany purchased the rest of Micronesia and held it until 1914. Japan then occupied Micronesia, annexing the islands completely by 1935, and governing them until after World War II. In 1947 the United Nations awarded the United States with trusteeship islands and atolls in Micronesia. Some of these islands and atolls were used militarily, including missile testing. Very little was done by the United States to help Micronesians advance economically, socially, and educationally besides employing significant numbers of Micronesians on American military bases in the Pacific.

Many GUAMANIANS and other Micronesians are still subsistence farmers, reliant on their environment for food, clothing, and shelter. They see emigrating to the United States an attractive way to improve their economic situation. Many use their experience of working on American military bases to help provide financial security once they have arrived in the United States. Statistics indicate that most Guamanians and other Micronesians live near military bases located on the United States' West Coast. Many reside in San Diego, Los Angeles, San Francisco, Seattle, and Tacoma.

Approximately 14 percent of Pacific Islanders in the United States are Micronesians, predominantly Guamanians of Chamorro ancestry. In 1990 Guamanians made up the third-largest group of Pacific Islanders in the United States (49,345). Other significant Micronesian groups are from the Mariana Islands, the Marshall Islands, and Palau.

Melanesians. The islanders inhabit the western region of the Pacific, settling in the area north of Australia but south of the equator principally in the Solomon Islands, Vanuatu, Fiji, Papua New Guinea, and New Caledonia.

Melanesians have distinct physical characteristics.

They tend to be short, dark-skinned people with curly hair. The word "Melanesian" comes from the Greek words *mela*, which means "black," and *nesos*, which means "island."

Melanesians did not have as much exposure to American influence in the Pacific as did the Polynesian and Micronesian islands. Therefore, there are not significant numbers of emigrants from Melanesia to the United States.

According to the 1990 U.S. census, FIJIANS make up the largest group of Melanesians in the United States (7,036). Melanesians constitute approximately 1 percent of the Pacific Islander population in the United States.—*Debbie Hippolite Wright*

SUGGESTED READINGS: • Barringer, H. R., R. W. Gardner, and M. J. Levin. *Asians and Pacific Islanders in the United States*. New York: Russell Sage Foundation, 1993. • Brower, Kenneth. *Micronesia: The Land, the People and the Sea*. Edited by Gregory Vitiello. Baton Rouge: Louisiana State University Press, 1981. • Ford, Douglas. *The Pacific Islanders*. New York: Chelsea House, 1989. • Johnson, Dwight L., Michael J. Levin, and Edna L. Paisano. *We, the Asian and Pacific Islander Americans*. Washington, D.C.: Government Printing Office, 1988. • Macpherson, Cluny, Bradd Shore, and Robert Franco, eds. *New Neighbors—Islanders in Adaptation*. Santa Cruz, Calif.: Center for South Pacific Studies, University of California, 1978.

Pacific Mail Steamship Company: Nineteenth century company that provided steamship service between San Francisco and Honolulu and between California and China, incorporated in 1848. The company became one of two lines allowed to carry Chinese laborers to Hawaii in the 1880's and later the largest to carry Chinese immigrants to the United States and Hawaii.

Pacific Times (*Taepyongyang Shi-sa*): Weekly Korean-language newspaper of the Hawaii-based KOREAN INDEPENDENCE LEAGUE (Choson Toknip-dan), established in 1919.

Page Law of 1875: U.S. legislation designed to prohibit the immigration of Chinese contract laborers and prostitutes to the United States. On February 10, 1875, California Congressman Horace F. Page presented a bill officially titled, "An Act Supplementary to the Acts in Relation to Immigration." Known as the "Page Law," this legislation expressly excluded prostitutes

Chinese Immigration by Sex, 1871-1910

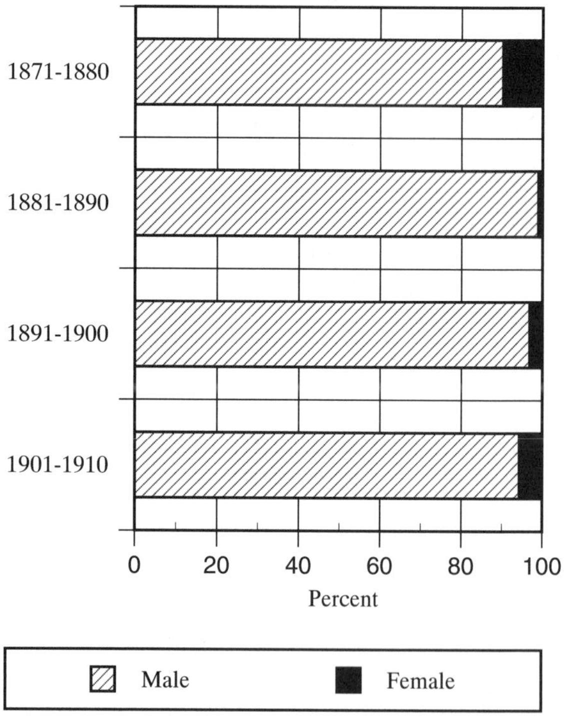

Source: Elmer Clarence Sandmeyer, *The Anti-Chinese Movement in California*. Urbana: University of Illinois Press, 1973.

from immigration to the United States, nullified their labor contracts, and made the importation of such women a felony. Those convicted of importing Chinese prostitutes were subject to a maximum prison term of five years and a fine of up to five thousand dollars. While the law also established much less severe penalties for individuals engaged in the COOLIE TRADE, the numbers of male immigrants rendered individual interrogation a logistical impossibility. Thus, its prohibition of contract labor proved merely symbolic, but the antiprostitute section functioned as an effective deterrent against female immigration.

In the years between the Page Law's enactment and exclusion (1875-1882), the average annual Chinese female immigration fell to one-third of its level for the previous seven-year period. Such a dramatic reduction was achieved through an elaborate cooperative network of intelligence gathering and interrogation, which included American and British consular officials at Hong Kong, that city's Tung Wah Hospital

Committee (an agency controlled by Chinese merchants), and port authorities in San Francisco. Together, they erected a formidable barrier against female immigration from China, which extended its focus far beyond prostitution.

A scarcity of surviving records obscures the actual occupations of Chinese women who sought to enter the United States from 1875 to 1882. Officials charged with enforcing the Page Law, however, clearly equated poverty with prostitution. Thus, even women who obtained certificates of good character in Hong Kong faced detainment and possible deportation upon their arrival in San Francisco. By refusing to acknowledge the legitimacy of these female immigrants, American customs officers converted the Page Law into a general exclusion of all but the dependents of wealthy Chinese merchants. This gender-specific exclusion law exacerbated an already dramatic shortage of women in the Chinese American community, preventing the establishment of immigrant families and preserving the United States' "bachelor Chinatowns."

Paigow: Chinese gambling game played with dominoes.

Paik, Hark-joon (b. 1935, Seoul, Korea): Judge. Immigrating to the United States as a student, he received a B.A. degree from Stanford University in 1958 and a J.D. degree from Stanford Law School in 1961. The first naturalized Korean American to become a California judge, he was appointed justice for the Superior Court of Monterey County in 1975. Recipient of the Freedom Foundation Award at Valley Forge, he coauthored the *California Complex Litigation Manual* (1991).

Paik, Naim June (b. July 20, 1932, Seoul, Korea): Video and performance artist. Paik was the youngest son of a family that owned a textile mill and two factories in northern Korea. The family's businesses were nationalized after the end of World War II; during the Korean War, Paik fled with his family first to Hong Kong and later to Tokyo. He enrolled in the University of Tokyo to study modern music, and in 1956 he was graduated with a degree in aesthetics, having completed his thesis on the works of the influential German composer Arnold Schoenberg.

Paik continued his studies of avant-garde music in Germany at the University of Munich and the Freiburg Conservatory, and in 1958 he met the famous American experimental composer John Cage at a music course in Darmstadt. Paik was strongly influenced by Cage's unpredictable public performances, which often included bizarre onstage action to accompany his unusual compositions.

Paik soon began performing what he called "action music"—collages of his own live piano playing, taped noises, and the sounds produced by such incongruous "instruments" as motorcycles and telephones. He supplemented his music with often outrageous onstage behavior; in one piece, he ran into the audience with a pair of scissors, cut off parts of Cage's tie and shirt, and lathered Cage's hair with shampoo before suddenly leaving the performance area. He then telephoned the performance hall to tell the audience that the show was over, thus becoming perhaps the first person to use the telephone as an artistic medium.

After earning notoriety for such antics, Cage began to work with the Fluxus group, a loose confederation of avant-garde artists influenced by the principles of Dadaism. He also became increasingly interested in video and television technology. In 1963, he staged a one-man exhibition at the Galerie Parnass in Wuppertal, West Germany, in which he displayed television sets that altered broadcast images and allowed for viewer interaction. In subsequent years, he continued to experiment with the use of video technology as an art form, producing such unusual videotapes as *Global Groove* (1973) and *Guadalcanal Requiem* (1977); he also continued to incorporate television sets in his museum exhibits. Many later video artists have been influenced by his work.

Pak, Ty (b. 1938, Korea): Writer and journalist. In 1960, after graduating from Seoul National University in South Korea with a law degree, he became a reporter for *The Korean Republic* and *Korea Times* in Korea until 1965, when he immigrated to the United States. After earning a Ph.D. degree in English literature at Bowling Green State University, he began teaching in the English department at the University of Hawaii. His fictional publications include *Guilt Payment* (1983), a collection of short stories.

Pak Un-sik (1861—1926): Historian. He was a major Korean figure during the 1920's, when the writing of nationalist histories of Korea flourished. Through his two books he hoped to ignite a new sense of national pride and self-respect among the Korean people, who had been under Japanese occupation since before 1910. *Hanguk tongsa* (the tragic history of Korea) and *Hanguk tongnip undong chi hyolsa* (the bloody history of the Korean independence movement) attacked Japan's aggression in Korea and lent spiritual support to the effort for independence, underscoring the importance of preserving the soul of the Korean people.

Pakistan, Islamic Republic of: Country located in South Asia on the Arabian Sea. It is bounded to the east and southeast by India, to the northeast by the People's Republic of China, to the north by Afghanistan and the Commonwealth of Independent States (formerly the Soviet Union), and to the west by Iran.

Pakistan's population in 1992 was 130,129,000 (with one of the highest growth rates in the world). ISLAM is the official religion, and only 2 percent or 3 percent of the population are non-Muslim. Most of the Muslims are of the Sunni sect, although a tiny minority (less than 5 percent) are Shia. Pakistan's currency is the Pakistani rupee. URDU, written in the Arabic script, is the official language, but PUNJABI, Sindhi, Pashto, and Baluchi are regional languages. English is widely spoken among the educated classes. The nation's capital city is Islamabad. The largest Pakistani city is Karachi, with the other major ones being Lahore, Rawalpindi, and Peshawar. Pakistan became independent in 1947, when India was partitioned by the British. It originally consisted of East and West Pakistan, which were separated by one thousand miles of Indian territory, but East Pakistan seceded in 1971 to become BANGLADESH. Pakistan is a populous country that does not have many natural resources and that has had difficulty maintaining a stable electoral system.

Geography. Pakistan, more than 307,000 square miles in size, is divided into four provinces—PUNJAB, Baluchistan, North-West Frontier Province, and Sind—and it administers a tribal area in the northwest. Nearly three-quarters of the people live in the rural areas, and about half work in agriculture. About 15 percent of the population works in manufacturing. The country's climate is hot and dry, with high average temperatures of seventy-five degrees Fahrenheit. The country consists

The Parliament House at Islamabad, capital of Pakistan. (Pakistani Consulate)

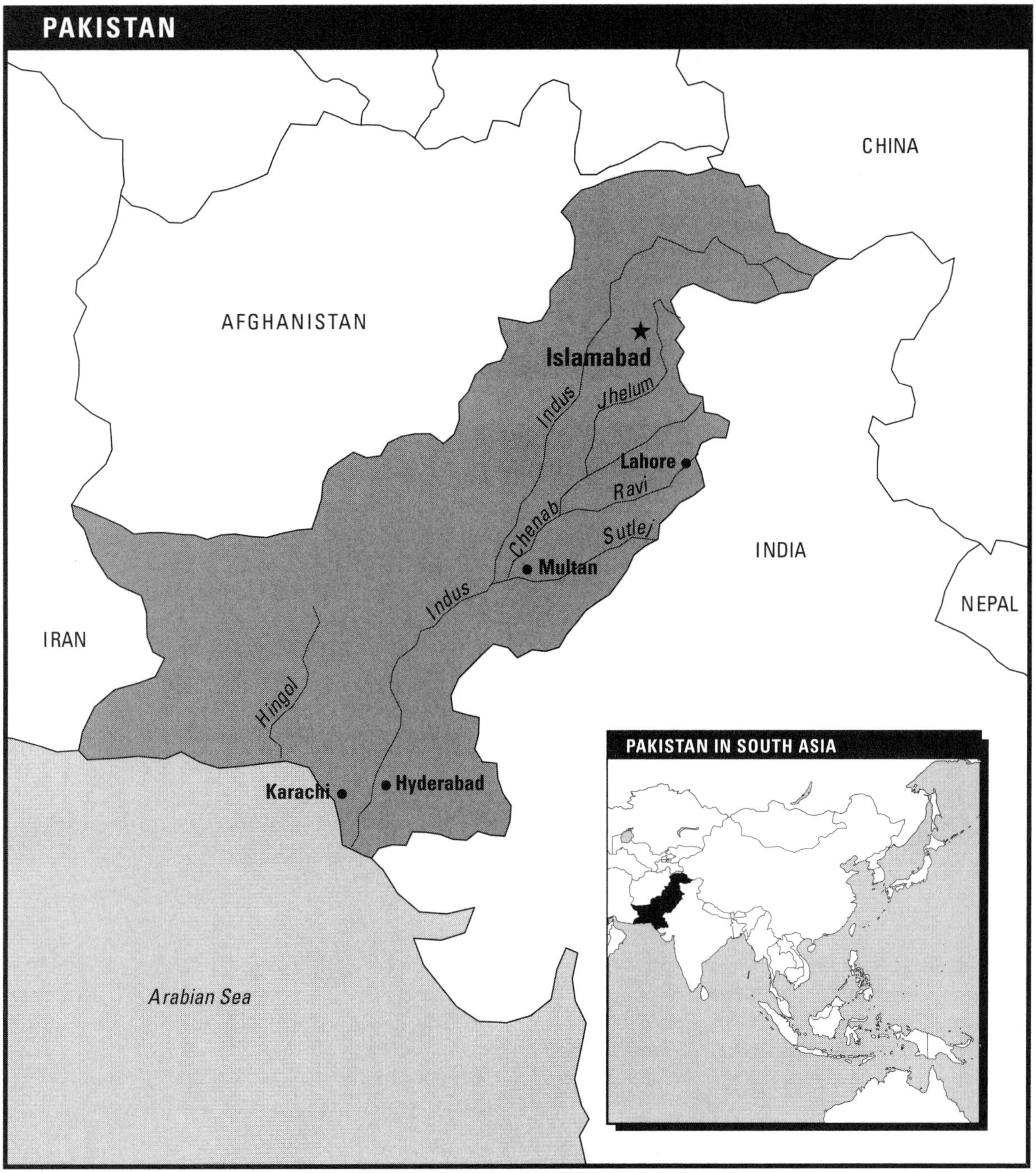

of plains along the Indus Valley that are densely populated where there is good irrigation; the rest is desert and arid highlands. The mountains in the north rise up two-thousand feet in the Himalayas and more than twenty thousand feet in the Hindu Kush and the Karakorams.

Ethnic Groups. The largest ethnic group in Pakistan, almost half of the population, are the Punjabis. The Sindhi and Pathans each account for about 12 percent of the population, while the Brahuis in Baluchistan account for less than 5 percent. Several million Afghans settled in the northwest during the Russian occupation of Afghanistan, but many, although not all, returned after the Russian withdrawal in 1989.

Economy. Agriculture provides about 25 percent of the national income but employs about half of the total

Kelash tribe, Chitral Valley, northern Pakistan. (Pakistani Consulate)

labor force, which toils mostly on irrigated land, especially in the PUNJAB, where the canal system has been highly developed. The Green Revolution of the 1960's dramatically improved Pakistan's agricultural production of wheat, as well as sugarcane, rice, and cotton. In addition to crops, livestock is important in rural areas. In 1947, the country had few industries but has developed its industrial base since then. Nevertheless, Pakistan suffers from a trade deficit with other nations, which is partially offset by the large amounts of remittances that expatriate workers send back to Pakistan. The most important industries are those connected with indigenous products such as cotton, sugar, and animal hides, while heavy industry has been developed to produce fertilizers, chemicals, and pharmaceuticals as well as steel and various kinds of machinery.

Hydroelectricity, with the building of the Mangla and Tarbela dams, has been developed to power these industries; there are also two nuclear power stations at Karachi and Chasma. Pakistan has engaged in a heavy program of drilling for oil but through the early 1990's had only developed natural gas fields. The railroad network in Pakistan is well developed, having been inherited from the British, who had developed it for military purposes. The road system is constantly being improved and provides access to all areas not covered by the railroad, although many of the roads in the rural areas are dirt roads. The major port in Pakistan is at Karachi, where the main exports are those connected with cotton products. Pakistan International Airlines is both international and domestic.

Education. Twenty universities exist in Pakistan for the small, highly educated urban elite. The University of Punjab in Lahore, the University of Karachi, and the Quaid-i-Azam University in Islamabad are the major ones. At the other end of the educational system, less than half the population attends free primary schools, and less than 25 percent attends secondary school. Much resistance for the education of girls is encountered, especially in the rural areas. Less than a quarter of the people are literate.

Cultural and Intellectual Life. The vibrant cultural and intellectual life of Pakistan is dominated by ISLAM, with Western influences strong among the elite. The predominant art form is poetry, which is written and often publicly recited both in Pakistan's classical language (Persian) and in URDU, while the regionally languages also have their own traditions. Pakistan's world-renowned poet is Muhammad Iqbal. Large numbers of newspapers and journals are produced in Pakistan both for regional and for national audiences, and the government-run radio and television stations heavily promote cultural events.

History. The demand for a separate country for the Muslims of South Asia was made in Lahore on March 23, 1940, under the leadership of Mohammed Ali Jinnah. The country became independent in 1947, and was under civilian leadership until the military coup led by General Mohammad Ayub Khan on October 7, 1958. He was overthrown in a coup by General Agha Mohammad Yahya Khan in March, 1969, who then held elections in 1970, when the East Pakistani Awami League under Sheihk Mujibur Rahman won a small majority. In West Pakistan, Zulfiqar Ali Bhutto won a majority. The West Pakistanis refused to give power to the East Pakistanis, and a civil war followed, which resulted in the independence of East Bengal under the name of BANGLADESH.

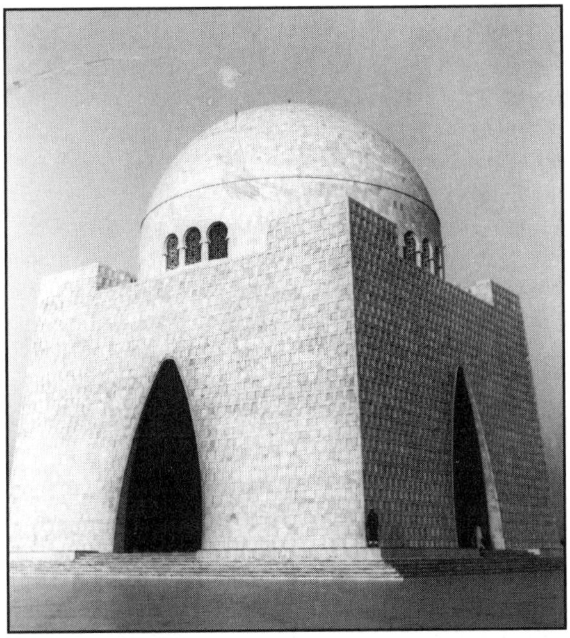

The Mausoleum of the Quaid-i-Azam, completed in 1971 and built according to the basic requirements of Islamic tradition. (Pakistani Consulate)

Zulfiqar Ali Bhutto became president of Pakistan in 1971, and he remained in power until 1977, when the military took power under General Mohammad Zia ul-Haq. Bhutto was executed in 1979, Zia died in a plane crash in 1988, and Pakistan returned to civilian rule first under Benazir Bhutto from 1988 to 1990, and then under Mian Mohammad Nawaz Sharif.—*Roger D. Long*

SUGGESTED READINGS: • Ahmed, Akbar S. *Pakistan Society: Islam, Ethnicity, and Leadership in South Asia*. New York: Oxford University Press, 1986. • Burki, Shahid Javed. *Pakistan: A Nation in the Making*. Boulder, Colo.: Westview Press, 1986. • Jalal, Ayesha. *The State of Martial Rule: The Origins of Pakistan's Political Economy of Defence*. Cambridge, England: Cambridge University Press, 1990. • Noman, Omar. *Pakistan: Political and Economic History Since 1947*. London: Kegan Paul, 1990.

Pali: Sacred language of the Theravada Buddhist canon, spoken during the time of the Buddha (Siddhartha Gautama), the father of BUDDHISM, who lived in the sixth century B.C.E. The dialect came into use at the insistence of the Buddha, who wanted his teachings spread in the language of the common people. As such, he opposed the use of SANSKRIT, a learned language, as the vehicle for his teachings. By the third century B.C.E., these teachings had been carried from India to Ceylon (now Sri Lanka). In time they were recorded in Pali in the form of the *Tripitaka*, the sacred scriptures of Theravada Buddhism. Both the language and the texts eventually found their way into major countries of Southeast Asia, where they are still used. By about the end of the fourteenth century C.E., the use of Pali in India had died out.

Palolo Chinese Home: Adult residential care facility, founded in 1917 and licensed by the State of Hawaii Department of Health. The Palolo Chinese Home was a result of the combined efforts of Chinese secular leaders and Christian ministers, the UNITED CHINESE SOCIETY, the Associated Charities of Hawaii, and the Territorial Legislature.

The major cause of the founding of the home was the serious problem of aged Chinese men, most of whom were without family. This situation was the result of both the sugar planters' policy of recruiting only Chinese male laborers and the decision of the Chinese SOJOURNERS to come without wives and children. Both the Chinese cultural tradition of filial piety and respect for the elderly and the Christian charitable belief in helping the needy led to the home's establishment.

The home began with 8 residents when it first opened. The number of residents peaked in 1937, when there were 165 of them. After World War II some residents found lodgings with friends or relatives, and others returned to China. From then on, the home's population declined gradually, and in 1990 there were 40 men and 31 women in residence. It remains open to the public regardless of race, religion, or sex.

Originally the home was simply "a place to live," but on January 15, 1940, the problem of lack of medical care was discussed in the Chinese Home Committee meeting. Since April 1, 1940, medical and nursing care have been provided along with recreational activities. The home gradually became a fairly well-equipped "care home." In April, 1961, the board of directors decided to join the Hawaii State Nursing Home Association.

The fact that the home was the earliest care facility for indigent aged Chinese in the United States meant that the first or second generation of Chinese in Hawaii enjoyed certain advantages in comparison with their compatriots on the U.S. mainland. There was less anti-Chinese agitation and discrimination in Hawaii, with Caucasians a minority. There was also a higher proportion of successful Chinese community leaders in Hawaii than on the mainland. This was a result of the greater educational, economic, and social opportunities in the multiethnic community of the Hawaiian Islands.

Therefore the Palolo Chinese Home can be regarded as an early effort by the Chinese immigrants to adapt to and integrate into the larger American society. The home still plays an active role in community service.

Pan Asian Repertory Theatre (New York, N.Y.): First Asian American theater company in New York City, founded in 1977. The company was created by Tisa Chang, an accomplished veteran dancer and actress. Frustrated by a performance climate that confined Asian stage representations to stereotype, Chang began in 1973 to reinterpret Asian forms for New York audiences. With encouragement from the highly regarded La Mama Experimental Theatre Club in New York, Chang created *Return of the Phoenix* (pr. 1973), a bilingual adaptation of a Beijing opera piece employing an Asian American cast. Company members from this highly successful project became the core members of her Chinese Theatre Group, which in 1977 became the Pan Asian Repertory Theatre.

The desire to transcend the stereotype remains central to the company's work. The company seeks at once to provide sustained and significant professional opportunities for Asian American theater artists while giving them "the chance to express themselves in a context that was not influenced by non-Asians' traditional images of them."

In its brief history the company has mounted more than fifty productions and some eighteen world premieres, while winning numerous awards, including a 1982-1983 season Obie Award for actor Ernest ABUBA in its production of R. A. SHIOMI's *Yellow Fever* (pr. 1982). The company generally offers a balanced season of some four pieces featuring new plays by Asian American playwrights, translations and adaptations of significant Asian works, and reinterpretations of Western classics, often through the use of Asian staging techniques. In 1987 the Pan Asian Repertory Theatre established a resident ensemble of Asian American actors.

Beyond its goal of nurturing Asian American theater talent, the company offers acting classes in traditional Asian performance techniques, maintains a Theatre for Youth Program, and tours its productions, both nationally and internationally, in a very active community outreach program.

Panchayat: Basic unit of local government designed for the rural population of India. In its simplest terms, a *panchayat* is the village's five-member ruling council responsible for protecting and enhancing rural economic interests and development.

By involving the villagers in *panchayati raj*, or rule, the central government believes that the rural populace, through participation in local affairs, can provide the springboard for economic development and national renewal.

The *panchayat* system is on a three-tier scale. Each *panchayat* elects one of its members to a second level known as a *panchayati samiti*. This second-tier association selects a chairperson or executive officer from its more or less fifty-member group. In turn, the association selects one of its members to a third-level group at the district level, called a *zila parishad*. Communication and decision making flows both ways, at least in theory, in this pyramid approach to local democratic rule.

The program was launched in the late 1950's largely

at the behest of Prime Minister Jawaharlal NEHRU, who was determined to tackle the deep-seated poverty of India, particularly in the rural areas. Nehru and others believed that the pace of rural reconstruction could be quickened through this program.

From the beginning, the program of involvement of the rural population in a national plan, largely centrally planned and controlled, has suffered from an almost staggering number of pressures in the rural countryside. These include tremendous population growth, illiteracy, a basic conservatism common in most rural areas, superstition, and an uneven program of irrigation and land reclamation, combined with limited energy, fertilizer, and water resources. An even more formidable obstacle facing the concept of local rule and local involvement in resolving serious economic problems is the increasing intensity and fragmentation of the political, linguistic, religious, and ethnic life of India. Violence in the country's political life has exacerbated the situation. *Panchayati raj* has fallen victim to a power struggle between the political parties, with each party splitting into smaller factions for control of the *panchayats*.

This competition for control is particularly important in the matter of patronage and the dispensing of significant resources for local development. Naturally, each of the competing political parties or groups wants credit for dispensing these limited resources.

The *panchayat* system is failing because of this intense struggle between the parties. Programs are slowed or halted, morale of the nonelected administrators of the development programs is severely diminished, corruption through the patronage system is endemic, and appropriate flow of information and decision making throughout *panchayati raj* has become erratic.

The *panchayat* system is laudable for its focus on involving the rural population in self-government and for addressing local problems with hoped-for local control and decision making in the utilization of the limited resources available to resolve the severe economic problems facing India. Unfortunately, *panchayati raj* is diminished through the intensity, severity, and fragmentation of the social, ethnic, religious, and political structure of India, as India continues to move away from the secular state envisioned by Nehru and other founders of the Republic.

Pancit: Chinese-influenced, Filipino fried food made with noodles, vegetables, shrimp, pork, chicken, or ham. There are many versions of this dish, including *pancit guisado*, which is made with fried noodles and mixed meats; *pancit luglog*, made with white noodles in a puddling-like sauce; and *pancit molo*, a clear noodle soup similar to Chinese wonton soup.

Pandit, Sakaram Ganesh (b. Ahmadabad, Gujarat State, India): Attorney. Although Pandit became a citizen of the United States in 1914, the U.S. Justice Department brought denaturalization proceedings against him in 1923 in the aftermath of the *UNITED STATES V. BHAGAT SINGH THIND* (1923) decision, which declared people of Asian Indian origin ineligible for citizenship. Arguing his own case, Pandit won a favorable legal opinion in 1924; however, federal authorities, through the appeals process, continued to challenge Pandit's right to citizenship. It was not until November, 1926, that the courts upheld the 1924 decision that Pandit should not be deprived of his U.S. citizenship.

Pandit received his education in Benares, India, earning an equivalent of a Ph.D. degree at a traditional Hindu college in 1904. He emigrated to the United States from England, arriving in California in 1909. Pandit applied for and received a certificate of naturalization in 1914. He thereafter studied law and was admitted to the California bar after passing the required examination in 1917. He practiced law in California state courts as well as U.S. district courts.

In 1919 Pandit represented a fellow Indian, Mohan Singh, who had applied for citizenship in Los Angeles. Naturalization examiners objected to Singh's petition on the grounds that Asian Indians were not "white," one of the requirements for eligibility for U.S. citizenship. Pandit countered the examiners' argument by citing several cases in which the courts had granted Asian Indians citizenship rights. He enumerated approximately twenty cases in California along with examples from other states such as New York, Washington, and Georgia where Asian Indians had become naturalized American citizens. Additionally, Pandit provided numerous instances where Asian Indians were classified as Caucasians in legal and anthropological texts. On the basis on Pandit's argument, the presiding judge declared Singh eligible for citizenship.

The U.S. Supreme Court's decision in *Thind* disallowed all previously granted citizenship to Asian Indians by determining that although they might be Caucasian by race, they were not "white" people by definition of the "common man." This decision stated that since Asian Indians were not "white" they were ineligible for U.S. citizenship. Following this ruling,

Not until 1946 would Congress, in the Luce-Celler Bill, extend naturalization to immigrant Asian Indians in the United States. (Frances M. Roberts)

the immigration service charged that Pandit and other naturalized Asian Indians had attained their citizenship papers illegally since they had never been eligible for naturalization.

For the next three years, Pandit fought to retain his citizenship and preserve his career and property rights. Pandit's denaturalization case also affected his American wife's legal status. Under the CABLE ACT of 1922, she was forced to forfeit her citizenship rights because of her marriage to an alien who was ineligible for U.S. citizenship.

In 1926 the U.S. Ninth Circuit Court of Appeals ruled in favor of Pandit, finding that he had not misrepresented himself in his application for naturalization. While the circuit court conceded that the lower court may have made an error in granting an Asian Indian naturalization, it held that Pandit's citizenship should not be invalidated since it went unquestioned by the government for so many years.

Pandit was among the few Asian Indians who successfully contested their denaturalization cases. Approximately sixty-five Asian Indian Americans lost their citizenship rights following the *Thind* decision in 1923. Asian Indians in the United States were not allowed to become naturalized citizens until 1946, when the U.S. Congress passed the LUCE-CELLER BILL making them eligible for naturalization and citizenship.

Paper sons: Chinese immigrants who, under the rule of derivative citizenship, took advantage of the destruction of birth records in the San Francisco earthquake and fire of 1906 to secure entry into the United States. The phrase thus describes a ruse to gain U.S. citizenship, beginning during the period when the Chinese and other Asians were singled out for exclusion from the country. Chinese immigrants had responded to the California gold rush of 1849 in large numbers. Later they were recruited to work on the building of the transcontinental railroad. Racism and economic competition, however, caused them to become scapegoats for the economic ills of the West after 1870, following completion of the railroad. In 1882, the first of many Chinese exclusion laws was passed prohibiting Chinese laborers from entering the country. (See CHINESE EXCLUSION ACT OF 1882.)

To circumvent the exclusion laws, prospective immigrants claimed that they were the sons of U.S. citizens and that they could not therefore be barred from entry. (The Constitution confers citizenship upon those born in the United States; foreign-born offspring of U.S. citizens derive American citizenship from their parents.)

The earthquake and subsequent destruction of government records made it possible for many Chinese to claim native-born citizenship. Having established their own status, they could then send for their sons (rarely daughters) back in China, thus circumventing the exclusion laws. Some enterprising "fathers" saw this loophole as a way to claim more sons, selling the extra slots.

Armed with crib papers, young men who purchased these additional slots would memorize the family history of their paper father and change their names and identities to conform to their paper families. U.S. immigration inspectors fought back, detaining the newcomers at the ports of entry and interrogating them at length, sometimes for weeks and even months. If the answers did not match those of other members of the "family," the hapless individual was deported. At the same time, the applicant put other members of the "family" at risk of deportation. Therefore, it was of utmost importance to memorize the most detailed and minute aspect of family history and lifestyle.

Once the paper son gained entry, he too could claim that his sons were entitled to enter the United States on the basis of derivative citizenship. This practice continued until the 1960's. Although Chinese exclusion had been repealed in 1943, the restrictive quota of 105 immigrants from China per year forced the Chinese to continue the ruse until a change in the immigration laws in 1965 made such deception unnecessary.

Chinese in America became the target of U.S. exclusionary laws starting in the nineteenth century. Here visitors to the Ellis Island Museum in New York, which opened in 1992, view a display. (Mary Pat Shaffer)

Parachute kids: Children from TAIWAN living in the United States while their affluent parents remain in Taiwan. Some of these "parachute kids"—so called because they are "dropped off" by their parents—stay with relatives; some are nominally under the care of "paper" aunts or uncles who assume the role of relatives when necessary (in dealing with school authorities, for example). Many high school age parachute kids, however, live by themselves or with siblings with no adult supervision.

For the parents of the parachute kids, education is the primary motivation. In Taiwan, only 8 percent of high school graduates are admitted to four-year colleges. The American system of higher education is much less competitive; at the same time, students who excel have access to world-class universities.

While many parachute kids do well in school and learn to function without their parents, school officials and Chinese American community leaders have expressed concern at the practice. They are concerned not only by the obvious cases in which students without supervision have become involved with drugs and crime but also by the larger question of the long-term effects of parental absence.

Park, Joseph (b. Oct. 13, 1906, Honolulu, Territory of Hawaii): Professor. Born to Korean immigrant parents, he became one of the leading American organic fluorine chemists. After receiving his doctorate from Ohio State University in 1937, he worked as a research supervisor for E. I. du Pont de Nemours and Company in 1944. Three years later he joined the faculty of the

University of Colorado, Boulder and became a professor of chemistry in 1953. In 1972 he became the first U.S.-born Korean to head the Institute of National Academic Sciences of the Republic of Korea.

Park Chan Ho (June 30, 1973, Kong Ju City, South Korea): Baseball player. Park, a righthanded pitcher, drew the attention of scouts for U.S. major-league teams with his impressive performances as an amateur in Korea. During Park's sophomore year at Ham Yang University, the Los Angeles Dodgers of the National League signed him to a lucrative contract, and in April, 1994, he became the first Korean to play in the major leagues.

Park Chung Hee (Sept. 30, 1917, near Taegu, Korea—Oct. 26, 1979, Seoul, South Korea): President of South Korea. A Japanese-trained brigadier general in the South Korean army, he staged a military coup on May 16, 1961, seizing power from Prime Minister Chang Myon. Through constitutional changes Park assured himself of a lifetime term in office. He was, however, assassinated in 1979 by Korean Central Intelligence Agency (KCIA) director Kim Jae Kyu.

Park presided over a period of significant economic growth. At the same time, his military regime was notorious for its oppressive domestic policies and for the "Koreagate" scandal of 1977, which involved the Korean government's illegal attempts to influence the U.S. Congress and extensive efforts to monitor and harass Korean Americans.

Park Yong-man. (The Korea Society/Los Angeles)

Park Yong-man (Pak Yong-man; 1881, Kangwon Province, Korea—Oct. 17, 1928, Beijing, China): Political activist. After engaging in anti-government activities and serving a prison sentence in Korea, Park came to the United States as a student in 1904, graduating from the University of Nebraska in 1909. Believing that Korean independence required direct military confrontation, Park established the KOREAN YOUTH MILITARY ACADEMY in Nebraska in 1909; four similar centers were established in California, Kansas, and Wyoming. In 1913 he consolidated these groups and others in Hawaii; this consolidated organization, officially established in 1914 as the Korean National Brigade, was based in Oahu, Hawaii, and numbered slightly more than three hundred cadets.

After the demonstrations that initiated the MARCH FIRST MOVEMENT, Park went to Shanghai, where he served briefly as minister of foreign affairs in the Korean provisional government in exile. He left after the arrival of Syngman RHEE, who dominated the provisional government and with whom Park had clashed strongly. Traveling to Manchuria, Park trained a corps of Korean exiles and continued to seek financial support for large-scale military action against the Japanese colonial regime in Korea. He was assassinated on October 17, 1928; his death was attributed to a rival faction in the independence movement.

Patel, Marilyn (b. Sept. 2, 1938, Amsterdam, N.Y.): Federal judge. She presided over and wrote the opinion in the U.S. District Court *coram nobis* case *Korematsu v. United States* (1984). The *coram nobis* cases were a concerted attempt by the Japanese American community to vacate the criminal convictions of three Japanese American men who had violated the U.S. government's World War II exclusion and curfew orders. On April 19 Patel vacated KOREMATSU's forty-year-old conviction.

Pathet Lao: Nationalist and revolutionary group in Laos. Founded in 1950, the Pathet Lao, or "Lao Nation," was the name for the military component of the Neo Lao Hak Sat, or the United Laotian Patriotic Front, which was the legal political wing of the group. In 1965, the Pathet Lao was renamed the "Lao People's Liberation Army." More widely, Pathet Lao refers to the political-military movement, predominantly communist and nationalist in nature, that took over full control of Laos and established the Laotian government in August, 1975, proclaiming in December of that year the LAO PEOPLE'S DEMOCRATIC REPUBLIC.

The Pathet Lao, as an almost indistinguishable military component from the political umbrella of the Neo Lao Hak Sat, has never been based on a personal following but rather is a tightly disciplined ideological party. In 1953, it gained control of the two northern provinces of Phong Saly and Sam Neua and began pursuing its goal of taking over Laos through a variety of military and political moves.

Conducting a civil and guerrilla war, the Pathet Lao, when it suited its purpose, joined coalition governments. More often than not, particularly when American influence supplanted the French, it resorted to military means to gain control of Laos.

In 1959, after the French had granted a degree of autonomy to Laos, an insurgent group under the general leadership of Prince Souphanouvong, who had participated in founding the Pathet Lao, continued to push for full independence from France. Several thousand guerrilla troops were organized by Souphanouvong and others, with training and military backing largely supplied by the VIET MINH.

When the Second Indochina War escalated in Vietnam in 1966, and with increasing American and South Vietnamese incursions into Laos by both air and ground, the Pathet Lao was increasingly militarily integrated into the North Vietnamese forces to protect the vital areas through which supplies and troops passed along the Ho Chi Minh Trail to the south.

Operation Lam Son, which was conducted in March and April of 1971 in Laos by South Vietnamese and American forces in an effort to interdict the Ho Chi Minh Trail, resulted in a heavy defeat for the allies at the hands of the North Vietnamese forces and the Pathet Lao. From this point until the Pathet Lao's takeover of the government in Laos in 1975, the effectiveness of the United States in forestalling a Communist takeover in Laos paralleled the American experience in South Vietnam.

In 1975, when the Pathet Lao achieved complete control over the country, the Lao People's Revolutionary Party became the only legal and recognized political force in Laos. From 1975 to 1986, the president of the Republic, whose role was largely titular and ceremonial, was Prince Souphanouvong.

Seen in the larger context of the national aspiration for independence that occurred in Southeast Asia after World War II (1939-1945), the role of the Pathet Lao in Laos was similar to the role of the Viet Minh forces in Vietnam.

Patterson, Wayne: Scholar. A professor of history at St. Norbert College, Patterson is a leading scholar in the field of Korean Studies. He has published widely on Korea, the Korean diaspora, and U.S.-Korea relations. Patterson received a B.A. degree in history (1968) from Swarthmore College, M.A. degrees in international relations (1969) and history (1974) from the University of Pennsylvania, and a Ph.D. degree in international relations (1977), also from the University of Pennsylvania. Among his books are *The Koreans in America, 1882-1974: A Chronology and Fact Book* (1974), with Hyung-chan KIM; *The Koreans in America* (1977), with Hyung-chan Kim; *The Two Koreas in World Politics* (1983), with Tae-Hwan Kwak and Edward Olsen; *One Hundred Years of Korean-American Relations, 1882-1992* (1986), with Yur-Bok Lee; and *The Korean Frontier in America: Immigration to Hawaii, 1896-1910* (1988).

Pearl Harbor, attack on: At about 6 A.M., Dec. 7, 1941, 230 miles north of Pearl Harbor, Hawaii, a Japanese naval fleet of thirty-one ships, including six aircraft carriers, began launching its attack planes. The attack was to begin an hour after Japan had served notice to the U.S. State Department that negotiations were ended, which would be 7 A.M. Hawaii time.

British, Dutch, and Americans had levied an embargo on oil shipments to Japan. Those responsible for the defense of Hawaii took it for granted that if, as expected, Japan went to war against those who had imposed the embargo, it would begin with nearby regions in Southeast Asia in possession of the essential oil.

Walter C. Short, Army commanding general for Hawaii, felt that he had more to fear from spies and saboteurs among the Japanese and those of Japanese ancestry in Hawaii than from a Japanese attack. Accordingly he had parked his war planes out in the open, wingtip to wingtip, where they could more easily be guarded against saboteurs.

In addition to the ships now launching the first wave

Captured Japanese aerial photograph snapped during the bombing. In the distance, smoke rises from Hickam Field. (National Archives)

of attacking planes, Japan had dispatched giant submarines to take strategic positions in Hawaiian waters. Eleven of these each carried a small plane; five carried midget submarines.

The preceding evening, officers aboard the giant submarines had launched the midget submarines ten miles from Pearl Harbor, charging them with the mission of stealing into the harbor and lying in wait there until the aerial attack began. They were then instructed to fire their torpedoes at the best targets.

At 6:45 A.M. the American destroyer *Ward*, patrolling outside Pearl Harbor, detected one of these midgets apparently seeking entrance, fired on it, and destroyed it. At 7:00 the *Ward* detected another midget and similarly destroyed it. The *Ward* promptly notified headquarters of each sinking.

At 7:02 at Opana Point, northern Oahu, Army radar operators detected what seemed to be an unusually large flight of planes coming from the north. They phoned this information to Army Intelligence at Fort Shafter. The lieutenant on duty there thought the planes either were from the American carrier *Enterprise* or were a large flight of American planes expected from the mainland. He told the radar operators not to worry about the flight.

At 7:40 the Japanese planes arrived over Oahu. A second wave of planes was halfway to the island. Of the hundreds of planes in the two-wave attack less than half had been assigned targets in Pearl Harbor. The function of the others was to gain air superiority so that the bombers could attack without American aerial interference.

The attackers had seen no American military planes en route, nor did they see any indication of American aerial alertness now. A reconnaissance flight had informed the Japanese that the American carriers, a prime target, were missing. The other major ships, as reported, were at hand, neatly moored. Nearly a hundred ships were in the harbor.

Japanese commander Fuchida Mitsuo gave the signal to attack and wired his superiors that he had achieved surprise. At 7:55 the Japanese attacked the

Hickam and Wheeler field air bases. They would attack most of the other air bases also. At 7:58 torpedo bombers attacked the ships in Pearl Harbor.

At 8:00 Japanese fighters strafed air bases with incendiary bullets, setting afire the neatly arrayed American planes. At 8:05 the Japanese level bombers attacked the battleships. At 8:10 the *Arizona* exploded, having been struck by a several-thousand-pound armor-piercing bomb that penetrated the deck and ignited the forward ammunition magazine. In less than nine minutes it sank with more than a thousand of her crew still aboard.

After about five minutes, American antiaircraft fire began to erupt.

At 8:25 the first attack wave began to retire. The second wave arrived at 8:40 and attacked at 8:45, continuing the damage, although less effectively against the now-alerted defenders and at greater cost to itself. The attack finally began to end at about 10:00.

The attackers lost all five of the midget submarines. They had also lost nine fighter planes, fifteen dive bombers, and five torpedo planes and their crews.

Offsetting this loss, the attackers had sunk or seriously damaged eighteen U.S. ships. They had taken numerous American lives aboard the battleships *Arizona*, *Oklahoma*, and *Utah* and the destroyers *Cassin* and *Downes*. They had sunk or caused to be beached the battleships *West Virginia*, *California*, and *Nevada* and the minelayer *Oglala*. They had damaged the battleships *Tennessee*, *Maryland*, and *Pennsylvania*, the cruisers *Helena*, *Honolulu*, and *Raleigh*; the destroyer *Shaw*, the seaplane tender *Curtiss*, and the repair ship *Vestal*.

The Japanese had destroyed 188 planes and damaged 159. U.S. military casualties exceeded three thousand, of which more than two thousand were fatalities. To this toll was the damage that the defenders inflicted on themselves during the attack—shooting down planes from the American carrier *Enterprise* as they came in to land, as well as the B-17's from the anticipated flight from the mainland. Americans were responsible for most of the dozens of civilians killed or wounded—most by antiaircraft shells with unset fuses that exploded on impact with the ground in nearby Honolulu—and for local fishermen machine-gunned by trigger-happy American fliers who, the morning

The USS Arizona, Tennessee, *and* West Virginia *all sustained extensive damage during the raid.* (Hawaii State Archives)

after the attack, mistook the fishermen for invaders.

The Japanese had immobilized the American Pacific Fleet and could proceed with their Far East operations without fear of American naval interference except for the threat of the missing American carriers.

In contrast to the meticulously executed attack, Japan's notice that it was breaking off diplomatic relations with the United States was delivered fifty-five minutes after the attack had begun.

Adm. Yamamoto Isoroku, Commander in Chief of the Japanese Combined Fleet and the officer who had inspired the attack, regarded reports of the missing carriers and bungled diplomatic note with pessimism. "I fear," he said, "we have only awakened the sleeping giant and filled him with a terrible resolve." He was right. Divided on the matter until that point, Congress the next day declared war against Japan.—*Allan Beekman*

SUGGESTED READINGS: • Beekman, Allan. *Crisis: The Japanese Attack on Pearl Harbor and Southeast Asia*. Honolulu, Hawaii: Heritage Press of the Pacific, 1992. • Feis, Herbert. *Road to Pearl Harbor*. New York: Atheneum, 1950. • Ike, Nobutake. *Japan's Decision for War: Records of the 1941 Policy Conferences*. Stanford, Calif.: Stanford University Press, 1967. • Lord, Walter. *Day of Infamy*. New York: Holt, 1957. • Prange, Gordon W. *At Dawn We Slept*. New York: Penguin Books, 1982. • Wohlstetter, Robert. *Pearl Harbor: Warning and Decision*. Stanford, Calif.: Stanford University Press, 1962.

Pearl River: Waterway in southern China, known in Chinese as the "Zhu Jiang." Its delta was the place of origin of most Chinese immigrants to America during the nineteenth century. The drainage area of the Pearl River and its associated smaller rivers takes up much of the Nan Ling region. The river flows from west to east.

Pearl River Delta: Delta located on the southern coast of China. On its north lies CANTON, the south's leading city, and on its southeast, facing Hong Kong, sits Shenzhen, China's most important Special Economic Zone.

The Pearl River Delta is a confluence of the Xi Jiang (West River), Bei Jiang (North River), and Dong Jiang (East River), with the West River being the longest. Because of these and other tributaries, the delta has been expanding toward the sea.

Cut by a large number of distributaries and by levee-protected flood canals, the delta is southern China's largest area of flat land. Fed by the heavy rainfall of the river basin, the Pearl River has the second largest runoff among China's rivers. It is also China's second longest navigable river. Precipitation on the delta is greatly affected by the monsoon climate. Rainfall is concentrated in the summer. Flooding is often a serious problem during the rainy season. Soil erosion is another problem in parts of the delta. On the positive side, the rich water resources are used for irrigation, fish farming, hydroelectric power generation, and river transportation.

The delta has an area of about eleven thousand square kilometers. It is the most important farming area in south China and probably one of the most productive agricultural ecosystems in the world. Major agricultural products include rice, sugarcane, and silkworm cocoons. With adequate water supply, rich soil, and a long growing season, three crops of rice and seven crops of silkworm cocoon are harvested annually. Its mulberry-silkworm-fish ecosystem interests scientists and scholars worldwide. The intensive agriculture also supports one of China's largest population clusters. Population density on the delta is about eight hundred people per square kilometer, with Han Chinese as the majority. The delta is also the place of origin of many overseas Chinese including many Chinese Americans, who make significant contributions to its development.

Major industries include textiles, food processing, and electronic appliances. The delta is world-famous for its silk products. It is also China's largest cane sugar production center. With roads leading to China's hinterland and foreign regions, the delta is one of China's most prosperous areas.

Pei, I. M. [Ieoh Ming] (b. Apr. 26, 1917, Canton, Guangdong Province, China): Architect. Pei is a founding partner of the architectural firm I. M. Pei & Partners (now Pei Cobb Freed & Partners). He was educated at St. John's Middle School in Shanghai before emigrating to the United States in 1935. His professional education in architecture started at Massachusetts Institute of Technology (MIT), from which he received a B.A. degree in 1940. He then earned a master's degree in architecture from Harvard, where he studied with Walter Gropius. Pei taught at Harvard as an assistant professor from 1945 to 1948. He was awarded traveling fellowships by both MIT and Harvard to study architecture in Europe.

In 1948 real estate developer William Zeckendorf offered Pei the post of director of architecture at the large firm of Webb & Knapp to design large-scale

I. M. Pei exhibits a model of the Regent Hotel in early 1989, to be erected along East 57th Street in New York City. (AP/Wide World Photos)

buildings. Among Pei's early important buildings were the Mile High Center, Denver, Colorado, and the Place Ville-Marie in Montreal, Canada. His personal architectural style was recognized in the design of the National Center for Atmospheric Research in Boulder, Colorado. In many of his projects he showed outstanding ability to design abstract forms with "cold" materials such as concrete, stone, glass, and metals with aesthetic interest.

Pei's design for the East Wing of the National Gallery of Art, Washington, D.C., is one of his best-known. There he used triangular forms to manage the space available next to the existing main building of the gallery. The John Fitzgerald Kennedy Library in Boston was built picturesquely by the seashore. Pei's other institutional buildings include churches, hospitals, schools, and municipal halls. His glass pyramid for the expansion of the Louvre in Paris tapers to a seventy-one-foot peak, while the seventy-two-story Bank of China in Hong Kong is the tallest building in Asia. Other designs include the Henry Luce church in Taiwan and the Fragrant Hill Hotel in Beijing.

Pei has been honored by many academic and professional institutions. He used the Pritzker Prize awarded to him in 1983 to establish a scholarship fund for Chinese students to study architecture in the United States. He was one of the twelve naturalized American citizens to receive the Medal of Liberty in 1986 from President Ronald Reagan at the rededication of the Statue of Liberty. The prestigious Gold Medal of the American Institute of Architects was presented to Pei in 1979.

Peking. *See* **Beijing**

Pele: In Hawaiian cultural tradition, the fire goddess who presides over a family of volcano gods on the Big Island of Hawaii. Accompanied by her siblings, Pele migrated to Hawaii from a distant homeland. Her origins are preserved in legend and *hula* by her worshipers.

Pensionado Act of 1903: Legislation enacted by the Second Philippine Commission, headed by William Howard Taft, that created a program for financing the studies of selected Filipino students in the United States. The program was established a year after U.S. president Theodore Roosevelt declared the "Philippine Insurrection" against the United States over, on July 4, 1902.

The idea for the program came from William Sutherland, a New Mexico A & M College professor of Spanish and Latin who served as one of Taft's Spanish secretaries. Sutherland believed that the *pensionado* (government scholar) program was an excellent way of reinforcing the task of the U.S. colonial government of creating "goodwill and confidence between Filipinos and Americans" and contributing to the "general purpose of bringing about better relations between us and our Filipino wards."

The first cohort of 100 *pensionados* was selected in 1903 from 20,000 applicants from 37 provinces of the Philippines by respective provincial governors and American school superintendents. Taft personally selected 25 students at large. The first batch of *pensionados* were all young "boys" of high-school age (four "girls" were chosen in 1904); they came from some of the top Philippine elite families, and many became national leaders upon their return. The criteria for selection were based on "unquestionable moral and physical qualifications, weight being given to social status"; an examination system was established the following year.

The first *pensionados* departed for the United States on October 10, 1903, accompanied by Sutherland and

William Howard Taft spearheaded the legislative effort that became the Pensionado Act of 1903. Taft served as the American colonial governor of the Philippines before serving as both U.S. president and, later, chief justice of the Supreme Court. (White House Historical Association)

his wife. The students spent their first winter in Southern California attending orientation and intensive oral English programs at various high schools. They attended a special summer school in 1904 in Santa Barbara. In August, they were taken to the St. Louis World's Fair, living for a month in the Philippine Reservation and working "as guides in the exhibition halls and as waiters in the mess hall." In the fall, "they were distributed to selected colleges and universities already prepared for their coming, according to the courses which had been assigned," Sutherland reported.

The *pensionado* program peaked in 1907 with 183 students. By then, it had become clear that the underlying purpose of the "pensionado movement" (as Sutherland referred to it) was "to prepare the Filipinos for their own promised self-government and independence and the discharge of their responsibilities in a world of independent nations" of which they were to become a part.

The recruitment of *pensionados*, however, was affected by changing political priorities. From 1908 to 1914, only two *pensionados* a year were selected. Recruitment stopped in 1915 and resumed in 1919 with 108 students going to 40 U.S. schools. In 1922, there were 147, 4 of whom received Ph.D. degrees and 19 of whom earned M.A. degrees. Recruitment was discontinued once more in 1928 and resumed in 1938.

The *pensionados* clearly pioneered the Filipino student movement abroad. Yet the total number of government-sponsored students was small compared to the many hundreds of self-supporting Filipino students who came in the 1920's and 1930's seeking to further their education in America. Many of these students never returned to the Philippines and played an active role in the development of Filipino American communities throughout the United States.

People Power (*lakas ng bayan*): Slogan associated in the minds of Filipinos with the Philippine revolution that began in February, 1986. The uprising succeeded in removing from power autocratic Philippine president Ferdinand MARCOS and giving the country a democratic foothold under new president Corazon AQUINO.

The Philippine revolution of 1986 began with the assassination of opposition leader Benigno S. Aquino, Jr., in 1983, which sparked protest against Marcos. Aquino's death placed his widow, Corazon, in the forefront of the campaign to regain democracy, and she was elected president in 1986. The elections were marred by widespread fraud and terrorism committed by the ruling party. Marcos was proclaimed president by the National Assembly, but Aquino led a nonviolent protest that had the support of millions of Filipinos,

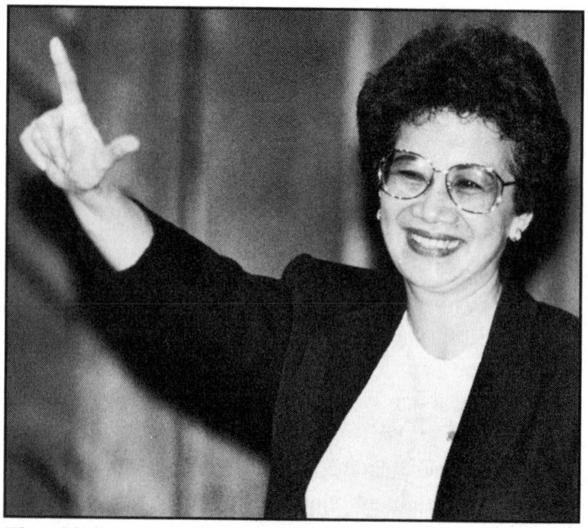

The Philippine revolution of 1986 propelled Corazon Aquino into power as the country's newest president. (AP/ Wide World Photos)

Supporters of opposition leader Corazon Aquino cheer anti-Marcos rebels as the latter move into the captured Philippine military headquarters in February, 1986. (AP/Wide World Photos)

including the Catholic bishops. On February 22, 1986, Minister of Defense Juan Ponce Enrile and Vice Chief of Staff Fidel V. Ramos led a military rebellion against Marcos. Archbishop Jaime Cardinal Sin appealed to the Filipino people to protect the two men. As thousands of civilians heeded the cardinal's call, Enrile and Ramos declared their allegiance to Corazon Aquino as the nation's president. This started the revolution.

It was a revolution without precedent. Men, women, and children—armed only with crucifixes, songs, and rosaries to signify their prayers—served as human barricades. Made invulnerable by their vulnerability, they resisted armed government troops and stopped tanks, thus disarming the Marcos forces. Aquino took her oath of office as president, and Marcos fled into exile in Honolulu, Hawaii, with the aid of the U.S. government.

The experience of People Power in the four-day revolution, which effected a dramatically peaceful transfer of political power and leadership, provided hope to many as a means of supporting the evolution of peaceful change. People Power, however, defies simple definition. From one perspective it was a civilian-based revolt of the military. From another perspective, and a more correct one, it was a military-backed civilian revolt, a triumph of the people over the forces of repression.

People v. Downer (1857): California Supreme Court ruling that declared the discriminatory state act of 1855 to be in violation of the California constitution. The act, or Passenger Tax, gave the state the right to collect a $50 head tax on every alien arriving by sea who was ineligible for American citizenship. This class-action lawsuit had been filed to collect $12,500 in Passenger Taxes from a shipping company for the privilege of bringing 250 Chinese into California.

The high court found that since the U.S. Congress alone has federal constitutional authority to regulate foreign commerce, the Passenger Tax must be repealed.

People v. Hall (1854): California Supreme Court ruling that a Chinese person may not testify against a white person in a California court of law. Reflective of anti-Chinese hostility soon after California entered the Union as a free state, *People v. Hall* involved a conviction for murder based on the testimony of Chinese witnesses. The opinion of the court, written by Chief Judge Hugh C. Murray, construed section 14 of the April 16, 1850 act, Section 14 regulates criminal proceedings and provides that "[n]o black or mulatto person, or Indian, shall be allowed to give evidence in favor of, or against a white man."

To Murray the key word in section 14 was "Indian." His historical analysis noted that the statute was a "transcript of those of older States" and that "[a]t the period from which this legislation dates," China along with India was known as the "Indies" and its people as "Indians." The North American continent was traversed by Asiatics; the name "Indian" was meant to apply not only to American Indians but also to "the whole of the Mongolian race."

It was clear to the court that the intent of the act "was to throw around the citizen a protection for life and property, which could only be secured by removing him above the corrupting influences of degraded castes": African Americans, "the Indian of Patagonia," and the "South Sea Islander," among others. All who are not white are disqualified under the statute from testifying in a California court of law against a person of the "highest caste." This must necessarily include the Chinese, because the word "'white' has a distinct signification, which . . . excludes black, yellow, and all other colors."

Murray then went on to excoriate the Chinese people. Naturally inferior, "incapable of progress . . . beyond a certain point," their language different, their color and "physical conformation" distinct, they do not recognize the laws of California. He found erroneous the suggestion that they had the "privilege of participating with us in administering the affairs of our Government" and of swearing "away the life of a citizen." He concluded that the legislature had no such intention. The Chinese under the Act of 1850 were therefore disqualified from testifying against a white person in a criminal or civil case.

People v. McGuire (1872): California Supreme Court ruling that upheld earlier supreme court decisions barring Chinese from testifying for or against white persons in courts of law. The defendant, McGuire, had been convicted of assaulting Sam Wah, a Chinese immigrant. At trial Wah gave testimony against McGuire, who objected on the basis that Chinese testimony was by law inadmissible in court. The trial judge, however, overruled his objection, and McGuire was eventually convicted. He then appealed to the high court.

California legal precedents established earlier (*PEOPLE V. HALL* and *People v. Brady*, both handed down in 1854) supported the defendant's argument. Sometime after these opinions were published, however, state lawmakers repealed all such prohibitory statutes as of January, 1873. In anticipation of the new law, the trial court had admitted Wah's testimony. The high court, however, reversed that decree and ordered that the defendant be given a new trial, reminding the lower court that its opinions are binding unless overturned.

Perahera: Buddhist festival peculiar to Sri Lanka, held annually in August. The occasion features a procession to the Temple of the Tooth in Kandy, central Sri Lanka, where the Buddha's tooth is enshrined. The marchers are led by monks, drummers, chanters, and gilded elephants. A significant and popular part of the procession are the *kandyan* dancers, who, wearing conical silver headpieces and glittering jewelry, thrill the audience with their musical storytelling and dancing.

Perez v. Sharp (1948): California Supreme Court decision. ANTIMISCEGENATION LAWS had been passed in California to prohibit intermarriage between Caucasians and the growing population of Chinese, Japanese, Filipinos, and other individuals of Asian descent. In the aftermath of World War II, many servicemen returned to the state with spouses of Asian descent and faced discrimination as a result of these laws. In *Perez v. Sharp*, the court ruled that state antimiscegenation laws banning intermarriage between Caucasians and racial minorities were unconstitutional because they violated the right of equal protection under the law. Such laws were based on racial distinctions that the court believed were abhorrent to a nation dedicated to freedom and the doctrine of equality for all individuals.

Perry, Matthew Calbraith (Apr. 10, 1794, South Kingstown, R.I.—Mar. 4, 1858, New York, N.Y.): American naval officer. Following a distinguished career in the Navy, with commissions in the United States, Africa, the Mediterranean, and the West Indies, and with wide public acclaim for leading the 1847 siege of Veracruz in Mexico, Perry was appointed by President Millard Fillmore in 1851 to lead a mission to reestablish American relations with Japan. His goal was to secure a safe harbor for shipwrecked American sailors and ports for both shipping supplies and trade.

Commodore Matthew Perry. (AP/Wide World Photos)

The mission raised much interest in the United States, since Japan, closed to international relations for more than two centuries, had rebuffed several earlier missions, including one by James Biddle in 1841.

Perry put together a fleet of several ships and established a beachhead by force at Naha in Okinawa, then sailed into the Edo (now Tokyo) Bay village of Uraga on July 8, 1853. His arrival caused immense consternation among the local population and Japanese officials, who had been monitoring the squadron's progress. Perry presented the American demands, then left for China to give the Japanese time to consider a response.

The debate in Japan during Perry's absence was intense, and the inability of the ruling TOKUGAWA family to respond forcefully helped stimulate a new opposition movement that would, in turn, lead to the overthrow of Tokugawa rule a decade and a half later. In the meantime, when Perry returned in February, 1854, the government had no option but to negotiate. The resultant TREATY OF KANAGAWA, signed on March 31, 1854, promised safekeeping for shipwrecked sailors, the opening of two refueling and supply ports, and the exchange of consuls. Perry failed to obtain the much-desired trade agreement but left satisfied, convinced that diplomatic representation would result in an early commercial treaty (as it did, in 1858). He returned to the United States in 1855 and described his experiences in the three-volume *Narrative of the Expedition of an American Squadron in the China Seas and Japan* (1856).

Phelan, James D. (Apr. 20, 1861, San Francisco, Calif.—Aug. 7, 1930, Saratoga, Calif.): Politician. He was mayor of San Francisco (1897-1902), U.S. senator from California (1915-1921), and a regent of the University of California (1898-1899). A champion of Chinese and Japanese exclusion, he supported California's ALIEN LAND LAW OF 1913; pushed for more stringent exclusionary legislation against the Japanese; used the slogan, "Keep California White," for his Senate reelection campaign; and once argued that Chinese exclusion was the only way to preserve Western civilization.

Philip II of Spain (May 21, 1527, Valladolid, Spain—Sept. 13, 1598, El Escorial, outside Madrid): King of Spain, from 1556 until 1598. The reigning monarch during the Spanish colonization of the Philippine Islands and from whom the archipelago derives its name, he was considered the most powerful monarch in Europe in the second half of the sixteenth century. His obsession with Catholicism and intolerance for other religions heavily affected religion in the Philippines where, out of all the countries in Asia, it is the only predominantly Christian one.

Philippine-American War (1899-1902): Fought between the United States and Filipino revolutionaries. The war was the United States' first overseas conflict and resulted in that country becoming a colonial power. Traditionally this event has been neglected by many historians and glossed over in history books. Only recently has it been recognized as a conflict that could be described as a prelude to the Vietnam War more than sixty years later. In both wars thousands of American troops were sent to Southeast Asia and were killed or wounded. Racism was a part of both wars.

For many years the Philippine-American War was referred to as the "Philippine Insurrection," a euphemism giving the impression that Filipinos were rebelling against a lawful authority. The American press referred to Filipino troops as "insurgents," "rebels," or "bandits." These terms tended to legitimize the American cause there. To the Filipinos, however, Americans

Admiral George Dewey. (Library of Congress)

Artist's rendering of the Battle of Manila Bay, May 1, 1898. (Library of Congress)

were fighting a war of conquest and imperialism, a continuation of three hundred years of harsh Spanish rule. Filipinos believed that they had been tricked into helping the United States defeat Spanish troops and that they were later denied their independence.

Continuation of War. The United States acquired the Philippines as a result of the Spanish-American War (1898). U.S. President William McKinley was reluctant to annex that country, although some historians have noted that he yielded to the wishes of expansionists who sought to make the United States an imperialist power such as England or France. Expansionists argued that if the U.S. government owned the Philippines, the former would have a key military outpost in the Pacific and the country would have a marketing outlet for exporting U.S. goods. Also many Americans believed it was their "manifest destiny to bring civilization and Christianity to [their] little brown brothers."

Filipino nationalists felt otherwise. The Philippines was basically already a Catholic nation, thanks to the Spaniards. It once had a written alphabet, which was abolished by the Spanish; and, since 1896, it had fought for independence from Spain. The Katipunan movement had prepared a written constitution and the Philippines was ready to become an independent nation before the Spanish-American War occurred.

After the battleship *Maine* exploded in Havana Harbor in Cuba in 1898, killing more than two hundred U.S. servicemen, American public opinion prompted McKinley to declare war. Admiral George Dewey's fleet was ordered to Manila Bay. The Battle of Manila Bay (May 1) between the weaker Spanish navy and Dewey's fleet was one-sided. After a mock battle, Spanish troops surrendered in Manila. Dewey's victory was heralded across the United States and around the world.

The United States had acquired Hawaii in 1898 but otherwise had no previous colonial experience. McKinley had trouble formulating policy for the Philippines. He said later that he had been inspired by "divine guidance," and that it would be "cowardly and dishonorable" to restore that nation to Spain and "bad business" to give the Philippines to France or Germany. McKinley's goal was "to educate the Philipinos (sic) and uplift and Christianize them. . . ." The U.S. government adopted a policy of "benevolent assimilation."

The Seeds of Revolution. Initially, when the Spanish-American war erupted, Filipinos were jubilant. They believed the U.S. government had no desire to annex their country. In fact, U.S. leaders had privately said as much. Emilio AGUINALDO, leader for independence, was in exile in Hong Kong when the war broke out. The U.S. government sought his help and provided a ship for his return to Manila. After Aguinaldo returned, Dewey and others were then vague about American intentions. Aguinaldo became suspicious and began arming Filipino soldiers with captured Spanish arms. Filipino troops occupied Manila. Dewey's fleet did not have enough troops to take over Manila, but more U.S. servicemen were added. An uneasy atmosphere developed as the two armies occupied the city. Aguinaldo did not want war with the United States.

On December 10, 1898, the United States and Spain signed the TREATY OF PARIS, which officially proclaimed that Spain had transferred sovereignty of the Philippines to the American government. Aguinaldo had sent a representative to the Paris conference and to the U.S. Senate to plead for independence. The missions failed. The Senate vote, narrowly passed, officially made the United States an imperialist nation despite opposition by the Anti-Imperialist League and other American critics.

Military forces on both sides were soon fighting because of an incident on February 3, 1899, when an American private killed a Filipino soldier on Balsahan Bridge in Manila. Aguinaldo wanted an investigation. American General Elwell Otis, however, ordered attacks on all Filipino troops. The war had begun.

More American troops were dispatched to Manila, and when the fighting started, the U.S. military had about 24,000 soldiers in the Philippines, about one-third the number of Filipino forces. Otis realized that he could win battles but could not hold territory won. Within one year more than 60,000 Americans were serving in the Philippines. Before the war was over, more than 126,000 servicemen had served in that country. Among the U.S. military forces were two regiments of African American "Buffalo Soldiers."

Devastation. As would happen in Vietnam decades later, U.S. forces not only had to fight native troops but also had to contend with tropical diseases, torrential rains, crushing heat, and the guerrilla warfare tactics of the Filipinos. The hot, humid climate took its toll on the

U.S. troops guard captured Filipino revolutionaries at the Walled City, circa 1899. (Library of Congress)

Americans. Stanley Karnow notes that about 30 percent or more of American troops were debilitated by the weather and tropical conditions. A military commander wrote that his men were "fighting under scorching sun almost as destructive and much harder to bear than the enemy's fire. . . ."

The Philippine-American War has been described as a brutal and racist one in which some American troops became dehumanized. Karnow has written: "The pervasive danger and doubt spurred the U.S. . . . to increasing brutality, especially after the nationalists switched to guerrilla warfare, with its deception and duplicity." Even early in the struggle, many Americans approved of any measures that halted the enemy. "No cruelty is too severe for these brainless monkeys, who can appreciate no sense of honor, kindness or justice," said one American soldier. Another soldier wrote that he wanted "to blow every nigger into nigger heaven." Still another serviceman wrote in a letter home that the Philippine islands would not be pacified until "the niggers are killed off like the [American] Indians." Some American troops had fought in the Civil War and the wars involving American Indians. Besides referring to Filipinos as "niggers," American troops also called them "gugus."

American general J. Franklin Bell, with a force of four thousand, utterly ravaged the townspeople of Batangas. Bell's troops took no prisoners and kept no records; women, children, prisoners, and suspects were all killed. An American correspondent wrote, "We are not dealing with a civilized people. The only thing they know is force, violence and brutality, and we give it to them."

In another incident, General Jacob Smith, outraged at the killing of forty American troops in a village on Samar Island, adopted a policy that the area "must be made a howling wilderness." His troops destroyed every village in the area and killed all people capable of fighting. American public opinion was outrage. Hearings were held, and Smith and his assistant went on trial. Both were acquitted, but their military careers were ruined.

A Costly Victory. Through a deceptive plan devised by American colonel Frederick Funston, AGUINALDO was caught by American troops who pretended they were captured prisoners and were taken to the Philippine leader's headquarters at Palanan, Isabela, on Luzon. Aguinaldo's capture led to the end of the war, and he took an oath of allegiance to the United States. He appealed to all Filipinos to "accept the sovereignty of the U.S." on April 1, 1901. He retired to his family mansion in Kawit and died in 1964. A few Filipino field commanders continued guerrilla warfare until April, 1902. The war officially ended on July 4, 1902.

In terms of human casualties, the Filipinos sustained a far heavier toll. The U.S. toll was 4,234 dead and 3,000 wounded, although countless others suffered and died at home as a result of diseases contracted in the Philippines. According to the U.S. military, some 20,000 Filipinos were killed, and possibly up to 200,000 civilians may have died from from famine and other war-related causes. Historians have noted that 90 percent of the number of carabao (water buffalo), an essential domestic animal for rural farmers, died during the war. The war cost U.S. taxpayers about $600 million, or approximately $4 billion in 1990 dollars.

After the war William Howard Taft became the first U.S. civil governor of the islands. Following the recommendations of the Taft Commission, the U.S. government set about preparing the Philippines for eventual democratic self-government.—*Donald L. Guimary*

SUGGESTED READINGS: • Agoncillo, Teodoro. *Introduction to Filipino History*. Quezon City: R. P. Garcia, 1985. • Graff, Henry, ed. *American Imperialism and the Philippine Insurrection*. Boston: Little, Brown, 1969. • Karnow, Stanley. *In Our Image: America's Empire in the Philippines*. New York: Random House, 1989. • Russell, Charles Edward. *The Outlook for the Philippines*. New York: Century, 1922.

Philippine Commission: American delegations preparing a Philippine colonial government. After the Spanish-American War (1898) and the U.S. military occupation of Manila, American president William McKinley sent a fact-finding mission and later a panel to organize the Philippines' political administration.

The first commission began its assignment of investigating conditions in the islands and deciding the necessary steps of action in 1899. McKinley had instituted the body in order to prevent war between Filipino and American forces. Chaired by Jacob G. Schurman of Cornell University, the commission's composition also included General Elwell Otis and Admiral George Dewey.

Despite Otis' opposition once the PHILIPPINE-AMERICAN WAR (1899-1902) started, the commission promised the Filipinos restricted self-government subject to Washington's supervision, including civil freedoms and competent rule. The Philippine revolutionary regime ignored the commission's pledge, but the commissioners did encourage some desertions.

To encourage more defections, the Schurman com-

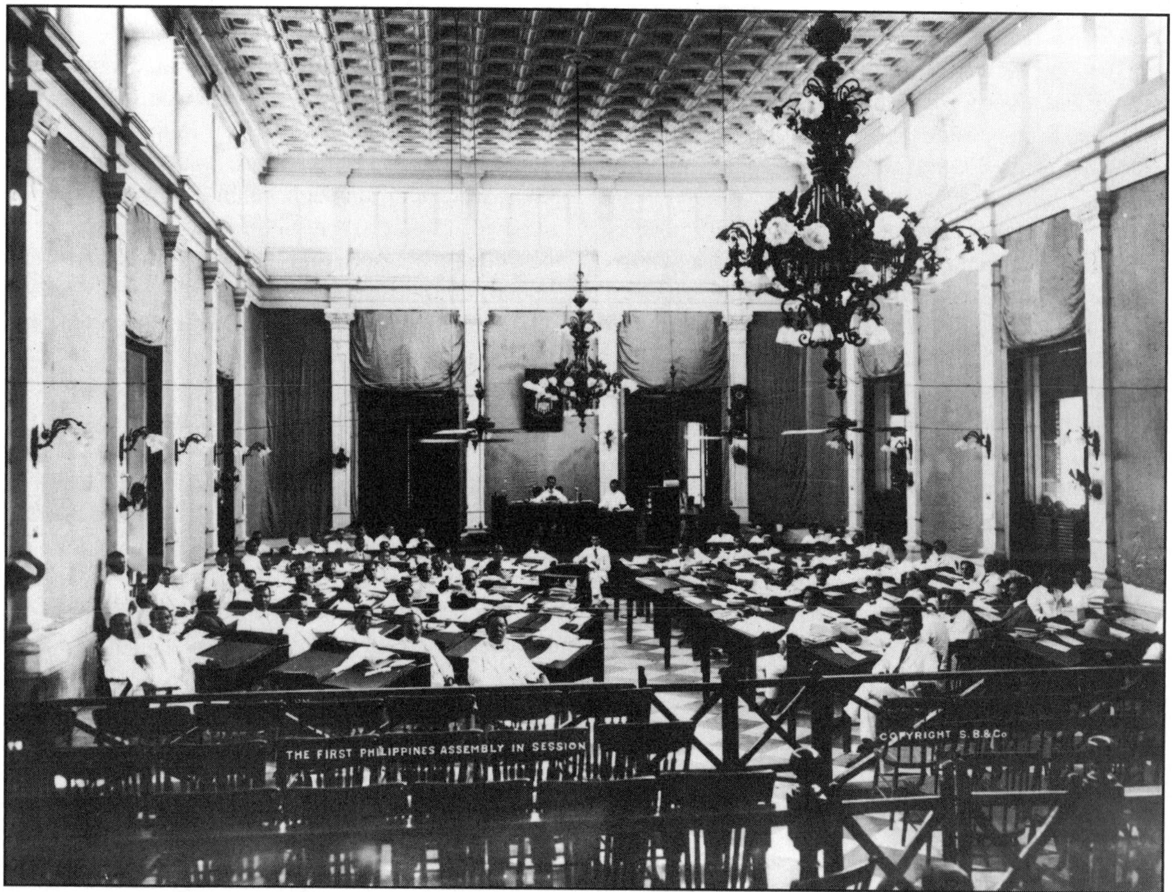

The First Philippine Assembly in session, 1907. Following the conclusion of the Philippine-American War in 1902, the U.S. government imposed on the Philippines a political restructuring based on limited national self-rule. (Library of Congress)

mission wanted a civilian rather than a military administration in Manila. Such a government would include an American-selected governor-general with veto authority, a cabinet appointed by him, a general advisory council elected through a limited vote, and a separate judicial branch. Although Schurman judged the Filipinos unready for independence, their colonial government could be self-sufficient, and its tariffs, taxation, and finances would be kept apart from those of the United States.

Most of Schurman's proposals were approved, and a second commission began its term of service in 1900. Chaired by William Howard Taft, the panel was instructed to allow a degree of Philippine self-rule. Taft, who was also opposed to independence, oversaw the installment of civil administration at all levels. While respectful of past Filipino statutes and practices, the commission instilled such American principles as the separation of power, responsible municipal governance, due process of law, deference for private property, and free public education.

In 1901 McKinley named Taft the Philippines' civil governor, an office retitled "governor-general" four years later. The commission, with three Filipino appointees, acted as a legislative body. Filipinos likewise served throughout the colonial government. Congressional passage of the first Philippine Organic Act in 1902 gave legal status to the Taft commission. With the commission as the upper house, elections determined membership in a lower body. Nevertheless the United States exercised dominant influence until Congress enacted the JONES ACT OF 1916.

Philippine Commonwealth: The ten-year transitional Philippine administration prior to independence. The TYDINGS-MCDUFFIE ACT OF 1934 provided for Filipino independence after an interim commonwealth period during which an American high commissioner replaced the governor-general in Manila. Under the tutelage of the United States, the commonwealth confronted serious challenges before attaining self-rule in 1946.

An elected body wrote the commonwealth's constitution in 1935. As in the United States, the charter divided powers between the legislative and executive branches but concentrated authority on the national level, specifically in the president's office. It also departed from the U.S. model by placing the state before the individual. It not only allowed government ownership and management of civic services and businesses but also mandated control of employment relations. Spanish legal influence survived. The authority of parents and educators was upheld. Moreover there was no provision for a jury system.

After the U.S. government and the Philippine electorate endorsed the constitution, Manuel QUEZON y Molina and Sergio Osmeña, running for the presidency and vice-presidency respectively, defeated Emilio AGUINALDO. Filipinos also elected representatives to a national assembly.

The commonwealth encountered economic problems. American quotas hurt Filipino imports while U.S. exports freely entered the Philippines. With landlords dominant, the commonwealth's effort to protect tenants under the law became impossible. Before President Quezon's limited attempts at enforcement, agrarian living standards had dropped and farm rebellion had broken out, most prominently the Sakdal uprising in 1935.

Military security preoccupied the commonwealth. Quezon brought U.S. Army General Douglas MacArthur into the Philippines to build up its military forces. MacArthur believed the islands were defensible and tried to develop a small yet mobile army supported by a large civilian reserve. Unfortunately personnel and political obstacles hampered his endeavor.

Japan's 1942 conquest of the Philippines resulted in the displacement of the commonwealth government. From Washington, D.C., Quezon promoted the Philippines' interests during World War II. Despite commonwealth membership in the United Nations and invitations to gatherings of the Pacific War Council, Quezon failed to change the European orientation of American military strategy. U.S. President Franklin D. Roosevelt did, however, accept the setting aside of the commonwealth constitution's term limitation, and Quezon remained president until his death in 1944.

When new president Osmeña returned to the Philippines with MacArthur's forces, the commonwealth faced the problems of collaboration, economic rehabilitation, and the timing of independence. MacArthur favored Manuel Roxas y Acuña for president, and the latter's victory in 1946 made him the final commonwealth chief executive.

Philippine Expressions: Filipiniana Bookshop: First full-service Philippine bookstore in the United States. Philippine Expressions was established in 1984 as a mail-order company; it operates the bookshop, which opened its doors in Beverly Hills, California, in 1989. In addition to serving the Filipino American community generally, the shop has become a well-equipped resource center for schools and libraries that promote multicultural education. Printed materials are sold in both English and TAGALOG, the two official languages of the Philippines, enabling Filipino American schoolchildren to read stories in their native language. The store also serves writers and scholars searching for otherwise hard-to-find publications—including those that must be shipped from the Philippines. In an effort to promote Philippine culture, as well as to boost the store's profile among the community at large, the Filipiniana Bookshop has in the past opened up its premises for public readings, lectures, and book-signings.

Philippine languages: These comprise a family of probably at least 100 languages spoken in the Philippine Islands. The two official languages of the country are PILIPINO/TAGALOG and English. Linguists, however, estimate that there are between 70 to 150 different languages spoken in the Philippines, on more than 7,000 islands covering almost 116,000 square miles (roughly the size of Arizona). In 1992 about 64 million people were living in the Philippines (about a fourth the size of the population of the United States).

Language Diversity in the Philippines. Because it is difficult to distinguish "language" from "dialect" in such an ethnically diverse area, it is difficult to estimate accurately the number of languages spoken in the Philippines, as well as to determine the exact number of speakers. While it is clear that TAGALOG is mutually unintelligible with, for example, Cebuano, it is not so obvious whether Cebuano and Hiligaynon are as distinct.

The Philippine languages are usually divided into three main families: Northern Philippine, the languages of northern Luzon; Central (Meso-) Philippine, the languages of central and southern Luzon, Mindoro, Leyte, Cebu, Samar, Panay, Negros, and Palawan; and Southern Philippine, the languages of Mindanao and the Sulu archipelago. Some scholars put the southern

The Major Languages of the Philippines, 1990

	Number of Speakers (in thousands)	Location
Austronesian, western branch		
Northern Philippine		
Agta	5	Luzon
Bontok	20	Luzon
Ga-dang	18	Luzon
Ibanag	300	Luzon
Ifugao	100	Luzon
Ilokano	7,000	northwest Luzon
Ilongot	3	Luzon
Isnag	12	northern Luzon
Itawit	15	Luzon
Itneg	20	Luzon
Kankanay	200	Luzon
Pangasinan	2,000	Luzon
Central (Meso-) Philippine		
Agutaynon	36	Palawan
Aklanon/Panay	400	north Panay
Bantuanan	50	Banton, Masbate
Batak	2	Palawan
Bikol	4,000	Luzon, Catanduanes
Bolinao	34	Luzon
Hanunoo	8	Mindoro
Hiligaynon/Panay	6,000	Visayas, Panay, Negros
Ivatan	30	Basco
Kalinga	100	Luzon
Kinaray-a/Hamtiknon	300	Iloilo, Panay
Masbateno	600	Masbate
Palawano	20	Palawan
Pampango/Kapampangan	2,000	northern Luzon
Sambal/Zambal	40	Luzon
Sebuano/Visayan	1,200	Cebu, Visayas
Tagalog/Filipino	36,000	the Philippines, Luzon
Waray-Samar/Leyete	3,000	Samar, Leyete
Southern Philippine		
Bagobo	17	Minanao
Bilaan	200	Mindanao
Binukid	100	Mindanao
Kagayanen	30	Cagayan
Magindanaon	1,000	Maguindanao, Mindanao, Iranun
Manobo	150	Mindanao
Maranao	500	Mindanao
Sama/Samal	250	Sulu Archipelago, Mindanao
Subanon	60	Mindanao
Tausug/Sulu	1,000	Sulu
Tiboli	60	Mindanao
Tiruray	35	Cotabato, Mindanao
Yakan	60	Sulu
Indo-European		
English	20,000	whole Philippines

Notes: (1) Austronesian is the modern term for Malayo-Polynesian languages. (2) Pilipino—a form of Tagalog—is the national language of the Philippines; only native speakers are listed in the above table. (3) English is also an official language of the Philippines. (4) Languages separated by slashes represent multiple names for a language or dialect variability; languages separated by hyphens represent composite linguistic groups composed of several different, though similar, languages. (5) Spellings—such as Cebuano vs. Sebuano, Bikol vs. Bicolano—and language names sometimes vary greatly in the Philippines; for example, some refer to Sebuano, Hilagaynon, and Samar collectively as Visayan.

Mindanao and the Samar (Sulu) languages into their own families.

The Structures of the Philippine Languages. The Philippine languages, though different from one another in many respects, are typologically rather uniform. The Philippine sound system is straightforward, with most languages having four or five vowels (usually *i*, *e*, *a*, *o*, or *u*). There is a voiceless series of "stop" sounds (*p*, *t*, *k*) and a voiced series (*b*, *d*, *g*). There are the nasal sounds *m*, *n*, and *ng*, as well as *s*, *h*, *r*, and *l*. Four of the major grammatical properties that characterize Philippine language syntax are infixing, case, topics and focus, and reduplication.

In English, prefixes and suffixes attached to root words are quite common. Most Philippine languages, however, also use "infixes," particles added to the middle of words to change meaning. For example, in Bontok the infix *-um-* can be added to adjective-roots to give the meaning "becoming." *Fikas* ("strong"), for example, can change to *f-um-ikas* ("becoming strong"), or *kilad* ("red") can become *k-um-ilad* ("becoming red").

Most Philippine languages use special devices called "case markers" to indicate the grammatical function of words in a sentence. In English generally it is word order that indicates the part of speech of each word. In a sentence such as, "The woman gives some rice to the child," one knows that "woman" is the subject because this word comes at the beginning of the sentence and before the verb "gives." In Tagalog, however, subjects take the prefix *ng-* to show this grammatical function. *Babae* ("woman"), for example, becomes *ng-babae* since the woman is the actor in this sentence. Likewise since something is given "to the child," the Tagalog word *bata* ("child") takes the direction-case marker *sa-* to show that this noun is acting as a receiver of the action (*bata* becomes *sa-bata*). There are often several dozen such particles in the Philippine languages. Because the parts of speech are clearly indicated by these markers, Philippine languages are not narrowly restricted to the subject-verb word order commonly found in English.

In Philippine languages it is not subject and predicate that determine the ultimate meaning of a sentence, but topic and comment. In English the common way to construct a sentence is by combining a subject with a predicate. Usually the subject contains some noun or noun phrase, while the predicate is composed of the verb and some optional complements such as a direct object or an indirect object.

A topic of a sentence is any noun phrase that is the focus of attention. This can be the "doer" of the action (the traditional English subject), but it is not necessarily restricted to it. The topic can also be the "location" of the action, the "beneficiary" of the action, the "instrument" used to perform the action, and so forth. The topic is usually distinguished by some special marker.

The focus of attention of a Tagalog sentence, for example, is marked with the topic prefix *ang-*. A neutral way to say, "The woman gives some rice to the child," in Tagalog would be *Mag-bibigay* ("gives") ng-babae ("woman") *ng-bigas* ("rice") *sa-bata* ("child"). Various centers of attention can be chosen, however, depending on what the speaker wants to communicate to the listener. In the example just given, if one wishes to make clear that it is the woman, and not someone else, who gives rice to the child, then the prefix *ang-* must be added to the word *-babae* to form the word *ang-babae*. The new sentence would therefore read: *"Mag-bibigay ang-babae ng-bigas sa-bata."*

Finally, most Philippine languages repeat all or part of a word to create a new form. For example, in Tagalog *araw* ("day," "sun") is reduplicated as *araw-araw*, meaning "everyday." *Isa* ("one") can reduplicate as *isa-isa*, meaning "one by one."

Pilipino, the National Language. When the Philippines won its independence after World War II, it was obvious that a *lingua franca* was necessary to develop a sense of nationalism among the scores of different ethnic groups throughout the islands. English had been the language of instruction in the school system, and almost all Filipino intellectuals and politicians were fluent in it. It was felt, however, that English still carried suggestions of American colonialism. Therefore the Manila/southern Luzon dialect of Tagalog—the speech around the new capital—was chosen to be the new national language. In the 1970's this version of TAGALOG became more standardized and formal, and its official name was changed to "PILIPINO."

Pilipino is now the language of instruction in the public school system, though English is still common in the universities. Most non-English media (newspapers, books, comics, for example) are usually in Pilipino, though occasionally Cebuano and Ilocano are found. Between twenty-five to thirty-six million Filipinos speak Pilipino as a first or fluent second language, and most people have at least some facility in it.—*James Stanlaw*

SUGGESTED READINGS: • LeBar, Frank, ed. *Ethnic Groups of Insular Southeast Asia, Vol. I.* New Haven, Conn.: HRAF Press, 1972. • McFarland, Curtis, comp. *A Linguistic Atlas of the Philippines.* Tokyo:

Institute for the Study of Languages and Cultures of Asia and Africa, 1980. • Ramos, Teresita. *Tagalog Structures*. Honolulu: University of Hawaii Press, 1971. • Reid, Lawrence. "Philippine Linguistics: The State of the Art, 1970-1980." In *Philippine Studies: Political Science, Economics, and Linguistics*, edited by Donn Hart. De Kalb: Northern Illinois University, Center for Southeast Asian Studies, 1981. • Schachter, Paul, and Fe T. Otanes. *Tagalog Reference Grammar*. Berkeley: University of California Press, 1972. • Walton, Charles. "A Philippine Language Tree." In *Anthropological Linguistics: An Introduction*. By Joseph H. Greenberg. New York: Random House, 1968.

Philippine News: National community news organization formed in 1961 and located in south San Francisco. The organization has improved the working conditions of Filipino immigrants and was instrumental in exposing ills that led to the eventual downfall of the Marcos regime in the Philippines. The *Philippine News*, the official publication of the organization, has an annual circulation of 120,000 across the United States.

Philippine Scouts: Filipino units of the U.S. regular army. From the PHILIPPINE-AMERICAN WAR (1899-1902) to World War II (1939-1945), the United States used native troops to pacify and defend the Philippines. One group of Filipino soldiers, the Scouts, won acclaim for its loyalty and *esprit de corps*.

During the Philippine-American War, General Arthur MacArthur favored arming Filipinos. Despite the misgivings of many American commanders, MacArthur needed replacements for departing U.S. volunteers and for future operations against Filipino revolutionaries.

By late 1900 the American military's practice of employing indigenous soldiers was proceeding successfully. Inhabitants of Ilocos Norte and Ilocos Sur saw duty as Scouts as early as 1899, when the United States garrisoned northern Luzon. Scout units were formed on Negros Island and from the anti-Tagalog town of Macabebe north of Manila. Yet American authorities opposed the enrollment of Tagalogs, and through 1902 most Filipino Scouts were Macabebes, ILOCANOS, and Visayans.

When the U.S. Congress remodeled the regular army in 1901, a provision for native soldiers to be named the Philippine Scouts was stipulated. The fifty Scout companies organized by 1903 were recognized as U.S. army units yet could only be utilized in the Philippine archipelago. With Americans commanding, Filipino enlistees served in the lower ranks.

By the time the Scouts totaled nearly seven thousand effectives in 1926, they had been deployed throughout the Philippines. Scout units battled Filipino Muslims on Jolo Island in Sulu. Scouts pursued remnants of Filipino revolutionaries that dispersed to the boondocks and were resorting to banditry. The Scouts also enforced quarantines during outbreaks of rinderpest.

Victorious Japanese troops capture Bataan, Philippines, circa 1942. (National Archives)

On the eve of the Pacific War, the Philippine Scouts were acknowledged as superior soldiers. Their recruits, outfitted with American equipment, were well trained. No other unit surpassed the Scouts in morale and sharpshooting.

Twelve thousand Scouts were deployed to meet the Japanese invasion of Luzon in December, 1941. The 26th Cavalry moved north to counter the Japanese landing near Lingayen Gulf, while the 45th and 57th Infantry Regiments retreated into the Bataan Peninsula and heroically resisted the Japanese siege until malnutrition and sickness forced the American garrison's surrender in April, 1942.